W9-BZL-277

150 Best

Low-Stress Jobs

Part of JIST's Best Jobs™ Series

The Editors @ JIST **and Laurence Shatkin, Ph.D.**

Foreword by Andrea Moselle, Senior Manager, Work/Life, AstraZeneca Pharmaceuticals

Also in JIST's Best Jobs Series

JIST
Works
America's Career Publisher®

150 Best Low-Stress Jobs

© 2008 by JIST Publishing

Published by JIST Works, an imprint of JIST Publishing
7321 Shadeland Station, Suite 200
Indianapolis, Indiana 46256-3923

Phone: 800-648-JIST   Fax: 877-454-7839
E-mail: info@jist.com   Web site: www.jist.com

Some Other Books by the Authors

The Editors at JIST

EZ Occupational Outlook Handbook

Salary Facts Handbook

Enhanced Occupational Outlook Handbook

Guide to America's Federal Jobs

Health-Care CareerVision Book and DVD

Laurence Shatkin

90-Minute College Major Matcher

Quantity discounts are available for JIST products. Have future editions of JIST books automatically delivered to you on publication through our convenient standing order program. Please call 800-648-JIST or visit www.jist.com for a free catalog and more information.

Visit www.jist.com for information on JIST, free job search information, tables of contents and sample pages, and ordering information on our many products.

Acquisitions Editor: Susan Pines
Development Editor: Stephanie Koutek
Copy Editor: Susan Shaw Dunn
Cover and Interior Designer: Aleata Halbig
Cover Illustration: Getty Images by Digital Vision
Proofreaders: Linda Seifert, Jeanne Clark
Indexer: Cheryl Lenser

Printed in the United States of America

13 12 11 10 09 08   9 8 7 6 5 4 3 2 1

Library of Congress Cataloging-in-Publication Data

150 best low-stress jobs / the editors at JIST and Laurence Shatkin, Ph.D.
        p. cm.
    Includes index.
    ISBN 978-1-59357-555-7 (alk. paper)
    1. Job hunting—United States. I. Shatkin, Laurence. II. JIST Publishing. III. Title: One hundred fifty low-stress jobs.
    HF5382.75.U6A17 2008
    331.702—dc22

                                            2008017930

We have been careful to provide accurate information throughout this book, but it is possible that errors and omissions have been introduced. Please consider this in making any career plans or other important decisions. Trust your own judgment above all else and in all things.

This Is a Big Book, But It Is Very Easy to Use

Does your job make you feel stressed out? This book can help you plan for a future in a less stressful job.

Workplace stress can ruin a major part of your day and can spill over to the rest of your life, harming your personal relationships. It can cause health problems and even lead to premature death.

You may feel you need to endure workplace stress to provide for your family or gain other rewards from your job. But wouldn't it be better to find a rewarding job with less stress? That's the purpose of this book.

Here you'll find lists of good jobs that avoid the most stress-producing aspects of work. The jobs on the lists are selected and ordered to emphasize those with the highest earnings and the highest demand for workers. Specialized lists arrange these jobs by the level of education or training required and by interest fields. You can also see lists of jobs that are low in specific stressful conditions.

Every job is described in detail later in the book, so you can explore the jobs that interest you the most. You'll learn the major work tasks, all the important skills, educational programs, and many other informative facts.

Using this book, you'll be surprised how quickly you'll get new ideas for careers that won't stress you out and can suit you in many other ways.

Some Things You Can Do with This Book

- Identify low-stress jobs that don't require you to get additional training or education, perhaps as options for retirement or a second career.
- Develop long-term career plans that may require additional training, education, or experience.
- Explore and select a training or educational program that relates to a career objective low in certain specific kinds of stress.
- Prepare for interviews by learning how to connect your work preferences (and stressors you want to avoid) to your career goal.

These are a few of the many ways you can use this book. We hope you find it as interesting to browse as we did to put together. We have tried to make it easy to use and as interesting as occupational information can be.

When you are done with this book, pass it along or tell someone else about it. We wish you well in your career and in your life.

Credits and Acknowledgments: While the authors created this book, it is based on the work of many others. The occupational information is based on data obtained from the U.S. Department of Labor and the U.S. Census Bureau. These sources provide the most authoritative occupational information available. The job titles and their related descriptions are from the O*NET database, which was developed by researchers and developers under the direction of the U.S. Department of Labor. They, in turn, were assisted by thousands of employers who provided details on the nature of work in the many thousands of job samplings used in the database's development. We used the most recent version of the O*NET database, release 12.0. We appreciate and thank the staff of the U.S. Department of Labor for their efforts and expertise in providing such a rich source of data.

Table of Contents

Summary of Major Sections

Introduction. A short overview to help you better understand and use the book. *Starts on page 1.*

Part I. Cures for Workplace Stress. Explains what workplace stress is, how it harms workers, and how you can cope with it. Challenge on the job can be stimulating and rewarding, but stress can be hazardous to your mental and physical health. Learn techniques that workers and their managers can use to defuse stress. *Starts on page 17.*

Part II. The Best Jobs Lists: Jobs Low in Stress. Very useful for exploring career options! Lists are arranged into easy-to-use groups. The first list presents the 150 best low-stress jobs overall. These jobs are selected to avoid major causes of stress and be outstanding in terms of earnings, job growth, and job openings. Additional lists give the 50 best-paying low-stress jobs, the 50 fastest-growing low-stress jobs, and the 50 low-stress jobs with the most openings. More-specialized lists follow, presenting the jobs lowest in overall stress and lowest in specific stressful features such as dealing with unpleasant or angry people, time pressure, and competition. You can also see lists of the best jobs that have a high concentration of certain kinds of workers (for example, workers in certain age brackets, part-time workers, or female workers) and lists with the jobs organized by level of education or training and by interest area. The column starting at right presents all the list titles. *Starts on page 25.*

Part III. Descriptions of the Best Low-Stress Jobs. Provides complete descriptions of the jobs that appear on the lists in Part II. Each description contains information on work tasks, skills, education and training required, earnings, projected growth, job duties, level of stress, most stressful aspects, related knowledge and courses, working conditions, and many other details. *Starts on page 141.*

Appendix A. Resources for Further Exploration. A helpful list of resources to learn more about low-stress careers. *Starts on page 403.*

Appendix B. The GOE Interest Areas and Work Groups. This list of the 16 GOE Interest Areas and Work Groups can help you narrow down your career interests. *Starts on page 405.*

Detailed Table of Contents

Table of Contents

Foreword

Workplace stress is a two-way street: It has a negative impact on business, and work can be a major source of stress for individuals. For many Americans, the amount and pace of work have been speeding up in response to a global economy and the introduction of technologies that can easily convert the anywhere-anytime workplace into the everywhere-all-the-time workplace. At the same time, a large and growing number of dual-earner families are struggling to manage the demands of work and personal life. Multiple studies indicate that the resulting stress negatively affects the mental and physical well-being of the workforce. Absenteeism increases, or employees who do come to work are thinking less clearly, making more mistakes, being less creative, or not getting along with co-workers. The consequence is lower productivity, which in turn affects the bottom line.

While it's probably not possible to create a completely stress-free workplace, companies like mine take these issues seriously. We look at ways to prevent stress whenever possible or manage it better. We are committed to taking steps both to create a work environment that is less stressful and to help our employees increase their resilience so that they can deal with change and manage the amount and pace of work. We also spend a lot of time making sure that the right person is in the right job. We know that when people are in a job that's not a good fit for them, it's stressful!

That's where a book like this one comes in. Dr. Shatkin notes that an aspect of a job that may be stressful for me is no problem at all for you, so *150 Best Low-Stress Jobs* analyzes each job on 11 different measures. The book recognizes that sometimes what makes a job stressful is the way an individual approaches the work, and therefore one chapter focuses on helping you find ways to avoid or cope with workplace stress. So, whether you are considering changing careers, finding a different job within your own workplace, or just trying to evaluate how you can lower your stress levels, you'll find valuable information.

Andrea Moselle
Senior Manager, Work/Life
AstraZeneca Pharmaceuticals

Introduction

Not everybody will want to read this introduction. You may want to skip this background information and go directly to Part I, which discusses workplace stress and its relationship to careers and health, or Part II, which lists the best low-stress jobs.

But if you want to understand how we put this book together, where the information comes from, and what makes a job "low-stress" and "best," this introduction can answer a lot of questions.

Where the Information Came From

The information we used in creating this book came mostly from databases created by the U.S. Department of Labor:

- We started with the job information included in the Standard Occupational Classification (SOC), the taxonomy that the federal government uses to classify and present information about all jobs. The U.S. Bureau of Labor Statistics uses SOC codes to report information on occupational earnings, projected growth, number of openings, and the number of self-employed workers. The Census Bureau uses SOC codes to report on the number of part-time workers, workers in various age brackets, and other characteristics of workers.

- We linked this SOC information to the job information included in the Department of Labor's O*NET (Occupational Information Network) database, which is now the primary source of detailed noneconomic information on occupations. The Labor Department updates the O*NET regularly, and we used the most recent one available: O*NET release 12. Data from the O*NET allowed us to determine the amount of stress that characterizes each job, among other topics. Because the O*NET taxonomy varies slightly from the SOC, we had to match O*NET job titles to similar SOC titles. In a few cases, two or more O*NET occupations matched a single SOC occupation, and we had to compute an average so that we could characterize the SOC occupation in terms of O*NET descriptors. Nevertheless, the information we report here is the most reliable data we could obtain.

- We used the Classification of Instructional Programs, a system developed by the U.S. Department of Education, to cross-reference the education or training programs related to each job.

Of course, information in a database format can be boring and even confusing, so we did many things to help make the data useful and present it to you in a form that is easy to understand.

How the Best Low-Stress Jobs Were Selected

It's important to understand that this book doesn't focus on the jobs with the lowest level of stress. Rather, we selected the 150 jobs by **eliminating those with the highest stress**. So a truly accurate title for this book might be *150 Not-High-Stress Jobs*—but we think you'll agree that the title *150 Low-Stress Jobs* is easier to understand.

We were able to determine the stress levels of various jobs because the O*NET database includes 11 relevant measures of work conditions that we felt would be stressful to the great majority of workers:

- The work-style measure Stress Tolerance is defined as accepting criticism and dealing calmly and effectively with high-stress situations.
- The work-context measure Consequence of Error means the seriousness of the result if the worker makes a mistake that cannot be readily corrected.
- The work-context measure Deal With Physically Aggressive People is defined as dealing with physical aggression of violent individuals.
- The work-context measure Deal With Unpleasant or Angry People is defined as dealing with unpleasant, angry, or discourteous individuals as part of the job requirements.
- The work-context measure Duration of Typical Work Week is based on the number of hours typically worked in one week.
- The work-context measure Frequency of Conflict Situations indicates how much the work involves people who are in conflict (not necessarily with the worker).
- The work-context measure Impact of Decisions on Co-workers or Company Results indicates how much the decisions an employee makes affect the results of co-workers, clients, or the company.
- The work-context measure Importance of Being Exact or Accurate means the necessity of being precise or highly accurate on the job.
- The work-context measure Level of Competition means competing or being aware of competitive pressures.
- The work-context measure Pace Determined by Speed of Equipment is defined as the extent to which the work pace is determined by the speed of equipment or machinery. (It doesn't refer to keeping busy at all times on the job.)
- The work-context measure Time Pressure means meeting strict deadlines.

The O*NET database also includes measures of workplace hazards, such as Exposure to Hazardous Conditions, but we didn't include such features among the set of stressors for this book because workers in hazardous environments are given equipment and training that let them do their jobs without fear. For example, one of the jobs you'll find among the 150 best low-stress jobs is Hazardous Materials Removal Workers. When these workers remove a hazardous substance such as asbestos, they wear appropriate safety gear and have enough training in safety procedures to have a healthy respect for asbestos rather than anxiety about it. In fact, supervisors of workers like these often need to remind workers to maintain careful procedures because daily familiarity with a hazard can reduce a worker's vigilance.

We followed this procedure to select the 150 jobs included in the lists in this book:

1. We began with the 801 civilian job titles in the SOC database. Of these, 726 are linked to O*NET jobs that have ratings for at least nine of the 11 stress-related factors.

2. We eliminated all occupations that were rated higher than 75 (on a scale from 0 to 100) on Stress Tolerance. This left 384 occupations.

3. Next, we eliminated all occupations that were rated higher than 85 on any of the other stress-related factors, with the exception of Duration of Typical Work Week. This left 242 occupations.

4. For the final round of elimination on the basis of stress, we removed all occupations that were rated higher than 87.5 on Duration of Typical Work Week. This left 205 occupations.

5. Of these, 192 occupations have the full range of information—economic topics, work tasks, skills, and work conditions—needed for a reasonably complete description in this book.

6. Next, we eliminated 32 jobs that cannot be considered best jobs because of their low economic rewards. Four of these are expected to employ fewer than 500 workers per year and to shrink rather than grow in workforce size. Another 28 jobs have annual earnings of less than $20,270, which means that 75 percent of workers earn more than the workers in these jobs.

7. We ranked the 160 remaining low-stress, high-reward jobs three times, based on these major criteria: median annual earnings, projected growth through 2016, and number of job openings projected per year.

8. We then added the three numerical rankings for each job to calculate its overall score.

9. To emphasize jobs that tend to pay more, are likely to grow more rapidly, and have more job openings, we selected the 150 job titles with the best total overall scores.

For example, the low-stress job with the best combined score for earnings, growth, and number of job openings is Computer Software Engineers, Applications, so this job is listed first even though it's not the best-paying job (which is Physicists) or the job with the most openings (which is Laborers and Freight, Stock, and Material Movers, Hand).

Why This Book Has More Than 150 Job Descriptions

We didn't think you would mind that this book actually provides information on more than 150 jobs. The jobs that are listed in Part II, as mentioned earlier, are based on the SOC taxonomy, but in Part III we describe these jobs on the basis of information from related low-stress jobs in the O*NET database. Several of the SOC job titles link to two or more low-stress O*NET job titles, which means that although we used 150 job titles to construct the lists, Part III actually has a total of 168 job descriptions.

Understand the Limits of the Data in This Book

In this book we use the most reliable and up-to-date information available on earnings, projected growth, number of openings, and other topics. The earnings and employment-projection data came from the U.S. Department of Labor's Bureau of Labor Statistics. As you look at the figures, keep in mind that they are estimates. They give you a general idea about the number of workers employed, annual earnings, rate of job growth, and annual job openings.

Understand that a problem with such data is that it describes an average. Just as there is no precisely average person, there is no such thing as a statistically average example of a particular job. We say this because data, while helpful, can also be misleading.

Take, for example, the yearly earnings information in this book. This is highly reliable data obtained from a very large U.S. working population sample by the Bureau of Labor Statistics. It tells us the average annual pay received as of May 2006 by people in various job titles (actually, it's the median annual pay, which means that half earned more and half less).

This sounds great, except that half of all people in that occupation earned less than that amount. For example, people who are new to the occupation or with only a few years of work experience often earn much less than the median amount. People who live in rural areas or who work for smaller employers typically earn less than those who do similar work in cities (where the cost of living is higher) or for bigger employers. People in certain areas of the country earn less than those in others. Other factors also influence how much you are likely to earn in a given job in your area. For example, the approximately 20,000 Computer Software Engineers, Applications, in the San Jose–Sunnyvale–Santa Clara, California, metropolitan area have median earnings of $100,630 (compared to a national average of $79,780), probably because they work where the red-hot high-tech industry is concentrated and they can collaborate productively with other workers. By comparison, the main industry in the Santa Fe, New Mexico, metropolitan area is state government; the 50 workers in the same occupation there earn only a median of $61,390—a good salary, but so much lower than that of their Silicon Valley colleagues.

Also keep in mind that the figures for job growth and number of openings are projections by labor economists—their best guesses about what we can expect between now and 2016. They are not guarantees. A major economic downturn, war, or technological breakthrough could change the actual outcome.

Finally, don't forget that the job market consists of both job openings and job *seekers*. The figures on job growth and openings don't tell you how many people will be competing with you to be hired. The Department of Labor doesn't publish figures on the supply of job candidates, so we are unable to tell you about the level of competition you can expect. Competition is an important issue that you should research for any tentative career goal. The *Occupational Outlook Handbook* provides informative statements for many occupations. You should speak to people who educate or train tomorrow's workers; they probably have a good idea of how many graduates find rewarding employment and how quickly. People in the workforce also can provide insights into this issue. Use your critical thinking skills to evaluate what people tell you. For example, educators or trainers may be trying to recruit you, whereas people in the workforce may be trying to discourage you from competing. Get a variety of opinions to balance out possible biases.

So, in reviewing the information in this book, please understand the limitations of the data. You need to use common sense in career decision making as in most other things in life. We hope that, by using that approach, you find the information helpful and interesting.

The Data Complexities

For those of you who like details, we present some of the complexities inherent in our sources of information and what we did to make sense of them here. You don't need to know this to use the book, so jump to the next section of the introduction if you are bored with details.

We include information on level of stress, earnings, projected growth, and number of job openings for each job throughout this book.

Level of Stress

The information in this book on the level of stress in various jobs was obtained from the O*NET database. The jobs sorted for the Part II lists, however, are SOC (Standard Occupational Classification) occupations rather than O*NET occupations. In some cases, a job on a list represents two or more O*NET jobs. For example, the SOC job Social Science Research Assistants is linked to two O*NET jobs, Social Science Research Assistants (rated 61.7 on Level of Stress Tolerance) and City and Regional Planning Aides (rated 83.3). These two O*NET jobs also have different ratings for the other stress-related features we used to create lists. As noted earlier in this introduction, we determined the ratings for SOC jobs such as Social Science Research Assistants by taking the average of the ratings for the related O*NET jobs. In the case of Social Science Research Assistants, the average for Level of Stress Tolerance comes to 72.5, which is low enough for us to retain this job on our list of the 150 best low-stress jobs. However, in Part III we don't include a description of one of the two linked jobs, City and Regional Planning Aides, because its rating for Stress Tolerance (83.3) is too high to meet our cutoff level (75).

Level of Stress Tolerance serves as an overall measure of the amount of stress workers are subjected to. The average rating for all jobs in O*NET is 75.2 (on a scale from 0 to 100), quite close to our cutoff level of 75. Because we eliminated all jobs rated above 75, the average rating for the jobs in this book is 64.8. (These are *weighted averages*, meaning that ratings of jobs with larger workforces are given proportionately greater weight.)

Another stress-related factor on which all jobs in O*NET are rated is Duration of Typical Work Week; we eliminated all jobs rated higher than 87.5 on this measure. (The scale ranges from 0 to 100, so our cutoff level isn't 87.5 *hours* per week.) The average rating for all jobs is 57.9. You may be surprised to learn that the average for the jobs in this book is actually slightly higher than average, 63.3. This probably occurred because we chose our list partly by emphasizing earnings and job outlook, and it happens that the low-stress jobs with the best economic rewards tend to require a slightly longer work week than is typical.

Following are the nine other stress-related factors that we used in selecting the jobs for this book. We eliminated all jobs rated higher than 85 on *any* of these measures, so the presence of just one of these stressors at a high level kept a job out of this book. The table shows the weighted average rating for all jobs and for the 150 jobs included in this book.

Stress-Related Factor	Average Rating for All Jobs	Average Rating for Jobs in This Book
Consequence of Error	42.9	43.9
Deal With Physically Aggressive People	15.9	9.2
Deal With Unpleasant or Angry People	54.4	43.2
Frequency of Conflict Situations	49.9	43.3
Impact of Decisions on Co-workers or Company Results	67.4	61.6
Importance of Being Exact or Accurate	75.9	73.8
Level of Competition	45.6	43.6
Pace Determined by Speed of Equipment	22.8	31.4
Time Pressure	67.6	68.3

Note that the jobs in this book are rated lower than average on most of these stress-related factors and are rated significantly higher on only one factor: Pace Determined by Speed of Equipment. Several otherwise low-stress jobs—such as Food Batchmakers, Bindery Workers, and Printing Machine Operators—require workers to keep pace with production machinery at a level above average, but still lower than the cutoff level of 85. If you have a particular objection to this or any other stress-related factor, you can look in Part II for the list of jobs low in that stressor. The job descriptions in Part III also identify the highest- and lowest-rated stress-related factors for each job, so you can steer clear of jobs where a particular stress-producing work condition dominates and seek those jobs where it's not a problem.

Earnings

The employment security agency of each state gathers information on earnings for various jobs and forwards it to the U.S. Bureau of Labor Statistics (BLS). This information is organized in standardized ways by a BLS program called Occupational Employment Statistics (OES). To keep the earnings for the various jobs and regions comparable, the OES screens out certain types of earnings and includes others, so the OES earnings we use in this book represent straight-time gross pay exclusive of premium pay. More specifically, the OES earnings include the job's base rate; cost-of-living allowances; guaranteed pay; hazardous-duty pay; incentive pay, including commissions and production bonuses; on-call pay; and tips, but don't include back pay, jury duty pay, overtime pay, severance pay, shift differentials, nonproduction bonuses, or tuition reimbursements. Also, self-employed workers aren't included in the estimates, and they can be a significant segment in certain occupations. When data on annual earnings for an occupation is highly unreliable, OES doesn't report a figure, which meant that we reluctantly had to exclude from this book a few occupations such as Hunters and Trappers. The median earnings for all workers in all occupations were $30,400 in May 2006. The 150 low-stress jobs in this book were chosen partly on the basis of good earnings, but their average (weighted to give greater emphasis to the jobs with the largest workforces) is only a little higher: $33,123.

The sad truth is that the highest-paying jobs tend to be stressful; if we created a list of the 150 best *high*-stress jobs (based on those that we eliminated from this book), the weighted average of their earnings would be $51,025.

The earnings data from the OES survey is reported under a system of job titles called the Standard Occupational Classification system, or SOC. These are the job titles we use in the lists in Part II, but in Part III we cross-reference these titles to O*NET job titles so we can provide O*NET-derived information on many useful topics. In some cases, an SOC title cross-references to more than one O*NET job title. For example, the SOC title Farm, Ranch, and Other Agricultural Managers, which we use in Part II, is linked to three jobs described in Part III: Aquacultural Managers; Crop and Livestock Managers; and Nursery and Greenhouse Managers. Because earnings data is available only for the combined job title Farm, Ranch, and Other Agricultural Managers, in Part III you will find the same earnings figure, $52,070, reported for all three kinds of agricultural managers. In reality, the earnings of these three kinds of agricultural managers probably vary, but this single figure of $52,070 is the best information available.

Projected Growth and Number of Job Openings

This information comes from the Office of Occupational Statistics and Employment Projections, a program within the Bureau of Labor Statistics that develops information about projected trends in the nation's labor market for the next ten years. The most recent projections available cover the years from 2006 to 2016. The projections are based on information about people moving into and out of occupations. The BLS uses data from various sources in projecting the growth and number of openings for each job title: Some data comes from the Census Bureau's Current Population Survey and some comes from an OES survey. The projections assume that there will be no major war, depression, or other economic upheaval.

Like the earnings figures, the figures on projected growth and job openings are reported according to the SOC classification, so again you will find that some of the SOC jobs that we use in Part II crosswalk to more than one O*NET job in Part III. To continue the example we used earlier, SOC reports growth (1.1 percent) and openings (18,101) for one occupation called Farm, Ranch, and Other Agricultural Managers, but in Part III of this book we report these figures separately for the occupations Aquacultural Managers, Crop and Livestock Managers, and Nursery and Greenhouse Managers. In Part III, when you see that the Aquacultural Managers job is described as having 1.1 percent projected growth and 18,101 projected job openings and the other two agricultural management jobs are described with the same two numbers, you should realize that the 1.1-percent rate of projected growth represents the *average* of these three occupations—one may actually experience higher growth than the other—and that these three occupations will *share* the 18,101 projected openings.

Although salary figures are fairly straightforward, you may not know what to make of job-growth figures. For example, is projected growth of 15 percent good or bad? Keep in mind that the average (mean) growth projected for all occupations by the Bureau of Labor Statistics is 10.4 percent. One-quarter of the SOC occupations have a growth projection of 1.1 percent or lower. Growth of 9.2 percent is the median, meaning that half of the occupations have more, half less. Only one-quarter of the occupations have growth projected at more than 14.6 percent.

Much of the job growth in our economy is happening for jobs that cause a lot of stress, such as jobs in health care that involve life-and-death decisions or jobs in the business world that can require working long hours. As a result, many of the fastest-growing jobs have been eliminated from this book. Therefore, even though the jobs in this book were selected as "best" partly on the basis of job growth, their mean growth is 4.7 percent, which is significantly lower than the mean for all jobs. Among these 150 jobs, the four jobs ranked 37th by projected growth have a figure of 10.9 percent, the job ranked 75th (the median) has a projected growth of 6.7 percent, and the job ranked 112th has a projected growth of –0.2 percent. Of the 150 jobs, one-quarter are expected to shrink in size.

The number of projected job openings for low-stress jobs is similar to the rate of job growth: lower than the national average for all occupations. The economy is expected to add an average of 26,923,474 job openings per year between 2006 and 2016, or an average of about 365,000 job openings per year for the 750 occupations that BLS studies. Some of these openings are newly created jobs (for example, when a new business opens or an existing business expands); others are replacement positions that open when a worker moves to another job, retires, or dies.

Some of the 150 occupations in this book are projected to provide a larger number of annual job openings than others, so you may wonder what an average number of openings might be. For these 150 occupations, the average number is 26,202. One-quarter of the occupations are projected to provide 2,657 openings or fewer. The median is 6,562. Only one-quarter of the occupations are projected to offer more than 17,920 openings.

However, keep in mind that figures for job openings depend on how BLS defines an occupation. For example, consider the occupation Stock Clerks and Order Fillers, which employs a very large workforce—1,704,921 in 2006—and is expected to provide 439,327 job openings per year, many of which will be replacement positions because of high turnover. The BLS regards this as one occupation, but O*NET divides it into four separate occupations: Marking Clerks; Order Fillers, Wholesale and Retail Sales; Stock Clerks, Sales Floor; and Stock Clerks—Stockroom, Warehouse, or Storage Yard. If the BLS employment-projection tables were to list these as four separate occupations and divide the 439,327 openings among them, the average number of openings for all occupations would be smaller. So it follows that because the way BLS defines occupations is somewhat arbitrary, any "average" figure for job openings is also somewhat arbitrary. Nevertheless, it is hard to avoid the conclusion that our economy is producing more job openings for high-stress jobs than for good low-stress jobs.

Perhaps you're wondering why we present figures on both job growth *and* number of openings. Aren't these two ways of saying the same thing? Actually, you need to know both. Consider the occupation Hydrologists, which is projected to grow at the outstanding rate of 24.3 percent. There should be lots of opportunities in such a fast-growing job, right? Not exactly. This is a tiny occupation, with only about 8,300 people currently employed, so even though it's growing rapidly, it won't create many new jobs (687 per year). Now consider Stock Clerks and Order Fillers. This occupation will be 7.7 percent *smaller* in 2016 than it was in 2006, held back by computer programs that automate many routine tasks. Nevertheless, this is a huge occupation that employs about 1.7 million workers, so even though it's shrinking in size, it's expected to take on 440,000 new workers each year as existing workers retire, die, or move on to other jobs. That's why we base our selection of the best jobs on both of these economic indicators and why you should pay attention to both when you scan our lists of best jobs.

How This Book Is Organized

The information in this book about best low-stress jobs moves from the general to the highly specific.

Part I. Cures for Workplace Stress

This part of the book defines workplace stress, explains how it is harmful to your mental and physical health, and provides pointers on how to avoid it or cope with it. If you're not yet ready to switch to one of the low-stress jobs included in this book, you may benefit from the coping strategies mentioned here.

Part II. The Best Jobs Lists

For many people, the 96 lists in Part II are the most interesting feature of the book. Here, you can see titles of the 150 jobs that avoid high stress and have the best combination of high salaries, fast growth, and plentiful job openings. You can see which jobs are best in terms of each of these factors combined and considered separately. Additional lists highlight jobs that avoid particular types of stress and jobs with a high percentage of female, male, part-time, and self-employed workers. Look in the Table of Contents for a complete list of lists. Although there are many lists, they're not difficult to understand because they have clear titles and are organized into groupings of related lists.

Depending on your situation, some of the lists in Part II will interest you more than others. For example, if you are young, you may be interested in the best-paying low-stress jobs that employ high percentages of people age 16–24. Other lists show jobs within interest groupings, personality types, levels of education, or other ways that you might find helpful in exploring your career options.

Whatever your situation, we suggest you use the lists that make sense for you to help explore career options. Following are the names of each group of lists along with short comments on each group. You will find additional information in a brief introduction provided at the beginning of each group of lists in Part II.

Best Low-Stress Jobs Overall: Jobs with the Highest Pay, Fastest Growth, and Most Openings

Four lists are in this group, and they are the ones that most people want to see first. The first list presents the top 150 low-stress job titles in order of their combined scores for earnings, growth, and number of job openings. All other lists in the book are based on these 150 jobs. The three additional lists in this group present the 50 jobs with the highest earnings, the 50 jobs projected to grow most rapidly, and the 50 jobs with the most openings.

Best Jobs with the Least Stress

The first of these two lists shows the 50 jobs that are rated lowest on an overall measure of stress. The second list shows the 20 jobs from this set that ranked highest on economic measures. The jobs on these two lists have very low stress but also have fairly low economic rewards. They illustrate the principle that you may need to tolerate some kinds of stress to hold a job with good income and job opportunities.

Best Jobs Low in Particular Stressful Features

This set consists of nine pairs of lists. In each pair, the first list shows the 50 jobs that have the least amount of a particular feature that contributes to stress, such as dealing with physically aggressive people. The second list shows the 20 jobs from this set that are best in terms of income, job growth, and job openings.

Best Low-Stress Jobs Lists by Demographic

This group of lists presents interesting information for various types of people based on data from the U.S. Census Bureau. The lists are arranged into groups for workers age 16–24, workers 55 and older, part-time workers, self-employed workers, women, and men. We created five lists for each group, basing the last four on the information in the first list:

◎ The low-stress jobs having the highest percentage of people of each type

◎ The 25 jobs with the highest combined scores for earnings, growth, and number of openings

◎ The 25 jobs with the highest earnings

◎ The 25 jobs with the highest growth rates

◎ The 25 jobs with the largest number of openings

Best Low-Stress Jobs Sorted by Education or Training Required

We created separate lists for each level of education, training, and experience as defined by the U.S. Department of Labor. We put each of the top 150 job titles into one of the lists based on the kind of preparation required for entry. Jobs within these lists are presented in order of their total combined scores for earnings, growth, and number of openings. The lists include low-stress jobs in these groupings:

◎ Short-term on-the-job training

◎ Moderate-term on-the-job training

◎ Long-term on-the-job training

◎ Work experience in a related job

◎ Postsecondary vocational training

◎ Associate degree

◎ Bachelor's degree

◎ Work experience plus degree

◎ Master's degree

◎ Doctoral degree

Best Low-Stress Jobs Sorted by Interests

These lists organize the 150 best jobs into groups based on interests. Within each list, jobs are presented in order of their total scores for earnings, growth, and number of openings. Here are the 16 interest areas used in these lists: Agriculture and Natural Resources; Architecture and Construction; Arts and Communication; Business and Administration; Education and Training; Finance and Insurance; Government and Public Administration; Health Science; Hospitality, Tourism, and Recreation; Human Service; Information Technology; Law and Public Safety; Manufacturing; Retail and Wholesale Sales and Service; Scientific Research, Engineering, and Mathematics; and Transportation, Distribution, and Logistics.

Best Low-Stress Jobs Sorted by Personality Types

These lists organize the 150 best jobs into six personality types described in the introduction to the lists: Realistic, Investigative, Artistic, Social, Enterprising, and Conventional. The jobs within each list are presented in order of their total scores for earnings, growth, and number of openings.

Bonus Lists: Jobs Rated Low on Factors That Are Stressful for Some People

These four pairs of lists show jobs that are low in certain features that don't bother many people but are intensely stressful to a limited number of people, such as public speaking. In each pair, the first list shows the 50 jobs with the lowest rating for the stressful feature; the second list shows the 20 best of these jobs, based on economic criteria.

Part III: Descriptions of the Best Low-Stress Jobs

This part contains 168 job descriptions and covers each of the 150 best low-stress jobs, using a format that is informative yet compact and easy to read. The descriptions contain statistics such as earnings and projected percent of growth; ratings of overall stress and specific sources of stress that are both high and low; lists such as major skills and work tasks; and key descriptors such as personality type and interest field. Because the jobs in this section are arranged in alphabetical order, you can easily find a job that you've identified from Part II and that you want to learn more about.

In some cases, a job title in Part II cross-references to two or more job titles in Part III. For example, if you look up Conservation Scientists in Part III, you'll find a note telling you to look at the descriptions for Soil and Water Conservationists, Range Managers, and Park Naturalists. That's why Part III has 168 descriptions rather than 150.

These differences between Part II jobs and Part III jobs sometimes appear to cause inconsistencies. For example, the SOC job Social Science Research Assistants does not appear on the Part II list of 50 jobs with the least frequent conflict situations because the job's rating on this stress factor is relatively high at 39.7. The rating of 39.7 for this SOC job represents the *average* of the ratings of *two* related O*NET jobs: Social Science Research Assistants (rated 28.7) and City and Regional Planning Aides (rated 50.7). In Part III, however, the job description of the O*NET job Social Science Research Assistants shows the job's rating for Frequency of Conflict Situations as 28.7—uninfluenced by the rating of its sister occupation City and Regional Planning Aides. Fortunately, these differences between Part II jobs and related Part III jobs are rare.

We used the most current information from a variety of government sources to create the descriptions. Although we've tried to make the descriptions easy to understand, the sample that follows—with an explanation of each of its parts—may help you better understand and use the descriptions.

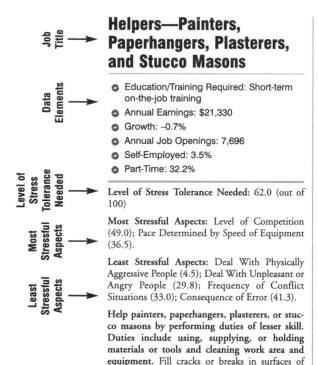

Job Title →

Helpers—Painters, Paperhangers, Plasterers, and Stucco Masons

Data Elements →

- Education/Training Required: Short-term on-the-job training
- Annual Earnings: $21,330
- Growth: –0.7%
- Annual Job Openings: 7,696
- Self-Employed: 3.5%
- Part-Time: 32.2%

Level of Stress Tolerance Needed →

Level of Stress Tolerance Needed: 62.0 (out of 100)

Most Stressful Aspects →

Most Stressful Aspects: Level of Competition (49.0); Pace Determined by Speed of Equipment (36.5).

Least Stressful Aspects →

Least Stressful Aspects: Deal With Physically Aggressive People (4.5); Deal With Unpleasant or Angry People (29.8); Frequency of Conflict Situations (33.0); Consequence of Error (41.3).

Summary Description and Tasks →

Help painters, paperhangers, plasterers, or stucco masons by performing duties of lesser skill. Duties include using, supplying, or holding materials or tools and cleaning work area and equipment. Fill cracks or breaks in surfaces of plaster articles or areas with putty or epoxy compounds. Clean work areas and equipment. Apply protective coverings such as masking tape to articles or areas that could be damaged or stained by work processes. Supply or hold tools and materials. Place articles to be stripped into stripping tanks. Pour specified amounts of chemical solutions into stripping tanks. Smooth surfaces of articles to be painted, using sanding and buffing tools and equipment. Mix plaster and carry it to plasterers. Perform support duties to assist painters, paperhangers, plasterers, or masons. Remove articles such as cabinets, metal furniture, and paint containers from stripping tanks after prescribed periods of time. Erect scaffolding.

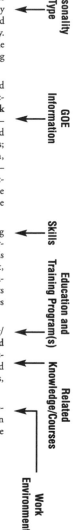

Personality Type →

Personality Type: Realistic. Realistic occupations frequently involve work activities that include practical, hands-on problems and solutions. They often deal with plants; animals; and real-world materials such as wood, tools, and machinery. Many of the occupations require working outside and do not involve a lot of paperwork or working closely with others.

GOE Information →

GOE—Interest Area: 02. Architecture and Construction. **Work Group:** 02.06. Construction Support/Labor. **Other Jobs in This Work Group:** Construction Laborers; Helpers—Brickmasons, Blockmasons, Stone-masons, and Tile and Marble Setters; Helpers—Carpenters; Helpers—Electricians; Helpers—Installation, Maintenance, and Repair Workers; Helpers—Pipelayers, Plumbers, Pipefitters, and Steamfitters; Helpers—Roofers; Highway Maintenance Workers; Septic Tank Servicers and Sewer Pipe Cleaners.

Skills →

Skills—Equipment Maintenance: Performing routine maintenance on equipment and determining when and what kind of maintenance is needed. **Installation:** Installing equipment, machines, wiring, or programs to meet specifications. **Quality Control Analysis:** Conducting tests and inspections of products, services, or processes to evaluate quality or performance.

Education and Training Program(s) →

Education and Training Program: Painting/Painter and Wall Coverer Training. **Related Knowledge/Course: Building and Construction:** Materials, methods, and the tools involved in the construction or repair of houses, buildings, or other structures such as highways and roads.

Related Knowledge/Courses →

Work Environment →

Work Environment: Outdoors; standing; climbing ladders, scaffolds, or poles; using hands on objects, tools, or controls; bending or twisting the body; repetitive motions.

Here are some details on each of the major parts of the job descriptions you will find in Part III:

- **Job Title:** This is the title for the job as defined by the U.S. Department of Labor and used in its O*NET database.

- **Data Elements:** The information comes from various U.S. Department of Labor and Census Bureau databases, as explained elsewhere in this introduction.

- **Level of Stress Tolerance Needed:** This figure is a measure of the overall level of stress on the job. The number is derived from the O*NET database and is expressed on a scale in which 0 is the lowest rating and 100 the highest. These ratings aren't percentages; they represent the level of stress tolerance needed for the job, not the amount of time spent exposed to stress. The average rating for all jobs in O*NET is 75.2. Only four jobs in Part III are rated higher than this average.

- **Most Stressful Aspects**: As many as four most stressful features of the job are listed here, based on the same O*NET ratings used to create the lists in Part II. The list includes only stressful features that are rated higher than the average for all jobs, and they are arranged in descending order of their ratings on a scale of 0 to 100.

- **Least Stressful Aspects**: This list is based on the same data as the list of Most Stressful Aspects, but it includes as many as four stressful features that are rated *lower* than the average for all jobs. They are arranged in ascending order of their ratings.

- **Summary Description and Tasks:** The boldfaced sentence provides a summary description of the occupation. It's followed by a listing of tasks that are generally performed by people who work in this job. This information comes from the O*NET database but where necessary has been edited to avoid exceeding 2,200 characters.

- **Personality Type:** The O*NET database assigns each job to its most closely related personality type. Our job descriptions include the name of the related personality type as well as a brief definition of this personality type.

- **GOE Information:** This information cross-references the Guide for Occupational Exploration (GOE), a system developed by the U.S. Department of Labor that organizes jobs based on interests. We use the groups from the *New Guide for Occupational Exploration*, Fourth Edition, as published by JIST. That book uses a set of interest areas based on the 16 career clusters developed by the U.S. Department of Education and used in various career information systems. Here, we include the major Interest Area the job fits into, its more-specific Work Group, and a list of related O*NET job titles that are in this same GOE Work Group. This information will help you identify other job titles that have similar interests or require similar skills, but note that not all jobs in a work group are low in stress. You can find a list of the GOE Interest Areas and Work Groups in the appendix.

- **Skills:** For each job, we included the skills whose level-of-performance scores exceeded the average for all jobs by the greatest amount and whose ratings on the importance scale were higher than very low. We included as many as six such skills for each job, and we ranked them by the extent to which their rating exceeds the average.

- **Education and Training Program(s):** This part of the job description provides the name of the educational or training program or programs for the job. It will help you identify sources of formal or informal training for a job that interests you. To get this information, we adapted a crosswalk created by the National Center for O*NET Development to connect information in the Classification of Instructional Programs (CIP) to the O*NET job titles used in this book. We made various changes to connect the O*NET job titles to the education or training programs related to them and modified the names of some education and training programs so that they would be more easily understood. In three cases, we abbreviated the listing of related programs for the sake of space; such entries end with "others."

- **Related Knowledge/Courses:** This entry can help you understand the most important knowledge areas required for a job and the types of courses or programs you will likely need to take to prepare for it. We used information in the Department of Labor's O*NET database for this entry. For each job, we identified any knowledge area with a rating that was higher than the average rating for that knowledge area for all jobs; then we listed as many as six in descending order.

- **Work Environment:** We included any work condition with a rating that exceeds the midpoint of the rating scale. The order doesn't indicate their frequency on the job. Consider whether you like these conditions and whether any of these conditions would make you uncomfortable. Keep in mind that when hazards are present (for example, contaminants), protective equipment and procedures are provided to keep you safe.

Getting all the information we used in the job descriptions wasn't a simple process, and it's not always perfect. Even so, we used the best and most recent sources of data we could find, and we think that our efforts will be helpful to many people.

PART I

Cures for Workplace Stress

The best cure for workplace stress is to avoid exposure to it in the first place. This book may help you identify jobs that are low in stress. Nevertheless, even the most laid-back job has occasional moments of stress, and almost all the jobs in this book have features that can be stressful at some times and for some people. (These features are identified in the job descriptions in Part III.)

Because job stress is a matter of concern to you—that's why you're reading this book—we thought it would be helpful to include a chapter about what workplace stress is and how to cope with it.

Workplace Stress Defined

To understand workplace stress, it helps to think about how stress differs from challenge. A workplace challenge puts a demand on you that temporarily goes beyond the routine level for your job. For example, a challenge may require that you think harder, be more creative, exert more physical strength, show more patience, put in extra hours, face more competition, pay extra attention to details, or speed up to meet a certain deadline. You willingly face a challenge because you understand that it is an exceptional part of your work and that you have a reasonable chance of meeting the demand. If you meet a challenge, you get a feeling of accomplishment and maybe even the recognition of your boss, co-workers, or customers. You can relax afterward, knowing that a similar demand won't arise for a while. Even if you don't meet the challenge, you still have the feeling that you might be able to tackle a similar demand in the future—besides, such challenges are the exception rather than the norm for your job.

But what if the demand greatly exceeds your abilities and you have good reason to expect to fail? And what if the demand is the normal level of expected work output rather than the exception? Then what you feel isn't challenge, but *stress*. The greater effort saps your energy; the demands on your patience leave you burnt out; the longer hours of work feel like a prison sentence; the competition and deadline pressure feel like a rat race. Instead of getting a sense of accomplishment, you feel frustrated and inadequate. You can't relax, even after successfully meeting one demand, because you know you will soon be hit with another that might overwhelm you. You feel as though your shortcomings are on display rather than your abilities, and you worry about losing your job—or about what will happen if you quit.

From this definition, it follows that workplace stress is, to some extent, subjective. Different people have different abilities, and a workplace task or situation that is simply challenging to Jill may be very stressful to Jack because it demands a level or type of performance that Jack can't meet or sustain. In some cases, the difference between challenge and stress is a matter of highly personal perceptions. For example, a job that requires workers to climb ladders would be mildly challenging to most people but extremely stressful to someone with a fear of heights. A job that requires a lot of work with the public would be attractive to extroverts but stressful to introverts.

A study by the National Institute for Occupational Safety and Health pointed out additional individual factors that can make the difference between a stressful work situation and a tolerable one: the balance between work and family life, which may be good or bad; having or lacking a support network of friends and co-workers; and having a relaxed and positive outlook as opposed to a tense and negative outlook.

Nevertheless, certain demands of work are stressful to almost everyone if they occur at a very high level. For example, only a few workaholics enjoy laboring for very long hours. Very few people enjoy spending most of the workday confronting physically aggressive people or being under constant time pressure. Most workers want to avoid being required to make life-or-death decisions routinely. Therefore, to create this book, we decided on a set of widely disliked stressors and put together a list of jobs in which these are *not* found at a high level. In the introduction you can read a detailed explanation of how we did this.

What's Wrong with Workplace Stress?

Many people seek challenge on the job, but when workplace demands exceed the level of challenge and become stress, they can be very destructive.

The human body reacts to a perceived threat by preparing to fight or flee: Sensory and cognitive abilities sharpen, the lungs take in more air, the heart beats faster, blood pressure rises, the spleen secretes extra red blood cells, digestion slows down, the liver pumps glucose into the bloodstream, fat is converted into energy, and energy is diverted from the immune and reproductive systems to other purposes. These responses are helpful for dealing with an occasional short-lived demand, especially one that results in a vigorous physical response. (Think of how our distant ancestors reacted to a crouching lion.) But if the demands occur constantly, the body's constant readiness for fighting or fleeing produces harmful effects, especially if this revved-up condition occurs in a sedentary job that offers minimal opportunities for physical response. It's like flooring your car's gas pedal and brake simultaneously.

Long-term stress produces harmful effects on many parts of our bodies. The hormones that stimulate the brain under stress can damage nerve cells over time, leading to memory loss, depression, sleep loss, or panic attacks. Continuously elevated blood pressure reduces the elasticity of the blood vessels, causing high blood pressure to become the normal state rather than a momentary response. Heart disease results. Decreased blood flow to the intestines can lead to ulcers and perhaps irritable bowel syndrome. The body's increased tolerance for elevated blood glucose levels can lead to diabetes. Fat is redistributed to the abdomen, where it can respond faster to the liver but where it is more dangerous to accumulate. The weakened immune system can leave the body vulnerable to infections. The reproductive system suffers, causing a decrease in potency or fertility.

One study found that health-care expenditures are nearly 50 percent greater for workers who report high levels of stress compared to workers who report low levels. The St. Paul Fire and Marine Insurance Company concluded that health complaints are more strongly associated with problems at work than with any other life stressors, more so than even financial problems or family problems. It is estimated that between 70 and 80 percent of all visits to physicians are for stress-related disorders. A study by the University of London found that unmanaged stress was a more dangerous risk factor for heart disease and cancer than cigarette smoking or high-cholesterol foods.

The harmful effects of stress on the body can be compounded by additional damage when stressed workers abuse alcohol. Research indicates that only a minority of workers react to job stress by turning to drink, but those who do are much more likely to be heavy drinkers.

Even worse, workplace stress sometimes reinforces itself. People who show up for work while sick, depressed, or hung over are less able to function well and are more likely to perceive a given job demand as stressful. They have a greater chance of being injured on the job. Stress-related illness also may keep them home from work. The business may suffer because of poor performance and absenteeism of stressed-out workers, and when the business is in trouble, the employees are likely to feel additional stress.

Workplace stress isn't a problem only for individual workers or their employers; it's a national problem. In a study by Northwestern National Life, 40 percent of workers reported their job as "very or extremely stressful," and 25 percent reported their job as the number-one stressor in their lives. These health problems add up: In the United States, about one million workers per day call in sick because of stress-related illness. Worker stress is estimated to cost American businesses between $50 billion and $150 billion each year in health expenses and lost productivity.

Home life also suffers. A survey by the Anxiety Disorders Association of America found that of workers who said that stress affects their work, 81 percent said it interferes with their relationship with their spouse or significant other and more than a third said it affects their relationship with their children.

Workplace stress affects people of all ages. Older workers who have endured many years of working in stressful situations may feel burnt out and may start to feel the accumulated harmful effects on their physical health. Changes in technology may place unexpected demands on their skills and make them anxious about their future employability. But young workers also suffer from stress. It used to be common to hear about "mid-life career changers," but nowadays one also hears the phrase "quarter-life career changers" because so many people in their 20s feel the need for a career change—most often because of stress. Many of these young workers were lured into an occupation by its high economic rewards and then discovered that they couldn't tolerate the stresses that the job imposed. Many promising careers are highly competitive or require long hours. Furthermore, some college graduates with excellent technical skills are poorly equipped with the social skills they need to interact with bosses, co-workers, and clients. And the effects of job stress start to appear long before these workers grow gray hair. One study found that young people in high-stress jobs were twice as likely to suffer serious depression or anxiety as those in low-stress jobs.

Some workers claim that they "thrive on stress," but they probably are using the word "stress" to refer to occasional workplace demands that they are capable of handling and that give them a sense of accomplishment. By definition, these are *challenges*, not true stressors. Or perhaps these stress-seekers are habitual procrastinators whose preferred working style is to postpone a task until the deadline is very close. Usually they adopt this strategy so that the fast turnaround time serves as an excuse for not doing the task perfectly. They are perfectionists who find it less stressful to work under time pressure than to admit to themselves and to others that they make mistakes even when they have lots of time to do the job. These workers would probably improve their health if they learned to accept their lack of perfection and abandoned their habit of scheduling work for the last minute.

Coping with Workplace Stress

Some people say, "Whatever doesn't kill me makes me stronger," but medical research about stress indicates that stress actually weakens the body, so a tough-guy attitude doesn't help. What can you do instead to cope with workplace stress?

Coping with workplace stress involves three main strategies: developing personal stress management techniques, imposing appropriate changes on the organization, or finding a less stressful job.

Developing Personal Stress Management Techniques

Earlier in this chapter, *workplace stress* was defined as a demand that a worker is unlikely to meet and that isn't an exceptional part of the job. Logically, it follows that one way a worker can cope with a stressor is to find a way to be able to meet the demand. For example, if you must operate unfamiliar equipment, use a level of mathematics you didn't learn in school, or deal with a new regulatory environment, you can get training or education that prepares you to handle these demands competently. If a co-worker is sexually harassing you, you can learn how to seek the protection of the relevant laws and personnel policies. In some cases, you can even cope with changes in the physical demands of your job through physical conditioning and retraining.

However, some workplace demands can't be overcome through education or training. Suppose that you work for a small business. A competitor offering the same service opens a business right across the street, dramatically raising the level of competition your employer faces. Also suppose that this competitor stays open for business 80 hours per week, causing your boss to ask you to work longer hours just to compete. With some additional education or training, you may be able to improve your productivity and the quality of the services your employer provides, thus making your employer more successful at competing with the newcomer. But these efforts probably will take some time to bear fruit and may not enable you to avoid working longer hours, so you can't avoid an increase in your level of workplace stress.

However, you can cope with increased workplace stress through a variety of stress management techniques:

- **Identify what's stressing you and set priorities:** You probably can't defuse every stressful aspect of your work—unless you quit, which creates new stresses. So focus on the most severe stressors that you have the greatest likelihood of being able to change. Avoid perfectionism, which is a self-imposed form of stress; accept the fact that you make mistakes and view them as opportunities for learning. Be realistic about the goals you set for yourself.

- **Speak up:** Don't suffer in silence. (One survey found that 60 percent of workers do.) Often, your boss or co-workers can make adjustments to your work situation that may reduce or eliminate stressors. The key is for you to avoid whining and make the case that reducing the stress will increase your productivity. Ask for the resources you need and show appreciation for the support you get. If you're self-employed, let your family know what's causing stress and enlist their help in reducing it or in making leisure time more rewarding.

- **Put up a fence between work and the rest of your life:** Avoid letting a cell phone or e-mail chain you to the workplace. Working partly at home can remove you from some office pressures, but it can also blur the line between work and free time. Cultivate friendships with people who aren't co-workers.

- **Get organized:** Sticking tightly (but not obsessively) to a schedule can help you separate work from leisure. It can prevent you from procrastinating and help you limit the amount of time you let yourself think about stressors. Deal with them when they're scheduled and then put them out of your thoughts. You can achieve a similar effect by reducing office clutter. Having dozens of papers lying around the office is like having dozens of voices nagging you to get tasks done and also makes it hard for you to find what you need. If you don't have a job description, ask your boss for one. It will help you set boundaries on what is expected of you.

- **Exercise regularly:** Leave time in your busy schedule for a workout of some kind. You may feel that stress leaves you too tired to exercise, but most people who take up a regular schedule of exercise find that it invigorates them. It also drains away stress-induced hormones and contributes to your long-term health.

- **Eat sensibly and get enough sleep:** Junk food and sleep deprivation can compound stress-related health problems. For example, caffeine and high-carbohydrate foods can increase the rush in blood sugar that stress produces.

◉ **Practice relaxation:** Meditation techniques—even something as simple as slow, rhythmic breathing in a quiet setting—can help you decompress. Some people get similar benefits from extended prayer or a midday nap. Many people believe that bringing a pet to work is helpful (if the employer allows it).

◉ **Build a social life:** Many people find the most rewarding time of the week is the time they spend with family and friends. Try to maximize these times. Social contacts distract you from workplace pressures and can provide support when you're feeling blue. Meet like-minded people through volunteer work, a night class, a book club, a faith community, or a sports league.

◉ **Maintain a sense of humor:** Try to find the humor in your situation. You can't be afraid of something while you're laughing at it. If you can't find any humor in your workplace, find it in your leisure time.

Imposing Appropriate Changes on the Organization

Managers can take steps to alleviate some stressful aspects of a workplace. If you're a manager, you may find some of these techniques useful. If you're not a manager, you—perhaps with the support of other stressed workers—may be able to suggest some of these ideas to the people in charge:

◉ **Redesign work tasks:** Find ways to lighten the workload, create rest breaks, and avoid long hours. Permit flexible hours so workers can deal with family needs. Assign tasks so that workers have some variety and a proportion of tasks that allow for creativity and independent judgment.

◉ **Redesign work roles:** Avoid making workers "wear too many hats." Match workers' assignments to their level of skill.

◉ **Improve communications:** Make clear what is expected of workers. Provide channels through which employees can communicate their concerns and participate in decision making. Keep workers informed about company trends that will affect their careers.

◉ **Improve the work environment:** Fix environmental problems such as overcrowding, excessive noise, inadequate lighting, bad ergonomics, and poor air quality. Make the environment more welcoming by installing lively artwork and potted plants. If uniforms or protective clothing are not needed on the job, allow workers to wear clothing that is casual (within limits) and comfortable.

◉ **Change expectations:** Recognize workers who do their jobs well; in response to a mistake, criticize the performance rather than the worker. Make sure workers feel no fear of violence or sexual harassment and expect that their rights will be defended. Make education and training available so that workers can adapt to change.

These may simply sound like all-around good management techniques, but note how they target stress by reducing demands on workers and preventing exceptional demands from being perceived as the norm. A pressure-cooker atmosphere in the office may *seem* to boost productivity, but it actually produces the opposite effect by increasing absenteeism, burnout, and employee turnover. It also results in higher health-care costs. A study by a health-management company that identified 11 modifiable health-risk factors among employees found that stress was the most costly risk factor—more so than tobacco or alcohol use, weight, high blood pressure, or high cholesterol.

Finding a Less Stressful Job

If your manager fails to reduce stress by following some of the pointers in the previous section, and if personal stress management techniques fail to alleviate the stress you feel on the job, you may decide that your best course of action is to leave your present job and find a less stressful situation. You won't be the only person who is doing this; one survey found that almost one in five respondents had quit a previous position because of job stress. Another estimate is that 40 percent of job turnover is caused by stress.

In some cases, simply moving to a different employer can remove certain stressors. For example, a worksite closer to home or a company with more liberal vacation hours may permit you to spend more time with your family. An employer with a policy of promoting from within may give you a greater feeling of recognition and fewer worries about your career. Even if your work tasks stay the same, your working environment may be more pleasant with a different boss or in a different industry. The clearer your understanding of what you find most stressful in your present job, the easier it will be for you to identify a new position that avoids these stressors. Try to find a way to ask about potential stressors in your interview for the new job and, if possible, speak about them to people working for your prospective employer.

On the other hand, changing employers may not help if what's stressing you is something essential to the nature of your occupation. Perhaps you've been able to tolerate the stressor for several years but have reached the point where you're ready to move on to a different occupation—a second career or a retirement job.

If so, you'll want to consider the jobs included in this book. The lists in Part II and the job descriptions in Part III will help you identify occupations in which you can avoid overall stress and also avoid specific stressful conditions such as time pressure, intense competition, or dealing with unpleasant or angry people. Although some low-stress jobs have low pay or gloomy employment outlook, in Parts II and III you can identify many low-stress jobs that promise good economic rewards.

So don't let yourself become a casualty of workplace stress. Turn the page and start scanning the lists of the best low-stress jobs.

PART II

The Best Jobs Lists: Jobs Low in Stress

This part contains many interesting lists, and it's a good place for you to start using the book. Here are some suggestions for using the lists to explore career options that avoid common causes of stress:

- The table of contents at the beginning of this book presents a complete listing of the list titles in this section. You can browse the lists or use the table of contents to find those that interest you most.

- We gave the lists clear titles, so most require little explanation. We provide comments for each group of lists.

- As you review the lists of jobs, one or more of the jobs may appeal to you enough that you want to seek additional information. As this happens, mark that job (or, if someone else will be using this book, write it on a separate sheet of paper) so that you can look up the description of the job in Part III.

- Keep in mind that all jobs in these lists meet our basic criteria for being included in this book, as explained in the introduction. All lists, therefore, contain jobs that offer lots of opportunities for low-stress work, with emphasis on occupations that have high pay, high growth, or large numbers of openings. These measures are easily quantified and are often presented in lists of best jobs in the newspapers and other media. While earnings, growth, and openings are important, you also should consider other factors in your career planning. Obviously, you are considering the amount of stress that characterizes the job; that's why you're reading this book. Other examples of factors to consider are location, liking the people you work with, and having opportunities to be creative. Many other factors that may help define the ideal job for you are difficult or impossible to quantify and thus aren't used in this book, so you will need to consider the importance of these issues yourself.

- All data used to create these lists comes from the U.S. Department of Labor and the Census Bureau. The earnings figures are based on the average annual pay received by full-time workers. Because the earnings represent the national averages, actual pay rates can vary greatly by location, amount of previous work experience, and other factors.

Some Details on the Lists

The sources of the information we used in constructing these lists are presented in this book's introduction. Here are some additional details on how we created the lists:

◉ Some jobs have the same scores for one or more data elements. For example, in the category of fastest-growing, two jobs—Fence Erectors and Operations Research Analysts—are expected to grow at the same rate, 10.6 percent. Therefore, we ordered these two jobs alphabetically, and their order has no other significance. There was no way to avoid these ties, so simply understand that the difference of several positions on a list may not mean as much as it seems.

◉ Likewise, it is unwise to place too much emphasis on small differences in outlook information—projections for job growth and job openings. For example, Refuse and Recyclable Material Collectors are projected to have 37,785 job openings per year, whereas 37,731 openings are projected for Helpers—Carpenters. This is a difference of only 54 jobs spread over the entire United States, and of course it is only a forecast. Before 2007, the Bureau of Labor Statistics rounded these projections to the nearest 1,000 and would have assigned these two occupations the same figure (38,000), which would have given Helpers—Carpenters the higher rank on the basis of alphabetical ordering. So, again, keep in mind that small differences of position on a list aren't very significant.

◉ Some job titles represent combinations of two or more closely related jobs. For example, here in Part II you will find a job called Farm, Ranch, and Other Agricultural Managers. The U.S. Department of Labor provides data on earnings, job growth, and job openings for Farm, Ranch, and Other Agricultural Managers, so this job title is useful for the purposes of these lists. In Part III, however, where you'll turn to find more detailed information about the jobs on these lists, you can find *separate* descriptions of the jobs Aquacultural Managers, Crop and Livestock Managers, and Nursery and Greenhouse Managers. That level of detail is more appropriate for that section of the book.

Best Low-Stress Jobs Overall: Jobs with the Highest Pay, Fastest Growth, and Most Openings

The four lists that follow are the most important lists in this book. The first list presents the jobs meeting the criteria for this book with the highest combined scores for pay, growth, and number of openings. These are very appealing lists because they represent low-stress jobs that have the very highest quantifiable measures from our labor market. The 150 jobs in the first list are the basis for all the job lists in Part II and are described in detail in Part III.

The three additional sets of lists present 50 jobs with the highest scores on each of three measures: annual earnings, projected percentage growth, and largest number of openings.

The 150 Best Low-Stress Jobs Overall

Most people want to see this list first. You can see the low-stress jobs with the highest overall combined ratings for earnings, projected growth, and number of openings. Some of these jobs actually are only moderately low in stress, but none of them is very stressful. (The section in the introduction on "How the Best Low-Stress Jobs Were Selected" explains in detail how we rated jobs to assemble this list.)

You'll notice a wide variety of jobs on the list. For example, among the top 25 you'll find jobs in high tech, scientific research, mechanical repair, engineering, construction, and health care. Some fields aren't well represented, however, because jobs in these fields tend to involve stressful situations. Thus, you'll find few jobs in management or classroom teaching.

A look at the list will clarify how we ordered the jobs. The occupation with the best total score was Computer Software Engineers, Applications, so it tops the list. Coming in at second place is another high-tech job, Computer Systems Analysts. Although it offers slightly more job openings than the top-ranked job, its average earnings are $10,000 less per year and its expected growth is 14 percent slower, so it therefore had a lower total score. The other occupations follow in descending order based on their total scores. Many jobs had tied scores and were simply listed one after another, so there are often only very small or even no differences between the scores of jobs that are near each other on the list. All other jobs lists in this book use these jobs as their source list. You can find descriptions for each of these jobs in Part III, beginning on page 141. If a job appeals to you, or if you're not sure what it is, find it alphabetically in Part III and read the description.

The 150 Best Low-Stress Jobs Overall

Job	Stress Rating	Annual Earnings	Percent Growth	Annual Openings
1. Computer Software Engineers, Applications	46.6	$79,780	44.6%	58,690
2. Computer Systems Analysts	50.7	$69,760	29.0%	63,166
3. Sales Managers	60.6	$91,560	10.2%	36,392
4. Civil Engineers	55.1	$68,600	18.0%	15,979
5. Environmental Scientists and Specialists, Including Health	45.2	$56,100	25.1%	6,961
6. Construction and Building Inspectors	54.4	$46,570	18.2%	12,606
7. Environmental Engineers	47.9	$69,940	25.4%	5,003
8. Carpenters	49.3	$36,550	10.3%	223,225
9. Bus and Truck Mechanics and Diesel Engine Specialists	54.5	$37,660	11.5%	25,428
10. Environmental Science and Protection Technicians, Including Health	54.5	$38,090	28.0%	8,404
11. Painters, Construction and Maintenance	49.5	$31,190	11.8%	101,140

(continued)

(continued)

The 150 Best Low-Stress Jobs Overall

Job	Stress Rating	Annual Earnings	Percent Growth	Annual Openings
12. Mobile Heavy Equipment Mechanics, Except Engines	56.3	$40,440	12.3%	11,037
13. Cement Masons and Concrete Finishers	53.0	$32,650	11.4%	34,625
14. Natural Sciences Managers	53.1	$100,080	11.4%	3,661
15. Industrial Machinery Mechanics	60.2	$41,050	9.0%	23,361
16. Tile and Marble Setters	48.5	$36,590	15.4%	9,066
17. Brickmasons and Blockmasons	52.4	$42,980	9.7%	17,569
18. Maintenance and Repair Workers, General	46.4	$31,910	10.1%	165,502
19. Operations Research Analysts	46.5	$64,650	10.6%	5,727
20. Water and Liquid Waste Treatment Plant and System Operators	53.9	$36,070	13.8%	9,575
21. Massage Therapists	37.2	$33,400	20.3%	9,193
22. Fitness Trainers and Aerobics Instructors	31.2	$25,910	26.8%	51,235
23. Civil Engineering Technicians	51.2	$40,560	10.2%	7,499
24. Sheet Metal Workers	53.4	$37,360	6.7%	31,677
25. Mechanical Engineers	55.9	$69,850	4.2%	12,394
26. Electrical Engineers	45.4	$75,930	6.3%	6,806
27. Industrial Engineering Technicians	60.8	$46,810	9.9%	6,172
28. Security and Fire Alarm Systems Installers	53.7	$34,810	20.2%	5,729
29. Librarians	46.7	$49,060	3.6%	18,945
30. Computer Programmers	51.6	$65,510	–4.1%	27,937
31. Telecommunications Line Installers and Repairers	56.5	$46,280	4.6%	14,719
32. Highway Maintenance Workers	43.4	$31,540	8.9%	24,774
33. Insurance Underwriters	46.7	$52,350	6.3%	6,880
34. Electrical and Electronic Engineering Technicians	52.3	$50,660	3.6%	12,583
35. Farm, Ranch, and Other Agricultural Managers	55.1	$52,070	1.1%	18,101
36. Landscaping and Groundskeeping Workers	42.7	$21,260	18.1%	307,138
37. Boilermakers	56.0	$46,960	14.0%	2,333
38. Hydrologists	46.9	$66,260	24.3%	687
39. Reinforcing Iron and Rebar Workers	50.6	$38,220	11.5%	4,502
40. Survey Researchers	39.4	$33,360	15.9%	4,959
41. Curators	34.0	$46,300	23.3%	1,416
42. Electronics Engineers, Except Computer	50.4	$81,050	3.7%	5,699
43. Welders, Cutters, Solderers, and Brazers	51.4	$31,400	5.1%	61,125
44. Commercial and Industrial Designers	49.4	$54,560	7.2%	4,777
45. Helpers—Pipelayers, Plumbers, Pipefitters, and Steamfitters	48.4	$23,910	11.9%	29,332

The 150 Best Low-Stress Jobs Overall

Job	Stress Rating	Annual Earnings	Percent Growth	Annual Openings
46. Occupational Health and Safety Specialists	56.9	$58,030	8.1%	3,440
47. Computer, Automated Teller, and Office Machine Repairers	54.2	$36,480	3.0%	22,330
48. Helpers—Carpenters	52.0	$23,060	11.7%	37,731
49. Locksmiths and Safe Repairers	52.3	$32,020	22.1%	3,545
50. Refuse and Recyclable Material Collectors	60.6	$28,970	7.4%	37,785
51. Social Science Research Assistants	47.5	$33,860	12.4%	3,571
52. Structural Iron and Steel Workers	59.3	$40,480	6.0%	6,969
53. Farmers and Ranchers	45.5	$37,130	–8.5%	129,552
54. Tree Trimmers and Pruners	59.0	$28,250	11.1%	9,621
55. Chemical Engineers	46.9	$78,860	7.9%	2,111
56. Set and Exhibit Designers	48.7	$41,820	17.8%	1,402
57. Marine Engineers and Naval Architects	51.4	$72,990	10.9%	495
58. Animal Trainers	36.8	$26,310	22.7%	6,713
59. Mathematicians	39.5	$86,930	10.2%	473
60. Library Technicians	42.8	$26,560	8.5%	29,075
61. Mechanical Engineering Technicians	46.8	$45,850	6.4%	3,710
62. Pipelayers	53.3	$30,330	8.7%	8,902
63. Millwrights	57.1	$45,630	5.8%	4,758
64. Excavating and Loading Machine and Dragline Operators	55.7	$32,930	8.3%	6,562
65. Tour Guides and Escorts	29.2	$20,420	21.2%	15,027
66. Health and Safety Engineers, Except Mining Safety Engineers and Inspectors	59.7	$66,290	9.6%	1,105
67. Physicists	45.1	$94,240	6.8%	1,302
68. Archivists	32.8	$40,730	14.4%	795
69. Bakers	36.8	$22,030	10.0%	31,442
70. Food Batchmakers	55.0	$23,100	10.9%	15,704
71. Zoologists and Wildlife Biologists	48.5	$53,300	8.7%	1,444
72. Motorcycle Mechanics	57.5	$30,050	12.5%	3,564
73. Geological and Petroleum Technicians	56.1	$46,160	8.6%	1,895
74. Hazardous Materials Removal Workers	58.5	$35,450	11.2%	1,933
75. Sociologists	45.8	$60,290	10.0%	403
76. Maintenance Workers, Machinery	55.6	$34,550	–1.1%	15,055
77. Stonemasons	45.4	$35,960	10.0%	2,657
78. Secretaries, Except Legal, Medical, and Executive	47.7	$27,450	1.2%	239,630

(continued)

(continued)

The 150 Best Low-Stress Jobs Overall

Job	Stress Rating	Annual Earnings	Percent Growth	Annual Openings
79. Insulation Workers, Floor, Ceiling, and Wall	43.5	$30,510	8.4%	6,580
80. Painters, Transportation Equipment	49.2	$35,680	8.4%	3,268
81. Tank Car, Truck, and Ship Loaders	65.3	$31,970	9.2%	4,519
82. Museum Technicians and Conservators	34.3	$34,340	15.9%	1,341
83. Helpers—Electricians	56.9	$23,760	6.8%	35,109
84. Septic Tank Servicers and Sewer Pipe Cleaners	54.9	$31,430	10.2%	3,156
85. Credit Analysts	44.5	$52,350	1.9%	3,180
86. Meat, Poultry, and Fish Cutters and Trimmers	50.1	$20,370	10.9%	17,920
87. Soil and Plant Scientists	46.6	$56,080	8.4%	850
88. Structural Metal Fabricators and Fitters	45.4	$30,290	–0.2%	20,746
89. Inspectors, Testers, Sorters, Samplers, and Weighers	51.1	$29,420	–7.0%	75,361
90. Multiple Machine Tool Setters, Operators, and Tenders, Metal and Plastic	60.5	$30,530	0.3%	15,709
91. Welding, Soldering, and Brazing Machine Setters, Operators, and Tenders	58.0	$30,980	3.0%	7,707
92. Political Scientists	47.5	$90,140	5.3%	318
93. Library Assistants, Clerical	36.5	$21,640	7.9%	18,961
94. Rail Car Repairers	46.7	$43,320	5.1%	1,989
95. Carpet Installers	50.2	$34,560	–1.2%	6,692
96. Conservation Scientists	52.4	$54,970	5.3%	1,161
97. Power Plant Operators	55.5	$55,000	2.7%	1,796
98. Funeral Attendants	41.1	$20,350	14.3%	6,034
99. Laborers and Freight, Stock, and Material Movers, Hand	55.7	$21,220	2.1%	630,487
100. Geographers	47.7	$62,990	6.1%	75
101. Travel Agents	54.9	$29,210	1.0%	13,128
102. Woodworking Machine Setters, Operators, and Tenders, Except Sawing	51.3	$23,940	6.4%	11,860
103. Word Processors and Typists	41.8	$29,430	–11.6%	32,279
104. Chemical Plant and System Operators	59.9	$49,080	–15.3%	5,620
105. Mixing and Blending Machine Setters, Operators, and Tenders	54.7	$29,330	–5.1%	18,661
106. Printing Machine Operators	59.0	$30,990	–5.7%	12,274
107. Butchers and Meat Cutters	54.4	$26,930	1.9%	14,503
108. Terrazzo Workers and Finishers	55.3	$31,630	10.9%	1,052
109. Electrical and Electronics Installers and Repairers, Transportation Equipment	46.5	$43,110	4.3%	1,663

The 150 Best Low-Stress Jobs Overall

Job	Stress Rating	Annual Earnings	Percent Growth	Annual Openings
110. Fiberglass Laminators and Fabricators	50.8	$25,980	6.2%	7,315
111. Rail-Track Laying and Maintenance Equipment Operators	56.6	$40,000	4.8%	1,817
112. Fence Erectors	45.2	$26,400	10.6%	2,812
113. Home Appliance Repairers	51.8	$33,860	1.5%	4,243
114. Packaging and Filling Machine Operators and Tenders	46.5	$22,990	–5.4%	79,540
115. Forest and Conservation Technicians	50.4	$30,880	–2.0%	5,946
116. Outdoor Power Equipment and Other Small Engine Mechanics	47.8	$26,910	5.5%	5,130
117. Stock Clerks and Order Fillers	48.5	$20,440	–7.7%	439,327
118. Cutting, Punching, and Press Machine Setters, Operators, and Tenders, Metal and Plastic	51.4	$26,340	–14.9%	30,635
119. Meter Readers, Utilities	49.1	$30,330	–10.3%	7,328
120. Sawing Machine Setters, Operators, and Tenders, Wood	54.3	$24,280	3.8%	6,086
121. Model Makers, Metal and Plastic	50.0	$42,050	–6.3%	1,801
122. Semiconductor Processors	56.8	$32,860	–12.9%	5,709
123. Electronic Home Entertainment Equipment Installers and Repairers	42.0	$29,980	3.0%	3,065
124. Mail Clerks and Mail Machine Operators, Except Postal Service	44.0	$23,810	–11.6%	27,889
125. Electromechanical Equipment Assemblers	42.4	$27,560	–9.1%	8,283
126. Chemical Equipment Operators and Tenders	60.4	$40,290	–3.9%	1,469
127. Segmental Pavers	57.2	$28,700	10.2%	152
128. Electrical and Electronic Equipment Assemblers	51.1	$25,560	–26.8%	26,595
129. Molders, Shapers, and Casters, Except Metal and Plastic	50.9	$25,010	1.3%	5,788
130. Electric Motor, Power Tool, and Related Repairers	58.5	$32,860	–4.2%	2,625
131. Metal-Refining Furnace Operators and Tenders	59.5	$32,640	–19.0%	5,496
132. Wellhead Pumpers	53.4	$36,150	–11.9%	2,517
133. File Clerks	41.8	$22,090	–41.3%	50,088
134. Animal Breeders	44.2	$27,090	4.4%	2,512
135. Helpers—Painters, Paperhangers, Plasterers, and Stucco Masons	44.9	$21,330	–0.7%	7,696
136. Logging Equipment Operators	53.6	$29,700	–1.3%	2,756
137. Separating, Filtering, Clarifying, Precipitating, and Still Machine Setters, Operators, and Tenders	60.4	$34,970	–3.2%	1,238
138. Floor Layers, Except Carpet, Wood, and Hard Tiles	39.4	$34,190	–12.2%	2,504

(continued)

(continued)

The 150 Best Low-Stress Jobs Overall

Job	Stress Rating	Annual Earnings	Percent Growth	Annual Openings
139. Helpers—Extraction Workers	55.6	$28,680	–0.2%	2,765
140. Rolling Machine Setters, Operators, and Tenders, Metal and Plastic	58.9	$31,050	–11.8%	3,075
141. Roustabouts, Oil and Gas	48.2	$25,700	–3.2%	4,800
142. Forest Fire Inspectors and Prevention Specialists	46.0	$32,940	2.1%	66
143. Crushing, Grinding, and Polishing Machine Setters, Operators, and Tenders	56.9	$28,080	–11.9%	5,357
144. Bindery Workers	51.0	$25,570	–21.8%	7,508
145. Audio-Visual Collections Specialists	38.5	$40,530	–13.8%	868
146. Cooks, Private Household	38.8	$22,870	8.8%	1,352
147. Gas Compressor and Gas Pumping Station Operators	56.5	$45,400	–17.5%	704
148. Grinding and Polishing Workers, Hand	47.6	$23,880	–7.1%	5,789
149. Food Cooking Machine Operators and Tenders	59.1	$21,280	–4.7%	6,714
150. Pourers and Casters, Metal	52.3	$29,570	–17.4%	4,459

The 50 Best-Paying Low-Stress Jobs

On the following list you'll find the 50 best-paying jobs that met our criteria for this book. This is an appealing list, for obvious reasons.

It shouldn't be a big surprise to learn that most of the highest-paying jobs require advanced levels of education, training, or experience. For example, a bachelor's degree or higher is needed for every one of the top 20 jobs. Although the top 20 jobs may not appeal to you for various reasons, you are likely to find others that will among the top 50 jobs with the highest earnings.

Keep in mind that the earnings reflect the national average for all workers in the occupation. This is an important consideration because starting pay in the job is usually a lot less than the pay that workers can earn with several years of experience. Earnings also vary significantly by region of the country, so actual pay in your area could be substantially different.

The 50 Best-Paying Low-Stress Jobs

Job	Annual Earnings
1. Natural Sciences Managers	$100,080
2. Physicists	$94,240
3. Sales Managers	$91,560
4. Political Scientists	$90,140
5. Mathematicians	$86,930
6. Electronics Engineers, Except Computer	$81,050
7. Computer Software Engineers, Applications	$79,780
8. Chemical Engineers	$78,860
9. Electrical Engineers	$75,930
10. Marine Engineers and Naval Architects	$72,990
11. Environmental Engineers	$69,940
12. Mechanical Engineers	$69,850
13. Computer Systems Analysts	$69,760
14. Civil Engineers	$68,600
15. Health and Safety Engineers, Except Mining Safety Engineers and Inspectors	$66,290
16. Hydrologists	$66,260
17. Computer Programmers	$65,510
18. Operations Research Analysts	$64,650
19. Geographers	$62,990
20. Sociologists	$60,290
21. Occupational Health and Safety Specialists	$58,030
22. Environmental Scientists and Specialists, Including Health	$56,100
23. Soil and Plant Scientists	$56,080
24. Power Plant Operators	$55,000
25. Conservation Scientists	$54,970
26. Commercial and Industrial Designers	$54,560
27. Zoologists and Wildlife Biologists	$53,300
28. Credit Analysts	$52,350
29. Insurance Underwriters	$52,350
30. Farm, Ranch, and Other Agricultural Managers	$52,070
31. Electrical and Electronic Engineering Technicians	$50,660
32. Chemical Plant and System Operators	$49,080
33. Librarians	$49,060
34. Boilermakers	$46,960
35. Industrial Engineering Technicians	$46,810
36. Construction and Building Inspectors	$46,570
37. Curators	$46,300

(continued)

(continued)

The 50 Best-Paying Low-Stress Jobs

Job	Annual Earnings
38. Telecommunications Line Installers and Repairers	$46,280
39. Geological and Petroleum Technicians	$46,160
40. Mechanical Engineering Technicians	$45,850
41. Millwrights	$45,630
42. Gas Compressor and Gas Pumping Station Operators	$45,400
43. Rail Car Repairers	$43,320
44. Electrical and Electronics Installers and Repairers, Transportation Equipment	$43,110
45. Brickmasons and Blockmasons	$42,980
46. Model Makers, Metal and Plastic	$42,050
47. Set and Exhibit Designers	$41,820
48. Industrial Machinery Mechanics	$41,050
49. Archivists	$40,730
50. Civil Engineering Technicians	$40,560

The 50 Fastest-Growing Low-Stress Jobs

From the list of the 150 best low-stress jobs, this list shows the 50 jobs that are projected to have the highest percentage increase in the numbers of people employed through 2016.

You'll find a wide variety of fields represented by the top 20 fastest-growing jobs, including high tech, engineering, and construction. Some jobs on the list are gritty and wouldn't appeal to many people—most conspicuously, Septic Tank Servicers and Sewer Pipe Cleaners. But the list also features the healthy lifestyle of Fitness Trainers and Aerobics Instructors, the intellectual challenges that engage Operations Research Analysts, the pleasant smells that surround Bakers, and the opportunities to work with animals experienced by Animal Trainers. These fast-growing jobs also cover a wide range of levels of training and education.

The 50 Fastest-Growing Low-Stress Jobs

Job	Percent Growth
1. Computer Software Engineers, Applications	44.6%
2. Computer Systems Analysts	29.0%
3. Environmental Science and Protection Technicians, Including Health	28.0%
4. Fitness Trainers and Aerobics Instructors	26.8%
5. Environmental Engineers	25.4%
6. Environmental Scientists and Specialists, Including Health	25.1%
7. Hydrologists	24.3%

The 50 Fastest-Growing Low-Stress Jobs

Job	Percent Growth
8. Curators	23.3%
9. Animal Trainers	22.7%
10. Locksmiths and Safe Repairers	22.1%
11. Tour Guides and Escorts	21.2%
12. Massage Therapists	20.3%
13. Security and Fire Alarm Systems Installers	20.2%
14. Construction and Building Inspectors	18.2%
15. Landscaping and Groundskeeping Workers	18.1%
16. Civil Engineers	18.0%
17. Set and Exhibit Designers	17.8%
18. Museum Technicians and Conservators	15.9%
19. Survey Researchers	15.9%
20. Tile and Marble Setters	15.4%
21. Archivists	14.4%
22. Funeral Attendants	14.3%
23. Boilermakers	14.0%
24. Water and Liquid Waste Treatment Plant and System Operators	13.8%
25. Motorcycle Mechanics	12.5%
26. Social Science Research Assistants	12.4%
27. Mobile Heavy Equipment Mechanics, Except Engines	12.3%
28. Helpers—Pipelayers, Plumbers, Pipefitters, and Steamfitters	11.9%
29. Painters, Construction and Maintenance	11.8%
30. Helpers—Carpenters	11.7%
31. Bus and Truck Mechanics and Diesel Engine Specialists	11.5%
32. Reinforcing Iron and Rebar Workers	11.5%
33. Cement Masons and Concrete Finishers	11.4%
34. Natural Sciences Managers	11.4%
35. Hazardous Materials Removal Workers	11.2%
36. Tree Trimmers and Pruners	11.1%
37. Food Batchmakers	10.9%
38. Marine Engineers and Naval Architects	10.9%
39. Meat, Poultry, and Fish Cutters and Trimmers	10.9%
40. Terrazzo Workers and Finishers	10.9%
41. Fence Erectors	10.6%
42. Operations Research Analysts	10.6%
43. Carpenters	10.3%
44. Civil Engineering Technicians	10.2%

(continued)

(continued)

The 50 Fastest-Growing Low-Stress Jobs

Job	Percent Growth
45. Mathematicians	10.2%
46. Sales Managers	10.2%
47. Segmental Pavers	10.2%
48. Septic Tank Servicers and Sewer Pipe Cleaners	10.2%
49. Maintenance and Repair Workers, General	10.1%
50. Bakers	10.0%

The 50 Low-Stress Jobs with the Most Openings

From the list of 150 best low-stress jobs, this list shows the 50 jobs that are projected to have the largest number of job openings per year through 2016.

Jobs with many openings present several advantages that may be attractive to you. Because there are many openings, these jobs can be easier to obtain, particularly for those just entering the job market. These jobs may also offer more opportunities to move from one employer to another with relative ease. Though some of these jobs have average or below-average pay, some also pay quite well and can provide good long-term career opportunities. This list is especially noteworthy because most of the jobs require only on-the-job training.

The 50 Low-Stress Jobs with the Most Openings

Job	Annual Openings
1. Laborers and Freight, Stock, and Material Movers, Hand	630,487
2. Stock Clerks and Order Fillers	439,327
3. Landscaping and Groundskeeping Workers	307,138
4. Secretaries, Except Legal, Medical, and Executive	239,630
5. Carpenters	223,225
6. Maintenance and Repair Workers, General	165,502
7. Farmers and Ranchers	129,552
8. Packaging and Filling Machine Operators and Tenders	79,540
9. Inspectors, Testers, Sorters, Samplers, and Weighers	75,361
10. Computer Systems Analysts	63,166
11. Welders, Cutters, Solderers, and Brazers	61,125
12. Computer Software Engineers, Applications	58,690
13. Fitness Trainers and Aerobics Instructors	51,235
14. File Clerks	50,088

The 50 Low-Stress Jobs with the Most Openings

Job	Annual Openings
15. Refuse and Recyclable Material Collectors	37,785
16. Helpers—Carpenters	37,731
17. Sales Managers	36,392
18. Helpers—Electricians	35,109
19. Cement Masons and Concrete Finishers	34,625
20. Word Processors and Typists	32,279
21. Sheet Metal Workers	31,677
22. Bakers	31,442
23. Cutting, Punching, and Press Machine Setters, Operators, and Tenders, Metal and Plastic	30,635
24. Helpers—Pipelayers, Plumbers, Pipefitters, and Steamfitters	29,332
25. Library Technicians	29,075
26. Computer Programmers	27,937
27. Mail Clerks and Mail Machine Operators, Except Postal Service	27,889
28. Electrical and Electronic Equipment Assemblers	26,595
29. Bus and Truck Mechanics and Diesel Engine Specialists	25,428
30. Highway Maintenance Workers	24,774
31. Industrial Machinery Mechanics	23,361
32. Computer, Automated Teller, and Office Machine Repairers	22,330
33. Structural Metal Fabricators and Fitters	20,746
34. Library Assistants, Clerical	18,961
35. Librarians	18,945
36. Mixing and Blending Machine Setters, Operators, and Tenders	18,661
37. Farm, Ranch, and Other Agricultural Managers	18,101
38. Meat, Poultry, and Fish Cutters and Trimmers	17,920
39. Brickmasons and Blockmasons	17,569
40. Civil Engineers	15,979
41. Multiple Machine Tool Setters, Operators, and Tenders, Metal and Plastic	15,709
42. Food Batchmakers	15,704
43. Maintenance Workers, Machinery	15,055
44. Tour Guides and Escorts	15,027
45. Telecommunications Line Installers and Repairers	14,719
46. Butchers and Meat Cutters	14,503
47. Travel Agents	13,128
48. Construction and Building Inspectors	12,606
49. Electrical and Electronic Engineering Technicians	12,583
50. Mechanical Engineers	12,394

Best Jobs with the Least Stress

It's an unfortunate truth that jobs with good economic rewards also tend to be stressful. To select the 150 jobs for this book, we eliminated the *most* stressful jobs, but then narrowed down the remaining jobs by focusing on those with high earnings and good job opportunities. As a result, the 150 occupations we ended up with aren't the most laid-back jobs in the economy.

If the overall level of workplace stress really is crucial to your satisfaction, you'll appreciate the following list, which isolates the 50 *least stressful* of the 150 jobs. We created the list by using the occupational ratings on an O*NET measure called Tolerance for Stress. This rating serves as a summary of all the workplace factors that may be stressful.

The 50 Jobs with the Least Stress

Job	Rating for Tolerance for Stress
1. Tour Guides and Escorts	29.2
2. Fitness Trainers and Aerobics Instructors	31.2
3. Archivists	32.8
4. Curators	34.0
5. Museum Technicians and Conservators	34.3
6. Library Assistants, Clerical	36.5
7. Animal Trainers	36.8
8. Bakers	36.8
9. Massage Therapists	37.2
10. Audio-Visual Collections Specialists	38.5
11. Cooks, Private Household	38.8
12. Floor Layers, Except Carpet, Wood, and Hard Tiles	39.4
13. Survey Researchers	39.4
14. Mathematicians	39.5
15. Funeral Attendants	41.1
16. File Clerks	41.8
17. Word Processors and Typists	41.8
18. Electronic Home Entertainment Equipment Installers and Repairers	42.0
19. Electromechanical Equipment Assemblers	42.4
20. Landscaping and Groundskeeping Workers	42.7
21. Library Technicians	42.8
22. Highway Maintenance Workers	43.4
23. Insulation Workers, Floor, Ceiling, and Wall	43.5
24. Mail Clerks and Mail Machine Operators, Except Postal Service	44.0

The 50 Jobs with the Least Stress

Job	Rating for Tolerance for Stress
25. Animal Breeders	44.2
26. Credit Analysts	44.5
27. Helpers—Painters, Paperhangers, Plasterers, and Stucco Masons	44.9
28. Physicists	45.1
29. Environmental Scientists and Specialists, Including Health	45.2
30. Fence Erectors	45.2
31. Electrical Engineers	45.4
32. Stonemasons	45.4
33. Structural Metal Fabricators and Fitters	45.4
34. Farmers and Ranchers	45.5
35. Sociologists	45.8
36. Forest Fire Inspectors and Prevention Specialists	46.0
37. Maintenance and Repair Workers, General	46.4
38. Electrical and Electronics Installers and Repairers, Transportation Equipment	46.5
39. Operations Research Analysts	46.5
40. Packaging and Filling Machine Operators and Tenders	46.5
41. Computer Software Engineers, Applications	46.6
42. Soil and Plant Scientists	46.6
43. Insurance Underwriters	46.7
44. Librarians	46.7
45. Rail Car Repairers	46.7
46. Mechanical Engineering Technicians	46.8
47. Chemical Engineers	46.9
48. Hydrologists	46.9
49. Political Scientists	47.5
50. Social Science Research Assistants	47.5

The preceding list serves as a good illustration of the principle that stress and economic rewards tend to go hand in hand. The list is dominated by jobs that, frankly, don't pay very well. In fact, the average wage for these 50 jobs is $35,293, which is not greatly higher than the average for all jobs, $30,400. They also have an average projected growth rate of 4.7 percent, which is considerably less than the average for all jobs, 13.0 percent.

But maybe you're willing to trade off high economic rewards for the sake of avoiding workplace stress. Or you may want to focus on the jobs on the following list, which extracts the 20 best jobs from the preceding list, sorted on the basis of their earnings, job growth, and job openings. The average wage for this more selective group of least-stressful jobs is a respectable $51,892, and the average job growth is a healthy 24.7 percent.

The 20 Best Jobs with the Least Stress

Job	Rating for Tolerance for Stress	Annual Earnings	Percent Growth	Annual Openings
1. Computer Software Engineers, Applications	46.6	$79,780	44.6%	58,690
2. Environmental Scientists and Specialists, Including Health	45.2	$56,100	25.1%	6,961
3. Fitness Trainers and Aerobics Instructors	31.2	$25,910	26.8%	51,235
4. Maintenance and Repair Workers, General	46.4	$31,910	10.1%	165,502
5. Operations Research Analysts	46.5	$64,650	10.6%	5,727
6. Massage Therapists	37.2	$33,400	20.3%	9,193
7. Hydrologists	46.9	$66,260	24.3%	687
8. Landscaping and Groundskeeping Workers	42.7	$21,260	18.1%	307,138
9. Curators	34.0	$46,300	23.3%	1,416
10. Electrical Engineers	45.4	$75,930	6.3%	6,806
11. Highway Maintenance Workers	43.4	$31,540	8.9%	24,774
12. Insurance Underwriters	46.7	$52,350	6.3%	6,880
13. Survey Researchers	39.4	$33,360	15.9%	4,959
14. Librarians	46.7	$49,060	3.6%	18,945
15. Mathematicians	39.5	$86,930	10.2%	473
16. Animal Trainers	36.8	$26,310	22.7%	6,713
17. Chemical Engineers	46.9	$78,860	7.9%	2,111
18. Farmers and Ranchers	45.5	$37,130	−8.5%	129,552
19. Social Science Research Assistants	47.5	$33,860	12.4%	3,571
20. Library Technicians	42.8	$26,560	8.5%	29,075

Best Jobs Low in Particular Stressful Features

The preceding two lists show what happens when you paint yourself into a corner by trying to eliminate all stress: You get a set of jobs that also are low in economic rewards. The following sets of lists invite you to try a different approach that can identify many more rewarding jobs. Rather than try to eliminate all stress, these lists focus on removing certain *specific* sources of stress that may particularly bother you. If you target the kinds of stress you want to avoid and accept other kinds of stress that you feel you can handle, you can find jobs with better economic payoffs.

For these lists, we identified 10 specific sources of on-the-job stress shared by a large number of people and then assembled 10 pairs of lists featuring jobs with only a small amount of these worrisome tendencies. All the jobs on these lists consist of subsets of the 150 best jobs.

In each set of lists, one list ranks the 50 jobs that are lowest in the specific stressful feature; the other list ranks the 20 best jobs from the first list, based on earnings, job growth, and job openings.

In all of these lists, we indicate how O*NET rates the stressful feature by using a number on a scale with 0 as the lowest level and 100 as the highest. Although these ratings resemble percentages, they don't represent the percentage of time that workers are engaged in the stressful activity or situation. Rather, they measure the level of the source of stress. In the introduction to each list we also indicate the average O*NET rating for *all* occupations on the stress-related factor. This is a weighted average, giving greater weight to occupations with a larger workforce.

Jobs with Least Frequent Conflict Situations

Some jobs exist mainly to resolve conflicts between people. As examples, think of the work done by judges, mediators, insurance adjusters, residential advisors, and mental health counselors. Because each party in a conflict wants and tries to win, the worker acting as referee between the contenders can come under considerable stress. So we compiled the following list of the 50 jobs with the *least* frequency of conflict situations, as rated by O*NET, to suggest jobs that let you avoid this kind of stress. This list is followed by a second list showing the 20 low-conflict jobs with the best economic rewards. The weighted average for this factor for all jobs is 49.9.

The 50 Jobs with the Least Frequent Conflict Situations

Job	Rating for Frequency of Conflict Situations
1. Grinding and Polishing Workers, Hand	19.7
2. Electronic Home Entertainment Equipment Installers and Repairers	20.2
3. Floor Layers, Except Carpet, Wood, and Hard Tiles	21.0
4. Curators	21.3
5. Cooks, Private Household	21.5
6. Farmers and Ranchers	22.2
7. Packaging and Filling Machine Operators and Tenders	22.5
8. Massage Therapists	23.0
9. Mathematicians	23.0
10. Bakers	23.5
11. Electromechanical Equipment Assemblers	23.5
12. Survey Researchers	23.8
13. Archivists	24.3
14. Helpers—Extraction Workers	25.5

(continued)

(continued)

The 50 Jobs with the Least Frequent Conflict Situations

Job	Rating for Frequency of Conflict Situations
15. Woodworking Machine Setters, Operators, and Tenders, Except Sawing	26.0
16. Carpet Installers	26.2
17. Tour Guides and Escorts	27.2
18. Molders, Shapers, and Casters, Except Metal and Plastic	27.3
19. Physicists	28.0
20. Electrical Engineers	28.3
21. Roustabouts, Oil and Gas	28.8
22. Model Makers, Metal and Plastic	29.0
23. Painters, Transportation Equipment	29.0
24. Credit Analysts	29.5
25. Logging Equipment Operators	30.3
26. Wellhead Pumpers	30.8
27. Mail Clerks and Mail Machine Operators, Except Postal Service	31.5
28. Stonemasons	32.0
29. Helpers—Painters, Paperhangers, Plasterers, and Stucco Masons	33.0
30. Animal Trainers	33.2
31. Funeral Attendants	33.2
32. Sawing Machine Setters, Operators, and Tenders, Wood	33.2
33. Welders, Cutters, Solderers, and Brazers	33.4
34. Computer Systems Analysts	33.7
35. Helpers—Pipelayers, Plumbers, Pipefitters, and Steamfitters	34.2
36. Pipelayers	34.2
37. Sociologists	34.5
38. Meter Readers, Utilities	34.8
39. Inspectors, Testers, Sorters, Samplers, and Weighers	35.5
40. Water and Liquid Waste Treatment Plant and System Operators	35.8
41. Museum Technicians and Conservators	36.0
42. Security and Fire Alarm Systems Installers	36.3
43. Geographers	36.5
44. Operations Research Analysts	36.5
45. Bindery Workers	37.3
46. Food Batchmakers	37.7
47. Structural Metal Fabricators and Fitters	37.7
48. Electrical and Electronics Installers and Repairers, Transportation Equipment	38.0
49. Commercial and Industrial Designers	38.2
50. Millwrights	38.2

The 20 Best Jobs with Low Frequency of Conflict Situations

Job	Rating for Frequency of Conflict Situations	Annual Earnings	Percent Growth	Annual Openings
1. Computer Systems Analysts	33.7	$69,760	29.0%	63,166
2. Water and Liquid Waste Treatment Plant and System Operators	35.8	$36,070	13.8%	9,575
3. Massage Therapists	23.0	$33,400	20.3%	9,193
4. Operations Research Analysts	36.5	$64,650	10.6%	5,727
5. Electrical Engineers	28.3	$75,930	6.3%	6,806
6. Security and Fire Alarm Systems Installers	36.3	$34,810	20.2%	5,729
7. Curators	21.3	$46,300	23.3%	1,416
8. Animal Trainers	33.2	$26,310	22.7%	6,713
9. Welders, Cutters, Solderers, and Brazers	33.4	$31,400	5.1%	61,125
10. Farmers and Ranchers	22.2	$37,130	−8.5%	129,552
11. Helpers—Pipelayers, Plumbers, Pipefitters, and Steamfitters	34.2	$23,910	11.9%	29,332
12. Commercial and Industrial Designers	38.2	$54,560	7.2%	4,777
13. Survey Researchers	23.8	$33,360	15.9%	4,959
14. Pipelayers	34.2	$30,330	8.7%	8,902
15. Tour Guides and Escorts	27.2	$20,420	21.2%	15,027
16. Mathematicians	23.0	$86,930	10.2%	473
17. Food Batchmakers	37.7	$23,100	10.9%	15,704
18. Bakers	23.5	$22,030	10.0%	31,442
19. Archivists	24.3	$40,730	14.4%	795
20. Millwrights	38.2	$45,630	5.8%	4,758

Jobs that Deal the Least with Physically Aggressive People

A job can be very stressful if you have to deal with people who are violent or physically aggressive. Police and prison guards are trained to respond appropriately, but the threat of violence and injury can take a toll on these and similar workers. A Gallup poll found that 10 percent of workers are concerned about an individual at work they fear could become violent. Of course, there are lots of jobs where violent encounters are unheard of. In fact, for all occupations, the average O*NET rating for Deal with Physically Aggressive People is only 15.9. The two following lists show the jobs rated lowest on this feature.

The 50 Jobs that Deal the Least with Physically Aggressive People

Job	Rating for Deal with Physically Aggressive People
1. Cooks, Private Household	0.0
2. Credit Analysts	0.0
3. Mathematicians	0.0
4. Set and Exhibit Designers	0.0
5. Computer Systems Analysts	0.2
6. Electronics Engineers, Except Computer	0.2
7. Floor Layers, Except Carpet, Wood, and Hard Tiles	0.2
8. Massage Therapists	0.5
9. Physicists	1.2
10. Electrical Engineers	1.5
11. Computer Software Engineers, Applications	1.8
12. Museum Technicians and Conservators	1.8
13. Marine Engineers and Naval Architects	1.9
14. File Clerks	2.0
15. Operations Research Analysts	2.0
16. Tour Guides and Escorts	2.0
17. Cement Masons and Concrete Finishers	2.3
18. Electromechanical Equipment Assemblers	2.3
19. Curators	2.5
20. Archivists	3.5
21. Audio-Visual Collections Specialists	3.5
22. Civil Engineering Technicians	3.5
23. Electronic Home Entertainment Equipment Installers and Repairers	3.5
24. Pourers and Casters, Metal	3.5
25. Bakers	3.7
26. Survey Researchers	3.7
27. Farmers and Ranchers	4.0
28. Semiconductor Processors	4.0
29. Geographers	4.2
30. Welders, Cutters, Solderers, and Brazers	4.3
31. Animal Trainers	4.5
32. Environmental Engineers	4.5
33. Helpers—Painters, Paperhangers, Plasterers, and Stucco Masons	4.5
34. Tile and Marble Setters	4.5
35. Woodworking Machine Setters, Operators, and Tenders, Except Sawing	4.5
36. Carpenters	4.7

The 50 Jobs that Deal the Least with Physically Aggressive People

Job	Rating for Deal with Physically Aggressive People
37. Bindery Workers	4.8
38. Civil Engineers	4.8
39. Commercial and Industrial Designers	4.8
40. Cutting, Punching, and Press Machine Setters, Operators, and Tenders, Metal and Plastic	4.8
41. Electrical and Electronics Installers and Repairers, Transportation Equipment	5.0
42. Electrical and Electronic Engineering Technicians	5.2
43. Chemical Engineers	5.3
44. Model Makers, Metal and Plastic	5.3
45. Word Processors and Typists	5.3
46. Zoologists and Wildlife Biologists	5.3
47. Chemical Plant and System Operators	5.5
48. Natural Sciences Managers	5.8
49. Soil and Plant Scientists	5.8
50. Wellhead Pumpers	6.0

The 20 Best Jobs Dealing Little with Physically Aggressive People

Job	Rating for Deal with Physically Aggressive People	Annual Earnings	Percent Growth	Annual Openings
1. Computer Software Engineers, Applications	1.8	$79,780	44.6%	58,690
2. Computer Systems Analysts	0.2	$69,760	29.0%	63,166
3. Civil Engineers	4.8	$68,600	18.0%	15,979
4. Environmental Engineers	4.5	$69,940	25.4%	5,003
5. Natural Sciences Managers	5.8	$100,080	11.4%	3,661
6. Carpenters	4.7	$36,550	10.3%	223,225
7. Operations Research Analysts	2.0	$64,650	10.6%	5,727
8. Massage Therapists	0.5	$33,400	20.3%	9,193
9. Tile and Marble Setters	4.5	$36,590	15.4%	9,066
10. Cement Masons and Concrete Finishers	2.3	$32,650	11.4%	34,625
11. Electrical Engineers	1.5	$75,930	6.3%	6,806
12. Electronics Engineers, Except Computer	0.2	$81,050	3.7%	5,699

(continued)

(continued)

The 20 Best Jobs Dealing Little with Physically Aggressive People

Job	Rating for Deal with Physically Aggressive People	Annual Earnings	Percent Growth	Annual Openings
13. Civil Engineering Technicians	3.5	$40,560	10.2%	7,499
14. Curators	2.5	$46,300	23.3%	1,416
15. Electrical and Electronic Engineering Technicians	5.2	$50,660	3.6%	12,583
16. Chemical Engineers	5.3	$78,860	7.9%	2,111
17. Farmers and Ranchers	4.0	$37,130	−8.5%	129,552
18. Tour Guides and Escorts	2.0	$20,420	21.2%	15,027
19. Animal Trainers	4.5	$26,310	22.7%	6,713
20. Commercial and Industrial Designers	4.8	$54,560	7.2%	4,777

Jobs that Deal the Least with Unpleasant or Angry People

Even jobs that avoid physical confrontations can be stressful if they involve dealing with people who are angry at you. As you might expect, many of the jobs that are lowest in this stressful situation are simply performed at some distance from the public and have very few interactions with people, unpleasant or otherwise. But others, such as Massage Therapists or Tour Guides and Escorts, put workers in constant contact with (usually friendly) people. The 50 jobs ranked *lowest* on Dealing with Unpleasant or Angry People are listed below. Their ratings compare favorably to the average rating for all occupations, 54.4.

The 50 Jobs that Deal the Least with Unpleasant or Angry People

Job	Rating for Dealing with Unpleasant or Angry People
1. Mathematicians	17.5
2. Electrical and Electronics Installers and Repairers, Transportation Equipment	18.8
3. Farmers and Ranchers	19.7
4. Computer Software Engineers, Applications	21.0
5. Operations Research Analysts	24.0
6. Museum Technicians and Conservators	24.5
7. Physicists	26.5
8. Massage Therapists	27.5

The 50 Jobs that Deal the Least with Unpleasant or Angry People

Job	Rating for Dealing with Unpleasant or Angry People
9. Sociologists	27.5
10. Tour Guides and Escorts	27.5
11. Cooks, Private Household	27.7
12. Curators	27.7
13. Molders, Shapers, and Casters, Except Metal and Plastic	27.8
14. Packaging and Filling Machine Operators and Tenders	28.3
15. Woodworking Machine Setters, Operators, and Tenders, Except Sawing	28.3
16. Helpers—Painters, Paperhangers, Plasterers, and Stucco Masons	29.8
17. Electromechanical Equipment Assemblers	30.0
18. Survey Researchers	30.0
19. Bindery Workers	30.3
20. File Clerks	30.3
21. Rail Car Repairers	30.3
22. Soil and Plant Scientists	30.8
23. Marine Engineers and Naval Architects	30.9
24. Archivists	31.0
25. Helpers—Pipelayers, Plumbers, Pipefitters, and Steamfitters	31.0
26. Floor Layers, Except Carpet, Wood, and Hard Tiles	31.3
27. Animal Breeders	31.5
28. Chemical Engineers	31.5
29. Tile and Marble Setters	31.5
30. Roustabouts, Oil and Gas	31.7
31. Carpet Installers	32.0
32. Mechanical Engineering Technicians	32.0
33. Geographers	32.2
34. Helpers—Extraction Workers	32.5
35. Animal Trainers	32.7
36. Electrical Engineers	32.7
37. Wellhead Pumpers	32.7
38. Structural Metal Fabricators and Fitters	33.0
39. Electrical and Electronic Engineering Technicians	33.5
40. Cement Masons and Concrete Finishers	33.7
41. Electronic Home Entertainment Equipment Installers and Repairers	33.7
42. Fiberglass Laminators and Fabricators	33.7
43. Stonemasons	33.7

(continued)

(continued)

The 50 Jobs that Deal the Least with Unpleasant or Angry People

Job	Rating for Dealing with Unpleasant or Angry People
44. Gas Compressor and Gas Pumping Station Operators	34.0
45. Hydrologists	34.0
46. Farm, Ranch, and Other Agricultural Managers	34.4
47. Carpenters	34.7
48. Mail Clerks and Mail Machine Operators, Except Postal Service	34.8
49. Model Makers, Metal and Plastic	35.0
50. Word Processors and Typists	35.5

The 20 Best Jobs Dealing Little with Unpleasant or Angry People

Job	Rating for Dealing with Unpleasant or Angry People	Annual Earnings	Percent Growth	Annual Openings
1. Computer Software Engineers, Applications	21.0	$79,780	44.6%	58,690
2. Carpenters	34.7	$36,550	10.3%	223,225
3. Operations Research Analysts	24.0	$64,650	10.6%	5,727
4. Tile and Marble Setters	31.5	$36,590	15.4%	9,066
5. Cement Masons and Concrete Finishers	33.7	$32,650	11.4%	34,625
6. Massage Therapists	27.5	$33,400	20.3%	9,193
7. Electrical Engineers	32.7	$75,930	6.3%	6,806
8. Hydrologists	34.0	$66,260	24.3%	687
9. Curators	27.7	$46,300	23.3%	1,416
10. Electrical and Electronic Engineering Technicians	33.5	$50,660	3.6%	12,583
11. Farm, Ranch, and Other Agricultural Managers	34.4	$52,070	1.1%	18,101
12. Chemical Engineers	31.5	$78,860	7.9%	2,111
13. Helpers—Pipelayers, Plumbers, Pipefitters, and Steamfitters	31.0	$23,910	11.9%	29,332
14. Survey Researchers	30.0	$33,360	15.9%	4,959
15. Animal Trainers	32.7	$26,310	22.7%	6,713
16. Farmers and Ranchers	19.7	$37,130	–8.5%	129,552
17. Physicists	26.5	$94,240	6.8%	1,302
18. Marine Engineers and Naval Architects	30.9	$72,990	10.9%	495
19. Mathematicians	17.5	$86,930	10.2%	473
20. Mechanical Engineering Technicians	32.0	$45,850	6.4%	3,710

Jobs with the Least Consequence of Error

One source of on-the-job stress is knowing that any mistakes you may make will have catastrophic results—for clients and customers (think of surgeons), for the environment (think of nuclear power reactor operators), or for the general public (think of air traffic controllers). Fortunately, there are plenty of good jobs in which errors can easily be corrected. The following list identifies the 50 jobs with the *lowest* ratings on the O*NET descriptor called Consequence of Error. The average rating for all occupations on this factor is 42.9.

The 50 Jobs with the Least Consequence of Error	
Job	Rating for Consequence of Error
1. Bakers	9.3
2. Library Technicians	12.5
3. Audio-Visual Collections Specialists	12.7
4. Fitness Trainers and Aerobics Instructors	15.3
5. Survey Researchers	16.0
6. Stonemasons	18.3
7. Library Assistants, Clerical	19.2
8. Librarians	21.5
9. Commercial and Industrial Designers	22.2
10. Electromechanical Equipment Assemblers	23.2
11. Tour Guides and Escorts	23.2
12. Curators	24.3
13. Floor Layers, Except Carpet, Wood, and Hard Tiles	25.0
14. Insulation Workers, Floor, Ceiling, and Wall	25.0
15. Political Scientists	26.2
16. Mathematicians	26.7
17. Stock Clerks and Order Fillers	27.3
18. Fence Erectors	27.5
19. Archivists	27.7
20. Carpenters	28.0
21. Animal Trainers	28.8
22. Secretaries, Except Legal, Medical, and Executive	30.0
23. Credit Analysts	31.0
24. Word Processors and Typists	32.7
25. Meter Readers, Utilities	33.0
26. Sociologists	33.0
27. Physicists	33.7

(continued)

(continued)

The 50 Jobs with the Least Consequence of Error

Job	Rating for Consequence of Error
28. Grinding and Polishing Workers, Hand	34.0
29. Home Appliance Repairers	34.5
30. Landscaping and Groundskeeping Workers	34.5
31. Computer, Automated Teller, and Office Machine Repairers	34.8
32. Cooks, Private Household	34.8
33. Insurance Underwriters	35.8
34. Environmental Engineers	36.0
35. Massage Therapists	36.3
36. Soil and Plant Scientists	36.3
37. Tile and Marble Setters	36.3
38. Electrical Engineers	36.5
39. Mail Clerks and Mail Machine Operators, Except Postal Service	36.5
40. Operations Research Analysts	36.5
41. Brickmasons and Blockmasons	37.0
42. Forest Fire Inspectors and Prevention Specialists	37.3
43. Painters, Transportation Equipment	37.3
44. Hazardous Materials Removal Workers	37.5
45. Carpet Installers	38.0
46. Sales Managers	38.0
47. Hydrologists	38.5
48. Locksmiths and Safe Repairers	38.5
49. Packaging and Filling Machine Operators and Tenders	39.2
50. Funeral Attendants	39.5

The 20 Best Jobs with Low Consequence of Error

Job	Rating for Consequence of Error	Annual Earnings	Percent Growth	Annual Openings
1. Sales Managers	38.0	$91,560	10.2%	36,392
2. Environmental Engineers	36.0	$69,940	25.4%	5,003
3. Carpenters	28.0	$36,550	10.3%	223,225
4. Fitness Trainers and Aerobics Instructors	15.3	$25,910	26.8%	51,235
5. Tile and Marble Setters	36.3	$36,590	15.4%	9,066

The 20 Best Jobs with Low Consequence of Error

Job	Rating for Consequence of Error	Annual Earnings	Percent Growth	Annual Openings
6. Operations Research Analysts	36.5	$64,650	10.6%	5,727
7. Massage Therapists	36.3	$33,400	20.3%	9,193
8. Brickmasons and Blockmasons	37.0	$42,980	9.7%	17,569
9. Hydrologists	38.5	$66,260	24.3%	687
10. Landscaping and Groundskeeping Workers	34.5	$21,260	18.1%	307,138
11. Curators	24.3	$46,300	23.3%	1,416
12. Electrical Engineers	36.5	$75,930	6.3%	6,806
13. Librarians	21.5	$49,060	3.6%	18,945
14. Insurance Underwriters	35.8	$52,350	6.3%	6,880
15. Animal Trainers	28.8	$26,310	22.7%	6,713
16. Computer, Automated Teller, and Office Machine Repairers	34.8	$36,480	3.0%	22,330
17. Mathematicians	26.7	$86,930	10.2%	473
18. Survey Researchers	16.0	$33,360	15.9%	4,959
19. Locksmiths and Safe Repairers	38.5	$32,020	22.1%	3,545
20. Commercial and Industrial Designers	22.2	$54,560	7.2%	4,777

Jobs with a Low Impact of Decisions on Co-workers or Company Results

Maybe you've heard the joke about the guy whose job it is to sort potatoes into bags of small, medium, and large spuds. His complaint about the job: "Decisions, decisions!" What makes the joke funny is that the decisions the man must make, though unending, are really of very little consequence. Great fortunes aren't riding on his ability to make extremely precise judgments about potato size. High-impact decisions, by contrast, can be stressful to make and can drain much of the enjoyment out of a job. That's why you may be interested in the jobs in the following set of lists, all of which have been rated very low for the impact of decisions on co-workers, clients, or company results. (All of them are rated lower than the average of 67.4 for all occupations.) Although some of these jobs are low-paying or low-status, many of the jobs near the top of the second list are quite rewarding.

The 50 Jobs with the Lowest Impact of Decisions on Co-workers or Company Results

Job	Rating for Impact of Decisions on Co-workers or Company Results
1. Mail Clerks and Mail Machine Operators, Except Postal Service	33.2
2. Reinforcing Iron and Rebar Workers	38.2
3. Electronic Home Entertainment Equipment Installers and Repairers	43.0
4. Cooks, Private Household	43.8
5. Archivists	44.2
6. Fiberglass Laminators and Fabricators	44.2
7. Landscaping and Groundskeeping Workers	44.7
8. Bakers	45.0
9. Cutting, Punching, and Press Machine Setters, Operators, and Tenders, Metal and Plastic	46.0
10. Curators	46.5
11. Library Assistants, Clerical	46.7
12. Structural Metal Fabricators and Fitters	47.0
13. Mixing and Blending Machine Setters, Operators, and Tenders	47.8
14. Meat, Poultry, and Fish Cutters and Trimmers	48.3
15. Sociologists	48.3
16. Word Processors and Typists	48.5
17. Electromechanical Equipment Assemblers	48.8
18. Insulation Workers, Floor, Ceiling, and Wall	49.3
19. Multiple Machine Tool Setters, Operators, and Tenders, Metal and Plastic	49.5
20. Inspectors, Testers, Sorters, Samplers, and Weighers	49.8
21. Museum Technicians and Conservators	50.0
22. Tour Guides and Escorts	50.2
23. Mathematicians	51.0
24. Rail Car Repairers	51.0
25. Bindery Workers	51.2
26. Highway Maintenance Workers	51.2
27. Electrical and Electronics Installers and Repairers, Transportation Equipment	52.2
28. Model Makers, Metal and Plastic	53.0
29. Welders, Cutters, Solderers, and Brazers	53.1
30. Roustabouts, Oil and Gas	53.8
31. Librarians	54.3
32. Semiconductor Processors	54.5
33. Electric Motor, Power Tool, and Related Repairers	55.0

The 50 Jobs with the Lowest Impact of Decisions on Co-workers or Company Results

Job	Rating for Impact of Decisions on Co-workers or Company Results
34. Pipelayers	55.0
35. Soil and Plant Scientists	56.0
36. Chemical Engineers	56.5
37. Food Batchmakers	56.5
38. Laborers and Freight, Stock, and Material Movers, Hand	56.5
39. Helpers—Carpenters	57.0
40. Pourers and Casters, Metal	57.0
41. Geographers	57.2
42. Electrical and Electronic Equipment Assemblers	57.7
43. Outdoor Power Equipment and Other Small Engine Mechanics	57.7
44. Secretaries, Except Legal, Medical, and Executive	57.7
45. Butchers and Meat Cutters	58.0
46. File Clerks	58.2
47. Fence Erectors	58.5
48. Political Scientists	58.7
49. Woodworking Machine Setters, Operators, and Tenders, Except Sawing	59.0
50. Electrical Engineers	59.2

The 20 Best Jobs with Low Impact of Decisions on Co-workers or Company Results

Job	Rating for Impact of Decisions on Co-workers or Company Results	Annual Earnings	Percent Growth	Annual Openings
1. Highway Maintenance Workers	51.2	$31,540	8.9%	24,774
2. Welders, Cutters, Solderers, and Brazers	53.1	$31,400	5.1%	61,125
3. Curators	46.5	$46,300	23.3%	1,416
4. Landscaping and Groundskeeping Workers	44.7	$21,260	18.1%	307,138
5. Electrical Engineers	59.2	$75,930	6.3%	6,806
6. Librarians	54.3	$49,060	3.6%	18,945

(continued)

(continued)

The 20 Best Jobs with Low Impact of Decisions on Co-workers or Company Results

Job	Rating for Impact of Decisions on Co-workers or Company Results	Annual Earnings	Percent Growth	Annual Openings
7. Reinforcing Iron and Rebar Workers	38.2	$38,220	11.5%	4,502
8. Helpers—Carpenters	57.0	$23,060	11.7%	37,731
9. Chemical Engineers	56.5	$78,860	7.9%	2,111
10. Mathematicians	51.0	$86,930	10.2%	473
11. Pipelayers	55.0	$30,330	8.7%	8,902
12. Museum Technicians and Conservators	50.0	$34,340	15.9%	1,341
13. Archivists	44.2	$40,730	14.4%	795
14. Bakers	45.0	$22,030	10.0%	31,442
15. Sociologists	48.3	$60,290	10.0%	403
16. Insulation Workers, Floor, Ceiling, and Wall	49.3	$30,510	8.4%	6,580
17. Secretaries, Except Legal, Medical, and Executive	57.7	$27,450	1.2%	239,630
18. Food Batchmakers	56.5	$23,100	10.9%	15,704
19. Soil and Plant Scientists	56.0	$56,080	8.4%	850
20. Inspectors, Testers, Sorters, Samplers, and Weighers	49.8	$29,420	–7.0%	75,361

Jobs with a Low Importance of Being Exact or Accurate

Some jobs have a low tolerance for error. For example, Computer Programmers who misplace just one comma in one line of code can see a whole program crash as a result. On the other hand, many jobs require a much lower level of accuracy and therefore are free of that source of workplace stress. You'll find such jobs on the following two lists. The average rating for all occupations on this stress-related factor is 75.9.

The 50 Jobs with the Lowest Importance of Being Exact or Accurate

Job	Rating for Importance of Being Exact or Accurate
1. Fitness Trainers and Aerobics Instructors	40.0
2. Insulation Workers, Floor, Ceiling, and Wall	41.0
3. Landscaping and Groundskeeping Workers	41.0
4. Animal Trainers	49.8
5. Tour Guides and Escorts	53.0
6. Audio-Visual Collections Specialists	54.8
7. Farmers and Ranchers	54.8
8. Logging Equipment Operators	56.5
9. Helpers—Painters, Paperhangers, Plasterers, and Stucco Masons	56.7
10. Rail Car Repairers	58.5
11. Bakers	58.7
12. Highway Maintenance Workers	58.7
13. Curators	59.8
14. Cooks, Private Household	61.0
15. Helpers—Extraction Workers	61.0
16. Animal Breeders	61.5
17. Roustabouts, Oil and Gas	62.0
18. Survey Researchers	62.0
19. Fence Erectors	63.0
20. Zoologists and Wildlife Biologists	63.0
21. Museum Technicians and Conservators	63.5
22. Meat, Poultry, and Fish Cutters and Trimmers	63.7
23. Mechanical Engineering Technicians	63.7
24. Structural Metal Fabricators and Fitters	63.7
25. Conservation Scientists	64.1
26. Hazardous Materials Removal Workers	65.0
27. Excavating and Loading Machine and Dragline Operators	65.2
28. Farm, Ranch, and Other Agricultural Managers	65.2
29. Stonemasons	65.8
30. Forest Fire Inspectors and Prevention Specialists	66.0
31. Segmental Pavers	67.0
32. Funeral Attendants	67.3
33. Food Batchmakers	68.0
34. Wellhead Pumpers	68.0
35. Maintenance and Repair Workers, General	68.5

(continued)

(continued)

The 50 Jobs with the Lowest Importance of Being Exact or Accurate

Job	Rating for Importance of Being Exact or Accurate
36. Natural Sciences Managers	69.0
37. Power Plant Operators	69.0
38. Forest and Conservation Technicians	69.2
39. Inspectors, Testers, Sorters, Samplers, and Weighers	69.5
40. Mail Clerks and Mail Machine Operators, Except Postal Service	69.7
41. Painters, Transportation Equipment	69.7
42. Brickmasons and Blockmasons	70.0
43. Archivists	70.5
44. Environmental Scientists and Specialists, Including Health	70.5
45. Metal-Refining Furnace Operators and Tenders	70.5
46. Mobile Heavy Equipment Mechanics, Except Engines	70.5
47. Fiberglass Laminators and Fabricators	70.7
48. Outdoor Power Equipment and Other Small Engine Mechanics	71.0
49. Bindery Workers	71.2
50. Home Appliance Repairers	71.5

The 20 Best Jobs with Low Importance of Being Exact or Accurate

Job	Rating for Importance of Being Exact or Accurate	Annual Earnings	Percent Growth	Annual Openings
1. Environmental Scientists and Specialists, Including Health	70.5	$56,100	25.1%	6,961
2. Mobile Heavy Equipment Mechanics, Except Engines	70.5	$40,440	12.3%	11,037
3. Brickmasons and Blockmasons	70.0	$42,980	9.7%	17,569
4. Natural Sciences Managers	69.0	$100,080	11.4%	3,661
5. Fitness Trainers and Aerobics Instructors	40.0	$25,910	26.8%	51,235
6. Maintenance and Repair Workers, General	68.5	$31,910	10.1%	165,502
7. Curators	59.8	$46,300	23.3%	1,416
8. Farm, Ranch, and Other Agricultural Managers	65.2	$52,070	1.1%	18,101
9. Landscaping and Groundskeeping Workers	41.0	$21,260	18.1%	307,138
10. Survey Researchers	62.0	$33,360	15.9%	4,959

The 20 Best Jobs with Low Importance of Being Exact or Accurate

Job	Rating for Importance of Being Exact or Accurate	Annual Earnings	Percent Growth	Annual Openings
11. Highway Maintenance Workers	58.7	$31,540	8.9%	24,774
12. Animal Trainers	49.8	$26,310	22.7%	6,713
13. Farmers and Ranchers	54.8	$37,130	–8.5%	129,552
14. Mechanical Engineering Technicians	63.7	$45,850	6.4%	3,710
15. Tour Guides and Escorts	53.0	$20,420	21.2%	15,027
16. Archivists	70.5	$40,730	14.4%	795
17. Bakers	58.7	$22,030	10.0%	31,442
18. Food Batchmakers	68.0	$23,100	10.9%	15,704
19. Hazardous Materials Removal Workers	65.0	$35,450	11.2%	1,933
20. Museum Technicians and Conservators	63.5	$34,340	15.9%	1,341

Jobs with a Short Work Week

A job with a long work week can interfere with family life and leave you little time for non-work activities that you enjoy. The long hours can turn a minor problem such as car troubles into a huge headache because you have such limited free time to deal with issues other than work.

It has been estimated that more than 26 percent of men and more than 11 percent of women worked 50 hours per week or more in 2000, and the trend is toward longer hours. If you want to avoid this source of stress, you'll be interested in the following two lists of low-stress jobs in which the typical work week is comparatively short.

You may wonder whether there's a way to use the rating numbers in these lists to calculate the average hours of the work week for the jobs. Unfortunately, there is no precise equivalence, because the O*NET data-gathering questionnaire doesn't ask job incumbents exactly *how many* hours they typically work in their current job. Instead, it asks whether they work less than 40 hours, 40 hours, or more than 40 hours. The rating for each occupation is based on the average of the responses to this three-point scale and is converted to a scale that ranges from 0 to 100. The average rating for all occupations is 57.9, and you may note that a few of the occupations in the following list are actually rated higher than this average.

The O*NET questionnaire also doesn't ask whether respondents are full-time or part-time workers, so many of these jobs have short work weeks because of a large showing of part-timers in the workforce. If you look at the list of jobs with a high percentage of part-time workers elsewhere in Part II, you'll find considerable overlap of job titles.

The 50 Jobs with the Shortest Work Week

Job	Rating for Duration of Typical Work Week
1. Fitness Trainers and Aerobics Instructors	4.0
2. Tour Guides and Escorts	7.0
3. Massage Therapists	11.5
4. Insurance Underwriters	28.0
5. Museum Technicians and Conservators	28.5
6. Social Science Research Assistants	30.5
7. Word Processors and Typists	30.5
8. Funeral Attendants	31.0
9. Library Assistants, Clerical	33.5
10. Cooks, Private Household	35.0
11. Library Technicians	38.5
12. Secretaries, Except Legal, Medical, and Executive	41.5
13. Animal Breeders	42.0
14. File Clerks	42.5
15. Archivists	44.0
16. Animal Trainers	44.5
17. Floor Layers, Except Carpet, Wood, and Hard Tiles	45.0
18. Forest Fire Inspectors and Prevention Specialists	46.0
19. Insulation Workers, Floor, Ceiling, and Wall	47.5
20. Bakers	48.0
21. Environmental Scientists and Specialists, Including Health	48.0
22. Curators	49.5
23. Audio-Visual Collections Specialists	50.0
24. Highway Maintenance Workers	50.0
25. Painters, Construction and Maintenance	50.0
26. Librarians	50.5
27. Helpers—Painters, Paperhangers, Plasterers, and Stucco Masons	52.5
28. Reinforcing Iron and Rebar Workers	52.5
29. Credit Analysts	53.0
30. Electronic Home Entertainment Equipment Installers and Repairers	53.5
31. Home Appliance Repairers	54.0
32. Meter Readers, Utilities	54.0
33. Computer, Automated Teller, and Office Machine Repairers	54.5
34. Helpers—Carpenters	54.5
35. Butchers and Meat Cutters	55.0
36. Mail Clerks and Mail Machine Operators, Except Postal Service	56.0

The 50 Jobs with the Shortest Work Week

Job	Rating for Duration of Typical Work Week
37. Tile and Marble Setters	56.0
38. Grinding and Polishing Workers, Hand	56.5
39. Electrical and Electronic Equipment Assemblers	57.0
40. Stonemasons	57.0
41. Electromechanical Equipment Assemblers	57.5
42. Fiberglass Laminators and Fabricators	58.0
43. Helpers—Pipelayers, Plumbers, Pipefitters, and Steamfitters	58.0
44. Landscaping and Groundskeeping Workers	58.0
45. Forest and Conservation Technicians	58.5
46. Packaging and Filling Machine Operators and Tenders	58.5
47. Carpenters	59.0
48. Computer Programmers	60.0
49. Printing Machine Operators	60.0
50. Helpers—Electricians	60.5

The 20 Best Jobs with a Short Work Week

Job	Rating for Duration of Typical Work Week	Annual Earnings	Percent Growth	Annual Openings
1. Carpenters	59.0	$36,550	10.3%	223,225
2. Environmental Scientists and Specialists, Including Health	48.0	$56,100	25.1%	6,961
3. Painters, Construction and Maintenance	50.0	$31,190	11.8%	101,140
4. Fitness Trainers and Aerobics Instructors	4.0	$25,910	26.8%	51,235
5. Tile and Marble Setters	56.0	$36,590	15.4%	9,066
6. Massage Therapists	11.5	$33,400	20.3%	9,193
7. Computer Programmers	60.0	$65,510	−4.1%	27,937
8. Curators	49.5	$46,300	23.3%	1,416
9. Librarians	50.5	$49,060	3.6%	18,945
10. Landscaping and Groundskeeping Workers	58.0	$21,260	18.1%	307,138
11. Highway Maintenance Workers	50.0	$31,540	8.9%	24,774
12. Computer, Automated Teller, and Office Machine Repairers	54.5	$36,480	3.0%	22,330

(continued)

(continued)

The 20 Best Jobs with a Short Work Week

Job	Rating for Duration of Typical Work Week	Annual Earnings	Percent Growth	Annual Openings
13. Insurance Underwriters	28.0	$52,350	6.3%	6,880
14. Helpers—Pipelayers, Plumbers, Pipefitters, and Steamfitters	58.0	$23,910	11.9%	29,332
15. Reinforcing Iron and Rebar Workers	52.5	$38,220	11.5%	4,502
16. Helpers—Carpenters	54.5	$23,060	11.7%	37,731
17. Archivists	44.0	$40,730	14.4%	795
18. Library Technicians	38.5	$26,560	8.5%	29,075
19. Secretaries, Except Legal, Medical, and Executive	41.5	$27,450	1.2%	239,630
20. Social Science Research Assistants	30.5	$33,860	12.4%	3,571

Jobs with a Low Level of Competition

One reason people call work a "rat race" is the element of competition. In some jobs, a few workers who can outproduce most others earn outstanding rewards, whereas less productive workers eventually drop out of the career. These highly competitive—and therefore stressful—kinds of jobs are conspicuous in sports and the arts, but also can be found in some business fields such as sales. Fortunately, many jobs don't tally the number of touchdowns, purchase orders, or widgets that workers produce and don't reward only a gifted few. We compiled a list of the 50 least competitive low-stress jobs and then sorted it to show the 20 with the best economic rewards. All are rated lower than the average of 45.6 for all occupations. Some of them pay well, and many promise good job opportunities.

The 50 Jobs with the Lowest Level of Competition

Job	Rating for Level of Competition
1. Tour Guides and Escorts	10.2
2. Library Technicians	17.5
3. Museum Technicians and Conservators	21.5
4. Archivists	23.5
5. Maintenance and Repair Workers, General	24.0
6. File Clerks	24.5
7. Library Assistants, Clerical	24.5
8. Highway Maintenance Workers	26.7
9. Packaging and Filling Machine Operators and Tenders	27.2

The 50 Jobs with the Lowest Level of Competition

Job	Rating for Level of Competition
10. Floor Layers, Except Carpet, Wood, and Hard Tiles	30.0
11. Mail Clerks and Mail Machine Operators, Except Postal Service	30.0
12. Electrical and Electronics Installers and Repairers, Transportation Equipment	30.5
13. Meter Readers, Utilities	30.5
14. Construction and Building Inspectors	30.8
15. Outdoor Power Equipment and Other Small Engine Mechanics	31.5
16. Environmental Scientists and Specialists, Including Health	31.7
17. Cutting, Punching, and Press Machine Setters, Operators, and Tenders, Metal and Plastic	32.0
18. Funeral Attendants	32.0
19. Pourers and Casters, Metal	32.0
20. Curators	32.2
21. Grinding and Polishing Workers, Hand	32.5
22. Fitness Trainers and Aerobics Instructors	33.0
23. Audio-Visual Collections Specialists	33.2
24. Librarians	34.5
25. Water and Liquid Waste Treatment Plant and System Operators	34.8
26. Animal Trainers	35.5
27. Secretaries, Except Legal, Medical, and Executive	36.0
28. Bakers	36.8
29. Rail-Track Laying and Maintenance Equipment Operators	36.8
30. Bus and Truck Mechanics and Diesel Engine Specialists	37.0
31. Chemical Plant and System Operators	37.3
32. Landscaping and Groundskeeping Workers	37.5
33. Farmers and Ranchers	37.7
34. Laborers and Freight, Stock, and Material Movers, Hand	38.0
35. Stock Clerks and Order Fillers	38.8
36. Electrical and Electronic Equipment Assemblers	39.0
37. Mechanical Engineering Technicians	39.0
38. Crushing, Grinding, and Polishing Machine Setters, Operators, and Tenders	39.2
39. Civil Engineering Technicians	40.2
40. Survey Researchers	40.5
41. Pipelayers	41.5
42. Welding, Soldering, and Brazing Machine Setters, Operators, and Tenders	41.5
43. Helpers—Pipelayers, Plumbers, Pipefitters, and Steamfitters	42.0
44. Rail Car Repairers	42.0

(continued)

(continued)

The 50 Jobs with the Lowest Level of Competition

Job	Rating for Level of Competition
45. Logging Equipment Operators	42.3
46. Electrical and Electronic Engineering Technicians	42.7
47. Geological and Petroleum Technicians	42.7
48. Electronic Home Entertainment Equipment Installers and Repairers	42.8
49. Painters, Construction and Maintenance	42.8
50. Word Processors and Typists	43.0

The 20 Best Jobs with a Low Level of Competition

Job	Rating for Level of Competition	Annual Earnings	Percent Growth	Annual Openings
1. Environmental Scientists and Specialists, Including Health	31.7	$56,100	25.1%	6,961
2. Construction and Building Inspectors	30.8	$46,570	18.2%	12,606
3. Maintenance and Repair Workers, General	24.0	$31,910	10.1%	165,502
4. Painters, Construction and Maintenance	42.8	$31,190	11.8%	101,140
5. Fitness Trainers and Aerobics Instructors	33.0	$25,910	26.8%	51,235
6. Bus and Truck Mechanics and Diesel Engine Specialists	37.0	$37,660	11.5%	25,428
7. Librarians	34.5	$49,060	3.6%	18,945
8. Water and Liquid Waste Treatment Plant and System Operators	34.8	$36,070	13.8%	9,575
9. Electrical and Electronic Engineering Technicians	42.7	$50,660	3.6%	12,583
10. Civil Engineering Technicians	40.2	$40,560	10.2%	7,499
11. Curators	32.2	$46,300	23.3%	1,416
12. Landscaping and Groundskeeping Workers	37.5	$21,260	18.1%	307,138
13. Highway Maintenance Workers	26.7	$31,540	8.9%	24,774
14. Farmers and Ranchers	37.7	$37,130	−8.5%	129,552
15. Survey Researchers	40.5	$33,360	15.9%	4,959
16. Helpers—Pipelayers, Plumbers, Pipefitters, and Steamfitters	42.0	$23,910	11.9%	29,332
17. Secretaries, Except Legal, Medical, and Executive	36.0	$27,450	1.2%	239,630
18. Animal Trainers	35.5	$26,310	22.7%	6,713
19. Archivists	23.5	$40,730	14.4%	795
20. Library Technicians	17.5	$26,560	8.5%	29,075

Jobs with Pace Least Determined by Speed of Equipment

One of the classic comedy moments of early TV was an episode of "I Love Lucy" in which Lucy and her pal Ethel struggled to keep up with an accelerating conveyer belt in a chocolate factory. Nowadays, many production tasks, such as wrapping chocolates, are being performed by robots that have no trouble keeping up with the pace of the assembly line. Nevertheless, some jobs still require workers to coordinate their tasks with machinery or other equipment, and not all of these jobs are in manufacturing. Chefs, mail sorters, and photographers are examples of workers who experience this kind of stress. If you want a job where the work pace is set by you, your boss, or your clients rather than by equipment, you may want to consider the jobs on the following two lists. Almost all are rated on this stress-related factor below the average of 22.8 for all occupations.

The 50 Jobs with Pace Least Determined by Speed of Equipment

Job	Rating for Pace Determined by Speed of Equipment
1. Massage Therapists	0.0
2. Political Scientists	0.0
3. Curators	0.5
4. Credit Analysts	0.7
5. Sociologists	0.7
6. Tour Guides and Escorts	0.7
7. Archivists	1.0
8. Environmental Scientists and Specialists, Including Health	1.0
9. Floor Layers, Except Carpet, Wood, and Hard Tiles	1.2
10. Physicists	1.5
11. Home Appliance Repairers	10.0
12. Occupational Health and Safety Specialists	10.5
13. Forest and Conservation Technicians	11.0
14. Computer Programmers	11.8
15. Locksmiths and Safe Repairers	11.8
16. Mechanical Engineering Technicians	11.8
17. Meter Readers, Utilities	12.0
18. Natural Sciences Managers	13.2
19. Outdoor Power Equipment and Other Small Engine Mechanics	13.7
20. Motorcycle Mechanics	14.3
21. Travel Agents	14.5

(continued)

(continued)

The 50 Jobs with Pace Least Determined by Speed of Equipment

Job	Rating for Pace Determined by Speed of Equipment
22. Librarians	14.8
23. Commercial and Industrial Designers	15.0
24. Security and Fire Alarm Systems Installers	15.0
25. Cooks, Private Household	15.3
26. Electronic Home Entertainment Equipment Installers and Repairers	16.2
27. Farm, Ranch, and Other Agricultural Managers	16.7
28. File Clerks	17.0
29. Secretaries, Except Legal, Medical, and Executive	17.0
30. Segmental Pavers	17.5
31. Carpenters	18.5
32. Maintenance and Repair Workers, General	18.5
33. Electronics Engineers, Except Computer	19.0
34. Word Processors and Typists	19.2
35. Carpet Installers	19.7
36. Environmental Science and Protection Technicians, Including Health	19.7
37. Operations Research Analysts	20.0
38. Survey Researchers	20.0
39. Rail Car Repairers	20.2
40. Computer Systems Analysts	20.3
41. Environmental Engineers	20.3
42. Boilermakers	20.8
43. Civil Engineering Technicians	21.3
44. Electrical and Electronic Engineering Technicians	21.4
45. Mechanical Engineers	21.5
46. Stonemasons	22.2
47. Stock Clerks and Order Fillers	22.3
48. Bakers	22.7
49. Electromechanical Equipment Assemblers	23.2
50. Bus and Truck Mechanics and Diesel Engine Specialists	24.8

The 20 Best Jobs with Pace Least Determined by Speed of Equipment

Job	Rating for Pace Determined by Speed of Equipment	Annual Earnings	Percent Growth	Annual Openings
1. Computer Systems Analysts	20.3	$69,760	29.0%	63,166
2. Environmental Engineers	20.3	$69,940	25.4%	5,003
3. Environmental Scientists and Specialists, Including Health	1.0	$56,100	25.1%	6,961
4. Environmental Science and Protection Technicians, Including Health	19.7	$38,090	28.0%	8,404
5. Carpenters	18.5	$36,550	10.3%	223,225
6. Bus and Truck Mechanics and Diesel Engine Specialists	24.8	$37,660	11.5%	25,428
7. Natural Sciences Managers	13.2	$100,080	11.4%	3,661
8. Operations Research Analysts	20.0	$64,650	10.6%	5,727
9. Mechanical Engineers	21.5	$69,850	4.2%	12,394
10. Massage Therapists	0.0	$33,400	20.3%	9,193
11. Maintenance and Repair Workers, General	18.5	$31,910	10.1%	165,502
12. Civil Engineering Technicians	21.3	$40,560	10.2%	7,499
13. Computer Programmers	11.8	$65,510	–4.1%	27,937
14. Librarians	14.8	$49,060	3.6%	18,945
15. Security and Fire Alarm Systems Installers	15.0	$34,810	20.2%	5,729
16. Electronics Engineers, Except Computer	19.0	$81,050	3.7%	5,699
17. Electrical and Electronic Engineering Technicians	21.4	$50,660	3.6%	12,583
18. Farm, Ranch, and Other Agricultural Managers	16.7	$52,070	1.1%	18,101
19. Curators	0.5	$46,300	23.3%	1,416
20. Commercial and Industrial Designers	15.0	$54,560	7.2%	4,777

Jobs with Low Time Pressure

Some workers are constantly faced with deadlines. They work with one eye on the clock because they are under pressure to complete their work tasks within a certain window of time. Journalists are famous for working like this, but did it occur to you that this kind of stress also affects florists, truck drivers, cooks, and insurance appraisers? A study by the Institute of Psychiatry at King's College London concluded that time pressure is the single most important cause of workplace stress and the illnesses that result from it. If you want a job where time pressure is minimal, the following two lists deserve your attention. All of the jobs are rated lower on time pressure than the average of 67.6 for all occupations. You'll find jobs in a variety of industries, some with outstanding economic rewards.

The 50 Jobs with the Lowest Time Pressure

Job	Rating for Time Pressure
1. Fitness Trainers and Aerobics Instructors	21.3
2. Mathematicians	34.2
3. Animal Trainers	36.5
4. Massage Therapists	36.8
5. Museum Technicians and Conservators	40.0
6. Archivists	43.0
7. Curators	43.3
8. Pourers and Casters, Metal	44.5
9. Highway Maintenance Workers	45.2
10. Library Assistants, Clerical	45.5
11. Computer Software Engineers, Applications	46.7
12. Tour Guides and Escorts	49.5
13. Mechanical Engineering Technicians	50.7
14. Logging Equipment Operators	51.5
15. Electrical Engineers	52.5
16. Audio-Visual Collections Specialists	53.3
17. Operations Research Analysts	54.3
18. Chemical Engineers	54.8
19. Helpers—Carpenters	54.8
20. Librarians	54.8
21. Sociologists	55.3
22. Civil Engineers	55.5
23. Power Plant Operators	56.0
24. Carpenters	56.4
25. Forest Fire Inspectors and Prevention Specialists	56.7
26. Survey Researchers	56.7
27. Bakers	57.0
28. Funeral Attendants	57.2
29. Hydrologists	57.2
30. Electronic Home Entertainment Equipment Installers and Repairers	57.7
31. Floor Layers, Except Carpet, Wood, and Hard Tiles	58.0
32. Soil and Plant Scientists	58.2
33. Forest and Conservation Technicians	58.5
34. Social Science Research Assistants	58.9
35. Rolling Machine Setters, Operators, and Tenders, Metal and Plastic	59.8
36. Environmental Scientists and Specialists, Including Health	60.5
37. Geographers	60.5

The 50 Jobs with the Lowest Time Pressure

Job	Rating for Time Pressure
38. Roustabouts, Oil and Gas	60.5
39. Water and Liquid Waste Treatment Plant and System Operators	60.5
40. Gas Compressor and Gas Pumping Station Operators	61.3
41. Excavating and Loading Machine and Dragline Operators	62.3
42. Physicists	62.3
43. Farm, Ranch, and Other Agricultural Managers	62.6
44. Environmental Engineers	62.7
45. Maintenance and Repair Workers, General	62.7
46. Structural Metal Fabricators and Fitters	62.7
47. Conservation Scientists	62.8
48. Political Scientists	63.0
49. Word Processors and Typists	63.0
50. Pipelayers	63.2

The 20 Best Jobs with Low Time Pressure

Job	Rating for Time Pressure	Annual Earnings	Percent Growth	Annual Openings
1. Computer Software Engineers, Applications	46.7	$79,780	44.6%	58,690
2. Civil Engineers	55.5	$68,600	18.0%	15,979
3. Environmental Engineers	62.7	$69,940	25.4%	5,003
4. Environmental Scientists and Specialists, Including Health	60.5	$56,100	25.1%	6,961
5. Carpenters	56.4	$36,550	10.3%	223,225
6. Fitness Trainers and Aerobics Instructors	21.3	$25,910	26.8%	51,235
7. Operations Research Analysts	54.3	$64,650	10.6%	5,727
8. Massage Therapists	36.8	$33,400	20.3%	9,193
9. Water and Liquid Waste Treatment Plant and System Operators	60.5	$36,070	13.8%	9,575
10. Maintenance and Repair Workers, General	62.7	$31,910	10.1%	165,502
11. Electrical Engineers	52.5	$75,930	6.3%	6,806
12. Hydrologists	57.2	$66,260	24.3%	687
13. Curators	43.3	$46,300	23.3%	1,416
14. Librarians	54.8	$49,060	3.6%	18,945
15. Highway Maintenance Workers	45.2	$31,540	8.9%	24,774

(continued)

(continued)

The 20 Best Jobs with Low Time Pressure

Job	Rating for Time Pressure	Annual Earnings	Percent Growth	Annual Openings
16. Survey Researchers	56.7	$33,360	15.9%	4,959
17. Chemical Engineers	54.8	$78,860	7.9%	2,111
18. Helpers—Carpenters	54.8	$23,060	11.7%	37,731
19. Farm, Ranch, and Other Agricultural Managers	62.6	$52,070	1.1%	18,101
20. Mathematicians	34.2	$86,930	10.2%	473

Best Low-Stress Jobs Lists by Demographic

We decided it would be interesting to include lists in this section that show what sorts of jobs different types of people are most likely to have. For example, what low-stress jobs have the highest percentage of men or young workers? We're not saying that men or young people should consider these jobs over others, but it is interesting information to know.

In some cases, the lists can give you ideas for jobs to consider that you might otherwise overlook. For example, perhaps women should consider some jobs that traditionally have high percentages of men in them. Or older workers might consider some jobs typically held by young people. Although these aren't obvious ways of using these lists, the lists may give you some good ideas on jobs to consider. The lists may also help you identify jobs that work well for others in your situation—for example, jobs with plentiful opportunities for part-time work, if that is something you want to do.

All lists in this section were created through a similar process. We began with the 150 best low-stress jobs. Next, we sorted those jobs in order of the primary criterion for each set of lists. For example, we sorted the 150 jobs based on the percentage of workers age 16 to 24 from highest to lowest percentage, and then selected the jobs with a high percentage (only 44 jobs with a percentage greater than 15). From this initial list of jobs with a high percentage of each type of worker, we created four more-specialized lists:

- ◎ 25 Best Jobs Overall (the subset of jobs that have the highest combined scores for earnings, growth rate, and number of openings)
- ◎ 25 Best-Paying Jobs
- ◎ 25 Fastest-Growing Jobs
- ◎ 25 Jobs with the Most Openings

Again, each of these four lists includes only jobs that have high percentages of different types of workers. The same basic process was used to create all the lists in this section. The lists are very interesting, and we hope you find them helpful.

Best Low-Stress Jobs with the Highest Percentage of Workers Age 16–24

These jobs have higher percentages (over 15 percent) of workers between the ages of 16 and 24. Young people are found in all jobs, but those with higher percentages of young people may present more opportunities for initial entry or upward mobility. Many jobs with the highest percentages of young people are learned through on-the-job training, such as construction jobs, but there is a wide variety of jobs in different fields among the top 43.

Best Low-Stress Jobs with the Highest Percentage of Workers Age 16–24

Job	Percent Age 16–24
1. Helpers—Carpenters	44.7%
2. Helpers—Electricians	44.7%
3. Helpers—Painters, Paperhangers, Plasterers, and Stucco Masons	44.7%
4. Helpers—Pipelayers, Plumbers, Pipefitters, and Steamfitters	44.7%
5. Library Technicians	43.5%
6. Cooks, Private Household	33.6%
7. Stock Clerks and Order Fillers	32.6%
8. Laborers and Freight, Stock, and Material Movers, Hand	31.9%
9. Fence Erectors	31.7%
10. Environmental Science and Protection Technicians, Including Health	30.8%
11. Forest and Conservation Technicians	30.8%
12. Social Science Research Assistants	30.8%
13. Fitness Trainers and Aerobics Instructors	29.1%
14. File Clerks	27.8%
15. Library Assistants, Clerical	26.7%
16. Landscaping and Groundskeeping Workers	26.6%
17. Tree Trimmers and Pruners	26.6%
18. Motorcycle Mechanics	25.9%
19. Outdoor Power Equipment and Other Small Engine Mechanics	25.9%
20. Animal Breeders	25.0%
21. Woodworking Machine Setters, Operators, and Tenders, Except Sawing	23.4%
22. Tour Guides and Escorts	22.6%
23. Mail Clerks and Mail Machine Operators, Except Postal Service	21.8%
24. Insulation Workers, Floor, Ceiling, and Wall	20.5%
25. Credit Analysts	20.0%
26. Security and Fire Alarm Systems Installers	20.0%
27. Tank Car, Truck, and Ship Loaders	20.0%

(continued)

(continued)

Best Low-Stress Jobs with the Highest Percentage of Workers Age 16–24

Job	Percent Age 16–24
28. Segmental Pavers	19.0%
29. Electronic Home Entertainment Equipment Installers and Repairers	18.2%
30. Packaging and Filling Machine Operators and Tenders	17.7%
31. Word Processors and Typists	17.7%
32. Locksmiths and Safe Repairers	17.4%
33. Food Batchmakers	17.1%
34. Carpet Installers	17.0%
35. Floor Layers, Except Carpet, Wood, and Hard Tiles	17.0%
36. Tile and Marble Setters	17.0%
37. Painters, Construction and Maintenance	16.8%
38. Animal Trainers	16.7%
39. Funeral Attendants	16.7%
40. Model Makers, Metal and Plastic	16.7%
41. Butchers and Meat Cutters	15.8%
42. Meat, Poultry, and Fish Cutters and Trimmers	15.8%
43. Carpenters	15.7%

The jobs in the following four lists are derived from the preceding list of the low-stress jobs with the highest percentage of workers age 16–24.

Best Low-Stress Jobs Overall with a High Percentage of Workers Age 16–24

Job	Percent Age 16–24	Annual Earnings	Percent Growth	Annual Openings
1. Environmental Science and Protection Technicians, Including Health	30.8%	$38,090	28.0%	8,404
2. Carpenters	15.7%	$36,550	10.3%	223,225
3. Painters, Construction and Maintenance	16.8%	$31,190	11.8%	101,140
4. Tile and Marble Setters	17.0%	$36,590	15.4%	9,066
5. Fitness Trainers and Aerobics Instructors	29.1%	$25,910	26.8%	51,235
6. Security and Fire Alarm Systems Installers	20.0%	$34,810	20.2%	5,729
7. Landscaping and Groundskeeping Workers	26.6%	$21,260	18.1%	307,138
8. Locksmiths and Safe Repairers	17.4%	$32,020	22.1%	3,545

Best Low-Stress Jobs Overall with a High Percentage of Workers Age 16–24

Job	Percent Age 16–24	Annual Earnings	Percent Growth	Annual Openings
9. Helpers—Pipelayers, Plumbers, Pipefitters, and Steamfitters	44.7%	$23,910	11.9%	29,332
10. Animal Trainers	16.7%	$26,310	22.7%	6,713
11. Social Science Research Assistants	30.8%	$33,860	12.4%	3,571
12. Helpers—Carpenters	44.7%	$23,060	11.7%	37,731
13. Tree Trimmers and Pruners	26.6%	$28,250	11.1%	9,621
14. Library Technicians	43.5%	$26,560	8.5%	29,075
15. Motorcycle Mechanics	25.9%	$30,050	12.5%	3,564
16. Food Batchmakers	17.1%	$23,100	10.9%	15,704
17. Tank Car, Truck, and Ship Loaders	20.0%	$31,970	9.2%	4,519
18. Tour Guides and Escorts	22.6%	$20,420	21.2%	15,027
19. Insulation Workers, Floor, Ceiling, and Wall	20.5%	$30,510	8.4%	6,580
20. Helpers—Electricians	44.7%	$23,760	6.8%	35,109
21. Carpet Installers	17.0%	$34,560	−1.2%	6,692
22. Credit Analysts	20.0%	$52,350	1.9%	3,180
23. Word Processors and Typists	17.7%	$29,430	−11.6%	32,279
24. Laborers and Freight, Stock, and Material Movers, Hand	31.9%	$21,220	2.1%	630,487
25. Butchers and Meat Cutters	15.8%	$26,930	1.9%	14,503

Best-Paying Low-Stress Jobs for Workers Age 16–24

Job	Percent Age 16–24	Annual Earnings
1. Credit Analysts	20.0%	$52,350
2. Model Makers, Metal and Plastic	16.7%	$42,050
3. Environmental Science and Protection Technicians, Including Health	30.8%	$38,090
4. Tile and Marble Setters	17.0%	$36,590
5. Carpenters	15.7%	$36,550
6. Security and Fire Alarm Systems Installers	20.0%	$34,810
7. Carpet Installers	17.0%	$34,560
8. Floor Layers, Except Carpet, Wood, and Hard Tiles	17.0%	$34,190
9. Social Science Research Assistants	30.8%	$33,860
10. Locksmiths and Safe Repairers	17.4%	$32,020

(continued)

(continued)

Best-Paying Low-Stress Jobs for Workers Age 16–24

Job	Percent Age 16–24	Annual Earnings
11. Tank Car, Truck, and Ship Loaders	20.0%	$31,970
12. Painters, Construction and Maintenance	16.8%	$31,190
13. Forest and Conservation Technicians	30.8%	$30,880
14. Insulation Workers, Floor, Ceiling, and Wall	20.5%	$30,510
15. Motorcycle Mechanics	25.9%	$30,050
16. Electronic Home Entertainment Equipment Installers and Repairers	18.2%	$29,980
17. Word Processors and Typists	17.7%	$29,430
18. Segmental Pavers	19.0%	$28,700
19. Tree Trimmers and Pruners	26.6%	$28,250
20. Animal Breeders	25.0%	$27,090
21. Butchers and Meat Cutters	15.8%	$26,930
22. Outdoor Power Equipment and Other Small Engine Mechanics	25.9%	$26,910
23. Library Technicians	43.5%	$26,560
24. Fence Erectors	31.7%	$26,400
25. Animal Trainers	16.7%	$26,310

Fastest-Growing Low-Stress Jobs for Workers Age 16–24

Job	Percent Age 16–24	Percent Growth
1. Environmental Science and Protection Technicians, Including Health	30.8%	28.0%
2. Fitness Trainers and Aerobics Instructors	29.1%	26.8%
3. Animal Trainers	16.7%	22.7%
4. Locksmiths and Safe Repairers	17.4%	22.1%
5. Tour Guides and Escorts	22.6%	21.2%
6. Security and Fire Alarm Systems Installers	20.0%	20.2%
7. Landscaping and Groundskeeping Workers	26.6%	18.1%
8. Tile and Marble Setters	17.0%	15.4%
9. Funeral Attendants	16.7%	14.3%
10. Motorcycle Mechanics	25.9%	12.5%
11. Social Science Research Assistants	30.8%	12.4%
12. Helpers—Pipelayers, Plumbers, Pipefitters, and Steamfitters	44.7%	11.9%
13. Painters, Construction and Maintenance	16.8%	11.8%
14. Helpers—Carpenters	44.7%	11.7%

Fastest-Growing Low-Stress Jobs for Workers Age 16–24

Job	Percent Age 16–24	Percent Growth
15. Tree Trimmers and Pruners	26.6%	11.1%
16. Food Batchmakers	17.1%	10.9%
17. Meat, Poultry, and Fish Cutters and Trimmers	15.8%	10.9%
18. Fence Erectors	31.7%	10.6%
19. Carpenters	15.7%	10.3%
20. Segmental Pavers	19.0%	10.2%
21. Tank Car, Truck, and Ship Loaders	20.0%	9.2%
22. Cooks, Private Household	33.6%	8.8%
23. Library Technicians	43.5%	8.5%
24. Insulation Workers, Floor, Ceiling, and Wall	20.5%	8.4%
25. Library Assistants, Clerical	26.7%	7.9%

Low-Stress Jobs with the Most Openings for Workers Age 16–24

Job	Percent Age 16–24	Annual Openings
1. Laborers and Freight, Stock, and Material Movers, Hand	31.9%	630,487
2. Stock Clerks and Order Fillers	32.6%	439,327
3. Landscaping and Groundskeeping Workers	26.6%	307,138
4. Carpenters	15.7%	223,225
5. Painters, Construction and Maintenance	16.8%	101,140
6. Packaging and Filling Machine Operators and Tenders	17.7%	79,540
7. Fitness Trainers and Aerobics Instructors	29.1%	51,235
8. File Clerks	27.8%	50,088
9. Helpers—Carpenters	44.7%	37,731
10. Helpers—Electricians	44.7%	35,109
11. Word Processors and Typists	17.7%	32,279
12. Helpers—Pipelayers, Plumbers, Pipefitters, and Steamfitters	44.7%	29,332
13. Library Technicians	43.5%	29,075
14. Mail Clerks and Mail Machine Operators, Except Postal Service	21.8%	27,889
15. Library Assistants, Clerical	26.7%	18,961
16. Meat, Poultry, and Fish Cutters and Trimmers	15.8%	17,920
17. Food Batchmakers	17.1%	15,704
18. Tour Guides and Escorts	22.6%	15,027
19. Butchers and Meat Cutters	15.8%	14,503

(continued)

(continued)

Low-Stress Jobs with the Most Openings for Workers Age 16–24

Job	Percent Age 16–24	Annual Openings
20. Woodworking Machine Setters, Operators, and Tenders, Except Sawing	23.4%	11,860
21. Tree Trimmers and Pruners	26.6%	9,621
22. Tile and Marble Setters	17.0%	9,066
23. Environmental Science and Protection Technicians, Including Health	30.8%	8,404
24. Helpers—Painters, Paperhangers, Plasterers, and Stucco Masons	44.7%	7,696
25. Animal Trainers	16.7%	6,713

Best Low-Stress Jobs with a High Percentage of Workers Age 55 and Over

We created the following list by identifying the best low-stress jobs that employ more than 15 percent of workers age 55 and over.

You may be surprised to note that 56 of the best 150 jobs meet this cutoff, whereas only 44 employ the same percentage of people age 16–24. You may be wondering why the older age bracket has a greater presence in low-stress jobs. There are a number of reasons:

- We selected our 150 best jobs partly by eliminating all jobs with annual earnings of less than $20,270, and a lot of entry-level jobs with high concentrations of young people were among those removed.

- Much of the growth in our economy is in fields that can often be stressful, such as health care, human service, and retail. That means a lot of young people who are entering the workforce are steered into stressful jobs.

- Some low-stress jobs have high concentrations of older workers who established themselves in those careers several decades ago, when those jobs held more promise than they do now (a good example is Farmers and Ranchers).

- Some jobs on the following list have a high concentration of older workers because their low level of stress permits workers to avoid burnout and postpone retirement. Many of these jobs might be good choices for someone planning a career change late in life, perhaps in retirement.

Best Low-Stress Jobs with the Highest Percentage of Workers Age 55 and Over

Job	Percent Age 55 and Over
1. Mathematicians	66.7%
2. Farmers and Ranchers	48.7%
3. Physicists	44.4%
4. Tour Guides and Escorts	41.9%
5. Funeral Attendants	41.7%
6. Model Makers, Metal and Plastic	33.3%
7. Industrial Machinery Mechanics	31.6%
8. Maintenance Workers, Machinery	31.6%
9. Farm, Ranch, and Other Agricultural Managers	30.1%
10. Librarians	28.9%
11. Marine Engineers and Naval Architects	28.6%
12. Travel Agents	28.4%
13. Animal Breeders	25.0%
14. Reinforcing Iron and Rebar Workers	25.0%
15. Construction and Building Inspectors	24.2%
16. Forest Fire Inspectors and Prevention Specialists	23.8%
17. Audio-Visual Collections Specialists	20.9%
18. Geographers	20.0%
19. Political Scientists	20.0%
20. Library Assistants, Clerical	19.8%
21. Secretaries, Except Legal, Medical, and Executive	19.5%
22. Archivists	19.4%
23. Curators	19.4%
24. Molders, Shapers, and Casters, Except Metal and Plastic	19.4%
25. Museum Technicians and Conservators	19.4%
26. Millwrights	19.2%
27. Logging Equipment Operators	19.0%
28. Rail-Track Laying and Maintenance Equipment Operators	18.2%
29. Bakers	18.0%
30. Civil Engineers	18.0%
31. Water and Liquid Waste Treatment Plant and System Operators	18.0%
32. Electric Motor, Power Tool, and Related Repairers	17.9%
33. Maintenance and Repair Workers, General	17.8%
34. Metal-Refining Furnace Operators and Tenders	17.6%
35. Pourers and Casters, Metal	17.6%

(continued)

(continued)

Best Low-Stress Jobs with the Highest Percentage of Workers Age 55 and Over

Job	Percent Age 55 and Over
36. Library Technicians	17.4%
37. Locksmiths and Safe Repairers	17.4%
38. Word Processors and Typists	17.4%
39. Conservation Scientists	17.2%
40. Health and Safety Engineers, Except Mining Safety Engineers and Inspectors	17.2%
41. Inspectors, Testers, Sorters, Samplers, and Weighers	17.2%
42. Excavating and Loading Machine and Dragline Operators	17.0%
43. Woodworking Machine Setters, Operators, and Tenders, Except Sawing	17.0%
44. Electrical and Electronic Equipment Assemblers	16.3%
45. Electromechanical Equipment Assemblers	16.3%
46. Mail Clerks and Mail Machine Operators, Except Postal Service	16.3%
47. File Clerks	16.0%
48. Structural Metal Fabricators and Fitters	16.0%
49. Bus and Truck Mechanics and Diesel Engine Specialists	15.9%
50. Refuse and Recyclable Material Collectors	15.9%
51. Geological and Petroleum Technicians	15.8%
52. Occupational Health and Safety Specialists	15.2%
53. Butchers and Meat Cutters	15.1%
54. Meat, Poultry, and Fish Cutters and Trimmers	15.1%
55. Mobile Heavy Equipment Mechanics, Except Engines	15.0%
56. Rail Car Repairers	15.0%

The jobs in the following four lists are derived from the preceding list of the low-stress jobs with the highest percentage of workers age 55 and over.

Best Low-Stress Jobs Overall for Workers Age 55 and Over

Job	Percent Age 55 and Over	Annual Earnings	Percent Growth	Annual Openings
1. Civil Engineers	18.0%	$68,600	18.0%	15,979
2. Construction and Building Inspectors	24.2%	$46,570	18.2%	12,606
3. Bus and Truck Mechanics and Diesel Engine Specialists	15.9%	$37,660	11.5%	25,428
4. Industrial Machinery Mechanics	31.6%	$41,050	9.0%	23,361
5. Maintenance and Repair Workers, General	17.8%	$31,910	10.1%	165,502

Best Low-Stress Jobs Overall for Workers Age 55 and Over

Job	Percent Age 55 and Over	Annual Earnings	Percent Growth	Annual Openings
6. Mobile Heavy Equipment Mechanics, Except Engines	15.0%	$40,440	12.3%	11,037
7. Curators	19.4%	$46,300	23.3%	1,416
8. Librarians	28.9%	$49,060	3.6%	18,945
9. Water and Liquid Waste Treatment Plant and System Operators	18.0%	$36,070	13.8%	9,575
10. Farm, Ranch, and Other Agricultural Managers	30.1%	$52,070	1.1%	18,101
11. Occupational Health and Safety Specialists	15.2%	$58,030	8.1%	3,440
12. Reinforcing Iron and Rebar Workers	25.0%	$38,220	11.5%	4,502
13. Marine Engineers and Naval Architects	28.6%	$72,990	10.9%	495
14. Locksmiths and Safe Repairers	17.4%	$32,020	22.1%	3,545
15. Mathematicians	66.7%	$86,930	10.2%	473
16. Refuse and Recyclable Material Collectors	15.9%	$28,970	7.4%	37,785
17. Health and Safety Engineers, Except Mining Safety Engineers and Inspectors	17.2%	$66,290	9.6%	1,105
18. Physicists	44.4%	$94,240	6.8%	1,302
19. Farmers and Ranchers	48.7%	$37,130	–8.5%	129,552
20. Geological and Petroleum Technicians	15.8%	$46,160	8.6%	1,895
21. Library Technicians	17.4%	$26,560	8.5%	29,075
22. Archivists	19.4%	$40,730	14.4%	795
23. Bakers	18.0%	$22,030	10.0%	31,442
24. Millwrights	19.2%	$45,630	5.8%	4,758
25. Tour Guides and Escorts	41.9%	$20,420	21.2%	15,027

Best-Paying Low-Stress Jobs for Workers Age 55 and Over

Job	Percent Age 55 and Over	Annual Earnings
1. Physicists	44.4%	$94,240
2. Political Scientists	20.0%	$90,140
3. Mathematicians	66.7%	$86,930
4. Marine Engineers and Naval Architects	28.6%	$72,990
5. Civil Engineers	18.0%	$68,600
6. Health and Safety Engineers, Except Mining Safety Engineers and Inspectors	17.2%	$66,290
7. Geographers	20.0%	$62,990
8. Occupational Health and Safety Specialists	15.2%	$58,030

(continued)

(continued)

Best-Paying Low-Stress Jobs for Workers Age 55 and Over

Job	Percent Age 55 and Over	Annual Earnings
9. Conservation Scientists	17.2%	$54,970
10. Farm, Ranch, and Other Agricultural Managers	30.1%	$52,070
11. Librarians	28.9%	$49,060
12. Construction and Building Inspectors	24.2%	$46,570
13. Curators	19.4%	$46,300
14. Geological and Petroleum Technicians	15.8%	$46,160
15. Millwrights	19.2%	$45,630
16. Rail Car Repairers	15.0%	$43,320
17. Model Makers, Metal and Plastic	33.3%	$42,050
18. Industrial Machinery Mechanics	31.6%	$41,050
19. Archivists	19.4%	$40,730
20. Audio-Visual Collections Specialists	20.9%	$40,530
21. Mobile Heavy Equipment Mechanics, Except Engines	15.0%	$40,440
22. Rail-Track Laying and Maintenance Equipment Operators	18.2%	$40,000
23. Reinforcing Iron and Rebar Workers	25.0%	$38,220
24. Bus and Truck Mechanics and Diesel Engine Specialists	15.9%	$37,660
25. Farmers and Ranchers	48.7%	$37,130

Fastest-Growing Low-Stress Jobs for Workers Age 55 and Over

Job	Percent Age 55 and Over	Percent Growth
1. Curators	19.4%	23.3%
2. Locksmiths and Safe Repairers	17.4%	22.1%
3. Tour Guides and Escorts	41.9%	21.2%
4. Construction and Building Inspectors	24.2%	18.2%
5. Civil Engineers	18.0%	18.0%
6. Museum Technicians and Conservators	19.4%	15.9%
7. Archivists	19.4%	14.4%
8. Funeral Attendants	41.7%	14.3%
9. Water and Liquid Waste Treatment Plant and System Operators	18.0%	13.8%
10. Mobile Heavy Equipment Mechanics, Except Engines	15.0%	12.3%
11. Bus and Truck Mechanics and Diesel Engine Specialists	15.9%	11.5%

150 Best Low-Stress Jobs © JIST Works

Fastest-Growing Low-Stress Jobs for Workers Age 55 and Over

Job	Percent Age 55 and Over	Percent Growth
12. Reinforcing Iron and Rebar Workers	25.0%	11.5%
13. Marine Engineers and Naval Architects	28.6%	10.9%
14. Meat, Poultry, and Fish Cutters and Trimmers	15.1%	10.9%
15. Mathematicians	66.7%	10.2%
16. Maintenance and Repair Workers, General	17.8%	10.1%
17. Bakers	18.0%	10.0%
18. Health and Safety Engineers, Except Mining Safety Engineers and Inspectors	17.2%	9.6%
19. Industrial Machinery Mechanics	31.6%	9.0%
20. Geological and Petroleum Technicians	15.8%	8.6%
21. Library Technicians	17.4%	8.5%
22. Excavating and Loading Machine and Dragline Operators	17.0%	8.3%
23. Occupational Health and Safety Specialists	15.2%	8.1%
24. Library Assistants, Clerical	19.8%	7.9%
25. Refuse and Recyclable Material Collectors	15.9%	7.4%

Low-Stress Jobs with the Most Openings for Workers Age 55 and Over

Job	Percent Age 55 and Over	Annual Openings
1. Secretaries, Except Legal, Medical, and Executive	19.5%	239,630
2. Maintenance and Repair Workers, General	17.8%	165,502
3. Farmers and Ranchers	48.7%	129,552
4. Inspectors, Testers, Sorters, Samplers, and Weighers	17.2%	75,361
5. File Clerks	16.0%	50,088
6. Refuse and Recyclable Material Collectors	15.9%	37,785
7. Word Processors and Typists	17.4%	32,279
8. Bakers	18.0%	31,442
9. Library Technicians	17.4%	29,075
10. Mail Clerks and Mail Machine Operators, Except Postal Service	16.3%	27,889
11. Electrical and Electronic Equipment Assemblers	16.3%	26,595
12. Bus and Truck Mechanics and Diesel Engine Specialists	15.9%	25,428
13. Industrial Machinery Mechanics	31.6%	23,361
14. Structural Metal Fabricators and Fitters	16.0%	20,746
15. Library Assistants, Clerical	19.8%	18,961

(continued)

(continued)

Low-Stress Jobs with the Most Openings for Workers Age 55 and Over

Job	Percent Age 55 and Over	Annual Openings
16. Librarians	28.9%	18,945
17. Farm, Ranch, and Other Agricultural Managers	30.1%	18,101
18. Meat, Poultry, and Fish Cutters and Trimmers	15.1%	17,920
19. Civil Engineers	18.0%	15,979
20. Maintenance Workers, Machinery	31.6%	15,055
21. Tour Guides and Escorts	41.9%	15,027
22. Butchers and Meat Cutters	15.1%	14,503
23. Travel Agents	28.4%	13,128
24. Construction and Building Inspectors	24.2%	12,606
25. Woodworking Machine Setters, Operators, and Tenders, Except Sawing	17.0%	11,860

Best Low-Stress Jobs with a High Percentage of Part-Time Workers

A wide variety of industries—including manufacturing, business, and construction—are also represented in the following lists of the low-stress jobs with high percentages (more than 20 percent) of part-time workers.

In some cases, people work part time because they want the freedom of time this arrangement can provide, but others may do so because they can't find full-time employment in these jobs. These folks may work in other full- or part-time jobs to make ends meet. If you want to work part time now or in the future, these lists will help you identify low-stress jobs that are more likely to provide that opportunity. If you want full-time work, the lists may also help you identify low-stress jobs for which such opportunities are more difficult to find. In either case, it's good information to know in advance.

The earnings estimates in the following lists are based on a survey of both part-time and full-time workers. On average, part-time workers earn about 10 percent less per hour than full-time workers.

Best Low-Stress Jobs with the Highest Percentage of Part-Time Workers

Job	Percent Part-Time Workers
1. Library Assistants, Clerical	70.0%
2. Funeral Attendants	59.3%
3. Library Technicians	58.3%
4. File Clerks	54.2%
5. Travel Agents	51.3%
6. Locksmiths and Safe Repairers	50.0%
7. Massage Therapists	48.3%
8. Cooks, Private Household	47.8%
9. Word Processors and Typists	44.9%
10. Stock Clerks and Order Fillers	44.2%
11. Fitness Trainers and Aerobics Instructors	44.1%
12. Food Batchmakers	41.2%
13. Rolling Machine Setters, Operators, and Tenders, Metal and Plastic	40.0%
14. Mail Clerks and Mail Machine Operators, Except Postal Service	39.4%
15. Laborers and Freight, Stock, and Material Movers, Hand	39.4%
16. Audio-Visual Collections Specialists	39.3%
17. Bakers	38.7%
18. Refuse and Recyclable Material Collectors	36.0%
19. Secretaries, Except Legal, Medical, and Executive	34.8%
20. Landscaping and Groundskeeping Workers	32.8%
21. Tree Trimmers and Pruners	32.8%
22. Meter Readers, Utilities	32.8%
23. Butchers and Meat Cutters	32.8%
24. Meat, Poultry, and Fish Cutters and Trimmers	32.8%
25. Archivists	32.4%
26. Curators	32.4%
27. Museum Technicians and Conservators	32.4%
28. Helpers—Carpenters	32.2%
29. Helpers—Electricians	32.2%
30. Helpers—Painters, Paperhangers, Plasterers, and Stucco Masons	32.2%
31. Helpers—Pipelayers, Plumbers, Pipefitters, and Steamfitters	32.2%
32. Commercial and Industrial Designers	32.0%
33. Set and Exhibit Designers	32.0%
34. Tour Guides and Escorts	31.4%
35. Excavating and Loading Machine and Dragline Operators	29.5%
36. Gas Compressor and Gas Pumping Station Operators	29.5%

(continued)

(continued)

Best Low-Stress Jobs with the Highest Percentage of Part-Time Workers

Job	Percent Part-Time Workers
37. Wellhead Pumpers	29.5%
38. Tank Car, Truck, and Ship Loaders	29.5%
39. Social Science Research Assistants	28.9%
40. Environmental Science and Protection Technicians, Including Health	28.9%
41. Forest and Conservation Technicians	28.9%
42. Occupational Health and Safety Specialists	28.9%
43. Animal Breeders	28.7%
44. Sawing Machine Setters, Operators, and Tenders, Wood	28.6%
45. Librarians	27.3%
46. Woodworking Machine Setters, Operators, and Tenders, Except Sawing	26.3%
47. Geological and Petroleum Technicians	25.2%
48. Marine Engineers and Naval Architects	25.0%
49. Survey Researchers	25.0%
50. Sociologists	25.0%
51. Geographers	25.0%
52. Political Scientists	25.0%
53. Multiple Machine Tool Setters, Operators, and Tenders, Metal and Plastic	25.0%
54. Animal Trainers	23.6%
55. Painters, Construction and Maintenance	21.9%
56. Credit Analysts	21.8%
57. Computer, Automated Teller, and Office Machine Repairers	21.1%
58. Civil Engineering Technicians	20.9%
59. Electrical and Electronic Engineering Technicians	20.9%
60. Industrial Engineering Technicians	20.9%
61. Mechanical Engineering Technicians	20.9%
62. Bindery Workers	20.5%

The jobs in the following four lists are derived from the preceding list of the low-stress jobs with the highest percentage of part-time workers.

Best Low-Stress Jobs Overall with a High Percentage of Part-Time Workers

Job	Percent Part-Time Workers	Annual Earnings	Percent Growth	Annual Openings
1. Environmental Science and Protection Technicians, Including Health	28.9%	$38,090	28.0%	8,404
2. Painters, Construction and Maintenance	21.9%	$31,190	11.8%	101,140
3. Fitness Trainers and Aerobics Instructors	44.1%	$25,910	26.8%	51,235
4. Massage Therapists	48.3%	$33,400	20.3%	9,193
5. Curators	32.4%	$46,300	23.3%	1,416
6. Landscaping and Groundskeeping Workers	32.8%	$21,260	18.1%	307,138
7. Librarians	27.3%	$49,060	3.6%	18,945
8. Civil Engineering Technicians	20.9%	$40,560	10.2%	7,499
9. Industrial Engineering Technicians	20.9%	$46,810	9.9%	6,172
10. Electrical and Electronic Engineering Technicians	20.9%	$50,660	3.6%	12,583
11. Helpers—Pipelayers, Plumbers, Pipefitters, and Steamfitters	32.2%	$23,910	11.9%	29,332
12. Survey Researchers	25.0%	$33,360	15.9%	4,959
13. Helpers—Carpenters	32.2%	$23,060	11.7%	37,731
14. Locksmiths and Safe Repairers	50.0%	$32,020	22.1%	3,545
15. Refuse and Recyclable Material Collectors	36.0%	$28,970	7.4%	37,785
16. Set and Exhibit Designers	32.0%	$41,820	17.8%	1,402
17. Animal Trainers	23.6%	$26,310	22.7%	6,713
18. Computer, Automated Teller, and Office Machine Repairers	21.1%	$36,480	3.0%	22,330
19. Marine Engineers and Naval Architects	25.0%	$72,990	10.9%	495
20. Commercial and Industrial Designers	32.0%	$54,560	7.2%	4,777
21. Social Science Research Assistants	28.9%	$33,860	12.4%	3,571
22. Occupational Health and Safety Specialists	28.9%	$58,030	8.1%	3,440
23. Tree Trimmers and Pruners	32.8%	$28,250	11.1%	9,621
24. Library Technicians	58.3%	$26,560	8.5%	29,075
25. Archivists	32.4%	$40,730	14.4%	795

Best-Paying Low-Stress Jobs with a High Percentage of Part-Time Workers

Job	Percent Part-Time Workers	Annual Earnings
1. Political Scientists	25.0%	$90,140
2. Marine Engineers and Naval Architects	25.0%	$72,990
3. Geographers	25.0%	$62,990
4. Sociologists	25.0%	$60,290
5. Occupational Health and Safety Specialists	28.9%	$58,030
6. Commercial and Industrial Designers	32.0%	$54,560
7. Credit Analysts	21.8%	$52,350
8. Electrical and Electronic Engineering Technicians	20.9%	$50,660
9. Librarians	27.3%	$49,060
10. Industrial Engineering Technicians	20.9%	$46,810
11. Curators	32.4%	$46,300
12. Geological and Petroleum Technicians	25.2%	$46,160
13. Mechanical Engineering Technicians	20.9%	$45,850
14. Gas Compressor and Gas Pumping Station Operators	29.5%	$45,400
15. Set and Exhibit Designers	32.0%	$41,820
16. Archivists	32.4%	$40,730
17. Civil Engineering Technicians	20.9%	$40,560
18. Audio-Visual Collections Specialists	39.3%	$40,530
19. Environmental Science and Protection Technicians, Including Health	28.9%	$38,090
20. Computer, Automated Teller, and Office Machine Repairers	21.1%	$36,480
21. Wellhead Pumpers	29.5%	$36,150
22. Museum Technicians and Conservators	32.4%	$34,340
23. Social Science Research Assistants	28.9%	$33,860
24. Massage Therapists	48.3%	$33,400
25. Survey Researchers	25.0%	$33,360

Fastest-Growing Low-Stress Jobs with a High Percentage of Part-Time Workers

Job	Percent Part-Time Workers	Percent Growth
1. Environmental Science and Protection Technicians, Including Health	28.9%	28.0%
2. Fitness Trainers and Aerobics Instructors	44.1%	26.8%

Fastest-Growing Low-Stress Jobs with a High Percentage of Part-Time Workers

Job	Percent Part-Time Workers	Percent Growth
3. Curators	32.4%	23.3%
4. Animal Trainers	23.6%	22.7%
5. Locksmiths and Safe Repairers	50.0%	22.1%
6. Tour Guides and Escorts	31.4%	21.2%
7. Massage Therapists	48.3%	20.3%
8. Landscaping and Groundskeeping Workers	32.8%	18.1%
9. Set and Exhibit Designers	32.0%	17.8%
10. Survey Researchers	25.0%	15.9%
11. Museum Technicians and Conservators	32.4%	15.9%
12. Archivists	32.4%	14.4%
13. Funeral Attendants	59.3%	14.3%
14. Social Science Research Assistants	28.9%	12.4%
15. Helpers—Pipelayers, Plumbers, Pipefitters, and Steamfitters	32.2%	11.9%
16. Painters, Construction and Maintenance	21.9%	11.8%
17. Helpers—Carpenters	32.2%	11.7%
18. Tree Trimmers and Pruners	32.8%	11.1%
19. Meat, Poultry, and Fish Cutters and Trimmers	32.8%	10.9%
20. Food Batchmakers	41.2%	10.9%
21. Marine Engineers and Naval Architects	25.0%	10.9%
22. Civil Engineering Technicians	20.9%	10.2%
23. Bakers	38.7%	10.0%
24. Sociologists	25.0%	10.0%
25. Industrial Engineering Technicians	20.9%	9.9%

Low-Stress Jobs with the Most Openings with a High Percentage of Part-Time Workers

Job	Percent Part-Time Workers	Annual Openings
1. Laborers and Freight, Stock, and Material Movers, Hand	39.4%	630,487
2. Stock Clerks and Order Fillers	44.2%	439,327
3. Landscaping and Groundskeeping Workers	32.8%	307,138

(continued)

(continued)

Low-Stress Jobs with the Most Openings with a High Percentage of Part-Time Workers

Job	Percent Part-Time Workers	Annual Openings
4. Secretaries, Except Legal, Medical, and Executive	34.8%	239,630
5. Painters, Construction and Maintenance	21.9%	101,140
6. Fitness Trainers and Aerobics Instructors	44.1%	51,235
7. File Clerks	54.2%	50,088
8. Refuse and Recyclable Material Collectors	36.0%	37,785
9. Helpers—Carpenters	32.2%	37,731
10. Helpers—Electricians	32.2%	35,109
11. Word Processors and Typists	44.9%	32,279
12. Bakers	38.7%	31,442
13. Helpers—Pipelayers, Plumbers, Pipefitters, and Steamfitters	32.2%	29,332
14. Library Technicians	58.3%	29,075
15. Mail Clerks and Mail Machine Operators, Except Postal Service	39.4%	27,889
16. Computer, Automated Teller, and Office Machine Repairers	21.1%	22,330
17. Library Assistants, Clerical	70.0%	18,961
18. Librarians	27.3%	18,945
19. Meat, Poultry, and Fish Cutters and Trimmers	32.8%	17,920
20. Multiple Machine Tool Setters, Operators, and Tenders, Metal and Plastic	25.0%	15,709
21. Food Batchmakers	41.2%	15,704
22. Tour Guides and Escorts	31.4%	15,027
23. Butchers and Meat Cutters	32.8%	14,503
24. Travel Agents	51.3%	13,128
25. Electrical and Electronic Engineering Technicians	20.9%	12,583

Best Low-Stress Jobs with a High Percentage of Self-Employed Workers

About 8 percent of all working people are self-employed. Although you may think of the self-employed as having similar jobs, they actually work in an enormous range of situations, fields, and work environments that you may not have considered.

Among the self-employed are people who own small or large businesses, as many animal trainers and locksmiths do; people working on a contract basis for one or more employers; people running home consulting or other businesses; and people in many other situations. They may go to the same worksite every day, as commercial and industrial designers do; visit multiple employers during the course of a week, as many models do; or do most of their work from home, as many craft artists do. Some work part time, others full time, some as a way to have fun, some so they can spend time with their kids or go to school.

The point is that there is an enormous range of situations, and one of them could make sense for you now or in the future.

The following list contains low-stress jobs in which more than 10 percent of the workers are self-employed.

Best Low-Stress Jobs with the Highest Percentage of Self-Employed Workers

Job	Percent Self-Employed Workers
1. Farmers and Ranchers	100.0%
2. Massage Therapists	64.0%
3. Animal Trainers	56.9%
4. Animal Breeders	50.2%
5. Carpet Installers	49.0%
6. Floor Layers, Except Carpet, Wood, and Hard Tiles	47.7%
7. Painters, Construction and Maintenance	42.2%
8. Tile and Marble Setters	33.8%
9. Carpenters	31.8%
10. Commercial and Industrial Designers	29.8%
11. Set and Exhibit Designers	29.8%
12. Tree Trimmers and Pruners	28.9%
13. Locksmiths and Safe Repairers	28.3%
14. Logging Equipment Operators	28.0%
15. Home Appliance Repairers	26.7%
16. Brickmasons and Blockmasons	24.5%
17. Molders, Shapers, and Casters, Except Metal and Plastic	24.2%
18. Fence Erectors	23.2%
19. Outdoor Power Equipment and Other Small Engine Mechanics	23.0%
20. Stonemasons	22.8%
21. Motorcycle Mechanics	21.9%
22. Landscaping and Groundskeeping Workers	20.5%
23. Tour Guides and Escorts	20.1%
24. Computer, Automated Teller, and Office Machine Repairers	19.7%
25. Soil and Plant Scientists	19.5%
26. Excavating and Loading Machine and Dragline Operators	14.9%

(continued)

(continued)

Best Low-Stress Jobs with the Highest Percentage of Self-Employed Workers

Job	Percent Self-Employed Workers
27. Travel Agents	13.4%
28. Electric Motor, Power Tool, and Related Repairers	12.5%
29. Marine Engineers and Naval Architects	12.4%
30. Electronic Home Entertainment Equipment Installers and Repairers	12.3%
31. Pipelayers	11.6%

The jobs in the following four lists are derived from the preceding list of the low-stress jobs with the highest percentage of self-employed workers. Where the following lists give earnings estimates, keep in mind that these figures are based on a survey that *doesn't include self-employed workers*. The median earnings for self-employed workers in these occupations may be significantly higher or lower.

Best Low-Stress Jobs Overall with a High Percentage of Self-Employed Workers

Job	Percent Self-Employed Workers	Annual Earnings	Percent Growth	Annual Openings
1. Carpenters	31.8%	$36,550	10.3%	223,225
2. Brickmasons and Blockmasons	24.5%	$42,980	9.7%	17,569
3. Tile and Marble Setters	33.8%	$36,590	15.4%	9,066
4. Massage Therapists	64.0%	$33,400	20.3%	9,193
5. Painters, Construction and Maintenance	42.2%	$31,190	11.8%	101,140
6. Computer, Automated Teller, and Office Machine Repairers	19.7%	$36,480	3.0%	22,330
7. Landscaping and Groundskeeping Workers	20.5%	$21,260	18.1%	307,138
8. Farmers and Ranchers	100.0%	$37,130	–8.5%	129,552
9. Commercial and Industrial Designers	29.8%	$54,560	7.2%	4,777
10. Locksmiths and Safe Repairers	28.3%	$32,020	22.1%	3,545
11. Set and Exhibit Designers	29.8%	$41,820	17.8%	1,402
12. Tour Guides and Escorts	20.1%	$20,420	21.2%	15,027
13. Animal Trainers	56.9%	$26,310	22.7%	6,713
14. Marine Engineers and Naval Architects	12.4%	$72,990	10.9%	495

Best Low-Stress Jobs Overall with a High Percentage of Self-Employed Workers

Job	Percent Self-Employed Workers	Annual Earnings	Percent Growth	Annual Openings
15. Tree Trimmers and Pruners	28.9%	$28,250	11.1%	9,621
16. Pipelayers	11.6%	$30,330	8.7%	8,902
17. Excavating and Loading Machine and Dragline Operators	14.9%	$32,930	8.3%	6,562
18. Motorcycle Mechanics	21.9%	$30,050	12.5%	3,564
19. Soil and Plant Scientists	19.5%	$56,080	8.4%	850
20. Stonemasons	22.8%	$35,960	10.0%	2,657
21. Carpet Installers	49.0%	$34,560	−1.2%	6,692
22. Home Appliance Repairers	26.7%	$33,860	1.5%	4,243
23. Travel Agents	13.4%	$29,210	1.0%	13,128
24. Fence Erectors	23.2%	$26,400	10.6%	2,812
25. Outdoor Power Equipment and Other Small Engine Mechanics	23.0%	$26,910	5.5%	5,130

Best-Paying Low-Stress Jobs with a High Percentage of Self-Employed Workers

Job	Percent Self-Employed Workers	Annual Earnings
1. Marine Engineers and Naval Architects	12.4%	$72,990
2. Soil and Plant Scientists	19.5%	$56,080
3. Commercial and Industrial Designers	29.8%	$54,560
4. Brickmasons and Blockmasons	24.5%	$42,980
5. Set and Exhibit Designers	29.8%	$41,820
6. Farmers and Ranchers	100.0%	$37,130
7. Tile and Marble Setters	33.8%	$36,590
8. Carpenters	31.8%	$36,550
9. Computer, Automated Teller, and Office Machine Repairers	19.7%	$36,480
10. Stonemasons	22.8%	$35,960
11. Carpet Installers	49.0%	$34,560
12. Floor Layers, Except Carpet, Wood, and Hard Tiles	47.7%	$34,190
13. Home Appliance Repairers	26.7%	$33,860

(continued)

(continued)

Best-Paying Low-Stress Jobs with a High Percentage of Self-Employed Workers

Job	Percent Self-Employed Workers	Annual Earnings
14. Massage Therapists	64.0%	$33,400
15. Excavating and Loading Machine and Dragline Operators	14.9%	$32,930
16. Electric Motor, Power Tool, and Related Repairers	12.5%	$32,860
17. Locksmiths and Safe Repairers	28.3%	$32,020
18. Painters, Construction and Maintenance	42.2%	$31,190
19. Pipelayers	11.6%	$30,330
20. Motorcycle Mechanics	21.9%	$30,050
21. Electronic Home Entertainment Equipment Installers and Repairers	12.3%	$29,980
22. Logging Equipment Operators	28.0%	$29,700
23. Travel Agents	13.4%	$29,210
24. Tree Trimmers and Pruners	28.9%	$28,250
25. Animal Breeders	50.2%	$27,090

Fastest-Growing Low-Stress Jobs with a High Percentage of Self-Employed Workers

Job	Percent Self-Employed Workers	Percent Growth
1. Animal Trainers	56.9%	22.7%
2. Locksmiths and Safe Repairers	28.3%	22.1%
3. Tour Guides and Escorts	20.1%	21.2%
4. Massage Therapists	64.0%	20.3%
5. Landscaping and Groundskeeping Workers	20.5%	18.1%
6. Set and Exhibit Designers	29.8%	17.8%
7. Tile and Marble Setters	33.8%	15.4%
8. Motorcycle Mechanics	21.9%	12.5%
9. Painters, Construction and Maintenance	42.2%	11.8%
10. Tree Trimmers and Pruners	28.9%	11.1%
11. Marine Engineers and Naval Architects	12.4%	10.9%
12. Fence Erectors	23.2%	10.6%

Fastest-Growing Low-Stress Jobs with a High Percentage of Self-Employed Workers

Job	Percent Self-Employed Workers	Percent Growth
13. Carpenters	31.8%	10.3%
14. Stonemasons	22.8%	10.0%
15. Brickmasons and Blockmasons	24.5%	9.7%
16. Pipelayers	11.6%	8.7%
17. Soil and Plant Scientists	19.5%	8.4%
18. Excavating and Loading Machine and Dragline Operators	14.9%	8.3%
19. Commercial and Industrial Designers	29.8%	7.2%
20. Outdoor Power Equipment and Other Small Engine Mechanics	23.0%	5.5%
21. Animal Breeders	50.2%	4.4%
22. Computer, Automated Teller, and Office Machine Repairers	19.7%	3.0%
23. Electronic Home Entertainment Equipment Installers and Repairers	12.3%	3.0%
24. Home Appliance Repairers	26.7%	1.5%
25. Molders, Shapers, and Casters, Except Metal and Plastic	24.2%	1.3%

Low-Stress Jobs with the Most Openings with a High Percentage of Self-Employed Workers

Job	Percent Self-Employed Workers	Annual Openings
1. Landscaping and Groundskeeping Workers	20.5%	307,138
2. Carpenters	31.8%	223,225
3. Farmers and Ranchers	100.0%	129,552
4. Painters, Construction and Maintenance	42.2%	101,140
5. Computer, Automated Teller, and Office Machine Repairers	19.7%	22,330
6. Brickmasons and Blockmasons	24.5%	17,569
7. Tour Guides and Escorts	20.1%	15,027
8. Travel Agents	13.4%	13,128
9. Tree Trimmers and Pruners	28.9%	9,621
10. Massage Therapists	64.0%	9,193
11. Tile and Marble Setters	33.8%	9,066
12. Pipelayers	11.6%	8,902
13. Animal Trainers	56.9%	6,713

(continued)

(continued)

Low-Stress Jobs with the Most Openings with a High Percentage of Self-Employed Workers		
Job	**Percent Self-Employed Workers**	**Annual Openings**
14. Carpet Installers	49.0%	6,692
15. Excavating and Loading Machine and Dragline Operators	14.9%	6,562
16. Molders, Shapers, and Casters, Except Metal and Plastic	24.2%	5,788
17. Outdoor Power Equipment and Other Small Engine Mechanics	23.0%	5,130
18. Commercial and Industrial Designers	29.8%	4,777
19. Home Appliance Repairers	26.7%	4,243
20. Motorcycle Mechanics	21.9%	3,564
21. Locksmiths and Safe Repairers	28.3%	3,545
22. Electronic Home Entertainment Equipment Installers and Repairers	12.3%	3,065
23. Fence Erectors	23.2%	2,812
24. Logging Equipment Operators	28.0%	2,756
25. Stonemasons	22.8%	2,657

Best Low-Stress Jobs Employing a High Percentage of Women

To create the eight lists that follow, we sorted the 150 best low-stress jobs according to the percentages of women and men in the workforce. We knew we would create some controversy when we first included the best jobs lists with high percentages (more than 70 percent) of men and women in an earlier *Best Jobs* book. But these lists aren't meant to restrict women or men from considering job options; our reason for including these lists is exactly the opposite. We hope the lists help people see possibilities that they might not otherwise have considered.

The fact is that jobs with high percentages of women or high percentages of men offer good opportunities for both men and women if they want to do one of these jobs. So we suggest that women browse the lists of low-stress jobs that employ high percentages of men and that men browse the lists of low-stress jobs with high percentages of women. There are jobs among both lists that pay well, and women or men who are interested in them and who have or can obtain the necessary education and training should consider them.

It is interesting to compare the two sets of low-stress jobs—those with the highest percentage of men and those with the highest percentage of women—in terms of the economic measures that we use to rank these lists. Sadly, the male-dominated jobs are significantly more rewarding on two of the three measures. The male-dominated jobs have higher average earnings than the female-dominated jobs ($36,551 compared to $29,284) and are growing faster (7.0 percent compared to –1.7 percent). That's right, the female-dominated low-stress jobs are actually *shrinking* on average. Fortunately, the female-dominated jobs have a much larger average number of projected job openings (43,330 compared to 26,123), mostly because of the very large number of openings for Secretaries, Except Legal, Medical, and Executive.

If you were to look at *all* the female-dominated occupations in the economy, not just the low-stress ones, you would find considerably better figures for job growth and openings. But many of these more rewarding jobs are in the high-stress fields of health care and classroom teaching. Women who want good opportunities in low-stress jobs may need to consider choosing occupations where they aren't in the great majority.

Best Low-Stress Jobs Employing the Highest Percentage of Women

Job	Percent Women
1. Secretaries, Except Legal, Medical, and Executive	96.8%
2. Word Processors and Typists	90.8%
3. Massage Therapists	86.0%
4. Librarians	84.8%
5. Library Assistants, Clerical	83.1%
6. File Clerks	80.2%
7. Travel Agents	76.5%
8. Insurance Underwriters	72.3%
9. Audio-Visual Collections Specialists	70.4%

The jobs in the following four lists are derived from the preceding list of the low-stress jobs employing the highest percentage of women.

Best Low-Stress Jobs Overall Employing a High Percentage of Women

Job	Percent Women	Annual Earnings	Percent Growth	Annual Openings
1. Librarians	84.8%	$49,060	3.6%	18,945
2. Insurance Underwriters	72.3%	$52,350	6.3%	6,880
3. Massage Therapists	86.0%	$33,400	20.3%	9,193
4. Secretaries, Except Legal, Medical, and Executive	96.8%	$27,450	1.2%	239,630
5. Library Assistants, Clerical	83.1%	$21,640	7.9%	18,961
6. Word Processors and Typists	90.8%	$29,430	–11.6%	32,279

(continued)

(continued)

Best Low-Stress Jobs Overall Employing a High Percentage of Women

Job	Percent Women	Annual Earnings	Percent Growth	Annual Openings
7. Travel Agents	76.5%	$29,210	1.0%	13,128
8. File Clerks	80.2%	$22,090	–41.3%	50,088
9. Audio-Visual Collections Specialists	70.4%	$40,530	–13.8%	868

Best-Paying Low-Stress Jobs Employing a High Percentage of Women

Job	Percent Women	Annual Earnings
1. Insurance Underwriters	72.3%	$52,350
2. Librarians	84.8%	$49,060
3. Audio-Visual Collections Specialists	70.4%	$40,530
4. Massage Therapists	86.0%	$33,400
5. Word Processors and Typists	90.8%	$29,430
6. Travel Agents	76.5%	$29,210
7. Secretaries, Except Legal, Medical, and Executive	96.8%	$27,450
8. File Clerks	80.2%	$22,090
9. Library Assistants, Clerical	83.1%	$21,640

Fastest-Growing Low-Stress Jobs Employing a High Percentage of Women

Job	Percent Women	Percent Growth
1. Massage Therapists	86.0%	20.3%
2. Library Assistants, Clerical	83.1%	7.9%
3. Insurance Underwriters	72.3%	6.3%
4. Librarians	84.8%	3.6%
5. Secretaries, Except Legal, Medical, and Executive	96.8%	1.2%
6. Travel Agents	76.5%	1.0%

Low-Stress Jobs with the Most Openings Employing a High Percentage of Women

Job	Percent Women	Annual Openings
1. Secretaries, Except Legal, Medical, and Executive	96.8%	239,630
2. File Clerks	80.2%	50,088
3. Word Processors and Typists	90.8%	32,279
4. Library Assistants, Clerical	83.1%	18,961
5. Librarians	84.8%	18,945
6. Travel Agents	76.5%	13,128
7. Massage Therapists	86.0%	9,193
8. Insurance Underwriters	72.3%	6,880
9. Audio-Visual Collections Specialists	70.4%	868

Best Low-Stress Jobs Employing a High Percentage of Men

If you haven't already read the intro to the previous group of lists, best low-stress jobs with high percentages of women, consider doing so. Much of the content there applies to these lists as well.

We didn't include these groups of lists with the assumption that men should consider low-stress jobs with high percentages of men or that women should consider low-stress jobs with high percentages of women. Instead, these lists are here because we think they are interesting and perhaps helpful in considering nontraditional career options. For example, some men would do very well in and enjoy some of the jobs with high percentages of women but may not have considered them seriously. In a similar way, some women would very much enjoy and do well in some jobs that traditionally have been held by high percentages of men. We hope that these lists help you consider options that you simply didn't seriously consider because of gender stereotypes.

In the jobs on the following lists, more than 70 percent of the workers are men. Notice that 95 jobs meet this cutoff, whereas only nine female-dominated jobs do. This huge imbalance shouldn't be surprising, because jobs working with things rather than people have traditionally had high concentrations of men, whereas women have traditionally been concentrated in jobs that have a lot of personal contact and the stress that comes with it. Nevertheless, increasing numbers of women are entering many of these jobs.

Best Low-Stress Jobs Employing the Highest Percentage of Men

Job	Percent Men
1. Helpers—Extraction Workers	100.0%
2. Rail-Track Laying and Maintenance Equipment Operators	100.0%
3. Reinforcing Iron and Rebar Workers	100.0%
4. Roustabouts, Oil and Gas	100.0%
5. Tank Car, Truck, and Ship Loaders	100.0%
6. Logging Equipment Operators	99.2%
7. Bus and Truck Mechanics and Diesel Engine Specialists	98.9%
8. Cement Masons and Concrete Finishers	98.5%
9. Mobile Heavy Equipment Mechanics, Except Engines	98.5%
10. Railcar Repairers	98.5%
11. Terrazzo Workers and Finishers	98.5%
12. Gas Compressor and Gas Pumping Station Operators	98.4%
13. Wellhead Pumpers	98.4%
14. Brickmasons and Blockmasons	98.2%
15. Stonemasons	98.2%
16. Motorcycle Mechanics	98.0%
17. Outdoor Power Equipment and Other Small Engine Mechanics	98.0%
18. Pipelayers	98.0%
19. Structural Iron and Steel Workers	97.9%
20. Fence Erectors	97.8%
21. Electric Motor, Power Tool, and Related Repairers	97.6%
22. Electronic Home Entertainment Equipment Installers and Repairers	97.4%
23. Carpenters	97.2%
24. Excavating and Loading Machine and Dragline Operators	97.0%
25. Carpet Installers	96.7%
26. Floor Layers, Except Carpet, Wood, and Hard Tiles	96.7%
27. Tile and Marble Setters	96.7%
28. Security and Fire Alarm Systems Installers	96.6%
29. Highway Maintenance Workers	96.3%
30. Septic Tank Servicers and Sewer Pipe Cleaners	96.2%
31. Water and Liquid Waste Treatment Plant and System Operators	96.2%
32. Industrial Machinery Mechanics	95.8%
33. Maintenance and Repair Workers, General	95.8%
34. Sheet Metal Workers	95.7%
35. Maintenance Workers, Machinery	94.9%
36. Home Appliance Repairers	94.7%
37. Boilermakers	94.5%

Best Low-Stress Jobs Employing the Highest Percentage of Men

Job	Percent Men
38. Mechanical Engineers	93.9%
39. Welders, Cutters, Solderers, and Brazers	93.8%
40. Welding, Soldering, and Brazing Machine Setters, Operators, and Tenders	93.8%
41. Helpers—Carpenters	93.4%
42. Helpers—Electricians	93.4%
43. Helpers—Painters, Paperhangers, Plasterers, and Stucco Masons	93.4%
44. Helpers—Pipelayers, Plumbers, Pipefitters, and Steamfitters	93.4%
45. Millwrights	93.4%
46. Structural Metal Fabricators and Fitters	93.4%
47. Segmental Pavers	92.8%
48. Chemical Plant and System Operators	92.3%
49. Insulation Workers, Floor, Ceiling, and Wall	92.3%
50. Locksmiths and Safe Repairers	92.0%
51. Telecommunications Line Installers and Repairers	91.8%
52. Landscaping and Groundskeeping Workers	91.5%
53. Tree Trimmers and Pruners	91.5%
54. Electrical Engineers	91.3%
55. Electronics Engineers, Except Computer	91.3%
56. Forest Fire Inspectors and Prevention Specialists	91.1%
57. Hazardous Materials Removal Workers	90.2%
58. Metal-Refining Furnace Operators and Tenders	90.2%
59. Pourers and Casters, Metal	90.2%
60. Physicists	90.0%
61. Painters, Construction and Maintenance	89.8%
62. Sawing Machine Setters, Operators, and Tenders, Wood	89.6%
63. Refuse and Recyclable Material Collectors	89.4%
64. Computer, Automated Teller, and Office Machine Repairers	89.0%
65. Crushing, Grinding, and Polishing Machine Setters, Operators, and Tenders	89.0%
66. Grinding and Polishing Workers, Hand	89.0%
67. Mixing and Blending Machine Setters, Operators, and Tenders	89.0%
68. Meter Readers, Utilities	88.6%
69. Civil Engineers	88.5%
70. Construction and Building Inspectors	88.5%
71. Chemical Equipment Operators and Tenders	87.9%
72. Separating, Filtering, Clarifying, Precipitating, and Still Machine Setters, Operators, and Tenders	87.9%

(continued)

(continued)

Best Low-Stress Jobs Employing the Highest Percentage of Men

Job	Percent Men
73. Power Plant Operators	87.0%
74. Model Makers, Metal and Plastic	84.2%
75. Conservation Scientists	83.7%
76. Chemical Engineers	83.3%
77. Laborers and Freight, Stock, and Material Movers, Hand	81.6%
78. Cutting, Punching, and Press Machine Setters, Operators, and Tenders, Metal and Plastic	81.2%
79. Molders, Shapers, and Casters, Except Metal and Plastic	81.1%
80. Rolling Machine Setters, Operators, and Tenders, Metal and Plastic	80.6%
81. Environmental Engineers	80.5%
82. Painters, Transportation Equipment	80.2%
83. Civil Engineering Technicians	79.2%
84. Electrical and Electronic Engineering Technicians	79.2%
85. Industrial Engineering Technicians	79.2%
86. Mechanical Engineering Technicians	79.2%
87. Printing Machine Operators	77.6%
88. Marine Engineers and Naval Architects	77.3%
89. Computer Software Engineers, Applications	77.2%
90. Health and Safety Engineers, Except Mining Safety Engineers and Inspectors	77.0%
91. Farm, Ranch, and Other Agricultural Managers	75.6%
92. Environmental Scientists and Specialists, Including Health	75.3%
93. Hydrologists	75.3%
94. Computer Programmers	75.2%
95. Farmers and Ranchers	72.3%

The jobs in the following four lists are derived from the preceding list of the low-stress jobs employing the highest percentage of men.

Best Low-Stress Jobs Overall Employing a High Percentage of Men

Job	Percent Men	Annual Earnings	Percent Growth	Annual Openings
1. Computer Software Engineers, Applications	77.2%	$79,780	44.6%	58,690
2. Civil Engineers	88.5%	$68,600	18.0%	15,979
3. Construction and Building Inspectors	88.5%	$46,570	18.2%	12,606

Best Low-Stress Jobs Overall Employing a High Percentage of Men

Job	Percent Men	Annual Earnings	Percent Growth	Annual Openings
4. Environmental Scientists and Specialists, Including Health	75.3%	$56,100	25.1%	6,961
5. Environmental Engineers	80.5%	$69,940	25.4%	5,003
6. Carpenters	97.2%	$36,550	10.3%	223,225
7. Bus and Truck Mechanics and Diesel Engine Specialists	98.9%	$37,660	11.5%	25,428
8. Mobile Heavy Equipment Mechanics, Except Engines	98.5%	$40,440	12.3%	11,037
9. Brickmasons and Blockmasons	98.2%	$42,980	9.7%	17,569
10. Industrial Machinery Mechanics	95.8%	$41,050	9.0%	23,361
11. Tile and Marble Setters	96.7%	$36,590	15.4%	9,066
12. Painters, Construction and Maintenance	89.8%	$31,190	11.8%	101,140
13. Cement Masons and Concrete Finishers	98.5%	$32,650	11.4%	34,625
14. Water and Liquid Waste Treatment Plant and System Operators	96.2%	$36,070	13.8%	9,575
15. Maintenance and Repair Workers, General	95.8%	$31,910	10.1%	165,502
16. Mechanical Engineers	93.9%	$69,850	4.2%	12,394
17. Civil Engineering Technicians	79.2%	$40,560	10.2%	7,499
18. Electrical Engineers	91.3%	$75,930	6.3%	6,806
19. Sheet Metal Workers	95.7%	$37,360	6.7%	31,677
20. Industrial Engineering Technicians	79.2%	$46,810	9.9%	6,172
21. Landscaping and Groundskeeping Workers	91.5%	$21,260	18.1%	307,138
22. Security and Fire Alarm Systems Installers	96.6%	$34,810	20.2%	5,729
23. Telecommunications Line Installers and Repairers	91.8%	$46,280	4.6%	14,719
24. Electrical and Electronic Engineering Technicians	79.2%	$50,660	3.6%	12,583
25. Computer Programmers	75.2%	$65,510	–4.1%	27,937

Best-Paying Low-Stress Jobs Employing a High Percentage of Men

Job	Percent Men	Annual Earnings
1. Physicists	90.0%	$94,240
2. Electronics Engineers, Except Computer	91.3%	$81,050
3. Computer Software Engineers, Applications	77.2%	$79,780
4. Chemical Engineers	83.3%	$78,860
5. Electrical Engineers	91.3%	$75,930
6. Marine Engineers and Naval Architects	77.3%	$72,990

(continued)

(continued)

Best-Paying Low-Stress Jobs Employing a High Percentage of Men

Job	Percent Men	Annual Earnings
7. Environmental Engineers	80.5%	$69,940
8. Mechanical Engineers	93.9%	$69,850
9. Civil Engineers	88.5%	$68,600
10. Health and Safety Engineers, Except Mining Safety Engineers and Inspectors	77.0%	$66,290
11. Hydrologists	75.3%	$66,260
12. Computer Programmers	75.2%	$65,510
13. Environmental Scientists and Specialists, Including Health	75.3%	$56,100
14. Power Plant Operators	87.0%	$55,000
15. Conservation Scientists	83.7%	$54,970
16. Farm, Ranch, and Other Agricultural Managers	75.6%	$52,070
17. Electrical and Electronic Engineering Technicians	79.2%	$50,660
18. Chemical Plant and System Operators	92.3%	$49,080
19. Boilermakers	94.5%	$46,960
20. Industrial Engineering Technicians	79.2%	$46,810
21. Construction and Building Inspectors	88.5%	$46,570
22. Telecommunications Line Installers and Repairers	91.8%	$46,280
23. Mechanical Engineering Technicians	79.2%	$45,850
24. Millwrights	93.4%	$45,630
25. Gas Compressor and Gas Pumping Station Operators	98.4%	$45,400

Fastest-Growing Low-Stress Jobs Employing a High Percentage of Men

Job	Percent Men	Percent Growth
1. Computer Software Engineers, Applications	77.2%	44.6%
2. Environmental Engineers	80.5%	25.4%
3. Environmental Scientists and Specialists, Including Health	75.3%	25.1%
4. Hydrologists	75.3%	24.3%
5. Locksmiths and Safe Repairers	92.0%	22.1%
6. Security and Fire Alarm Systems Installers	96.6%	20.2%
7. Construction and Building Inspectors	88.5%	18.2%
8. Landscaping and Groundskeeping Workers	91.5%	18.1%
9. Civil Engineers	88.5%	18.0%
10. Tile and Marble Setters	96.7%	15.4%
11. Boilermakers	94.5%	14.0%

Fastest-Growing Low-Stress Jobs Employing a High Percentage of Men

Job	Percent Men	Percent Growth
12. Water and Liquid Waste Treatment Plant and System Operators	96.2%	13.8%
13. Motorcycle Mechanics	98.0%	12.5%
14. Mobile Heavy Equipment Mechanics, Except Engines	98.5%	12.3%
15. Helpers—Pipelayers, Plumbers, Pipefitters, and Steamfitters	93.4%	11.9%
16. Painters, Construction and Maintenance	89.8%	11.8%
17. Helpers—Carpenters	93.4%	11.7%
18. Bus and Truck Mechanics and Diesel Engine Specialists	98.9%	11.5%
19. Reinforcing Iron and Rebar Workers	100.0%	11.5%
20. Cement Masons and Concrete Finishers	98.5%	11.4%
21. Hazardous Materials Removal Workers	90.2%	11.2%
22. Tree Trimmers and Pruners	91.5%	11.1%
23. Marine Engineers and Naval Architects	77.3%	10.9%
24. Terrazzo Workers and Finishers	98.5%	10.9%
25. Fence Erectors	97.8%	10.6%

Low-Stress Jobs with the Most Openings Employing a High Percentage of Men

Job	Percent Men	Annual Openings
1. Laborers and Freight, Stock, and Material Movers, Hand	81.6%	630,487
2. Landscaping and Groundskeeping Workers	91.5%	307,138
3. Carpenters	97.2%	223,225
4. Maintenance and Repair Workers, General	95.8%	165,502
5. Farmers and Ranchers	72.3%	129,552
6. Painters, Construction and Maintenance	89.8%	101,140
7. Welders, Cutters, Solderers, and Brazers	93.8%	61,125
8. Computer Software Engineers, Applications	77.2%	58,690
9. Refuse and Recyclable Material Collectors	89.4%	37,785
10. Helpers—Carpenters	93.4%	37,731
11. Helpers—Electricians	93.4%	35,109
12. Cement Masons and Concrete Finishers	98.5%	34,625
13. Sheet Metal Workers	95.7%	31,677
14. Cutting, Punching, and Press Machine Setters, Operators, and Tenders, Metal and Plastic	81.2%	30,635

(continued)

(continued)

Low-Stress Jobs with the Most Openings Employing a High Percentage of Men

Job	Percent Men	Annual Openings
15. Helpers—Pipelayers, Plumbers, Pipefitters, and Steamfitters	93.4%	29,332
16. Computer Programmers	75.2%	27,937
17. Bus and Truck Mechanics and Diesel Engine Specialists	98.9%	25,428
18. Highway Maintenance Workers	96.3%	24,774
19. Industrial Machinery Mechanics	95.8%	23,361
20. Computer, Automated Teller, and Office Machine Repairers	89.0%	22,330
21. Structural Metal Fabricators and Fitters	93.4%	20,746
22. Mixing and Blending Machine Setters, Operators, and Tenders	89.0%	18,661
23. Farm, Ranch, and Other Agricultural Managers	75.6%	18,101
24. Brickmasons and Blockmasons	98.2%	17,569
25. Civil Engineers	88.5%	15,979

Best Low-Stress Jobs Sorted by Education or Training Required

The lists in this section organize the 150 best low-stress jobs into groups based on the education or training typically required for entry. Unlike in many of the previous sections, here we don't include separate lists for highest pay, growth, or number of openings. Instead, we provide one list that includes all the best low-stress jobs that fit into each of the education levels and ranks them by their total combined score for earnings, growth, and number of openings.

These lists can help you identify a job with higher earnings or upward mobility but with a similar level of education to the job you now hold. For example, you will find jobs within the same level of education that require similar skills, yet one pays significantly better than the other, is projected to grow more rapidly, or has significantly more job openings per year. This information can help you leverage your present skills and experience into jobs that might provide better long-term career opportunities.

You can also use these lists to explore possible job options if you were to get additional training, education, or work experience. For example, you can use these lists to identify low-stress occupations that offer high potential and then look into the education or training required to get the jobs that interest you most.

The lists can also help you when you plan your education. For example, you might be thinking about a construction job but you aren't sure what kind of work you want to do.

The lists show that Hazardous Materials Removal Workers need moderate-term on-the-job training and earn $35,450, while Terrazzo Workers and Finishers need long-term on-the-job training but earn an average of $31,630. If you want higher earnings without lengthy training, this information might make a difference in your choice.

The Education Levels

The U.S. Department of Labor defines the training and education levels used in this set of lists as follows:

- **Short-term on-the-job training:** You can work in these occupations and achieve an average level of performance within a few days or weeks through on-the-job training.

- **Moderate-term on-the-job training:** Occupations that require this type of training can be performed adequately after a one- to 12-month period of combined on-the-job and informal training. Typically, untrained workers observe experienced workers perform tasks and are gradually moved into progressively more difficult assignments.

- **Long-term on-the-job training:** This training requires more than 12 months of on-the-job training or combined work experience and formal classroom instruction. This includes occupations that use formal apprenticeships for training workers that may take up to four years. It also includes intensive occupation-specific, employer-sponsored training such as police academies. Furthermore, it includes occupations that require natural talent that must be developed over many years.

- **Work experience in a related occupation:** This type of job requires experience in a related occupation. For example, police detectives are selected based on their experience as police patrol officers.

- **Postsecondary vocational training:** This requirement can vary from training that involves a few months but is usually less than one year. In a few instances, as many as four years of training could be required.

- **Associate degree:** This degree usually requires two years of full-time academic work beyond high school.

- **Bachelor's degree:** This degree requires approximately four to five years of full-time academic work beyond high school.

- **Work experience plus degree:** Jobs in this category are often management-related and require some experience in a related nonmanagerial position.

- **Master's degree:** Completion of a master's degree usually requires one to two years of full-time study beyond the bachelor's degree.

- **Doctoral degree:** This degree normally requires two or more years of full-time academic work beyond the bachelor's degree.

In other books in the *Best Jobs* series, we also include a list of jobs that require a first professional degree, but none of the jobs in this book require that level of education. Evidently working at the professional level (for example, as a dentist or lawyer) tends to be stressful.

Another Warning About the Data

We warned you in the introduction to use caution in interpreting the data we use, and we want to do it again here. The occupational data we use is the most accurate available anywhere, but it has its limitations. The education or training requirements for entry into a job are those typically required as a minimum—but some people working in those jobs may have considerably more or different credentials. For example, although an associate degree is considered the usual requirement for Semiconductor Processors, two-thirds of the people working in this occupation have no formal education beyond high school. On the other hand, Fitness Trainers and Aerobics Instructors usually need to have completed only postsecondary vocational training, but over half of these workers are college graduates.

In a similar way, you need to be cautious about assuming that more education or training always leads to higher income. It is true that people with jobs that require long-term on-the-job training typically earn more than people with jobs that require short-term on-the-job training. (For the jobs in this book, the difference is an average of $37,411 versus an average of $21,799.) However, some people with short-term on-the-job training do earn more than the average for the highest-paying occupations listed in this book; furthermore, some people with long-term on-the-job training earn much less than the average shown in this book—this is particularly true early in a person's career.

So as you browse the following lists, please use them as a way to be encouraged rather than discouraged. Education and training are very important for success in the labor market of the future, but so are ability, drive, initiative, and—yes—luck.

Having said this, we encourage you to get as much education and training as you can. You used to be able to get your schooling and then close the schoolbooks forever, but this isn't a good attitude to have now. You will probably need to continue learning new things throughout your working life. This can be done by going to school, which is a good thing for many people to do. But other workers may learn through workshops, adult education programs, certification programs, employer training, professional conferences, Internet training, or reading related books and magazines. Upgrading your computer skills—and other technical skills—is particularly important in our rapidly changing workplace, and you avoid doing so at your peril.

Best Low-Stress Jobs Requiring Short-Term On-the-Job Training

Job	Annual Earnings	Percent Growth	Annual Openings
1. Refuse and Recyclable Material Collectors	$28,970	7.4%	37,785
2. Helpers—Pipelayers, Plumbers, Pipefitters, and Steamfitters	$23,910	11.9%	29,332
3. Landscaping and Groundskeeping Workers	$21,260	18.1%	307,138
4. Helpers—Carpenters	$23,060	11.7%	37,731
5. Tree Trimmers and Pruners	$28,250	11.1%	9,621

Best Low-Stress Jobs Requiring Short-Term On-the-Job Training

Job	Annual Earnings	Percent Growth	Annual Openings
6. Helpers—Electricians	$23,760	6.8%	35,109
7. Food Batchmakers	$23,100	10.9%	15,704
8. Laborers and Freight, Stock, and Material Movers, Hand	$21,220	2.1%	630,487
9. Packaging and Filling Machine Operators and Tenders	$22,990	–5.4%	79,540
10. Library Assistants, Clerical	$21,640	7.9%	18,961
11. Helpers—Extraction Workers	$28,680	–0.2%	2,765
12. Electromechanical Equipment Assemblers	$27,560	–9.1%	8,283
13. Mail Clerks and Mail Machine Operators, Except Postal Service	$23,810	–11.6%	27,889
14. Meter Readers, Utilities	$30,330	–10.3%	7,328
15. Stock Clerks and Order Fillers	$20,440	–7.7%	439,327
16. Electrical and Electronic Equipment Assemblers	$25,560	–26.8%	26,595
17. Meat, Poultry, and Fish Cutters and Trimmers	$20,370	10.9%	17,920
18. File Clerks	$22,090	–41.3%	50,088
19. Bindery Workers	$25,570	–21.8%	7,508
20. Funeral Attendants	$20,350	14.3%	6,034
21. Helpers—Painters, Paperhangers, Plasterers, and Stucco Masons	$21,330	–0.7%	7,696
22. Food Cooking Machine Operators and Tenders	$21,280	–4.7%	6,714

Best Low-Stress Jobs Requiring Moderate-Term On-the-Job Training

Job	Annual Earnings	Percent Growth	Annual Openings
1. Cement Masons and Concrete Finishers	$32,650	11.4%	34,625
2. Painters, Construction and Maintenance	$31,190	11.8%	101,140
3. Maintenance and Repair Workers, General	$31,910	10.1%	165,502
4. Highway Maintenance Workers	$31,540	8.9%	24,774
5. Locksmiths and Safe Repairers	$32,020	22.1%	3,545
6. Maintenance Workers, Machinery	$34,550	–1.1%	15,055
7. Excavating and Loading Machine and Dragline Operators	$32,930	8.3%	6,562
8. Hazardous Materials Removal Workers	$35,450	11.2%	1,933
9. Painters, Transportation Equipment	$35,680	8.4%	3,268
10. Pipelayers	$30,330	8.7%	8,902
11. Carpet Installers	$34,560	–1.2%	6,692
12. Tank Car, Truck, and Ship Loaders	$31,970	9.2%	4,519

(continued)

(continued)

Best Low-Stress Jobs Requiring Moderate-Term On-the-Job Training

Job	Annual Earnings	Percent Growth	Annual Openings
13. Animal Trainers	$26,310	22.7%	6,713
14. Insulation Workers, Floor, Ceiling, and Wall	$30,510	8.4%	6,580
15. Multiple Machine Tool Setters, Operators, and Tenders, Metal and Plastic	$30,530	0.3%	15,709
16. Secretaries, Except Legal, Medical, and Executive	$27,450	1.2%	239,630
17. Septic Tank Servicers and Sewer Pipe Cleaners	$31,430	10.2%	3,156
18. Structural Metal Fabricators and Fitters	$30,290	–0.2%	20,746
19. Tour Guides and Escorts	$20,420	21.2%	15,027
20. Rail-Track Laying and Maintenance Equipment Operators	$40,000	4.8%	1,817
21. Inspectors, Testers, Sorters, Samplers, and Weighers	$29,420	–7.0%	75,361
22. Printing Machine Operators	$30,990	–5.7%	12,274
23. Word Processors and Typists	$29,430	–11.6%	32,279
24. Mixing and Blending Machine Setters, Operators, and Tenders	$29,330	–5.1%	18,661
25. Fiberglass Laminators and Fabricators	$25,980	6.2%	7,315
26. Chemical Equipment Operators and Tenders	$40,290	–3.9%	1,469
27. Woodworking Machine Setters, Operators, and Tenders, Except Sawing	$23,940	6.4%	11,860
28. Fence Erectors	$26,400	10.6%	2,812
29. Separating, Filtering, Clarifying, Precipitating, and Still Machine Setters, Operators, and Tenders	$34,970	–3.2%	1,238
30. Wellhead Pumpers	$36,150	–11.9%	2,517
31. Outdoor Power Equipment and Other Small Engine Mechanics	$26,910	5.5%	5,130
32. Metal-Refining Furnace Operators and Tenders	$32,640	–19.0%	5,496
33. Segmental Pavers	$28,700	10.2%	152
34. Cutting, Punching, and Press Machine Setters, Operators, and Tenders, Metal and Plastic	$26,340	–14.9%	30,635
35. Sawing Machine Setters, Operators, and Tenders, Wood	$24,280	3.8%	6,086
36. Molders, Shapers, and Casters, Except Metal and Plastic	$25,010	1.3%	5,788
37. Gas Compressor and Gas Pumping Station Operators	$45,400	–17.5%	704
38. Floor Layers, Except Carpet, Wood, and Hard Tiles	$34,190	–12.2%	2,504
39. Logging Equipment Operators	$29,700	–1.3%	2,756
40. Rolling Machine Setters, Operators, and Tenders, Metal and Plastic	$31,050	–11.8%	3,075
41. Crushing, Grinding, and Polishing Machine Setters, Operators, and Tenders	$28,080	–11.9%	5,357
42. Roustabouts, Oil and Gas	$25,700	–3.2%	4,800
43. Pourers and Casters, Metal	$29,570	–17.4%	4,459
44. Grinding and Polishing Workers, Hand	$23,880	–7.1%	5,789

Best Low-Stress Jobs Requiring Long-Term On-the-Job Training

Job	Annual Earnings	Percent Growth	Annual Openings
1. Boilermakers	$46,960	14.0%	2,333
2. Brickmasons and Blockmasons	$42,980	9.7%	17,569
3. Carpenters	$36,550	10.3%	223,225
4. Mobile Heavy Equipment Mechanics, Except Engines	$40,440	12.3%	11,037
5. Industrial Machinery Mechanics	$41,050	9.0%	23,361
6. Tile and Marble Setters	$36,590	15.4%	9,066
7. Telecommunications Line Installers and Repairers	$46,280	4.6%	14,719
8. Sheet Metal Workers	$37,360	6.7%	31,677
9. Water and Liquid Waste Treatment Plant and System Operators	$36,070	13.8%	9,575
10. Reinforcing Iron and Rebar Workers	$38,220	11.5%	4,502
11. Millwrights	$45,630	5.8%	4,758
12. Bakers	$22,030	10.0%	31,442
13. Structural Iron and Steel Workers	$40,480	6.0%	6,969
14. Chemical Plant and System Operators	$49,080	−15.3%	5,620
15. Farmers and Ranchers	$37,130	−8.5%	129,552
16. Motorcycle Mechanics	$30,050	12.5%	3,564
17. Power Plant Operators	$55,000	2.7%	1,796
18. Rail Car Repairers	$43,320	5.1%	1,989
19. Stonemasons	$35,960	10.0%	2,657
20. Butchers and Meat Cutters	$26,930	1.9%	14,503
21. Model Makers, Metal and Plastic	$42,050	−6.3%	1,801
22. Terrazzo Workers and Finishers	$31,630	10.9%	1,052
23. Home Appliance Repairers	$33,860	1.5%	4,243
24. Cooks, Private Household	$22,870	8.8%	1,352

Best Low-Stress Jobs Requiring Work Experience in a Related Occupation

Job	Annual Earnings	Percent Growth	Annual Openings
1. Construction and Building Inspectors	$46,570	18.2%	12,606
2. Animal Breeders	$27,090	4.4%	2,512
3. Forest Fire Inspectors and Prevention Specialists	$32,940	2.1%	66

Best Low-Stress Jobs Requiring Postsecondary Vocational Training

Job	Annual Earnings	Percent Growth	Annual Openings
1. Bus and Truck Mechanics and Diesel Engine Specialists	$37,660	11.5%	25,428
2. Massage Therapists	$33,400	20.3%	9,193
3. Welders, Cutters, Solderers, and Brazers	$31,400	5.1%	61,125
4. Fitness Trainers and Aerobics Instructors	$25,910	26.8%	51,235
5. Computer, Automated Teller, and Office Machine Repairers	$36,480	3.0%	22,330
6. Security and Fire Alarm Systems Installers	$34,810	20.2%	5,729
7. Library Technicians	$26,560	8.5%	29,075
8. Electrical and Electronics Installers and Repairers, Transportation Equipment	$43,110	4.3%	1,663
9. Welding, Soldering, and Brazing Machine Setters, Operators, and Tenders	$30,980	3.0%	7,707
10. Electronic Home Entertainment Equipment Installers and Repairers	$29,980	3.0%	3,065
11. Travel Agents	$29,210	1.0%	13,128
12. Electric Motor, Power Tool, and Related Repairers	$32,860	–4.2%	2,625

Best Low-Stress Jobs Requiring an Associate Degree

Job	Annual Earnings	Percent Growth	Annual Openings
1. Electrical and Electronic Engineering Technicians	$50,660	3.6%	12,583
2. Environmental Science and Protection Technicians, Including Health	$38,090	28.0%	8,404
3. Industrial Engineering Technicians	$46,810	9.9%	6,172
4. Civil Engineering Technicians	$40,560	10.2%	7,499
5. Geological and Petroleum Technicians	$46,160	8.6%	1,895
6. Mechanical Engineering Technicians	$45,850	6.4%	3,710
7. Social Science Research Assistants	$33,860	12.4%	3,571
8. Forest and Conservation Technicians	$30,880	–2.0%	5,946
9. Semiconductor Processors	$32,860	–12.9%	5,709

Best Low-Stress Jobs Requiring a Bachelor's Degree

Job	Annual Earnings	Percent Growth	Annual Openings
1. Computer Software Engineers, Applications	$79,780	44.6%	58,690
2. Computer Systems Analysts	$69,760	29.0%	63,166
3. Civil Engineers	$68,600	18.0%	15,979
4. Environmental Engineers	$69,940	25.4%	5,003
5. Electrical Engineers	$75,930	6.3%	6,806
6. Electronics Engineers, Except Computer	$81,050	3.7%	5,699
7. Chemical Engineers	$78,860	7.9%	2,111
8. Mechanical Engineers	$69,850	4.2%	12,394
9. Computer Programmers	$65,510	–4.1%	27,937
10. Marine Engineers and Naval Architects	$72,990	10.9%	495
11. Occupational Health and Safety Specialists	$58,030	8.1%	3,440
12. Health and Safety Engineers, Except Mining Safety Engineers and Inspectors	$66,290	9.6%	1,105
13. Insurance Underwriters	$52,350	6.3%	6,880
14. Survey Researchers	$33,360	15.9%	4,959
15. Commercial and Industrial Designers	$54,560	7.2%	4,777
16. Set and Exhibit Designers	$41,820	17.8%	1,402
17. Zoologists and Wildlife Biologists	$53,300	8.7%	1,444
18. Museum Technicians and Conservators	$34,340	15.9%	1,341
19. Soil and Plant Scientists	$56,080	8.4%	850
20. Conservation Scientists	$54,970	5.3%	1,161
21. Credit Analysts	$52,350	1.9%	3,180
22. Audio-Visual Collections Specialists	$40,530	–13.8%	868

Best Low-Stress Jobs Requiring Work Experience Plus Degree

Job	Annual Earnings	Percent Growth	Annual Openings
1. Natural Sciences Managers	$100,080	11.4%	3,661
2. Sales Managers	$91,560	10.2%	36,392
3. Farm, Ranch, and Other Agricultural Managers	$52,070	1.1%	18,101

Best Low-Stress Jobs Requiring a Master's Degree

Job	Annual Earnings	Percent Growth	Annual Openings
1. Environmental Scientists and Specialists, Including Health	$56,100	25.1%	6,961
2. Hydrologists	$66,260	24.3%	687
3. Operations Research Analysts	$64,650	10.6%	5,727
4. Curators	$46,300	23.3%	1,416
5. Librarians	$49,060	3.6%	18,945
6. Political Scientists	$90,140	5.3%	318
7. Archivists	$40,730	14.4%	795
8. Sociologists	$60,290	10.0%	403
9. Geographers	$62,990	6.1%	75

Best Low-Stress Jobs Requiring a Doctoral Degree

Job	Annual Earnings	Percent Growth	Annual Openings
1. Physicists	$94,240	6.8%	1,302
2. Mathematicians	$86,930	10.2%	473

Best Low-Stress Jobs Sorted by Interests

This group of lists organizes the 150 best low-stress jobs into 16 interest areas. You can use these lists to identify jobs quickly based on your interests. Within each interest area, jobs are listed in order of their combined score on earnings, job growth, and job openings, from highest to lowest.

Find the interest area or areas that appeal to you most and review the low-stress jobs in those areas. When you find jobs you want to explore in more detail, look up their descriptions in Part III. You can also review interest areas in which you have had past experience, education, or training to see whether other jobs in those areas would meet your current requirements.

As you scan the following lists, you may notice that one of the interest areas has *no* jobs listed—Law and Public Safety—and three others include only one job each—Human Service; Retail and Wholesale Sales and Service; and Transportation, Distribution, and Logistics. These interest areas are dominated by human contact, responsibilities, and deadlines, and any low-stress jobs they may include tend not to have sufficient economic rewards to earn a place in this book. But keep in mind that this book is based on averages. If you have the right skills and are really motivated, you may be able to find a rewarding low-stress position in these sparsely represented interest areas. That's one reason we describe all 16 interest areas below. Another reason is that you can more easily decide on your most important interests in the context of the complete classification scheme.

NOTE: The 16 interest areas used in these lists are those used in the *New Guide for Occupational Exploration*, Fourth Edition, published by JIST. The original GOE was developed by the U.S. Department of Labor as an intuitive way to assist in career exploration. The 16 interest areas used in the *New GOE* are based on the 16 career clusters developed by the U.S. Department of Education's Office of Vocational and Adult Education around 1999 that many states now use to organize their career-oriented programs and career information.

Descriptions for the 16 Interest Areas

Brief descriptions follow for the 16 interest areas we use in the lists. The descriptions are from the *New Guide for Occupational Exploration,* Fourth Edition. Some of them refer to jobs (as examples) that aren't included in this book.

Also note that we put each of the 150 best jobs into only one interest area list, the one it fit into best. However, many jobs could be included in more than one list, so consider reviewing a variety of these interest areas to find jobs that you might otherwise overlook.

For a detailed outline of the interest areas that shows the work groups classified into each interest area, see the appendix.

- **Agriculture and Natural Resources:** *An interest in working with plants, animals, forests, or mineral resources for agriculture, horticulture, conservation, extraction, and other purposes.* You can satisfy this interest by working in farming, landscaping, forestry, fishing, mining, and related fields. You may like doing physical work outdoors, such as on a farm or ranch, in a forest, or on a drilling rig. If you have a scientific curiosity, you could study plants and animals or analyze biological or rock samples in a lab. If you have management ability, you could own, operate, or manage a fish hatchery, a landscaping business, or a greenhouse.

- **Architecture and Construction:** *An interest in designing, assembling, and maintaining components of buildings and other structures.* You may want to be part of the team of architects, drafters, and others who design buildings and render the plans. If construction interests you, you can find fulfillment in the many building projects being undertaken at all times. If you like to organize and plan, you can find careers in managing these projects. Or you can play a more direct role in putting up and finishing buildings by doing jobs such as plumbing, carpentry, masonry, painting, or roofing, either as a skilled craftsworker or as a helper. You can prepare the building site by operating heavy equipment or install, maintain, and repair vital building equipment and systems such as electricity and heating.

- **Arts and Communication:** *An interest in creatively expressing feelings or ideas, in communicating news or information, or in performing.* You can satisfy this interest in creative, verbal, or performing activities. For example, if you enjoy literature, perhaps writing or editing would appeal to you. Journalism and public relations are other fields for people who like to use their writing or speaking skills. Do you prefer to work in the performing arts? If so, you could direct or perform in drama, music, or dance. If you especially enjoy the visual arts, you could create paintings, sculpture, or ceramics or design products or visual displays. A flair for technology might lead you to specialize in photography, broadcast production, or dispatching.

- **Business and Administration:** *An interest in making a business organization or function run smoothly.* You can satisfy this interest by working in a position of leadership or by specializing in a function that contributes to the overall effort in a business, a nonprofit organization, or a government agency. If you especially enjoy working with people, you may find fulfillment from working in human resources. An interest in numbers may lead you to consider accounting, finance, budgeting, billing, or financial record-keeping. A job as an administrative assistant may interest you if you like a variety of tasks in a busy environment. If you are good with details and word processing, you may enjoy a job as a secretary or data entry keyer. Or perhaps you would do well as the manager of a business.

- **Education and Training:** *An interest in helping people learn.* You can satisfy this interest by teaching students, who may be preschoolers, retirees, or any age in between. You may specialize in a particular academic field or work with learners of a particular age, with a particular interest, or with a particular learning problem. Working in a library or museum may give you an opportunity to expand people's understanding of the world.

- **Finance and Insurance:** *An interest in helping businesses and people be assured of a financially secure future.* You can satisfy this interest by working in a financial or insurance business in a leadership or support role. If you like gathering and analyzing information, you may find fulfillment as an insurance adjuster or financial analyst. Or you may deal with information at the clerical level as a banking or insurance clerk or in person-to-person situations providing customer service. Another way to interact with people is to sell financial or insurance services that will meet their needs.

- **Government and Public Administration:** *An interest in helping a government agency serve the needs of the public.* You can satisfy this interest by working in a position of leadership or by specializing in a function that contributes to the role of government. You may help protect the public by working as an inspector or examiner to enforce standards. If you enjoy using clerical skills, you could work as a clerk in a law court or government office. Or perhaps you prefer the top-down perspective of a government executive or urban planner.

- **Health Science:** *An interest in helping people and animals be healthy.* You can satisfy this interest by working on a health-care team as a doctor, therapist, or nurse. You might specialize in one of the many different parts of the body (such as the teeth or eyes) or in one of the many different types of care. Or you may want to be a generalist who deals with the whole patient. If you like technology, you might find satisfaction working with X rays or new diagnostic methods. You might work with healthy people, helping them eat right. If you enjoy working with animals, you might care for them and keep them healthy.

- **Hospitality, Tourism, and Recreation:** *An interest in catering to the personal wishes and needs of others so that they can enjoy a clean environment, good food and drink, comfortable lodging away from home, and recreation.* You can satisfy this interest by providing services for the convenience, care, and pampering of others in hotels, restaurants, airplanes, beauty parlors, and so on. You may want to use your love of cooking as a chef. If you like working with people, you may want to provide personal services by being a travel guide, a flight attendant, a concierge, a hairdresser, or a waiter. You may want to work in cleaning and building services if you like a clean environment. If you enjoy sports or games, you could work for an athletic team or casino.

◎ **Human Service:** *An interest in improving people's social, mental, emotional, or spiritual well-being.* You can satisfy this interest as a counselor, social worker, or religious worker who helps people sort out their complicated lives or solve personal problems. You may work as a caretaker for very young people or the elderly. Or you may interview people to help identify the social services they need.

◎ **Information Technology:** *An interest in designing, developing, managing, and supporting information systems.* You can satisfy this interest by working with hardware, software, multimedia, or integrated systems. If you like to use your organizational skills, you might work as a systems or database administrator. Or you can solve complex problems as a software engineer or systems analyst. If you enjoy getting your hands on the hardware, you might find work servicing computers, peripherals, and information-intense machines such as cash registers and ATMs.

◎ **Law and Public Safety:** *An interest in upholding people's rights or in protecting people and property by using authority, inspecting, or investigating.* You can satisfy this interest by working in law, law enforcement, fire fighting, the military, and related fields. For example, if you enjoy mental challenge and intrigue, you could investigate crimes or fires for a living. If you enjoy working with verbal skills and research skills, you may want to defend citizens in court or research deeds, wills, and other legal documents. If you want to help people in critical situations, you may want to fight fires, work as a police officer, or become a paramedic. Or, if you want more routine work in public safety, perhaps a job in guarding, patrolling, or inspecting would appeal to you. If you have management ability, you could seek a leadership position in law enforcement and the protective services. Work in the military gives you a chance to use technical and leadership skills while serving your country.

◎ **Manufacturing:** *An interest in processing materials into intermediate or final products or maintaining and repairing products by using machines or hand tools.* You can satisfy this interest by working in one of many industries that mass-produce goods or by working for a utility that distributes electric power or other resources. You might enjoy manual work, using your hands or hand tools in highly skilled jobs such as assembling engines or electronic equipment. If you enjoy making machines run efficiently or fixing them when they break down, you could seek a job installing or repairing such devices as copiers, aircraft engines, cars, or watches. Perhaps you prefer to set up or operate machines used to manufacture products made of food, glass, or paper. You may enjoy cutting and grinding metal and plastic parts to desired shapes and measurements. Or you may want to operate equipment in systems that provide water and process wastewater. You may like inspecting, sorting, counting, or weighing products. Another option is to work with your hands and machinery to move boxes and freight in a warehouse. If leadership appeals to you, you could manage people engaged in production and repair.

- **Retail and Wholesale Sales and Service:** *An interest in bringing others to a particular point of view by personal persuasion and by sales and promotional techniques.* You can satisfy this interest in various jobs that involve persuasion and selling. If you like using knowledge of science, you may enjoy selling pharmaceutical, medical, or electronic products or services. Real estate offers several kinds of sales jobs as well. If you like speaking on the phone, you could work as a telemarketer. Or you may enjoy selling apparel and other merchandise in a retail setting. If you prefer to help people, you may want a job in customer service.

- **Scientific Research, Engineering, and Mathematics:** *An interest in discovering, collecting, and analyzing information about the natural world; in applying scientific research findings to problems in medicine, the life sciences, human behavior, and the natural sciences; in imagining and manipulating quantitative data; and in applying technology to manufacturing, transportation, and other economic activities.* You can satisfy this interest by working with the knowledge and processes of the sciences. You may enjoy researching and developing new knowledge in mathematics, or perhaps solving problems in the physical, life, or social sciences would appeal to you. You may want to study engineering and help create new machines, processes, and structures. If you want to work with scientific equipment and procedures, you could seek a job in a research or testing laboratory.

- **Transportation, Distribution, and Logistics:** *An interest in operations that move people or materials.* You can satisfy this interest by managing a transportation service, by helping vehicles keep on their assigned schedules and routes, or by driving or piloting a vehicle. If you enjoy taking responsibility, perhaps managing a rail line would appeal to you. If you work well with details and can take pressure on the job, you might consider being an air traffic controller. Or would you rather get out on the highway, on the water, or up in the air? If so, then you could drive a truck from state to state, be employed on a ship, or fly a crop duster over a cornfield. If you prefer to stay closer to home, you could drive a delivery van, taxi, or school bus. You can use your physical strength to load freight and arrange it so it gets to its destination in one piece.

Best Low-Stress Jobs for People Interested in Agriculture and Natural Resources

Job	Annual Earnings	Percent Growth	Annual Openings
1. Environmental Engineers	$69,940	25.4%	5,003
2. Environmental Science and Protection Technicians, Including Health	$38,090	28.0%	8,404
3. Farm, Ranch, and Other Agricultural Managers	$52,070	1.1%	18,101
4. Landscaping and Groundskeeping Workers	$21,260	18.1%	307,138
5. Tree Trimmers and Pruners	$28,250	11.1%	9,621
6. Zoologists and Wildlife Biologists	$53,300	8.7%	1,444
7. Excavating and Loading Machine and Dragline Operators	$32,930	8.3%	6,562
8. Farmers and Ranchers	$37,130	–8.5%	129,552

Best Low-Stress Jobs for People Interested in Agriculture and Natural Resources

Job	Annual Earnings	Percent Growth	Annual Openings
9. Geological and Petroleum Technicians	$46,160	8.6%	1,895
10. Soil and Plant Scientists	$56,080	8.4%	850
11. Conservation Scientists	$54,970	5.3%	1,161
12. Forest and Conservation Technicians	$30,880	–2.0%	5,946
13. Helpers—Extraction Workers	$28,680	–0.2%	2,765
14. Logging Equipment Operators	$29,700	–1.3%	2,756
15. Wellhead Pumpers	$36,150	–11.9%	2,517
16. Roustabouts, Oil and Gas	$25,700	–3.2%	4,800

Best Low-Stress Jobs for People Interested in Architecture and Construction

Job	Annual Earnings	Percent Growth	Annual Openings
1. Carpenters	$36,550	10.3%	223,225
2. Tile and Marble Setters	$36,590	15.4%	9,066
3. Boilermakers	$46,960	14.0%	2,333
4. Painters, Construction and Maintenance	$31,190	11.8%	101,140
5. Cement Masons and Concrete Finishers	$32,650	11.4%	34,625
6. Brickmasons and Blockmasons	$42,980	9.7%	17,569
7. Security and Fire Alarm Systems Installers	$34,810	20.2%	5,729
8. Reinforcing Iron and Rebar Workers	$38,220	11.5%	4,502
9. Maintenance and Repair Workers, General	$31,910	10.1%	165,502
10. Sheet Metal Workers	$37,360	6.7%	31,677
11. Helpers—Carpenters	$23,060	11.7%	37,731
12. Helpers—Pipelayers, Plumbers, Pipefitters, and Steamfitters	$23,910	11.9%	29,332
13. Telecommunications Line Installers and Repairers	$46,280	4.6%	14,719
14. Structural Iron and Steel Workers	$40,480	6.0%	6,969
15. Hazardous Materials Removal Workers	$35,450	11.2%	1,933
16. Highway Maintenance Workers	$31,540	8.9%	24,774
17. Stonemasons	$35,960	10.0%	2,657
18. Helpers—Electricians	$23,760	6.8%	35,109
19. Septic Tank Servicers and Sewer Pipe Cleaners	$31,430	10.2%	3,156
20. Pipelayers	$30,330	8.7%	8,902

(continued)

(continued)

Best Low-Stress Jobs for People Interested in Architecture and Construction

Job	Annual Earnings	Percent Growth	Annual Openings
21. Terrazzo Workers and Finishers	$31,630	10.9%	1,052
22. Rail-Track Laying and Maintenance Equipment Operators	$40,000	4.8%	1,817
23. Carpet Installers	$34,560	−1.2%	6,692
24. Fence Erectors	$26,400	10.6%	2,812
25. Insulation Workers, Floor, Ceiling, and Wall	$30,510	8.4%	6,580
26. Segmental Pavers	$28,700	10.2%	152
27. Floor Layers, Except Carpet, Wood, and Hard Tiles	$34,190	−12.2%	2,504
28. Helpers—Painters, Paperhangers, Plasterers, and Stucco Masons	$21,330	−0.7%	7,696

Best Low-Stress Jobs for People Interested in Arts and Communication

Job	Annual Earnings	Percent Growth	Annual Openings
1. Commercial and Industrial Designers	$54,560	7.2%	4,777
2. Set and Exhibit Designers	$41,820	17.8%	1,402

Best Low-Stress Jobs for People Interested in Business and Administration

Job	Annual Earnings	Percent Growth	Annual Openings
1. Operations Research Analysts	$64,650	10.6%	5,727
2. Secretaries, Except Legal, Medical, and Executive	$27,450	1.2%	239,630
3. Industrial Engineering Technicians	$46,810	9.9%	6,172
4. Stock Clerks and Order Fillers	$20,440	−7.7%	439,327
5. Meter Readers, Utilities	$30,330	−10.3%	7,328
6. Word Processors and Typists	$29,430	−11.6%	32,279
7. Mail Clerks and Mail Machine Operators, Except Postal Service	$23,810	−11.6%	27,889
8. File Clerks	$22,090	−41.3%	50,088

Best Low-Stress Jobs for People Interested in Education and Training

Job	Annual Earnings	Percent Growth	Annual Openings
1. Curators	$46,300	23.3%	1,416
2. Fitness Trainers and Aerobics Instructors	$25,910	26.8%	51,235
3. Librarians	$49,060	3.6%	18,945
4. Library Technicians	$26,560	8.5%	29,075
5. Museum Technicians and Conservators	$34,340	15.9%	1,341
6. Archivists	$40,730	14.4%	795
7. Library Assistants, Clerical	$21,640	7.9%	18,961
8. Audio-Visual Collections Specialists	$40,530	−13.8%	868

Best Low-Stress Jobs for People Interested in Finance and Insurance

Job	Annual Earnings	Percent Growth	Annual Openings
1. Insurance Underwriters	$52,350	6.3%	6,880
2. Survey Researchers	$33,360	15.9%	4,959
3. Credit Analysts	$52,350	1.9%	3,180

Best Low-Stress Jobs for People Interested in Government and Public Administration

Job	Annual Earnings	Percent Growth	Annual Openings
1. Construction and Building Inspectors	$46,570	18.2%	12,606
2. Occupational Health and Safety Specialists	$58,030	8.1%	3,440
3. Forest Fire Inspectors and Prevention Specialists	$32,940	2.1%	66

Best Low-Stress Jobs for People Interested in Health Science

Job	Annual Earnings	Percent Growth	Annual Openings
1. Massage Therapists	$33,400	20.3%	9,193
2. Animal Trainers	$26,310	22.7%	6,713
3. Animal Breeders	$27,090	4.4%	2,512

Best Low-Stress Jobs for People Interested in Hospitality, Tourism, and Recreation

Job	Annual Earnings	Percent Growth	Annual Openings
1. Tour Guides and Escorts	$20,420	21.2%	15,027
2. Butchers and Meat Cutters	$26,930	1.9%	14,503
3. Travel Agents	$29,210	1.0%	13,128
4. Cooks, Private Household	$22,870	8.8%	1,352

Best Low-Stress Jobs for People Interested in Human Service

Job	Annual Earnings	Percent Growth	Annual Openings
1. Funeral Attendants	$20,350	14.3%	6,034

Best Low-Stress Jobs for People Interested in Information Technology

Job	Annual Earnings	Percent Growth	Annual Openings
1. Computer Software Engineers, Applications	$79,780	44.6%	58,690
2. Computer Systems Analysts	$69,760	29.0%	63,166
3. Computer Programmers	$65,510	–4.1%	27,937
4. Computer, Automated Teller, and Office Machine Repairers	$36,480	3.0%	22,330

None of the best low-stress jobs is associated with the Law and Public Safety interest area.

Best Low-Stress Jobs for People Interested in Manufacturing

Job	Annual Earnings	Percent Growth	Annual Openings
1. Bus and Truck Mechanics and Diesel Engine Specialists	$37,660	11.5%	25,428
2. Industrial Machinery Mechanics	$41,050	9.0%	23,361
3. Mobile Heavy Equipment Mechanics, Except Engines	$40,440	12.3%	11,037
4. Water and Liquid Waste Treatment Plant and System Operators	$36,070	13.8%	9,575
5. Welders, Cutters, Solderers, and Brazers	$31,400	5.1%	61,125
6. Refuse and Recyclable Material Collectors	$28,970	7.4%	37,785
7. Millwrights	$45,630	5.8%	4,758

Best Low-Stress Jobs for People Interested in Manufacturing

Job	Annual Earnings	Percent Growth	Annual Openings
8. Maintenance Workers, Machinery	$34,550	−1.1%	15,055
9. Locksmiths and Safe Repairers	$32,020	22.1%	3,545
10. Bakers	$22,030	10.0%	31,442
11. Painters, Transportation Equipment	$35,680	8.4%	3,268
12. Structural Metal Fabricators and Fitters	$30,290	−0.2%	20,746
13. Tank Car, Truck, and Ship Loaders	$31,970	9.2%	4,519
14. Food Batchmakers	$23,100	10.9%	15,704
15. Multiple Machine Tool Setters, Operators, and Tenders, Metal and Plastic	$30,530	0.3%	15,709
16. Rail Car Repairers	$43,320	5.1%	1,989
17. Meat, Poultry, and Fish Cutters and Trimmers	$20,370	10.9%	17,920
18. Welding, Soldering, and Brazing Machine Setters, Operators, and Tenders	$30,980	3.0%	7,707
19. Motorcycle Mechanics	$30,050	12.5%	3,564
20. Power Plant Operators	$55,000	2.7%	1,796
21. Inspectors, Testers, Sorters, Samplers, and Weighers	$29,420	−7.0%	75,361
22. Electrical and Electronics Installers and Repairers, Transportation Equipment	$43,110	4.3%	1,663
23. Woodworking Machine Setters, Operators, and Tenders, Except Sawing	$23,940	6.4%	11,860
24. Chemical Plant and System Operators	$49,080	−15.3%	5,620
25. Fiberglass Laminators and Fabricators	$25,980	6.2%	7,315
26. Printing Machine Operators	$30,990	−5.7%	12,274
27. Home Appliance Repairers	$33,860	1.5%	4,243
28. Mixing and Blending Machine Setters, Operators, and Tenders	$29,330	−5.1%	18,661
29. Packaging and Filling Machine Operators and Tenders	$22,990	−5.4%	79,540
30. Outdoor Power Equipment and Other Small Engine Mechanics	$26,910	5.5%	5,130
31. Cutting, Punching, and Press Machine Setters, Operators, and Tenders, Metal and Plastic	$26,340	−14.9%	30,635
32. Chemical Equipment Operators and Tenders	$40,290	−3.9%	1,469
33. Model Makers, Metal and Plastic	$42,050	−6.3%	1,801
34. Sawing Machine Setters, Operators, and Tenders, Wood	$24,280	3.8%	6,086
35. Semiconductor Processors	$32,860	−12.9%	5,709
36. Electric Motor, Power Tool, and Related Repairers	$32,860	−4.2%	2,625
37. Electronic Home Entertainment Equipment Installers and Repairers	$29,980	3.0%	3,065
38. Separating, Filtering, Clarifying, Precipitating, and Still Machine Setters, Operators, and Tenders	$34,970	−3.2%	1,238

(continued)

(continued)

Best Low-Stress Jobs for People Interested in Manufacturing

Job	Annual Earnings	Percent Growth	Annual Openings
39. Molders, Shapers, and Casters, Except Metal and Plastic	$25,010	1.3%	5,788
40. Electromechanical Equipment Assemblers	$27,560	−9.1%	8,283
41. Electrical and Electronic Equipment Assemblers	$25,560	−26.8%	26,595
42. Metal-Refining Furnace Operators and Tenders	$32,640	−19.0%	5,496
43. Gas Compressor and Gas Pumping Station Operators	$45,400	−17.5%	704
44. Rolling Machine Setters, Operators, and Tenders, Metal and Plastic	$31,050	−11.8%	3,075
45. Food Cooking Machine Operators and Tenders	$21,280	−4.7%	6,714
46. Crushing, Grinding, and Polishing Machine Setters, Operators, and Tenders	$28,080	−11.9%	5,357
47. Grinding and Polishing Workers, Hand	$23,880	−7.1%	5,789
48. Bindery Workers	$25,570	−21.8%	7,508
49. Pourers and Casters, Metal	$29,570	−17.4%	4,459

Best Low-Stress Jobs for People Interested in Retail and Wholesale Sales and Service

Job	Annual Earnings	Percent Growth	Annual Openings
1. Sales Managers	$91,560	10.2%	36,392

Best Low-Stress Jobs for People Interested in Scientific Research, Engineering, and Mathematics

Job	Annual Earnings	Percent Growth	Annual Openings
1. Civil Engineers	$68,600	18.0%	15,979
2. Natural Sciences Managers	$100,080	11.4%	3,661
3. Environmental Scientists and Specialists, Including Health	$56,100	25.1%	6,961
4. Physicists	$94,240	6.8%	1,302
5. Electrical Engineers	$75,930	6.3%	6,806
6. Mathematicians	$86,930	10.2%	473
7. Chemical Engineers	$78,860	7.9%	2,111
8. Hydrologists	$66,260	24.3%	687

Best Low-Stress Jobs for People Interested in Scientific Research, Engineering, and Mathematics

Job	Annual Earnings	Percent Growth	Annual Openings
9. Civil Engineering Technicians	$40,560	10.2%	7,499
10. Marine Engineers and Naval Architects	$72,990	10.9%	495
11. Mechanical Engineers	$69,850	4.2%	12,394
12. Electronics Engineers, Except Computer	$81,050	3.7%	5,699
13. Social Science Research Assistants	$33,860	12.4%	3,571
14. Health and Safety Engineers, Except Mining Safety Engineers and Inspectors	$66,290	9.6%	1,105
15. Electrical and Electronic Engineering Technicians	$50,660	3.6%	12,583
16. Political Scientists	$90,140	5.3%	318
17. Mechanical Engineering Technicians	$45,850	6.4%	3,710
18. Sociologists	$60,290	10.0%	403
19. Geographers	$62,990	6.1%	75

Best Low-Stress Jobs for People Interested in Transportation, Distribution, and Logistics

Job	Annual Earnings	Percent Growth	Annual Openings
1. Laborers and Freight, Stock, and Material Movers, Hand	$21,220	2.1%	630,487

Best Low-Stress Jobs Sorted by Personality Types

These lists organize the 150 best low-stress jobs into groups matching six personality types. The personality types are Realistic, Investigative, Artistic, Social, Enterprising, and Conventional. This system was developed by John Holland and is used in the *Self-Directed Search* (SDS) and other career assessment inventories and information systems.

If you have used one of these career inventories or systems, the lists will help you identify jobs that most closely match these personality types. Even if you haven't used one of these systems, the concept of personality types and the jobs that are related to them can help you identify low-stress jobs that most closely match the type of person you are.

We've ranked the low-stress jobs within each personality type based on their total combined scores for earnings, growth, and annual job openings. Like the job lists for education levels, there is only one list for each personality type. Note that each job is listed in the one personality type it most closely matches, even though it might also fit into others. Consider reviewing the jobs for more than one personality type so you don't overlook possible jobs that would interest you.

Also, note that we didn't have data to crosswalk 11 of the 150 best jobs to their related personality type, so the following best jobs don't appear on the lists in this section:

Conservation Scientists

Cooks, Private Household

Environmental Engineers

Fiberglass Laminators and Fabricators

Forest and Conservation Technicians

Massage Therapists

Security and Fire Alarm Systems Installers

Segmental Pavers

Social Science Research Assistants

Stock Clerks and Order Fillers

Survey Researchers

It should come as no surprise that the smallest list in this set, with only three jobs, is the list for the Enterprising personality type. Enterprising jobs often involve responsibility, deadlines, and risk-taking—very stressful conditions.

Descriptions of the Six Personality Types

Following are brief descriptions for each of the six personality types used in the lists. Select the two or three descriptions that most closely describe you and then use the lists to identify jobs that best fit these personality types.

- **Realistic:** These occupations frequently involve work activities that include practical, hands-on problems and solutions. They often deal with plants; animals; and real-world materials such as wood, tools, and machinery. Many of these occupations require working outside and don't involve a lot of paperwork or working closely with others.

- **Investigative:** These occupations frequently involve working with ideas and require an extensive amount of thinking. These occupations can involve searching for facts and figuring out problems mentally.

- **Artistic:** These occupations frequently involve working with forms, designs, and patterns. They often require self-expression, and the work can be done without following a clear set of rules.

- **Social:** These occupations frequently involve working with, communicating with, and teaching people. These occupations often involve helping or providing service to others.

⊙ **Enterprising:** These occupations frequently involve starting up and carrying out projects. These occupations can involve leading people and making many decisions. They sometimes require risk taking and often deal with business.

⊙ **Conventional:** These occupations frequently involve following set procedures and routines. These occupations can include working with data and details more than with ideas. Usually there is a clear line of authority to follow.

Best Low-Stress Jobs for People with a Realistic Personality Type

Job	Annual Earnings	Percent Growth	Annual Openings
1. Civil Engineers	$68,600	18.0%	15,979
2. Carpenters	$36,550	10.3%	223,225
3. Bus and Truck Mechanics and Diesel Engine Specialists	$37,660	11.5%	25,428
4. Mobile Heavy Equipment Mechanics, Except Engines	$40,440	12.3%	11,037
5. Industrial Machinery Mechanics	$41,050	9.0%	23,361
6. Brickmasons and Blockmasons	$42,980	9.7%	17,569
7. Painters, Construction and Maintenance	$31,190	11.8%	101,140
8. Cement Masons and Concrete Finishers	$32,650	11.4%	34,625
9. Tile and Marble Setters	$36,590	15.4%	9,066
10. Water and Liquid Waste Treatment Plant and System Operators	$36,070	13.8%	9,575
11. Maintenance and Repair Workers, General	$31,910	10.1%	165,502
12. Sheet Metal Workers	$37,360	6.7%	31,677
13. Civil Engineering Technicians	$40,560	10.2%	7,499
14. Mechanical Engineers	$69,850	4.2%	12,394
15. Telecommunications Line Installers and Repairers	$46,280	4.6%	14,719
16. Electrical and Electronic Engineering Technicians	$50,660	3.6%	12,583
17. Boilermakers	$46,960	14.0%	2,333
18. Landscaping and Groundskeeping Workers	$21,260	18.1%	307,138
19. Reinforcing Iron and Rebar Workers	$38,220	11.5%	4,502
20. Highway Maintenance Workers	$31,540	8.9%	24,774
21. Computer, Automated Teller, and Office Machine Repairers	$36,480	3.0%	22,330
22. Welders, Cutters, Solderers, and Brazers	$31,400	5.1%	61,125
23. Structural Iron and Steel Workers	$40,480	6.0%	6,969
24. Helpers—Carpenters	$23,060	11.7%	37,731
25. Helpers—Pipelayers, Plumbers, Pipefitters, and Steamfitters	$23,910	11.9%	29,332
26. Marine Engineers and Naval Architects	$72,990	10.9%	495
27. Farmers and Ranchers	$37,130	–8.5%	129,552
28. Refuse and Recyclable Material Collectors	$28,970	7.4%	37,785
29. Locksmiths and Safe Repairers	$32,020	22.1%	3,545

(continued)

(continued)

Best Low-Stress Jobs for People with a Realistic Personality Type

Job	Annual Earnings	Percent Growth	Annual Openings
30. Millwrights	$45,630	5.8%	4,758
31. Mechanical Engineering Technicians	$45,850	6.4%	3,710
32. Tree Trimmers and Pruners	$28,250	11.1%	9,621
33. Geological and Petroleum Technicians	$46,160	8.6%	1,895
34. Excavating and Loading Machine and Dragline Operators	$32,930	8.3%	6,562
35. Bakers	$22,030	10.0%	31,442
36. Food Batchmakers	$23,100	10.9%	15,704
37. Hazardous Materials Removal Workers	$35,450	11.2%	1,933
38. Pipelayers	$30,330	8.7%	8,902
39. Maintenance Workers, Machinery	$34,550	−1.1%	15,055
40. Stonemasons	$35,960	10.0%	2,657
41. Helpers—Electricians	$23,760	6.8%	35,109
42. Motorcycle Mechanics	$30,050	12.5%	3,564
43. Painters, Transportation Equipment	$35,680	8.4%	3,268
44. Meat, Poultry, and Fish Cutters and Trimmers	$20,370	10.9%	17,920
45. Tank Car, Truck, and Ship Loaders	$31,970	9.2%	4,519
46. Rail Car Repairers	$43,320	5.1%	1,989
47. Insulation Workers, Floor, Ceiling, and Wall	$30,510	8.4%	6,580
48. Septic Tank Servicers and Sewer Pipe Cleaners	$31,430	10.2%	3,156
49. Structural Metal Fabricators and Fitters	$30,290	−0.2%	20,746
50. Multiple Machine Tool Setters, Operators, and Tenders, Metal and Plastic	$30,530	0.3%	15,709
51. Power Plant Operators	$55,000	2.7%	1,796
52. Laborers and Freight, Stock, and Material Movers, Hand	$21,220	2.1%	630,487
53. Chemical Plant and System Operators	$49,080	−15.3%	5,620
54. Electrical and Electronics Installers and Repairers, Transportation Equipment	$43,110	4.3%	1,663
55. Inspectors, Testers, Sorters, Samplers, and Weighers	$29,420	−7.0%	75,361
56. Carpet Installers	$34,560	−1.2%	6,692
57. Welding, Soldering, and Brazing Machine Setters, Operators, and Tenders	$30,980	3.0%	7,707
58. Rail-Track Laying and Maintenance Equipment Operators	$40,000	4.8%	1,817
59. Terrazzo Workers and Finishers	$31,630	10.9%	1,052
60. Woodworking Machine Setters, Operators, and Tenders, Except Sawing	$23,940	6.4%	11,860
61. Butchers and Meat Cutters	$26,930	1.9%	14,503
62. Home Appliance Repairers	$33,860	1.5%	4,243

Best Low-Stress Jobs for People with a Realistic Personality Type

Job	Annual Earnings	Percent Growth	Annual Openings
63. Mixing and Blending Machine Setters, Operators, and Tenders	$29,330	–5.1%	18,661
64. Printing Machine Operators	$30,990	–5.7%	12,274
65. Fence Erectors	$26,400	10.6%	2,812
66. Packaging and Filling Machine Operators and Tenders	$22,990	–5.4%	79,540
67. Outdoor Power Equipment and Other Small Engine Mechanics	$26,910	5.5%	5,130
68. Model Makers, Metal and Plastic	$42,050	–6.3%	1,801
69. Cutting, Punching, and Press Machine Setters, Operators, and Tenders, Metal and Plastic	$26,340	–14.9%	30,635
70. Chemical Equipment Operators and Tenders	$40,290	–3.9%	1,469
71. Sawing Machine Setters, Operators, and Tenders, Wood	$24,280	3.8%	6,086
72. Semiconductor Processors	$32,860	–12.9%	5,709
73. Electronic Home Entertainment Equipment Installers and Repairers	$29,980	3.0%	3,065
74. Electric Motor, Power Tool, and Related Repairers	$32,860	–4.2%	2,625
75. Electrical and Electronic Equipment Assemblers	$25,560	–26.8%	26,595
76. Forest Fire Inspectors and Prevention Specialists	$32,940	2.1%	66
77. Wellhead Pumpers	$36,150	–11.9%	2,517
78. Metal-Refining Furnace Operators and Tenders	$32,640	–19.0%	5,496
79. Separating, Filtering, Clarifying, Precipitating, and Still Machine Setters, Operators, and Tenders	$34,970	–3.2%	1,238
80. Electromechanical Equipment Assemblers	$27,560	–9.1%	8,283
81. Gas Compressor and Gas Pumping Station Operators	$45,400	–17.5%	704
82. Molders, Shapers, and Casters, Except Metal and Plastic	$25,010	1.3%	5,788
83. Animal Breeders	$27,090	4.4%	2,512
84. Helpers—Painters, Paperhangers, Plasterers, and Stucco Masons	$21,330	–0.7%	7,696
85. Floor Layers, Except Carpet, Wood, and Hard Tiles	$34,190	–12.2%	2,504
86. Helpers—Extraction Workers	$28,680	–0.2%	2,765
87. Logging Equipment Operators	$29,700	–1.3%	2,756
88. Roustabouts, Oil and Gas	$25,700	–3.2%	4,800
89. Rolling Machine Setters, Operators, and Tenders, Metal and Plastic	$31,050	–11.8%	3,075
90. Crushing, Grinding, and Polishing Machine Setters, Operators, and Tenders	$28,080	–11.9%	5,357
91. Food Cooking Machine Operators and Tenders	$21,280	–4.7%	6,714
92. Bindery Workers	$25,570	–21.8%	7,508
93. Grinding and Polishing Workers, Hand	$23,880	–7.1%	5,789
94. Pourers and Casters, Metal	$29,570	–17.4%	4,459

Best Low-Stress Jobs for People with an Investigative Personality Type

Job	Annual Earnings	Percent Growth	Annual Openings
1. Computer Software Engineers, Applications	$79,780	44.6%	58,690
2. Computer Systems Analysts	$69,760	29.0%	63,166
3. Natural Sciences Managers	$100,080	11.4%	3,661
4. Environmental Scientists and Specialists, Including Health	$56,100	25.1%	6,961
5. Environmental Science and Protection Technicians, Including Health	$38,090	28.0%	8,404
6. Operations Research Analysts	$64,650	10.6%	5,727
7. Electrical Engineers	$75,930	6.3%	6,806
8. Physicists	$94,240	6.8%	1,302
9. Mathematicians	$86,930	10.2%	473
10. Chemical Engineers	$78,860	7.9%	2,111
11. Hydrologists	$66,260	24.3%	687
12. Electronics Engineers, Except Computer	$81,050	3.7%	5,699
13. Computer Programmers	$65,510	–4.1%	27,937
14. Health and Safety Engineers, Except Mining Safety Engineers and Inspectors	$66,290	9.6%	1,105
15. Industrial Engineering Technicians	$46,810	9.9%	6,172
16. Political Scientists	$90,140	5.3%	318
17. Archivists	$40,730	14.4%	795
18. Zoologists and Wildlife Biologists	$53,300	8.7%	1,444
19. Sociologists	$60,290	10.0%	403
20. Soil and Plant Scientists	$56,080	8.4%	850
21. Geographers	$62,990	6.1%	75

Best Low-Stress Jobs for People with an Artistic Personality Type

Job	Annual Earnings	Percent Growth	Annual Openings
1. Commercial and Industrial Designers	$54,560	7.2%	4,777
2. Curators	$46,300	23.3%	1,416
3. Librarians	$49,060	3.6%	18,945
4. Set and Exhibit Designers	$41,820	17.8%	1,402
5. Museum Technicians and Conservators	$34,340	15.9%	1,341

Best Low-Stress Jobs for People with a Social Personality Type

Job	Annual Earnings	Percent Growth	Annual Openings
1. Fitness Trainers and Aerobics Instructors	$25,910	26.8%	51,235
2. Animal Trainers	$26,310	22.7%	6,713
3. Tour Guides and Escorts	$20,420	21.2%	15,027
4. Occupational Health and Safety Specialists	$58,030	8.1%	3,440
5. Funeral Attendants	$20,350	14.3%	6,034

Best Low-Stress Jobs for People with an Enterprising Personality Type

Job	Annual Earnings	Percent Growth	Annual Openings
1. Sales Managers	$91,560	10.2%	36,392
2. Farm, Ranch, and Other Agricultural Managers	$52,070	1.1%	18,101
3. Travel Agents	$29,210	1.0%	13,128

Best Low-Stress Jobs for People with a Conventional Personality Type

Job	Annual Earnings	Percent Growth	Annual Openings
1. Construction and Building Inspectors	$46,570	18.2%	12,606
2. Insurance Underwriters	$52,350	6.3%	6,880
3. Library Technicians	$26,560	8.5%	29,075
4. Secretaries, Except Legal, Medical, and Executive	$27,450	1.2%	239,630
5. Social Science Research Assistants	$33,860	12.4%	3,571
6. Credit Analysts	$52,350	1.9%	3,180
7. Word Processors and Typists	$29,430	–11.6%	32,279
8. Library Assistants, Clerical	$21,640	7.9%	18,961
9. Meter Readers, Utilities	$30,330	–10.3%	7,328
10. Mail Clerks and Mail Machine Operators, Except Postal Service	$23,810	–11.6%	27,889
11. File Clerks	$22,090	–41.3%	50,088
12. Audio-Visual Collections Specialists	$40,530	–13.8%	868

Bonus Lists: Jobs Rated Low on Factors That Are Stressful for Some People

The 150 jobs in this book were chosen because they are comparatively low in certain features that most people consider stressful: dealing with physically aggressive people, competition, time pressure, and so forth. However, some other factors in the workplace are highly stressful for a limited number of people. For example, public speaking is something that some people enjoy and many tolerate doing, but a few people find it terrifying and will avoid any job that requires it. The number of people with this fear may be small, but their discomfort can be so intense that a book about low-stress jobs would be incomplete without suggesting ways to avoid these sources of workplace anxiety.

We assembled four sets of lists based on these very particular stress factors: Public Speaking; Cramped Work Space, Awkward Positions; Exposure to High Places; and Pressure to Compromise Moral Values. The jobs on these lists consist of subsets of the 150 best jobs. In each set of lists, one list ranks the 50 jobs that are lowest in the stressful feature; the other list ranks the 20 best jobs from the first list, based on earnings, job growth, and job openings.

As in the lists based on the more universally acknowledged stressful features, we use a figure from 0 to 100 to indicate how O*NET rates the feature in question.

Jobs with the Least Public Speaking

Fear of public speaking always ranks at or near the top on lists of the most common phobias. Not everyone who dislikes public speaking suffers from a phobia or social anxiety, but for some people it is still stressful enough that they want to avoid it in their work. For these podium-shy people we compiled the following two lists of jobs that require little or no public speaking. You may notice that these lists overlap heavily with the list of best jobs for the Realistic personality type.

The 50 Jobs with the Least Public Speaking

Job	Rating for Public Speaking
1. Outdoor Power Equipment and Other Small Engine Mechanics	0.0
2. Packaging and Filling Machine Operators and Tenders	0.7
3. Tile and Marble Setters	0.7
4. Floor Layers, Except Carpet, Wood, and Hard Tiles	1.0
5. Stonemasons	1.0
6. Insulation Workers, Floor, Ceiling, and Wall	1.2

The 50 Jobs with the Least Public Speaking

Job	Rating for Public Speaking
7. Chemical Equipment Operators and Tenders	1.5
8. Logging Equipment Operators	1.5
9. Credit Analysts	1.8
10. Home Appliance Repairers	2.3
11. Electric Motor, Power Tool, and Related Repairers	3.2
12. Fence Erectors	3.7
13. Mobile Heavy Equipment Mechanics, Except Engines	4.0
14. Landscaping and Groundskeeping Workers	4.8
15. Locksmiths and Safe Repairers	5.3
16. Woodworking Machine Setters, Operators, and Tenders, Except Sawing	5.3
17. Food Batchmakers	5.5
18. File Clerks	5.8
19. Electrical and Electronics Installers and Repairers, Transportation Equipment	6.0
20. Cement Masons and Concrete Finishers	6.3
21. Multiple Machine Tool Setters, Operators, and Tenders, Metal and Plastic	7.0
22. Tank Car, Truck, and Ship Loaders	7.0
23. Electromechanical Equipment Assemblers	7.7
24. Welders, Cutters, Solderers, and Brazers	8.1
25. Brickmasons and Blockmasons	8.5
26. Meter Readers, Utilities	8.5
27. Farmers and Ranchers	8.8
28. Structural Metal Fabricators and Fitters	8.8
29. Metal-Refining Furnace Operators and Tenders	9.0
30. Carpet Installers	9.5
31. Bus and Truck Mechanics and Diesel Engine Specialists	9.7
32. Telecommunications Line Installers and Repairers	9.7
33. Construction and Building Inspectors	10.0
34. Helpers—Pipelayers, Plumbers, Pipefitters, and Steamfitters	10.0
35. Electronic Home Entertainment Equipment Installers and Repairers	10.2
36. Painters, Construction and Maintenance	10.5
37. Rail Car Repairers	10.5
38. Terrazzo Workers and Finishers	10.5
39. Maintenance and Repair Workers, General	11.0
40. Structural Iron and Steel Workers	11.0
41. Model Makers, Metal and Plastic	11.3

(continued)

(continued)

The 50 Jobs with the Least Public Speaking

Job	Rating for Public Speaking
42. Bindery Workers	11.5
43. Industrial Machinery Mechanics	11.8
44. Insurance Underwriters	11.8
45. Rolling Machine Setters, Operators, and Tenders, Metal and Plastic	11.8
46. Electrical and Electronic Engineering Technicians	11.9
47. Pipelayers	12.0
48. Security and Fire Alarm Systems Installers	12.0
49. Bakers	12.5
50. Food Cooking Machine Operators and Tenders	12.5

The 20 Best Jobs with Low Public Speaking

Job	Rating for Public Speaking	Annual Earnings	Percent Growth	Annual Openings
1. Construction and Building Inspectors	10.0	$46,570	18.2%	12,606
2. Bus and Truck Mechanics and Diesel Engine Specialists	9.7	$37,660	11.5%	25,428
3. Brickmasons and Blockmasons	8.5	$42,980	9.7%	17,569
4. Mobile Heavy Equipment Mechanics, Except Engines	4.0	$40,440	12.3%	11,037
5. Cement Masons and Concrete Finishers	6.3	$32,650	11.4%	34,625
6. Industrial Machinery Mechanics	11.8	$41,050	9.0%	23,361
7. Painters, Construction and Maintenance	10.5	$31,190	11.8%	101,140
8. Maintenance and Repair Workers, General	11.0	$31,910	10.1%	165,502
9. Tile and Marble Setters	0.7	$36,590	15.4%	9,066
10. Telecommunications Line Installers and Repairers	9.7	$46,280	4.6%	14,719
11. Electrical and Electronic Engineering Technicians	11.9	$50,660	3.6%	12,583
12. Insurance Underwriters	11.8	$52,350	6.3%	6,880
13. Security and Fire Alarm Systems Installers	12.0	$34,810	20.2%	5,729
14. Landscaping and Groundskeeping Workers	4.8	$21,260	18.1%	307,138
15. Farmers and Ranchers	8.8	$37,130	–8.5%	129,552
16. Helpers—Pipelayers, Plumbers, Pipefitters, and Steamfitters	10.0	$23,910	11.9%	29,332
17. Welders, Cutters, Solderers, and Brazers	8.1	$31,400	5.1%	61,125
18. Structural Iron and Steel Workers	11.0	$40,480	6.0%	6,969

The 20 Best Jobs with Low Public Speaking

Job	Rating for Public Speaking	Annual Earnings	Percent Growth	Annual Openings
19. Locksmiths and Safe Repairers	5.3	$32,020	22.1%	3,545
20. Credit Analysts	1.8	$52,350	1.9%	3,180

Jobs with the Least Cramped Work Space, Awkward Positions

Many people have a fear of confined spaces (claustrophobia) and would experience a great amount of emotional stress if required to work in a mineshaft or under the dashboard of a car. Some other people find it physically difficult to work doubled over or in other awkward positions, and their discomfort in such a work situation would also produce stress. With these people in mind, we assembled the following lists of the best low-stress jobs rated low on this feature.

The 50 Jobs with the Least Cramped Work Space, Awkward Positions

Job	Rating for Cramped Work Space, Awkward Positions
1. Fitness Trainers and Aerobics Instructors	0.2
2. Computer Software Engineers, Applications	1.0
3. Mathematicians	1.0
4. Operations Research Analysts	2.0
5. Sociologists	2.8
6. Political Scientists	3.2
7. Packaging and Filling Machine Operators and Tenders	6.5
8. Library Assistants, Clerical	6.7
9. Geographers	7.5
10. Computer Programmers	7.7
11. Travel Agents	8.5
12. Credit Analysts	9.0
13. Social Science Research Assistants	9.8
14. Word Processors and Typists	10.0
15. Tour Guides and Escorts	10.2
16. Industrial Engineering Technicians	10.5

(continued)

(continued)

The 50 Jobs with the Least Cramped Work Space, Awkward Positions

Job	Rating for Cramped Work Space, Awkward Positions
17. Survey Researchers	10.5
18. Electrical Engineers	11.3
19. File Clerks	11.5
20. Environmental Engineers	12.0
21. Commercial and Industrial Designers	12.5
22. Animal Trainers	12.7
23. Insurance Underwriters	13.0
24. Grinding and Polishing Workers, Hand	13.5
25. Secretaries, Except Legal, Medical, and Executive	13.5
26. Electronics Engineers, Except Computer	13.7
27. Funeral Attendants	14.3
28. Meat, Poultry, and Fish Cutters and Trimmers	14.5
29. Inspectors, Testers, Sorters, Samplers, and Weighers	15.0
30. Forest Fire Inspectors and Prevention Specialists	17.0
31. Hydrologists	17.0
32. Bakers	17.3
33. Librarians	17.3
34. Segmental Pavers	17.5
35. Civil Engineers	17.8
36. Computer Systems Analysts	17.8
37. Mail Clerks and Mail Machine Operators, Except Postal Service	17.8
38. Massage Therapists	17.8
39. Civil Engineering Technicians	18.0
40. Physicists	18.3
41. Environmental Scientists and Specialists, Including Health	18.5
42. Sales Managers	18.8
43. Model Makers, Metal and Plastic	19.2
44. Audio-Visual Collections Specialists	19.5
45. Geological and Petroleum Technicians	20.9
46. Chemical Engineers	21.3
47. Curators	22.0
48. Mechanical Engineers	22.5
49. Cooks, Private Household	23.2
50. Crushing, Grinding, and Polishing Machine Setters, Operators, and Tenders	23.2

The 20 Best Jobs with Low Cramped Work Space, Awkward Positions

Job	Rating for Cramped Work Space, Awkward Positions	Annual Earnings	Percent Growth	Annual Openings
1. Computer Software Engineers, Applications	1.0	$79,780	44.6%	58,690
2. Computer Systems Analysts	17.8	$69,760	29.0%	63,166
3. Sales Managers	18.8	$91,560	10.2%	36,392
4. Civil Engineers	17.8	$68,600	18.0%	15,979
5. Environmental Engineers	12.0	$69,940	25.4%	5,003
6. Environmental Scientists and Specialists, Including Health	18.5	$56,100	25.1%	6,961
7. Fitness Trainers and Aerobics Instructors	0.2	$25,910	26.8%	51,235
8. Massage Therapists	17.8	$33,400	20.3%	9,193
9. Operations Research Analysts	2.0	$64,650	10.6%	5,727
10. Electrical Engineers	11.3	$75,930	6.3%	6,806
11. Hydrologists	17.0	$66,260	24.3%	687
12. Mechanical Engineers	22.5	$69,850	4.2%	12,394
13. Civil Engineering Technicians	18.0	$40,560	10.2%	7,499
14. Computer Programmers	7.7	$65,510	–4.1%	27,937
15. Mathematicians	1.0	$86,930	10.2%	473
16. Chemical Engineers	21.3	$78,860	7.9%	2,111
17. Electronics Engineers, Except Computer	13.7	$81,050	3.7%	5,699
18. Curators	22.0	$46,300	23.3%	1,416
19. Animal Trainers	12.7	$26,310	22.7%	6,713
20. Industrial Engineering Technicians	10.5	$46,810	9.9%	6,172

Jobs with the Least Exposure to High Places

Are you frightened of heights? This common anxiety would cause you to rule out such jobs as Roofers or Flight Attendants. The following two lists feature low-stress jobs that let you keep your feet planted on, or close to, terra firma.

The 50 Jobs with the Least Exposure to High Places

Job	Rating for Exposure to High Places
1. Computer Programmers	0.0
2. Computer Software Engineers, Applications	0.0

(continued)

(continued)

The 50 Jobs with the Least Exposure to High Places

Job	Rating for Exposure to High Places
3. Cooks, Private Household	0.0
4. Credit Analysts	0.0
5. Electromechanical Equipment Assemblers	0.0
6. File Clerks	0.0
7. Fitness Trainers and Aerobics Instructors	0.0
8. Insurance Underwriters	0.0
9. Massage Therapists	0.0
10. Mathematicians	0.0
11. Political Scientists	0.0
12. Social Science Research Assistants	0.0
13. Sociologists	0.0
14. Survey Researchers	0.0
15. Travel Agents	0.0
16. Word Processors and Typists	0.0
17. Library Technicians	0.2
18. Bindery Workers	0.5
19. Operations Research Analysts	1.0
20. Industrial Engineering Technicians	1.5
21. Mail Clerks and Mail Machine Operators, Except Postal Service	1.5
22. Librarians	2.0
23. Grinding and Polishing Workers, Hand	2.3
24. Bakers	2.5
25. Library Assistants, Clerical	2.5
26. Commercial and Industrial Designers	2.8
27. Inspectors, Testers, Sorters, Samplers, and Weighers	3.0
28. Floor Layers, Except Carpet, Wood, and Hard Tiles	3.2
29. Outdoor Power Equipment and Other Small Engine Mechanics	3.2
30. Semiconductor Processors	3.5
31. Electrical and Electronic Equipment Assemblers	3.7
32. Civil Engineers	4.0
33. Cutting, Punching, and Press Machine Setters, Operators, and Tenders, Metal and Plastic	4.0
34. Electronics Engineers, Except Computer	4.2
35. Funeral Attendants	4.2
36. Home Appliance Repairers	4.5
37. Audio-Visual Collections Specialists	5.3

The 50 Jobs with the Least Exposure to High Places

Job	Rating for Exposure to High Places
38. Computer Systems Analysts	5.3
39. Fiberglass Laminators and Fabricators	5.3
40. Archivists	5.5
41. Carpet Installers	5.8
42. Woodworking Machine Setters, Operators, and Tenders, Except Sawing	6.0
43. Geographers	6.5
44. Animal Trainers	7.0
45. Electrical Engineers	7.2
46. Soil and Plant Scientists	7.5
47. Computer, Automated Teller, and Office Machine Repairers	7.7
48. Secretaries, Except Legal, Medical, and Executive	7.7
49. Tour Guides and Escorts	7.7
50. Model Makers, Metal and Plastic	8.5

The 20 Best Jobs with Low Exposure to High Places

Job	Rating for Exposure to High Places	Annual Earnings	Percent Growth	Annual Openings
1. Computer Software Engineers, Applications	0.0	$79,780	44.6%	58,690
2. Computer Systems Analysts	5.3	$69,760	29.0%	63,166
3. Civil Engineers	4.0	$68,600	18.0%	15,979
4. Fitness Trainers and Aerobics Instructors	0.0	$25,910	26.8%	51,235
5. Massage Therapists	0.0	$33,400	20.3%	9,193
6. Operations Research Analysts	1.0	$64,650	10.6%	5,727
7. Electrical Engineers	7.2	$75,930	6.3%	6,806
8. Computer Programmers	0.0	$65,510	–4.1%	27,937
9. Industrial Engineering Technicians	1.5	$46,810	9.9%	6,172
10. Insurance Underwriters	0.0	$52,350	6.3%	6,880
11. Librarians	2.0	$49,060	3.6%	18,945
12. Mathematicians	0.0	$86,930	10.2%	473
13. Library Technicians	0.2	$26,560	8.5%	29,075
14. Computer, Automated Teller, and Office Machine Repairers	7.7	$36,480	3.0%	22,330
15. Electronics Engineers, Except Computer	4.2	$81,050	3.7%	5,699

(continued)

(continued)

The 20 Best Jobs with Low Exposure to High Places

Job	Rating for Exposure to High Places	Annual Earnings	Percent Growth	Annual Openings
16. Animal Trainers	7.0	$26,310	22.7%	6,713
17. Secretaries, Except Legal, Medical, and Executive	7.7	$27,450	1.2%	239,630
18. Bakers	2.5	$22,030	10.0%	31,442
19. Commercial and Industrial Designers	2.8	$54,560	7.2%	4,777
20. Inspectors, Testers, Sorters, Samplers, and Weighers	3.0	$29,420	–7.0%	75,361

Jobs with the Least Pressure to Compromise Moral Values

Some jobs that are otherwise low in stress are known for situations where workers are asked to "look the other way." For example, Construction and Building Inspectors may be urged to ignore defective installations, or Credit Analysts may be pressured to bend the rules for certain clients. Fortunately, many of the low-stress jobs rarely put workers into morally compromising situations, and we were able to prepare lists of the jobs that are least likely to create this kind of stress.

Note that eight of the best low-stress jobs aren't rated for this feature in the O*NET database, so we can't determine whether they should be on the following list. These jobs are Cooks, Private Household; Environmental Engineers; Fiberglass Laminators and Fabricators; Forest and Conservation Technicians; Massage Therapists; Security and Fire Alarm Systems Installers; Segmental Pavers; and Survey Researchers.

The 50 Jobs with the Least Pressure to Compromise Moral Values

Job	Rating for Pressure to Compromise Moral Values
1. Multiple Machine Tool Setters, Operators, and Tenders, Metal and Plastic	6.2
2. Welding, Soldering, and Brazing Machine Setters, Operators, and Tenders	7.7
3. Crushing, Grinding, and Polishing Machine Setters, Operators, and Tenders	9.5
4. Cutting, Punching, and Press Machine Setters, Operators, and Tenders, Metal and Plastic	9.5
5. Food Cooking Machine Operators and Tenders	9.5
6. Logging Equipment Operators	9.5
7. Mixing and Blending Machine Setters, Operators, and Tenders	9.5

The 50 Jobs with the Least Pressure to Compromise Moral Values

Job	Rating for Pressure to Compromise Moral Values
8. Painters, Transportation Equipment	9.5
9. Separating, Filtering, Clarifying, Precipitating, and Still Machine Setters, Operators, and Tenders	9.5
10. Molders, Shapers, and Casters, Except Metal and Plastic	11.8
11. Bindery Workers	12.5
12. Fence Erectors	12.5
13. Grinding and Polishing Workers, Hand	12.5
14. Highway Maintenance Workers	12.5
15. Metal-Refining Furnace Operators and Tenders	12.5
16. Packaging and Filling Machine Operators and Tenders	12.5
17. Painters, Construction and Maintenance	12.5
18. Rail-Track Laying and Maintenance Equipment Operators	12.5
19. Sawing Machine Setters, Operators, and Tenders, Wood	12.5
20. Semiconductor Processors	12.5
21. Structural Metal Fabricators and Fitters	12.5
22. Woodworking Machine Setters, Operators, and Tenders, Except Sawing	12.5
23. Chemical Equipment Operators and Tenders	14.0
24. Electric Motor, Power Tool, and Related Repairers	15.0
25. Welders, Cutters, Solderers, and Brazers	15.6
26. Bakers	15.8
27. Brickmasons and Blockmasons	15.8
28. Cement Masons and Concrete Finishers	15.8
29. Electrical and Electronic Equipment Assemblers	15.8
30. Industrial Machinery Mechanics	15.8
31. Library Technicians	15.8
32. Maintenance and Repair Workers, General	15.8
33. Museum Technicians and Conservators	15.8
34. Outdoor Power Equipment and Other Small Engine Mechanics	15.8
35. Reinforcing Iron and Rebar Workers	15.8
36. Rolling Machine Setters, Operators, and Tenders, Metal and Plastic	15.8
37. Sheet Metal Workers	15.8
38. Stonemasons	15.8
39. Structural Iron and Steel Workers	15.8
40. Terrazzo Workers and Finishers	15.8
41. Tile and Marble Setters	15.8

(continued)

(continued)

The 50 Jobs with the Least Pressure to Compromise Moral Values

Job	Rating for Pressure to Compromise Moral Values
42. Printing Machine Operators	16.3
43. Computer, Automated Teller, and Office Machine Repairers	17.3
44. Audio-Visual Collections Specialists	18.7
45. Boilermakers	18.7
46. Carpenters	18.7
47. Electrical and Electronics Installers and Repairers, Transportation Equipment	18.7
48. Electromechanical Equipment Assemblers	18.7
49. File Clerks	18.7
50. Helpers—Electricians	18.7

The 20 Best Jobs with Low Pressure to Compromise Moral Values

Job	Rating for Pressure to Compromise Moral Values	Annual Earnings	Percent Growth	Annual Openings
1. Carpenters	18.7	$36,550	10.3%	223,225
2. Industrial Machinery Mechanics	15.8	$41,050	9.0%	23,361
3. Painters, Construction and Maintenance	12.5	$31,190	11.8%	101,140
4. Cement Masons and Concrete Finishers	15.8	$32,650	11.4%	34,625
5. Maintenance and Repair Workers, General	15.8	$31,910	10.1%	165,502
6. Brickmasons and Blockmasons	15.8	$42,980	9.7%	17,569
7. Tile and Marble Setters	15.8	$36,590	15.4%	9,066
8. Sheet Metal Workers	15.8	$37,360	6.7%	31,677
9. Boilermakers	18.7	$46,960	14.0%	2,333
10. Reinforcing Iron and Rebar Workers	15.8	$38,220	11.5%	4,502
11. Highway Maintenance Workers	12.5	$31,540	8.9%	24,774
12. Welders, Cutters, Solderers, and Brazers	15.6	$31,400	5.1%	61,125
13. Structural Iron and Steel Workers	15.8	$40,480	6.0%	6,969
14. Computer, Automated Teller, and Office Machine Repairers	17.3	$36,480	3.0%	22,330
15. Library Technicians	15.8	$26,560	8.5%	29,075
16. Museum Technicians and Conservators	15.8	$34,340	15.9%	1,341

The 20 Best Jobs with Low Pressure to Compromise Moral Values

Job	Rating for Pressure to Compromise Moral Values	Annual Earnings	Percent Growth	Annual Openings
17. Stonemasons	15.8	$35,960	10.0%	2,657
18. Painters, Transportation Equipment	9.5	$35,680	8.4%	3,268
19. Bakers	15.8	$22,030	10.0%	31,442
20. Helpers—Electricians	18.7	$23,760	6.8%	35,109

PART III

Descriptions of the Best Low-Stress Jobs

This part provides descriptions for all the jobs included in one or more of the lists in Part II. The book's introduction gives more details on how to use and interpret the job descriptions, but here is some additional information:

- Job descriptions are arranged in alphabetical order by job title. This approach allows you to find a description quickly if you know its correct title from one of the lists in Part II.

- In some cases, a job title that appears in Part II is linked to two or more different job titles in Part III. For example, if you look for the job title Carpenters, you will find it listed here alphabetically, but a note will tell you to see the descriptions for Construction Carpenters and Rough Carpenters. Because these job titles are also listed alphabetically, you can find the descriptions easily.

- Consider the job descriptions in this section as a first step in career exploration. When you find a job that interests you, turn to the appendix for suggestions about resources for further exploration.

- If you are using this section to browse for interesting options, we suggest that you begin with the table of contents. Part II features many interesting lists that will help you identify job titles to explore in more detail. If you have not browsed the lists in Part II, consider spending some time there. The lists are interesting and will help you identify job titles you can find described in the material that follows. The job titles in Part III are also listed in the table of contents.

Animal Breeders

- ◎ Education/Training Required: Work experience in a related occupation
- ◎ Annual Earnings: $27,090
- ◎ Growth: 4.4%
- ◎ Annual Job Openings: 2,512
- ◎ Self-Employed: 50.2%
- ◎ Part-Time: 28.7%

Level of Stress Tolerance Needed: 49.5 (out of 100)

Most Stressful Aspects: Impact of Decisions on Co-workers or Company Results (77.3); Level of Competition (58.2).

Least Stressful Aspects: Pace Determined by Speed of Equipment (5.0); Deal With Physically Aggressive People (8.5); Deal With Unpleasant or Angry People (31.5); Consequence of Error (40.8).

Breed animals, including cattle, goats, horses, sheep, swine, poultry, dogs, cats, or pet birds. Select and breed animals according to their genealogy, characteristics, and offspring. May require a knowledge of artificial insemination techniques and equipment use. May involve keeping records on heats, birth intervals, or pedigree. Feed and water animals and clean and disinfect pens, cages, yards, and hutches. Examine animals to detect symptoms of illness or injury. Place vaccines in drinking water, inject vaccines, or dust air with vaccine powder to protect animals from diseases. Select animals to be bred and semen specimens to be used according to knowledge of animals, genealogies, traits, and desired offspring characteristics. Treat minor injuries and ailments and contact veterinarians to obtain treatment for animals with serious illnesses or injuries. Observe animals in heat to detect approach of estrus and exercise animals to induce or hasten estrus if necessary. Record animal characteristics such as weights, growth patterns, and diets. Exhibit animals at shows. Build hutches, pens, and fenced yards. Clip or shear hair on animals. Attach rubber collecting sheaths to genitals of tethered bull and stimulate animal's organ to induce ejaculation. Package and label semen to be used for artificial insemination, recording information such as the date, source, quality, and concentration. Prepare containers of semen for freezing and storage or shipment, placing them in dry ice or liquid nitrogen. Maintain logs of semen specimens used and animals bred. Arrange for sale of animals and eggs to hospitals, research centers, pet shops, and food-processing plants. Measure specified amounts of semen into calibrated syringes and insert syringes into inseminating guns. Inject prepared animal semen into female animals for breeding purposes by inserting nozzle of syringe into vagina and depressing syringe plunger. Adjust controls to maintain specific building temperatures required for animals' health and safety. Examine semen microscopically to assess and record density and motility of gametes and dilute semen with prescribed diluents according to formulas. Brand, tattoo, or tag animals to allow animal identification. Perform procedures such as animal dehorning or castration.

Personality Type: Realistic. Realistic occupations frequently involve work activities that include practical, hands-on problems and solutions. They often deal with plants; animals; and real-world materials such as wood, tools, and machinery. Many of the occupations require working outside and do not involve a lot of paperwork or working closely with others.

GOE—Interest Area: 08. Health Science. **Work Group:** 08.05. Animal Care. **Other Jobs in This Work Group:** Animal Trainers; Nonfarm Animal Caretakers; Veterinarians; Veterinary Assistants and Laboratory Animal Caretakers; Veterinary Technologists and Technicians.

Skills—Management of Financial Resources: Determining how money will be spent to get the work done and accounting for these expenditures. **Equipment Maintenance:** Performing routine maintenance on equipment and determining when and what kind of maintenance is needed. **Repairing:** Repairing machines or systems, using the needed tools. **Quality Control Analysis:** Conducting tests and inspections of products, services, or processes to evaluate quality or performance. **Monitoring:** Monitoring/assessing performance of yourself, other individuals, or organizations to make improvements or take corrective action. **Science:** Using scientific rules and methods to solve problems.

Education and Training Programs: Agricultural and Domestic Animal Services, Other; Animal/Livestock Husbandry and Production; Horse Husbandry/Equine Science and Management. **Related Knowledge/Courses: Biology:** Plant and animal organisms, their tissues, cells, functions, interdependencies, and interactions with each other and the environment. **Sales and Marketing:** Principles and methods for showing, promoting, and selling products or services. This includes marketing strategy and tactics, product demonstration, sales techniques, and sales control systems. **Food Production:** Techniques and equipment for planting, growing, and harvesting food products (both plant and animal) for consumption, including storage/handling techniques. **Production and Processing:** Raw materials, production processes, quality control, costs, and other techniques for maximizing the effective manufacture and distribution of goods. **Medicine and Dentistry:** The information and techniques needed to diagnose and treat human injuries, diseases, and deformities. This includes symptoms, treatment alternatives, drug properties and interactions, and preventive health-care measures. **Transportation:** Principles and methods for moving people or goods by air, rail, sea, or road, including the relative costs and benefits.

Work Environment: Outdoors; noisy; very hot or cold; contaminants; standing; using hands on objects, tools, or controls.

Animal Trainers

- Education/Training Required: Moderate-term on-the-job training
- Annual Earnings: $26,310
- Growth: 22.7%
- Annual Job Openings: 6,713
- Self-Employed: 56.9%
- Part-Time: 23.6%

Level of Stress Tolerance Needed: 68.8 (out of 100)

Most Stressful Aspects: None greater than average.

Least Stressful Aspects: Pace Determined by Speed of Equipment (3.5); Deal With Physically Aggressive People (4.5); Consequence of Error (28.8); Deal With Unpleasant or Angry People (32.7).

Train animals for riding, harness, security, performance, or obedience or assisting persons with disabilities. Accustom animals to human voice and contact and condition them to respond to commands. Train animals according to prescribed standards for show or competition. May train animals to carry pack loads or work as part of pack team. Observe animals' physical conditions to detect illness or unhealthy conditions requiring medical care. Cue or signal animals during performances. Administer prescribed medications to animals. Evaluate animals to determine their temperaments, abilities, and aptitude for training. Feed and exercise animals and provide other general care such as cleaning and maintaining holding and performance areas. Talk to and interact with animals to familiarize them to human voices and contact. Conduct training programs to develop and maintain desired animal behaviors for competition, entertainment, obedience, security, riding, and related areas. Keep records documenting animal health, diet, and behavior. Advise animal owners regarding the purchase of specific animals. Instruct jockeys in handling specific horses during races. Train horses or other equines for riding, harness, show, racing, or other work, using knowledge of breed characteristics, training methods, performance standards, and the peculiarities of each animal. Use oral, spur, rein, and hand commands to condition horses to carry riders or to pull horse-drawn equipment. Place tack or harnesses on horses to accustom them to the feel of equipment. Train dogs in human-assistance or property protection duties. Retrain horses to break bad habits, such as kicking, bolting, and resisting bridling and grooming. Train and rehearse animals, according to scripts, for motion picture, television, film, stage, or circus performances. Organize and conduct animal shows. Arrange for mating of stallions and mares and assist mares during foaling.

Personality Type: Social. Social occupations frequently involve working with, communicating with, and teaching people. These occupations often involve helping or providing service to others.

GOE—Interest Area: 08. Health Science. **Work Group:** 08.05. Animal Care. **Other Jobs in This Work Group:** Animal Breeders; Nonfarm Animal Caretakers; Veterinarians; Veterinary Assistants and Laboratory Animal Caretakers; Veterinary Technologists and Technicians.

Skills—Management of Financial Resources: Determining how money will be spent to get the work done and accounting for these expenditures. **Persuasion:** Persuading others to change their minds or behavior. **Service Orientation:** Actively looking for ways to help people.

Instructing: Teaching others how to do something. **Learning Strategies:** Selecting and using training/instructional methods and procedures appropriate for the situation when learning or teaching new things. **Monitoring:** Monitoring/assessing performance of yourself, other individuals, or organizations to make improvements or take corrective action.

Education and Training Programs: Animal Training; Equestrian/Equine Studies. **Related Knowledge/Courses: Sales and Marketing:** Principles and methods for showing, promoting, and selling products or services. This includes marketing strategy and tactics, product demonstration, sales techniques, and sales control systems. **Biology:** Plant and animal organisms, their tissues, cells, functions, interdependencies, and interactions with each other and the environment. **Economics and Accounting:** Economic and accounting principles and practices, the financial markets, banking, and the analysis and reporting of financial data. **Communications and Media:** Media production, communication, and dissemination techniques and methods. This includes alternative ways to inform and entertain via written, oral, and visual media. **Customer and Personal Service:** Principles and processes for providing customer and personal services. This includes customer needs assessment, meeting quality standards for services, and evaluation of customer satisfaction. **Clerical Practices:** Administrative and clerical procedures and systems such as word processing, managing files and records, stenography and transcription, designing forms, and other office procedures and terminology.

Work Environment: Outdoors; noisy; standing; walking and running; using hands on objects, tools, or controls; repetitive motions.

Aquacultural Managers

- Education/Training Required: Work experience plus degree
- Annual Earnings: $52,070
- Growth: 1.1%
- Annual Job Openings: 18,101
- Self-Employed: 0.0%
- Part-Time: 12.1%

Our sources did not provide separate job openings data for this occupation. The job openings listed here are shared with Crop and Livestock Managers and with Nursery and Greenhouse Managers.

Level of Stress Tolerance Needed: 75.0 (out of 100)

Most Stressful Aspects: Duration of Typical Work Week (82.5); Impact of Decisions on Co-workers or Company Results (75.0); Time Pressure (72.5); Level of Competition (56.5).

Least Stressful Aspects: Deal With Physically Aggressive People (13.7); Pace Determined by Speed of Equipment (21.8); Deal With Unpleasant or Angry People (37.0); Frequency of Conflict Situations (49.3).

Direct and coordinate, through subordinate supervisory personnel, activities of workers engaged in fish hatchery production for corporations, cooperatives, or other owners. Grow fish and shellfish as cash crops or for release into fresh water or salt water. Supervise and train aquaculture and fish hatchery support workers. Collect and record growth, production, and environmental data. Conduct and supervise stock examinations to identify diseases or parasites. Account for and disburse funds. Devise and participate in activities to improve fish hatching and growth rates and to prevent disease in hatcheries. Monitor environments to ensure maintenance of optimum conditions for aquatic life. Direct and monitor trapping and spawning of fish, egg incubation, and fry rearing, applying knowledge of management and fish culturing techniques. Coordinate the selection and maintenance of brood stock. Direct and monitor the transfer of mature fish to lakes, ponds, streams, or commercial tanks. Determine, administer, and execute policies relating to operations administration and standards and facility maintenance. Determine how to allocate resources and how to respond to unanticipated problems such as insect infestation, drought, and fire. Collect information regarding techniques for fish collection and fertilization, spawn incubation, and treatment of spawn and fry. Operate and maintain cultivating and harvesting equipment. Confer with biologists, fish pathologists, and other fishery personnel to obtain data concerning fish habits, diseases, food, and environmental requirements. Prepare reports required by state and federal laws. Identify environmental requirements of a particular species and select and oversee the preparation of sites for species cultivation. Scuba dive to inspect sea farm operations. Design and construct pens, floating stations, and collector strings or fences for sea farms.

Personality Type: Enterprising. Enterprising occupations frequently involve starting up and carrying out projects. These occupations can involve leading people and making many decisions. They sometimes require risk taking and often deal with business.

GOE—Interest Area: 01. Agriculture and Natural Resources. **Work Group:** 01.01. Managerial Work in Agriculture and Natural Resources. **Other Jobs in This Work Group:** Crop and Livestock Managers; Farm Labor Contractors; Farm, Ranch, and Other Agricultural Managers; Farmers and Ranchers; First-Line Supervisors/Managers of Agricultural Crop and Horticultural Workers; First-Line Supervisors/Managers of Animal Husbandry and Animal Care Workers; First-Line Supervisors/Managers of Aquacultural Workers; First-Line Supervisors/Managers of Construction Trades and Extraction Workers; First-Line Supervisors/Managers of Farming, Fishing, and Forestry Workers; First-Line Supervisors/Managers of Landscaping, Lawn Service, and Groundskeeping Workers; First-Line Supervisors/Managers of Logging Workers; Nursery and Greenhouse Managers; Park Naturalists; Purchasing Agents and Buyers, Farm Products.

Skills—Management of Financial Resources: Determining how money will be spent to get the work done and accounting for these expenditures. **Management of Material Resources:** Obtaining and seeing to the appropriate use of equipment, facilities, and materials needed to do certain work. **Technology Design:** Generating or adapting equipment and technology to serve user needs. **Science:** Using scientific rules and methods to solve problems. **Management of Personnel Resources:** Motivating, developing, and directing people as they work, identifying the best people for the job. **Systems Evaluation:** Identifying measures or indicators of system performance and the actions needed to improve or correct performance, relative to the goals of the system.

Education and Training Programs: Agribusiness/Agricultural Business Operations; Agricultural Business and Management, General; Agricultural Business and Manage-ment, Other; Agricultural Production Opera-tions, General; Agricultural Production Operations, Other; Animal/Livestock Husbandry and Production; Crop Production; Farm/Farm and Ranch Management. **Related Knowledge/Courses: Food Production:** Techniques and equipment for planting, growing, and harvesting food products (both plant and animal) for consumption, including storage/handling techniques. **Biology:** Plant and animal organisms, their tissues, cells,

functions, interdependencies, and interactions with each other and the environment. **Engineering and Technology:** The practical application of engineering science and technology. This includes applying principles, techniques, procedures, and equipment to the design and production of various goods and services. **Building and Construction:** Materials, methods, and the tools involved in the construction or repair of houses, buildings, or other structures such as highways and roads. **Chemistry:** The chemical composition, structure, and properties of substances and of the chemical processes and transformations that they undergo. This includes uses of chemicals, their danger signs, production techniques, and disposal methods. **Mechanical Devices:** Machines and tools, including their designs, uses, repair, and maintenance.

Work Environment: More often outdoors than indoors; noisy; very hot or cold; standing; using hands on objects, tools, or controls.

Archivists

- ◎ Education/Training Required: Master's degree
- ◎ Annual Earnings: $40,730
- ◎ Growth: 14.4%
- ◎ Annual Job Openings: 795
- ◎ Self-Employed: 1.3%
- ◎ Part-Time: 32.4%

Level of Stress Tolerance Needed: 48.0 (out of 100)

Most Stressful Aspects: None greater than average.

Least Stressful Aspects: Pace Determined by Speed of Equipment (1.0); Deal With Physically

Aggressive People (3.5); Level of Competition (23.5); Frequency of Conflict Situations (24.3).

Appraise, edit, and direct safekeeping of permanent records and historically valuable documents. Participate in research activities based on archival materials. Create and maintain accessible, retrievable computer archives and databases, incorporating current advances in electric information storage technology. Organize archival records and develop classification systems to facilitate access to archival materials. Authenticate and appraise historical documents and archival materials. Provide reference services and assistance for users needing archival materials. Direct activities of workers who assist in arranging, cataloging, exhibiting, and maintaining collections of valuable materials. Prepare archival records, such as document descriptions, to allow easy access to information. Preserve records, documents, and objects by copying records to film, videotape, audiotape, disk, or computer formats as necessary. Establish and administer policy guidelines concerning public access and use of materials. Locate new materials and direct their acquisition and display. Research and record the origins and historical significance of archival materials. Specialize in an area of history or technology, researching topics or items relevant to collections to determine what should be retained or acquired. Coordinate educational and public outreach programs such as tours, workshops, lectures, and classes. Select and edit documents for publication and display, applying knowledge of subject, literary expression, and presentation techniques.

Personality Type: Investigative. Investigative occupations frequently involve working with ideas and require an extensive amount of thinking. These occupations can involve searching for facts and figuring out problems mentally.

GOE—Interest Area: 05. Education and Training. **Work Group:** 05.05. Archival and Museum Services. **Other Jobs in This Work Group:** Audio-Visual Collections Specialists; Curators; Museum Technicians and Conservators.

Skills—Programming: Writing computer programs for various purposes. **Writing:** Communicating effectively in writing as appropriate for the needs of the audience. **Reading Comprehension:** Understanding written sentences and paragraphs in work-related documents. **Quality Control Analysis:** Conducting tests and inspections of products, services, or processes to evaluate quality or performance. **Operations Analysis:** Analyzing needs and product requirements to create a design. **Persuasion:** Persuading others to change their minds or behavior.

Education and Training Programs: Art History, Criticism and Conservation; Cultural Resource Management and Policy Analysis; Historic Preservation and Conservation; Historic Preservation and Conservation, Other; Museology/Museum Studies; Public/Applied History and Archival Administration. **Related Knowledge/Courses: Clerical Practices:** Administrative and clerical procedures and systems such as word processing, managing files and records, stenography and transcription, designing forms, and other office procedures and terminology. **History and Archeology:** Historical events and their causes, indicators, and effects on civilizations and cultures. **Computers and Electronics:** Circuit boards, processors, chips, electronic equipment, and computer hardware and software, including applications and programming. **English Language:** Structure and content of the English language, including meaning and spelling of words, rules of composition, and grammar. **Administration and Management:** Business and management principles involved in strategic planning, resource allocation, human resources modeling, leadership technique, production methods, and coordination of people and resources. **Customer and Personal Service:** Principles and processes for providing customer and personal services. This includes customer needs assessment, meeting quality standards for services, and evaluation of customer satisfaction.

Work Environment: Indoors; sitting.

Audio-Visual Collections Specialists

- ◎ Education/Training Required: Bachelor's degree
- ◎ Annual Earnings: $40,530
- ◎ Growth: –13.8%
- ◎ Annual Job Openings: 868
- ◎ Self-Employed: 4.3%
- ◎ Part-Time: 39.3%

Level of Stress Tolerance Needed: 74.8 (out of 100)

Most Stressful Aspects: None greater than average.

Least Stressful Aspects: Pace Determined by Speed of Equipment (3.5); Deal With Physically Aggressive People (3.5); Consequence of Error (12.7); Level of Competition (33.2).

Prepare, plan, and operate audiovisual teaching aids for use in education. May record, catalog, and file audiovisual materials. Set up, adjust, and operate audiovisual equipment such as cameras, film and slide projectors, and recording equipment for meetings, events, classes, seminars, and videoconferences. Offer presentations and workshops on the role of multimedia in effective presentations. Attend conventions and conferences, read trade journals, and communicate with industry insiders to keep abreast of industry developments. Instruct users in the selection, use, and design of audiovisual materials and assist them in the preparation of instructional materials and the rehearsal of presentations. Maintain hardware and software, including computers, scanners, color copiers, and color laser printers. Confer with teachers to select course materials and to determine which training aids are best suited to particular grade levels. Perform simple maintenance tasks such as cleaning monitors and lenses and changing batteries and light bulbs. Develop manuals, texts, workbooks, or related materials for use in conjunction with production materials. Determine formats, approaches, content, levels, and mediums necessary to meet production objectives effectively and within budgetary constraints. Direct and coordinate activities of assistants and other personnel during production. Acquire, catalog, and maintain collections of audiovisual material such as films, videotapes and audiotapes, photographs, and software programs. Narrate presentations and productions. Construct and position properties, sets, lighting equipment, and other equipment. Develop preproduction ideas and incorporate them into outlines, scripts, storyboards, and graphics. Plan and prepare audiovisual teaching aids and methods for use in school systems. Produce rough and finished graphics and graphic designs. Locate and secure settings, properties, effects, and other production necessities.

Personality Type: Conventional. Conventional occupations frequently involve following set procedures and routines. These occupations can include working with data and details more than with ideas. Usually there is a clear line of authority to follow.

GOE—Interest Area: 05. Education and Training. **Work Group:** 05.05. Archival and Museum Services. **Other Jobs in This Work Group:** Archivists; Curators; Museum Technicians and Conservators.

Skills—Troubleshooting: Determining causes of operating errors and deciding what to do about them. **Installation:** Installing equipment, machines, wiring, or programs to meet specifications. **Technology Design:** Generating or adapting equipment and technology to serve user needs. **Equipment Selection:** Determining the tools and equipment needed to do a job. **Instructing:** Teaching others how to do something. **Operations Analysis:** Analyzing needs and product requirements to create a design.

Education and Training Program: Educational/Instructional Media Design. **Related Knowledge/Courses: Education and Training:** Principles and methods for curriculum and training design, teaching and instruction for individuals and groups, and the measurement of training effects. **Communications and Media:** Media production, communication, and dissemination techniques and methods. This includes alternative ways to inform and entertain via written, oral, and visual media. **Telecommunications:** Transmission, broadcasting, switching, control, and operation of telecommunications systems. **Computers and Electronics:** Circuit boards, processors, chips, electronic equipment, and computer hardware and software, including applications and programming. **Customer and Personal Service:** Principles and processes for providing customer and personal services. This includes customer needs assessment, meeting quality standards for services, and evaluation of customer satisfaction. **Clerical Practices:** Administrative and clerical procedures and systems such as word processing, managing files and records, stenography and transcription, designing forms, and other office procedures and terminology.

Work Environment: Indoors; sitting; using hands on objects, tools, or controls.

Bakers

- Education/Training Required: Long-term on-the-job training
- Annual Earnings: $22,030
- Growth: 10.0%
- Annual Job Openings: 31,442
- Self-Employed: 4.3%
- Part-Time: 38.7%

Level of Stress Tolerance Needed: 64.0 (out of 100)

Most Stressful Aspects: None greater than average.

Least Stressful Aspects: Deal With Physically Aggressive People (3.7); Consequence of Error (9.3); Pace Determined by Speed of Equipment (22.7); Frequency of Conflict Situations (23.5).

Mix and bake ingredients according to recipes to produce breads, rolls, cookies, cakes, pies, pastries, or other baked goods. Observe color of products being baked and adjust oven temperatures, humidity, and conveyor speeds accordingly. Set oven temperatures and place items into hot ovens for baking. Combine measured ingredients in bowls of mixing, blending, or cooking machinery. Measure and weigh flour and other ingredients to prepare batters, doughs, fillings, and icings, using scales and graduated containers. Roll, knead, cut, and shape dough to form sweet rolls, pie crusts, tarts, cookies, and other products. Place dough in pans, in molds, or on sheets and bake in production ovens or on grills. Check the quality of raw materials to ensure that standards and specifications are met. Adapt the quantity of ingredients to match the amount of items to be baked. Apply glazes, icings, or other toppings to baked goods, using spatulas or brushes. Check equipment to ensure that it meets health and safety regulations and perform maintenance or cleaning as necessary. Decorate baked goods such as cakes and pastries. Set time and speed controls for mixing machines, blending machines, or steam kettles so that ingredients will be mixed or cooked according to instructions. Prepare and maintain inventory and production records. Direct and coordinate bakery deliveries. Order and receive supplies and equipment. Operate slicing and wrapping machines. Develop new recipes for baked goods.

Personality Type: Realistic. Realistic occupations frequently involve work activities that include practical, hands-on problems and solutions. They often deal with plants; animals; and real-world materials such as wood, tools, and machinery. Many of the occupations require working outside and do not involve a lot of paperwork or working closely with others.

GOE—Interest Area: 13. Manufacturing. **Work Group:** 13.03. Production Work, Assorted Materials Processing. **Other Jobs in This Work Group:** Cementing and Gluing Machine Operators and Tenders; Chemical Equipment Operators and Tenders; Cleaning, Washing, and Metal Pickling Equipment Operators and Tenders; Coating, Painting, and Spraying Machine Setters, Operators, and Tenders; Cooling and Freezing Equipment Operators and Tenders; Cutting and Slicing Machine Setters, Operators, and Tenders; Extruding and Forming Machine Setters, Operators, and Tenders, Synthetic and Glass Fibers; Extruding, Forming, Pressing, and Compacting Machine Setters, Operators, and Tenders; Food and Tobacco Roasting, Baking, and Drying Machine Operators and Tenders; Food Batchmakers; Food Cooking Machine Operators and Tenders; Furnace, Kiln, Oven, Drier, and Kettle Operators and Tenders; Heat Treating Equipment Setters, Operators, and Tenders, Metal and Plastic; Helpers—Production Workers; Meat, Poultry, and Fish Cutters and Trimmers; Metal-Refining Furnace Operators and Tenders; Mixing and Blending Machine Setters, Operators, and Tenders; Packaging and Filling Machine Operators and Tenders; Plating and Coating Machine Setters, Operators, and Tenders, Metal and Plastic; Pourers and Casters, Metal; Sawing Machine Setters, Operators, and Tenders, Wood; Separating, Filtering, Clarifying, Precipitating, and Still Machine Setters, Operators, and Tenders; Sewing Machine Operators; Shoe Machine Operators and Tenders; Slaughterers and Meat Packers; Team Assemblers; Textile Bleaching and Dyeing Machine Operators and Tenders; Tire Builders; Woodworking Machine Setters, Operators, and Tenders, Except Sawing.

Skills—Systems Evaluation: Identifying measures or indicators of system performance and the actions needed to improve or correct performance, relative to the goals of the system. **Quality Control Analysis:** Conducting tests and inspections of products, services, or processes to evaluate quality or performance. **Equipment Maintenance:** Performing routine maintenance on equipment and determining when and what kind of maintenance is needed. **Operation and Control:** Controlling operations of equipment or systems. **Management of Personnel Resources:** Motivating, developing, and directing people as they work, identifying the best people for the job. **Systems Analysis:** Determining how a system should work and how changes in conditions, operations, and the environment will affect outcomes.

Education and Training Program: Baking and Pastry Arts/Baker/Pastry Chef Training. **Related Knowledge/Courses: Food Production:** Techniques and equipment for planting, growing, and harvesting food products (both plant and animal) for consumption, including storage/handling techniques. **Production and**

Processing: Raw materials, production processes, quality control, costs, and other techniques for maximizing the effective manufacture and distribution of goods. **Personnel and Human Resources:** Principles and procedures for personnel recruitment, selection, training, compensation and benefits, labor relations and negotiation, and personnel information systems. **Mathematics:** Arithmetic, algebra, geometry, calculus, statistics, and their applications. **Sales and Marketing:** Principles and methods for showing, promoting, and selling products or services. This includes marketing strategy and tactics, product demonstration, sales techniques, and sales control systems. **Administration and Management:** Business and management principles involved in strategic planning, resource allocation, human resources modeling, leadership technique, production methods, and coordination of people and resources.

Work Environment: Indoors; very hot or cold; minor burns, cuts, bites, or stings; standing; walking and running; using hands on objects, tools, or controls.

Bindery Workers

- Education/Training Required: Short-term on-the-job training
- Annual Earnings: $25,570
- Growth: –21.8%
- Annual Job Openings: 7,508
- Self-Employed: 1.3%
- Part-Time: 20.5%

Level of Stress Tolerance Needed: 51.7 (out of 100)

Most Stressful Aspects: Pace Determined by Speed of Equipment (83.2); Time Pressure (80.0); Duration of Typical Work Week (64.0); Consequence of Error (43.3).

Least Stressful Aspects: Deal With Physically Aggressive People (4.8); Deal With Unpleasant or Angry People (30.3); Frequency of Conflict Situations (37.3); Level of Competition (43.5).

Set up or operate binding machines that produce books and other printed materials. Read work orders to determine setup specifications and instructions. Examine stitched, collated, bound, and unbound product samples for defects such as imperfect bindings, ink spots, torn or loose pages, and loose and uncut threads. Start machines and make trial runs to verify accuracy of machine setups. Set up, or set up and operate, machines that perform binding operations such as pressing, folding, and trimming on books and related articles. Move controls to adjust and activate bindery machines. Observe and monitor machine operations to detect malfunctions and to determine whether adjustments are needed. Install and adjust bindery machine devices, such as knives, guides, rollers, rounding forms, creasing rams, and clamps, to accommodate sheets, signatures, or books of specified sizes, using hand tools. Maintain records of daily production, using specified forms. Fill machine paper feeds. Lubricate and clean machine parts and make minor repairs to keep machines in working condition. Feed books and related articles such as periodicals and pamphlets into binding machines, following specifications. Remove printed material or finished products from machines or conveyors, wrap products in plastic, and stack them on pallets or skids or pack them in boxes. Clean work areas and maintain equipment and workstations, using hand tools. Stock supplies such as signatures, books, or paper. Punch holes in paper sheets and fasten sheets, signatures, or other material, using hand or machine punches or staplers. Set machine controls to adjust lengths and thicknesses of folds, stitches, or cuts, to synchronize speed of feeding devices and stitching, and to adjust tension on creasing blades and folding rollers. Record production sheet information such as the amount of time spent on specific tasks. Fill glue reservoirs, turn switches to activate heating elements, and adjust flow of glue and speed of conveyors. Secure reels of stitching wire on spindles and thread wire through feeding, cutting, stitch-forming, and driving mechanisms to load stitcher heads for stapling. Open machines and remove and replace damaged covers and books, using hand tools.

Personality Type: Realistic. Realistic occupations frequently involve work activities that include practical, hands-on problems and solutions. They often deal with plants; animals; and real-world materials such as wood, tools, and machinery. Many of the occupations require working outside and do not involve a lot of paperwork or working closely with others.

GOE—Interest Area: 13. Manufacturing. **Work Group:** 13.08. Graphic Arts Production. **Other Jobs in This Work Group:** Desktop Publishers; Etchers and Engravers; Job Printers; Photographic Process Workers; Photographic Processing Machine Operators; Prepress Technicians and Workers; Printing Machine Operators.

Skills—Operation and Control: Controlling operations of equipment or systems. **Quality Control Analysis:** Conducting tests and inspections of products, services, or processes to evaluate quality or performance. **Equipment Maintenance:** Performing routine maintenance on equipment and determining when and what kind of maintenance is needed. **Operation Monitoring:** Watching gauges, dials, or other indicators to make sure a machine is working properly. **Repairing:** Repairing machines or systems, using the needed tools. **Systems Analysis:** Determining how a system should work and how changes in conditions, operations, and the environment will affect outcomes.

Education and Training Programs: No related CIP programs; this job is learned through informal short-term on-the-job training. **Related Knowledge/Courses: Production and Processing:** Raw materials, production processes, quality control, costs, and other techniques for maximizing the effective manufacture and distribution of goods. **Mechanical Devices:** Machines and tools, including their designs, uses, repair, and maintenance.

Work Environment: Noisy; contaminants; standing; using hands on objects, tools, or controls; bending or twisting the body; repetitive motions.

Boilermakers

- Education/Training Required: Long-term on-the-job training
- Annual Earnings: $46,960
- Growth: 14.0%
- Annual Job Openings: 2,333
- Self-Employed: 0.2%
- Part-Time: 10.0%

Level of Stress Tolerance Needed: 72.5 (out of 100)

Most Stressful Aspects: Duration of Typical Work Week (80.5); Impact of Decisions on Co-workers or Company Results (75.5); Time Pressure (73.0); Level of Competition (64.5).

Least Stressful Aspects: Deal With Physically Aggressive People (12.3); Pace Determined by Speed of Equipment (20.8); Deal With Unpleasant or Angry People (45.0); Frequency of Conflict Situations (46.7).

Construct, assemble, maintain, and repair stationary steam boilers and boiler house auxiliaries. Align structures or plate sections to assemble boiler frame tanks or vats, following

blueprints. **Work involves use of hand and power tools, plumb bobs, levels, wedges, dogs, or turnbuckles. Assist in testing assembled vessels. Direct cleaning of boilers and boiler furnaces. Inspect and repair boiler fittings, such as safety valves, regulators, automatic-control mechanisms, water columns, and auxiliary machines.** Bolt or arc-weld pressure vessel structures and parts together, using wrenches and welding equipment. Examine boilers, pressure vessels, tanks, and vats to locate defects such as leaks, weak spots, and defective sections so that they can be repaired. Repair or replace defective pressure vessel parts, such as safety valves and regulators, using torches, jacks, caulking hammers, power saws, threading dies, welding equipment, and metalworking machinery. Inspect assembled vessels and individual components, such as tubes, fittings, valves, controls, and auxiliary mechanisms, to locate any defects. Attach rigging and signal crane or hoist operators to lift heavy frame and plate sections and other parts into place. Bell, bead with power hammers, or weld pressure vessel tube ends to ensure leakproof joints. Lay out plate, sheet steel, or other heavy metal and locate and mark bending and cutting lines, using protractors, compasses, and drawing instruments or templates. Install manholes, handholes, taps, tubes, valves, gauges, and feedwater connections in drums of water tube boilers, using hand tools. Study blueprints to determine locations, relationships, and dimensions of parts. Straighten or reshape bent pressure vessel plates and structure parts, using hammers, jacks, and torches. Shape seams, joints, and irregular edges of pressure vessel sections and structural parts to attain specified fit of parts, using cutting torches, hammers, files, and metalworking machines. Position, align, and secure structural parts and related assemblies to boiler frames, tanks, or vats of pressure vessels, following blueprints. Locate and mark reference points for columns or plates on boiler foundations, following blueprints and using straightedges, squares, transits, and measuring instruments. Shape and fabricate parts, such as stacks, uptakes, and chutes, to adapt pressure vessels, heat exchangers, and piping to premises, using heavy-metalworking machines such as brakes, rolls, and drill presses. Clean pressure vessel equipment, using scrapers, wire brushes, and cleaning solvents.

Personality Type: Realistic. Realistic occupations frequently involve work activities that include practical, hands-on problems and solutions. They often deal with plants; animals; and real-world materials such as wood, tools, and machinery. Many of the occupations require working outside and do not involve a lot of paperwork or working closely with others.

GOE—Interest Area: 02. Architecture and Construction. **Work Group:** 02.04. Construction Crafts. **Other Jobs in This Work Group:** Brickmasons and Blockmasons; Carpet Installers; Cement Masons and Concrete Finishers; Commercial Divers; Construction Carpenters; Crane and Tower Operators; Drywall and Ceiling Tile Installers; Electricians; Fence Erectors; Floor Layers, Except Carpet, Wood, and Hard Tiles; Floor Sanders and Finishers; Glaziers; Hazardous Materials Removal Workers; Insulation Workers, Floor, Ceiling, and Wall; Insulation Workers, Mechanical; Manufactured Building and Mobile Home Installers; Operating Engineers and Other Construction Equipment Operators; Painters, Construction and Maintenance; Paperhangers; Paving, Surfacing, and Tamping Equipment Operators; Pile-Driver Operators; Pipe Fitters and Steamfitters; Pipelayers; Plasterers and Stucco Masons; Plumbers; Plumbers, Pipefitters, and Steamfitters; Rail-Track Laying and Maintenance Equipment Operators; Refractory Materials Repairers, Except Brickmasons; Reinforcing Iron and

Rebar Workers; Riggers; Roofers; Rough Carpenters; Security and Fire Alarm Systems Installers; Segmental Pavers; Sheet Metal Workers; Stone Cutters and Carvers, Manufacturing; Stonemasons; Structural Iron and Steel Workers; Tapers; Terrazzo Workers and Finishers; Tile and Marble Setters.

Skills—Repairing: Repairing machines or systems, using the needed tools. **Installation:** Installing equipment, machines, wiring, or programs to meet specifications. **Equipment Maintenance:** Performing routine maintenance on equipment and determining when and what kind of maintenance is needed. **Operation Monitoring:** Watching gauges, dials, or other indicators to make sure a machine is working properly. **Mathematics:** Using mathematics to solve problems. **Troubleshooting:** Determining causes of operating errors and deciding what to do about them.

Education and Training Program: Boilermaking/Boilermaker Training. **Related Knowledge/ Courses: Building and Construction:** Materials, methods, and the tools involved in the construction or repair of houses, buildings, or other structures such as highways and roads. **Mechanical Devices:** Machines and tools, including their designs, uses, repair, and maintenance. **Engineering and Technology:** The practical application of engineering science and technology. This includes applying principles, techniques, procedures, and equipment to the design and production of various goods and services. **Design:** Design techniques, tools, and principles involved in production of precision technical plans, blueprints, drawings, and models. **Physics:** Physical principles, laws, their interrelationships, and applications to understanding fluid, material, and atmospheric dynamics, and mechanical, electrical, atomic, and subatomic structures and processes. **Transportation:** Principles and methods for moving people or goods by air, rail, sea, or road, including the relative costs and benefits.

Work Environment: Noisy; very hot or cold; contaminants; minor burns, cuts, bites, or stings; standing; using hands on objects, tools, or controls.

Brickmasons and Blockmasons

- Education/Training Required: Long-term on-the-job training
- Annual Earnings: $42,980
- Growth: 9.7%
- Annual Job Openings: 17,569
- Self-Employed: 24.5%
- Part-Time: 16.8%

Level of Stress Tolerance Needed: 60.0 (out of 100)

Most Stressful Aspects: Duration of Typical Work Week (73.0); Time Pressure (72.3); Level of Competition (60.5); Pace Determined by Speed of Equipment (30.5).

Least Stressful Aspects: Consequence of Error (37.0); Deal With Unpleasant or Angry People (44.5); Frequency of Conflict Situations (48.3); Impact of Decisions on Co-workers or Company Results (64.5).

Lay and bind building materials, such as brick, structural tile, concrete block, cinderblock, glass block, and terra-cotta block, with mortar and other substances to construct or repair walls, partitions, arches, sewers, and other structures. Construct corners by fastening in plumb position a corner pole or building a corner pyramid of bricks and filling in between the corners, using a line from corner to corner to guide each course, or layer, of brick. Measure distance from reference points and mark guidelines to lay out work, using plumb bobs and levels. Fasten or fuse brick or other building material to structure with wire clamps, anchor holes, torch, or cement. Calculate angles and courses and determine vertical and horizontal alignment of courses. Break or cut bricks, tiles, or blocks to size, using trowel edge, hammer, or power saw. Remove excess mortar with trowels and hand tools and finish mortar joints with jointing tools for a sealed, uniform appearance. Interpret blueprints and drawings to determine specifications and to calculate the materials required. Apply and smooth mortar or other mixture over work surface. Mix specified amounts of sand, clay, dirt, or mortar powder with water to form refractory mixtures. Examine brickwork or structure to determine need for repair. Clean working surface to remove scale, dust, soot, or chips of brick and mortar, using broom, wire brush, or scraper. Lay and align bricks, blocks, or tiles to build or repair structures or high-temperature equipment, such as cupola, kilns, ovens, or furnaces. Remove burned or damaged brick or mortar, using sledgehammer, crowbar, chipping gun, or chisel. Spray or spread refractory material over brickwork to protect against deterioration.

Personality Type: Realistic. Realistic occupations frequently involve work activities that include practical, hands-on problems and solutions. They often deal with plants; animals; and real-world materials such as wood, tools, and machinery. Many of the occupations require working outside and do not involve a lot of paperwork or working closely with others.

GOE—Interest Area: 02. Architecture and Construction. **Work Group:** 02.04. Construction Crafts. **Other Jobs in This Work Group:** Boilermakers; Carpet Installers; Cement Masons and Concrete Finishers; Commercial Divers; Construction Carpenters; Crane and Tower Operators; Drywall and Ceiling Tile Installers; Electricians; Fence Erectors; Floor Layers, Except Carpet, Wood, and Hard Tiles; Floor Sanders and Finishers; Glaziers; Hazardous Materials Removal Workers; Insulation Workers, Floor, Ceiling, and Wall; Insulation Workers, Mechanical; Manufactured Building and Mobile Home Installers; Operating Engineers and Other Construction Equipment Operators; Painters, Construction and Maintenance; Paperhangers; Paving, Surfacing, and Tamping Equipment Operators; Pile-Driver Operators; Pipe Fitters and Steamfitters; Pipelayers; Plasterers and Stucco Masons; Plumbers; Plumbers, Pipefitters, and Steamfitters; Rail-Track Laying and Maintenance Equipment Operators; Refractory Materials Repairers, Except Brickmasons; Reinforcing Iron and Rebar Workers; Riggers; Roofers; Rough Carpenters; Security and Fire Alarm Systems Installers; Segmental Pavers; Sheet Metal Workers; Stone Cutters and Carvers, Manufacturing; Stonemasons; Structural Iron and Steel Workers; Tapers; Terrazzo Workers and Finishers; Tile and Marble Setters.

Skills—Equipment Maintenance: Performing routine maintenance on equipment and determining when and what kind of maintenance is needed. **Mathematics:** Using mathematics to solve problems. **Installation:** Installing equipment, machines, wiring, or programs to meet specifications.

Education and Training Program: Mason Training/Masonry. **Related Knowledge/Courses: Building and Construction:** Materials, methods, and the tools involved in the construction or repair of houses, buildings, or other structures such as highways and roads. **Design:** Design techniques, tools, and principles involved in production of precision technical plans, blueprints, drawings, and models. **Mechanical Devices:** Machines and tools, including their designs, uses, repair, and maintenance. **Production and Processing:** Raw materials, production processes, quality control, costs, and other techniques for maximizing the effective manufacture and distribution of goods. **Public Safety and Security:** Relevant equipment, policies, procedures, and strategies to promote effective local, state, or national security operations for the protection of people, data, property, and institutions. **Mathematics:** Arithmetic, algebra, geometry, calculus, statistics, and their applications.

Work Environment: Outdoors; very hot or cold; hazardous equipment; standing; using hands on objects, tools, or controls; bending or twisting the body.

Bus and Truck Mechanics and Diesel Engine Specialists

- Education/Training Required: Postsecondary vocational training
- Annual Earnings: $37,660
- Growth: 11.5%
- Annual Job Openings: 25,428
- Self-Employed: 5.8%
- Part-Time: 7.3%

Level of Stress Tolerance Needed: 66.3 (out of 100)

Most Stressful Aspects: Importance of Being Exact or Accurate (83.2); Impact of Decisions on Co-workers or Company Results (77.3); Time Pressure (73.8); Consequence of Error (69.2).

Least Stressful Aspects: Deal With Physically Aggressive People (11.8); Level of Competition (37.0); Frequency of Conflict Situations (44.7); Deal With Unpleasant or Angry People (46.5).

Diagnose, adjust, repair, or overhaul trucks, buses, and all types of diesel engines. Includes mechanics working primarily with automobile diesel engines. Use hand tools such as screwdrivers, pliers, wrenches, pressure gauges, and precision instruments, as well as power tools such as pneumatic wrenches, lathes, welding equipment, and jacks and hoists. Inspect brake systems, steering mechanisms, wheel bearings, and other important parts to ensure that they are in proper operating condition. Perform routine maintenance such as changing oil, checking batteries, and lubricating equipment and machinery. Adjust and reline brakes, align wheels, tighten bolts and screws, and reassemble equipment. Raise trucks, buses, and heavy parts or equipment, using hydraulic jacks or hoists. Test drive trucks and buses to diagnose malfunctions or to ensure that they are working properly. Inspect, test, and listen to defective equipment to diagnose malfunctions, using test instruments such as handheld computers, motor analyzers, chassis charts, and pressure gauges. Examine and adjust protective guards, loose bolts, and specified safety devices. Inspect and verify dimensions and clearances of parts to ensure conformance to factory specifications. Specialize in repairing and maintaining parts of the engine, such as fuel injection systems. Attach test instruments to equipment and read dials and gauges to diagnose malfunctions. Rewire ignition systems, lights, and instrument panels. Recondition and replace parts, pistons, bearings, gears, and valves. Repair and adjust seats, doors, and windows and install and repair accessories. Inspect, repair, and maintain automotive and mechanical equipment and machinery such as pumps and compressors. Disassemble and overhaul internal combustion engines, pumps, generators, transmissions, clutches, and differential units. Rebuild gas or diesel engines. Align front ends and suspension systems. Operate valve-grinding machines to grind and reset valves.

Personality Type: Realistic. Realistic occupations frequently involve work activities that include practical, hands-on problems and solutions. They often deal with plants; animals; and real-world materials such as wood, tools, and machinery. Many of the occupations require working outside and do not involve a lot of paperwork or working closely with others.

GOE—Interest Area: 13. Manufacturing. **Work Group:** 13.14. Vehicle and Facility Mechanical Work. **Other Jobs in This Work Group:** Aircraft Mechanics and Service Technicians; Aircraft Structure, Surfaces, Rigging, and Systems Assemblers; Automotive Body and Related Repairers; Automotive Glass Installers and Repairers; Automotive Master Mechanics; Automotive Service Technicians and Mechanics; Automotive Specialty Technicians; Farm Equipment Mechanics; Fiberglass Laminators and Fabricators; Mobile Heavy Equipment Mechanics, Except Engines; Motorboat Mechanics; Motorcycle Mechanics; Outdoor Power Equipment and Other Small Engine Mechanics; Rail Car Repairers; Recreational Vehicle Service Technicians; Tire Repairers and Changers.

Skills—Repairing: Repairing machines or systems, using the needed tools. **Equipment Maintenance:** Performing routine maintenance on equipment and determining when and what kind of maintenance is needed. **Troubleshooting:** Determining causes of operating errors and deciding what to do about them. **Installation:**

Installing equipment, machines, wiring, or programs to meet specifications. **Science:** Using scientific rules and methods to solve problems. **Technology Design:** Generating or adapting equipment and technology to serve user needs.

Education and Training Programs: Diesel Mechanics Technology/Technician Training; Medium/Heavy Vehicle and Truck Technology/Technician Training. **Related Knowledge/Courses: Mechanical Devices:** Machines and tools, including their designs, uses, repair, and maintenance. **Transportation:** Principles and methods for moving people or goods by air, rail, sea, or road, including the relative costs and benefits. **Public Safety and Security:** Relevant equipment, policies, procedures, and strategies to promote effective local, state, or national security operations for the protection of people, data, property, and institutions. **Physics:** Physical principles, laws, their interrelationships, and applications to understanding fluid, material, and atmospheric dynamics, and mechanical, electrical, atomic, and subatomic structures and processes. **Engineering and Technology:** The practical application of engineering science and technology. This includes applying principles, techniques, procedures, and equipment to the design and production of various goods and services. **Law and Government:** Laws, legal codes, court procedures, precedents, government regulations, executive orders, agency rules, and the democratic political process.

Work Environment: Noisy; very bright or dim lighting; contaminants; hazardous equipment; minor burns, cuts, bites, or stings; using hands on objects, tools, or controls.

Butchers and Meat Cutters

- ◉ Education/Training Required: Long-term on-the-job training
- ◉ Annual Earnings: $26,930
- ◉ Growth: 1.9%
- ◉ Annual Job Openings: 14,503
- ◉ Self-Employed: 1.1%
- ◉ Part-Time: 32.8%

Level of Stress Tolerance Needed: 55.8 (out of 100)

Most Stressful Aspects: Importance of Being Exact or Accurate (80.5); Time Pressure (72.5); Deal With Unpleasant or Angry People (65.8); Consequence of Error (61.3).

Least Stressful Aspects: Deal With Physically Aggressive People (9.3); Frequency of Conflict Situations (44.2); Duration of Typical Work Week (55.0); Impact of Decisions on Co-workers or Company Results (58.0).

Cut, trim, or prepare consumer-sized portions of meat for use or sale in retail establishments. Wrap, weigh, label, and price cuts of meat. Prepare and place meat cuts and products in display counter so they will appear attractive and catch the shopper's eye. Prepare special cuts of meat ordered by customers. Cut, trim, bone, tie, and grind meats, such as beef, pork, poultry, and fish, to prepare meat in cooking form. Receive, inspect, and store meat upon delivery to ensure meat quality. Shape, lace, and tie roasts, using boning knife, skewer, and twine. Estimate requirements and order or requisition meat supplies to maintain inventories. Supervise other butchers or meat cutters. Record quantity of meat received and issued to cooks and keep records of meat sales. Negotiate with representatives from supply companies to determine order details. Cure, smoke, tenderize, and preserve meat. Total sales and collect money from customers.

Personality Type: Realistic. Realistic occupations frequently involve work activities that include practical, hands-on problems and solutions. They often deal with plants; animals; and real-world materials such as wood, tools, and machinery. Many of the occupations require working outside and do not involve a lot of paperwork or working closely with others.

GOE—Interest Area: 09. Hospitality, Tourism, and Recreation. **Work Group:** 09.04. Food and Beverage Preparation. **Other Jobs in This Work Group:** Chefs and Head Cooks; Cooks, Fast Food; Cooks, Institution and Cafeteria; Cooks, Private Household; Cooks, Restaurant; Cooks, Short Order; Dishwashers; Food Preparation Workers.

Skills—None met the criteria.

Education and Training Program: Meat Cutting/Meat Cutter Training. **Related Knowledge/Courses: Food Production:** Techniques and equipment for planting, growing, and harvesting food products (both plant and animal) for consumption, including storage/handling techniques. **Production and Processing:** Raw materials, production processes, quality control, costs, and other techniques for maximizing the effective manufacture and distribution of goods. **Mechanical Devices:** Machines and tools, including their designs, uses, repair, and maintenance. **Sales and Marketing:** Principles and methods for showing, promoting, and selling products or services. This includes marketing strategy and tactics, product demonstration, sales techniques, and sales control systems.

Work Environment: Indoors; very hot or cold; hazardous equipment; standing; using hands on objects, tools, or controls; repetitive motions.

Carpet Installers

- Education/Training Required: Moderate-term on-the-job training
- Annual Earnings: $34,560
- Growth: –1.2%
- Annual Job Openings: 6,692
- Self-Employed: 49.0%
- Part-Time: 16.8%

Level of Stress Tolerance Needed: 68.3 (out of 100)

Most Stressful Aspects: Time Pressure (84.5); Importance of Being Exact or Accurate (84.2); Impact of Decisions on Co-workers or Company Results (68.0); Duration of Typical Work Week (64.0).

Least Stressful Aspects: Deal With Physically Aggressive People (9.0); Pace Determined by Speed of Equipment (19.7); Frequency of Conflict Situations (26.2); Deal With Unpleasant or Angry People (32.0).

Lay and install carpet from rolls or blocks on floors. Install padding and trim flooring materials. Join edges of carpet and seam edges where necessary by sewing or by using tape with glue and heated carpet iron. Cut and trim carpet to fit along wall edges, openings, and projections, finishing the edges with a wall trimmer. Roll out, measure, mark, and cut carpeting to size with a carpet knife, following floor sketches and allowing extra carpet for final fitting. Inspect the surface to be covered to determine its condition and correct any imperfections that might show through carpet or cause carpet to wear unevenly. Plan the layout of the carpet, allowing for expected traffic patterns and placing seams for best appearance and longest wear. Stretch carpet to align with walls and ensure a smooth surface and press carpet in place over tack strips or use staples, tape, tacks, or glue to hold carpet in place. Take measurements and study floor sketches to calculate the area to be carpeted and the amount of material needed. Cut carpet padding to size and install padding, following prescribed method. Install carpet on some floors by using adhesive, following prescribed method. Nail tack strips around area to be carpeted or use old strips to attach edges of new carpet. Fasten metal treads across door openings or where carpet meets flooring to hold carpet in place. Measure, cut, and install tackless strips along the baseboard or wall. Draw building diagrams and record dimensions. Move furniture from area to be carpeted and remove old carpet and padding. Cut and bind material.

Personality Type: Realistic. Realistic occupations frequently involve work activities that include practical, hands-on problems and solutions. They often deal with plants; animals; and real-world materials such as wood, tools, and machinery. Many of the occupations require working outside and do not involve a lot of paperwork or working closely with others.

GOE—Interest Area: 02. Architecture and Construction. **Work Group:** 02.04. Construction Crafts. **Other Jobs in This Work Group:** Boilermakers; Brickmasons and Blockmasons; Cement Masons and Concrete Finishers; Commercial Divers; Construction Carpenters; Crane and Tower Operators; Drywall and Ceiling Tile Installers; Electricians; Fence Erectors; Floor Layers, Except Carpet, Wood, and Hard Tiles; Floor Sanders and Finishers; Glaziers; Hazardous Materials Removal Workers; Insulation Workers, Floor, Ceiling, and Wall; Insulation Workers, Mechanical; Manufactured Building and Mobile Home Installers; Operating Engineers and Other Construction Equipment Operators; Painters, Construction and Maintenance; Paperhangers; Paving, Surfacing, and Tamping Equipment

Operators; Pile-Driver Operators; Pipe Fitters and Steamfitters; Pipelayers; Plasterers and Stucco Masons; Plumbers; Plumbers, Pipefitters, and Steamfitters; Rail-Track Laying and Maintenance Equipment Operators; Refractory Materials Repairers, Except Brickmasons; Reinforcing Iron and Rebar Workers; Riggers; Roofers; Rough Carpenters; Security and Fire Alarm Systems Installers; Segmental Pavers; Sheet Metal Workers; Stone Cutters and Carvers, Manufacturing; Stonemasons; Structural Iron and Steel Workers; Tapers; Terrazzo Workers and Finishers; Tile and Marble Setters.

Skills—Installation: Installing equipment, machines, wiring, or programs to meet specifications. **Repairing:** Repairing machines or systems, using the needed tools. **Equipment Selection:** Determining the kind of tools and equipment needed to do a job. **Management of Personnel Resources:** Motivating, developing, and directing people as they work, identifying the best people for the job. **Mathematics:** Using mathematics to solve problems. **Equipment Maintenance:** Performing routine maintenance on equipment and determining when and what kind of maintenance is needed.

Education and Training Program: Construction Trades, Other. **Related Knowledge/ Courses: Building and Construction:** Materials, methods, and the tools involved in the construction or repair of houses, buildings, or other structures such as highways and roads. **Public Safety and Security:** Relevant equipment, policies, procedures, and strategies to promote effective local, state, or national security operations for the protection of people, data, property, and institutions. **Sales and Marketing:** Principles and methods for showing, promoting, and selling products or services. This includes marketing strategy and tactics, product demonstration, sales techniques, and sales control systems.

Transportation: Principles and methods for moving people or goods by air, rail, sea, or road, including the relative costs and benefits. **Mechanical Devices:** Machines and tools, including their designs, uses, repair, and maintenance. **Design:** Design techniques, tools, and principles involved in production of precision technical plans, blueprints, drawings, and models.

Work Environment: Minor burns, cuts, bites, or stings; standing; walking and running; kneeling, crouching, stooping, or crawling; using hands on objects, tools, or controls; bending or twisting the body.

Cement Masons and Concrete Finishers

- Education/Training Required: Moderate-term on-the-job training
- Annual Earnings: $32,650
- Growth: 11.4%
- Annual Job Openings: 34,625
- Self-Employed: 2.0%
- Part-Time: 16.8%

Level of Stress Tolerance Needed: 40.5 (out of 100)

Most Stressful Aspects: Duration of Typical Work Week (82.5); Impact of Decisions on Co-workers or Company Results (82.2); Time Pressure (70.0); Consequence of Error (55.5).

Least Stressful Aspects: Deal With Physically Aggressive People (2.3); Deal With Unpleasant or Angry People (33.7); Frequency of Conflict Situations (41.5); Importance of Being Exact or Accurate (71.7).

Smooth and finish surfaces of poured concrete, such as floors, walks, sidewalks, roads, or curbs,

using a variety of hand and power tools. **Align forms for sidewalks, curbs, or gutters; patch voids; and use saws to cut expansion joints.** Check forms that hold concrete to see that they are properly constructed. Set forms that hold concrete to desired pitch and depth and align them. Spread, level, and smooth concrete, using rake, shovel, hand or power trowel, hand or power screed, and float. Mold expansion joints and edges, using edging tools, jointers, and straightedge. Monitor how wind, heat, or cold affect curing of concrete throughout entire process. Signal truck driver to position truck to facilitate pouring concrete and move chute to direct concrete on forms. Produce rough concrete surface, using broom. Operate power vibrator to compact concrete. Direct casting of concrete and supervise laborers who use shovels or special tools to spread it. Mix cement, sand, and water to produce concrete, grout, or slurry, using hoe, trowel, tamper, scraper, or concrete-mixing machine. Cut out damaged areas, drill holes for reinforcing rods, and position reinforcing rods to repair concrete, using power saw and drill. Wet surface to prepare for bonding, fill holes and cracks with grout or slurry, and use trowel to smooth. Wet concrete surface and rub with stone to smooth surface and obtain specified finish. Clean chipped area with wire brush, and feel and observe surface to determine whether it is rough or uneven. Apply hardening and sealing compounds to cure surface of concrete and waterproof or restore surface. Chip, scrape, and grind high spots, ridges, and rough projections to finish concrete, using pneumatic chisels, power grinders, or hand tools. Spread roofing paper on surface of foundation and spread concrete onto roofing paper with trowel to form terrazzo base. Build wooden molds and clamp molds around area to be repaired, using hand tools. Sprinkle colored marble or stone chips, powdered steel, or coloring powder over surface to produce prescribed finish. Cut metal division strips and press them into terrazzo base so that top edges form desired design or pattern. Fabricate concrete beams, columns, and panels. Waterproof or restore concrete surfaces, using appropriate compounds.

Personality Type: Realistic. Realistic occupations frequently involve work activities that include practical, hands-on problems and solutions. They often deal with plants; animals; and real-world materials such as wood, tools, and machinery. Many of the occupations require working outside and do not involve a lot of paperwork or working closely with others.

GOE—Interest Area: 02. Architecture and Construction. **Work Group:** 02.04. Construction Crafts. **Other Jobs in This Work Group:** Boilermakers; Brickmasons and Blockmasons; Carpet Installers; Commercial Divers; Construction Carpenters; Crane and Tower Operators; Drywall and Ceiling Tile Installers; Electricians; Fence Erectors; Floor Layers, Except Carpet, Wood, and Hard Tiles; Floor Sanders and Finishers; Glaziers; Hazardous Materials Removal Workers; Insulation Workers, Floor, Ceiling, and Wall; Insulation Workers, Mechanical; Manufactured Building and Mobile Home Installers; Operating Engineers and Other Construction Equipment Operators; Painters, Construction and Maintenance; Paperhangers; Paving, Surfacing, and Tamping Equipment Operators; Pile-Driver Operators; Pipe Fitters and Steamfitters; Pipelayers; Plasterers and Stucco Masons; Plumbers; Plumbers, Pipefitters, and Steamfitters; Rail-Track Laying and Maintenance Equipment Operators; Refractory Materials Repairers, Except Brickmasons; Reinforcing Iron and Rebar Workers; Riggers; Roofers; Rough Carpenters; Security and Fire Alarm Systems Installers; Segmental Pavers; Sheet Metal Workers; Stone Cutters and Carvers, Manufacturing; Stonemasons;

Structural Iron and Steel Workers; Tapers; Terrazzo Workers and Finishers; Tile and Marble Setters.

Skills—Mathematics: Using mathematics to solve problems. **Installation:** Installing equipment, machines, wiring, or programs to meet specifications. **Repairing:** Repairing machines or systems, using the needed tools. **Equipment Maintenance:** Performing routine maintenance on equipment and determining when and what kind of maintenance is needed. **Equipment Selection:** Determining the tools and equipment needed to do a job. **Coordination:** Adjusting actions in relation to others' actions.

Education and Training Program: Concrete Finishing/Concrete Finisher Training. **Related Knowledge/Courses: Building and Construction:** Materials, methods, and the tools involved in the construction or repair of houses, buildings, or other structures such as highways and roads. **Public Safety and Security:** Relevant equipment, policies, procedures, and strategies to promote effective local, state, or national security operations for the protection of people, data, property, and institutions. **Mechanical Devices:** Machines and tools, including their designs, uses, repair, and maintenance. **Design:** Design techniques, tools, and principles involved in production of precision technical plans, blueprints, drawings, and models. **Engineering and Technology:** The practical application of engineering science and technology. This includes applying principles, techniques, procedures, and equipment to the design and production of various goods and services. **Mathematics:** Arithmetic, algebra, geometry, calculus, statistics, and their applications.

Work Environment: Outdoors; noisy; hazardous equipment; standing; using hands on objects, tools, or controls; bending or twisting the body.

Chemical Engineers

- Education/Training Required: Bachelor's degree
- Annual Earnings: $78,860
- Growth: 7.9%
- Annual Job Openings: 2,111
- Self-Employed: 1.9%
- Part-Time: 4.8%

Level of Stress Tolerance Needed: 64.7 (out of 100)

Most Stressful Aspects: Duration of Typical Work Week (79.0); Consequence of Error (50.7); Level of Competition (48.8).

Least Stressful Aspects: Deal With Physically Aggressive People (5.3); Pace Determined by Speed of Equipment (9.3); Deal With Unpleasant or Angry People (31.5); Frequency of Conflict Situations (42.0).

Design chemical plant equipment and devise processes for manufacturing chemicals and products, such as gasoline, synthetic rubber, plastics, detergents, cement, paper, and pulp, by applying principles and technology of chemistry, physics, and engineering. Perform tests throughout stages of production to determine degree of control over variables, including temperature, density, specific gravity, and pressure. Develop safety procedures to be employed by workers operating equipment or working in close proximity to ongoing chemical reactions. Determine most effective arrangement of operations such as mixing, crushing, heat transfer, distillation, and drying. Prepare estimate of production costs and production progress reports for management. Direct activities of workers who operate or who are engaged in constructing and improving absorption, evaporation, or electromagnetic equipment. Perform laboratory studies of steps in manufacture of new product and test proposed process in small-scale operation such as a pilot plant. Develop processes to separate components of liquids or gases or generate electrical currents by using controlled chemical processes. Conduct research to develop new and improved chemical manufacturing processes. Design measurement and control systems for chemical plants based on data collected in laboratory experiments and in pilot plant operations. Design and plan layout of equipment.

Personality Type: Investigative. Investigative occupations frequently involve working with ideas and require an extensive amount of thinking. These occupations can involve searching for facts and figuring out problems mentally.

GOE—Interest Area: 15. Scientific Research, Engineering, and Mathematics. **Work Group:** 15.07. Research and Design Engineering. **Other Jobs in This Work Group:** Aerospace Engineers; Biomedical Engineers; Civil Engineers; Computer Hardware Engineers; Electrical Engineers; Electronics Engineers, Except Computer; Marine Architects; Marine Engineers; Marine Engineers and Naval Architects; Materials Engineers; Mechanical Engineers; Nuclear Engineers.

Skills—Science: Using scientific rules and methods to solve problems. **Technology Design:** Generating or adapting equipment and technology to serve user needs. **Programming:** Writing computer programs for various purposes. **Troubleshooting:** Determining causes of operating errors and deciding what to do about them. **Systems Analysis:** Determining how a system should work and how changes in conditions, operations, and the environment will affect outcomes. **Systems Evaluation:** Identifying measures or indicators of system performance and the actions needed to improve or correct performance, relative to the goals of the system.

Education and Training Program: Chemical Engineering. **Related Knowledge/Courses: Engineering and Technology:** The practical application of engineering science and technology. This includes applying principles, techniques, procedures, and equipment to the design and production of various goods and services. **Chemistry:** The chemical composition, structure, and properties of substances and of the chemical processes and transformations that they undergo. This includes uses of chemicals, their danger signs, production techniques, and disposal methods. **Physics:** Physical principles, laws, their interrelationships, and applications to understanding fluid, material, and atmospheric dynamics, and mechanical, electrical, atomic, and subatomic structures and processes. **Design:** Design techniques, tools, and principles involved in production of precision technical plans, blueprints, drawings, and models. **Production and Processing:** Raw materials, production processes, quality control, costs, and other techniques for maximizing the effective manufacture and distribution of goods. **Mathematics:** Arithmetic, algebra, geometry, calculus, statistics, and their applications.

Work Environment: Indoors; noisy; hazardous conditions; sitting.

Chemical Equipment Operators and Tenders

- Education/Training Required: Moderate-term on-the-job training
- Annual Earnings: $40,290
- Growth: –3.9%
- Annual Job Openings: 1,469
- Self-Employed: 1.1%
- Part-Time: 15.8%

Level of Stress Tolerance Needed: 75.0 (out of 100)

Most Stressful Aspects: Impact of Decisions on Co-workers or Company Results (82.7); Importance of Being Exact or Accurate (79.5); Duration of Typical Work Week (79.0); Consequence of Error (70.7).

Least Stressful Aspects: Deal With Physically Aggressive People (14.0); Frequency of Conflict Situations (44.2); Deal With Unpleasant or Angry People (46.2).

Operate or tend equipment to control chemical changes or reactions in the processing of industrial or consumer products. Equipment used includes devulcanizers, steam-jacketed kettles, and reactor vessels. Adjust controls to regulate temperature, pressure, feed, and flow of liquids and gases and times of prescribed reactions according to knowledge of equipment and processes. Observe safety precautions to prevent fires and explosions. Monitor gauges, recording instruments, flowmeters, or products to ensure that specified conditions are maintained. Control and operate equipment in which chemical changes or reactions take place during the processing of industrial or consumer products. Measure, weigh, and mix chemical ingredients according to specifications. Inspect equipment or units to detect leaks and malfunctions, shutting equipment down if necessary. Patrol work areas to detect leaks and equipment malfunctions and to monitor operating conditions. Test product samples for specific gravity, chemical characteristics, pH levels, and concentrations or viscosities or send them to laboratories for testing. Draw samples of products at specified stages so that analyses can be performed. Record operational data such as temperatures, pressures, ingredients used, processing times, or test results. Notify maintenance engineers of equipment malfunctions. Add treating or neutralizing agents to products and pump products through filters or centrifuges to remove impurities or to precipitate products. Open valves or start pumps, agitators, reactors, blowers, or automatic feed of materials. Read plant specifications to determine products, ingredients, and prescribed modifications of plant procedures. Drain equipment and pump water or other solutions through to flush and clean tanks and equipment. Make minor repairs and lubricate and maintain equipment, using hand tools. Flush or clean equipment, using steam hoses or mechanical reamers. Observe colors and consistencies of products and compare them to instrument readings and to laboratory and standard test results. Implement appropriate industrial emergency response procedures. Dump or scoop prescribed solid, granular, or powdered materials into equipment. Estimate materials required for production and manufacturing of products.

Personality Type: Realistic. Realistic occupations frequently involve work activities that include practical, hands-on problems and solutions. They often deal with plants; animals; and real-world materials such as wood, tools, and machinery. Many of the occupations require working outside and do not involve a lot of paperwork or working closely with others.

GOE—Interest Area: 13. Manufacturing. **Work Group:** 13.03. Production Work, Assorted Materials Processing. **Other Jobs in This Work Group:** Bakers; Cementing and Gluing Machine Operators and Tenders; Cleaning, Washing, and Metal Pickling Equipment Operators and Tenders; Coating, Painting, and Spraying Machine Setters, Operators, and Tenders; Cooling and Freezing Equipment Operators and Tenders; Cutting and Slicing Machine Setters, Operators, and Tenders; Extruding and Forming Machine Setters, Operators, and Tenders, Synthetic and Glass Fibers; Extruding, Forming, Pressing, and Compacting Machine Setters, Operators, and Tenders; Food and Tobacco

Roasting, Baking, and Drying Machine Operators and Tenders; Food Batchmakers; Food Cooking Machine Operators and Tenders; Furnace, Kiln, Oven, Drier, and Kettle Operators and Tenders; Heat Treating Equipment Setters, Operators, and Tenders, Metal and Plastic; Helpers—Production Workers; Meat, Poultry, and Fish Cutters and Trimmers; Metal-Refining Furnace Operators and Tenders; Mixing and Blending Machine Setters, Operators, and Tenders; Packaging and Filling Machine Operators and Tenders; Plating and Coating Machine Setters, Operators, and Tenders, Metal and Plastic; Pourers and Casters, Metal; Sawing Machine Setters, Operators, and Tenders, Wood; Separating, Filtering, Clarifying, Precipitating, and Still Machine Setters, Operators, and Tenders; Sewing Machine Operators; Shoe Machine Operators and Tenders; Slaughterers and Meat Packers; Team Assemblers; Textile Bleaching and Dyeing Machine Operators and Tenders; Tire Builders; Woodworking Machine Setters, Operators, and Tenders, Except Sawing.

Skills—Operation Monitoring: Watching gauges, dials, or other indicators to make sure a machine is working properly. **Operation and Control:** Controlling operations of equipment or systems. **Troubleshooting:** Determining causes of operating errors and deciding what to do about them. **Equipment Maintenance:** Performing routine maintenance on equipment and determining when and what kind of maintenance is needed. **Repairing:** Repairing machines or systems, using the needed tools. **Science:** Using scientific rules and methods to solve problems.

Education and Training Program: Chemical Technology/Technician. **Related Knowledge/Courses: Chemistry:** The chemical composition, structure, and properties of substances and of the chemical processes and transformations that they undergo. This includes uses of chemi-

cals, their danger signs, production techniques, and disposal methods. **Mechanical Devices:** Machines and tools, including their designs, uses, repair, and maintenance. **Production and Processing:** Raw materials, production processes, quality control, costs, and other techniques for maximizing the effective manufacture and distribution of goods. **Public Safety and Security:** Relevant equipment, policies, procedures, and strategies to promote effective local, state, or national security operations for the protection of people, data, property, and institutions.

Work Environment: More often outdoors than indoors; noisy; very hot or cold; contaminants; hazardous conditions.

Chemical Plant and System Operators

- Education/Training Required: Long-term on-the-job training
- Annual Earnings: $49,080
- Growth: –15.3%
- Annual Job Openings: 5,620
- Self-Employed: 0.1%
- Part-Time: 1.3%

Level of Stress Tolerance Needed: 70.0 (out of 100)

Most Stressful Aspects: Consequence of Error (83.2); Importance of Being Exact or Accurate (83.2); Impact of Decisions on Co-workers or Company Results (79.3); Duration of Typical Work Week (73.5).

Least Stressful Aspects: Deal With Physically Aggressive People (5.5); Level of Competition (37.3); Deal With Unpleasant or Angry People (43.0); Frequency of Conflict Situations (45.5).

Control or operate an entire chemical process or system of machines. Move control settings to make necessary adjustments on equipment units affecting speeds of chemical reactions, quality, and yields. Monitor recording instruments, flowmeters, panel lights, and other indicators and listen for warning signals to verify conformity of process conditions. Control or operate chemical processes or systems of machines, using panelboards, control boards, or semi-automatic equipment. Record operating data such as process conditions, test results, and instrument readings. Confer with technical and supervisory personnel to report or resolve conditions affecting safety, efficiency, and product quality. Draw samples of products and conduct quality control tests to monitor processing and to ensure that standards are met. Regulate or shut down equipment during emergency situations as directed by supervisory personnel. Start pumps to wash and rinse reactor vessels; to exhaust gases and vapors; to regulate the flow of oil, steam, air, and perfume to towers; and to add products to converter or blending vessels. Interpret chemical reactions visible through sight glasses or on television monitors and review laboratory test reports for process adjustments. Patrol work areas to ensure that solutions in tanks and troughs are not in danger of overflowing. Notify maintenance, stationary-engineering, and other auxiliary personnel to correct equipment malfunctions and to adjust power, steam, water, or air supplies. Direct workers engaged in operating machinery that regulates the flow of materials and products. Inspect operating units such as towers, soap-spray storage tanks, scrubbers, collectors, and driers to ensure that all are functioning and to maintain maximum efficiency. Turn valves to regulate flow of products or byproducts through agitator tanks, storage drums, or neutralizer tanks. Calculate material requirements or yields according to formulas. Gauge tank levels, using calibrated rods. Repair and replace damaged equipment. Defrost frozen valves, using steam hoses. Supervise the cleaning of towers, strainers, and spray tips.

Personality Type: Realistic. Realistic occupations frequently involve work activities that include practical, hands-on problems and solutions. They often deal with plants; animals; and real-world materials such as wood, tools, and machinery. Many of the occupations require working outside and do not involve a lot of paperwork or working closely with others.

GOE—Interest Area: 13. Manufacturing. **Work Group:** 13.16. Utility Operation and Energy Distribution. **Other Jobs in This Work Group:** Gas Compressor and Gas Pumping Station Operators; Gas Plant Operators; Nuclear Power Reactor Operators; Petroleum Pump System Operators, Refinery Operators, and Gaugers; Power Distributors and Dispatchers; Power Plant Operators; Ship Engineers; Stationary Engineers and Boiler Operators; Water and Liquid Waste Treatment Plant and System Operators.

Skills—Operation Monitoring: Watching gauges, dials, or other indicators to make sure a machine is working properly. **Operation and Control:** Controlling operations of equipment or systems. **Troubleshooting:** Determining causes of operating errors and deciding what to do about them. **Systems Analysis:** Determining how a system should work and how changes in conditions, operations, and the environment will affect outcomes. **Equipment Maintenance:** Performing routine maintenance on equipment and determining when and what kind of maintenance is needed. **Science:** Using scientific rules and methods to solve problems.

Education and Training Program: Chemical Technology/Technician Training. **Related Knowledge/Courses: Production and Processing:** Raw materials, production processes, quality control, costs, and other techniques for maximizing the effective manufacture and distribution of goods. **Chemistry:** The chemical composition, structure, and properties of substances and of the chemical processes and transformations that they undergo. This includes uses of chemicals, their danger signs, production techniques, and disposal methods. **Mechanical Devices:** Machines and tools, including their designs, uses, repair, and maintenance. **Physics:** Physical principles, laws, their interrelationships, and applications to understanding fluid, material, and atmospheric dynamics, and mechanical, electrical, atomic, and subatomic structures and processes. **Engineering and Technology:** The practical application of engineering science and technology. This includes applying principles, techniques, procedures, and equipment to the design and production of various goods and services. **Public Safety and Security:** Relevant equipment, policies, procedures, and strategies to promote effective local, state, or national security operations for the protection of people, data, property, and institutions.

Work Environment: More often indoors than outdoors; noisy; very hot or cold; contaminants; hazardous conditions.

City and Regional Planning Aides

- ◉ Education/Training Required: Associate degree
- ◉ Annual Earnings: $33,860
- ◉ Growth: 12.4%
- ◉ Annual Job Openings: 3,571
- ◉ Self-Employed: 1.7%
- ◉ Part-Time: 28.9%

Our sources did not provide separate job openings data for this occupation. The job openings listed here are shared with Social Science Research Assistants.

Level of Stress Tolerance Needed: 83.2 (out of 100)

Most Stressful Aspects: Importance of Being Exact or Accurate (77.8); Impact of Decisions on Co-workers or Company Results (75.3); Duration of Typical Work Week (69.0); Time Pressure (69.0).

Least Stressful Aspects: Pace Determined by Speed of Equipment (6.5).

Compile data from various sources, such as maps, reports, and field and file investigations, for use by city planner in making planning studies. Prepare, maintain, and update files and records, including land-use data and statistics. Respond to public inquiries and complaints. Research, compile, analyze, and organize information from maps, reports, investigations, and books for use in reports and special projects. Prepare, develop, and maintain maps and databases. Serve as liaison between planning department and other departments and agencies. Prepare reports, using statistics, charts, and graphs, to illustrate planning studies in areas such as population, land use, or zoning. Participate in and support team planning efforts. Provide and process zoning and project permits and applications. Perform clerical duties such as composing, typing, and proofreading documents; scheduling appointments and meetings; handling mail; and posting public notices. Conduct interviews, surveys, and site inspections concerning factors that affect land usage, such as zoning, traffic flow, and housing. Perform code enforcement tasks. Inspect sites and review plans for minor development permit applications.

Personality Type: Conventional. Conventional occupations frequently involve following set procedures and routines. These occupations can include working with data and details more than with ideas. Usually there is a clear line of authority to follow.

GOE—Interest Area: 07. Government and Public Administration. **Work Group:** 07.02. Public Planning. **Other Jobs in This Work Group:** Urban and Regional Planners.

Skills—Service Orientation: Actively looking for ways to help people. **Coordination:** Adjusting actions in relation to others' actions. **Writing:** Communicating effectively in writing as appropriate for the needs of the audience. **Social Perceptiveness:** Being aware of others' reactions and understanding why they react as they do. **Persuasion:** Persuading others to change their minds or behavior. **Complex Problem Solving:** Identifying complex problems and reviewing related information to develop and evaluate options and implement solutions.

Education and Training Program: Social Sciences, General. **Related Knowledge/Courses: Geography:** Principles and methods for describing the features of land, sea, and air masses, including their physical characteristics, locations, interrelationships, and distribution of plant, animal, and human life. **Design:** Design techniques, tools, and principles involved in production of precision technical plans, blueprints, drawings, and models. **Law and Government:** Laws, legal codes, court procedures, precedents, government regulations, executive orders, agency rules, and the democratic political process. **Clerical Practices:** Administrative and clerical procedures and systems such as word processing, managing files and records, stenography and transcription, designing forms, and other office procedures and terminology. **English Language:** The structure and content of the English language,

including the meaning and spelling of words, rules of composition, and grammar. **Building and Construction:** Materials, methods, and the tools involved in the construction or repair of houses, buildings, or other structures such as highways and roads.

Work Environment: Indoors; noisy; sitting.

Civil Engineering Technicians

- Education/Training Required: Associate degree
- Annual Earnings: $40,560
- Growth: 10.2%
- Annual Job Openings: 7,499
- Self-Employed: 0.9%
- Part-Time: 20.9%

Level of Stress Tolerance Needed: 56.7 (out of 100)

Most Stressful Aspects: Importance of Being Exact or Accurate (79.8); Impact of Decisions on Co-workers or Company Results (79.0); Time Pressure (70.2); Duration of Typical Work Week (68.0).

Least Stressful Aspects: Deal With Physically Aggressive People (3.5); Pace Determined by Speed of Equipment (21.3); Level of Competition (40.2); Deal With Unpleasant or Angry People (42.3).

Apply theory and principles of civil engineering in planning, designing, and overseeing construction and maintenance of structures and facilities under the direction of engineering staff or physical scientists. Calculate dimensions, square footage, profile and component specifications, and material quantities, using calculator or computer. Draft detailed dimensional drawings and design layouts for projects and to ensure conformance to specifications. Analyze proposed site factors and design maps, graphs, tracings, and diagrams to illustrate findings. Read and review project blueprints and structural specifications to determine dimensions of structure or system and material requirements. Prepare reports and document project activities and data. Confer with supervisor to determine project details such as plan preparation, acceptance testing, and evaluation of field conditions. Inspect project site and evaluate contractor work to detect design malfunctions and ensure conformance to design specifications and applicable codes. Plan and conduct field surveys to locate new sites and analyze details of project sites. Develop plans and estimate costs for installation of systems, utilization of facilities, or construction of structures. Report maintenance problems occurring at project site to supervisor and negotiate changes to resolve system conflicts. Conduct materials test and analysis, using tools and equipment and applying engineering knowledge. Respond to public suggestions and complaints. Evaluate facility to determine suitability for occupancy and square footage availability.

Personality Type: Realistic. Realistic occupations frequently involve work activities that include practical, hands-on problems and solutions. They often deal with plants; animals; and real-world materials such as wood, tools, and machinery. Many of the occupations require working outside and do not involve a lot of paperwork or working closely with others.

GOE—Interest Area: 15. Scientific Research, Engineering, and Mathematics. **Work Group:** 15.09. Engineering Technology. **Other Jobs in This Work Group:** Aerospace Engineering and Operations Technicians; Cartographers and Photogrammetrists; Electrical and Electronic Engineering Technicians; Electrical and Elec-

tronics Drafters; Electrical Drafters; Electrical Engineering Technicians; Electro-Mechanical Technicians; Electronic Drafters; Electronics Engineering Technicians; Environmental Engineering Technicians; Mapping Technicians; Mechanical Drafters; Mechanical Engineering Technicians; Surveying and Mapping Technicians; Surveying Technicians.

Skills—Mathematics: Using mathematics to solve problems. **Science:** Using scientific rules and methods to solve problems. **Operations Analysis:** Analyzing needs and product requirements to create a design. **Writing:** Communicating effectively in writing as appropriate for the needs of the audience. **Complex Problem Solving:** Identifying complex problems and reviewing related information to develop and evaluate options and implement solutions. **Reading Comprehension:** Understanding written sentences and paragraphs in work-related documents.

Education and Training Programs: Civil Engineering Technology/Technician Training; Construction Engineering Technology/Technician Training. **Related Knowledge/Courses: Building and Construction:** Materials, methods, and the tools involved in the construction or repair of houses, buildings, or other structures such as highways and roads. **Design:** Design techniques, tools, and principles involved in production of precision technical plans, blueprints, drawings, and models. **Engineering and Technology:** The practical application of engineering science and technology. This includes applying principles, techniques, procedures, and equipment to the design and production of various goods and services. **Mathematics:** Arithmetic, algebra, geometry, calculus, statistics, and their applications. **Computers and Electronics:** Circuit boards, processors, chips, electronic equipment, and computer hardware and software, including applications and programming. **Transportation:** Principles and methods for moving people or goods by air, rail, sea, or road, including the relative costs and benefits.

Work Environment: More often indoors than outdoors; sitting.

Civil Engineers

- ◎ Education/Training Required: Bachelor's degree
- ◎ Annual Earnings: $68,600
- ◎ Growth: 18.0%
- ◎ Annual Job Openings: 15,979
- ◎ Self-Employed: 4.9%
- ◎ Part-Time: 13.3%

Level of Stress Tolerance Needed: 73.3 (out of 100)

Most Stressful Aspects: Duration of Typical Work Week (90.0); Importance of Being Exact or Accurate (83.7); Impact of Decisions on Co-workers or Company Results (75.3); Frequency of Conflict Situations (73.0).

Least Stressful Aspects: Deal With Physically Aggressive People (4.8); Pace Determined by Speed of Equipment (5.5); Deal With Unpleasant or Angry People (47.3); Time Pressure (55.5).

Perform engineering duties in planning, designing, and overseeing construction and maintenance of building structures and facilities, such as roads, railroads, airports, bridges, harbors, channels, dams, irrigation projects, pipelines, power plants, water and sewage systems, and waste disposal units. Includes architectural, structural, traffic, ocean, and geo-technical engineers. Analyze survey reports, maps, drawings, blueprints, aerial photography, and other topographical or geologic data to plan projects. Plan and design transportation or hydraulic systems and structures, following construction and government standards and using design software and drawing tools. Compute load and grade requirements, water flow rates, and material stress factors to determine design specifications. Inspect project sites to monitor progress and ensure conformance to design specifications and safety or sanitation standards. Direct construction, operations, and maintenance activities at project site. Direct or participate in surveying to lay out installations and establish reference points, grades, and elevations to guide construction. Estimate quantities and cost of materials, equipment, or labor to determine project feasibility. Prepare or present public reports on topics such as bid proposals, deeds, environmental impact statements, or property and right-of-way descriptions. Test soils and materials to determine the adequacy and strength of foundations, concrete, asphalt, or steel. Provide technical advice regarding design, construction, or program modifications and structural repairs to industrial and managerial personnel. Conduct studies of traffic patterns or environmental conditions to identify engineering problems and assess the potential impact of projects.

Personality Type: Realistic. Realistic occupations frequently involve work activities that include practical, hands-on problems and solutions. They often deal with plants; animals; and real-world materials such as wood, tools, and machinery. Many of the occupations require working outside and do not involve a lot of paperwork or working closely with others.

GOE—Interest Area: 15. Scientific Research, Engineering, and Mathematics. **Work Group:** 15.07. Research and Design Engineering. **Other Jobs in This Work Group:** Aerospace Engineers; Biomedical Engineers; Chemical Engineers;

Computer Hardware Engineers; Electrical Engineers; Electronics Engineers, Except Computer; Marine Architects; Marine Engineers; Marine Engineers and Naval Architects; Materials Engineers; Mechanical Engineers; Nuclear Engineers.

Skills—Science: Using scientific rules and methods to solve problems. **Mathematics:** Using mathematics to solve problems. **Operations Analysis:** Analyzing needs and product requirements to create a design. **Negotiation:** Bringing others together and trying to reconcile differences. **Coordination:** Adjusting actions in relation to others' actions. **Persuasion:** Persuading others to change their minds or behavior.

Education and Training Programs: Civil Engineering, General; Civil Engineering, Other; Transportation and Highway Engineering; Water Resources Engineering. **Related Knowledge/Courses: Engineering and Technology:** The practical application of engineering science and technology. This includes applying principles, techniques, procedures, and equipment to the design and production of various goods and services. **Design:** Design techniques, tools, and principles involved in production of precision technical plans, blueprints, drawings, and models. **Building and Construction:** Materials, methods, and the tools involved in the construction or repair of houses, buildings, or other structures such as highways and roads. **Physics:** Physical principles, laws, their interrelationships, and applications to understanding fluid, material, and atmospheric dynamics, and mechanical, electrical, atomic, and subatomic structures and processes. **Mathematics:** Arithmetic, algebra, geometry, calculus, statistics, and their applications. **Transportation:** Principles and methods for moving people or goods by air, rail, sea, or road, including the relative costs and benefits.

Work Environment: More often outdoors than indoors; very hot or cold; contaminants; hazardous equipment; sitting.

Commercial and Industrial Designers

- Education/Training Required: Bachelor's degree
- Annual Earnings: $54,560
- Growth: 7.2%
- Annual Job Openings: 4,777
- Self-Employed: 29.8%
- Part-Time: 32.0%

Level of Stress Tolerance Needed: 70.7 (out of 100)

Most Stressful Aspects: Importance of Being Exact or Accurate (84.2); Time Pressure (83.2); Duration of Typical Work Week (68.5); Level of Competition (58.0).

Least Stressful Aspects: Deal With Physically Aggressive People (4.8); Pace Determined by Speed of Equipment (15.0); Consequence of Error (22.2); Deal With Unpleasant or Angry People (36.8).

Develop and design manufactured products, such as cars, home appliances, and children's toys. Combine artistic talent with research on product use, marketing, and materials to create the most functional and appealing product design. Prepare sketches of ideas, detailed drawings, illustrations, artwork, or blueprints, using drafting instruments, paints and brushes, or computer-aided design equipment. Direct and coordinate the fabrication of models or samples and the drafting of working drawings and specification sheets from sketches. Modify and refine designs, using working models, to conform with customer specifications, production limitations, or changes in design trends. Coordinate the look and function of product lines. Confer with engineering, marketing, production, or sales departments, or with customers, to establish and evaluate design concepts for manufactured products. Present designs and reports to customers or design committees for approval and discuss need for modification. Evaluate feasibility of design ideas based on factors such as appearance, safety, function, serviceability, budget, production costs/methods, and market characteristics. Read publications, attend showings, and study competing products and design styles and motifs to obtain perspective and generate design concepts. Research production specifications, costs, production materials, and manufacturing methods and provide cost estimates and itemized production requirements. Design graphic material for use as ornamentation, illustration, or advertising on manufactured materials and packaging or containers. Develop manufacturing procedures and monitor the manufacture of their designs in a factory to improve operations and product quality. Supervise assistants' work throughout the design process. Fabricate models or samples in paper, wood, glass, fabric, plastic, metal, or other materials, using hand or power tools. Investigate product characteristics such as the product's safety and handling qualities; its market appeal; how efficiently it can be produced; and ways of distributing, using, and maintaining it. Develop industrial standards and regulatory guidelines. Participate in new product planning or market research, including studying the potential need for new products. Advise corporations on issues involving corporate image projects or problems.

Personality Type: Artistic. Artistic occupations frequently involve working with forms, designs, and patterns. They often require self-expression, and the work can be done without following a clear set of rules.

GOE—Interest Area: 03. Arts and Communication. **Work Group:** 03.05. Design. **Other Jobs in This Work Group:** Fashion Designers; Floral Designers; Graphic Designers; Interior Designers; Merchandise Displayers and Window Trimmers; Set and Exhibit Designers.

Skills—Technology Design: Generating or adapting equipment and technology to serve user needs. **Operations Analysis:** Analyzing needs and product requirements to create a design. **Quality Control Analysis:** Conducting tests and inspections of products, services, or processes to evaluate quality or performance. **Troubleshooting:** Determining causes of operating errors and deciding what to do about them. **Systems Evaluation:** Identifying measures or indicators of system performance and the actions needed to improve or correct performance, relative to the goals of the system. **Installation:** Installing equipment, machines, wiring, or programs to meet specifications.

Education and Training Programs: Commercial and Advertising Art; Design and Applied Arts, Other; Design and Visual Communications, General; Industrial Design. **Related Knowledge/Courses: Design:** Design techniques, tools, and principles involved in production of precision technical plans, blueprints, drawings, and models. **Engineering and Technology:** The practical application of engineering science and technology. This includes applying principles, techniques, procedures, and equipment to the design and production of various goods and services. **Mathematics:** Arithmetic, algebra, geometry, calculus, statistics, and their applications. **Physics:** Physical principles, laws, their interrelationships, and applications to understanding fluid, material, and atmospheric dynamics, and mechanical, electrical, atomic, and subatomic structures and processes. **Mechanical Devices:** Machines and tools, including their designs, uses, repair, and maintenance. **Production and Processing:** Raw materials, production processes, quality control, costs, and other techniques for maximizing the effective manufacture and distribution of goods.

Work Environment: Indoors; sitting; using hands on objects, tools, or controls; repetitive motions.

Computer Programmers

- ◎ Education/Training Required: Bachelor's degree
- ◎ Annual Earnings: $65,510
- ◎ Growth: –4.1%
- ◎ Annual Job Openings: 27,937
- ◎ Self-Employed: 3.9%
- ◎ Part-Time: 11.5%

Level of Stress Tolerance Needed: 64.5 (out of 100)

Most Stressful Aspects: Importance of Being Exact or Accurate (84.7); Time Pressure (69.7); Duration of Typical Work Week (60.0); Consequence of Error (59.0).

Least Stressful Aspects: Pace Determined by Speed of Equipment (11.8); Deal With Physically Aggressive People (14.0); Deal With Unpleasant or Angry People (36.8); Impact of Decisions on Co-workers or Company Results (60.5).

Convert project specifications and statements of problems and procedures into detailed logical flow charts for coding into computer language. Develop and write computer programs to store, locate, and retrieve specific documents, data, and information. May program Web sites. Correct errors by making appropriate changes and rechecking the program to ensure that the desired results are produced. Conduct trial runs of programs and software applications to be sure that they will produce the desired information and that the instructions are correct. Compile and write documentation of program development and subsequent revisions, inserting comments in the coded instructions so others can understand the program. Write, update, and maintain computer programs or software packages to handle specific jobs such as tracking inventory, storing or retrieving data, or controlling other equipment. Consult with managerial, engineering, and technical personnel to clarify program intent, identify problems, and suggest changes. Perform or direct revision, repair, or expansion of existing programs to increase operating efficiency or adapt to new requirements. Write, analyze, review, and rewrite programs, using workflow chart and diagram and applying knowledge of computer capabilities, subject matter, and symbolic logic. Write or contribute to instructions or manuals to guide end users. Investigate whether networks, workstations, the system's central processing unit, or peripheral equipment are responding to a program's instructions. Prepare detailed workflow charts and diagrams that describe input, output, and logical operation and convert them into a series of instructions coded in a computer language. Perform systems analysis and programming tasks to maintain and control the use of computer systems software as a systems programmer. Consult with and assist computer operators or system analysts to define and resolve problems in running computer programs. Assign, coordinate, and review work and activities of programming personnel. Collaborate with computer manufacturers and other users to develop new programming methods. Train subordinates in programming and program coding.

Personality Type: Investigative. Investigative occupations frequently involve working with ideas and require an extensive amount of thinking. These occupations can involve searching for facts and figuring out problems mentally.

GOE—Interest Area: 11. Information Technology. Work Group: 11.02. Information Technology Specialties. Other Jobs in This Work Group: Computer and Information Scientists, Research; Computer Operators; Computer Security Specialists; Computer Software Engineers, Applications; Computer Software Engineers, Systems Software; Computer Support Specialists; Computer Systems Analysts; Computer Systems Engineers/Architects; Database Administrators; Network Designers; Network Systems and Data Communications Analysts; Software Quality Assurance Engineers and Testers; Web Administrators; Web Developers.

Skills—Programming: Writing computer programs for various purposes. Operations Analysis: Analyzing needs and product requirements to create a design. Technology Design: Generating or adapting equipment and technology to serve user needs. Systems Analysis: Determining how a system should work and how changes in conditions, operations, and the environment will affect outcomes. Troubleshooting: Determining causes of operating errors and deciding what to do about them. Installation: Installing equipment, machines, wiring, or programs to meet specifications.

Education and Training Programs: Artificial Intelligence and Robotics; Bioinformatics; Computer Graphics; Computer Programming, Specific Applications; Computer Programming, Vendor/Product Certification; Computer Programming/Programmer, General; E-Commerce/Electronic Commerce; Management Information Systems, General; Medical Informatics; Medical Office Computer Specialist/Assistant Training; Web Page, Digital/Multimedia and Information Resources Design; Web/Multimedia Management and Webmaster Training. Related Knowledge/Courses: Computers and Electronics: Circuit boards, processors, chips, electronic equipment, and computer hardware and software, including applications and programming. Design: Design techniques, tools, and principles involved in production of precision technical plans, blueprints, drawings, and models. Mathematics: Arithmetic, algebra, geometry, calculus, statistics, and their applications. Telecommunications: Transmission, broadcasting, switching, control, and operation of telecommunications systems. Economics and Accounting: Economic and accounting principles and practices, the financial markets, banking, and the analysis and reporting of financial data. Engineering and Technology: The practical application of engineering science and technology. This includes applying principles, techniques, procedures, and equipment to the design and production of various goods and services.

Work Environment: Indoors; sitting; using hands on objects, tools, or controls; repetitive motions.

Computer Software Engineers, Applications

- Education/Training Required: Bachelor's degree
- Annual Earnings: $79,780
- Growth: 44.6%
- Annual Job Openings: 58,690
- Self-Employed: 2.0%
- Part-Time: 13.1%

Level of Stress Tolerance Needed: 68.5 (out of 100)

Most Stressful Aspects: Importance of Being Exact or Accurate (79.8); Duration of Typical Work Week (67.0); Level of Competition (57.7); Consequence of Error (55.3).

Least Stressful Aspects: Deal With Physically Aggressive People (1.8); Pace Determined by Speed of Equipment (7.5); Deal With Unpleasant or Angry People (21.0); Frequency of Conflict Situations (46.7).

Develop, create, and modify general computer applications software or specialized utility programs. Analyze user needs and develop software solutions. Design software or customize software for client use with the aim of optimizing operational efficiency. May analyze and design databases within an application area, working individually or coordinating database development as part of a team. Confer with systems analysts, engineers, programmers, and others to design system and to obtain information on project limitations and capabilities, performance requirements, and interfaces. Modify existing software to correct errors, allow it to adapt to new hardware, or improve its performance. Analyze user needs and software requirements to determine feasibility of design within time and cost constraints. Consult with customers about software system design and maintenance. Coordinate software system installation and monitor equipment functioning to ensure specifications are met. Design, develop, and modify software systems, using scientific analysis and mathematical models to predict and measure outcome and consequences of design. Develop and direct software system testing and validation procedures, programming, and documentation. Analyze information to determine, recommend, and plan computer specifications and layouts and peripheral equipment modifications. Supervise the work of programmers, technologists, and technicians and other engineering and scientific personnel. Obtain and evaluate information on factors such as reporting formats required, costs, and security needs to determine hardware configuration. Determine system performance standards. Train users to use new or modified equipment. Store, retrieve, and manipulate data for analysis of system capabilities and requirements. Specify power supply requirements and configuration. Recommend purchase of equipment to control dust, temperature, and humidity in area of system installation.

Personality Type: Investigative. Investigative occupations frequently involve working with ideas and require an extensive amount of thinking. These occupations can involve searching for facts and figuring out problems mentally.

GOE—Interest Area: 11. Information Technology. **Work Group:** 11.02. Information Technology Specialties. **Other Jobs in This Work Group:** Computer and Information Scientists, Research; Computer Operators; Computer Programmers; Computer Security Specialists; Computer Software Engineers, Systems Software; Computer Support Specialists; Computer Systems Analysts; Computer Systems Engineers/Architects; Database Administrators; Network Designers; Network Systems and Data Communications Analysts; Software Quality Assurance Engineers and Testers; Web Administrators; Web Developers.

Skills—Programming: Writing computer programs for various purposes. **Troubleshooting:** Determining causes of operating errors and deciding what to do about them. **Technology Design:** Generating or adapting equipment and technology to serve user needs. **Systems Analysis:** Determining how a system should work and how changes in conditions, operations, and the environment will affect outcomes. **Quality Control Analysis:** Conducting tests and inspections of products, services, or processes to evaluate quality or performance. **Operations Analysis:** Analyzing needs and product requirements to create a design.

Education and Training Programs: Artificial Intelligence and Robotics; Bioinformatics; Computer Engineering Technologies/Technician Training, Other; Computer Engineering, General; Computer Science; Computer Software Engineering; Information Technology; Medical Illustration and Informatics, Other; Medical Informatics. **Related Knowledge/ Courses: Computers and Electronics:** Circuit boards, processors, chips, electronic equipment, and computer hardware and software, including applications and programming. **Telecommunications:** Transmission, broadcasting, switching, control, and operation of telecommunications systems. **Engineering and Technology:** The practical application of engineering science and technology. This includes applying principles, techniques, procedures, and equipment to the design and production of various goods and services. **Design:** Design techniques, tools, and principles involved in production of precision technical plans, blueprints, drawings, and models. **Mathematics:** Arithmetic, algebra, geometry, calculus, statistics, and their applications. **Physics:** Physical principles, laws, their interrelationships, and applications to understanding fluid, material, and atmospheric dynamics, and mechanical, electrical, atomic, and subatomic structures and processes.

Work Environment: Indoors; sitting; using hands on objects, tools, or controls; repetitive motions.

Computer Systems Analysts

- Education/Training Required: Bachelor's degree
- Annual Earnings: $69,760
- Growth: 29.0%
- Annual Job Openings: 63,166
- Self-Employed: 5.8%
- Part-Time: 13.0%

Level of Stress Tolerance Needed: 68.3 (out of 100)

Most Stressful Aspects: Importance of Being Exact or Accurate (81.0); Impact of Decisions on Co-workers or Company Results (74.5); Duration of Typical Work Week (73.5); Consequence of Error (63.2).

Least Stressful Aspects: Deal With Physically Aggressive People (0.2); Pace Determined by Speed of Equipment (2.3); Frequency of Conflict Situations (33.7); Deal With Unpleasant or Angry People (45.0).

Analyze science, engineering, business, and all other data-processing problems for application to electronic data processing systems. Analyze user requirements, procedures, and problems to automate or improve existing systems and review computer system capabilities, workflow, and scheduling limitations. May analyze or recommend commercially available software. May supervise computer programmers. Provide staff and users with assistance solving computer-related problems, such as malfunctions and program problems. Test, maintain, and monitor computer programs and systems, including coordinating the installation of computer programs and systems. Use object-oriented programming languages as well as client and server applications development processes and

C

multimedia and Internet technology. Confer with clients regarding the nature of the information processing or computation needs a computer program is to address. Coordinate and link the computer systems within an organization to increase compatibility and so information can be shared. Consult with management to ensure agreement on system principles. Expand or modify system to serve new purposes or improve workflow. Interview or survey workers, observe job performance, or perform the job to determine what information is processed and how it is processed. Determine computer software or hardware needed to set up or alter system. Train staff and users to work with computer systems and programs. Analyze information processing or computation needs and plan and design computer systems, using techniques such as structured analysis, data modeling, and information engineering. Assess the usefulness of pre-developed application packages and adapt them to a user environment. Define the goals of the system and devise flow charts and diagrams describing logical operational steps of programs. Develop, document, and revise system design procedures, test procedures, and quality standards. Review and analyze computer printouts and performance indicators to locate code problems; correct errors by correcting codes. Recommend new equipment or software packages. Read manuals, periodicals, and technical reports to learn how to develop programs that meet staff and user requirements. Supervise computer programmers or other systems analysts or serve as project leaders for particular systems projects. Utilize the computer in the analysis and solution of business problems such as development of integrated production and inventory control and cost analysis systems.

Personality Type: Investigative. Investigative occupations frequently involve working with ideas and require an extensive amount of think-

ing. These occupations can involve searching for facts and figuring out problems mentally.

GOE—Interest Area: 11. Information Technology. **Work Group:** 11.02. Information Technology Specialties. **Other Jobs in This Work Group:** Computer and Information Scientists, Research; Computer Operators; Computer Programmers; Computer Security Specialists; Computer Software Engineers, Applications; Computer Software Engineers, Systems Software; Computer Support Specialists; Computer Systems Engineers/Architects; Database Administrators; Network Designers; Network Systems and Data Communications Analysts; Software Quality Assurance Engineers and Testers; Web Administrators; Web Developers.

Skills—Installation: Installing equipment, machines, wiring, or programs to meet specifications. **Quality Control Analysis:** Conducting tests and inspections of products, services, or processes to evaluate quality or performance. **Systems Analysis:** Determining how a system should work and how changes in conditions, operations, and the environment will affect outcomes. **Programming:** Writing computer programs for various purposes. **Technology Design:** Generating or adapting equipment and technology to serve user needs. **Troubleshooting:** Determining causes of operating errors and deciding what to do about them.

Education and Training Programs: Computer and Information Sciences, General; Computer Systems Analysis/Analyst Training; Information Technology; Web/Multimedia Management and Webmaster Training. **Related Knowledge/ Courses: Computers and Electronics:** Circuit boards, processors, chips, electronic equipment, and computer hardware and software, including applications and programming. **Telecommunications:** Transmission, broadcasting, switching, control, and operation of telecommunications systems. **Design:** Design techniques, tools, and principles involved in production of precision technical plans, blueprints, drawings, and models. **Customer and Personal Service:** Principles and processes for providing customer and personal services. This includes customer needs assessment, meeting quality standards for services, and evaluation of customer satisfaction. **Law and Government:** Laws, legal codes, court procedures, precedents, government regulations, executive orders, agency rules, and the democratic political process. **Communications and Media:** Media production, communication, and dissemination techniques and methods. This includes alternative ways to inform and entertain via written, oral, and visual media.

Work Environment: Indoors; sitting.

Computer, Automated Teller, and Office Machine Repairers

- Education/Training Required: Postsecondary vocational training
- Annual Earnings: $36,480
- Growth: 3.0%
- Annual Job Openings: 22,330
- Self-Employed: 19.7%
- Part-Time: 21.1%

Level of Stress Tolerance Needed: 67.0 (out of 100)

Most Stressful Aspects: Importance of Being Exact or Accurate (77.8); Time Pressure (75.0); Level of Competition (73.5); Impact of Decisions on Co-workers or Company Results (69.7).

Least Stressful Aspects: Deal With Physically Aggressive People (15.0); Consequence of Error (34.8); Frequency of Conflict Situations (43.3); Deal With Unpleasant or Angry People (53.5).

Repair, maintain, or install computers; word-processing systems; automated teller machines; and electronic office machines, such as duplicating and fax machines. Converse with customers to determine details of equipment problems. Reassemble machines after making repairs or replacing parts. Travel to customers' stores or offices to service machines or to provide emergency repair service. Reinstall software programs or adjust settings on existing software to fix machine malfunctions. Advise customers concerning equipment operation, maintenance, and programming. Assemble machines according to specifications, using hand tools, power tools, and measuring devices. Test new systems to ensure that they are in working order. Operate machines to test functioning of parts and mechanisms. Maintain records of equipment maintenance work and repairs. Install and configure new equipment, including operating software and peripheral equipment. Maintain parts inventories and order any additional parts needed for repairs. Update existing equipment, performing tasks such as installing updated circuit boards or additional memory. Test components and circuits of faulty equipment to locate defects, using oscilloscopes, signal generators, ammeters, voltmeters, or special diagnostic software programs. Align, adjust, and calibrate equipment according to specifications. Repair, adjust, or replace electrical and mechanical components and parts, using hand tools, power tools, and soldering or welding equipment. Complete repair bills, shop records, time cards, and expense reports. Disassemble machine to examine parts such as wires, gears, and bearings for wear and defects, using hand tools, power tools, and measuring devices. Clean, oil, and adjust mechanical parts to maintain machines' operating efficiency and to prevent breakdowns. Enter information into computers to copy programs from one electronic component to another or to draw, modify, or store schematics. Read specifications such as blueprints, charts, and schematics to determine machine settings and adjustments. Lay cable and hook up electrical connections between machines, power sources, and phone lines. Analyze equipment performance records to assess equipment functioning.

Personality Type: Realistic. Realistic occupations frequently involve work activities that include practical, hands-on problems and solutions. They often deal with plants; animals; and real-world materials such as wood, tools, and machinery. Many of the occupations require working outside and do not involve a lot of paperwork or working closely with others.

GOE—Interest Area: 11. Information Technology. **Work Group:** 11.03. Digital Equipment Repair. **Other Jobs in This Work Group:** Coin, Vending, and Amusement Machine Servicers and Repairers.

Skills—Installation: Installing equipment, machines, wiring, or programs to meet specifications. **Repairing:** Repairing machines or systems, using the needed tools. **Troubleshooting:** Determining causes of operating errors and deciding what to do about them. **Equipment Maintenance:** Performing routine maintenance on equipment and determining when and what kind of maintenance is needed. **Management of Material Resources:** Obtaining and seeing to the appropriate use of equipment, facilities, and materials needed to do certain work. **Programming:** Writing computer programs for various purposes.

Education and Training Programs: Business Machine Repair; Computer Installation and Repair Technology/Technician Training. **Related Knowledge/Courses: Computers and**

Electronics: Circuit boards, processors, chips, electronic equipment, and computer hardware and software, including applications and programming. **Telecommunications:** Transmission, broadcasting, switching, control, and operation of telecommunications systems. **Mechanical Devices:** Machines and tools, including their designs, uses, repair, and maintenance. **Customer and Personal Service:** Principles and processes for providing customer and personal services. This includes customer needs assessment, meeting quality standards for services, and evaluation of customer satisfaction. **Engineering and Technology:** The practical application of engineering science and technology. This includes applying principles, techniques, procedures, and equipment to the design and production of various goods and services. **Sales and Marketing:** Principles and methods for showing, promoting, and selling products or services. This includes marketing strategy and tactics, product demonstration, sales techniques, and sales control systems.

Work Environment: Indoors; sitting; using hands on objects, tools, or controls; repetitive motions.

Construction and Building Inspectors

- Education/Training Required: Work experience in a related occupation
- Annual Earnings: $46,570
- Growth: 18.2%
- Annual Job Openings: 12,606
- Self-Employed: 9.4%
- Part-Time: 11.9%

Level of Stress Tolerance Needed: 70.2 (out of 100)

Most Stressful Aspects: Time Pressure (78.0); Importance of Being Exact or Accurate (77.8); Impact of Decisions on Co-workers or Company Results (70.7); Frequency of Conflict Situations (64.7).

Least Stressful Aspects: Deal With Physically Aggressive People (7.7); Level of Competition (30.8); Consequence of Error (41.0).

Inspect structures, using engineering skills to determine structural soundness and compliance with specifications, building codes, and other regulations. Inspections may be general in nature or may be limited to a specific area, such as electrical systems or plumbing. Use survey instruments; metering devices; tape measures; and test equipment, such as concrete strength measurers, to perform inspections. Inspect bridges, dams, highways, buildings, wiring, plumbing, electrical circuits, sewers, heating systems, and foundations during and after construction for structural quality, general safety, and conformance to specifications and codes. Maintain daily logs and supplement inspection records with photographs. Review and interpret plans, blueprints, site layouts, specifications, and construction methods to ensure compliance to legal requirements and safety regulations. Inspect and monitor construction sites to ensure adherence to safety standards, building codes, and specifications. Measure dimensions and verify level, alignment, and elevation of structures and fixtures to ensure compliance to building plans and codes. Issue violation notices and stop-work orders, conferring with owners, violators, and authorities to explain regulations and recommend rectifications. Issue permits for construction, relocation, demolition, and occupancy. Approve and sign plans that meet required specifications. Compute estimates of work completed or of needed renovations or upgrades and approve payment for contractors. Monitor installation of plumbing, wiring, equipment, and appliances to ensure that installation is performed properly and is in compliance with applicable regulations. Examine lifting and conveying devices, such as elevators, escalators, moving sidewalks, lifts and hoists, inclined railways, ski lifts, and amusement rides, to ensure safety and proper functioning. Train, direct, and supervise other construction inspectors. Evaluate premises for cleanliness, including proper garbage disposal and lack of vermin infestation.

Personality Type: Conventional. Conventional occupations frequently involve following set procedures and routines. These occupations can include working with data and details more than with ideas. Usually there is a clear line of authority to follow.

GOE—Interest Area: 07. Government and Public Administration. **Work Group:** 07.03. Regulations Enforcement. **Other Jobs in This Work Group:** Agricultural Inspectors; Aviation Inspectors; Compliance Officers, Except Agriculture, Construction, Health and Safety, and Transportation; Environmental Compliance Inspectors; Equal Opportunity Representatives and Officers; Financial Examiners; Fire Inspectors; Fish and Game Wardens; Forest Fire Inspectors and Prevention Specialists; Freight and Cargo Inspectors; Government Property Inspectors and Investigators; Immigration and Customs Inspectors; Licensing Examiners and Inspectors; Nuclear Monitoring Technicians; Occupational Health and Safety Specialists; Occupational Health and Safety Technicians; Tax Examiners, Collectors, and Revenue Agents; Transportation Vehicle, Equipment, and Systems Inspectors, Except Aviation.

Skills—Mathematics: Using mathematics to solve problems. **Persuasion:** Persuading others to change their minds or behavior. **Quality Control Analysis:** Conducting tests and inspections of products, services, or processes to evaluate quality or performance. **Reading Comprehension:** Understanding written sentences and paragraphs in work-related documents. **Science:** Using scientific rules and methods to solve problems. **Installation:** Installing equipment, machines, wiring, or programs to meet specifications.

Education and Training Program: Building/Home/Construction Inspection/Inspector Training. **Related Knowledge/Courses: Building and Construction:** Materials, methods, and the tools involved in the construction or repair of houses, buildings, or other structures such as highways and roads. **Design:** Design techniques, tools, and principles involved in production of precision technical plans, blueprints, drawings, and models. **Engineering and Technology:** The practical application of engineering science and technology. This includes applying principles, techniques, procedures, and equipment to the design and production of various goods and services. **Public Safety and Security:** Relevant equipment, policies, procedures, and strategies to promote effective local, state, or national security operations for the protection of people, data, property, and institutions. **Mechanical Devices:** Machines and tools, including their designs, uses, repair, and maintenance. **Computers and Electronics:** Circuit boards, processors, chips, electronic equipment, and computer hardware and software, including applications and programming.

Work Environment: More often outdoors than indoors; noisy; contaminants; hazardous equipment; standing.

Construction Carpenters

- Education/Training Required: Long-term on-the-job training
- Annual Earnings: $36,550
- Growth: 10.3%
- Annual Job Openings: 223,225
- Self-Employed: 31.8%
- Part-Time: 15.9%

Our sources did not provide separate job openings data for this occupation. The job openings listed here are shared with Rough Carpenters.

Level of Stress Tolerance Needed: 73.3 (out of 100)

Most Stressful Aspects: Importance of Being Exact or Accurate (78.0); Level of Competition (64.2); Duration of Typical Work Week (59.0).

Least Stressful Aspects: Deal With Physically Aggressive People (4.0); Pace Determined by Speed of Equipment (19.2); Consequence of Error (20.2); Deal With Unpleasant or Angry People (27.5).

Construct, erect, install, and repair structures and fixtures of wood, plywood, and wallboard, using carpenter's hand tools and power tools. Measure and mark cutting lines on materials, using ruler, pencil, chalk, and marking gauge. Follow established safety rules and regulations and maintain a safe and clean environment. Verify trueness of structure, using plumb bob and level. Shape or cut materials to specified measurements, using hand tools, machines, or power saw. Study specifications in blueprints, sketches, or building plans to prepare project layout and determine dimensions and materials required. Assemble and fasten materials to make framework or props, using hand tools and wood screws, nails, dowel pins, or glue. Build or repair cabinets, doors, frameworks, floors, and other wooden fixtures used in buildings, using wood-working machines, carpenter's hand tools, and power tools. Erect scaffolding and ladders for assembling structures above ground level. Remove damaged or defective parts or sections of structures and repair or replace, using hand tools. Install structures and fixtures, such as windows, frames, floorings, and trim, or hardware, using carpenter's hand and power tools. Select and order lumber and other required materials. Maintain records, document actions, and present written progress reports. Finish surfaces of woodwork or wallboard in houses and buildings, using paint, hand tools, and paneling. Prepare cost estimates for clients or employers. Arrange for subcontractors to deal with special areas such as heating and electrical wiring work. Inspect ceiling or floor tile, wall coverings, siding, glass, or woodwork to detect broken or damaged structures. Work with or remove hazardous material. Construct forms and chutes for pouring concrete. Cover subfloors with building paper to keep out moisture and lay hardwood, parquet, and wood-strip-block floors by nailing floors to subfloor or cementing them to mastic or asphalt base. Fill cracks and other defects in plaster or plasterboard and sand patch, using patching plaster, trowel, and sanding tool. Perform minor plumbing, welding, or concrete mixing work. Apply shock-absorbing, sound-deadening, and decorative paneling to ceilings and walls.

Personality Type: Realistic. Realistic occupations frequently involve work activities that include practical, hands-on problems and solutions. They often deal with plants; animals; and real-world materials such as wood, tools, and machinery. Many of the occupations require working outside and do not involve a lot of paperwork or working closely with others.

GOE—Interest Area: 02. Architecture and Construction. **Work Group:** 02.04. Construction Crafts. **Other Jobs in This Work Group:** Boilermakers; Brickmasons and Blockmasons; Carpet Installers; Cement Masons and Concrete Finishers; Commercial Divers; Crane and Tower Operators; Drywall and Ceiling Tile Installers; Electricians; Fence Erectors; Floor Layers, Except Carpet, Wood, and Hard Tiles; Floor Sanders and Finishers; Glaziers; Hazardous Materials Removal Workers; Insulation Workers, Floor, Ceiling, and Wall; Insulation Workers, Mechanical; Manufactured Building and Mobile Home Installers; Operating Engineers and Other Construction Equipment Operators; Painters, Construction and Maintenance; Paperhangers; Paving, Surfacing, and Tamping Equipment Operators; Pile-Driver Operators; Pipe Fitters and Steamfitters; Pipelayers; Plasterers and Stucco Masons; Plumbers; Plumbers, Pipefitters, and Steamfitters; Rail-Track Laying and Maintenance Equipment Operators; Refractory Materials Repairers, Except Brickmasons; Reinforcing Iron and Rebar Workers; Riggers; Roofers; Rough Carpenters; Security and Fire Alarm Systems Installers; Segmental Pavers; Sheet Metal Workers; Stone Cutters and Carvers, Manufacturing; Stonemasons; Structural Iron and Steel Workers; Tapers; Terrazzo Workers and Finishers; Tile and Marble Setters.

Skills—Management of Personnel Resources: Motivating, developing, and directing people as they work, identifying the best people for the job. **Management of Material Resources:** Obtaining and seeing to the appropriate use of equipment, facilities, and materials needed to do certain work. **Management of Financial Resources:** Determining how money will be spent to get the work done and accounting for these expenditures. **Repairing:** Repairing

C

machines or systems, using the needed tools. **Equipment Maintenance:** Performing routine maintenance on equipment and determining when and what kind of maintenance is needed. **Quality Control Analysis:** Conducting tests and inspections of products, services, or processes to evaluate quality or performance.

Education and Training Program: Carpentry/ Carpenter Training. **Related Knowledge/ Courses: Building and Construction:** Materials, methods, and the tools involved in the construction or repair of houses, buildings, or other structures such as highways and roads. **Mechanical Devices:** Machines and tools, including their designs, uses, repair, and maintenance. **Design:** Design techniques, tools, and principles involved in production of precision technical plans, blueprints, drawings, and models. **Engineering and Technology:** The practical application of engineering science and technology. This includes applying principles, techniques, procedures, and equipment to the design and production of various goods and services. **Production and Processing:** Raw materials, production processes, quality control, costs, and other techniques for maximizing the effective manufacture and distribution of goods. **Public Safety and Security:** Relevant equipment, policies, procedures, and strategies to promote effective local, state, or national security operations for the protection of people, data, property, and institutions.

Work Environment: Outdoors; noisy; hazardous equipment; standing; walking and running; using hands on objects, tools, or controls.

Cooks, Private Household

- Education/Training Required: Long-term on-the-job training
- Annual Earnings: $22,870
- Growth: 8.8%
- Annual Job Openings: 1,352
- Self-Employed: 0.0%
- Part-Time: 47.8%

Level of Stress Tolerance Needed: 59.8 (out of 100)

Most Stressful Aspects: Time Pressure (76.8); Level of Competition (51.7).

Least Stressful Aspects: Deal With Physically Aggressive People (0.0); Pace Determined by Speed of Equipment (15.3); Frequency of Conflict Situations (21.5); Deal With Unpleasant or Angry People (27.7).

Prepare meals in private homes. Plan menus according to employers' needs and diet restrictions. Shop for or order food and kitchen supplies and equipment. Peel, wash, trim, and cook vegetables and meats and bake breads and pastries. Prepare meals in private homes according to employers' recipes or tastes, handling all meals for the family and possibly for other household staff. Stock, organize, and clean kitchens and cooking utensils. Specialize in preparing fancy dishes or food for special diets. Create and explore new cuisines. Direct the operation and organization of kitchens and all food-related activities, including the presentation and serving of food. Plan and prepare food for parties, holiday meals, luncheons, special functions, and other social events. Serve meals and snacks to employing families and their guests. Travel with employers to vacation homes to provide meal preparation at those locations.

Personality Type: No data available.

GOE—**Interest Area:** 09. Hospitality, Tourism, and Recreation. **Work Group:** 09.04. Food and Beverage Preparation. **Other Jobs in This Work Group:** Butchers and Meat Cutters; Chefs and Head Cooks; Cooks, Fast Food; Cooks, Institution and Cafeteria; Cooks, Restaurant; Cooks, Short Order; Dishwashers; Food Preparation Workers.

Skills—Management of Financial Resources: Determining how money will be spent to get the work done and accounting for these expenditures. **Management of Material Resources:** Obtaining and seeing to the appropriate use of equipment, facilities, and materials needed to do certain work. **Time Management:** Managing one's own time and the time of others. **Equipment Selection:** Determining the kind of tools and equipment needed to do a job. **Quality Control Analysis:** Conducting tests and inspections of products, services, or processes to evaluate quality or performance. **Service Orientation:** Actively looking for ways to help people.

Education and Training Programs: Culinary Arts/Chef Training; Food Preparation/Professional Cooking/Kitchen Assistant Training. **Related Knowledge/Courses: Food Production:** Techniques and equipment for planting, growing, and harvesting food products (both plant and animal) for consumption, including storage/handling techniques. **Sales and Marketing:** Principles and methods for showing, promoting, and selling products or services. This includes marketing strategy and tactics, product demonstration, sales techniques, and sales control systems. **Production and Processing:** Raw materials, production processes, quality control, costs, and other techniques for maximizing the effective manufacture and distribution of goods. **Clerical Practices:** Administrative and clerical procedures and systems such as word processing, managing files and records, stenography and transcription, designing forms, and other office procedures and terminology. **Customer and**

Personal Service: Principles and processes for providing customer and personal services. This includes customer needs assessment, meeting quality standards for services, and evaluation of customer satisfaction. **Economics and Accounting:** Economic and accounting principles and practices, the financial markets, banking, and the analysis and reporting of financial data.

Work Environment: Indoors; minor burns, cuts, bites, or stings; standing; using hands on objects, tools, or controls; repetitive motions.

Credit Analysts

- Education/Training Required: Bachelor's degree
- Annual Earnings: $52,350
- Growth: 1.9%
- Annual Job Openings: 3,180
- Self-Employed: 0.0%
- Part-Time: 21.8%

Level of Stress Tolerance Needed: 73.8 (out of 100)

Most Stressful Aspects: Importance of Being Exact or Accurate (84.0); Time Pressure (70.2).

Least Stressful Aspects: Deal With Physically Aggressive People (0.0); Pace Determined by Speed of Equipment (0.7); Frequency of Conflict Situations (29.5); Consequence of Error (31.0).

Analyze current credit data and financial statements of individuals or firms to determine the degree of risk involved in extending credit or lending money. Prepare reports with this credit information for use in decision making. Evaluate customer records and recommend payment plans based on earnings, savings data, payment history, and purchase activity. Confer with credit association and other business representatives to exchange credit information. Complete loan applications, including credit analyses and summaries of loan requests, and submit to loan committees for approval. Generate financial ratios, using computer programs, to evaluate customers' financial status. Review individual or commercial customer files to identify and select delinquent accounts for collection. Compare liquidity, profitability, and credit histories of establishments being evaluated with those of similar establishments in the same industries and geographic locations. Consult with customers to resolve complaints and verify financial and credit transactions. Analyze financial data such as income growth, quality of management, and market share to determine expected profitability of loans.

Personality Type: Conventional. Conventional occupations frequently involve following set procedures and routines. These occupations can include working with data and details more than with ideas. Usually, there is a clear line of authority to follow.

GOE—Interest Area: 06. Finance and Insurance. **Work Group:** 06.02. Finance/Insurance Investigation and Analysis. **Other Jobs in This Work Group:** Appraisers and Assessors of Real Estate; Appraisers, Real Estate; Assessors; Claims Adjusters, Examiners, and Investigators; Claims Examiners, Property and Casualty Insurance; Cost Estimators; Financial Analysts; Insurance Adjusters, Examiners, and Investigators; Insurance Appraisers, Auto Damage; Insurance Underwriters; Loan Counselors; Loan Officers; Market Research Analysts; Survey Researchers.

Skills—Speaking: Talking to others to convey information effectively. **Writing:** Communicating effectively in writing as appropriate for the needs of the audience. **Operations Analysis:** Analyzing needs and product requirements to create a design. **Systems Evaluation:** Identifying measures or indicators of system performance and the actions needed to improve or correct performance, relative to the goals of the system. **Negotiation:** Bringing others together and trying to reconcile differences. **Active Listening:** Giving full attention to what other people are saying, taking time to understand the points being made, asking questions as appropriate, and not interrupting at inappropriate times.

Education and Training Programs: Accounting; Credit Management; Finance, General. **Related Knowledge/Courses: Economics and Accounting:** Economic and accounting principles and practices, the financial markets, banking, and the analysis and reporting of financial data. **Clerical Practices:** Administrative and clerical procedures and systems such as word processing, managing files and records, stenography and transcription, designing forms, and other office procedures and terminology. **Mathematics:** Arithmetic, algebra, geometry, calculus, statistics, and their applications. **Law and Government:** Laws, legal codes, court procedures, precedents, government regulations, executive orders, agency rules, and the democratic political process. **Administration and Management:** Business and management principles involved in strategic planning, resource allocation, human resources modeling, leadership technique, production methods, and coordination of people and resources. **English Language:** The structure and content of the English language, including the meaning and spelling of words, rules of composition, and grammar.

Work Environment: Indoors; sitting; repetitive motions.

Crop and Livestock Managers

- Education/Training Required: Work experience plus degree
- Annual Earnings: $52,070
- Growth: 1.1%
- Annual Job Openings: 18,101
- Self-Employed: 0.0%
- Part-Time: 12.1%

Our sources did not provide separate job openings data for this occupation. The job openings listed here are shared with Aquacultural Managers and with Nursery and Greenhouse Managers.

Level of Stress Tolerance Needed: 66.5 (out of 100)

Most Stressful Aspects: Duration of Typical Work Week (89.5); Impact of Decisions on Co-workers or Company Results (73.3); Level of Competition (63.0).

Least Stressful Aspects: Pace Determined by Speed of Equipment (3.5); Deal With Physically Aggressive People (8.5); Deal With Unpleasant or Angry People (38.0); Consequence of Error (42.0).

Direct and coordinate, through subordinate supervisory personnel, activities of workers engaged in agricultural crop production for corporations, cooperatives, or other owners. Record information such as production figures, farm management practices, and parent stock data and prepare financial and operational reports. Confer with buyers to arrange for the sale of crops. Contract with farmers or independent owners for raising of crops or for management of crop production. Evaluate financial statements and make budget proposals. Analyze soil to determine types and quantities of fertiliz-er required for maximum production. Purchase machinery, equipment, and supplies, such as tractors, seed, fertilizer, and chemicals. Analyze market conditions to determine acreage allocations. Direct and coordinate worker activities such as planting, irrigation, chemical application, harvesting, and grading. Inspect orchards and fields to determine maturity dates of crops or to estimate potential crop damage from weather. Hire, discharge, transfer, and promote workers. Enforce applicable safety regulations. Negotiate with bank officials to obtain credit. Plan and direct development and production of hybrid plant varieties with high yields or with disease or insect resistance. Inspect equipment to ensure proper functioning. Determine procedural changes in drying, grading, storage, and shipment processes in order to provide greater efficiency and accuracy. Coordinate growing activities with activities of related departments such as engineering, equipment maintenance, and packing.

Personality Type: Enterprising. Enterprising occupations frequently involve starting up and carrying out projects. These occupations can involve leading people and making many decisions. They sometimes require risk taking and often deal with business.

GOE—Interest Area: 01. Agriculture and Natural Resources. **Work Group:** 01.01. Managerial Work in Agriculture and Natural Resources. **Other Jobs in This Work Group:** Aquacultural Managers; Farm Labor Contractors; Farm, Ranch, and Other Agricultural Managers; Farmers and Ranchers; First-Line Supervisors/Managers of Agricultural Crop and Horticultural Workers; First-Line Supervisors/Managers of Animal Husbandry and Animal Care Workers; First-Line Supervisors/Managers of Aquacultural Workers; First-Line Supervisors/Managers of Construction Trades and Extraction Workers; First-Line

Supervisors/Managers of Farming, Fishing, and Forestry Workers; First-Line Supervisors/Managers of Landscaping, Lawn Service, and Groundskeeping Workers; First-Line Supervisors/Managers of Logging Workers; Nursery and Greenhouse Managers; Park Naturalists; Purchasing Agents and Buyers, Farm Products.

Skills—Management of Financial Resources: Determining how money will be spent to get the work done and accounting for these expenditures. **Negotiation:** Bringing others together and trying to reconcile differences. **Management of Material Resources:** Obtaining and seeing to the appropriate use of equipment, facilities, and materials needed to do certain work. **Management of Personnel Resources:** Motivating, developing, and directing people as they work, identifying the best people for the job. **Persuasion:** Persuading others to change their minds or behavior. **Judgment and Decision Making:** Considering the relative costs and benefits of potential actions to choose the most appropriate one.

Education and Training Programs: Agribusiness/Agricultural Business Operations; Agricultural Animal Breeding; Agricultural Production Operations, General; Agronomy and Crop Science; Animal Nutrition; Animal Sciences, General; Crop Production; Dairy Husbandry and Production; Dairy Science; Farm and Ranch Management; Equine Science and Management; Horticultural Science; Livestock Management; Plant Protection and Integrated Pest Management; Plant Sciences, General; Poultry Science; Range Science and Management; others. **Related Knowledge/Courses: Food Production:** Techniques and equipment for planting, growing, and harvesting food products (both plant and animal) for consumption, including storage/handling techniques. **Biology:** Plant and animal organisms,

their tissues, cells, functions, interdependencies, and interactions with each other and the environment. **Economics and Accounting:** Economic and accounting principles and practices, the financial markets, banking, and the analysis and reporting of financial data. **Geography:** Principles and methods for describing the features of land, sea, and air masses, including their physical characteristics, locations, interrelationships, and distribution of plant, animal, and human life. **Sales and Marketing:** Principles and methods for showing, promoting, and selling products or services. This includes marketing strategy and tactics, product demonstration, sales techniques, and sales control systems. **Chemistry:** The chemical composition, structure, and properties of substances and of the chemical processes and transformations that they undergo. This includes uses of chemicals, their danger signs, production techniques, and disposal methods.

Work Environment: More often indoors than outdoors; sitting.

Crushing, Grinding, and Polishing Machine Setters, Operators, and Tenders

- ◎ Education/Training Required: Moderate-term on-the-job training
- ◎ Annual Earnings: $28,080
- ◎ Growth: –11.9%
- ◎ Annual Job Openings: 5,357
- ◎ Self-Employed: 0.9%
- ◎ Part-Time: 15.8%

Level of Stress Tolerance Needed: 66.5 (out of 100)

Most Stressful Aspects: Time Pressure (83.2); Duration of Typical Work Week (81.5); Importance of Being Exact or Accurate (77.0); Pace Determined by Speed of Equipment (66.8).

Least Stressful Aspects: Deal With Physically Aggressive People (14.0); Deal With Unpleasant or Angry People (39.0); Level of Competition (39.2); Frequency of Conflict Situations (46.2).

Set up, operate, or tend machines to crush, grind, or polish materials such as coal, glass, grain, stone, food, or rubber. Read work orders to determine production specifications and information. Observe operation of equipment to ensure continuity of flow, safety, and efficient operation and to detect malfunctions. Move controls to start, stop, or adjust machinery and equipment that crushes, grinds, polishes, or blends materials. Record data from operations, testing, and production on specified forms. Examine materials, ingredients, or products visually or with hands to ensure conformance to established standards. Weigh or measure materials, ingredients, or products at specified intervals to ensure conformance to requirements. Clean, adjust, and maintain equipment, using hand tools. Notify supervisors of needed repairs. Set mill gauges to specified fineness of grind. Reject defective products and readjust equipment to eliminate problems. Clean work areas. Transfer materials, supplies, and products between work areas, using moving equipment and hand tools. Dislodge and clear jammed materials or other items from machinery and equipment, using hand tools. Inspect chains, belts, and scrolls for signs of wear. Tend accessory equipment such as pumps and conveyors to move materials or ingredients through production processes. Test samples of materials or products to ensure compliance with specifications, using test equipment. Collect samples of materials or products for laboratory testing. Mark bins as to types of mixtures stored. Turn valves to regulate the moisture contents of materials. Load materials into machinery and equipment, using hand tools. Add or mix chemicals and ingredients for processing, using hand tools or other devices. Break mixtures to size, using picks.

Personality Type: Realistic. Realistic occupations frequently involve work activities that include practical, hands-on problems and solutions. They often deal with plants; animals; and real-world materials such as wood, tools, and machinery. Many of the occupations require working outside and do not involve a lot of paperwork or working closely with others.

GOE—Interest Area: 13. Manufacturing. **Work Group:** 13.02. Machine Setup and Operation. **Other Jobs in This Work Group:** Cutting, Punching, and Press Machine Setters, Operators, and Tenders, Metal and Plastic; Drilling and Boring Machine Tool Setters, Operators, and Tenders, Metal and Plastic; Extruding and Drawing Machine Setters, Operators, and Tenders, Metal and Plastic; Forging Machine Setters, Operators, and Tenders, Metal and Plastic; Grinding, Lapping, Polishing, and Buffing Machine Tool Setters, Operators, and Tenders, Metal and Plastic; Lathe and Turning Machine Tool Setters, Operators, and Tenders, Metal and Plastic; Milling and Planing Machine Setters, Operators, and Tenders, Metal and Plastic; Multiple Machine Tool Setters, Operators, and Tenders, Metal and Plastic; Paper Goods Machine Setters, Operators, and Tenders; Rolling Machine Setters, Operators, and Tenders, Metal and Plastic; Textile Cutting Machine Setters, Operators, and Tenders; Textile Knitting and Weaving Machine Setters, Operators, and Tenders; Textile Winding, Twisting, and Drawing Out Machine Setters, Operators, and Tenders.

Skills—Operation Monitoring: Watching gauges, dials, or other indicators to make sure a machine is working properly. **Equipment Maintenance:** Performing routine maintenance on equipment and determining when and what kind of maintenance is needed. **Operation and Control:** Controlling operations of equipment or systems. **Installation:** Installing equipment, machines, wiring, or programs to meet specifications. **Repairing:** Repairing machines or systems, using the needed tools. **Quality Control Analysis:** Conducting tests and inspections of products, services, or processes to evaluate quality or performance.

Education and Training Programs: No related CIP programs; this job is learned through informal moderate-term on-the-job training. **Related Knowledge/Courses: Mechanical Devices:** Machines and tools, including their designs, uses, repair, and maintenance. **Production and Processing:** Raw materials, production processes, quality control, costs, and other techniques for maximizing the effective manufacture and distribution of goods. **Chemistry:** The chemical composition, structure, and properties of substances and of the chemical processes and transformations that they undergo. This includes uses of chemicals, their danger signs, production techniques, and disposal methods. **Engineering and Technology:** The practical application of engineering science and technology. This includes applying principles, techniques, procedures, and equipment to the design and production of various goods and services. **Design:** Design techniques, tools, and principles involved in production of precision technical plans, blueprints, drawings, and models. **Physics:** Physical principles, laws, their interrelationships, and applications to understanding fluid, material, and atmospheric dynamics, and mechanical, electrical, atomic, and subatomic structures and processes.

Work Environment: Noisy; very hot or cold; contaminants; hazardous equipment; standing; using hands on objects, tools, or controls.

Curators

- Education/Training Required: Master's degree
- Annual Earnings: $46,300
- Growth: 23.3%
- Annual Job Openings: 1,416
- Self-Employed: 1.3%
- Part-Time: 32.4%

Level of Stress Tolerance Needed: 67.0 (out of 100)

Most Stressful Aspects: None greater than average.

Least Stressful Aspects: Pace Determined by Speed of Equipment (0.5); Deal With Physically Aggressive People (2.5); Frequency of Conflict Situations (21.3); Consequence of Error (24.3).

Administer affairs of museum and conduct research programs. Direct instructional, research, and public service activities of institution. Plan and organize the acquisition, storage, and exhibition of collections and related materials, including the selection of exhibition themes and designs. Develop and maintain an institution's registration, cataloging, and basic record-keeping systems, using computer databases. Provide information from the institution's holdings to other curators and to the public. Inspect premises to assess the need for repairs and to ensure that climate and pest-control issues are addressed. Train and supervise curatorial, fiscal, technical, research, and clerical staff, as well as volunteers or interns. Negotiate and authorize purchase, sale, exchange, or loan of collections. Plan and conduct special research projects in area of interest or expertise. Conduct or organize tours, workshops, and instructional sessions to acquaint individuals with an institution's facilities and materials. Confer with the board of directors to formulate and interpret policies, to determine budget requirements, and to plan overall operations. Attend meetings, conventions, and civic events to promote use of institution's services, to seek financing, and to maintain community alliances. Schedule events and organize details, including refreshment, entertainment, decorations, and the collection of any fees. Write and review grant proposals, journal articles, institutional reports, and publicity materials. Study, examine, and test acquisitions to authenticate their origin, composition, and history and to assess their current value. Arrange insurance coverage for objects on loan or for special exhibits and recommend changes in coverage for the entire collection. Establish specifications for reproductions and oversee their manufacture or select items from commercially available replica sources.

Personality Type: Artistic. Artistic occupations frequently involve working with forms, designs, and patterns. They often require self-expression, and the work can be done without following a clear set of rules.

GOE—Interest Area: 05. Education and Training. **Work Group:** 05.05. Archival and Museum Services. **Other Jobs in This Work Group:** Archivists; Audio-Visual Collections Specialists; Museum Technicians and Conservators.

Skills—Management of Financial Resources: Determining how money will be spent to get the work done and accounting for these expenditures. **Management of Personnel Resources:** Motivating, developing, and directing people as they work, identifying the best people for the job. **Writing:** Communicating effectively in writing as appropriate for the needs of the audience. **Time Management:** Managing one's own time and the time of others. **Speaking:** Talking to others to convey information effectively. **Persuasion:** Persuading others to change their minds or behavior.

Education and Training Programs: Art History, Criticism and Conservation; Museology/Museum Studies; Public/Applied History and Archival Administration. **Related Knowledge/Courses: Fine Arts:** Theory and techniques required to compose, produce, and perform works of music, dance, visual arts, drama, and sculpture. **History and Archeology:** Historical events and their causes, indicators, and effects on civilizations and cultures. **Clerical Practices:** Administrative and clerical procedures and systems such as word processing, managing files and records, stenography and transcription, designing forms, and other office procedures and terminology. **Sociology and Anthropology:** Group behavior and dynamics, societal trends and influences, human migrations, ethnicity, cultures, and their history and origins. **Philosophy and Theology:** Different philosophical systems and religions. This includes their basic principles, values, ethics, ways of thinking, customs, practices, and impact on human culture. **Geography:** Principles and methods for describing features of land, sea, and air masses, including physical characteristics, locations, interrelationships, and distribution of plant, animal, and human life.

Work Environment: Indoors; sitting.

Cutting, Punching, and Press Machine Setters, Operators, and Tenders, Metal and Plastic

- ◉ Education/Training Required: Moderate-term on-the-job training
- ◉ Annual Earnings: $26,340
- ◉ Growth: –14.9%
- ◉ Annual Job Openings: 30,635
- ◉ Self-Employed: 0.5%
- ◉ Part-Time: 6.3%

Level of Stress Tolerance Needed: 61.3 (out of 100)

Most Stressful Aspects: Importance of Being Exact or Accurate (76.5); Time Pressure (75.3); Pace Determined by Speed of Equipment (74.0); Duration of Typical Work Week (69.5).

Least Stressful Aspects: Deal With Physically Aggressive People (4.8); Level of Competition (32.0); Deal With Unpleasant or Angry People (38.2); Frequency of Conflict Situations (42.5).

Set up, operate, or tend machines to saw, cut, shear, slit, punch, crimp, notch, bend, or straighten metal or plastic material. Measure completed workpieces to verify conformance to specifications, using micrometers, gauges, calipers, templates, or rulers. Examine completed workpieces for defects such as chipped edges and marred surfaces and sort defective pieces according to types of flaws. Read work orders and production schedules to determine specifications such as materials to be used, locations of cutting lines, and dimensions and tolerances. Load workpieces, plastic material, or chemical solutions into machines. Start machines, monitor their operations, and record operational data. Test and adjust machine speeds and actions according to product specifications by using gauges and hand tools. Install, align, and lock specified punches, dies, cutting blades, or other fixtures in rams or beds of machines, using gauges, templates, feelers, shims, and hand tools. Clean and lubricate machines. Position, align, and secure workpieces against fixtures or stops on machine beds or on dies. Scribe reference lines on workpieces as guides for cutting operations according to blueprints, templates, sample parts, or specifications. Set blade tensions, heights, and angles to perform prescribed cuts, using wrenches. Adjust ram strokes of presses to specified lengths, using hand tools. Place workpieces on cutting tables manually or using hoists, cranes, or sledges. Position guides, stops, holding blocks, or other fixtures to secure and direct workpieces, using hand tools and measuring devices. Thread ends of metal coils from reels through slitters and secure ends on recoilers. Turn valves to start flow of coolant against cutting areas and to start airflow that blows cuttings away from kerfs. Set stops on machine beds; change dies; and adjust components, such as rams or power presses, when making multiple or successive passes. Lubricate workpieces with oil. Replace defective blades or wheels, using hand tools. Mark identifying data on workpieces. Turn controls to set cutting speeds, feed rates, and table angles for specified operations.

Personality Type: Realistic. Realistic occupations frequently involve work activities that include practical, hands-on problems and solutions. They often deal with plants; animals; and real-world materials such as wood, tools, and machinery. Many of the occupations require working outside and do not involve a lot of paperwork or working closely with others.

GOE—Interest Area: 13. Manufacturing. **Work Group:** 13.02. Machine Setup and Operation. **Other Jobs in This Work Group:** Crushing, Grinding, and Polishing Machine Setters,

Operators, and Tenders; Drilling and Boring Machine Tool Setters, Operators, and Tenders, Metal and Plastic; Extruding and Drawing Machine Setters, Operators, and Tenders, Metal and Plastic; Forging Machine Setters, Operators, and Tenders, Metal and Plastic; Grinding, Lapping, Polishing, and Buffing Machine Tool Setters, Operators, and Tenders, Metal and Plastic; Lathe and Turning Machine Tool Setters, Operators, and Tenders, Metal and Plastic; Milling and Planing Machine Setters, Operators, and Tenders, Metal and Plastic; Multiple Machine Tool Setters, Operators, and Tenders, Metal and Plastic; Paper Goods Machine Setters, Operators, and Tenders; Rolling Machine Setters, Operators, and Tenders, Metal and Plastic; Textile Cutting Machine Setters, Operators, and Tenders; Textile Knitting and Weaving Machine Setters, Operators, and Tenders; Textile Winding, Twisting, and Drawing Out Machine Setters, Operators, and Tenders.

Skills—Quality Control Analysis: Conducting tests and inspections of products, services, or processes to evaluate quality or performance. **Operation Monitoring:** Watching gauges, dials, or other indicators to make sure a machine is working properly. **Operation and Control:** Controlling operations of equipment or systems. **Repairing:** Repairing machines or systems, using the needed tools. **Equipment Maintenance:** Performing routine maintenance on equipment and determining when and what kind of maintenance is needed. **Troubleshooting:** Determining causes of operating errors and deciding what to do about them.

Education and Training Programs: No related CIP programs; this job is learned through informal moderate-term on-the-job training. **Related Knowledge/Courses:** **Production and Processing:** Raw materials, production process-es, quality control, costs, and other techniques for maximizing the effective manufacture and distribution of goods. **Mechanical Devices:** Machines and tools, including their designs, uses, repair, and maintenance.

Work Environment: Noisy; contaminants; minor burns, cuts, bites, or stings; standing; using hands on objects, tools, or controls; repetitive motions.

Electric Motor, Power Tool, and Related Repairers

- Education/Training Required: Postsecondary vocational training
- Annual Earnings: $32,860
- Growth: –4.2%
- Annual Job Openings: 2,625
- Self-Employed: 12.5%
- Part-Time: 13.3%

Level of Stress Tolerance Needed: 63.7 (out of 100)

Most Stressful Aspects: Duration of Typical Work Week (81.0); Importance of Being Exact or Accurate (78.3); Time Pressure (72.3); Consequence of Error (63.7).

Least Stressful Aspects: Impact of Equipment Decisions on Co-workers or Company Results (55.0).

Repair, maintain, or install electric motors, wiring, or switches. Measure velocity, horsepower, revolutions per minute (rpm), amperage, circuitry, and voltage of units or parts to diagnose problems, using ammeters, voltmeters, wattmeters, and other testing devices. Record repairs required, parts used, and labor time.

E

Reassemble repaired electric motors to specified requirements and ratings, using hand tools and electrical meters. Maintain stocks of parts. Repair and rebuild defective mechanical parts in electric motors, generators, and related equipment, using hand tools and power tools. Rewire electrical systems and repair or replace electrical accessories. Inspect electrical connections, wiring, relays, charging resistance boxes, and storage batteries, following wiring diagrams. Read service guides to find information needed to perform repairs. Inspect and test equipment to locate damage or worn parts and diagnose malfunctions or read work orders or schematic drawings to determine required repairs. Solder, wrap, and coat wires to ensure proper insulation. Assemble electrical parts such as alternators, generators, starting devices, and switches, following schematic drawings and using hand, machine, and power tools. Lubricate moving parts. Remove and replace defective parts such as coil leads, carbon brushes, and wires, using soldering equipment. Disassemble defective equipment so that repairs can be made, using hand tools. Lift units or parts such as motors or generators, using cranes or chain hoists, or signal crane operators to lift heavy parts or subassemblies. Weld, braze, or solder electrical connections. Reface, ream, and polish commutators and machine parts to specified tolerances, using machine tools. Adjust working parts, such as fan belts, contacts, and springs, using hand tools and gauges. Clean cells, cell assemblies, glassware, leads, electrical connections, and battery poles, using scrapers, steam, water, emery cloths, power grinders, or acid. Scrape and clean units or parts, using cleaning solvents and equipment such as buffing wheels. Rewind coils on cores in slots or make replacement coils, using coil-winding machines.

Personality Type: Realistic. Realistic occupations frequently involve work activities that include practical, hands-on problems and solutions. They often deal with plants; animals; and real-world materials such as wood, tools, and machinery. Many of the occupations require working outside and do not involve a lot of paperwork or working closely with others.

GOE—Interest Area: 13. Manufacturing. **Work Group:** 13.12. Electrical and Electronic Repair. **Other Jobs in This Work Group:** Avionics Technicians; Electrical and Electronics Installers and Repairers, Transportation Equipment; Electrical and Electronics Repairers, Commercial and Industrial Equipment; Electronic Equipment Installers and Repairers, Motor Vehicles; Electronic Home Entertainment Equipment Installers and Repairers; Radio Mechanics.

Skills—Installation: Installing equipment, machines, wiring, or programs to meet specifications. **Repairing:** Repairing machines or systems, using the needed tools. **Troubleshooting:** Determining causes of operating errors and deciding what to do about them. **Equipment Maintenance:** Performing routine maintenance on equipment and determining when and what kind of maintenance is needed. **Technology Design:** Generating or adapting equipment and technology to serve user needs. **Operation Monitoring:** Watching gauges, dials, or other indicators to make sure a machine is working properly.

Education and Training Program: Electrical/Electronics Equipment Installation and Repair, General. **Related Knowledge/Courses: Mechanical Devices:** Machines and tools, including their designs, uses, repair, and maintenance. **Engineering and Technology:** The practical application of engineering science and technology. This includes applying principles, techniques, procedures, and equipment to the design and production of various goods and services. **Design:** Design techniques, tools, and principles involved in production of precision technical plans, blueprints, drawings, and models. **Production and Processing:** Raw materials, production processes, quality control, costs, and other techniques for maximizing the effective manufacture and distribution of goods.

Work Environment: Noisy; contaminants; hazardous conditions; hazardous equipment; standing; using hands on objects, tools, or controls.

Electrical and Electronic Equipment Assemblers

- Education/Training Required: Short-term on-the-job training
- Annual Earnings: $25,560
- Growth: –26.8%
- Annual Job Openings: 26,595
- Self-Employed: 0.0%
- Part-Time: 16.2%

Level of Stress Tolerance Needed: 61.3 (out of 100)

Most Stressful Aspects: Importance of Being Exact or Accurate (84.0); Time Pressure (73.5); Consequence of Error (46.0); Pace Determined by Speed of Equipment (44.5).

Least Stressful Aspects: Deal With Physically Aggressive People (10.2); Level of Competition (39.0); Frequency of Conflict Situations (41.3); Deal With Unpleasant or Angry People (47.5).

Assemble or modify electrical or electronic equipment, such as computers, test equipment telemetering systems, electric motors, and batteries. Inspect and test wiring installations, assemblies, and circuits for resistance factors and for operation and record results. Assemble electrical or electronic systems and support structures and install components, units, subassemblies, wiring, and assembly casings, using rivets, bolts, and soldering and microwelding equipment. Adjust, repair, or replace electrical or electronic component parts to correct defects and to ensure conformance to specifications. Clean parts, using cleaning solutions, air hoses, and cloths. Read and interpret schematic drawings, diagrams, blueprints, specifications, work orders, and reports to determine materials requirements and assembly instructions. Mark and tag components so that stock inventory can be tracked and identified. Position, align, and adjust workpieces and electrical parts to facilitate wiring and assembly. Pack finished assemblies for shipment and transport them to storage areas, using hoists or handtrucks. Confer with supervisors or engineers to plan and review work activities and to resolve production problems. Explain assembly procedures or techniques to other workers. Measure and adjust voltages to specified values to determine operational accuracy of instruments. Fabricate and form parts, coils, and structures according to specifications, using drills, calipers, cutters, and saws. Drill and tap holes in specified equipment locations to mount control units and to provide openings for elements, wiring, and instruments. Complete, review, and maintain production, time, and component waste reports. Paint structures as specified, using paint sprayers. Instruct customers in the installation, repair, and maintenance of products. Distribute materials, supplies, and subassemblies to work areas.

Personality Type: Realistic. Realistic occupations frequently involve work activities that include practical, hands-on problems and solutions. They often deal with plants; animals; and real-world materials such as wood, tools, and machinery. Many of the occupations require working outside and do not involve a lot of paperwork or working closely with others.

GOE—Interest Area: 13. Manufacturing. **Work Group:** 13.06. Production Precision Work.

Other Jobs in This Work Group: Bookbinders; Dental Laboratory Technicians; Electromechanical Equipment Assemblers; Engine and Other Machine Assemblers; Gem and Diamond Workers; Jewelers; Jewelers and Precious Stone and Metal Workers; Medical Appliance Technicians; Molding, Coremaking, and Casting Machine Setters, Operators, and Tenders, Metal and Plastic; Ophthalmic Laboratory Technicians; Precious Metal Workers; Semiconductor Processors; Timing Device Assemblers, Adjusters, and Calibrators.

Skills—Quality Control Analysis: Conducting tests and inspections of products, services, or processes to evaluate quality or performance. **Installation:** Installing equipment, machines, wiring, or programs to meet specifications. **Equipment Selection:** Determining the kind of tools and equipment needed to do a job. **Systems Evaluation:** Identifying measures or indicators of system performance and the actions needed to improve or correct performance, relative to the goals of the system. **Repairing:** Repairing machines or systems, using the needed tools. **Programming:** Writing computer programs for various purposes.

Education and Training Programs: Communications Systems Installation and Repair Technology; Industrial Electronics Technology/Technician Training. **Related Knowledge/Course: Production and Processing:** Raw materials, production processes, quality control, costs, and other techniques for maximizing the effective manufacture and distribution of goods.

Work Environment: Indoors; contaminants; hazardous equipment; sitting; using hands on objects, tools, or controls; repetitive motions.

Electrical and Electronics Installers and Repairers, Transportation Equipment

- Education/Training Required: Postsecondary vocational training
- Annual Earnings: $43,110
- Growth: 4.3%
- Annual Job Openings: 1,663
- Self-Employed: 0.0%
- Part-Time: 15.2%

Level of Stress Tolerance Needed: 60.3 (out of 100)

Most Stressful Aspects: Duration of Typical Work Week (77.5); Time Pressure (69.7); Consequence of Error (54.8); Pace Determined by Speed of Equipment (32.2).

Least Stressful Aspects: Deal With Physically Aggressive People (5.0); Deal With Unpleasant or Angry People (18.8); Level of Competition (30.5); Frequency of Conflict Situations (38.0).

Install, adjust, or maintain mobile electronics communication equipment, including sound, sonar, security, navigation, and surveillance systems on trains, watercraft, or other mobile equipment. Inspect and test electrical systems and equipment to locate and diagnose malfunctions, using visual inspections, testing devices, and computer software. Reassemble and test equipment after repairs. Splice wires with knives or cutting pliers and solder connections to fixtures, outlets, and equipment. Install new fuses, electrical cables, or power sources as required. Locate and remove or repair circuit defects such as blown fuses or malfunctioning transistors. Adjust, repair, or replace defective wiring and relays in ignition, lighting, air-conditioning, and safety control systems, using electrician's tools.

Refer to schematics and manufacturers' specifications that show connections and provide instructions on how to locate problems. Maintain equipment service records. Cut openings and drill holes for fixtures, outlet boxes, and fuse holders, using electric drills and routers. Measure, cut, and install frameworks and conduit to support and connect wiring, control panels, and junction boxes, using hand tools. Install electrical equipment such as air-conditioning, heating, or ignition systems and components such as generator brushes and commutators, using hand tools. Install fixtures, outlets, terminal boards, switches, and wall boxes, using hand tools. Repair or rebuild equipment such as starters, generators, distributors, or door controls, using electrician's tools. Confer with customers to determine the nature of malfunctions. Estimate costs of repairs based on parts and labor requirements.

Personality Type: Realistic. Realistic occupations frequently involve work activities that include practical, hands-on problems and solutions. They often deal with plants; animals; and real-world materials such as wood, tools, and machinery. Many of the occupations require working outside and do not involve a lot of paperwork or working closely with others.

GOE—Interest Area: 13. Manufacturing. **Work Group:** 13.12. Electrical and Electronic Repair. **Other Jobs in This Work Group:** Avionics Technicians; Electric Motor, Power Tool, and Related Repairers; Electrical and Electronics Repairers, Commercial and Industrial Equipment; Electronic Equipment Installers and Repairers, Motor Vehicles; Electronic Home Entertainment Equipment Installers and Repairers; Radio Mechanics.

Skills—Installation: Installing equipment, machines, wiring, or programs to meet specifications. **Repairing:** Repairing machines or systems, using the needed tools. **Troubleshooting:** Determining causes of operating errors and deciding what to do about them. **Complex Problem Solving:** Identifying complex problems and reviewing related information to develop and evaluate options and implement solutions. **Operation Monitoring:** Watching gauges, dials, or other indicators to make sure a machine is working properly. **Equipment Selection:** Determining the kind of tools and equipment needed to do a job.

Education and Training Program: Automobile/Automotive Mechanics Technology/Technician Training. **Related Knowledge/Courses: Mechanical Devices:** Machines and tools, including their designs, uses, repair, and maintenance. **Engineering and Technology:** The practical application of engineering science and technology. This includes applying principles, techniques, procedures, and equipment to the design and production of various goods and services. **Building and Construction:** Materials, methods, and the tools involved in the construction or repair of houses, buildings, or other structures such as highways and roads. **Physics:** Physical principles, laws, their interrelationships, and applications to understanding fluid, material, and atmospheric dynamics, and mechanical, electrical, atomic, and subatomic structures and processes. **Design:** Design techniques, tools, and principles involved in production of precision technical plans, blueprints, drawings, and models. **Production and Processing:** Raw materials, production processes, quality control, costs, and other techniques for maximizing the effective manufacture and distribution of goods.

Work Environment: Outdoors; contaminants; hazardous conditions; standing; using hands on objects, tools, or controls; repetitive motions.

E

Electrical Engineering Technicians

- Education/Training Required: Associate degree
- Annual Earnings: $50,660
- Growth: 3.6%
- Annual Job Openings: 12,583
- Self-Employed: 0.9%
- Part-Time: 20.9%

Our sources did not provide separate job openings data for this occupation. The job openings listed here are shared with Electronics Engineering Technicians.

Level of Stress Tolerance Needed: 52.0 (out of 100)

Most Stressful Aspects: Importance of Being Exact or Accurate (86.7); Duration of Typical Work Week (79.5); Impact of Decisions on Co-workers or Company Results (79.5); Consequence of Error (59.5).

Least Stressful Aspects: Deal With Physically Aggressive People (7.7); Pace Determined by Speed of Equipment (18.5); Deal With Unpleasant or Angry People (38.5); Frequency of Conflict Situations (43.0).

Apply electrical theory and related knowledge to test and modify developmental or operational electrical machinery and electrical control equipment and circuitry in industrial or commercial plants and laboratories. Usually work under direction of engineering staff. Assemble electrical and electronic systems and prototypes according to engineering data and knowledge of electrical principles, using hand tools and measuring instruments. Provide technical assistance and resolution when electrical or engineering problems are encountered before, during, and after construction. Install and maintain electrical control systems and solid state equipment. Modify electrical prototypes, parts, assemblies, and systems to correct functional deviations. Set up and operate test equipment to evaluate performance of developmental parts, assemblies, or systems under simulated operating conditions and record results. Collaborate with electrical engineers and other personnel to identify, define, and solve developmental problems. Build, calibrate, maintain, troubleshoot, and repair electrical instruments or testing equipment. Analyze and interpret test information to resolve design-related problems. Write commissioning procedures for electrical installations. Prepare project cost and work-time estimates. Evaluate engineering proposals, shop drawings, and design comments for sound electrical engineering practice and conformance with established safety and design criteria and recommend approval or disapproval. Draw or modify diagrams and write engineering specifications to clarify design details and functional criteria of experimental electronics units. Conduct inspections for quality control and assurance programs, reporting findings and recommendations. Prepare contracts and initiate, review, and coordinate modifications to contract specifications and plans throughout the construction process. Plan, schedule, and monitor work of support personnel to assist supervisor. Review existing electrical engineering criteria to identify necessary revisions, deletions, or amendments to outdated material. Perform supervisory duties such as recommending work assignments, approving leaves, and completing performance evaluations. Plan method and sequence of operations for developing and testing experimental electronic and electrical equipment. Visit construction sites to observe conditions impacting design and to identify solutions to technical design problems involving electrical systems equipment that arise during construction.

Personality Type: Realistic. Realistic occupations frequently involve work activities that include practical, hands-on problems and solutions. They often deal with plants; animals; and real-world materials such as wood, tools, and machinery. Many of the occupations require working outside and do not involve a lot of paperwork or working closely with others.

GOE—Interest Area: 15. Scientific Research, Engineering, and Mathematics. **Work Group:** 15.09. Engineering Technology. **Other Jobs in This Work Group:** Aerospace Engineering and Operations Technicians; Cartographers and Photogrammetrists; Civil Engineering Technicians; Electrical and Electronic Engineering Technicians; Electrical and Electronics Drafters; Electrical Drafters; Electro-Mechanical Technicians; Electronic Drafters; Electronics Engineering Technicians; Environmental Engineering Technicians; Mapping Technicians; Mechanical Drafters; Mechanical Engineering Technicians; Surveying and Mapping Technicians; Surveying Technicians.

Skills—Repairing: Repairing machines or systems, using the needed tools. **Installation:** Installing equipment, machines, wiring, or programs to meet specifications. **Troubleshooting:** Determining causes of operating errors and deciding what to do about them. **Science:** Using scientific rules and methods to solve problems. **Mathematics:** Using mathematics to solve problems. **Technology Design:** Generating or adapting equipment and technology to serve user needs.

Education and Training Programs: Computer Engineering Technology/Technician Training; Computer Technology/Computer Systems Technology; Electrical and Electronic Engineering Technologies/Technician Training, Other; Electrical, Electronic and Communications Engineering Technology/Technician Training; Telecommunications Technology/Technician Training. **Related Knowledge/Courses: Engineering and Technology:** The practical application of engineering science and technology. This includes applying principles, techniques, procedures, and equipment to the design and production of various goods and services. **Design:** Design techniques, tools, and principles involved in production of precision technical plans, blueprints, drawings, and models. **Computers and Electronics:** Circuit boards, processors, chips, electronic equipment, and computer hardware and software, including applications and programming. **Physics:** Physical principles, laws, their interrelationships, and applications to understanding fluid, material, and atmospheric dynamics, and mechanical, electrical, atomic, and subatomic structures and processes. **Mechanical Devices:** Machines and tools, including their designs, uses, repair, and maintenance. **Telecommunications:** Transmission, broadcasting, switching, control, and operation of telecommunications systems.

Work Environment: Indoors; noisy; sitting; using hands on objects, tools, or controls.

Electrical Engineers

- Education/Training Required: Bachelor's degree
- Annual Earnings: $75,930
- Growth: 6.3%
- Annual Job Openings: 6,806
- Self-Employed: 2.1%
- Part-Time: 14.3%

Level of Stress Tolerance Needed: 75.0 (out of 100)

Most Stressful Aspects: Importance of Being Exact or Accurate (81.3); Duration of Typical

Work Week (67.0); Level of Competition (59.5).

Least Stressful Aspects: Deal With Physically Aggressive People (1.5); Pace Determined by Speed of Equipment (5.8); Frequency of Conflict Situations (28.3); Deal With Unpleasant or Angry People (32.7).

Design, develop, test, or supervise the manufacturing and installation of electrical equipment, components, or systems for commercial, industrial, military, or scientific use. Confer with engineers, customers, and others to discuss existing or potential engineering projects and products. Design, implement, maintain, and improve electrical instruments, equipment, facilities, components, products, and systems for commercial, industrial, and domestic purposes. Operate computer-assisted engineering and design software and equipment to perform engineering tasks. Direct and coordinate manufacturing, construction, installation, maintenance, support, documentation, and testing activities to ensure compliance with specifications, codes, and customer requirements. Perform detailed calculations to compute and establish manufacturing, construction, and installation standards and specifications. Inspect completed installations and observe operations to ensure conformance to design and equipment specifications and compliance with operational and safety standards. Plan and implement research methodology and procedures to apply principles of electrical theory to engineering projects. Prepare specifications for purchase of materials and equipment. Supervise and train project team members as necessary. Investigate and test vendors' and competitors' products. Oversee project production efforts to assure projects are completed satisfactorily, on time, and within budget. Prepare and study technical drawings, specifications of electrical systems, and topographical maps to ensure that installation and operations conform to standards and customer requirements. Investigate customer or public complaints, determine nature and extent of problem, and recommend remedial measures. Plan layout of electric-power-generating plants and distribution lines and stations. Assist in developing capital project programs for new equipment and major repairs. Develop budgets, estimating labor, material, and construction costs. Compile data and write reports regarding existing and potential engineering studies and projects. Collect data relating to commercial and residential development, population, and power system interconnection to determine operating efficiency of electrical systems. Conduct field surveys and study maps, graphs, diagrams, and other data to identify and correct power system problems.

Personality Type: Investigative. Investigative occupations frequently involve working with ideas and require an extensive amount of thinking. These occupations can involve searching for facts and figuring out problems mentally.

GOE—Interest Area: 15. Scientific Research, Engineering, and Mathematics. **Work Group:** 15.07. Research and Design Engineering. **Other Jobs in This Work Group:** Aerospace Engineers; Biomedical Engineers; Chemical Engineers; Civil Engineers; Computer Hardware Engineers; Electronics Engineers, Except Computer; Marine Architects; Marine Engineers; Marine Engineers and Naval Architects; Materials Engineers; Mechanical Engineers; Nuclear Engineers.

Skills—Systems Analysis: Determining how a system should work and how changes in conditions, operations, and the environment will affect outcomes. **Technology Design:** Generating or adapting equipment and technology to serve user needs. **Science:** Using scientific rules and methods to solve problems. **Troubleshooting:** Determining causes of operating errors and deciding what to do about them. **Systems Evaluation:** Identifying measures or indicators of system performance and the actions needed to improve or correct performance, relative to the goals of the system. **Equipment Selection:** Determining the kind of tools and equipment needed to do a job.

Education and Training Program: Electrical, Electronics and Communications Engineering. **Related Knowledge/Courses: Engineering and Technology:** The practical application of engineering science and technology. This includes applying principles, techniques, procedures, and equipment to the design and production of various goods and services. **Design:** Design techniques, tools, and principles involved in production of precision technical plans, blueprints, drawings, and models. **Physics:** Physical principles, laws, their interrelationships, and applications to understanding fluid, material, and atmospheric dynamics, and mechanical, electrical, atomic, and subatomic structures and processes. **Telecommunications:** Transmission, broadcasting, switching, control, and operation of telecommunications systems. **Computers and Electronics:** Circuit boards, processors, chips, electronic equipment, and computer hardware and software, including applications and programming. **Mathematics:** Arithmetic, algebra, geometry, calculus, statistics, and their applications.

Work Environment: Indoors; sitting.

Electromechanical Equipment Assemblers

- Education/Training Required: Short-term on-the-job training
- Annual Earnings: $27,560
- Growth: –9.1%
- Annual Job Openings: 8,283
- Self-Employed: 0.0%
- Part-Time: 16.2%

Level of Stress Tolerance Needed: 63.2 (out of 100)

Most Stressful Aspects: Importance of Being Exact or Accurate (77.8); Time Pressure (70.7); Level of Competition (46.0); Pace Determined by Speed of Equipment (23.2).

Least Stressful Aspects: Deal With Physically Aggressive People (2.3); Consequence of Error (23.2); Frequency of Conflict Situations (23.5); Deal With Unpleasant or Angry People (30.0).

Assemble or modify electromechanical equipment or devices, such as servomechanisms, gyros, dynamometers, magnetic drums, tape drives, brakes, control linkage, actuators, and appliances. Clean and lubricate parts and subassemblies, using grease paddles or oilcans. Operate small cranes to transport or position large parts. Disassemble units to replace parts or to crate them for shipping. Assemble parts or units and position, align, and fasten units to assemblies, subassemblies, or frames, using hand tools and power tools. Connect cables, tubes, and wiring according to specifications. Drill, tap, ream, countersink, and spot-face bolt holes in parts, using drill presses and portable power drills. File, lap, and buff parts to fit, using hand and power tools. Inspect, test, and adjust completed units to ensure that units meet specifications, tolerances, and customer order

E

requirements. Measure parts to determine tolerances, using precision measuring instruments such as micrometers, calipers, and verniers. Position, align, and adjust parts for proper fit and assembly. Read blueprints and specifications to determine component parts and assembly sequences of electromechanical units. Attach name plates and mark identifying information on parts. Operate or tend automated assembling equipment, such as robotics and fixed automation equipment. Pack or fold insulation between panels.

Personality Type: Realistic. Realistic occupations frequently involve work activities that include practical, hands-on problems and solutions. They often deal with plants; animals; and real-world materials such as wood, tools, and machinery. Many of the occupations require working outside and do not involve a lot of paperwork or working closely with others.

GOE—Interest Area: 13. Manufacturing. **Work Group:** 13.06. Production Precision Work. **Other Jobs in This Work Group:** Bookbinders; Dental Laboratory Technicians; Electrical and Electronic Equipment Assemblers; Engine and Other Machine Assemblers; Gem and Diamond Workers; Jewelers; Jewelers and Precious Stone and Metal Workers; Medical Appliance Technicians; Molding, Coremaking, and Casting Machine Setters, Operators, and Tenders, Metal and Plastic; Ophthalmic Laboratory Technicians; Precious Metal Workers; Semiconductor Processors; Timing Device Assemblers, Adjusters, and Calibrators.

Skills—Installation: Installing equipment, machines, wiring, or programs to meet specifications. **Repairing:** Repairing machines or systems, using the needed tools. **Quality Control Analysis:** Conducting tests and inspections of products, services, or processes to evaluate quality or performance. **Troubleshooting:** Determining causes of operating errors and deciding

what to do about them. **Equipment Maintenance:** Performing routine maintenance on equipment and determining when and what kind of maintenance is needed. **Operation Monitoring:** Watching gauges, dials, or other indicators to make sure a machine is working properly.

Education and Training Programs: Electromechanical and Instrumentation and Maintenance Technologies/Technician Training, Other; Electromechanical Technology/Electromechanical Engineering Technology; Robotics Technology/Technician Training. **Related Knowledge/Courses: Production and Processing:** Raw materials, production processes, quality control, costs, and other techniques for maximizing the effective manufacture and distribution of goods. **Mechanical Devices:** Machines and tools, including their designs, uses, repair, and maintenance. **Engineering and Technology:** The practical application of engineering science and technology. This includes applying principles, techniques, procedures, and equipment to the design and production of various goods and services. **Design:** Design techniques, tools, and principles involved in production of precision technical plans, blueprints, drawings, and models. **Sales and Marketing:** Principles and methods for showing, promoting, and selling products or services. This includes marketing strategy and tactics, product demonstration, sales techniques, and sales control systems. **Administration and Management:** Business and management principles involved in strategic planning, resource allocation, human resources modeling, leadership technique, production methods, and coordination of people and resources.

Work Environment: Indoors; noisy; contaminants; standing; using hands on objects, tools, or controls; repetitive motions.

Electronic Home Entertainment Equipment Installers and Repairers

- Education/Training Required: Postsecondary vocational training
- Annual Earnings: $29,980
- Growth: 3.0%
- Annual Job Openings: 3,065
- Self-Employed: 12.3%
- Part-Time: 8.7%

Level of Stress Tolerance Needed: 70.5 (out of 100)

Most Stressful Aspects: Importance of Being Exact or Accurate (79.5).

Least Stressful Aspects: Deal With Physically Aggressive People (3.5); Pace Determined by Speed of Equipment (16.2); Frequency of Conflict Situations (20.2); Deal With Unpleasant or Angry People (33.7).

Repair, adjust, or install audio or television receivers, stereo systems, camcorders, video systems, or other electronic home entertainment equipment. Read and interpret electronic circuit diagrams, function block diagrams, specifications, engineering drawings, and service manuals. Install, service, and repair electronic equipment or instruments such as televisions, radios, and videocassette recorders. Position or mount speakers and wire speakers to consoles. Calibrate and test equipment and locate circuit and component faults, using hand and power tools and measuring and testing instruments such as resistance meters and oscilloscopes. Compute cost estimates for labor and materials. Disassemble entertainment equipment and repair or replace loose, worn, or defective components and wiring, using hand tools and sol-

dering irons. Make service calls to repair units in customers' homes or return units to shops for major repairs. Tune or adjust equipment and instruments to obtain optimum visual or auditory reception according to specifications, manuals, and drawings. Instruct customers on the safe and proper use of equipment. Keep records of work orders and test and maintenance reports. Confer with customers to determine the nature of problems or to explain repairs.

Personality Type: Realistic. Realistic occupations frequently involve work activities that include practical, hands-on problems and solutions. They often deal with plants; animals; and real-world materials such as wood, tools, and machinery. Many of the occupations require working outside and do not involve a lot of paperwork or working closely with others.

GOE—Interest Area: 13. Manufacturing. **Work Group:** 13.12. Electrical and Electronic Repair. **Other Jobs in This Work Group:** Avionics Technicians; Electric Motor, Power Tool, and Related Repairers; Electrical and Electronics Installers and Repairers, Transportation Equipment; Electrical and Electronics Repairers, Commercial and Industrial Equipment; Electronic Equipment Installers and Repairers, Motor Vehicles; Radio Mechanics.

Skills—Installation: Installing equipment, machines, wiring, or programs to meet specifications. **Troubleshooting:** Determining causes of operating errors and deciding what to do about them. **Repairing:** Repairing machines or systems, using the needed tools. **Systems Evaluation:** Identifying measures or indicators of system performance and the actions needed to improve or correct performance, relative to the goals of the system. **Technology Design:** Generating or adapting equipment and technology to serve user needs. **Operation Monitoring:** Watching gauges, dials, or other indicators to make sure a machine is working properly.

E

Education and Training Program: Communications Systems Installation and Repair Technology. **Related Knowledge/Courses: Telecommunications:** Transmission, broadcasting, switching, control, and operation of telecommunications systems. **Engineering and Technology:** The practical application of engineering science and technology. This includes applying principles, techniques, procedures, and equipment to the design and production of various goods and services. **Computers and Electronics:** Circuit boards, processors, chips, electronic equipment, and computer hardware and software, including applications and programming. **Mechanical Devices:** Machines and tools, including their designs, uses, repair, and maintenance. **Physics:** Physical principles, laws, their interrelationships, and applications to understanding fluid, material, and atmospheric dynamics, and mechanical, electrical, atomic, and subatomic structures and processes. **Design:** Design techniques, tools, and principles involved in production of precision technical plans, blueprints, drawings, and models.

Work Environment: Indoors; hazardous conditions; standing; using hands on objects, tools, or controls.

Electronics Engineering Technicians

- Education/Training Required: Associate degree
- Annual Earnings: $50,660
- Growth: 3.6%
- Annual Job Openings: 12,583
- Self-Employed: 0.9%
- Part-Time: 20.9%

Our sources did not provide separate job openings data for this occupation. The job openings listed here are shared with Electrical Engineering Technicians.

Level of Stress Tolerance Needed: 69.5 (out of 100)

Most Stressful Aspects: Importance of Being Exact or Accurate (81.0); Time Pressure (79.8); Duration of Typical Work Week (70.5); Pace Determined by Speed of Equipment (24.3).

Least Stressful Aspects: Deal With Physically Aggressive People (2.8); Deal With Unpleasant or Angry People (28.5); Level of Competition (39.7); Consequence of Error (41.0).

Lay out, build, test, troubleshoot, repair, and modify developmental and production electronic components, parts, equipment, and systems, such as computer equipment, missile control instrumentation, electron tubes, test equipment, and machine tool numerical controls, applying principles and theories of electronics, electrical circuitry, engineering mathematics, electronic and electrical testing, and physics. Usually work under direction of engineering staff. Test electronics units, using standard test equipment, and analyze results to evaluate performance and determine need for adjustment. Perform preventative maintenance and calibration of equipment and systems. Read blueprints, wiring diagrams, schematic drawings, and engineering instructions for assembling electronics units, applying knowledge of electronic theory and components. Identify and resolve equipment malfunctions, working with manufacturers and field representatives as necessary to procure replacement parts. Maintain system logs and manuals to document testing and operation of equipment. Assemble, test, and maintain circuitry or electronic components according to engineering instructions, technical manuals, and knowledge of electronics, using hand and power tools. Adjust and replace defective or improperly functioning circuitry and electronics components, using hand tools and soldering iron. Procure parts and maintain inventory and related documentation. Maintain working knowledge of state-of-the-art tools or software by reading or attending conferences, workshops, or other training. Provide user applications and engineering support and recommendations for new and existing equipment with regard to installation, upgrades, and enhancement. Write reports and record data on testing techniques, laboratory equipment, and specifications to assist engineers. Provide customer support and education, working with users to identify needs, determine sources of problems, and provide information on product use. Design basic circuitry and draft sketches for clarification of details and design documentation under engineers' direction, using drafting instruments and computer-aided design (CAD) equipment. Build prototypes from rough sketches or plans. Develop and upgrade preventative maintenance procedures for components, equipment, parts, and systems. Fabricate parts, such as coils, terminal boards, and chassis, using bench lathes, drills, or other machine tools. Research equipment and component needs, sources, competitive prices, delivery times, and ongoing operational costs. Write computer or microprocessor software programs.

Personality Type: Realistic. Realistic occupations frequently involve work activities that include practical, hands-on problems and solutions. They often deal with plants; animals; and real-world materials such as wood, tools, and machinery. Many of the occupations require working outside and do not involve a lot of paperwork or working closely with others.

GOE—Interest Area: 15. Scientific Research, Engineering, and Mathematics. **Work Group:** 15.09. Engineering Technology. **Other Jobs in This Work Group:** Aerospace Engineering and Operations Technicians; Cartographers and Photogrammetrists; Civil Engineering Technicians; Electrical and Electronic Engineering Technicians; Electrical and Electronics Drafters; Electrical Drafters; Electrical Engineering Technicians; Electro-Mechanical Technicians; Electronic Drafters; Environmental Engineering Technicians; Mapping Technicians; Mechanical Drafters; Mechanical Engineering Technicians; Surveying and Mapping Technicians; Surveying Technicians.

Skills—Repairing: Repairing machines or systems, using the needed tools. **Installation:** Installing equipment, machines, wiring, or programs to meet specifications. **Equipment Maintenance:** Performing routine maintenance on equipment and determining when and what kind of maintenance is needed. **Troubleshooting:** Determining causes of operating errors and deciding what to do about them. **Operation Monitoring:** Watching gauges, dials, or other indicators to make sure a machine is working properly. **Technology Design:** Generating or adapting equipment and technology to serve user needs.

Education and Training Programs: Computer Engineering Technology/Technician Training; Electrical and Electronic Engineering Technologies/Technician Training, Other; Electrical, Electronic and Communications Engineering Technology/Technician Training; Telecommunications Technology/Technician Training. **Related Knowledge/Courses: Engineering and Technology:** The practical application of engineering science and technology. This includes applying principles, techniques, procedures, and equipment to the design and production of various goods and services. **Mechanical Devices:** Machines and tools, including their designs, uses, repair, and maintenance. **Computers and**

Electronics: Circuit boards, processors, chips, electronic equipment, and computer hardware and software, including applications and programming. **Design:** Design techniques, tools, and principles involved in production of precision technical plans, blueprints, drawings, and models. **Telecommunica-tions:** Transmission, broadcasting, switching, control, and operation of telecommunications systems. **Mathematics:** Arithmetic, algebra, geometry, calculus, statistics, and their applications.

Work Environment: Indoors; contaminants; hazardous conditions; hazardous equipment; sitting; using hands on objects, tools, or controls.

Electronics Engineers, Except Computer

- ◎ Education/Training Required: Bachelor's degree
- ◎ Annual Earnings: $81,050
- ◎ Growth: 3.7%
- ◎ Annual Job Openings: 5,699
- ◎ Self-Employed: 2.2%
- ◎ Part-Time: 14.3%

Level of Stress Tolerance Needed: 73.0 (out of 100)

Most Stressful Aspects: Duration of Typical Work Week (68.0); Level of Competition (55.8); Consequence of Error (51.0).

Least Stressful Aspects: Deal With Physically Aggressive People (0.2); Pace Determined by Speed of Equipment (19.0); Deal With Unpleasant or Angry People (38.0); Frequency of Conflict Situations (42.8).

Research, design, develop, and test electronic components and systems for commercial, industrial, military, or scientific use, utilizing knowledge of electronic theory and materials properties. **Design electronic circuits and components for use in fields such as telecommunications, aerospace guidance and propulsion control, acoustics, or instruments and controls.** Design electronic components, software, products, or systems for commercial, industrial, medical, military, or scientific applications. Provide technical support and instruction to staff or customers regarding equipment standards, assisting with specific, difficult in-service engineering. Operate computer-assisted engineering and design software and equipment to perform engineering tasks. Analyze system requirements, capacity, cost, and customer needs to determine feasibility of project and develop system plan. Confer with engineers, customers, vendors, or others to discuss existing and potential engineering projects or products. Review and evaluate work of others inside and outside the organization to ensure effectiveness, technical adequacy, and compatibility in the resolution of complex engineering problems. Determine material and equipment needs and order supplies. Inspect electronic equipment, instruments, products, and systems to ensure conformance to specifications, safety standards, and applicable codes and regulations. Evaluate operational systems, prototypes, and proposals and recommend repair or design modifications based on factors such as environment, service, cost, and system capabilities. Prepare documentation containing information such as confidential descriptions and specifications of proprietary hardware and software, product development and introduction schedules, product costs, and information about product performance weaknesses. Direct and coordinate activities concerned with manufacture, construction, installation, maintenance, operation, and modification of electronic equipment, products, and systems. Develop and perform operational, maintenance, and testing procedures for electronic products, components, equipment, and systems. Plan and develop applications and modifications for electronic properties used in components, products, and systems to improve technical performance. Plan and implement research, methodology, and procedures to apply principles of electronic theory to engineering projects. Prepare engineering sketches and specifications for construction, relocation, and installation of equipment, facilities, products, and systems.

Personality Type: Investigative. Investigative occupations frequently involve working with ideas and require an extensive amount of thinking. These occupations can involve searching for facts and figuring out problems mentally.

GOE—Interest Area: 15. Scientific Research, Engineering, and Mathematics. **Work Group:** 15.07. Research and Design Engineering. **Other Jobs in This Work Group:** Aerospace Engineers; Biomedical Engineers; Chemical Engineers; Civil Engineers; Computer Hardware Engineers; Electrical Engineers; Marine Architects; Marine Engineers; Marine Engineers and Naval Architects; Materials Engineers; Mechanical Engineers; Nuclear Engineers.

Skills—Troubleshooting: Determining causes of operating errors and deciding what to do about them. **Installation:** Installing equipment, machines, wiring, or programs to meet specifications. **Technology Design:** Generating or adapting equipment and technology to serve user needs. **Science:** Using scientific rules and methods to solve problems. **Operations Analysis:** Analyzing needs and product requirements to create a design. **Systems Evaluation:** Identifying measures or indicators of system performance and the actions needed to improve or correct performance, relative to the goals of the system.

Education and Training Program: Electrical, Electronics and Communications Engineering. **Related Knowledge/Courses: Engineering and**

Technology: The practical application of engineering science and technology. This includes applying principles, techniques, procedures, and equipment to the design and production of various goods and services. **Design:** Design techniques, tools, and principles involved in production of precision technical plans, blueprints, drawings, and models. **Computers and Electronics:** Circuit boards, processors, chips, electronic equipment, and computer hardware and software, including applications and programming. **Physics:** Physical principles, laws, their interrelationships, and applications to understanding fluid, material, and atmospheric dynamics, and mechanical, electrical, atomic, and subatomic structures and processes. **Telecommunications:** Transmission, broadcasting, switching, control, and operation of telecommunications systems. **Production and Processing:** Raw materials, production processes, quality control, costs, and other techniques for maximizing the effective manufacture and distribution of goods.

Work Environment: Indoors; noisy; sitting.

Environmental Engineers

- Education/Training Required: Bachelor's degree
- Annual Earnings: $69,940
- Growth: 25.4%
- Annual Job Openings: 5,003
- Self-Employed: 2.7%
- Part-Time: 13.3%

Level of Stress Tolerance Needed: 74.8 (out of 100)

Most Stressful Aspects: Importance of Being Exact or Accurate (78.5); Impact of Decisions on Co-workers or Company Results (67.8); Duration of Typical Work Week (66.5).

Least Stressful Aspects: Pace Determined by Speed of Equipment (2.3); Deal With Physically Aggressive People (4.5); Consequence of Error (36.0); Deal With Unpleasant or Angry People (41.3).

Design, plan, or perform engineering duties in the prevention, control, and remediation of environmental health hazards, utilizing various engineering disciplines. Work may include waste treatment, site remediation, or pollution control technology. Prepare, review, and update environmental investigation and recommendation reports. Collaborate with environmental scientists, planners, hazardous waste technicians, engineers, and other specialists and experts in law and business to address environmental problems. Obtain, update, and maintain plans, permits, and standard operating procedures. Provide technical-level support for environmental remediation and litigation projects, including remediation system design and determination of regulatory applicability. Monitor progress of environmental improvement programs. Inspect industrial and municipal facilities and programs to evaluate operational effectiveness and ensure compliance with environmental regulations. Provide administrative support for projects by collecting data, providing project documentation, training staff, and performing other general administrative duties. Develop proposed project objectives and targets and report to management on progress in attaining them. Advise corporations and government agencies of procedures to follow in cleaning up contaminated sites to protect people and the environment. Advise industries and government agencies about environmental policies and standards. Inform company employees and other interested parties of environmental issues. Assess the existing or potential environmental impact of land-use projects on air, water, and land. Assist in budget implementation, forecasts, and administration. Develop site-specific health and safety protocols, such as spill contingency plans and methods for loading and transporting waste. Coordinate and manage environmental protection programs and projects, assigning and evaluating work. Serve as liaison with federal, state, and local agencies and officials on issues pertaining to solid and hazardous waste program requirements. Design systems, processes, and equipment for control, management, and remediation of water, air, and soil quality. Prepare hazardous waste manifests and land disposal restriction notifications. Serve on teams conducting multimedia inspections at complex facilities, providing assistance with planning, quality assurance, safety inspection protocols, and sampling.

Personality Type: No data available.

GOE—Interest Area: 01. Agriculture and Natural Resources. **Work Group:** 01.02. Resource Science/Engineering for Plants, Animals, and the Environment. **Other Jobs in This Work Group:** Agricultural Engineers; Animal Scientists; Conservation Scientists; Foresters; Mining and Geological Engineers, Including Mining Safety Engineers; Petroleum Engineers; Range Managers; Soil and Plant Scientists; Soil and Water Conservationists; Zoologists and Wildlife Biologists.

Skills—Science: Using scientific rules and methods to solve problems. **Management of Financial Resources:** Determining how money will be spent to get the work done, and accounting for these expenditures. **Mathematics:** Using mathematics to solve problems. **Writing:** Communicating effectively in writing as appropriate for the needs of the audience. **Systems Analysis:** Determining how a system should work and how changes in conditions, operations, and the environment will affect outcomes. **Technology Design:** Generating or adapting equipment and technology to serve user needs.

Education and Training Program: Environmental/Environmental Health Engineering. **Related Knowledge/Courses: Biology:** Plant and animal organisms, their tissues, cells, functions, interdependencies, and interactions with each other and the environment. **Chemistry:** The chemical composition, structure, and properties of substances and of the chemical processes and transformations that they undergo. This includes uses of chemicals, their danger signs, production techniques, and disposal methods. **Engineering and Technology:** The practical application of engineering science and technology. This includes applying principles, techniques, procedures, and equipment to the design and production of various goods and services. **Education and Training:** Principles and methods for curriculum and training design, teaching and instruction for individuals and groups, and the measurement of training effects. **Law and Government:** Laws, legal codes, court procedures, precedents, government regulations, executive orders, agency rules, and the democratic political process. **Design:** Design techniques, tools, and principles involved in production of precision technical plans, blueprints, drawings, and models.

Work Environment: Indoors; sitting.

Environmental Science and Protection Technicians, Including Health

- ◎ Education/Training Required: Associate degree
- ◎ Annual Earnings: $38,090
- ◎ Growth: 28.0%
- ◎ Annual Job Openings: 8,404
- ◎ Self-Employed: 1.5%
- ◎ Part-Time: 28.9%

Level of Stress Tolerance Needed: 74.8 (out of 100)

Most Stressful Aspects: Importance of Being Exact or Accurate (81.0); Duration of Typical Work Week (74.0); Impact of Decisions on Coworkers or Company Results (73.8); Time Pressure (68.5).

Least Stressful Aspects: Deal With Physically Aggressive People (9.0); Pace Determined by Speed of Equipment (19.7); Deal With Unpleasant or Angry People (44.5).

Perform laboratory and field tests to monitor the environment and investigate sources of pollution, including those that affect health. Under direction of an environmental scientist or specialist, may collect samples of gases, soil, water, and other materials for testing and take corrective actions as assigned. Record test data and prepare reports, summaries, and charts that interpret test results. Collect samples of gases, soils, water, industrial wastewater, and asbestos products to conduct tests on pollutant levels and identify sources of pollution. Respond to and investigate hazardous conditions or spills or outbreaks of disease or food poisoning, collecting samples for analysis. Provide information and technical and program assistance to government representatives, employers, and the general public on the issues of public health, environmental protection, or workplace safety. Calibrate microscopes and test instruments. Make recommendations to control or eliminate unsafe conditions at workplaces or public facilities. Inspect sanitary conditions at public facilities. Prepare samples or photomicrographs for testing and analysis. Calculate amount of pollutant in samples or compute air pollution or gas flow in industrial processes, using chemical and mathematical formulas. Initiate procedures to close down or fine establishments violating environmental or health regulations. Determine amounts and kinds of chemicals to use in destroying harmful organisms and removing impurities from purification systems. Discuss test results and analyses with customers. Maintain files such as hazardous waste databases, chemical usage data, personnel exposure information, and diagrams showing equipment locations. Perform statistical analysis of environmental data. Set up equipment or stations to monitor and collect pollutants from sites such as smokestacks, manufacturing plants, or mechanical equipment. Distribute permits, closure plans, and cleanup plans. Inspect workplaces to ensure the absence of health and safety hazards such as high noise levels, radiation, or potential lighting hazards. Weigh, analyze, and measure collected sample particles, such as lead, coal dust, or rock, to determine concentration of pollutants. Examine and analyze material for presence and concentration of contaminants such as asbestos, using variety of microscopes. Develop testing procedures or direct activities of workers in laboratory.

Personality Type: Investigative. Investigative occupations frequently involve working with ideas and require an extensive amount of thinking. These occupations can involve searching for facts and figuring out problems mentally.

GOE—Interest Area: 01. Agriculture and Natural Resources. **Work Group:** 01.03. Resource Technologies for Plants, Animals, and the Environment. **Other Jobs in This Work Group:** Agricultural and Food Science Technicians; Agricultural Technicians; Food Science Technicians; Food Scientists and Technologists; Geological and Petroleum Technicians; Geological Sample Test Technicians; Geophysical Data Technicians.

Skills—Science: Using scientific rules and methods to solve problems. **Persuasion:** Persuading others to change their minds or behavior. **Mathematics:** Using mathematics to solve problems. **Quality Control Analysis:** Conducting tests and inspections of products, services, or processes to evaluate quality or performance. **Reading Comprehension:** Understanding written sentences and paragraphs in work-related documents. **Active Learning:** Understanding the implications of new information for both current and future problem solving and decision making.

Education and Training Programs: Environmental Science; Environmental Studies; Physical Science Technologies/Technician Training, Other; Science Technologies/Technician Training, Other. **Related Knowledge/Courses: Biology:** Plant and animal organisms, their tissues, cells, functions, interdependencies, and interactions with each other and the environment. **Engineering and Technology:** The practical application of engineering science and technology. This includes applying principles, techniques, procedures, and equipment to the design and production of various goods and services. **Physics:** Physical principles, laws, their interrelationships, and applications to understanding fluid, material, and atmospheric dynamics, and mechanical, electrical, atomic, and subatomic structures and processes. **Chemistry:** The chemical composition, structure, and properties of substances and of the chemical processes and transformations that they undergo. This includes uses of chemicals, their danger signs, production techniques, and disposal methods. **Building and Construction:** Materials, methods, and the tools involved in the construction or repair of houses, buildings, or other structures such as highways and roads. **Design:** Design techniques, tools, and principles involved in production of precision technical plans, blueprints, drawings, and models.

Work Environment: More often indoors than outdoors; noisy; very hot or cold; contaminants; sitting.

Environmental Scientists and Specialists, Including Health

- Education/Training Required: Master's degree
- Annual Earnings: $56,100
- Growth: 25.1%
- Annual Job Openings: 6,961
- Self-Employed: 2.2%
- Part-Time: 12.4%

Level of Stress Tolerance Needed: 74.3 (out of 100)

Most Stressful Aspects: Frequency of Conflict Situations (50.5); Consequence of Error (45.0).

Least Stressful Aspects: Pace Determined by Speed of Equipment (1.0); Deal With Physically Aggressive People (7.2); Level of Competition (31.7); Deal With Unpleasant or Angry People (44.7).

Conduct research or perform investigation for the purpose of identifying, abating, or eliminating sources of pollutants or hazards that affect either the environment or the health of the population. Utilizing knowledge of various scientific disciplines, may collect, synthesize, study, report, and take action based on data derived from measurements or observations of air, food, soil, water, and other sources. Conduct environmental audits and inspections and investigations of violations. Evaluate violations or problems discovered during inspections to determine appropriate regulatory actions or to provide advice on the development and prosecution of regulatory cases. Communicate scientific and technical information through oral briefings, written documents, workshops, conferences, and public hearings. Review and implement environmental technical standards, guidelines, policies, and formal regulations that meet all appropriate requirements. Provide technical guidance, support, and oversight to environmental programs, industry, and the public. Provide advice on proper standards and regulations or the development of policies, strategies, and codes of practice for environmental management. Analyze data to determine validity, quality, and scientific significance and to interpret correlations between human activities and environmental effects. Collect, synthesize, and analyze data derived from pollution emission measurements, atmospheric monitoring, meteorological and mineralogical information, and soil or water samples. Determine data collection methods to be employed in research projects and surveys. Prepare charts or graphs from data samples, providing summary information on the environmental relevance of the data. Develop the technical portions of legal documents, administrative orders, or consent decrees. Investigate and report on accidents affecting the environment. Monitor environmental impacts of development activities. Supervise environmental technologists and technicians. Develop programs designed to obtain the most productive, non-damaging use of land. Research

E

sources of pollution to determine their effects on the environment and to develop theories or methods of pollution abatement or control. Monitor effects of pollution and land degradation and recommend means of prevention or control. Design and direct studies to obtain technical environmental information about planned projects. Conduct applied research on topics such as waste control and treatment and pollution control methods.

Personality Type: Investigative. Investigative occupations frequently involve working with ideas and require an extensive amount of thinking. These occupations can involve searching for facts and figuring out problems mentally.

GOE—Interest Area: 15. Scientific Research, Engineering, and Mathematics. **Work Group:** 15.03. Life Sciences. **Other Jobs in This Work Group:** Biochemists and Biophysicists; Biologists; Epidemiologists; Medical Scientists, Except Epidemiologists; Microbiologists.

Skills—Science: Using scientific rules and methods to solve problems. **Service Orientation:** Actively looking for ways to help people. **Negotiation:** Bringing others together and trying to reconcile differences. **Reading Comprehension:** Understanding written sentences and paragraphs in work-related documents. **Coordination:** Adjusting actions in relation to others' actions. **Complex Problem Solving:** Identifying complex problems and reviewing related information to develop and evaluate options and implement solutions.

Education and Training Programs: Environmental Science; Environmental Studies. **Related Knowledge/Courses: Biology:** Plant and animal organisms, their tissues, cells, functions, interdependencies, and interactions with each other and the environment. **Geography:** Principles and methods for describing the features of land, sea, and air masses, including their physical characteristics, locations, interrelation-

ships, and distribution of plant, animal, and human life. **Chemistry:** The chemical composition, structure, and properties of substances and of the chemical processes and transformations that they undergo. This includes uses of chemicals, their danger signs, production techniques, and disposal methods. **Law and Government:** Laws, legal codes, court procedures, precedents, government regulations, executive orders, agency rules, and the democratic political process. **Engineering and Technology:** The practical application of engineering science and technology. This includes applying principles, techniques, procedures, and equipment to the design and production of various goods and services. **Physics:** Physical principles, laws, their interrelationships, and applications to understanding fluid, material, and atmospheric dynamics, and mechanical, electrical, atomic, and subatomic structures and processes.

Work Environment: More often indoors than outdoors; noisy; sitting.

Excavating and Loading Machine and Dragline Operators

- Education/Training Required: Moderate-term on-the-job training
- Annual Earnings: $32,930
- Growth: 8.3%
- Annual Job Openings: 6,562
- Self-Employed: 14.9%
- Part-Time: 29.5%

Level of Stress Tolerance Needed: 63.2 (out of 100)

Most Stressful Aspects: Duration of Typical Work Week (77.0); Pace Determined by Speed of Equipment (70.7); Consequence of Error (53.0); Frequency of Conflict Situations (51.7).

Least Stressful Aspects: Deal With Physically Aggressive People (11.8); Level of Competition (43.8); Deal With Unpleasant or Angry People (52.2); Impact of Decisions on Co-workers or Company Results (61.3).

Operate or tend machinery equipped with scoops, shovels, or buckets to excavate and load loose materials. Move levers, depress foot pedals, and turn dials to operate power machinery such as power shovels, stripping shovels, scraper loaders, or backhoes. Set up and inspect equipment prior to operation. Observe hand signals, grade stakes, and other markings when operating machines so that work can be performed to specifications. Become familiar with digging plans, machine capabilities and limitations, and efficient and safe digging procedures in a given application. Operate machinery to perform activities such as backfilling excavations, vibrating or breaking rock or concrete, and making winter roads. Create and maintain inclines and ramps and handle slides, mud, and pit cleanings and maintenance. Lubricate, adjust, and repair machinery and replace parts such as gears, bearings, and bucket teeth. Move materials over short distances, such as around a construction site, factory, or warehouse. Measure and verify levels of rock or gravel, bases, and other excavated material. Receive written or oral instructions regarding material movement or excavation. Adjust dig face angles for varying overburden depths and set lengths. Drive machines to worksites. Perform manual labor to prepare or finish sites, such as shoveling materials by hand. Direct ground workers engaged in activities such as moving stakes or markers or changing positions of towers. Direct workers engaged in placing blocks and outriggers to prevent machines from capsizing when lifting heavy loads.

Personality Type: Realistic. Realistic occupations frequently involve work activities that include practical, hands-on problems and solutions. They often deal with plants; animals; and real-world materials such as wood, tools, and machinery. Many of the occupations require working outside and do not involve a lot of paperwork or working closely with others.

GOE—Interest Area: 01. Agriculture and Natural Resources. **Work Group:** 01.08. Mining and Drilling. **Other Jobs in This Work Group:** Continuous Mining Machine Operators; Derrick Operators, Oil and Gas; Earth Drillers, Except Oil and Gas; Explosives Workers, Ordnance Handling Experts, and Blasters; Helpers—Extraction Workers; Loading Machine Operators, Underground Mining; Mine Cutting and Channeling Machine Operators; Rock Splitters, Quarry; Roof Bolters, Mining; Rotary Drill Operators, Oil and Gas; Roustabouts, Oil and Gas; Service Unit Operators, Oil, Gas, and Mining; Shuttle Car Operators; Wellhead Pumpers.

Skills—Repairing: Repairing machines or systems, using the needed tools. **Operation Monitoring:** Watching gauges, dials, or other indicators to make sure a machine is working properly. **Operation and Control:** Controlling operations of equipment or systems. **Equipment Maintenance:** Performing routine maintenance on equipment and determining when and what kind of maintenance is needed. **Installation:** Installing equipment, machines, wiring, or programs to meet specifications. **Systems Analysis:** Determining how a system should work and how changes in conditions, operations, and the environment will affect outcomes.

Education and Training Program: Construction/Heavy Equipment/Earthmoving Equipment Operation. **Related Knowledge/Courses: Building and Construction:** Materials, methods, and the tools involved in the construction or repair of houses, buildings, or other structures such as highways and roads. **Mechanical Devices:** Machines and tools, including their designs, uses, repair, and maintenance. **Transportation:** Principles and methods for moving people or goods by air, rail, sea, or road, including the relative costs and benefits. **Production and Processing:** Raw materials, production processes, quality control, costs, and other techniques for maximizing the effective manufacture and distribution of goods. **Public Safety and Security:** Relevant equipment, policies, procedures, and strategies to promote effective local, state, or national security operations for the protection of people, data, property, and institutions. **Engineering and Technology:** The practical application of engineering science and technology. This includes applying principles, techniques, procedures, and equipment to the design and production of various goods and services.

Work Environment: Outdoors; noisy; contaminants; whole-body vibration; sitting; using hands on objects, tools, or controls.

Farmers and Ranchers

- Education/Training Required: Long-term on-the-job training
- Annual Earnings: $37,130
- Growth: –8.5%
- Annual Job Openings: 129,552
- Self-Employed: 100.0%
- Part-Time: 18.2%

Level of Stress Tolerance Needed: 69.7 (out of 100)

Most Stressful Aspects: Duration of Typical Work Week (84.5); Pace Determined by Speed of Equipment (39.0).

Least Stressful Aspects: Deal With Physically Aggressive People (4.0); Deal With Unpleasant or Angry People (19.7); Frequency of Conflict Situations (22.2); Level of Competition (37.7).

On an ownership or rental basis, operate farms, ranches, greenhouses, nurseries, timber tracts, or other agricultural production establishments that produce crops, horticultural specialties, livestock, poultry, finfish, shellfish, or animal specialties. May plant, cultivate, harvest, perform post-harvest activities on, and market crops and livestock; may hire, train, and supervise farm workers or supervise a farm labor contractor; may prepare cost, production, and other records. May maintain and operate machinery and perform physical work. Monitor crops as they grow in order to ensure that they are growing properly and are free from diseases and contaminants. Select animals for market and provide transportation of livestock to market. Select and purchase supplies and equipment such as seed, fertilizers, and farm machinery. Remove lower-quality or older animals from herds and purchase other livestock to replace culled animals. Purchase and store livestock feed. Plan crop activities based on factors such as crop maturity and weather conditions. Negotiate and arrange with buyers for the sale, storage, and shipment of crops. Determine types and quantities of crops or livestock to be raised according to factors such as market conditions, federal program availability, and soil conditions. Milk cows, using milking machinery. Maintain pastures or grazing lands to ensure that animals have enough feed, employing pasture-conservation measures such as arranging rotational grazing. Install and shift irrigation systems to irrigate fields evenly or according to crop need. Harvest crops and collect specialty products such as royal jelly, wax, pollen, and honey from bee colonies. Evaluate product marketing alternatives and then promote and market farm products, acting as the sales agent for livestock and crops. Assist in animal births and care for newborn livestock. Breed and raise stock such as cattle, poultry, and honeybees, using recognized breeding practices to ensure continued improvement in stock. Clean and disinfect buildings and yards and remove manure. Clean and sanitize milking equipment, storage tanks, collection cups, and cows' udders or ensure that procedures are followed to maintain sanitary conditions for handling of milk. Clean, grade, and package crops for marketing. Control the spread of disease and parasites in herds by using vaccination and medication and by separating sick animals. Destroy diseased or superfluous crops. Perform crop production duties such as planning, tilling, planting, fertilizing, cultivating, spraying, and harvesting. Set up and operate farm machinery to cultivate, harvest, and haul crops.

Personality Type: Realistic. Realistic occupations frequently involve work activities that include practical, hands-on problems and solutions. They often deal with plants; animals; and real-world materials such as wood, tools, and machinery. Many of the occupations require working outside and do not involve a lot of paperwork or working closely with others.

GOE—Interest Area: 01. Agriculture and Natural Resources. **Work Group:** 01.01. Managerial Work in Agriculture and Natural Resources. **Other Jobs in This Work Group:** Aquacultural Managers; Crop and Livestock Managers; Farm Labor Contractors; Farm, Ranch, and Other Agricultural Managers; First-Line Supervisors/Managers of Agricultural Crop and Horticultural Workers; First-Line Supervisors/Managers of Animal Husbandry and Animal Care Workers; First-Line Supervisors/Managers of Aquacultural Workers; First-Line Supervisors/Managers of Construction Trades and Extraction Workers; First-Line Supervisors/Managers of Farming, Fishing, and Forestry Workers; First-Line Supervisors/Managers of Landscaping, Lawn Service, and Groundskeeping Workers; First-Line Supervisors/Managers of Logging Workers; Nursery and Greenhouse Managers; Park Naturalists; Purchasing Agents and Buyers, Farm Products.

Skills—Repairing: Repairing machines or systems, using the needed tools. **Management of Financial Resources:** Determining how money will be spent to get the work done, and accounting for these expenditures. **Equipment Maintenance:** Performing routine maintenance on equipment and determining when and what kind of maintenance is needed. **Operation Monitoring:** Watching gauges, dials, or other indicators to make sure a machine is working properly. **Installation:** Installing equipment, machines, wiring, or programs to meet specifications. **Management of Material Resources:** Obtaining and seeing to the appropriate use of equipment, facilities, and materials needed to do certain work.

Education and Training Programs: Agribusiness/Agricultural Business Operations; Agricultural Animal Breeding; Agricultural Business and Management, General; Agronomy and Crop Science; Animal Nutrition; Animal Sciences, General; Aquaculture; Crop Production; Dairy Science; Farm/Farm and Ranch Management; Greenhouse Operations and Management; Horticultural Science; Livestock Management; Ornamental Horticulture; Plant Nursery Operations and Management; Poultry Science; Range Science and Management; others. **Related Knowledge/Courses: Food Production:** Techniques and equipment for planting, growing, and harvesting food products (both plant and animal) for consumption, including storage/handling techniques. **Building and Construction:** Materials, methods, and the tools involved in the construction or repair of houses, buildings, or other structures such as highways and roads. **Biology:** Plant and animal organisms, their tissues, cells, functions, interdependencies, and interactions with each other and the environment. **Mechanical Devices:** Machines and tools, including their designs, uses, repair, and maintenance. **Sales and Marketing:** Principles and methods for showing, promoting, and selling products or services. This includes marketing strategy and tactics, product demonstration, sales techniques, and sales control systems. **Economics and Accounting:** Economic and accounting principles and practices, the financial markets, banking, and the analysis and reporting of financial data.

Work Environment: Outdoors; noisy; very hot or cold; contaminants; hazardous equipment; using hands on objects, tools, or controls.

Fence Erectors

- ◎ Education/Training Required: Moderate-term on-the-job training
- ◎ Annual Earnings: $26,400
- ◎ Growth: 10.6%
- ◎ Annual Job Openings: 2,812
- ◎ Self-Employed: 23.2%
- ◎ Part-Time: 15.0%

Level of Stress Tolerance Needed: 48.8 (out of 100)

Most Stressful Aspects: Time Pressure (71.0); Duration of Typical Work Week (64.5); Pace Determined by Speed of Equipment (26.0).

Least Stressful Aspects: Deal With Physically Aggressive People (7.2); Consequence of Error (27.5); Deal With Unpleasant or Angry People (42.8); Frequency of Conflict Situations (42.8).

Erect and repair metal and wooden fences and fence gates around highways, industrial establishments, residences, or farms, using hand and power tools. Insert metal tubing through rail supports. Discuss fencing needs with customers and estimate and quote prices. Weld metal parts

together, using portable gas welding equipment. Stretch wire, wire mesh, or chain link fencing between posts and attach fencing to frames. Set metal or wooden posts in upright positions in postholes. Nail top and bottom rails to fence posts or insert them in slots on posts. Nail pointed slats to rails to construct picket fences. Mix and pour concrete around bases of posts or tamp soil into postholes to embed posts. Blast rock formations and rocky areas with dynamite to facilitate posthole digging. Make rails for fences by sawing lumber or by cutting metal tubing to required lengths. Establish the location for a fence and gather information needed to ensure that there are no electric cables or water lines in the area. Erect alternate panel, basket weave, and louvered fences. Construct and repair barriers, retaining walls, trellises, and other types of fences, walls, and gates. Align posts, using lines or by sighting, and verify vertical alignment of posts, using plumb bobs or spirit levels. Assemble gates and fasten gates into position, using hand tools. Attach fence rail supports to posts, using hammers and pliers. Complete top fence rails of metal fences by connecting tube sections, using metal sleeves. Attach rails or tension wire along bottoms of posts to form fencing frames. Measure and lay out fence lines and mark posthole positions, following instructions, drawings, or specifications. Dig postholes, using spades, posthole diggers, or power-driven augers.

Personality Type: Realistic. Realistic occupations frequently involve work activities that include practical, hands-on problems and solutions. They often deal with plants; animals; and real-world materials such as wood, tools, and machinery. Many of the occupations require working outside and do not involve a lot of paperwork or working closely with others.

GOE—Interest Area: 02. Architecture and Construction. **Work Group:** 02.04. Construction Crafts. **Other Jobs in This Work Group:**

Boilermakers; Brickmasons and Blockmasons; Carpet Installers; Cement Masons and Concrete Finishers; Commercial Divers; Construction Carpenters; Crane and Tower Operators; Drywall and Ceiling Tile Installers; Electricians; Floor Layers, Except Carpet, Wood, and Hard Tiles; Floor Sanders and Finishers; Glaziers; Hazardous Materials Removal Workers; Insulation Workers, Floor, Ceiling, and Wall; Insulation Workers, Mechanical; Manufactured Building and Mobile Home Installers; Operating Engineers and Other Construction Equipment Operators; Painters, Construction and Maintenance; Paperhangers; Paving, Surfacing, and Tamping Equipment Operators; Pile-Driver Operators; Pipe Fitters and Steamfitters; Pipelayers; Plasterers and Stucco Masons; Plumbers; Plumbers, Pipefitters, and Steamfitters; Rail-Track Laying and Maintenance Equipment Operators; Refractory Materials Repairers, Except Brickmasons; Reinforcing Iron and Rebar Workers; Riggers; Roofers; Rough Carpenters; Security and Fire Alarm Systems Installers; Segmental Pavers; Sheet Metal Workers; Stone Cutters and Carvers, Manufacturing; Stonemasons; Structural Iron and Steel Workers; Tapers; Terrazzo Workers and Finishers; Tile and Marble Setters.

Skills—Installation: Installing equipment, machines, wiring, or programs to meet specifications. **Repairing:** Repairing machines or systems, using the needed tools. **Equipment Maintenance:** Performing routine maintenance on equipment and determining when and what kind of maintenance is needed. **Management of Material Resources:** Obtaining and seeing to the appropriate use of equipment, facilities, and materials needed to do certain work. **Management of Personnel Resources:** Motivating, developing, and directing people as they work, identifying the best people for the job.

Equipment Selection: Determining the kind of tools and equipment needed to do a job.

Education and Training Program: Construction Trades, Other. **Related Knowledge/Courses: Building and Construction:** Materials, methods, and the tools involved in the construction or repair of houses, buildings, or other structures such as highways and roads. **Sales and Marketing:** Principles and methods for showing, promoting, and selling products or services. This includes marketing strategy and tactics, product demonstration, sales techniques, and sales control systems.

Work Environment: Outdoors; very hot or cold; minor burns, cuts, bites, or stings; standing; walking and running; using hands on objects, tools, or controls.

Fiberglass Laminators and Fabricators

- Education/Training Required: Moderate-term on-the-job training
- Annual Earnings: $25,980
- Growth: 6.2%
- Annual Job Openings: 7,315
- Self-Employed: 1.6%
- Part-Time: 16.2%

Level of Stress Tolerance Needed: 61.0 (out of 100)

Most Stressful Aspects: Time Pressure (70.7); Pace Determined by Speed of Equipment (60.0); Duration of Typical Work Week (58.0); Consequence of Error (58.0).

Least Stressful Aspects: Deal With Physically Aggressive People (7.0); Deal With Unpleasant or Angry People (33.7); Impact of Decisions on

Co-workers or Company Results (44.2); Frequency of Conflict Situations (45.7).

Laminate layers of fiberglass on molds to form boat decks and hulls, bodies for golf carts or automobiles, or other products. Apply lacquers and waxes to mold surfaces to facilitate assembly and removal of laminated parts. Check all dies, templates, and cutout patterns to be used in the manufacturing process to ensure that they conform to dimensional data, photographs, blueprints, samples, and customer specifications. Check completed products for conformance to specifications and for defects by measuring with rulers or micrometers, by checking them visually, or by tapping them to detect bubbles or dead spots. Cure materials by letting them set at room temperature, placing them under heat lamps, or baking them in ovens. Inspect, clean, and assemble molds before beginning work. Mask off mold areas that are not to be laminated, using cellophane, wax paper, masking tape, or special sprays containing mold-release substances. Mix catalysts into resins and saturate cloth and mats with mixtures, using brushes. Pat or press layers of saturated mat or cloth into place on molds, using brushes or hands, and smooth out wrinkles and air bubbles with hands or squeegees. Release air bubbles and smooth seams, using rollers. Repair or modify damaged or defective glass-fiber parts, checking thicknesses, densities, and contours to ensure a close fit after repair. Select precut fiberglass mats, cloth, and wood-bracing materials as required by projects being assembled. Spray chopped fiberglass, resins, and catalysts onto prepared molds or dies using pneumatic spray guns with chopper attachments. Trim cured materials by sawing them with diamond-impregnated cutoff wheels. Trim excess materials from molds, using hand shears or trimming knives. Bond wood reinforcing strips to decks and cabin structures of watercraft, using resin-saturated fiberglass. Apply layers of plastic resin to mold surfaces prior to placement of fiberglass mats, repeating layers until products have the desired thicknesses and plastics have jelled.

Personality Type: No data available.

GOE—Interest Area: 13. Manufacturing. **Work Group:** 13.14. Vehicle and Facility Mechanical Work. **Other Jobs in This Work Group:** Aircraft Mechanics and Service Technicians; Aircraft Structure, Surfaces, Rigging, and Systems Assemblers; Automotive Body and Related Repairers; Automotive Glass Installers and Repairers; Automotive Master Mechanics; Automotive Service Technicians and Mechanics; Automotive Specialty Technicians; Bus and Truck Mechanics and Diesel Engine Specialists; Farm Equipment Mechanics; Mobile Heavy Equipment Mechanics, Except Engines; Motorboat Mechanics; Motorcycle Mechanics; Outdoor Power Equipment and Other Small Engine Mechanics; Rail Car Repairers; Recreational Vehicle Service Technicians; Tire Repairers and Changers.

Skills—Repairing: Repairing machines or systems, using the needed tools. **Operation and Control:** Controlling operations of equipment or systems.

Education and Training Program: Marine Maintenance/Fitter and Ship Repair Technology/Technician Training. **Related Knowledge/Courses: Chemistry:** The chemical composition, structure, and properties of substances and of the chemical processes and transformations that they undergo. This includes uses of chemicals, their danger signs, production techniques, and disposal methods. **Production and Processing:** Raw materials, production processes, quality control, costs, and other techniques for maximizing the effective manufacture and distribution of goods. **Building and Construction:** Materials, methods, and the tools involved in the construction or repair of houses, buildings, or other structures such as highways and roads. **Mechanical Devices:** Machines and tools, including their designs, uses, repair, and maintenance. **Engineering and Technology:** The practical application of engineering science and technology. This includes applying principles, techniques, procedures, and equipment to the design and production of various goods and services. **Design:** Design techniques, tools, and principles involved in production of precision technical plans, blueprints, drawings, and models.

Work Environment: Noisy; contaminants; hazardous conditions; standing; using hands on objects, tools, or controls; repetitive motions.

File Clerks

- ◎ Education/Training Required: Short-term on-the-job training
- ◎ Annual Earnings: $22,090
- ◎ Growth: –41.3%
- ◎ Annual Job Openings: 50,088
- ◎ Self-Employed: 1.7%
- ◎ Part-Time: 54.2%

Level of Stress Tolerance Needed: 42.5 (out of 100)

Most Stressful Aspects: Time Pressure (79.8).

Least Stressful Aspects: Deal With Physically Aggressive People (2.0); Pace Determined by Speed of Equipment (17.0); Level of Competition (24.5); Deal With Unpleasant or Angry People (30.3).

File correspondence, cards, invoices, receipts, and other records in alphabetical or numerical order or according to the filing system used. Locate and remove material from file when requested. Keep records of materials filed or removed, using logbooks or computers. Add new material to file records and create new records as necessary. Perform general office duties such as typing, operating office machines, and sorting mail. Track materials removed from files to ensure that borrowed files are returned. Gather materials to be filed from departments and employees. Sort or classify information according to guidelines such as content; purpose; user criteria; or chronological, alphabetical, or numerical order. Find and retrieve information from files in response to requests from authorized users. Scan or read incoming materials to determine how and where they should be classified or filed. Place materials into storage receptacles, such as file cabinets, boxes, bins, or drawers, according to classification and identification information. Assign and record or stamp identification numbers or codes to index materials for filing. Answer questions about records and files. Modify and improve filing systems or implement new filing systems. Perform periodic inspections of materials or files to ensure correct placement, legibility, and proper condition. Eliminate outdated or unnecessary materials, destroying them or transferring them to inactive storage according to file maintenance guidelines or legal requirements. Enter document identification codes into systems to determine locations of documents to be retrieved. Operate mechanized files that rotate to bring needed records to a particular location. Design forms related to filing systems. Retrieve documents stored in microfilm or microfiche and place them in viewers for reading.

Personality Type: Conventional. Conventional occupations frequently involve following set procedures and routines. These occupations can include working with data and details more than with ideas. Usually, there is a clear line of authority to follow.

GOE—Interest Area: 04. Business and Administration. **Work Group:** 04.07. Records and Materials Processing. **Other Jobs in This Work Group:** Correspondence Clerks; Human

Resources Assistants, Except Payroll and Timekeeping; Marking Clerks; Meter Readers, Utilities; Office Clerks, General; Order Fillers, Wholesale and Retail Sales; Postal Service Clerks; Postal Service Mail Sorters, Processors, and Processing Machine Operators; Procurement Clerks; Production, Planning, and Expediting Clerks; Shipping, Receiving, and Traffic Clerks; Stock Clerks and Order Fillers; Stock Clerks, Sales Floor; Stock Clerks—Stockroom, Warehouse, or Storage Yard; Weighers, Measurers, Checkers, and Samplers, Recordkeeping.

Skills—None met the criteria.

Education and Training Program: General Office Occupations and Clerical Services. **Related Knowledge/Courses: Clerical Practices:** Administrative and clerical procedures and systems such as word processing, managing files and records, stenography and transcription, designing forms, and other office procedures and terminology. **Computers and Electronics:** Circuit boards, processors, chips, electronic equipment, and computer hardware and software, including applications and programming. **English Language:** The structure and content of the English language, including the meaning and spelling of words, rules of composition, and grammar.

Work Environment: Indoors; sitting; using hands on objects, tools, or controls; repetitive motions.

Fire-Prevention and Protection Engineers

◎ Education/Training Required: Bachelor's degree
◎ Annual Earnings: $66,290
◎ Growth: 9.6%
◎ Annual Job Openings: 1,105
◎ Self-Employed: 1.1%
◎ Part-Time: 14.3%

Our sources did not provide separate job openings data for this occupation. The job openings listed here are shared with Industrial Safety and Health Engineers and with Product Safety Engineers.

Level of Stress Tolerance Needed: 68.8 (out of 100)

Most Stressful Aspects: Duration of Typical Work Week (93.0); Importance of Being Exact or Accurate (78.5); Time Pressure (75.0); Impact of Decisions on Co-workers or Company Results (68.5).

Least Stressful Aspects: Deal With Physically Aggressive People (7.5); Pace Determined by Speed of Equipment (9.0); Deal With Unpleasant or Angry People (41.8).

Research causes of fires, determine fire protection methods, and design or recommend materials or equipment such as structural components or fire-detection equipment to assist organizations in safeguarding life and property against fire, explosion, and related hazards. Design fire-detection equipment, alarm systems, and fire-extinguishing devices and systems. Inspect buildings or building designs to determine fire protection system requirements and potential problems in areas such as water supplies, exit locations, and construction materials. Advise architects, builders, and other construction personnel on fire prevention equipment and techniques and on fire code and standard interpretation and compliance. Prepare and write reports detailing specific fire prevention and protection issues, such as work performed and proposed review schedules. Determine causes of fires and ways in which they could have been prevented. Direct the purchase, modification, installation, maintenance, and operation of fire protection systems. Consult with authorities to discuss safety regulations and to recommend changes as necessary. Develop plans for the prevention of destruction by fire, wind, and water. Study the relationships between ignition sources and materials to determine how fires start. Attend workshops, seminars, or conferences to present or obtain information regarding fire prevention and protection. Develop training materials and conduct training sessions on fire protection. Evaluate fire department performance and the laws and regulations affecting fire prevention or fire safety. Conduct research on fire retardants and the fire safety of materials and devices.

Personality Type: Investigative. Investigative occupations frequently involve working with ideas and require an extensive amount of thinking. These occupations can involve searching for facts and figuring out problems mentally.

GOE—Interest Area: 15. Scientific Research, Engineering, and Mathematics. **Work Group:** 15.08. Industrial and Safety Engineering. **Other Jobs in This Work Group:** Health and Safety Engineers, Except Mining Safety Engineers and Inspectors; Industrial Engineers; Industrial Safety and Health Engineers; Product Safety Engineers.

Skills—Science: Using scientific rules and methods to solve problems. **Management of Financial Resources:** Determining how money will be spent to get the work done, and account-

ing for these expenditures. **Operations Analysis:** Analyzing needs and product requirements to create a design. **Mathematics:** Using mathematics to solve problems. **Management of Personnel Resources:** Motivating, developing, and directing people as they work, identifying the best people for the job. **Systems Analysis:** Determining how a system should work and how changes in conditions, operations, and the environment will affect outcomes.

Education and Training Program: Environmental/Environmental Health Engineering. **Related Knowledge/Courses: Design:** Design techniques, tools, and principles involved in production of precision technical plans, blueprints, drawings, and models. **Engineering and Technology:** The practical application of engineering science and technology. This includes applying principles, techniques, procedures, and equipment to the design and production of various goods and services. **Building and Construction:** Materials, methods, and the tools involved in the construction or repair of houses, buildings, or other structures such as highways and roads. **Physics:** Physical principles, laws, their interrelationships, and applications to understanding fluid, material, and atmospheric dynamics, and mechanical, electrical, atomic, and subatomic structures and processes. **Chemistry:** The chemical composition, structure, and properties of substances and of the chemical processes and transformations that they undergo. This includes uses of chemicals, their danger signs, production techniques, and disposal methods. **Public Safety and Security:** Relevant equipment, policies, procedures, and strategies to promote effective local, state, or national security operations for the protection of people, data, property, and institutions.

Work Environment: Indoors; sitting.

Fitness Trainers and Aerobics Instructors

- Education/Training Required: Postsecondary vocational training
- Annual Earnings: $25,910
- Growth: 26.8%
- Annual Job Openings: 51,235
- Self-Employed: 7.6%
- Part-Time: 44.1%

Level of Stress Tolerance Needed: 64.2 (out of 100)

Most Stressful Aspects: None greater than average.

Least Stressful Aspects: Pace Determined by Speed of Equipment (3.0); Duration of Typical Work Week (4.0); Deal With Physically Aggressive People (11.5); Consequence of Error (15.3).

Instruct or coach groups or individuals in exercise activities and the fundamentals of sports. Demonstrate techniques and methods of participation. Observe participants and inform them of corrective measures necessary to improve their skills. Explain and enforce safety rules and regulations governing sports, recreational activities, and the use of exercise equipment. Offer alternatives during classes to accommodate different levels of fitness. Plan routines, choose appropriate music, and choose different movements for each set of muscles, depending on participants' capabilities and limitations. Observe participants and inform them of corrective measures necessary for skill improvement. Teach proper breathing techniques used during physical exertion. Teach and demonstrate use of gymnastic and training equipment such as trampolines and weights. Instruct participants in maintaining exertion levels to maximize benefits from exercise routines. Maintain fitness equipment. Conduct therapeutic, recreational, or athletic activities. Monitor participants' progress and adapt programs as needed. Evaluate individuals' abilities, needs, and physical conditions and develop suitable training programs to meet any special requirements. Plan physical education programs to promote development of participants' physical attributes and social skills. Provide students with information and resources regarding nutrition, weight control, and lifestyle issues. Administer emergency first aid, wrap injuries, treat minor chronic disabilities, or refer injured persons to physicians. Advise clients about proper clothing and shoes. Wrap ankles, fingers, wrists, or other body parts with synthetic skin, gauze, or adhesive tape to support muscles and ligaments. Teach individual and team sports to participants through instruction and demonstration, utilizing knowledge of sports techniques and of participants' physical capabilities. Promote health clubs through membership sales and record member information. Organize, lead, and referee indoor and outdoor games such as volleyball, baseball, and basketball. Maintain equipment inventories and select, store, or issue equipment as needed. Organize and conduct competitions and tournaments. Advise participants in use of heat or ultraviolet treatments and hot baths. Massage body parts to relieve soreness, strains, and bruises.

Personality Type: Social. Social occupations frequently involve working with, communicating with, and teaching people. These occupations often involve helping or providing service to others.

GOE—Interest Area: 05. Education and Training. **Work Group:** 05.06. Counseling, Health, and Fitness Education. **Other Jobs in This Work Group:** Educational, Vocational, and School Counselors; Health Educators.

Skills—**Instructing:** Teaching others how to do something. **Equipment Selection:** Determining the kind of tools and equipment needed to do a job. **Monitoring:** Monitoring/assessing performance of yourself, other individuals, or organizations to make improvements or take corrective action. **Service Orientation:** Actively looking for ways to help people. **Coordination:** Adjusting actions in relation to others' actions. **Social Perceptiveness:** Being aware of others' reactions and understanding why they react as they do.

Education and Training Programs: Health and Physical Education, General; Physical Education Teaching and Coaching; Sport and Fitness Administration/Management. **Related Knowledge/Courses: Customer and Personal Service:** Principles and processes for providing customer and personal services. This includes customer needs assessment, meeting quality standards for services, and evaluation of customer satisfaction. **Psychology:** Human behavior and performance; individual differences in ability, personality, and interests; learning and motivation; psychological research methods; and the assessment and treatment of behavioral and affective disorders. **Sociology and Anthropology:** Group behavior and dynamics, societal trends and influences, human migrations, ethnicity, cultures and their history and origins. **Education and Training:** Principles and methods for curriculum and training design, teaching and instruction for individuals and groups, and the measurement of training effects. **Sales and Marketing:** Principles and methods for showing, promoting, and selling products or services. This includes marketing strategy and tactics, product demonstration, sales techniques, and sales control systems. **Personnel and Human Resources:** Principles and procedures for personnel recruitment, selection, training, compensation and benefits, labor relations and negotiation, and personnel information systems.

Work Environment: Indoors; standing; walking and running; repetitive motions.

Floor Layers, Except Carpet, Wood, and Hard Tiles

- Education/Training Required: Moderate-term on-the-job training
- Annual Earnings: $34,190
- Growth: –12.2%
- Annual Job Openings: 2,504
- Self-Employed: 47.7%
- Part-Time: 16.8%

Level of Stress Tolerance Needed: 58.2 (out of 100)

Most Stressful Aspects: Impact of Decisions on Co-workers or Company Results (84.0); Importance of Being Exact or Accurate (79.8).

Least Stressful Aspects: Deal With Physically Aggressive People (0.2); Pace Determined by Speed of Equipment (1.2); Frequency of Conflict Situations (21.0); Consequence of Error (25.0).

Apply blocks, strips, or sheets of shock-absorbing, sound-deadening, or decorative coverings to floors. Sweep, scrape, sand, or chip dirt and irregularities to clean base surfaces, correcting imperfections that may show through the covering. Cut flooring material to fit around obstructions. Inspect surface to be covered to ensure that it is firm and dry. Trim excess covering materials, tack edges, and join sections of covering material to form tight joint. Form a smooth foundation by stapling plywood or Masonite over the floor or by brushing waterproof compound onto surface and filling cracks with plaster, putty, or grout to seal pores.

Measure and mark guidelines on surfaces or foundations, using chalk lines and dividers. Cut covering and foundation materials according to blueprints and sketches. Roll and press sheet wall and floor covering into cement base to smooth and finish surface, using hand roller. Apply adhesive cement to floor or wall material to join and adhere foundation material. Determine traffic areas and decide location of seams. Lay out, position, and apply shock-absorbing, sound-deadening, or decorative coverings to floors, walls, and cabinets, following guidelines to keep courses straight and create designs. Remove excess cement to clean finished surface. Disconnect and remove appliances, light fixtures, and worn floor and wall covering from floors, walls, and cabinets. Heat and soften floor covering materials to patch cracks or fit floor coverings around irregular surfaces, using blowtorch.

Personality Type: Realistic. Realistic occupations frequently involve work activities that include practical, hands-on problems and solutions. They often deal with plants; animals; and real-world materials such as wood, tools, and machinery. Many of the occupations require working outside and do not involve a lot of paperwork or working closely with others.

GOE—Interest Area: 02. Architecture and Construction. **Work Group:** 02.04. Construction Crafts. **Other Jobs in This Work Group:** Boilermakers; Brickmasons and Blockmasons; Carpet Installers; Cement Masons and Concrete Finishers; Commercial Divers; Construction Carpenters; Crane and Tower Operators; Drywall and Ceiling Tile Installers; Electricians; Fence Erectors; Floor Sanders and Finishers; Glaziers; Hazardous Materials Removal Workers; Insulation Workers, Floor, Ceiling, and Wall; Insulation Workers, Mechanical; Manufactured Building and Mobile Home Installers; Operating Engineers and Other Construction Equipment Operators; Painters, Construction and Maintenance; Paperhangers; Paving, Surfacing, and Tamping Equipment Operators; Pile-Driver Operators; Pipe Fitters and Steamfitters; Pipelayers; Plasterers and Stucco Masons; Plumbers; Plumbers, Pipefitters, and Steamfitters; Rail-Track Laying and Maintenance Equipment Operators; Refractory Materials Repairers, Except Brickmasons; Reinforcing Iron and Rebar Workers; Riggers; Roofers; Rough Carpenters; Security and Fire Alarm Systems Installers; Segmental Pavers; Sheet Metal Workers; Stone Cutters and Carvers, Manufacturing; Stonemasons; Structural Iron and Steel Workers; Tapers; Terrazzo Workers and Finishers; Tile and Marble Setters.

Skills—Installation: Installing equipment, machines, wiring, or programs to meet specifications. **Repairing:** Repairing machines or systems, using the needed tools. **Equipment Selection:** Determining the kind of tools and equipment needed to do a job. **Equipment Maintenance:** Performing routine maintenance on equipment and determining when and what kind of maintenance is needed. **Mathematics:** Using mathematics to solve problems. **Operations Analysis:** Analyzing needs and product requirements to create a design.

Education and Training Program: Construction Trades, Other. **Related Knowledge/ Courses: Building and Construction:** Materials, methods, and the tools involved in the construction or repair of houses, buildings, or other structures such as highways and roads. **Design:** Design techniques, tools, and principles involved in production of precision technical plans, blueprints, drawings, and models. **Mechanical Devices:** Machines and tools, including their designs, uses, repair, and maintenance. **Production and Processing:** Raw materials, production processes, quality control, costs, and other techniques for maximizing the effective manufacture and distribution of goods.

Mathematics: Arithmetic, algebra, geometry, calculus, statistics, and their applications. **Transportation:** Principles and methods for moving people or goods by air, rail, sea, or road, including the relative costs and benefits.

Work Environment: Indoors; contaminants; cramped work space, awkward positions; kneeling, crouching, stooping, or crawling; using hands on objects, tools, or controls; bending or twisting the body.

Food Batchmakers

- Education/Training Required: Short-term on-the-job training
- Annual Earnings: $23,100
- Growth: 10.9%
- Annual Job Openings: 15,704
- Self-Employed: 1.7%
- Part-Time: 41.2%

Level of Stress Tolerance Needed: 55.3 (out of 100)

Most Stressful Aspects: Duration of Typical Work Week (76.5); Pace Determined by Speed of Equipment (75.3); Time Pressure (74.5); Consequence of Error (57.0).

Least Stressful Aspects: Deal With Physically Aggressive People (14.0); Frequency of Conflict Situations (37.7); Level of Competition (43.5); Deal With Unpleasant or Angry People (46.2).

Set up and operate equipment that mixes or blends ingredients used in the manufacturing of food products. Includes candy makers and cheese makers. Record production and test data for each food product batch, such as the ingredients used, temperature, test results, and time cycle. Observe gauges and thermometers to determine whether the mixing chamber temperature is within specified limits and turn valves to control the temperature. Clean and sterilize vats and factory processing areas. Press switches and turn knobs to start, adjust, and regulate equipment such as beaters, extruders, discharge pipes, and salt pumps. Observe and listen to equipment to detect possible malfunctions, such as leaks or plugging, and report malfunctions or undesirable tastes to supervisors. Set up, operate, and tend equipment that cooks, mixes, blends, or processes ingredients in the manufacturing of food products according to formulas or recipes. Mix or blend ingredients according to recipes by using a paddle or an agitator or by controlling vats that heat and mix ingredients. Select and measure or weigh ingredients, using English or metric measures and balance scales. Follow recipes to produce food products of specified flavor, texture, clarity, bouquet, or color. Turn valve controls to start equipment and to adjust operation to maintain product quality. Determine mixing sequences, based on knowledge of temperature effects and of the solubility of specific ingredients. Fill processing or cooking containers, such as kettles, rotating cookers, pressure cookers, or vats, with ingredients by opening valves, by starting pumps or injectors, or by hand. Give directions to other workers who are assisting in the batchmaking process. Homogenize or pasteurize material to prevent separation or to obtain prescribed butterfat content, using a homogenizing device. Inspect vats after cleaning to ensure that fermentable residue has been removed. Examine, feel, and taste product samples during production to evaluate quality, color, texture, flavor, and bouquet and document the results. Test food product samples for moisture content, acidity level, specific gravity, or butterfat content and continue processing until desired levels are reached. Formulate or modify recipes for specific kinds of food products.

Personality Type: Realistic. Realistic occupations frequently involve work activities that include practical, hands-on problems and solutions. They often deal with plants; animals; and real-world materials such as wood, tools, and machinery. Many of the occupations require working outside and do not involve a lot of paperwork or working closely with others.

GOE—Interest Area: 13. Manufacturing. **Work Group:** 13.03. Production Work, Assorted Materials Processing. **Other Jobs in This Work Group:** Bakers; Cementing and Gluing Machine Operators and Tenders; Chemical Equipment Operators and Tenders; Cleaning, Washing, and Metal Pickling Equipment Operators and Tenders; Coating, Painting, and Spraying Machine Setters, Operators, and Tenders; Cooling and Freezing Equipment Operators and Tenders; Cutting and Slicing Machine Setters, Operators, and Tenders; Extruding and Forming Machine Setters, Operators, and Tenders, Synthetic and Glass Fibers; Extruding, Forming, Pressing, and Compacting Machine Setters, Operators, and Tenders; Food and Tobacco Roasting, Baking, and Drying Machine Operators and Tenders; Food Cooking Machine Operators and Tenders; Furnace, Kiln, Oven, Drier, and Kettle Operators and Tenders; Heat Treating Equipment Setters, Operators, and Tenders, Metal and Plastic; Helpers—Production Workers; Meat, Poultry, and Fish Cutters and Trimmers; Metal-Refining Furnace Operators and Tenders; Mixing and Blending Machine Setters, Operators, and Tenders; Packaging and Filling Machine Operators and Tenders; Plating and Coating Machine Setters, Operators, and Tenders, Metal and Plastic; Pourers and Casters, Metal; Sawing Machine Setters, Operators, and Tenders, Wood; Separating, Filtering, Clarifying, Precipitating, and Still Machine Setters, Operators, and Tenders; Sewing Machine Operators; Shoe Machine Operators and Tenders; Slaughterers and Meat Packers; Team Assemblers; Textile Bleaching and Dyeing Machine Operators and Tenders; Tire Builders; Woodworking Machine Setters, Operators, and Tenders, Except Sawing.

Skills—Operation Monitoring: Watching gauges, dials, or other indicators to make sure a machine is working properly. **Operation and Control:** Controlling operations of equipment or systems. **Equipment Maintenance:** Performing routine maintenance on equipment and determining when and what kind of maintenance is needed. **Quality Control Analysis:** Conducting tests and inspections of products, services, or processes to evaluate quality or performance. **Repairing:** Repairing machines or systems, using the needed tools. **Troubleshooting:** Determining causes of operating errors and deciding what to do about them.

Education and Training Programs: Agricultural and Food Products Processing; Foodservice Systems Administration/Management. **Related Knowledge/Courses: Production and Processing:** Raw materials, production processes, quality control, costs, and other techniques for maximizing the effective manufacture and distribution of goods. **Public Safety and Security:** Relevant equipment, policies, procedures, and strategies to promote effective local, state, or national security operations for the protection of people, data, property, and institutions. **Chemistry:** The chemical composition, structure, and properties of substances and of the chemical processes and transformations that they undergo. This includes uses of chemicals, their danger signs, production techniques, and disposal methods. **Mathematics:** Arithmetic, algebra, geometry, calculus, statistics, and their applications.

Work Environment: Noisy; contaminants; standing; using hands on objects, tools, or controls; bending or twisting the body; repetitive motions.

Food Cooking Machine Operators and Tenders

- Education/Training Required: Short-term on-the-job training
- Annual Earnings: $21,280
- Growth: −4.7%
- Annual Job Openings: 6,714
- Self-Employed: 0.2%
- Part-Time: 12.5%

Level of Stress Tolerance Needed: 66.0 (out of 100)

Most Stressful Aspects: Importance of Being Exact or Accurate (84.5); Pace Determined by Speed of Equipment (78.5); Time Pressure (75.0); Impact of Decisions on Co-workers or Company Results (68.3).

Least Stressful Aspects: Deal With Physically Aggressive People (8.8); Deal With Unpleasant or Angry People (42.5); Frequency of Conflict Situations (47.3).

Operate or tend cooking equipment, such as steam cooking vats, deep-fry cookers, pressure cookers, kettles, and boilers, to prepare food products. Record production and test data, such as processing steps, temperature and steam readings, cooking time, batches processed, and test results. Listen for malfunction alarms and shut down equipment and notify supervisors when necessary. Collect and examine product samples during production to test them for quality, color, content, consistency, viscosity, acidity, or specific gravity. Observe gauges, dials, and product characteristics and adjust controls to maintain appropriate temperature, pressure, and flow of ingredients. Read work orders, recipes, or formulas to determine cooking times and temperatures and ingredient specifications. Clean, wash, and sterilize equipment and cooking area, using water hoses, cleaning or sterilizing solutions, or rinses. Set temperature, pressure, and time controls and start conveyers, machines, or pumps. Tend or operate and control equipment such as kettles, cookers, vats and tanks, and boilers to cook ingredients or prepare products for further processing. Measure or weigh ingredients, using scales or measuring containers. Admit required amounts of water, steam, cooking oils, or compressed air into equipment, such as by opening water valves to cool mixtures to the desired consistency. Remove cooked material or products from equipment. Notify or signal other workers to operate equipment or when processing is complete. Turn valves or start pumps to add ingredients or drain products from equipment and to transfer products for storage, cooling, or further processing. Place products on conveyors or carts and monitor product flow. Pour, dump, or load prescribed quantities of ingredients or products into cooking equipment manually or by using a hoist. Activate agitators and paddles to mix or stir ingredients, stopping machines when ingredients are thoroughly mixed. Operate auxiliary machines and equipment such as grinders, canners, and molding presses to prepare or further process products.

Personality Type: Realistic. Realistic occupations frequently involve work activities that include practical, hands-on problems and solutions. They often deal with plants; animals; and real-world materials such as wood, tools, and machinery. Many of the occupations require working outside and do not involve a lot of paperwork or working closely with others.

GOE—Interest Area: 13. Manufacturing. **Work Group:** 13.03. Production Work, Assorted Materials Processing. **Other Jobs in This Work Group:** Bakers; Cementing and Gluing Machine Operators and Tenders; Chemical Equipment Operators and Tenders; Cleaning, Washing, and Metal Pickling Equipment Operators and Tenders; Coating, Painting, and Spraying

Machine Setters, Operators, and Tenders; Cooling and Freezing Equipment Operators and Tenders; Cutting and Slicing Machine Setters, Operators, and Tenders; Extruding and Forming Machine Setters, Operators, and Tenders, Synthetic and Glass Fibers; Extruding, Forming, Pressing, and Compacting Machine Setters, Operators, and Tenders; Food and Tobacco Roasting, Baking, and Drying Machine Operators and Tenders; Food Batchmakers; Furnace, Kiln, Oven, Drier, and Kettle Operators and Tenders; Heat Treating Equipment Setters, Operators, and Tenders, Metal and Plastic; Helpers—Production Workers; Meat, Poultry, and Fish Cutters and Trimmers; Metal-Refining Furnace Operators and Tenders; Mixing and Blending Machine Setters, Operators, and Tenders; Packaging and Filling Machine Operators and Tenders; Plating and Coating Machine Setters, Operators, and Tenders, Metal and Plastic; Pourers and Casters, Metal; Sawing Machine Setters, Operators, and Tenders, Wood; Separating, Filtering, Clarifying, Precipitating, and Still Machine Setters, Operators, and Tenders; Sewing Machine Operators; Shoe Machine Operators and Tenders; Slaughterers and Meat Packers; Team Assemblers; Textile Bleaching and Dyeing Machine Operators and Tenders; Tire Builders; Woodworking Machine Setters, Operators, and Tenders, Except Sawing.

Skills—Operation Monitoring: Watching gauges, dials, or other indicators to make sure a machine is working properly. **Quality Control Analysis:** Conducting tests and inspections of products, services, or processes to evaluate quality or performance. **Operation and Control:** Controlling operations of equipment or systems. **Operations Analysis:** Analyzing needs and product requirements to create a design. **Management of Personnel Resources:**

Motivating, developing, and directing people as they work, identifying the best people for the job. **Systems Evaluation:** Identifying measures or indicators of system performance and the actions needed to improve or correct performance, relative to the goals of the system.

Education and Training Program: Agricultural and Food Products Processing. **Related Knowledge/Courses: Food Production:** Techniques and equipment for planting, growing, and harvesting food products (both plant and animal) for consumption, including storage/handling techniques. **Production and Processing:** Raw materials, production processes, quality control, costs, and other techniques for maximizing the effective manufacture and distribution of goods. **Chemistry:** The chemical composition, structure, and properties of substances and of the chemical processes and transformations that they undergo. This includes uses of chemicals, their danger signs, production techniques, and disposal methods.

Work Environment: Noisy; very hot or cold; minor burns, cuts, bites, or stings; standing; walking and running; using hands on objects, tools, or controls.

Forest and Conservation Technicians

- Education/Training Required: Associate degree
- Annual Earnings: $30,880
- Growth: –2.0%
- Annual Job Openings: 5,946
- Self-Employed: 1.7%
- Part-Time: 28.9%

Level of Stress Tolerance Needed: 70.2 (out of 100)

Most Stressful Aspects: Impact of Decisions on Co-workers or Company Results (68.0); Consequence of Error (61.5); Duration of Typical Work Week (58.5); Frequency of Conflict Situations (53.3).

Least Stressful Aspects: Pace Determined by Speed of Equipment (11.0); Level of Competition (43.5); Deal With Unpleasant or Angry People (44.2); Time Pressure (58.5).

Compile data pertaining to size, content, condition, and other characteristics of forest tracts under direction of foresters; train and lead forest workers in forest propagation and fire prevention and suppression. May assist conservation scientists in managing, improving, and protecting rangelands and wildlife habitats and help provide technical assistance regarding the conservation of soil, water, and related natural resources. Train and lead forest and conservation workers in seasonal activities such as planting tree seedlings, putting out forest fires, and maintaining recreational facilities. Monitor activities of logging companies and contractors. Select and mark trees for thinning or logging, drawing detailed plans that include access roads. Thin and space trees and control weeds and undergrowth, using manual tools and chemicals, or supervise workers performing these tasks. Manage forest protection activities, including fire control, fire crew training, and coordination of fire detection and public education programs. Survey, measure, and map access roads and forest areas such as burns, cut-over areas, experimental plots, and timber sales sections. Patrol park or forest areas to protect resources and prevent damage. Provide information about, and enforce, regulations such as those concerning environmental protection, resource utilization, fire safety, and accident prevention. Keep records of the amount and condi-

tion of logs taken to mills. Supervise forest nursery operations, timber harvesting, land-use activities such as livestock grazing, and disease- or insect-control programs. Issue fire permits, timber permits, and other forest-use licenses. Develop and maintain computer databases. Measure distances, clean site lines, and record data to help survey crews. Plan and supervise construction of access routes and forest roads. Provide forestry education and general information, advice, and recommendations to woodlot owners, community organizations, and the general public. Perform reforestation, or forest renewal, including nursery and silviculture operations, site preparation, seeding and tree planting programs, cone collection, and tree improvement. Conduct laboratory or field experiments with plants, animals, insects, diseases, and soils. Provide technical support to forestry research programs in areas such as tree improvement, seed orchard operations, insect and disease surveys, or experimental forestry and forest engineering research. Inspect trees and collect samples of plants, seeds, foliage, bark, and roots to locate insect and disease damage.

Personality Type: No data available.

GOE—Interest Area: 01. Agriculture and Natural Resources. **Work Group:** 01.06. Forestry and Logging. **Other Jobs in This Work Group:** Fallers; Forest and Conservation Workers; Log Graders and Scalers; Logging Equipment Operators.

Skills—Management of Financial Resources: Determining how money will be spent to get the work done and accounting for these expenditures. **Science:** Using scientific rules and methods to solve problems. **Operations Analysis:** Analyzing needs and product requirements to create a design. **Management of Personnel Resources:** Motivating, developing, and directing people as they work, identifying the best people for the job. **Equipment Selection:**

F

Determining the kind of tools and equipment needed to do a job. **Mathematics:** Using mathematics to solve problems.

Education and Training Programs: Forest Management/Forest Resources Management; Forest Resources Production and Management; Forest Sciences and Biology; Forest Technology/ Technician Training; Forestry, General; Forestry, Other; Land Use Planning and Management/Development; Natural Resources and Conservation, Other; Natural Resources Management and Policy, Other; Natural Resources/Conservation, General; Urban Forestry; Water, Wetlands, and Marine Resources Management. **Related Knowledge/ Courses: Biology:** Plant and animal organisms, their tissues, cells, functions, interdependencies, and interactions with each other and the environment. **Geography:** Principles and methods for describing the features of land, sea, and air masses, including their physical characteristics, locations, interrelationships, and distribution of plant, animal, and human life. **Mechanical Devices:** Machines and tools, including their designs, uses, repair, and maintenance. **Law and Government:** Laws, legal codes, court procedures, precedents, government regulations, executive orders, agency rules, and the democratic political process. **Building and Construction:** Materials, methods, and the tools involved in the construction or repair of houses, buildings, or other structures such as highways and roads. **Transportation:** Principles and methods for moving people or goods by air, rail, sea, or road, including the relative costs and benefits.

Work Environment: Outdoors; very hot or cold; contaminants; hazardous equipment; minor burns, cuts, bites, or stings; walking and running.

Forest Fire Inspectors and Prevention Specialists

- Education/Training Required: Work experience in a related occupation
- Annual Earnings: $32,940
- Growth: 2.1%
- Annual Job Openings: 66
- Self-Employed: 0.0%
- Part-Time: 3.6%

Level of Stress Tolerance Needed: 53.5 (out of 100)

Most Stressful Aspects: Impact of Decisions on Co-workers or Company Results (71.0); Level of Competition (57.5); Frequency of Conflict Situations (55.5); Deal With Physically Aggressive People (16.0).

Least Stressful Aspects: Pace Determined by Speed of Equipment (6.3); Consequence of Error (37.3); Deal With Unpleasant or Angry People (39.7); Duration of Typical Work Week (46.0).

Enforce fire regulations and inspect for forest fire hazards. Report forest fires and weather conditions. Relay messages about emergencies, accidents, locations of crew and personnel, and fire hazard conditions. Direct crews working on firelines during forest fires. Estimate sizes and characteristics of fires and report findings to base camps by radio or telephone. Administer regulations regarding sanitation, fire prevention, violation corrections, and related forest regulations. Extinguish smaller fires with portable extinguishers, shovels, and axes. Locate forest fires on area maps, using azimuth sighters and known landmarks. Maintain records and logbooks. Examine and inventory firefighting equipment such as axes, fire hoses, shovels, pumps, buckets, and fire extinguishers to determine amount and condition. Direct maintenance and repair of firefighting equipment or requisition new equipment. Restrict public access and recreational use of forest lands during critical fire seasons. Patrol assigned areas, looking for forest fires, hazardous conditions, and weather phenomena. Compile and report meteorological data, such as temperature, relative humidity, wind direction and velocity, and types of cloud formations. Inspect campsites to ensure that campers are in compliance with forest-use regulations. Inspect forest tracts and logging areas for fire hazards such as accumulated wastes or mishandling of combustibles and recommend appropriate fire prevention measures.

Personality Type: Realistic. Realistic occupations frequently involve work activities that include practical, hands-on problems and solutions. They often deal with plants; animals; and real-world materials such as wood, tools, and machinery. Many of the occupations require working outside and do not involve a lot of paperwork or working closely with others.

GOE—Interest Area: 07. Government and Public Administration. **Work Group:** 07.03. Regulations Enforcement. **Other Jobs in This Work Group:** Agricultural Inspectors; Aviation Inspectors; Compliance Officers, Except Agriculture, Construction, Health and Safety, and Transportation; Construction and Building Inspectors; Environmental Compliance Inspectors; Equal Opportunity Representatives and Officers; Financial Examiners; Fire Inspectors; Fish and Game Wardens; Freight and Cargo Inspectors; Government Property Inspectors and Investigators; Immigration and Customs Inspectors; Licensing Examiners and Inspectors; Nuclear Monitoring Technicians; Occupational Health and Safety Specialists; Occupational Health and Safety Technicians; Tax Examiners, Collectors, and Revenue Agents; Transportation Vehicle, Equipment, and Systems Inspectors, Except Aviation.

Skills—Management of Personnel Resources: Motivating, developing, and directing people as they work, identifying the best people for the job. **Equipment Maintenance:** Performing routine maintenance on equipment and determining when and what kind of maintenance is needed. **Science:** Using scientific rules and methods to solve problems. **Repairing:** Repairing machines or systems, using the needed tools. **Service Orientation:** Actively looking for ways to help people. **Technology Design:** Generating or adapting equipment and technology to serve user needs.

Education and Training Program: Fire Science/Firefighting. **Related Knowledge/Courses: Geography:** Principles and methods for describing the features of land, sea, and air masses, including their physical characteristics, locations, interrelationships, and distribution of plant, animal, and human life. **Biology:** Plant and animal organisms, their tissues, cells, functions, interdependencies, and interactions with each other and the environment. **Law and Government:** Laws, legal codes, court procedures, precedents, government regulations, executive orders, agency rules, and the democratic political process. **Telecommunications:** Transmission, broadcasting, switching, control, and operation of telecommunications systems. **Public Safety and Security:** Relevant equipment, policies, procedures, and strategies to promote effective local, state, or national security operations for the protection of people, data, property, and institutions. **Education and Training:** Principles and methods for curriculum and training design, teaching and instruction for individuals and groups, and the measurement of training effects.

Work Environment: More often outdoors than indoors; very hot or cold.

Funeral Attendants

- Education/Training Required: Short-term on-the-job training
- Annual Earnings: $20,350
- Growth: 14.3%
- Annual Job Openings: 6,034
- Self-Employed: 0.6%
- Part-Time: 59.3%

Level of Stress Tolerance Needed: 71.0 (out of 100)

Most Stressful Aspects: None greater than average.

Least Stressful Aspects: Pace Determined by Speed of Equipment (6.7); Deal With Physically Aggressive People (10.5); Duration of Typical Work Week (31.0); Level of Competition (32.0).

Perform variety of tasks during funeral, such as placing casket in parlor or chapel prior to service, arranging floral offerings or lights around casket, directing or escorting mourners, closing casket, and issuing and storing funeral equipment. Perform various tasks during funerals to assist funeral directors and to ensure that services run smoothly and as planned. Greet people at the funeral home. Offer assistance to mourners as they enter or exit limousines. Close caskets at appropriate point in services. Transfer the deceased to funeral homes. Obtain burial permits and register deaths. Direct or escort mourners to parlors or chapels in which wakes or funerals are being held. Place caskets in parlors or chapels prior to wakes or funerals. Clean and drive funeral vehicles such as cars or hearses in funeral processions. Carry flowers to hearses or limousines for transportation to places of interment. Clean funeral parlors and chapels. Arrange floral offerings or lights around caskets. Provide advice to mourners on how to make charitable donations in honor of the deceased. Perform general maintenance duties for funeral homes. Issue and store funeral equipment. Assist with cremations and with the processing and packaging of cremated remains. Act as pallbearers.

Personality Type: Social. Social occupations frequently involve working with, communicating with, and teaching people. These occupations often involve helping or providing service to others.

GOE—Interest Area: 10. Human Service. **Work Group:** 10.03. Child/Personal Care and Services. **Other Jobs in This Work Group:** Child Care Workers; Nannies; Personal and Home Care Aides.

Skills—Social Perceptiveness: Being aware of others' reactions and understanding why they react as they do. **Service Orientation:** Actively looking for ways to help people.

Education and Training Program: Funeral Service and Mortuary Science, General. **Related Knowledge/Courses: Philosophy and Theology:** Different philosophical systems and religions. This includes their basic principles, values, ethics, ways of thinking, customs, practices, and their impact on human culture. **Transportation:** Principles and methods for moving people or goods by air, rail, sea, or road, including the relative costs and benefits. **Customer and Personal Service:** Principles and processes for providing customer and personal services. This includes customer needs assessment, meeting quality standards for services, and evaluation of customer satisfaction. **Psychology:** Human behavior and performance; individual differences in ability, personality, and interests; learning and motivation; psychological research methods; and the assessment and treatment of behavioral and affective disorders. **Law and Government:** Laws, legal codes, court procedures, precedents, government regulations, executive orders, agency rules, and the democratic political process. **Clerical Practices:** Administrative and clerical procedures and systems such as word processing, managing files and records, stenography and transcription, designing forms, and other office procedures and terminology.

Work Environment: More often indoors than outdoors; standing.

Gas Compressor and Gas Pumping Station Operators

- Education/Training Required: Moderate-term on-the-job training
- Annual Earnings: $45,400
- Growth: –17.5%
- Annual Job Openings: 704
- Self-Employed: 3.5%
- Part-Time: 29.5%

Level of Stress Tolerance Needed: 75.0 (out of 100)

Most Stressful Aspects: Importance of Being Exact or Accurate (80.3); Duration of Typical Work Week (74.0); Consequence of Error (66.5); Pace Determined by Speed of Equipment (61.8).

Least Stressful Aspects: Deal With Physically Aggressive People (15.3); Deal With Unpleasant or Angry People (34.0); Frequency of Conflict Situations (43.3); Impact of Decisions on Coworkers or Company Results (61.0).

Operate steam, gas, electric motor, or internal combustion engine–driven compressors. Transmit, compress, or recover gases such as butane, nitrogen, hydrogen, and natural gas. Turn knobs or switches to regulate pressures. Take samples of gases and conduct chemical tests to determine gas quality and sulfur or moisture content or send samples to laboratories for analysis. Submit daily reports on facility operations. Record instrument readings and operational changes in operating logs. Maintain each station by performing general housekeeping duties such as painting, washing, and cleaning. Clean, lubricate, and adjust equipment and replace filters and gaskets, using hand tools. Respond to problems by adjusting control room equipment or instructing other personnel to adjust equipment at problem locations or in other control areas. Read gas meters and maintain records of the amounts of gas received and dispensed from holders. Operate power-driven pumps that transfer liquids, semi-liquids, gases, or powdered materials. Move controls and turn valves to start compressor engines, pumps, and auxiliary equipment. Monitor meters and pressure gauges to determine consumption rate variations, temperatures, and pressures. Adjust valves and equipment to obtain specified performance. Connect pipelines between pumps and containers that are being filled or emptied.

Personality Type: Realistic. Realistic occupations frequently involve work activities that include practical, hands-on problems and solutions. They often deal with plants; animals; and real-world materials such as wood, tools, and machinery. Many of the occupations require working outside and do not involve a lot of paperwork or working closely with others.

GOE—Interest Area: 13. Manufacturing. **Work Group:** 13.16. Utility Operation and Energy Distribution. **Other Jobs in This Work Group:** Chemical Plant and System Operators; Gas Plant Operators; Nuclear Power Reactor Operators; Petroleum Pump System Operators, Refinery Operators, and Gaugers; Power Distributors and Dispatchers; Power Plant Operators; Ship Engineers; Stationary Engineers and Boiler Operators; Water and Liquid Waste Treatment Plant and System Operators.

Skills—Operation Monitoring: Watching gauges, dials, or other indicators to make sure a machine is working properly. **Equipment Maintenance:** Performing routine maintenance on equipment and determining when and what kind of maintenance is needed. **Operation and Control:** Controlling operations of equipment or systems. **Repairing:** Repairing machines or systems, using the needed tools. **Installation:** Installing equipment, machines, wiring, or programs to meet specifications. **Quality Control Analysis:** Conducting tests and inspections of products, services, or processes to evaluate quality or performance.

Education and Training Programs: No related CIP programs; this job is learned through informal moderate-term on-the-job training. **Related Knowledge/Courses: Mechanical Devices:** Machines and tools, including their designs, uses, repair, and maintenance. **Physics:** Physical principles, laws, their interrelationships, and applications to understanding fluid, material, and atmospheric dynamics, and mechanical, electrical, atomic, and subatomic structures and processes. **Public Safety and Security:** Relevant equipment, policies, procedures, and strategies to promote effective local, state, or national security operations for the protection of people, data, property, and institutions. **Design:** Design techniques, tools, and principles involved in production of precision technical plans, blueprints, drawings, and models. **Production and Processing:** Raw materials, production processes, quality control, costs, and other techniques for maximizing the effective manufacture and distribution of goods. **Engineering and Technology:** The practical application of engineering science and technology. This includes applying principles, techniques, procedures, and equipment to the design and production of various goods and services.

Work Environment: More often outdoors than indoors; noisy; very hot or cold; contaminants; hazardous conditions.

Geographers

- Education/Training Required: Master's degree
- Annual Earnings: $62,990
- Growth: 6.1%
- Annual Job Openings: 75
- Self-Employed: 5.3%
- Part-Time: 25.0%

Level of Stress Tolerance Needed: 63.5 (out of 100)

Most Stressful Aspects: Duration of Typical Work Week (83.5); Importance of Being Exact or Accurate (81.3); Level of Competition (59.5).

Least Stressful Aspects: Deal With Physically Aggressive People (4.2); Pace Determined by Speed of Equipment (6.3); Deal With Unpleasant or Angry People (32.2); Frequency of Conflict Situations (36.5).

Study nature and use of areas of earth's surface, relating and interpreting interactions of physical and cultural phenomena. Conduct research on physical aspects of a region, including land forms, climates, soils, plants, and animals, and conduct research on the spatial implications of human activities within a given area, including social characteristics, economic activities, and political organization, as well as researching interdependence between regions at scales ranging from local to global. Create and modify maps, graphs, or diagrams, using geographical information software and related equipment and principles of cartography such as coordinate

systems, longitude, latitude, elevation, topography, and map scales. Write and present reports of research findings. Develop, operate, and maintain geographical information (GIS) computer systems, including hardware, software, plotters, digitizers, printers, and video cameras. Locate and obtain existing geographic information databases. Analyze geographic distributions of physical and cultural phenomena on local, regional, continental, or global scales. Teach geography. Gather and compile geographic data from sources including censuses, field observations, satellite imagery, aerial photographs, and existing maps. Conduct fieldwork at outdoor sites. Study the economic, political, and cultural characteristics of a specific region's population. Provide consulting services in fields including resource development and management, business location and market area analysis, environmental hazards, regional cultural history, and urban social planning. Collect data on physical characteristics of specified areas, such as geological formations, climates, and vegetation, using surveying or meteorological equipment. Provide geographical information systems support to the private and public sectors.

Personality Type: Investigative. Investigative occupations frequently involve working with ideas and require an extensive amount of thinking. These occupations can involve searching for facts and figuring out problems mentally.

GOE—Interest Area: 15. Scientific Research, Engineering, and Mathematics. **Work Group:** 15.02. Physical Sciences. **Other Jobs in This Work Group:** Astronomers; Atmospheric and Space Scientists; Chemists; Geoscientists, Except Hydrologists and Geographers; Hydrologists; Materials Scientists; Physicists.

Skills—Programming: Writing computer programs for various purposes. **Science:** Using scientific rules and methods to solve problems. **Complex Problem Solving:** Identifying complex problems and reviewing related information to develop and evaluate options and implement solutions. **Writing:** Communicating effectively in writing as appropriate for the needs of the audience. **Management of Financial Resources:** Determining how money will be spent to get the work done, and accounting for these expenditures. **Reading Comprehension:** Understanding written sentences and paragraphs in work-related documents.

Education and Training Program: Geography. **Related Knowledge/Courses: Geography:** Principles and methods for describing the features of land, sea, and air masses, including their physical characteristics, locations, interrelationships, and distribution of plant, animal, and human life. **Sociology and Anthropology:** Group behavior and dynamics, societal trends and influences, human migrations, ethnicity, cultures and their history and origins. **History and Archeology:** Historical events and their causes, indicators, and effects on civilizations and cultures. **Biology:** Plant and animal organisms, their tissues, cells, functions, interdependencies, and interactions with each other and the environment. **Education and Training:** Principles and methods for curriculum and training design, teaching and instruction for individuals and groups, and the measurement of training effects. **Philosophy and Theology:** Different philosophical systems and religions. This includes their basic principles, values, ethics, ways of thinking, customs, practices, and their impact on human culture.

Work Environment: Indoors; sitting.

Geological Sample Test Technicians

- ◎ Education/Training Required: Associate degree
- ◎ Annual Earnings: $46,160
- ◎ Growth: 8.6%
- ◎ Annual Job Openings: 1,895
- ◎ Self-Employed: 0.0%
- ◎ Part-Time: 25.2%

Our sources did not provide separate job openings data for this occupation. The job openings listed here are shared with Geophysical Data Technicians.

Level of Stress Tolerance Needed: 68.0 (out of 100)

Most Stressful Aspects: Importance of Being Exact or Accurate (82.5); Duration of Typical Work Week (82.0); Impact of Decisions on Co-workers or Company Results (80.8); Consequence of Error (69.2).

Least Stressful Aspects: Deal With Physically Aggressive People (6.5); Frequency of Conflict Situations (32.2); Level of Competition (32.7); Deal With Unpleasant or Angry People (50.0).

Test and analyze geological samples, crude oil, or petroleum products to detect presence of petroleum, gas, or mineral deposits indicating potential for exploration and production or to determine physical and chemical properties to ensure that products meet quality standards. Test and analyze samples in order to determine their content and characteristics, using laboratory apparatus and testing equipment. Collect and prepare solid and fluid samples for analysis. Assemble, operate, and maintain field and laboratory testing, measuring, and mechanical equipment, working as part of a crew when required. Compile and record testing and operational data for review and further analysis. Adjust and repair testing, electrical, and mechanical equipment and devices. Supervise well exploration and drilling activities and well completions. Inspect engines for wear and defective parts, using equipment and measuring devices. Prepare notes, sketches, geological maps, and cross sections. Participate in geological, geophysical, geochemical, hydrographic, or oceanographic surveys; prospecting field trips; exploratory drilling; well logging; or underground mine survey programs. Plot information from aerial photographs, well logs, section descriptions, and other databases. Assess the environmental impacts of development projects on subsurface materials. Collaborate with hydrogeologists to evaluate groundwater and well circulation. Prepare, transcribe, and/or analyze seismic, gravimetric, well log, or other geophysical and survey data. Participate in the evaluation of possible mining locations.

Personality Type: Realistic. Realistic occupations frequently involve work activities that include practical, hands-on problems and solutions. They often deal with plants; animals; and real-world materials such as wood, tools, and machinery. Many of the occupations require working outside and do not involve a lot of paperwork or working closely with others.

GOE—Interest Area: 01. Agriculture and Natural Resources. **Work Group:** 01.03. Resource Technologies for Plants, Animals, and the Environment. **Other Jobs in This Work Group:** Agricultural and Food Science Technicians; Agricultural Technicians; Environmental Science and Protection Technicians, Including Health; Food Science Technicians; Food Scientists and Technologists; Geological and Petroleum Technicians; Geophysical Data Technicians.

Skills—**Science:** Using scientific rules and methods to solve problems. **Operation Monitoring:** Watching gauges, dials, or other indicators to make sure a machine is working properly. **Equipment Maintenance:** Performing routine maintenance on equipment and determining when and what kind of maintenance is needed. **Quality Control Analysis:** Conducting tests and inspections of products, services, or processes to evaluate quality or performance. **Mathematics:** Using mathematics to solve problems. **Operation and Control:** Controlling operations of equipment or systems.

Education and Training Program: Petroleum Technology/Technician Training. **Related Knowledge/Courses: Chemistry:** The chemical composition, structure, and properties of substances and of the chemical processes and transformations that they undergo. This includes uses of chemicals, their danger signs, production techniques, and disposal methods. **Geography:** Principles and methods for describing the features of land, sea, and air masses, including their physical characteristics, locations, interrelationships, and distribution of plant, animal, and human life. **Physics:** Physical principles, laws, their interrelationships, and applications to understanding fluid, material, and atmospheric dynamics, and mechanical, electrical, atomic, and subatomic structures and processes. **Mechanical Devices:** Machines and tools, including their designs, uses, repair, and maintenance. **Mathematics:** Arithmetic, algebra, geometry, calculus, statistics, and their applications. **Computers and Electronics:** Circuit boards, processors, chips, electronic equipment, and computer hardware and software, including applications and programming.

Work Environment: Indoors; noisy; contaminants; more often standing than sitting; using hands on objects, tools, or controls.

Geophysical Data Technicians

- Education/Training Required: Associate degree
- Annual Earnings: $46,160
- Growth: 8.6%
- Annual Job Openings: 1,895
- Self-Employed: 0.0%
- Part-Time: 25.2%

Our sources did not provide separate job openings data for this occupation. The job openings listed here are shared with Geological Sample Test Technicians.

Level of Stress Tolerance Needed: 67.5 (out of 100)

Most Stressful Aspects: Importance of Being Exact or Accurate (86.0); Duration of Typical Work Week (71.0); Impact of Decisions on Co-workers or Company Results (70.0); Time Pressure (69.7).

Least Stressful Aspects: Deal With Physically Aggressive People (14.8); Pace Determined by Speed of Equipment (16.7); Deal With Unpleasant or Angry People (41.3); Frequency of Conflict Situations (48.0).

Measure, record, and evaluate geological data, using sonic, electronic, electrical, seismic, or gravity-measuring instruments to prospect for oil or gas. May collect and evaluate core samples and cuttings. Prepare notes, sketches, geological maps, and cross-sections. Read and study reports to compile information and data for geological and geophysical prospecting. Interview individuals and research public databases to obtain information. Assemble, maintain, and distribute information for library or record systems. Operate and adjust equipment and apparatus used to obtain geological data. Plan and direct activities of workers who operate equipment to collect data. Set up or direct setup of instruments used to collect geological data. Record readings to compile data used in prospecting for oil or gas. Supervise oil, water, and gas well-drilling activities. Collect samples and cuttings, using equipment and hand tools. Develop and print photographic recordings of information, using equipment. Measure geological characteristics used in prospecting for oil or gas, using measuring instruments. Evaluate and interpret core samples and cuttings and other geological data used in prospecting for oil or gas. Diagnose and repair malfunctioning instruments and equipment, using manufacturers' manuals and hand tools. Prepare and attach packing instructions to shipping containers. Develop and design packing materials and handling procedures for shipping of objects.

Personality Type: Realistic. Realistic occupations frequently involve work activities that include practical, hands-on problems and solutions. They often deal with plants; animals; and real-world materials such as wood, tools, and machinery. Many of the occupations require working outside and do not involve a lot of paperwork or working closely with others.

GOE—Interest Area: 01. Agriculture and Natural Resources. **Work Group:** 01.03. Resource Technologies for Plants, Animals, and the Environment. **Other Jobs in This Work Group:** Agricultural and Food Science Technicians; Agricultural Technicians; Environmental Science and Protection Technicians, Including Health; Food Science Technicians; Food Scientists and Technologists; Geological and Petroleum Technicians; Geological Sample Test Technicians.

Skills—Science: Using scientific rules and methods to solve problems. **Mathematics:** Using mathematics to solve problems. **Technology Design:** Generating or adapting equipment and technology to serve user needs. **Operations Analysis:** Analyzing needs and product requirements to create a design. **Operation Monitoring:** Watching gauges, dials, or other indicators to make sure a machine is working properly. **Persuasion:** Persuading others to change their minds or behavior.

Education and Training Program: Petroleum Technology/Technician Training. **Related Knowledge/Courses: Geography:** Principles and methods for describing the features of land, sea, and air masses, including their physical characteristics, locations, interrelationships, and distribution of plant, animal, and human life. **Engineering and Technology:** The practical application of engineering science and technology. This includes applying principles, techniques, procedures, and equipment to the design and production of various goods and services. **Physics:** Physical principles, laws, their interrelationships, and applications to understanding fluid, material, and atmospheric dynamics, and mechanical, electrical, atomic, and subatomic structures and processes. **Computers and Electronics:** Circuit boards, processors, chips, electronic equipment, and computer hardware and software, including applications and programming. **Mathematics:** Arithmetic, algebra, geometry, calculus, statistics, and their applications. **Chemistry:** The chemical composition, structure, and properties of substances and of the chemical processes and transformations that they undergo. This includes uses of chemicals, their danger signs, production techniques, and disposal methods.

Work Environment: Indoors; sitting.

Glass Blowers, Molders, Benders, and Finishers

- ◎ Education/Training Required: Moderate-term on-the-job training
- ◎ Annual Earnings: $25,010
- ◎ Growth: 1.3%
- ◎ Annual Job Openings: 5,788
- ◎ Self-Employed: 24.2%
- ◎ Part-Time: 19.0%

Our sources did not provide separate job openings data for this occupation. The job openings listed here are shared with Molding and Casting Workers; Potters, Manufacturing; and Stone Cutters and Carvers, Manufacturing.

Level of Stress Tolerance Needed: 76.3 (out of 100)

Most Stressful Aspects: Importance of Being Exact or Accurate (86.7); Pace Determined by Speed of Equipment (63.7); Duration of Typical Work Week (59.5); Consequence of Error (49.0).

Least Stressful Aspects: Deal With Physically Aggressive People (2.8); Deal With Unpleasant or Angry People (23.5); Frequency of Conflict Situations (30.3); Level of Competition (45.2).

Shape molten glass according to patterns. Place electrodes in tube ends and heat them with glass burners to fuse them into place. Inspect, weigh, and measure products to verify conformance to specifications, using instruments such as micrometers, calipers, magnifiers, and rulers. Heat glass to pliable stage, using gas flames or ovens and rotating glass to heat it uniformly. Place rubber hoses on ends of tubing and charge tubing with gas. Design and create glass objects, using blowpipes and artisans' hand tools and equipment. Repair broken scrolls by replacing them with new sections of tubing. Set up and adjust machine-press stroke lengths and pressures and regulate oven temperatures according to glass types to be processed. Shape, bend, or join sections of glass, using paddles, pressing and flattening hand tools, or cork. Spray or swab molds with oil solutions to prevent adhesion of glass. Strike necks of finished articles to separate articles from blowpipes. Superimpose bent tubing on asbestos patterns to ensure accuracy. Place glass into dies or molds of presses and control presses to form products such as glassware components or optical blanks. Operate electric kilns that heat glass sheets and molds to the shape and curve of metal jigs. Determine types and quantities of glass required to fabricate products. Dip ends of blowpipes into molten glass to collect gobs on pipe heads or cut gobs from molten glass, using shears. Record manufacturing information such as quantities, sizes, and types of goods produced. Operate and maintain finishing machines to grind, drill, sand, bevel, decorate, wash, or polish glass or glass products. Develop sketches of glass products into blueprint specifications, applying knowledge of glass technology and glass blowing. Blow tubing into specified shapes to prevent glass from collapsing, using compressed air or own breath, or blow and rotate gathers in molds or on boards to obtain final shapes. Cut lengths of tubing to specified sizes, using files or cutting wheels.

Personality Type: Realistic. Realistic occupations frequently involve work activities that include practical, hands-on problems and solutions. They often deal with plants; animals; and real-world materials such as wood, tools, and machinery. Many of the occupations require working outside and do not involve a lot of paperwork or working closely with others.

GOE—Interest Area: 13. Manufacturing. **Work Group:** 13.09. Hands-On Work, Assorted

Materials. **Other Jobs in This Work Group:** Coil Winders, Tapers, and Finishers; Cutters and Trimmers, Hand; Fabric and Apparel Patternmakers; Grinding and Polishing Workers, Hand; Molding and Casting Workers; Painters, Transportation Equipment; Painting, Coating, and Decorating Workers; Sewers, Hand.

Skills—Operation Monitoring: Watching gauges, dials, or other indicators to make sure a machine is working properly. **Repairing:** Repairing machines or systems, using the needed tools. **Equipment Maintenance:** Performing routine maintenance on equipment and determining when and what kind of maintenance is needed. **Installation:** Installing equipment, machines, wiring, or programs to meet specifications. **Quality Control Analysis:** Conducting tests and inspections of products, services, or processes to evaluate quality or performance. **Troubleshooting:** Determining causes of operating errors and deciding what to do about them.

Education and Training Program: Crafts/Craft Design, Folk Art and Artisanry. **Related Knowledge/Courses: Production and Processing:** Raw materials, production processes, quality control, costs, and other techniques for maximizing the effective manufacture and distribution of goods. **Mechanical Devices:** Machines and tools, including their designs, uses, repair, and maintenance. **Design:** Design techniques, tools, and principles involved in production of precision technical plans, blueprints, drawings, and models. **Chemistry:** The chemical composition, structure, and properties of substances and of the chemical processes and transformations that they undergo. This includes uses of chemicals, their danger signs, production techniques, and disposal methods. **Physics:** Physical principles, laws, their interrelationships, and applications to understanding fluid, material, and atmospheric dynamics, and

mechanical, electrical, atomic, and subatomic structures and processes. **Engineering and Technology:** The practical application of engineering science and technology. This includes applying principles, techniques, procedures, and equipment to the design and production of various goods and services.

Work Environment: Noisy; very hot or cold; contaminants; minor burns, cuts, bites, or stings; standing; using hands on objects, tools, or controls.

Grinding and Polishing Workers, Hand

- Education/Training Required: Moderate-term on-the-job training
- Annual Earnings: $23,880
- Growth: –7.1%
- Annual Job Openings: 5,789
- Self-Employed: 0.9%
- Part-Time: 15.8%

Level of Stress Tolerance Needed: 57.2 (out of 100)

Most Stressful Aspects: Importance of Being Exact or Accurate (82.7); Time Pressure (70.2); Pace Determined by Speed of Equipment (62.5).

Least Stressful Aspects: Deal With Physically Aggressive People (8.0); Frequency of Conflict Situations (19.7); Level of Competition (32.5); Consequence of Error (34.0).

Grind, sand, or polish, using hand tools or hand-held power tools, a variety of metal, wood, stone, clay, plastic, or glass objects. Clean brass particles from files by drawing file cards through file grooves. Wash grit from stone, using hoses. Verify quality of finished workpieces by inspecting them, comparing them to templates, measuring their dimensions, or testing them in working machinery. Transfer equipment, objects, or parts to specified work areas, using moving devices. Spread emery powder or other polishing compounds on stone or wet stone surfaces, using hoses; then guide buffing wheels over stone to polish surfaces. Sharpen abrasive grinding tools, using machines and hand tools. Repair and maintain equipment, objects, or parts, using hand tools. Record product and processing data on specified forms. Fill cracks or imperfections in marble with wax that matches the stone color. Apply solutions and chemicals to equipment, objects, or parts, using hand tools. Study blueprints or layouts to determine how to lay out workpieces or saw out templates. Select files or other abrasives according to materials, sizes and shapes of workpieces, amount of stock to be removed, finishes specified, and steps in finishing processes. Mark defects such as knotholes, cracks, and splits for repair. Grind, sand, clean, or polish objects or parts to correct defects or to prepare surfaces for further finishing, using hand tools and power tools. Move controls to adjust, start, or stop equipment during grinding and polishing processes. Measure and mark equipment, objects, or parts to ensure grinding and polishing standards are met. Load and adjust workpieces onto equipment or work tables, using hand tools. Remove completed workpieces from equipment or work tables, using hand tools, and place workpieces in containers. File grooved, contoured, and irregular surfaces of metal objects, such as metalworking dies and machine parts, to conform to templates, other parts, layouts, or blueprint specifications. Trim, scrape, or deburr objects or parts, using chisels, scrapers, and other hand tools and equipment.

Personality Type: Realistic. Realistic occupations frequently involve work activities that include practical, hands-on problems and solutions. They often deal with plants; animals; and real-world materials such as wood, tools, and machinery. Many of the occupations require working outside and do not involve a lot of paperwork or working closely with others.

GOE—Interest Area: 13. Manufacturing. **Work Group:** 13.09. Hands-On Work, Assorted Materials. **Other Jobs in This Work Group:** Coil Winders, Tapers, and Finishers; Cutters and Trimmers, Hand; Fabric and Apparel Patternmakers; Glass Blowers, Molders, Benders, and Finishers; Molding and Casting Workers; Painters, Transportation Equipment; Painting, Coating, and Decorating Workers; Sewers, Hand.

Skills—Repairing: Repairing machines or systems, using the needed tools. **Installation:** Installing equipment, machines, wiring, or programs to meet specifications. **Equipment Maintenance:** Performing routine maintenance on equipment and determining when and what kind of maintenance is needed. **Management of Material Resources:** Obtaining and seeing to the appropriate use of equipment, facilities, and materials needed to do certain work. **Equipment Selection:** Determining the kind of tools and equipment needed to do a job. **Management of Financial Resources:** Determining how money will be spent to get the work done, and accounting for these expenditures.

Education and Training Programs: No related CIP programs; this job is learned through informal moderate-term on-the-job training. **Related Knowledge/Courses: Production and Processing:** Raw materials, production processes, quality control, costs, and other techniques for maximizing the effective manufacture and distribution of goods. **Transportation:** Principles and methods for moving people or goods by air, rail, sea, or road, including the relative costs and benefits.

Work Environment: Noisy; contaminants; hazardous equipment; standing; using hands on objects, tools, or controls; repetitive motions.

Hazardous Materials Removal Workers

- Education/Training Required: Moderate-term on-the-job training
- Annual Earnings: $35,450
- Growth: 11.2%
- Annual Job Openings: 1,933
- Self-Employed: 1.6%
- Part-Time: 16.7%

Level of Stress Tolerance Needed: 74.5 (out of 100)

Most Stressful Aspects: Duration of Typical Work Week (85.0); Time Pressure (84.7); Impact of Decisions on Co-workers or Company Results (71.2); Level of Competition (62.3).

Least Stressful Aspects: Deal With Physically Aggressive People (11.8); Consequence of Error (37.5); Frequency of Conflict Situations (45.7); Deal With Unpleasant or Angry People (51.7).

Identify, remove, pack, transport, or dispose of hazardous materials, including asbestos, lead-based paint, waste oil, fuel, transmission fluid, radioactive materials, contaminated soil, and so on. Specialized training and certification in hazardous materials handling or a confined entry permit are generally required. May operate earth-moving equipment or trucks. Follow prescribed safety procedures and comply with federal laws regulating waste-disposal methods. Record numbers of containers stored at disposal sites and specify amounts and types of equipment and waste disposed. Drive trucks or other heavy equipment to convey contaminated waste to designated sea or ground locations. Operate machines and equipment to remove, package, store, or transport loads of waste materials. Load and unload materials into containers and onto trucks, using hoists or forklifts. Clean contaminated equipment or areas for reuse, using detergents and solvents, sandblasters, filter pumps, and steam cleaners. Construct scaffolding or build containment areas before beginning abatement or decontamination work. Remove asbestos or lead from surfaces, using hand and power tools such as scrapers, vacuums, and high-pressure sprayers. Unload baskets of irradiated elements onto packaging machines that automatically insert fuel elements into canisters and secure lids. Apply chemical compounds to lead-based paint, allow compounds to dry; then scrape the hazardous material into containers for removal or storage. Identify asbestos, lead, or other hazardous materials that need to be removed, using monitoring devices. Pull tram cars along underwater tracks and position cars to receive irradiated fuel elements; then pull loaded cars to mechanisms that automatically unload elements onto underwater tables. Package, store, and move irradiated fuel elements in the underwater storage basin of a nuclear reactor plant, using machines and equipment. Organize and track the locations of hazardous items in landfills. Operate cranes to move and load baskets, casks, and canisters. Manipulate handgrips of mechanical arms to place irradiated fuel elements into baskets. Mix and pour concrete into forms to encase waste material for disposal.

Personality Type: Realistic. Realistic occupations frequently involve work activities that include practical, hands-on problems and solutions. They often deal with plants; animals; and real-world materials such as wood, tools, and machinery. Many of the occupations require working outside and do not involve a lot of paperwork or working closely with others.

GOE—Interest Area: 02. Architecture and Construction. **Work Group:** 02.04. Construction Crafts. **Other Jobs in This Work Group:** Boilermakers; Brickmasons and Blockmasons; Carpet Installers; Cement Masons and Concrete Finishers; Commercial Divers; Construction Carpenters; Crane and Tower Operators; Drywall and Ceiling Tile Installers; Electricians; Fence Erectors; Floor Layers, Except Carpet, Wood, and Hard Tiles; Floor Sanders and Finishers; Glaziers; Insulation Workers, Floor, Ceiling, and Wall; Insulation Workers, Mechanical; Manufactured Building and Mobile Home Installers; Operating Engineers and Other Construction Equipment Operators; Painters, Construction and Maintenance; Paperhangers; Paving, Surfacing, and Tamping Equipment Operators; Pile-Driver Operators; Pipe Fitters and Steamfitters; Pipelayers; Plasterers and Stucco Masons; Plumbers; Plumbers, Pipefitters, and Steamfitters; Rail-Track Laying and Maintenance Equipment Operators; Refractory Materials Repairers, Except Brickmasons; Reinforcing Iron and Rebar Workers; Riggers; Roofers; Rough Carpenters; Security and Fire Alarm Systems Installers; Segmental Pavers; Sheet Metal Workers; Stone Cutters and Carvers, Manufacturing; Stonemasons; Structural Iron and Steel Workers; Tapers; Terrazzo Workers and Finishers; Tile and Marble Setters.

Skills—Operation Monitoring: Watching gauges, dials, or other indicators to make sure a machine is working properly. **Equipment Maintenance:** Performing routine maintenance on equipment and determining when and what kind of maintenance is needed. **Repairing:** Repairing machines or systems, using the needed tools. **Operation and Control:** Controlling operations of equipment or systems.

Troubleshooting: Determining causes of operating errors and deciding what to do about them. **Science:** Using scientific rules and methods to solve problems.

Education and Training Programs: Construction Trades, Other; Hazardous Materials Management and Waste Technology/Technician Training; Mechanic and Repair Technologies/Technician Training, Other. **Related Knowledge/Courses: Chemistry:** The chemical composition, structure, and properties of substances and of the chemical processes and transformations that they undergo. This includes uses of chemicals, their danger signs, production techniques, and disposal methods. **Mechanical Devices:** Machines and tools, including their designs, uses, repair, and maintenance. **Building and Construction:** Materials, methods, and the tools involved in the construction or repair of houses, buildings, or other structures such as highways and roads. **Transportation:** Principles and methods for moving people or goods by air, rail, sea, or road, including the relative costs and benefits. **Physics:** Physical principles, laws, their interrelationships, and applications to understanding fluid, material, and atmospheric dynamics, and mechanical, electrical, atomic, and subatomic structures and processes. **Public Safety and Security:** Relevant equipment, policies, procedures, and strategies to promote effective local, state, or national security operations for the protection of people, data, property, and institutions.

Work Environment: Outdoors; very hot or cold; contaminants; hazardous conditions; using hands on objects, tools, or controls; repetitive motions.

Helpers—Carpenters

- ◎ Education/Training Required: Short-term on-the-job training
- ◎ Annual Earnings: $23,060
- ◎ Growth: 11.7%
- ◎ Annual Job Openings: 37,731
- ◎ Self-Employed: 3.2%
- ◎ Part-Time: 32.2%

Level of Stress Tolerance Needed: 43.0 (out of 100)

Most Stressful Aspects: Consequence of Error (73.8); Frequency of Conflict Situations (52.7); Level of Competition (46.0); Pace Determined by Speed of Equipment (41.0).

Least Stressful Aspects: Deal With Unpleasant or Angry People (52.7); Duration of Typical Work Week (54.5); Time Pressure (54.8); Impact of Decisions on Co-workers or Company Results (57.0).

Help carpenters by performing duties of lesser skill. Duties include using, supplying, or holding materials or tools and cleaning work area and equipment. Position and hold timbers, lumber, and paneling in place for fastening or cutting. Erect scaffolding, shoring, and braces. Select tools, equipment, and materials from storage and transport items to worksite. Fasten timbers or lumber with glue, screws, pegs, or nails and install hardware. Clean work areas, machines, and equipment to maintain a clean and safe jobsite. Align, straighten, plumb, and square forms for installation. Hold plumb bobs, sighting rods, and other equipment to aid in establishing reference points and lines. Cut timbers, lumber, or paneling to specified dimensions and drill holes in timbers or lumber. Smooth and sand surfaces to remove ridges, tool marks, glue, or caulking. Perform tie spacing layout; then measure, mark, drill, and cut.

Secure stakes to grids for construction of footings, nail scabs to footing forms, and vibrate and float concrete. Construct forms; then assist in raising them to the required elevation. Install handrails under the direction of a carpenter. Glue and clamp edges or joints of assembled parts. Cut and install insulating or sound-absorbing material. Cut tile or linoleum to fit and spread adhesives on flooring to install tile or linoleum. Cover surfaces with laminated-plastic covering material.

Personality Type: Realistic. Realistic occupations frequently involve work activities that include practical, hands-on problems and solutions. They often deal with plants; animals; and real-world materials such as wood, tools, and machinery. Many of the occupations require working outside and do not involve a lot of paperwork or working closely with others.

GOE—Interest Area: 02. Architecture and Construction. **Work Group:** 02.06. Construction Support/Labor. **Other Jobs in This Work Group:** Construction Laborers; Helpers—Brickmasons, Blockmasons, Stonemasons, and Tile and Marble Setters; Helpers—Electricians; Helpers—Installation, Maintenance, and Repair Workers; Helpers—Painters, Paperhangers, Plasterers, and Stucco Masons; Helpers—Pipelayers, Plumbers, Pipefitters, and Steamfitters; Helpers—Roofers; Highway Maintenance Workers; Septic Tank Servicers and Sewer Pipe Cleaners.

Skills—Installation: Installing equipment, machines, wiring, or programs to meet specifications. **Repairing:** Repairing machines or systems, using the needed tools. **Equipment Maintenance:** Performing routine maintenance on equipment and determining when and what kind of maintenance is needed. **Management of Material Resources:** Obtaining and seeing to the appropriate use of equipment, facilities, and materials needed to do certain work.

Troubleshooting: Determining causes of operating errors and deciding what to do about them. **Mathematics:** Using mathematics to solve problems.

Education and Training Program: Carpentry/Carpenter Training. **Related Knowledge/Courses: Building and Construction:** Materials, methods, and the tools involved in the construction or repair of houses, buildings, or other structures such as highways and roads. **Design:** Design techniques, tools, and principles involved in production of precision technical plans, blueprints, drawings, and models. **Engineering and Technology:** The practical application of engineering science and technology. This includes applying principles, techniques, procedures, and equipment to the design and production of various goods and services.

Work Environment: Noisy; very hot or cold; hazardous equipment; standing; walking and running; using hands on objects, tools, or controls.

Helpers—Electricians

- ◎ Education/Training Required: Short-term on-the-job training
- ◎ Annual Earnings: $23,760
- ◎ Growth: 6.8%
- ◎ Annual Job Openings: 35,109
- ◎ Self-Employed: 2.9%
- ◎ Part-Time: 32.2%

Level of Stress Tolerance Needed: 66.8 (out of 100)

Most Stressful Aspects: Importance of Being Exact or Accurate (78.5); Time Pressure (76.0); Impact of Decisions on Co-workers or Company Results (67.8); Consequence of Error (61.3).

Least Stressful Aspects: None less than average.

Help electricians by performing duties of lesser skill. Duties include using, supplying, or holding materials or tools and cleaning work area and equipment. Trace out short circuits in wiring, using test meter. Measure, cut, and bend wire and conduit, using measuring instruments and hand tools. Maintain tools, vehicles, and equipment and keep parts and supplies in order. Drill holes and pull or push wiring through openings, using hand and power tools. Perform semi-skilled and unskilled laboring duties related to the installation, maintenance, and repair of a wide variety of electrical systems and equipment. Disassemble defective electrical equipment, replace defective or worn parts, and reassemble equipment, using hand tools. Transport tools, materials, equipment, and supplies to worksite by hand; handtruck; or heavy, motorized truck. Examine electrical units for loose connections and broken insulation and tighten connections, using hand tools. Strip insulation from wire ends, using wire-stripping pliers, and attach wires to terminals for subsequent soldering. Construct controllers and panels, using power drills, drill presses, taps, saws, and punches. Thread conduit ends, connect couplings, and fabricate and secure conduit support brackets, using hand tools. String transmission lines or cables through ducts or conduits, under the ground, through equipment, or to towers. Clean work area and wash parts. Erect electrical system components and barricades and rig scaffolds, hoists, and shoring. Install copper-clad ground rods, using a manual post driver. Raise, lower, or position equipment, tools, and materials, using hoist, hand line, or block and tackle. Dig trenches or holes for installation of conduit or supports. Requisition materials, using warehouse requisition or release forms. Bolt component parts together to form tower assemblies, using hand tools. Paint a variety of objects related to electrical functions. Operate cutting torches and welding equipment while working with conduit and metal components to construct devices associated with electrical functions. Break up concrete, using air hammer, to facilitate installation, construction, or repair of equipment. Solder electrical connections, using soldering iron. Trim trees and clear undergrowth along right-of-way.

Personality Type: Realistic. Realistic occupations frequently involve work activities that include practical, hands-on problems and solutions. They often deal with plants; animals; and real-world materials such as wood, tools, and machinery. Many of the occupations require working outside and do not involve a lot of paperwork or working closely with others.

GOE—Interest Area: 02. Architecture and Construction. **Work Group:** 02.06. Construction Support/Labor. **Other Jobs in This Work Group:** Construction Laborers; Helpers—Brickmasons, Blockmasons, Stone-masons, and Tile and Marble Setters; Helpers—Carpenters; Helpers—Installation, Maintenance, and Repair Workers; Helpers—Painters, Paperhangers, Plasterers, and Stucco Masons; Helpers—Pipelayers, Plumbers, Pipe-fitters, and Steamfitters; Helpers—Roofers; Highway Maintenance Workers; Septic Tank Servicers and Sewer Pipe Cleaners.

Skills—Installation: Installing equipment, machines, wiring, or programs to meet specifications. **Troubleshooting:** Determining causes of operating errors and deciding what to do about them. **Repairing:** Repairing machines or systems, using the needed tools. **Mathematics:** Using mathematics to solve problems. **Complex Problem Solving:** Identifying complex problems and reviewing related information to develop and evaluate options and implement solutions. **Equipment Selection:** Determining the kind of tools and equipment needed to do a job.

Education and Training Program: Electrician Training. **Related Knowledge/Courses: Building and Construction:** Materials, methods, and the tools involved in the construction or repair of houses, buildings, or other structures such as highways and roads. **Mechanical Devices:** Machines and tools, including their designs, uses, repair, and maintenance. **Design:** Design techniques, tools, and principles involved in production of precision technical plans, blueprints, drawings, and models. **Engineering and Technology:** The practical application of engineering science and technology. This includes applying principles, techniques, procedures, and equipment to the design and production of various goods and services. **Mathematics:** Arithmetic, algebra, geometry, calculus, statistics, and their applications. **Public Safety and Security:** Relevant equipment, policies, procedures, and strategies to promote effective local, state, or national security operations for the protection of people, data, property, and institutions.

Work Environment: Outdoors; very hot or cold; contaminants; high places; standing; using hands on objects, tools, or controls.

Helpers—Extraction Workers

- Education/Training Required: Short-term on-the-job training
- Annual Earnings: $28,680
- Growth: –0.2%
- Annual Job Openings: 2,765
- Self-Employed: 0.0%
- Part-Time: 4.9%

Level of Stress Tolerance Needed: 60.8 (out of 100)

Most Stressful Aspects: Consequence of Error (78.8); Duration of Typical Work Week (77.5); Pace Determined by Speed of Equipment (77.0); Impact of Decisions on Co-workers or Company Results (73.5).

Least Stressful Aspects: Deal With Physically Aggressive People (7.5); Frequency of Conflict Situations (25.5); Deal With Unpleasant or Angry People (32.5); Level of Competition (44.2).

Help extraction craft workers, such as earth drillers, blasters and explosives workers, derrick operators, and mining machine operators, by performing duties of lesser skill. Duties include supplying equipment or cleaning work area. Set up and adjust equipment used to excavate geological materials. Load materials into well holes or into equipment, using hand tools. Repair and maintain automotive and drilling equipment, using hand tools. Dig trenches. Collect and examine geological matter, using hand tools and testing devices. Unload materials, devices, and machine parts, using hand tools. Signal workers to start geological material extraction or boring. Clean and prepare sites for excavation or boring. Observe and monitor equipment operation during the extraction process to detect any problems. Drive moving equipment to transport materials and parts to excavation sites. Dismantle extracting and boring equipment used for excavation, using hand tools. Clean up work areas and remove debris after extraction activities are complete. Organize materials to prepare for use. Provide assistance to extraction craft workers such as earth drillers and derrick operators.

Personality Type: Realistic. Realistic occupations frequently involve work activities that include practical, hands-on problems and solutions. They often deal with plants; animals; and real-world materials such as wood, tools, and machinery. Many of the occupations require

working outside and do not involve a lot of paperwork or working closely with others.

GOE—Interest Area: 01. Agriculture and Natural Resources. **Work Group:** 01.08. Mining and Drilling. **Other Jobs in This Work Group:** Continuous Mining Machine Operators; Derrick Operators, Oil and Gas; Earth Drillers, Except Oil and Gas; Excavating and Loading Machine and Dragline Operators; Explosives Workers, Ordnance Handling Experts, and Blasters; Loading Machine Operators, Underground Mining; Mine Cutting and Channeling Machine Operators; Rock Splitters, Quarry; Roof Bolters, Mining; Rotary Drill Operators, Oil and Gas; Roustabouts, Oil and Gas; Service Unit Operators, Oil, Gas, and Mining; Shuttle Car Operators; Wellhead Pumpers.

Skills—Equipment Maintenance: Performing routine maintenance on equipment and determining when and what kind of maintenance is needed. **Repairing:** Repairing machines or systems, using the needed tools. **Operation Monitoring:** Watching gauges, dials, or other indicators to make sure a machine is working properly.

Education and Training Programs: No related CIP programs; this job is learned through informal short-term on-the-job training. **Related Knowledge/Courses: Mechanical Devices:** Machines and tools, including their designs, uses, repair, and maintenance. **Building and Construction:** Materials, methods, and the tools involved in the construction or repair of houses, buildings, or other structures such as highways and roads. **Engineering and Technology:** The practical application of engineering science and technology. This includes applying principles, techniques, procedures, and equipment to the design and production of various goods and services. **Public Safety and Security:** Relevant equipment, policies, procedures, and strategies to promote effective local, state, or national security operations for the protection of people, data, property, and institutions. **Law and Government:** Laws, legal codes, court procedures, precedents, government regulations, executive orders, agency rules, and the democratic political process. **Production and Processing:** Raw materials, production processes, quality control, costs, and other techniques for maximizing the effective manufacture and distribution of goods.

Work Environment: Noisy; very bright or dim lighting; cramped work space, awkward positions; hazardous equipment; standing; using hands on objects, tools, or controls.

Helpers—Painters, Paperhangers, Plasterers, and Stucco Masons

- Education/Training Required: Short-term on-the-job training
- Annual Earnings: $21,330
- Growth: –0.7%
- Annual Job Openings: 7,696
- Self-Employed: 3.5%
- Part-Time: 32.2%

Level of Stress Tolerance Needed: 62.0 (out of 100)

Most Stressful Aspects: Level of Competition (49.0); Pace Determined by Speed of Equipment (36.5).

Least Stressful Aspects: Deal With Physically Aggressive People (4.5); Deal With Unpleasant or Angry People (29.8); Frequency of Conflict Situations (33.0); Consequence of Error (41.3).

Help painters, paperhangers, plasterers, or stucco masons by performing duties of lesser skill. Duties include using, supplying, or holding materials or tools and cleaning work area and equipment. Fill cracks or breaks in surfaces of plaster articles or areas with putty or epoxy compounds. Clean work areas and equipment. Apply protective coverings such as masking tape to articles or areas that could be damaged or stained by work processes. Supply or hold tools and materials. Place articles to be stripped into stripping tanks. Pour specified amounts of chemical solutions into stripping tanks. Smooth surfaces of articles to be painted, using sanding and buffing tools and equipment. Mix plaster and carry it to plasterers. Perform support duties to assist painters, paperhangers, plasterers, or masons. Remove articles such as cabinets, metal furniture, and paint containers from stripping tanks after prescribed periods of time. Erect scaffolding.

Personality Type: Realistic. Realistic occupations frequently involve work activities that include practical, hands-on problems and solutions. They often deal with plants; animals; and real-world materials such as wood, tools, and machinery. Many of the occupations require working outside and do not involve a lot of paperwork or working closely with others.

GOE—Interest Area: 02. Architecture and Construction. **Work Group:** 02.06. Construction Support/Labor. **Other Jobs in This Work Group:** Construction Laborers; Helpers—Brickmasons, Blockmasons, Stonemasons, and Tile and Marble Setters; Helpers—Carpenters; Helpers—Electricians; Helpers—Installation, Maintenance, and Repair Workers; Helpers—Pipelayers, Plumbers, Pipefitters, and Steamfitters; Helpers—Roofers; Highway Maintenance Workers; Septic Tank Servicers and Sewer Pipe Cleaners.

Skills—Equipment Maintenance: Performing routine maintenance on equipment and determining when and what kind of maintenance is needed. **Installation:** Installing equipment, machines, wiring, or programs to meet specifications. **Quality Control Analysis:** Conducting tests and inspections of products, services, or processes to evaluate quality or performance.

Education and Training Program: Painting/ Painter and Wall Coverer Training. **Related Knowledge/Course: Building and Construction:** Materials, methods, and the tools involved in the construction or repair of houses, buildings, or other structures such as highways and roads.

Work Environment: Outdoors; standing; climbing ladders, scaffolds, or poles; using hands on objects, tools, or controls; bending or twisting the body; repetitive motions.

Helpers—Pipelayers, Plumbers, Pipefitters, and Steamfitters

- Education/Training Required: Short-term on-the-job training
- Annual Earnings: $23,910
- Growth: 11.9%
- Annual Job Openings: 29,332
- Self-Employed: 2.9%
- Part-Time: 32.2%

Level of Stress Tolerance Needed: 73.0 (out of 100)

Most Stressful Aspects: Time Pressure (71.0); Duration of Typical Work Week (58.0); Consequence of Error (48.0); Pace Determined by Speed of Equipment (32.7).

Least Stressful Aspects: Deal With Physically Aggressive People (7.5); Deal With Unpleasant or Angry People (31.0); Frequency of Conflict Situations (34.2); Level of Competition (42.0).

Help plumbers, pipefitters, steamfitters, or pipelayers by performing duties of lesser skill. Duties include using, supplying, or holding materials or tools and cleaning work area and equipment. Assist plumbers by performing rough-ins, repairing and replacing fixtures, and locating and repairing leaking or broken pipes. Cut or drill holes in walls or floors to accommodate the passage of pipes. Measure, cut, thread, and assemble new pipe, placing the assembled pipe in hangers or other supports. Mount brackets and hangers on walls and ceilings to hold pipes and set sleeves or inserts to provide support for pipes. Requisition tools and equipment, select type and size of pipe, and collect and transport materials and equipment to worksite. Fit or assist in fitting valves, couplings, or assemblies to tanks, pumps, or systems, using hand tools. Assist pipe fitters in the layout, assembly, and installation of piping for air, ammonia, gas, and water systems. Excavate and grade ditches and lay and join pipe for water and sewer service. Cut pipe and lift up to fitters. Disassemble and remove damaged or worn pipe. Clean shop, work area, and machines, using solvent and rags. Install gas burners to convert furnaces from wood, coal, or oil. Immerse pipe in chemical solution to remove dirt, oil, and scale. Clean and renew steam traps. Fill pipes with sand or resin to prevent distortion and hold pipes during bending and installation.

Personality Type: Realistic. Realistic occupations frequently involve work activities that include practical, hands-on problems and solutions. They often deal with plants; animals; and real-world materials such as wood, tools, and machinery. Many of the occupations require working outside and do not involve a lot of paperwork or working closely with others.

GOE—Interest Area: 02. Architecture and Construction. **Work Group:** 02.06. Construction Support/Labor. **Other Jobs in This Work Group:** Construction Laborers; Helpers—

Brickmasons, Blockmasons, Stonemasons, and Tile and Marble Setters; Helpers—Carpenters; Helpers—Electricians; Helpers—Installation, Maintenance, and Repair Workers; Helpers—Painters, Paperhangers, Plasterers, and Stucco Masons; Helpers—Roofers; Highway Maintenance Workers; Septic Tank Servicers and Sewer Pipe Cleaners.

Skills—Installation: Installing equipment, machines, wiring, or programs to meet specifications. **Repairing:** Repairing machines or systems, using the needed tools. **Equipment Maintenance:** Performing routine maintenance on equipment and determining when and what kind of maintenance is needed. **Troubleshooting:** Determining causes of operating errors and deciding what to do about them. **Mathematics:** Using mathematics to solve problems. **Quality Control Analysis:** Conducting tests and inspections of products, services, or processes to evaluate quality or performance.

Education and Training Program: Plumbing Technology/Plumber Training. **Related Knowledge/Courses: Building and Construction:** Materials, methods, and the tools involved in the construction or repair of houses, buildings, or other structures such as highways and roads. **Mechanical Devices:** Machines and tools, including their designs, uses, repair, and maintenance. **Design:** Design techniques, tools, and principles involved in production of precision technical plans, blueprints, drawings, and models. **Public Safety and Security:** Relevant equipment, policies, procedures, and strategies to promote effective local, state, or national security operations for the protection of people, data, property, and institutions. **Engineering and Technology:** The practical application of engineering science and technology. This includes applying principles, techniques, procedures, and equipment to the design and production of various goods and services. **Law and Government:**

Laws, legal codes, court procedures, precedents, government regulations, executive orders, agency rules, and the democratic political process.

Work Environment: Outdoors; noisy; contaminants; hazardous equipment; standing; using hands on objects, tools, or controls.

Highway Maintenance Workers

- Education/Training Required: Moderate-term on-the-job training
- Annual Earnings: $31,540
- Growth: 8.9%
- Annual Job Openings: 24,774
- Self-Employed: 0.9%
- Part-Time: 14.6%

Level of Stress Tolerance Needed: 60.0 (out of 100)

Most Stressful Aspects: Consequence of Error (47.8); Pace Determined by Speed of Equipment (43.3); Deal With Physically Aggressive People (18.3).

Least Stressful Aspects: Level of Competition (26.7); Deal With Unpleasant or Angry People (37.0); Frequency of Conflict Situations (38.7); Time Pressure (45.2).

Maintain highways, municipal and rural roads, airport runways, and rights-of-way. Duties include patching broken or eroded pavement and repairing guardrails, highway markers, and snow fences. May also mow or clear brush from along road or plow snow from roadway. Flag motorists to warn them of obstacles or repair work ahead. Set out signs and cones around work areas to divert traffic. Drive trucks or tractors with adjustable attachments to sweep debris

from paved surfaces, mow grass and weeds, and remove snow and ice. Dump, spread, and tamp asphalt, using pneumatic tampers, to repair joints and patch broken pavement. Drive trucks to transport crews and equipment to worksites. Inspect, clean, and repair drainage systems, bridges, tunnels, and other structures. Haul and spread sand, gravel, and clay to fill washouts and repair road shoulders. Erect, install, or repair guardrails, road shoulders, berms, highway markers, warning signals, and highway lighting, using hand tools and power tools. Remove litter and debris from roadways, including debris from rock slides and mudslides. Clean and clear debris from culverts, catch basins, drop inlets, ditches, and other drain structures. Perform roadside landscaping work, such as clearing weeds and brush and planting and trimming trees. Paint traffic control lines and place pavement traffic messages by hand or using machines. Inspect markers to verify accurate installation. Apply poisons along roadsides and in animal burrows to eliminate unwanted roadside vegetation and rodents. Measure and mark locations for installation of markers, using tape, string, or chalk. Apply oil to road surfaces, using sprayers. Blend compounds to form adhesive mixtures used for marker installation. Place and remove snow fences used to prevent the accumulation of drifting snow on highways.

Personality Type: Realistic. Realistic occupations frequently involve work activities that include practical, hands-on problems and solutions. They often deal with plants; animals; and real-world materials such as wood, tools, and machinery. Many of the occupations require working outside and do not involve a lot of paperwork or working closely with others.

GOE—Interest Area: 02. Architecture and Construction. **Work Group:** 02.06. Construction Support/Labor. **Other Jobs in This Work Group:** Construction Laborers; Helpers—

Brickmasons, Blockmasons, Stonemasons, and Tile and Marble Setters; Helpers—Carpenters; Helpers—Electricians; Helpers—Installation, Maintenance, and Repair Workers; Helpers—Painters, Paperhangers, Plasterers, and Stucco Masons; Helpers—Pipelayers, Plumbers, Pipefitters, and Steamfitters; Helpers—Roofers; Septic Tank Servicers and Sewer Pipe Cleaners.

Skills—Equipment Maintenance: Performing routine maintenance on equipment and determining when and what kind of maintenance is needed. **Repairing:** Repairing machines or systems, using the needed tools. **Installation:** Installing equipment, machines, wiring, or programs to meet specifications. **Operation and Control:** Controlling operations of equipment or systems. **Management of Material Resources:** Obtaining and seeing to the appropriate use of equipment, facilities, and materials needed to do certain work. **Troubleshooting:** Determining causes of operating errors and deciding what to do about them.

Education and Training Program: Construction/Heavy Equipment/Earthmoving Equipment Operation. **Related Knowledge/Courses: Building and Construction:** Materials, methods, and the tools involved in the construction or repair of houses, buildings, or other structures such as highways and roads. **Transportation:** Principles and methods for moving people or goods by air, rail, sea, or road, including the relative costs and benefits. **Mechanical Devices:** Machines and tools, including their designs, uses, repair, and maintenance. **Public Safety and Security:** Relevant equipment, policies, procedures, and strategies to promote effective local, state, or national security operations for the protection of people, data, property, and institutions. **Customer and Personal Service:** Principles and processes for providing customer and personal services. This includes customer needs assessment, meeting quality standards for services, and evaluation of customer satisfaction. **Geography:** Principles and methods for describing the features of land, sea, and air masses, including their physical characteristics, locations, interrelationships, and distribution of plant, animal, and human life.

Work Environment: Outdoors; noisy; very hot or cold; contaminants; hazardous equipment; using hands on objects, tools, or controls.

Home Appliance Repairers

- ◉ Education/Training Required: Long-term on-the-job training
- ◉ Annual Earnings: $33,860
- ◉ Growth: 1.5%
- ◉ Annual Job Openings: 4,243
- ◉ Self-Employed: 26.7%
- ◉ Part-Time: 17.5%

Level of Stress Tolerance Needed: 73.5 (out of 100)

Most Stressful Aspects: Impact of Decisions on Co-workers or Company Results (79.3); Time Pressure (77.8); Deal With Unpleasant or Angry People (65.8); Level of Competition (47.8).

Least Stressful Aspects: Deal With Physically Aggressive People (8.8); Pace Determined by Speed of Equipment (10.0); Consequence of Error (34.5); Frequency of Conflict Situations (47.3).

Repair, adjust, or install all types of electric or gas household appliances, such as refrigerators, washers, dryers, and ovens. Clean, lubricate, and touch up minor defects on newly installed or repaired appliances. Observe and test operation of appliances following installation and make any initial installation adjustments as necessary. Level refrigerators, adjust doors, and connect water lines to water pipes for ice makers

and water dispensers, using hand tools. Level washing machines and connect hoses to water pipes, using hand tools. Maintain stocks of parts used in on-site installation, maintenance, and repair of appliances. Instruct customers regarding operation and care of appliances and provide information such as emergency service numbers. Provide repair cost estimates and recommend whether appliance repair or replacement is a better choice. Conserve, recover, and recycle refrigerants used in cooling systems. Contact supervisors or offices to receive repair assignments. Install gas pipes and water lines to connect appliances to existing gas lines or plumbing. Record maintenance and repair work performed on appliances. Respond to emergency calls for problems such as gas leaks. Assemble new or reconditioned appliances. Disassemble and reinstall existing kitchen cabinets or assemble and install prefabricated kitchen cabinets and trim in conjunction with appliance installation. Hang steel supports from beams or joists to hold hoses, vents, and gas pipes in place. Install appliances such as refrigerators, washing machines, and stoves. Set appliance thermostats and check to ensure that they are functioning properly. Refer to schematic drawings, product manuals, and troubleshooting guides to diagnose and repair problems. Clean and reinstall parts. Disassemble appliances so that problems can be diagnosed and repairs can be made. Light and adjust pilot lights on gas stoves and examine valves and burners for gas leakage and specified flame. Test and examine gas pipelines and equipment to locate leaks and faulty connections and to determine the pressure and flow of gas. Take measurements to determine whether appliances will fit in installation locations; perform minor carpentry work when necessary to ensure proper installation. Measure, cut, and thread pipe and connect it to feeder lines and equipment or appliances, using rules and hand tools. Reassemble units after repairs are made, making adjustments and cleaning and lubricating parts as needed.

Personality Type: Realistic. Realistic occupations frequently involve work activities that include practical, hands-on problems and solutions. They often deal with plants; animals; and real-world materials such as wood, tools, and machinery. Many of the occupations require working outside and do not involve a lot of paperwork or working closely with others.

GOE—Interest Area: 13. Manufacturing. **Work Group:** 13.13. Machinery Repair. **Other Jobs in This Work Group:** Bicycle Repairers; Control and Valve Installers and Repairers, Except Mechanical Door; Industrial Machinery Mechanics; Locksmiths and Safe Repairers; Maintenance Workers, Machinery; Mechanical Door Repairers; Millwrights; Signal and Track Switch Repairers.

Skills—Repairing: Repairing machines or systems, using the needed tools. **Installation:** Installing equipment, machines, wiring, or programs to meet specifications. **Troubleshooting:** Determining causes of operating errors and deciding what to do about them. **Technology Design:** Generating or adapting equipment and technology to serve user needs. **Systems Analysis:** Determining how a system should work and how changes in conditions, operations, and the environment will affect outcomes. **Equipment Maintenance:** Performing routine maintenance on equipment and determining when and what kind of maintenance is needed.

Education and Training Programs: Appliance Installation and Repair Technology/Technician; Electrical/Electronics Equipment Installation and Repair, General; Home Furnishings and Equipment Installers. **Related Knowledge/ Courses: Sales and Marketing:** Principles and methods for showing, promoting, and selling products or services. This includes marketing strategy and tactics, product demonstration, sales techniques, and sales control systems. **Mechanical Devices:** Machines and tools, including their designs, uses, repair, and maintenance. **Customer and Personal Service:** Principles and processes for providing customer and personal services. This includes customer needs assessment, meeting quality standards for services, and evaluation of customer satisfaction. **Physics:** Physical principles, laws, their interrelationships, and applications to understanding fluid, material, and atmospheric dynamics, and mechanical, electrical, atomic, and subatomic structures and processes. **Economics and Accounting:** Economic and accounting principles and practices, the financial markets, banking, and the analysis and reporting of financial data. **Engineering and Technology:** The practical application of engineering science and technology. This includes applying principles, techniques, procedures, and equipment to the design and production of various goods and services.

Work Environment: Indoors; contaminants; cramped work space, awkward positions; standing; using hands on objects, tools, or controls; bending or twisting the body.

Hydrologists

- Education/Training Required: Master's degree
- Annual Earnings: $66,260
- Growth: 24.3%
- Annual Job Openings: 687
- Self-Employed: 2.4%
- Part-Time: 12.4%

Level of Stress Tolerance Needed: 59.8 (out of 100)

Most Stressful Aspects: Duration of Typical Work Week (82.0); Importance of Being Exact or Accurate (76.0); Level of Competition (55.3).

Least Stressful Aspects: Pace Determined by Speed of Equipment (3.5); Deal With Physically Aggressive People (9.3); Deal With Unpleasant or Angry People (34.0); Consequence of Error (38.5).

Research the distribution, circulation, and physical properties of underground and surface waters; study the form and intensity of precipitation, its rate of infiltration into the soil, its movement through the earth, and its return to the ocean and atmosphere. Study and document quantities, distribution, disposition, and development of underground and surface waters. Draft final reports describing research results, including illustrations, appendices, maps, and other attachments. Coordinate and supervise the work of professional and technical staff, including research assistants, technologists, and technicians. Prepare hydrogeologic evaluations of known or suspected hazardous waste sites and land treatment and feedlot facilities. Design and conduct scientific hydrogeological investigations to ensure that accurate and appropriate information is available for use in water resource management decisions. Study public water supply issues, including flood and drought risks, water quality, wastewater, and impacts on wetland habitats. Collect and analyze water samples as part of field investigations and/or to validate data from automatic monitors. Apply research findings to help minimize the environmental impacts of pollution, water-borne diseases, erosion, and sedimentation. Measure and graph phenomena such as lake levels, stream flows, and changes in water volumes. Investigate complaints or conflicts related to the alteration of public waters, gathering information, recommending alternatives, informing participants of progress, and preparing draft orders. Develop or modify methods of conducting hydrologic studies. Answer questions and provide technical assistance and information to contractors and/or the public regarding issues such as well drilling, code requirements, hydrology, and geology. Install, maintain, and calibrate instruments such as those that monitor water levels, rainfall, and sediments. Evaluate data and provide recommendations regarding the feasibility of municipal projects such as hydroelectric power plants, irrigation systems, flood warning systems, and waste treatment facilities. Conduct short-term and long-term climate assessments and study storm occurrences. Study and analyze the physical aspects of the Earth in terms of the hydrological components, including atmosphere, hydrosphere, and interior structure. Conduct research and communicate information to promote the conservation and preservation of water resources.

Personality Type: Investigative. Investigative occupations frequently involve working with ideas and require an extensive amount of thinking. These occupations can involve searching for facts and figuring out problems mentally.

GOE—Interest Area: 15. Scientific Research, Engineering, and Mathematics. **Work Group:** 15.02. Physical Sciences. **Other Jobs in This Work Group:** Astronomers; Atmospheric and Space Scientists; Chemists; Geographers; Geoscientists, Except Hydrologists and Geographers; Materials Scientists; Physicists.

Skills—Science: Using scientific rules and methods to solve problems. **Programming:** Writing computer programs for various purposes. **Management of Financial Resources:** Determining how money will be spent to get the work done and accounting for these expenditures. **Mathematics:** Using mathematics to solve problems. **Management of Personnel Resources:** Motivating, developing, and directing people as they work, identifying the best people for the job. **Systems Analysis:** Determining how a system should work and how changes in conditions, operations, and the environment will affect outcomes.

Education and Training Programs: Geology/ Earth Science, General; Hydrology and Water Resources Science; Oceanography, Chemical and Physical. **Related Knowledge/Courses: Geography:** Principles and methods for describing the features of land, sea, and air masses, including their physical characteristics, locations, interrelationships, and distribution of plant, animal, and human life. **Physics:** Physical principles, laws, their interrelationships, and applications to understanding fluid, material, and atmospheric dynamics, and mechanical, electrical, atomic, and subatomic structures and processes. **Engineering and Technology:** The practical application of engineering science and technology. This includes applying principles, techniques, procedures, and equipment to the design and production of various goods and services. **Biology:** Plant and animal organisms, their tissues, cells, functions, interdependencies, and interactions with each other and the environment. **Chemistry:** The chemical composition, structure, and properties of substances and of the chemical processes and transformations that they undergo. This includes uses of chemicals, their danger signs, production techniques, and disposal methods. **Mathematics:** Arithmetic, algebra, geometry, calculus, statistics, and their applications.

Work Environment: More often indoors than outdoors; sitting.

Industrial Engineering Technicians

- Education/Training Required: Associate degree
- Annual Earnings: $46,810
- Growth: 9.9%
- Annual Job Openings: 6,172
- Self-Employed: 0.8%
- Part-Time: 20.9%

Level of Stress Tolerance Needed: 72.3 (out of 100)

Most Stressful Aspects: Duration of Typical Work Week (81.5); Time Pressure (78.8); Importance of Being Exact or Accurate (78.5); Impact of Decisions on Co-workers or Company Results (77.0).

Least Stressful Aspects: Deal With Physically Aggressive People (14.3).

Apply engineering theory and principles to problems of industrial layout or manufacturing production, usually under the direction of engineering staff. May study and record time, motion, method, and speed involved in performance of production, maintenance, clerical, and other worker operations for such purposes as establishing standard production rates or improving efficiency. Recommend revision to methods of operation, material handling, equipment layout, or other changes to increase production or improve standards. Study time, motion, methods, and speed involved in maintenance, production, and other operations to establish standard production rate and improve efficiency. Interpret engineering drawings, schematic diagrams, or formulas and confer with management or engineering staff to determine quality and reliability standards. Recommend modifications to existing quality or production standards to achieve optimum quality within limits of equipment capability. Aid in planning work assignments in accordance with worker performance, machine capacity, production schedules, and anticipated delays. Observe workers using equipment to verify that equipment is being operated and maintained according to quality assurance standards. Observe workers operating equipment or performing tasks to determine time involved and fatigue rate, using timing devices. Prepare charts, graphs, and diagrams to illustrate workflow, routing, floor layouts, material handling, and machine utilization. Evaluate data and write reports to validate or indicate deviations from existing standards. Read worker logs, product processing sheets, and specification sheets to verify that records adhere to quality assurance specifications. Prepare graphs or charts of data or enter data into computer for analysis. Record test data, applying statistical quality control procedures. Select products for tests at specified stages in production process and test products for performance characteristics and adherence to specifications. Compile and evaluate statistical data to determine and maintain quality and reliability of products.

Personality Type: Investigative. Investigative occupations frequently involve working with ideas and require an extensive amount of thinking. These occupations can involve searching for facts and figuring out problems mentally.

GOE—Interest Area: 04. Business and Administration. **Work Group:** 04.05. Accounting, Auditing, and Analytical Support. **Other Jobs in This Work Group:** Accountants; Accountants and Auditors; Auditors; Budget Analysts; Logisticians; Management Analysts; Operations Research Analysts.

Skills—Operations Analysis: Analyzing needs and product requirements to create a design. **Technology Design:** Generating or adapting equipment and technology to serve user needs. **Repairing:** Repairing machines or systems, using the needed tools. **Systems Evaluation:** Identifying measures or indicators of system performance and the actions needed to improve or correct performance, relative to the goals of the system. **Systems Analysis:** Determining how a system should work and how changes in conditions, operations, and the environment will affect outcomes. **Troubleshooting:** Determining causes of operating errors and deciding what to do about them.

Education and Training Programs: Engineering/Industrial Management; Industrial Production Technologies/Technician Training, Other; Industrial Technology/Technician Training; Manufacturing Technology/Technician Training. **Related Knowledge/Courses: Production and Processing:** Raw materials, production processes, quality control, costs, and other techniques for maximizing the effective manufacture and distribution of goods. **Engineering and Technology:** The practical application of engineering science and technology. This includes applying principles, techniques, procedures, and equipment to the design and production of various goods and services. **Design:** Design techniques, tools, and principles involved in production of precision technical plans, blueprints, drawings, and models. **Clerical Practices:** Administrative and clerical procedures and systems such as word processing, managing files and records, stenography and transcription, designing forms, and other office procedures and terminology. **Mathematics:** Arithmetic, algebra, geometry, calculus, statistics, and their applications. **Mechanical Devices:** Machines and tools, including their designs, uses, repair, and maintenance.

Work Environment: Indoors; noisy; contaminants; hazardous equipment; standing; walking and running.

Industrial Machinery Mechanics

- Education/Training Required: Long-term on-the-job training
- Annual Earnings: $41,050
- Growth: 9.0%
- Annual Job Openings: 23,361
- Self-Employed: 2.5%
- Part-Time: 2.4%

Level of Stress Tolerance Needed: 73.5 (out of 100)

Most Stressful Aspects: Duration of Typical Work Week (87.5); Time Pressure (83.2); Impact of Decisions on Co-workers or Company Results (69.7); Pace Determined by Speed of Equipment (62.3).

Least Stressful Aspects: Deal With Unpleasant or Angry People (52.5); Importance of Being Exact or Accurate (72.3).

Repair, install, adjust, or maintain industrial production and processing machinery or refinery and pipeline distribution systems. Disassemble machinery and equipment to remove parts and make repairs. Repair and replace broken or malfunctioning components of machinery and equipment. Examine parts for defects such as breakage and excessive wear. Repair and maintain the operating condition of industrial production and processing machinery and equipment. Reassemble equipment after completion of inspections, testing, or repairs. Observe and test the operation of machinery and equipment to diagnose malfunctions, using voltmeters and other testing devices. Operate newly repaired machinery and equipment to verify the adequacy of repairs. Clean, lubricate, and adjust parts, equipment, and machinery. Analyze test results, machine error messages, and information obtained from operators to diagnose equipment problems. Record repairs and maintenance performed. Study blueprints and manufacturers' manuals to determine correct installation and operation of machinery. Record parts and materials used and order or requisition new parts and materials as necessary. Cut and weld metal to repair broken metal parts, fabricate new parts, and assemble new equipment. Demonstrate equipment functions and features to machine operators. Enter codes and instructions to program computer-controlled machinery.

Personality Type: Realistic. Realistic occupations frequently involve work activities that include practical, hands-on problems and solutions. They often deal with plants; animals; and real-world materials such as wood, tools, and machinery. Many of the occupations require working outside and do not involve a lot of paperwork or working closely with others.

GOE—Interest Area: 13. Manufacturing. **Work Group:** 13.13. Machinery Repair. **Other Jobs in This Work Group:** Bicycle Repairers; Control and Valve Installers and Repairers, Except Mechanical Door; Home Appliance Repairers; Locksmiths and Safe Repairers; Maintenance Workers, Machinery; Mechanical Door Repairers; Millwrights; Signal and Track Switch Repairers.

Skills—Repairing: Repairing machines or systems, using the needed tools. **Installation:** Installing equipment, machines, wiring, or programs to meet specifications. **Equipment Maintenance:** Performing routine maintenance on equipment and determining when and what kind of maintenance is needed. **Operation Monitoring:** Watching gauges, dials, or other indicators to make sure a machine is working properly. **Troubleshooting:** Determining causes of operating errors and deciding what to do about them. **Technology Design:** Generating or adapting equipment and technology to serve user needs.

Education and Training Programs: Heavy/Industrial Equipment Maintenance Technologies, Other; Industrial Mechanics and Maintenance Technology. **Related Knowledge/Courses: Mechanical Devices:** Machines and tools, including their designs, uses, repair, and maintenance. **Engineering and Technology:** The practical application of engineering science and technology. This includes applying principles, techniques, procedures, and equipment to the design and production of various goods and services. **Building and Construction:** Materials, methods, and the tools involved in the construction or repair of houses, buildings, or other structures such as highways and roads. **Design:** Design techniques, tools, and principles involved in production of precision technical plans, blueprints, drawings, and models. **Chemistry:** The chemical composition, structure, and properties of substances and of the chemical processes and transformations that they undergo. This includes uses of chemicals, their danger signs, production techniques, and disposal methods. **Physics:** Physical principles, laws, their interrelationships, and applications to understanding fluid, material, and atmospheric dynamics, and mechanical, electrical, atomic, and subatomic structures and processes.

Work Environment: Noisy; contaminants; hazardous conditions; hazardous equipment; standing; using hands on objects, tools, or controls.

Industrial Safety and Health Engineers

- Education/Training Required: Bachelor's degree
- Annual Earnings: $66,290
- Growth: 9.6%
- Annual Job Openings: 1,105
- Self-Employed: 1.1%
- Part-Time: 14.3%

Our sources did not provide separate job openings data for this occupation. The job openings listed here are shared with Fire-Prevention and Protection Engineers and with Product Safety Engineers.

Level of Stress Tolerance Needed: 75.0 (out of 100)

Most Stressful Aspects: Duration of Typical Work Week (92.0); Impact of Decisions on Coworkers or Company Results (84.2); Consequence of Error (59.8); Frequency of Conflict Situations (56.5).

Least Stressful Aspects: Pace Determined by Speed of Equipment (9.7); Deal With Unpleasant or Angry People (49.3); Time Pressure (62.5); Importance of Being Exact or Accurate (74.3).

Plan, implement, and coordinate safety programs requiring application of engineering principles and technology to prevent or correct unsafe environmental working conditions. Investigate industrial accidents, injuries, or occupational diseases to determine causes and preventive measures. Report or review findings from accident investigations, facilities inspections, or environmental testing. Maintain and apply knowledge of current policies, regulations, and industrial processes. Inspect facilities, machinery, and safety equipment to identify and correct potential hazards and to ensure safety regulation compliance. Conduct or coordinate worker training in areas such as safety laws and regulations, hazardous condition monitoring, and use of safety equipment. Review employee safety programs to determine their adequacy. Interview employers and employees to obtain information about work environments and workplace incidents. Review plans and specifications for construction of new machinery or equipment to determine whether all safety requirements have been met. Compile, analyze, and interpret statistical data related to occupational illnesses and accidents. Interpret safety regulations for others interested in industrial safety, such as safety engineers, labor representatives, and safety inspectors. Recommend process and product safety features that will reduce employees' exposure to chemical, physical, and biological work hazards. Conduct or direct testing of air quality, noise, temperature, or radiation levels to verify compliance with health and safety regulations. Provide technical advice and guidance to organizations on how to handle health-related problems and make needed changes. Confer with medical professionals to assess health risks and to develop ways to manage health issues and concerns. Install safety devices on machinery or direct device installation. Maintain liaisons with outside organizations such as fire departments, mutual aid societies, and rescue teams so that emergency responses can be facilitated. Evaluate adequacy of actions taken to correct health inspection violations. Write and revise safety regulations and codes. Check floors of plants to ensure that they are strong enough to support heavy machinery. Plan and conduct industrial hygiene research.

Personality Type: Investigative. Investigative occupations frequently involve working with ideas and require an extensive amount of thinking. These occupations can involve searching for facts and figuring out problems mentally.

GOE—Interest Area: 15. Scientific Research, Engineering, and Mathematics. **Work Group:** 15.08. Industrial and Safety Engineering. **Other Jobs in This Work Group:** Fire-Prevention and Protection Engineers; Health and Safety Engineers, Except Mining Safety Engineers and Inspectors; Industrial Engineers; Product Safety Engineers.

Skills—Management of Financial Resources: Determining how money will be spent to get the work done and accounting for these expenditures. **Science:** Using scientific rules and methods to solve problems. **Systems Analysis:** Determining how a system should work and how changes in conditions, operations, and the environment will affect outcomes. **Persuasion:** Persuading others to change their minds or behavior. **Management of Personnel Resources:** Motivating, developing, and directing people as they work, identifying the best people for the job. **Systems Evaluation:** Identifying measures or indicators of system performance and the actions needed to improve or correct performance, relative to the goals of the system.

Education and Training Program: Environmental/Environmental Health Engineering. **Related Knowledge/Courses: Building and Construction:** Materials, methods, and the tools involved in the construction or repair of houses, buildings, or other structures such as highways and roads. **Physics:** Physical principles, laws, their interrelationships, and applications to understanding fluid, material, and atmospheric dynamics, and mechanical, electrical, atomic, and subatomic structures and processes. **Chemistry:** The chemical composition, structure, and properties of substances and of the chemical processes and transformations that they undergo. This includes uses of chemicals, their danger signs, production techniques, and disposal methods. **Biology:** Plant and animal organisms, their tissues, cells, functions, interdependencies, and interactions with each other and the environment. **Engineering and Technology:** The practical application of engineering science and technology. This includes applying principles, techniques, procedures, and equipment to the design and production of various goods and services. **Education and Training:** Principles and methods for curriculum and training design, teaching and instruction for individuals and groups, and the measurement of training effects.

Work Environment: More often indoors than outdoors; noisy; sitting.

Inspectors, Testers, Sorters, Samplers, and Weighers

- Education/Training Required: Moderate-term on-the-job training
- Annual Earnings: $29,420
- Growth: –7.0%
- Annual Job Openings: 75,361
- Self-Employed: 1.5%
- Part-Time: 12.0%

Level of Stress Tolerance Needed: 60.5 (out of 100)

Most Stressful Aspects: Duration of Typical Work Week (72.0); Consequence of Error (60.3); Pace Determined by Speed of Equipment (40.0); Deal With Physically Aggressive People (16.2).

Least Stressful Aspects: Frequency of Conflict Situations (35.5); Level of Competition (44.7); Deal With Unpleasant or Angry People (48.5); Impact of Decisions on Co-workers or Company Results (49.8).

Inspect, test, sort, sample, or weigh nonagricultural raw materials or processed, machined, fabricated, or assembled parts or products for defects, wear, and deviations from specifications. May use precision measuring instruments and complex test equipment. Discard or reject products, materials, and equipment not meeting specifications. Analyze and interpret blueprints, data, manuals, and other materials to determine specifications, inspection and testing procedures, adjustment and certification methods, formulas, and measuring instruments required. Inspect, test, or measure materials, products, installations, and work for conformance to specifications. Notify supervisors and other personnel of production problems and assist in identifying and correcting these problems. Discuss inspection results with those responsible for products and recommend necessary corrective actions. Record inspection or test data, such as weights, temperatures, grades, or moisture content and quantities inspected or graded. Mark items with details such as grade and acceptance or rejection status. Observe and monitor production operations and equipment to ensure conformance to specifications and make or order necessary process or assembly adjustments. Measure dimensions of products to verify conformance to specifications, using measuring instruments such as rulers, calipers, gauges, or micrometers. Analyze test data and make computations as necessary to determine test results. Collect or select samples for testing or for use as models. Check arriving materials to ensure that they match purchase orders and submit discrepancy reports when problems are found. Compare colors, shapes, textures, or grades of products or materials with color charts, templates, or samples to verify conformance to standards. Write test and inspection reports describing results, recommendations, and needed repairs. Read dials and meters to verify that equipment is functioning at specified levels. Remove defects, such as chips and burrs, and lap corroded or pitted surfaces. Clean, maintain, repair, and calibrate measuring instruments and test equipment such as dial indicators, fixed gauges, and height gauges. Adjust, clean, or repair products or processing equipment to correct defects found during inspections. Stack and arrange tested products for further processing, shipping, or packaging and transport products to other workstations as necessary.

Personality Type: Realistic. Realistic occupations frequently involve work activities that include practical, hands-on problems and solutions. They often deal with plants; animals; and real-world materials such as wood, tools, and machinery. Many of the occupations require working outside and do not involve a lot of paperwork or working closely with others.

GOE—Interest Area: 13. Manufacturing. **Work Group:** 13.07. Production Quality Control. **Other Jobs in This Work Group:** Graders and Sorters, Agricultural Products.

Skills—Quality Control Analysis: Conducting tests and inspections of products, services, or processes to evaluate quality or performance. **Operation Monitoring:** Watching gauges, dials, or other indicators to make sure a machine is working properly. **Operation and Control:** Controlling operations of equipment or systems. **Repairing:** Repairing machines or systems, using the needed tools. **Systems Evaluation:** Identifying measures or indicators of system performance and the actions needed to improve or correct performance, relative to the goals of the system.

Education and Training Program: Quality Control Technology/Technician. **Related Knowledge/Course: Production and Processing:** Raw materials, production processes, quality control, costs, and other techniques

for maximizing the effective manufacture and distribution of goods.

Work Environment: Noisy; standing; using hands on objects, tools, or controls; repetitive motions.

Insulation Workers, Floor, Ceiling, and Wall

- Education/Training Required: Moderate-term on-the-job training
- Annual Earnings: $30,510
- Growth: 8.4%
- Annual Job Openings: 6,580
- Self-Employed: 1.3%
- Part-Time: 16.8%

Level of Stress Tolerance Needed: 51.2 (out of 100)

Most Stressful Aspects: Time Pressure (69.7); Level of Competition (63.7); Pace Determined by Speed of Equipment (27.5).

Least Stressful Aspects: Deal With Physically Aggressive People (14.8); Consequence of Error (25.0); Frequency of Conflict Situations (40.0); Importance of Being Exact or Accurate (41.0).

Line and cover structures with insulating materials. May work with batt, roll, or blown insulation materials. Distribute insulating materials evenly into small spaces within floors, ceilings, or walls, using blowers and hose attachments or cement mortars. Cover and line structures with blown or rolled forms of materials to insulate against cold, heat, or moisture, using saws, knives, rasps, trowels, blowers, and other tools and implements. Move controls, buttons, or levers to start blowers and regulate flow of materials through nozzles. Remove old insulation such as asbestos, following safety procedures.

Read blueprints and select appropriate insulation, based on space characteristics and the heat-retaining or -excluding characteristics of the material. Prepare surfaces for insulation application by brushing or spreading on adhesives, cement, or asphalt or by attaching metal pins to surfaces. Measure and cut insulation for covering surfaces, using tape measures, hand saws, power saws, knives, or scissors. Fit, wrap, staple, or glue insulating materials to structures or surfaces, using hand tools or wires. Fill blower hoppers with insulating materials. Cover, seal, or finish insulated surfaces or access holes with plastic covers, canvas strips, sealants, tape, cement, or asphalt mastic.

Personality Type: Realistic. Realistic occupations frequently involve work activities that include practical, hands-on problems and solutions. They often deal with plants; animals; and real-world materials such as wood, tools, and machinery. Many of the occupations require working outside and do not involve a lot of paperwork or working closely with others.

GOE—Interest Area: 02. Architecture and Construction. **Work Group:** 02.04. Construction Crafts. **Other Jobs in This Work Group:** Boilermakers; Brickmasons and Blockmasons; Carpet Installers; Cement Masons and Concrete Finishers; Commercial Divers; Construction Carpenters; Crane and Tower Operators; Drywall and Ceiling Tile Installers; Electricians; Fence Erectors; Floor Layers, Except Carpet, Wood, and Hard Tiles; Floor Sanders and Finishers; Glaziers; Hazardous Materials Removal Workers; Insulation Workers, Mechanical; Manufactured Building and Mobile Home Installers; Operating Engineers and Other Construction Equipment Operators; Painters, Construction and Maintenance; Paperhangers; Paving, Surfacing, and Tamping Equipment Operators; Pile-Driver Operators; Pipe Fitters and Steamfitters; Pipelayers; Plasterers and Stucco Masons; Plumbers; Plumbers, Pipefitters, and Steamfitters; Rail-Track Laying and Maintenance Equipment Operators; Refractory Materials Repairers, Except Brickmasons; Reinforcing Iron and Rebar Workers; Riggers; Roofers; Rough Carpenters; Security and Fire Alarm Systems Installers; Segmental Pavers; Sheet Metal Workers; Stone Cutters and Carvers, Manufacturing; Stonemasons; Structural Iron and Steel Workers; Tapers; Terrazzo Workers and Finishers; Tile and Marble Setters.

Skills—Installation: Installing equipment, machines, wiring, or programs to meet specifications. **Management of Material Resources:** Obtaining and seeing to the appropriate use of equipment, facilities, and materials needed to do certain work. **Repairing:** Repairing machines or systems, using the needed tools. **Mathematics:** Using mathematics to solve problems. **Equipment Maintenance:** Performing routine maintenance on equipment and determining when and what kind of maintenance is needed.

Education and Training Program: Construction Trades, Other. **Related Knowledge/Courses: Building and Construction:** Materials, methods, and the tools involved in the construction or repair of houses, buildings, or other structures such as highways and roads. **Production and Processing:** Raw materials, production processes, quality control, costs, and other techniques for maximizing the effective manufacture and distribution of goods. **Transportation:** Principles and methods for moving people or goods by air, rail, sea, or road, including the relative costs and benefits. **Personnel and Human Resources:** Principles and procedures for personnel recruitment, selection, training, compensation and benefits, labor relations and negotiation, and personnel information systems. **Design:** Design techniques, tools, and principles involved in production of precision technical plans, blueprints, drawings, and models. **Economics and Accounting:** Economic and accounting principles and practices, the financial markets, banking, and the analysis and reporting of financial data.

Work Environment: Outdoors; contaminants; standing; using hands on objects, tools, or controls; bending or twisting the body; repetitive motions.

Insurance Underwriters

- ◉ Education/Training Required: Bachelor's degree
- ◉ Annual Earnings: $52,350
- ◉ Growth: 6.3%
- ◉ Annual Job Openings: 6,880
- ◉ Self-Employed: 0.0%
- ◉ Part-Time: 16.7%

Level of Stress Tolerance Needed: 65.2 (out of 100)

Most Stressful Aspects: Time Pressure (77.0); Importance of Being Exact or Accurate (76.8); Impact of Decisions on Co-workers or Company Results (67.8); Level of Competition (50.7).

Least Stressful Aspects: Pace Determined by Speed of Equipment (8.3); Duration of Typical Work Week (28.0); Consequence of Error (35.8); Frequency of Conflict Situations (43.0).

Review individual applications for insurance to evaluate degree of risk involved and determine acceptance of applications. Examine documents to determine degree of risk from such factors as applicant financial standing and value and condition of property. Decline excessive risks. Write to field representatives, medical personnel, and others to obtain further information, quote rates, or explain company underwriting policies.

Evaluate possibility of losses due to catastrophe or excessive insurance. Decrease value of policy when risk is substandard and specify applicable endorsements or apply rating to ensure safe profitable distribution of risks, using reference materials. Review company records to determine amount of insurance in force on single risk or group of closely related risks. Authorize reinsurance of policy when risk is high.

Personality Type: Conventional. Conventional occupations frequently involve following set procedures and routines. These occupations can include working with data and details more than with ideas. Usually, there is a clear line of authority to follow.

GOE—Interest Area: 06. Finance and Insurance. **Work Group:** 06.02. Finance/Insurance Investigation and Analysis. **Other Jobs in This Work Group:** Appraisers and Assessors of Real Estate; Appraisers, Real Estate; Assessors; Claims Adjusters, Examiners, and Investigators; Claims Examiners, Property and Casualty Insurance; Cost Estimators; Credit Analysts; Financial Analysts; Insurance Adjusters, Examiners, and Investigators; Insurance Appraisers, Auto Damage; Loan Counselors; Loan Officers; Market Research Analysts; Survey Researchers.

Skills—Writing: Communicating effectively in writing as appropriate for the needs of the audience. **Service Orientation:** Actively looking for ways to help people. **Speaking:** Talking to others to convey information effectively. **Active Listening:** Giving full attention to what other people are saying, taking time to understand the points being made, asking questions as appropriate, and not interrupting at inappropriate times. **Active Learning:** Understanding the implications of new information for both current and future problem solving and decision making. **Learning Strategies:** Selecting and using training/instructional methods and procedures appropriate for the situation when learning or teaching new things.

Education and Training Program: Insurance. **Related Knowledge/Courses: Clerical Practices:** Administrative and clerical procedures and systems such as word processing, managing files and records, stenography and transcription, designing forms, and other office procedures and terminology. **Customer and Personal Service:** Principles and processes for providing customer and personal services. This includes customer needs assessment, meeting quality standards for services, and evaluation of customer satisfaction. **Sales and Marketing:** Principles and methods for showing, promoting, and selling products or services. This includes marketing strategy and tactics, product demonstration, sales techniques, and sales control systems. **Economics and Accounting:** Economic and accounting principles and practices, the financial markets, banking, and the analysis and reporting of financial data. **Computers and Electronics:** Circuit boards, processors, chips, electronic equipment, and computer hardware and software, including applications and programming. **Law and Government:** Laws, legal codes, court procedures, precedents, government regulations, executive orders, agency rules, and the democratic political process.

Work Environment: Indoors; sitting; using hands on objects, tools, or controls; repetitive motions.

Laborers and Freight, Stock, and Material Movers, Hand

- ◉ Education/Training Required: Short-term on-the-job training
- ◉ Annual Earnings: $21,220
- ◉ Growth: 2.1%
- ◉ Annual Job Openings: 630,487
- ◉ Self-Employed: 1.1%
- ◉ Part-Time: 39.4%

Level of Stress Tolerance Needed: 67.3 (out of 100)

Most Stressful Aspects: Time Pressure (83.5); Importance of Being Exact or Accurate (79.0); Duration of Typical Work Week (73.5); Deal With Unpleasant or Angry People (56.7).

Least Stressful Aspects: Deal With Physically Aggressive People (14.0); Level of Competition (38.0); Impact of Decisions on Co-workers or Company Results (56.5).

Manually move freight, stock, or other materials or perform other unskilled general labor. Includes all unskilled manual laborers not elsewhere classified. Attach identifying tags to containers or mark them with identifying information. Read work orders or receive oral instructions to determine work assignments and material and equipment needs. Record numbers of units handled and moved, using daily production sheets or work tickets. Move freight, stock, and other materials to and from storage and production areas, loading docks, delivery vehicles, ships, and containers by hand or by using trucks, tractors, and other equipment. Sort cargo before loading and unloading. Assemble product containers and crates, using hand tools and precut lumber. Load and unload ship cargo, using winches and other hoisting devices. Connect hoses and operate equipment to move liquid materials into and out of storage tanks on vessels. Pack containers and repack damaged containers. Carry needed tools and supplies from storage or trucks and return them after use. Install protective devices, such as bracing, padding, or strapping, to prevent shifting or damage to items being transported. Maintain equipment storage areas to ensure that inventory is protected. Attach slings, hooks, and other devices to lift cargo and guide loads. Carry out general yard duties such as performing shunting on railway lines. Adjust controls to guide, position, and move equipment such as cranes, booms, and cameras. Guide loads being lifted to prevent swinging. Adjust or replace equipment parts such as rollers, belts, plugs, and caps, using hand tools. Stack cargo in locations such as transit sheds or in holds of ships as directed, using pallets or cargo boards. Connect electrical equipment to power sources so that it can be tested before use. Set up the equipment needed to produce special lighting and sound effects during performances. Bundle and band material such as fodder and tobacco leaves, using banding machines. Rig and dismantle props and equipment such as frames, scaffolding, platforms, or backdrops, using hand tools. Check out, rent, or requisition all equipment needed for productions or for set construction. Direct spouts and position receptacles such as bins, carts, and containers so that they can be loaded.

Personality Type: Realistic. Realistic occupations frequently involve work activities that include practical, hands-on problems and solutions. They often deal with plants; animals; and real-world materials such as wood, tools, and machinery. Many of the occupations require working outside and do not involve a lot of paperwork or working closely with others.

GOE—Interest Area: 16. Transportation, Distribution, and Logistics. **Work Group:** 16.07. Transportation Support Work. **Other Jobs in This Work Group:** Bridge and Lock Tenders; Cargo and Freight Agents; Cleaners of Vehicles and Equipment; Railroad Brake, Signal, and Switch Operators; Traffic Technicians.

Skills—None met the criteria.

Education and Training Programs: No related CIP programs; this job is learned through informal short-term on-the-job training. **Related Knowledge/Courses: Transportation:** Principles and methods for moving people or goods by air, rail, sea, or road, including the relative costs and benefits. **Public Safety and Security:** Relevant equipment, policies, procedures, and strategies to promote effective local, state, or national security operations for the protection of people, data, property, and institutions. **Production and Processing:** Raw materials, production processes, quality control, costs, and other techniques for maximizing the effective manufacture and distribution of goods.

Work Environment: Outdoors; noisy; very hot or cold; contaminants; standing; using hands on objects, tools, or controls.

Landscaping and Groundskeeping Workers

- Education/Training Required: Short-term on-the-job training
- Annual Earnings: $21,260
- Growth: 18.1%
- Annual Job Openings: 307,138
- Self-Employed: 20.5%
- Part-Time: 32.8%

Level of Stress Tolerance Needed: 47.0 (out of 100)

Most Stressful Aspects: Pace Determined by Speed of Equipment (58.7); Duration of Typical Work Week (58.0).

Least Stressful Aspects: Deal With Physically Aggressive People (6.7); Consequence of Error (34.5); Deal With Unpleasant or Angry People (36.5); Level of Competition (37.5).

Landscape or maintain grounds of property, using hand or power tools or equipment. Workers typically perform a variety of tasks, which may include any combination of the following: sod laying, mowing, trimming, planting, watering, fertilizing, digging, raking, sprinkler installation, and installation of mortarless segmental concrete masonry wall units. Operate powered equipment such as mowers, tractors, twin-axle vehicles, snowblowers, chain saws, electric clippers, sod cutters, and pruning saws. Mow and edge lawns, using power mowers and edgers. Shovel snow from walks, driveways, and parking lots and spread salt in those areas. Care for established lawns by mulching; aerating; weeding; grubbing and removing thatch; and trimming and edging around flower beds, walks, and walls. Use hand tools such as shovels, rakes, pruning saws, saws, hedge and brush trimmers, and axes. Prune and trim trees, shrubs, and hedges, using shears, pruners, or chain saws. Maintain and repair tools; equipment; and structures such as buildings, greenhouses, fences, and benches, using hand and power tools. Gather and remove litter. Mix and spray or spread fertilizers, herbicides, or insecticides onto grass, shrubs, and trees, using hand or automatic sprayers or spreaders. Provide proper upkeep of sidewalks, driveways, parking lots, fountains, planters, burial sites, and other grounds features. Water lawns, trees, and plants, using portable sprinkler systems, hoses, or watering cans. Trim and pick flowers and clean flowerbeds. Rake, mulch, and compost leaves. Plant seeds, bulbs, foliage, flowering plants, grass, ground covers, trees, and shrubs and apply mulch for protection, using gardening tools. Follow planned landscaping designs to determine where to lay sod, sow grass, or plant flowers and foliage. Decorate gardens with stones and plants. Maintain irrigation systems, including winterizing the systems and starting them up in spring. Care for natural turf fields, making sure the underlying soil has the required composition to allow proper drainage and to support the grasses used on the fields. Use irrigation methods to adjust the amount of water consumption and to prevent waste. Haul or spread topsoil and spread straw over seeded soil to hold soil in place. Advise customers on plant selection and care. Care for artificial turf fields, periodically removing the turf and replacing cushioning pads and vacuuming and disinfecting the turf after use to prevent the growth of harmful bacteria.

Personality Type: Realistic. Realistic occupations frequently involve work activities that include practical, hands-on problems and solutions. They often deal with plants; animals; and real-world materials such as wood, tools, and machinery. Many of the occupations require working outside and do not involve a lot of paperwork or working closely with others.

GOE—Interest Area: 01. Agriculture and Natural Resources. **Work Group:** 01.05. Nursery, Groundskeeping, and Pest Control. **Other Jobs in This Work Group:** Nursery Workers; Pest Control Workers; Pesticide Handlers, Sprayers, and Applicators, Vegetation; Tree Trimmers and Pruners.

Skills—Equipment Maintenance: Performing routine maintenance on equipment and determining when and what kind of maintenance is needed. **Repairing:** Repairing machines or systems, using the needed tools. **Operation**

Monitoring: Watching gauges, dials, or other indicators to make sure a machine is working properly. **Installation:** Installing equipment, machines, wiring, or programs to meet specifications.

Education and Training Programs: Landscaping and Groundskeeping; Turf and Turfgrass Management. **Related Knowledge/Course: Mechanical Devices:** Machines and tools, including their designs, uses, repair, and maintenance.

Work Environment: Outdoors; noisy; very hot or cold; contaminants; standing; using hands on objects, tools, or controls.

Librarians

- Education/Training Required: Master's degree
- Annual Earnings: $49,060
- Growth: 3.6%
- Annual Job Openings: 18,945
- Self-Employed: 0.6%
- Part-Time: 27.3%

Level of Stress Tolerance Needed: 74.8 (out of 100)

Most Stressful Aspects: Importance of Being Exact or Accurate (80.5); Deal With Physically Aggressive People (28.3).

Least Stressful Aspects: Pace Determined by Speed of Equipment (14.8); Consequence of Error (21.5); Level of Competition (34.5); Frequency of Conflict Situations (47.8).

Administer libraries and perform related library services. Work in a variety of settings, including public libraries, schools, colleges and universities, museums, corporations, government agencies, law firms, non-profit organiza- tions, and health-care providers. **Tasks may include selecting, acquiring, cataloging, classifying, circulating, and maintaining library materials and furnishing reference, bibliographical, and readers' advisory services. May perform in-depth, strategic research and synthesize, analyze, edit, and filter information. May set up or work with databases and information systems to catalogue and access information.** Search standard reference materials, including online sources and the Internet, to answer patrons' reference questions. Analyze patrons' requests to determine needed information and assist in furnishing or locating that information. Teach library patrons to search for information by using databases. Keep records of circulation and materials. Supervise budgeting, planning, and personnel activities. Check books in and out of the library. Explain use of library facilities, resources, equipment, and services and provide information about library policies. Review and evaluate resource material, such as book reviews and catalogs, to select and order print, audiovisual, and electronic resources. Code, classify, and catalog books, publications, films, audiovisual aids, and other library materials based on subject matter or standard library classification systems. Locate unusual or unique information in response to specific requests. Direct and train library staff in duties such as receiving, shelving, researching, cataloging, and equipment use. Respond to customer complaints, taking action as necessary. Organize collections of books, publications, documents, audiovisual aids, and other reference materials for convenient access. Develop library policies and procedures. Evaluate materials to determine outdated or unused items to be discarded. Develop information access aids such as indexes and annotated bibliographies, Web pages, electronic pathfinders, and online tutorials. Plan and deliver client-centered programs and services such as special services for corporate clients, storytelling for children, newsletters, or programs for special groups. Compile lists of books, periodicals, articles, and audiovisual materials on particular subjects. Arrange for interlibrary loans of materials not available in a particular library. Assemble and arrange display materials. Confer with teachers, parents, and community organizations to develop, plan, and conduct programs in reading, viewing, and communication skills. Compile lists of overdue materials and notify borrowers that their materials are overdue.

Personality Type: Artistic. Artistic occupations frequently involve working with forms, designs, and patterns. They often require self-expression, and the work can be done without following a clear set of rules.

GOE—Interest Area: 05. Education and Training. **Work Group:** 05.04. Library Services. **Other Jobs in This Work Group:** Library Assistants, Clerical; Library Technicians.

Skills—Management of Financial Resources: Determining how money will be spent to get the work done, and accounting for these expenditures. **Management of Material Resources:** Obtaining and seeing to the appropriate use of equipment, facilities, and materials needed to do certain work. **Learning Strategies:** Selecting and using training/instructional methods and procedures appropriate for the situation when learning or teaching new things. **Systems Evaluation:** Identifying measures or indicators of system performance and the actions needed to improve or correct performance, relative to the goals of the system. **Service Orientation:** Actively looking for ways to help people. **Persuasion:** Persuading others to change their minds or behavior.

Education and Training Programs: Library Science, Other; Library Science/Librarianship; School Librarian/School Library Media Specialist Training. **Related Knowledge/ Courses: Communications and Media:** Media production, communication, and dissemination techniques and methods. This includes alternative ways to inform and entertain via written, oral, and visual media. **Clerical Practices:** Administrative and clerical procedures and systems such as word processing, managing files and records, stenography and transcription, designing forms, and other office procedures and terminology. **Customer and Personal Service:** Principles and processes for providing customer and personal services. This includes customer needs assessment, meeting quality standards for services, and evaluation of customer satisfaction. **Personnel and Human Resources:** Principles and procedures for personnel recruitment, selection, training, compensation and benefits, labor relations and negotiation, and personnel information systems. **English Language:** The structure and content of the English language, including the meaning and spelling of words, rules of composition, and grammar. **Computers and Electronics:** Circuit boards, processors, chips, electronic equipment, and computer hardware and software, including applications and programming.

Work Environment: Indoors; sitting; using hands on objects, tools, or controls; repetitive motions.

Library Assistants, Clerical

- Education/Training Required: Short-term on-the-job training
- Annual Earnings: $21,640
- Growth: 7.9%
- Annual Job Openings: 18,961
- Self-Employed: 0.3%
- Part-Time: 70.0%

Level of Stress Tolerance Needed: 58.2 (out of 100)

Most Stressful Aspects: Importance of Being Exact or Accurate (76.3).

Least Stressful Aspects: Deal With Physically Aggressive People (6.5); Pace Determined by Speed of Equipment (9.7); Consequence of Error (19.2); Level of Competition (24.5).

Compile records; sort and shelve books; and issue and receive library materials such as pictures, cards, slides, and microfilm. Locate library materials for loan and replace material in shelving area, stacks, or files according to identification number and title. Register patrons to permit them to borrow books, periodicals, and other library materials. Lend and collect books, periodicals, videotapes, and other materials at circulation desks. Enter and update patrons' records on computers. Process new materials, including books, audiovisual materials, and computer software. Sort books, publications, and other items according to established procedure and return them to shelves, files, or other designated storage areas. Locate library materials for patrons, including books, periodicals, tape cassettes, Braille volumes, and pictures. Instruct patrons on how to use reference sources, card catalogs, and automated information systems. Inspect returned books for condition and due-date status and compute any applicable fines. Answer routine inquiries and refer patrons in need of professional assistance to librarians. Maintain records of items received, stored, issued, and returned and file catalog cards according to system used. Perform clerical activities such as filing, typing, word processing, photocopying and mailing out material, and mail sorting. librarians in the maintenance of collections of books, periodicals, magazines, newspapers, and audiovisual and other materials. Take action to deal with disruptive or problem patrons. Classify and catalog items according to content and purpose. Register new patrons and issue borrower identification cards that permit patrons to borrow books and other materials. Send out notices and accept fine payments for lost or overdue books. Operate small branch libraries under the direction of off-site librarian supervisors. Prepare, store, and retrieve classification and catalog information, lecture notes, or other information related to stored documents, using computers. Schedule and supervise clerical workers, volunteers, and student assistants. Operate and maintain audiovisual equipment. Review records, such as microfilm and issue cards, to identify titles of overdue materials and delinquent borrowers. Select substitute titles when requested materials are unavailable, following criteria such as age, education, and interests. Repair books, using mending tape, paste, and brushes.

Personality Type: Conventional. Conventional occupations frequently involve following set procedures and routines. These occupations can include working with data and details more than with ideas. Usually, there is a clear line of authority to follow.

GOE—Interest Area: 05. Education and Training. **Work Group:** 05.04. Library Services. **Other Jobs in This Work Group:** Librarians; Library Technicians.

Skills—Service Orientation: Actively looking for ways to help people.

Education and Training Program: Library Assistant/Technician Training. **Related Knowledge/Courses: Clerical Practices:** Administrative and clerical procedures and systems such as word processing, managing files and records, stenography and transcription, designing forms, and other office procedures and terminology. **Computers and Electronics:** Circuit boards, processors, chips, electronic equipment, and computer hardware and software, including applications and programming.

Work Environment: Indoors; sitting; using hands on objects, tools, or controls; repetitive motions.

Library Technicians

- ⦿ Education/Training Required: Postsecondary vocational training
- ⦿ Annual Earnings: $26,560
- ⦿ Growth: 8.5%
- ⦿ Annual Job Openings: 29,075
- ⦿ Self-Employed: 0.0%
- ⦿ Part-Time: 58.3%

Level of Stress Tolerance Needed: 68.5 (out of 100)

Most Stressful Aspects: Importance of Being Exact or Accurate (78.8); Frequency of Conflict Situations (55.3).

Least Stressful Aspects: Pace Determined by Speed of Equipment (3.2); Deal With Physically Aggressive People (12.0); Consequence of Error (12.5); Level of Competition (17.5).

Assist librarians by helping readers in the use of library catalogs, databases, and indexes to locate books and other materials and by answering questions that require only brief consultation of standard reference. Compile records; sort and shelve books; remove or repair damaged books; register patrons; check materials in and out of the circulation process. Replace materials in shelving area (stacks) or files. Includes bookmobile drivers who operate bookmobiles or light trucks that pull trailers to specific locations on a predetermined schedule and assist with providing services in mobile libraries. Reserve, circulate, renew, and discharge books and other materials. Enter and update patrons' records on computers. Provide assistance to teachers and students by locating materials and helping to complete special projects. Guide patrons in finding and using library resources, including reference materials, audiovisual equipment, computers, and electronic resources. Answer routine reference inquiries and refer patrons needing further assistance to librarians. Train other staff, volunteers, or student assistants, and schedule and supervise their work. Sort books, publications, and other items according to procedure and return them to shelves, files, or other designated storage areas. Conduct reference searches, using printed materials and in-house and online databases. Deliver and retrieve items throughout the library by hand or by using pushcart. Take actions to halt disruption of library activities by problem patrons. Process interlibrary loans for patrons. Process print and non-print library materials to prepare them for inclusion in library collections. Retrieve information from central databases for storage in a library's computer. Organize and maintain periodicals and reference materials. Compile and maintain records relating to circulation, materials, and equipment. Collect fines and respond to complaints about fines. Issue identification cards to borrowers. Verify bibliographical data for materials, including author, title, publisher, publication date, and edition. Review subject matter of materials to be classified and select classification numbers and headings according to classification systems. Send out notices about lost or overdue books. Prepare order slips for materials to be acquired, checking prices and figuring costs. Design, customize, and maintain databases, Web pages, and local area networks. Operate and maintain audiovisual equipment such as projectors, tape recorders, and videocassette recorders. File catalog cards according to system used. Prepare volumes for binding. Conduct children's programs and other specialized programs such as library tours. Compose explanatory summaries of contents of books and other reference materials.

Personality Type: Conventional. Conventional occupations frequently involve following set procedures and routines. These occupations can include working with data and details more than with ideas. Usually, there is a clear line of authority to follow.

GOE—Interest Area: 05. Education and Training. **Work Group:** 05.04. Library Services. **Other Jobs in This Work Group:** Librarians; Library Assistants, Clerical.

Skills—Service Orientation: Actively looking for ways to help people. **Reading Comprehension:** Understanding written sentences and paragraphs in work-related documents.

Education and Training Program: Library Assistant/Technician Training. **Related Knowledge/Courses:** **Clerical Practices:** Administrative and clerical procedures and systems such as word processing, managing files and records, stenography and transcription, designing forms, and other office procedures and terminology. **Computers and Electronics:** Circuit boards, processors, chips, electronic equipment, and computer hardware and software, including applications and programming. **Customer and Personal Service:** Principles and processes for providing customer and personal services. This includes customer needs assessment, meeting quality standards for services, and evaluation of customer satisfaction. **English Language:** The structure and content of the English language, including the meaning and spelling of words, rules of composition, and grammar. **Administration and Management:** Business and management principles involved in strategic planning, resource allocation, human resources modeling, leadership technique, production methods, and coordination of people and resources. **Education and Training:** Principles and methods for curriculum and training design, teaching and instruction for

individuals and groups, and the measurement of training effects.

Work Environment: Indoors; sitting; using hands on objects, tools, or controls; repetitive motions.

Locksmiths and Safe Repairers

- Education/Training Required: Moderate-term on-the-job training
- Annual Earnings: $32,020
- Growth: 22.1%
- Annual Job Openings: 3,545
- Self-Employed: 28.3%
- Part-Time: 50.0%

Level of Stress Tolerance Needed: 68.5 (out of 100)

Most Stressful Aspects: Duration of Typical Work Week (76.0); Impact of Decisions on Co-workers or Company Results (72.3); Deal With Unpleasant or Angry People (55.3); Level of Competition (47.3).

Least Stressful Aspects: Pace Determined by Speed of Equipment (11.8); Consequence of Error (38.5); Frequency of Conflict Situations (45.0); Time Pressure (67.0).

Repair and open locks, make keys, change locks and safe combinations, and install and repair safes. Cut new or duplicate keys, using keycutting machines. Keep records of company locks and keys. Insert new or repaired tumblers into locks to change combinations. Move picklocks in cylinders to open door locks without keys. Disassemble mechanical or electrical locking devices and repair or replace worn tumblers, springs, and other parts, using hand tools.

Repair and adjust safes, vault doors, and vault components, using hand tools, lathes, drill presses, and welding and acetylene cutting apparatus. Install safes, vault doors, and deposit boxes according to blueprints, using equipment such as powered drills, taps, dies, truck cranes, and dollies. Open safe locks by drilling. Remove interior and exterior finishes on safes and vaults and spray on new finishes.

Personality Type: Realistic. Realistic occupations frequently involve work activities that include practical, hands-on problems and solutions. They often deal with plants; animals; and real-world materials such as wood, tools, and machinery. Many of the occupations require working outside and do not involve a lot of paperwork or working closely with others.

GOE—Interest Area: 13. Manufacturing. **Work Group:** 13.13. Machinery Repair. **Other Jobs in This Work Group:** Bicycle Repairers; Control and Valve Installers and Repairers, Except Mechanical Door; Home Appliance Repairers; Industrial Machinery Mechanics; Maintenance Workers, Machinery; Mechanical Door Repairers; Millwrights; Signal and Track Switch Repairers.

Skills—Installation: Installing equipment, machines, wiring, or programs to meet specifications. **Repairing:** Repairing machines or systems, using the needed tools. **Equipment Maintenance:** Performing routine maintenance on equipment and determining when and what kind of maintenance is needed. **Troubleshooting:** Determining causes of operating errors and deciding what to do about them. **Equipment Selection:** Determining the kind of tools and equipment needed to do a job. **Service Orientation:** Actively looking for ways to help people.

Education and Training Program: Locksmithing and Safe Repair. **Related Knowledge/Courses: Sales and Marketing:** Principles and methods for showing, promoting, and selling products or services. This includes marketing strategy and tactics, product demonstration, sales techniques, and sales control systems. **Clerical Practices:** Administrative and clerical procedures and systems such as word processing, managing files and records, stenography and transcription, designing forms, and other office procedures and terminology. **Customer and Personal Service:** Principles and processes for providing customer and personal services. This includes customer needs assessment, meeting quality standards for services, and evaluation of customer satisfaction. **Administration and Management:** Business and management principles involved in strategic planning, resource allocation, human resources modeling, leadership technique, production methods, and coordination of people and resources. **Mechanical Devices:** Machines and tools, including their designs, uses, repair, and maintenance. **Public Safety and Security:** Relevant equipment, policies, procedures, and strategies to promote effective local, state, or national security operations for the protection of people, data, property, and institutions.

Work Environment: More often outdoors than indoors; noisy; very bright or dim lighting; standing; using hands on objects, tools, or controls.

Logging Equipment Operators

- Education/Training Required: Moderate-term on-the-job training
- Annual Earnings: $29,700
- Growth: –1.3%
- Annual Job Openings: 2,756
- Self-Employed: 28.0%
- Part-Time: 13.4%

Level of Stress Tolerance Needed: 60.0 (out of 100)

Most Stressful Aspects: Impact of Decisions on Co-workers or Company Results (82.2); Duration of Typical Work Week (81.0); Consequence of Error (75.0); Pace Determined by Speed of Equipment (61.8).

Least Stressful Aspects: Deal With Physically Aggressive People (8.8); Frequency of Conflict Situations (30.3); Deal With Unpleasant or Angry People (40.5); Level of Competition (42.3).

Drive logging tractor or wheeled vehicle equipped with one or more accessories, such as bulldozer blade, frontal shear, grapple, logging arch, cable winches, hoisting rack, or crane boom, to fell tree; to skid, load, unload, or stack logs; or to pull stumps or clear brush. Inspect equipment for safety before use and perform necessary basic maintenance tasks. Drive straight or articulated tractors equipped with accessories such as bulldozer blades, grapples, logging arches, cable winches, and crane booms to skid, load, unload, or stack logs; pull stumps; or clear brush. Drive crawler or wheeled tractors to drag or transport logs from felling sites to log landing areas for processing and loading. Drive tractors for the purpose of building or repairing logging and skid roads. Grade logs according to characteristics such as knot size and straightness and according to established industry or company standards. Control hydraulic tractors equipped with tree clamps and booms to lift, swing, and bunch sheared trees. Drive and maneuver tractors and tree harvesters to shear the tops off of trees, cut and limb the trees, and then cut the logs into desired lengths. Fill out required job or shift report forms. Calculate total board feet, cordage, or other wood measurement units, using conversion tables.

Personality Type: Realistic. Realistic occupations frequently involve work activities that include practical, hands-on problems and solutions. They often deal with plants; animals; and real-world materials such as wood, tools, and machinery. Many of the occupations require working outside and do not involve a lot of paperwork or working closely with others.

GOE—Interest Area: 01. Agriculture and Natural Resources. **Work Group:** 01.06. Forestry and Logging. **Other Jobs in This Work Group:** Fallers; Forest and Conservation Technicians; Forest and Conservation Workers; Log Graders and Scalers.

Skills—Repairing: Repairing machines or systems, using the needed tools. **Equipment Maintenance:** Performing routine maintenance on equipment and determining when and what kind of maintenance is needed. **Operation Monitoring:** Watching gauges, dials, or other indicators to make sure a machine is working properly. **Troubleshooting:** Determining causes of operating errors and deciding what to do about them. **Operation and Control:** Controlling operations of equipment or systems. **Installation:** Installing equipment, machines, wiring, or programs to meet specifications.

Education and Training Program: Forest Resources Production and Management. **Related Knowledge/Courses: Mechanical Devices:** Machines and tools, including their designs, uses, repair, and maintenance. **Transportation:** Principles and methods for moving people or goods by air, rail, sea, or road, including the relative costs and benefits. **Production and Processing:** Raw materials, production processes, quality control, costs, and other techniques for maximizing the effective manufacture and distribution of goods.

Work Environment: Outdoors; noisy; contaminants; hazardous equipment; sitting; using hands on objects, tools, or controls.

Mail Clerks and Mail Machine Operators, Except Postal Service

- ◎ Education/Training Required: Short-term on-the-job training
- ◎ Annual Earnings: $23,810
- ◎ Growth: –11.6%
- ◎ Annual Job Openings: 27,889
- ◎ Self-Employed: 0.8%
- ◎ Part-Time: 39.4%

Level of Stress Tolerance Needed: 58.2 (out of 100)

Most Stressful Aspects: Time Pressure (76.0).

Least Stressful Aspects: Deal With Physically Aggressive People (7.0); Level of Competition (30.0); Frequency of Conflict Situations (31.5); Impact of Decisions on Co-workers or Company Results (33.2).

Prepare incoming and outgoing mail for distribution. Use hand or mail-handling machines to time-stamp, open, read, sort, and route incoming mail and address, seal, stamp, fold, stuff, and affix postage to outgoing mail or packages. Duties may also include keeping necessary records and completed forms. Release packages or letters to customers upon presentation of written notices or other identification. Sell mail products and accept payment for products and mailing charges. Place incoming or outgoing letters or packages into sacks or bins based on destination or type and place identifying tags on sacks or bins. Lift and unload containers of mail or parcels onto equipment for transportation to sortation stations. Inspect mail machine output for defects; determine how to eliminate causes of any defects. Use equipment such as forklifts and automated "trains" to move containers of mail. Remove containers of sorted mail/parcels and transfer them to designated areas according to established procedures. Operate computer-controlled keyboards or voice recognition equipment to direct items according to established routing schemes. Wrap packages or bundles by hand or by using tying machines. Accept and check containers of mail or parcels from large-volume mailers, couriers, and contractors. Start machines that automatically feed plates, stencils, or tapes through mechanisms and observe machine operations to detect any malfunctions. Sort and route incoming mail and collect outgoing mail, using carts as necessary. Insert material for printing or addressing into loading racks on machines; select type or die sizes; and position plates, stencils, or tapes in machine magazines. Affix postage to packages or letters by hand or stamp materials, using postage meters. Adjust guides, rollers, loose-card inserters, weighing machines, and tying arms, using rules and hand tools. Contact delivery or courier services to arrange delivery of letters and parcels. Fold letters or circulars and insert them in envelopes. Stamp dates and times of receipt of incoming mail. Operate embossing machines or typewriters to make corrections, additions, and changes to address plates. Remove from machines printed materials such as labeled articles, postmarked envelopes or tape, and folded sheets. Seal or open envelopes by hand or by using machines. Mail merchandise samples or promotional literature in response to requests. Determine manner in which mail is to be sent and prepare it for delivery to mailing facilities. Read production orders to determine types and sizes of items scheduled for printing and mailing. Add ink, fill paste reservoirs, and change machine ribbons when necessary.

Personality Type: Conventional. Conventional occupations frequently involve following set procedures and routines. These occupations can include working with data and details more than with ideas. Usually, there is a clear line of authority to follow.

GOE—Interest Area: 04. Business and Administration. **Work Group:** 04.08. Clerical Machine Operation. **Other Jobs in This Work Group:** Billing, Posting, and Calculating Machine Operators; Data Entry Keyers; Office Machine Operators, Except Computer; Switchboard Operators, Including Answering Service; Word Processors and Typists.

Skills—Operation Monitoring: Watching gauges, dials, or other indicators to make sure a machine is working properly. **Operation and Control:** Controlling operations of equipment or systems.

Education and Training Programs: No related CIP programs; this job is learned through informal short-term on-the-job training. **Related Knowledge/Course: Production and Processing:** Raw materials, production processes, quality control, costs, and other techniques for maximizing the effective manufacture and distribution of goods.

Work Environment: Indoors; standing; using hands on objects, tools, or controls; repetitive motions.

Maintenance and Repair Workers, General

- Education/Training Required: Moderate-term on-the-job training
- Annual Earnings: $31,910
- Growth: 10.1%
- Annual Job Openings: 165,502
- Self-Employed: 1.5%
- Part-Time: 14.1%

Level of Stress Tolerance Needed: 68.8 (out of 100)

Perform work involving the skills of two or more maintenance or craft occupations to keep machines, mechanical equipment, or the structure of an establishment in repair. Duties may involve pipe fitting; boiler making; insulating; welding; machining; carpentry; repairing electrical or mechanical equipment; installing, aligning, and balancing new equipment; and repairing buildings, floors, or stairs. Repair or replace defective equipment parts, using hand tools and power tools, and reassemble equipment. Perform routine preventive maintenance to ensure that machines continue to run smoothly, building systems operate efficiently, and the physical condition of buildings does not deteriorate. Inspect drives, motors, and belts; check fluid levels; replace filters; and perform other maintenance actions, following checklists. Use tools ranging from common hand and power tools, such as hammers, hoists, saws, drills, and wrenches, to precision measuring instruments and electrical and electronic testing devices. Assemble, install, or repair wiring, electrical and electronic components, pipe systems and plumbing, machinery, and equipment. Diagnose mechanical problems and determine how to correct them, checking blueprints, repair manuals, and parts catalogs as necessary. Inspect,

M

operate, and test machinery and equipment to diagnose machine malfunctions. Record maintenance and repair work performed and the costs of the work. Clean and lubricate shafts, bearings, gears, and other parts of machinery. Dismantle devices to gain access to and remove defective parts, using hoists, cranes, hand tools, and power tools. Plan and lay out repair work, using diagrams, drawings, blueprints, maintenance manuals, and schematic diagrams. Adjust functional parts of devices and control instruments, using hand tools, levels, plumb bobs, and straightedges. Order parts, supplies, and equipment from catalogs and suppliers or obtain them from storerooms. Paint and repair roofs, windows, doors, floors, woodwork, plaster, drywall, and other parts of building structures. Operate cutting torches or welding equipment to cut or join metal parts. Align and balance new equipment after installation. Inspect used parts to determine changes in dimensional requirements, using rules, calipers, micrometers, and other measuring instruments. Set up and operate machine tools to repair or fabricate machine parts, jigs and fixtures, and tools. Maintain and repair specialized equipment and machinery found in cafeterias, laundries, hospitals, stores, offices, and factories.

Personality Type: Realistic. Realistic occupations frequently involve work activities that include practical, hands-on problems and solutions. They often deal with plants; animals; and real-world materials such as wood, tools, and machinery. Many of the occupations require working outside and do not involve a lot of paperwork or working closely with others.

GOE—Interest Area: 02. Architecture and Construction. **Work Group:** 02.05. Systems and Equipment Installation, Maintenance, and Repair. **Other Jobs in This Work Group:** Electrical and Electronics Repairers, Powerhouse, Substation, and Relay; Electrical Power-Line Installers and Repairers; Elevator Installers and Repairers; Heating and Air Conditioning Mechanics and Installers; Refrigeration Mechanics and Installers; Telecommunications Equipment Installers and Repairers, Except Line Installers; Telecommunications Line Installers and Repairers.

Skills—Equipment Maintenance: Performing routine maintenance on equipment and determining when and what kind of maintenance is needed. **Installation:** Installing equipment, machines, wiring, or programs to meet specifications. **Repairing:** Repairing machines or systems, using the needed tools. **Troubleshooting:** Determining causes of operating errors and deciding what to do about them. **Operation Monitoring:** Watching gauges, dials, or other indicators to make sure a machine is working properly. **Operation and Control:** Controlling operations of equipment or systems.

Education and Training Program: Building/ Construction Site Management/Manager Training. **Related Knowledge/Courses: Building and Construction:** Materials, methods, and the tools involved in the construction or repair of houses, buildings, or other structures such as highways and roads. **Mechanical Devices:** Machines and tools, including their designs, uses, repair, and maintenance. **Design:** Design techniques, tools, and principles involved in production of precision technical plans, blueprints, drawings, and models. **Physics:** Physical principles, laws, their interrelationships, and applications to understanding fluid, material, and atmospheric dynamics, and mechanical, electrical, atomic, and subatomic structures and processes. **Engineering and Technology:** The practical application of engineering science and technology. This includes applying principles, techniques, procedures, and equipment to the design and production of various goods and services. **Public Safety and Security:** Relevant equipment, policies, procedures, and strategies to promote effective local, state, or national security operations for the protection of people, data, property, and institutions.

Work Environment: Indoors; noisy; minor burns, cuts, bites, or stings; standing; walking and running; using hands on objects, tools, or controls.

Maintenance Workers, Machinery

- Education/Training Required: Moderate-term on-the-job training
- Annual Earnings: $34,550
- Growth: –1.1%
- Annual Job Openings: 15,055
- Self-Employed: 0.0%
- Part-Time: 12.5%

Level of Stress Tolerance Needed: 50.0 (out of 100)

Most Stressful Aspects: Importance of Being Exact or Accurate (80.8); Time Pressure (80.0); Impact of Decisions on Co-workers or Company Results (77.8); Duration of Typical Work Week (74.0).

Least Stressful Aspects: Deal With Physically Aggressive People (9.5); Deal With Unpleasant or Angry People (37.0); Frequency of Conflict Situations (39.7).

Lubricate machinery, change parts, or perform other routine machinery maintenance. Reassemble machines after the completion of repair or maintenance work. Start machines and observe mechanical operation to determine efficiency and to detect problems. Inspect or test damaged machine parts and mark defective areas or advise supervisors of repair needs. Lubricate or apply adhesives or other materials to machines, machine parts, or other equipment according to specified procedures. Install, replace, or change machine parts and attachments according to production specifications. Dismantle machines and remove parts for repair, using hand tools, chain falls, jacks, cranes, or hoists. Record production, repair, and machine maintenance information. Read work orders and specifications to determine machines and equipment requiring repair or maintenance. Set up and operate machines and adjust controls to regulate operations. Collaborate with other workers to repair or move machines, machine parts, or equipment. Inventory and requisition machine parts, equipment, and other supplies so that stock can be maintained and replenished. Transport machine parts, tools, equipment, and other material between work areas and storage, using cranes, hoists, or dollies. Collect and discard worn machine parts and other refuse to maintain machinery and work areas. Clean machines and machine parts, using cleaning solvents, cloths, air guns, hoses, vacuums, or other equipment. Replace or repair metal, wood, leather, glass, or other lining in machines or in equipment compartments or containers. Remove hardened material from machines or machine parts, using abrasives, power and hand tools, jackhammers, sledgehammers, or other equipment. Measure, mix, prepare, and test chemical solutions used to clean or repair machinery and equipment. Replace, empty, or replenish machine and equipment containers such as gas tanks or boxes.

Personality Type: Realistic. Realistic occupations frequently involve work activities that include practical, hands-on problems and solutions. They often deal with plants; animals; and real-world materials such as wood, tools, and machinery. Many of the occupations require working outside and do not involve a lot of paperwork or working closely with others.

GOE—Interest Area: 13. Manufacturing. **Work Group:** 13.13. Machinery Repair. **Other Jobs in**

M

This Work Group: Bicycle Repairers; Control and Valve Installers and Repairers, Except Mechanical Door; Home Appliance Repairers; Industrial Machinery Mechanics; Locksmiths and Safe Repairers; Mechanical Door Repairers; Millwrights; Signal and Track Switch Repairers.

Skills—Installation: Installing equipment, machines, wiring, or programs to meet specifications. **Repairing:** Repairing machines or systems, using the needed tools. **Equipment Maintenance:** Performing routine maintenance on equipment and determining when and what kind of maintenance is needed. **Troubleshooting:** Determining causes of operating errors and deciding what to do about them. **Operation Monitoring:** Watching gauges, dials, or other indicators to make sure a machine is working properly. **Operation and Control:** Controlling operations of equipment or systems.

Education and Training Programs: Heavy/Industrial Equipment Maintenance Technologies, Other; Industrial Mechanics and Maintenance Technology. **Related Knowledge/Courses: Mechanical Devices:** Machines and tools, including their designs, uses, repair, and maintenance. **Building and Construction:** Materials, methods, and the tools involved in the construction or repair of houses, buildings, or other structures such as highways and roads. **Engineering and Technology:** The practical application of engineering science and technology. This includes applying principles, techniques, procedures, and equipment to the design and production of various goods and services. **Physics:** Physical principles, laws, their interrelationships, and applications to understanding fluid, material, and atmospheric dynamics, and mechanical, electrical, atomic, and subatomic structures and processes. **Chemistry:** The chemical composition, structure, and properties of substances and of the chemical processes and transformations that they undergo. This includes uses of chemicals, their danger signs,

production techniques, and disposal methods. **Design:** Design techniques, tools, and principles involved in production of precision technical plans, blueprints, drawings, and models.

Work Environment: Noisy; very hot or cold; contaminants; hazardous equipment; standing; using hands on objects, tools, or controls.

Marine Architects

- Education/Training Required: Bachelor's degree
- Annual Earnings: $72,990
- Growth: 10.9%
- Annual Job Openings: 495
- Self-Employed: 12.4%
- Part-Time: 25.0%

Our sources did not provide separate job openings data for this occupation. The job openings listed here are shared with Marine Engineers.

Level of Stress Tolerance Needed: 62.3 (out of 100)

Most Stressful Aspects: Importance of Being Exact or Accurate (79.3); Impact of Decisions on Co-workers or Company Results (73.8); Duration of Typical Work Week (62.0); Level of Competition (55.5).

Least Stressful Aspects: Pace Determined by Speed of Equipment (0.7); Deal With Physically Aggressive People (1.8); Deal With Unpleasant or Angry People (26.0); Frequency of Conflict Situations (39.7).

Design and oversee construction and repair of marine craft and floating structures such as ships, barges, tugs, dredges, submarines, torpedoes, floats, and buoys. May confer with marine engineers. Design complete hull and superstructure according to specifications and

test data and in conformity with standards of safety, efficiency, and economy. Design layout of craft interior, including cargo space, passenger compartments, ladder wells, and elevators. Study design proposals and specifications to establish basic characteristics of craft, such as size, weight, speed, propulsion, displacement, and draft. Confer with marine engineering personnel to establish arrangement of boiler room equipment and propulsion machinery, heating and ventilating systems, refrigeration equipment, piping, and other functional equipment. Evaluate performance of craft during dock and sea trials to determine design changes and conformance with national and international standards. Oversee construction and testing of prototype in model basin and develop sectional and waterline curves of hull to establish center of gravity, ideal hull form, and buoyancy and stability data.

Personality Type: Realistic. Realistic occupations frequently involve work activities that include practical, hands-on problems and solutions. They often deal with plants; animals; and real-world materials such as wood, tools, and machinery. Many of the occupations require working outside and do not involve a lot of paperwork or working closely with others.

GOE—Interest Area: 15. Scientific Research, Engineering, and Mathematics. **Work Group:** 15.07. Research and Design Engineering. **Other Jobs in This Work Group:** Aerospace Engineers; Biomedical Engineers; Chemical Engineers; Civil Engineers; Computer Hardware Engineers; Electrical Engineers; Electronics Engineers, Except Computer; Marine Engineers; Marine Engineers and Naval Architects; Materials Engineers; Mechanical Engineers; Nuclear Engineers.

Skills—Science: Using scientific rules and methods to solve problems. **Mathematics:** Using mathematics to solve problems. **Operations Analysis:** Analyzing needs and product requirements to create a design. **Technology Design:** Generating or adapting equipment and technology to serve user needs. **Complex Problem Solving:** Identifying complex problems and reviewing related information to develop and evaluate options and implement solutions. **Systems Analysis:** Determining how a system should work and how changes in conditions, operations, and the environment will affect outcomes.

Education and Training Program: Naval Architecture and Marine Engineering. **Related Knowledge/Courses: Engineering and Technology:** The practical application of engineering science and technology. This includes applying principles, techniques, procedures, and equipment to the design and production of various goods and services. **Design:** Design techniques, tools, and principles involved in production of precision technical plans, blueprints, drawings, and models. **Physics:** Physical principles, laws, their interrelationships, and applications to understanding fluid, material, and atmospheric dynamics, and mechanical, electrical, atomic, and subatomic structures and processes. **Building and Construction:** Materials, methods, and the tools involved in the construction or repair of houses, buildings, or other structures such as highways and roads. **Mechanical Devices:** Machines and tools, including their designs, uses, repair, and maintenance. **Production and Processing:** Raw materials, production processes, quality control, costs, and other techniques for maximizing the effective manufacture and distribution of goods.

Work Environment: Indoors; sitting.

Marine Engineers

- Education/Training Required: Bachelor's degree
- Annual Earnings: $72,990
- Growth: 10.9%
- Annual Job Openings: 495
- Self-Employed: 12.4%
- Part-Time: 25.0%

Our sources did not provide separate job openings data for this occupation. The job openings listed here are shared with Marine Architects.

Level of Stress Tolerance Needed: 71.7 (out of 100)

Most Stressful Aspects: Impact of Decisions on Co-workers or Company Results (86.0); Importance of Being Exact or Accurate (83.0); Duration of Typical Work Week (75.0); Time Pressure (68.8).

Least Stressful Aspects: Deal With Physically Aggressive People (2.0); Pace Determined by Speed of Equipment (8.0); Deal With Unpleasant or Angry People (35.8); Frequency of Conflict Situations (46.5).

Design, develop, and take responsibility for the installation of ship machinery and related equipment, including propulsion machines and power supply systems. Prepare, or direct the preparation of, product or system layouts and detailed drawings and schematics. Inspect marine equipment and machinery in order to draw up work requests and job specifications. Conduct analytical, environmental, operational, or performance studies in order to develop designs for products such as marine engines, equipment, and structures. Design and oversee testing, installation, and repair of marine apparatus and equipment. Prepare plans, estimates, design and construction schedules, and contract specifications, including any special provisions. Investigate and observe tests on machinery and equipment for compliance with standards. Coordinate activities with regulatory bodies in order to ensure repairs and alterations are at minimum cost consistent with safety. Prepare technical reports for use by engineering, management, or sales personnel. Conduct environmental, operational, or performance tests on marine machinery and equipment. Maintain contact with, and formulate reports for, contractors and clients to ensure completion of work at minimum cost. Evaluate operation of marine equipment during acceptance testing and shakedown cruises. Analyze data in order to determine feasibility of product proposals. Determine conditions under which tests are to be conducted, as well as sequences and phases of test operations. Procure materials needed to repair marine equipment and machinery. Confer with research personnel to clarify or resolve problems and to develop or modify designs. Review work requests and compare them with previous work completed on ships to ensure that costs are economically sound. Act as liaisons between ships' captains and shore personnel to ensure that schedules and budgets are maintained and that ships are operated safely and efficiently. Perform monitoring activities to ensure that ships comply with international regulations and standards for lifesaving equipment and pollution preventatives. Check, test, and maintain automatic controls and alarm systems. Supervise other engineers and crewmembers and train them for routine and emergency duties.

Personality Type: Realistic. Realistic occupations frequently involve work activities that include practical, hands-on problems and solutions. They often deal with plants; animals; and real-world materials such as wood, tools, and machinery. Many of the occupations require working outside and do not involve a lot of paperwork or working closely with others.

GOE—**Interest Area:** 15. Scientific Research, Engineering, and Mathematics. **Work Group:** 15.07. Research and Design Engineering. **Other Jobs in This Work Group:** Aerospace Engineers; Biomedical Engineers; Chemical Engineers; Civil Engineers; Computer Hardware Engineers; Electrical Engineers; Electronics Engineers, Except Computer; Marine Architects; Marine Engineers and Naval Architects; Materials Engineers; Mechanical Engineers; Nuclear Engineers.

Skills—Science: Using scientific rules and methods to solve problems. **Technology Design:** Generating or adapting equipment and technology to serve user needs. **Installation:** Installing equipment, machines, wiring, or programs to meet specifications. **Mathematics:** Using mathematics to solve problems. **Operations Analysis:** Analyzing needs and product requirements to create a design. **Systems Analysis:** Determining how a system should work and how changes in conditions, operations, and the environment will affect outcomes.

Education and Training Program: Naval Architecture and Marine Engineering. **Related Knowledge/Courses: Engineering and Technology:** The practical application of engineering science and technology. This includes applying principles, techniques, procedures, and equipment to the design and production of various goods and services. **Design:** Design techniques, tools, and principles involved in production of precision technical plans, blueprints, drawings, and models. **Physics:** Physical principles, laws, their interrelationships, and applications to understanding fluid, material, and atmospheric dynamics, and mechanical, electrical, atomic, and subatomic structures and processes. **Mechanical Devices:** Machines and tools, including their designs, uses, repair, and maintenance. **Building and Construction:** Materials, methods, and the tools involved in the construction or repair of houses, buildings,

or other structures such as highways and roads. **Computers and Electronics:** Circuit boards, processors, chips, electronic equipment, and computer hardware and software, including applications and programming.

Work Environment: Outdoors; noisy; sitting.

Marking Clerks

- ◎ Education/Training Required: Short-term on-the-job training
- ◎ Annual Earnings: $20,440
- ◎ Growth: –7.7%
- ◎ Annual Job Openings: 439,327
- ◎ Self-Employed: 0.2%
- ◎ Part-Time: 44.2%

Our sources did not provide separate job openings data for this occupation. The job openings listed here are shared with Order Fillers, Wholesale and Retail Sales; Stock Clerks, Sales Floor; and Stock Clerks— Stockroom, Warehouse, or Storage Yard.

Level of Stress Tolerance Needed: 63.2 (out of 100)

Most Stressful Aspects: Frequency of Conflict Situations (59.8); Deal With Unpleasant or Angry People (57.5).

Least Stressful Aspects: Deal With Physically Aggressive People (8.8); Pace Determined by Speed of Equipment (9.7); Consequence of Error (25.7); Level of Competition (41.3).

Print and attach price tickets to articles of merchandise, using one or several methods, such as marking price on tickets by hand or using ticket-printing machine. Put price information on tickets, marking by hand or using ticket-printing machine. Compare printed price tickets with entries on purchase orders to verify accuracy and notify supervisor of discrepancies. Pin,

M

paste, sew, tie, or staple tickets, tags, or labels to article. Record number and types of articles marked and pack articles in boxes. Mark selling price by hand on boxes containing merchandise. Record price, buyer, and grade of product on tickets attached to products auctioned. Keep records of production, returned goods, and related transactions. Indicate item size, style, color, and inspection results on tags, tickets, and labels, using rubber stamp or writing instrument. Change the price of books in a warehouse.

Personality Type: Conventional. Conventional occupations frequently involve following set procedures and routines. These occupations can include working with data and details more than with ideas. Usually, there is a clear line of authority to follow.

GOE—Interest Area: 04. Business and Administration. **Work Group:** 04.07. Records and Materials Processing. **Other Jobs in This Work Group:** Correspondence Clerks; File Clerks; Human Resources Assistants, Except Payroll and Timekeeping; Meter Readers, Utilities; Office Clerks, General; Order Fillers, Wholesale and Retail Sales; Postal Service Clerks; Postal Service Mail Sorters, Processors, and Processing Machine Operators; Procurement Clerks; Production, Planning, and Expediting Clerks; Shipping, Receiving, and Traffic Clerks; Stock Clerks and Order Fillers; Stock Clerks, Sales Floor; Stock Clerks—Stockroom, Warehouse, or Storage Yard; Weighers, Measurers, Checkers, and Samplers, Recordkeeping.

Skills—Monitoring: Monitoring/assessing performance of yourself, other individuals, or organizations to make improvements or take corrective action. **Mathematics:** Using mathematics to solve problems.

Education and Training Program: Retailing and Retail Operations. **Related Knowledge/**

Courses: Production and Processing: Raw materials, production processes, quality control, costs, and other techniques for maximizing the effective manufacture and distribution of goods. **Sales and Marketing:** Principles and methods for showing, promoting, and selling products or services. This includes marketing strategy and tactics, product demonstration, sales techniques, and sales control systems. **Mathematics:** Arithmetic, algebra, geometry, calculus, statistics, and their applications.

Work Environment: Indoors; standing; walking and running; using hands on objects, tools, or controls; bending or twisting the body; repetitive motions.

Massage Therapists

- ◎ Education/Training Required: Postsecondary vocational training
- ◎ Annual Earnings: $33,400
- ◎ Growth: 20.3%
- ◎ Annual Job Openings: 9,193
- ◎ Self-Employed: 64.0%
- ◎ Part-Time: 48.3%

Level of Stress Tolerance Needed: 63.5 (out of 100)

Most Stressful Aspects: Importance of Being Exact or Accurate (83.0); Impact of Decisions on Co-workers or Company Results (75.3); Level of Competition (52.2).

Least Stressful Aspects: Pace Determined by Speed of Equipment (0.0); Deal With Physically Aggressive People (0.5); Duration of Typical Work Week (11.5); Frequency of Conflict Situations (23.0).

Massage customers for hygienic or remedial purposes. Confer with clients about their medical histories and any problems with stress or pain to determine whether massage would be helpful. Apply finger and hand pressure to specific points of the body. Massage and knead the muscles and soft tissues of the human body to provide courses of treatment for medical conditions and injuries or wellness maintenance. Maintain treatment records. Provide clients with guidance and information about techniques for postural improvement and stretching, strengthening, relaxation, and rehabilitative exercises. Assess clients' soft tissue condition, joint quality and function, muscle strength, and range of motion. Develop and propose client treatment plans that specify which types of massage are to be used. Refer clients to other types of therapists when necessary. Use complementary aids, such as infrared lamps, wet compresses, ice, and whirlpool baths, to promote clients' recovery, relaxation, and well-being. Treat clients in own offices or travel to clients' offices and homes. Consult with other health-care professionals such as physiotherapists, chiropractors, physicians, and psychologists to develop treatment plans for clients. Prepare and blend oils and apply the blends to clients' skin.

Personality Type: No data available.

GOE—Interest Area: 08. Health Science. **Work Group:** 08.07. Medical Therapy. **Other Jobs in This Work Group:** Audiologists; Occupational Therapist Aides; Occupational Therapist Assistants; Occupational Therapists; Physical Therapist Aides; Physical Therapist Assistants; Physical Therapists; Radiation Therapists; Recreational Therapists; Respiratory Therapists; Respiratory Therapy Technicians; Speech-Language Pathologists.

Skills—Service Orientation: Actively looking for ways to help people. **Active Listening:** Giving full attention to what other people are saying, taking time to understand the points being made, asking questions as appropriate, and not interrupting at inappropriate times.

Education and Training Programs: Asian Bodywork Therapy; Massage Therapy/ Therapeutic Massage; Somatic Bodywork; Somatic Bodywork and Related Therapeutic Services, Other. **Related Knowledge/Courses: Therapy and Counseling:** Principles, methods, and procedures for diagnosis, treatment, and rehabilitation of physical and mental dysfunctions, and for career counseling and guidance. **Psychology:** Human behavior and performance; individual differences in ability, personality, and interests; learning and motivation; psychological research methods; and the assessment and treatment of behavioral and affective disorders. **Sales and Marketing:** Principles and methods for showing, promoting, and selling products or services. This includes marketing strategy and tactics, product demonstration, sales techniques, and sales control systems. **Medicine and Dentistry:** The information and techniques needed to diagnose and treat human injuries, diseases, and deformities. This includes symptoms, treatment alternatives, drug properties and interactions, and preventive health-care measures. **Chemistry:** The chemical composition, structure, and properties of substances and of the chemical processes and transformations that they undergo. This includes uses of chemicals, their danger signs, production techniques, and disposal methods. **English Language:** The structure and content of the English language, including the meaning and spelling of words, rules of composition, and grammar.

Work Environment: Indoors; standing; using hands on objects, tools, or controls; repetitive motions.

M

Mathematicians

- ◎ Education/Training Required: Doctoral degree
- ◎ Annual Earnings: $86,930
- ◎ Growth: 10.2%
- ◎ Annual Job Openings: 473
- ◎ Self-Employed: 0.0%
- ◎ Part-Time: 2.3%

Level of Stress Tolerance Needed: 41.8 (out of 100)

Most Stressful Aspects: Duration of Typical Work Week (83.5); Importance of Being Exact or Accurate (81.5); Level of Competition (70.2).

Least Stressful Aspects: Deal With Physically Aggressive People (0.0); Pace Determined by Speed of Equipment (4.8); Deal With Unpleasant or Angry People (17.5); Frequency of Conflict Situations (23.0).

Conduct research in fundamental mathematics or in application of mathematical techniques to science, management, and other fields. Solve or direct solutions to problems in various fields by mathematical methods. Apply mathematical theories and techniques to the solution of practical problems in business, engineering, the sciences, or other fields. Develop computational methods for solving problems that occur in areas of science and engineering or that come from applications in business or industry. Maintain knowledge in the field by reading professional journals, talking with other mathematicians, and attending professional conferences. Perform computations and apply methods of numerical analysis to data. Develop mathematical or statistical models of phenomena to be used for analysis or for computational simulation. Assemble sets of assumptions and explore the consequences of each set. Address the relationships of quantities, magnitudes, and forms through the use of numbers and symbols. Develop new principles and new relationships between existing mathematical principles to advance mathematical science. Design, analyze, and decipher encryption systems designed to transmit military, political, financial, or law-enforcement-related information in code. Conduct research to extend mathematical knowledge in traditional areas, such as algebra, geometry, probability, and logic.

Personality Type: Investigative. Investigative occupations frequently involve working with ideas, and require an extensive amount of thinking. These occupations can involve searching for facts and figuring out problems mentally.

GOE—Interest Area: 15. Scientific Research, Engineering, and Mathematics. **Work Group:** 15.06. Mathematics and Data Analysis. **Other Jobs in This Work Group:** Actuaries; Mathematical Technicians; Social Science Research Assistants; Statistical Assistants; Statisticians.

Skills—Programming: Writing computer programs for various purposes. **Mathematics:** Using mathematics to solve problems. **Science:** Using scientific rules and methods to solve problems. **Complex Problem Solving:** Identifying complex problems and reviewing related information to develop and evaluate options and implement solutions. **Critical Thinking:** Using logic and reasoning to identify the strengths and weaknesses of alternative solutions, conclusions, or approaches to problems. **Reading Comprehension:** Understanding written sentences and paragraphs in work-related documents.

Education and Training Programs: Algebra and Number Theory; Analysis and Functional Analysis; Applied Mathematics; Applied Mathematics, Other; Computational Mathematics; Geometry/Geometric Analysis; Logic;

Mathematical Statistics and Probability; Mathematics and Statistics, Other; Mathematics, General; Mathematics, Other; Topology and Foundations. **Related Knowledge/Courses: Mathematics:** Arithmetic, algebra, geometry, calculus, statistics, and their applications. **Physics:** Physical principles, laws, their interrelationships, and applications to understanding fluid, material, and atmospheric dynamics, and mechanical, electrical, atomic, and subatomic structures and processes. **Computers and Electronics:** Circuit boards, processors, chips, electronic equipment, and computer hardware and software, including applications and programming. **Engineering and Technology:** The practical application of engineering science and technology. This includes applying principles, techniques, procedures, and equipment to the design and production of various goods and services. **English Language:** The structure and content of the English language, including the meaning and spelling of words, rules of composition, and grammar.

Work Environment: Indoors; sitting.

Meat, Poultry, and Fish Cutters and Trimmers

- Education/Training Required: Short-term on-the-job training
- Annual Earnings: $20,370
- Growth: 10.9%
- Annual Job Openings: 17,920
- Self-Employed: 1.1%
- Part-Time: 32.8%

Level of Stress Tolerance Needed: 56.0 (out of 100)

Most Stressful Aspects: Pace Determined by Speed of Equipment (63.0); Duration of Typical Work Week (60.5); Consequence of Error (43.5).

Least Stressful Aspects: Deal With Physically Aggressive People (12.7); Frequency of Conflict Situations (41.5); Level of Competition (44.2); Impact of Decisions on Co-workers or Company Results (48.3).

Use hand tools to perform routine cutting and trimming of meat, poultry, and fish. Use knives, cleavers, meat saws, band saws, or other equipment to perform meat cutting and trimming. Clean, trim, slice, and section carcasses for future processing. Cut and trim meat to prepare for packing. Remove parts, such as skin, feathers, scales, or bones, from carcass. Inspect meat products for defects, bruises, or blemishes and remove them along with any excess fat. Produce hamburger meat and meat trimmings. Process primal parts into cuts that are ready for retail use. Obtain and distribute specified meat or carcass. Separate meats and byproducts into specified containers and seal containers. Weigh meats and tag containers for weight and contents. Clean and salt hides. Prepare sausages, luncheon meats, hot dogs, and other fabricated meat products, using meat trimmings and hamburger meat. Prepare ready-to-heat foods by filleting meat or fish or cutting it into bite-sized pieces, preparing and adding vegetables, or applying sauces or breading.

Personality Type: Realistic. Realistic occupations frequently involve work activities that include practical, hands-on problems and solutions. They often deal with plants; animals; and real-world materials such as wood, tools, and machinery. Many of the occupations require working outside and do not involve a lot of paperwork or working closely with others.

GOE—Interest Area: 13. Manufacturing. **Work Group:** 13.03. Production Work, Assorted Materials Processing. **Other Jobs in This Work**

M

Group: Bakers; Cementing and Gluing Machine Operators and Tenders; Chemical Equipment Operators and Tenders; Cleaning, Washing, and Metal Pickling Equipment Operators and Tenders; Coating, Painting, and Spraying Machine Setters, Operators, and Tenders; Cooling and Freezing Equipment Operators and Tenders; Cutting and Slicing Machine Setters, Operators, and Tenders; Extruding and Forming Machine Setters, Operators, and Tenders, Synthetic and Glass Fibers; Extruding, Forming, Pressing, and Compacting Machine Setters, Operators, and Tenders; Food and Tobacco Roasting, Baking, and Drying Machine Operators and Tenders; Food Batchmakers; Food Cooking Machine Operators and Tenders; Furnace, Kiln, Oven, Drier, and Kettle Operators and Tenders; Heat Treating Equipment Setters, Operators, and Tenders, Metal and Plastic; Helpers—Production Workers; Metal-Refining Furnace Operators and Tenders; Mixing and Blending Machine Setters, Operators, and Tenders; Packaging and Filling Machine Operators and Tenders; Plating and Coating Machine Setters, Operators, and Tenders, Metal and Plastic; Pourers and Casters, Metal; Sawing Machine Setters, Operators, and Tenders, Wood; Separating, Filtering, Clarifying, Precipitating, and Still Machine Setters, Operators, and Tenders; Sewing Machine Operators; Shoe Machine Operators and Tenders; Slaughterers and Meat Packers; Team Assemblers; Textile Bleaching and Dyeing Machine Operators and Tenders; Tire Builders; Woodworking Machine Setters, Operators, and Tenders, Except Sawing.

Skills—None met the criteria.

Education and Training Program: Meat Cutting/Meat Cutter Training. **Related Knowledge/Courses: Food Production:** Techniques and equipment for planting, growing, and harvesting food products (both plant and animal) for consumption, including storage/handling techniques. **Production and Processing:** Raw materials, production processes, quality control, costs, and other techniques for maximizing the effective manufacture and distribution of goods. **Mechanical Devices:** Machines and tools, including their designs, uses, repair, and maintenance.

Work Environment: Indoors; very hot or cold; hazardous equipment; standing; using hands on objects, tools, or controls; repetitive motions.

Mechanical Engineering Technicians

- Education/Training Required: Associate degree
- Annual Earnings: $45,850
- Growth: 6.4%
- Annual Job Openings: 3,710
- Self-Employed: 0.8%
- Part-Time: 20.9%

Level of Stress Tolerance Needed: 57.0 (out of 100)

Most Stressful Aspects: Impact of Decisions on Co-workers or Company Results (74.5); Consequence of Error (68.8); Duration of Typical Work Week (68.0).

Least Stressful Aspects: Deal With Physically Aggressive People (7.0); Pace Determined by Speed of Equipment (11.8); Deal With Unpleasant or Angry People (32.0); Level of Competition (39.0).

Apply theory and principles of mechanical engineering to modify, develop, and test machinery and equipment under direction of engineering staff or physical scientists. Prepare parts sketches and write work orders and

purchase requests to be furnished by outside contractors. Draft detail drawing or sketch for drafting room completion or to request parts fabrication by machine, sheet, or wood shops. Review project instructions and blueprints to ascertain test specifications, procedures, and objectives and test nature of technical problems such as redesign. Review project instructions and specifications to identify, modify, and plan requirements fabrication, assembly, and testing. Devise, fabricate, and assemble new or modified mechanical components for products such as industrial machinery or equipment and measuring instruments. Discuss changes in design, method of manufacture and assembly, and drafting techniques and procedures with staff and coordinate corrections. Set up and conduct tests of complete units and components under operational conditions to investigate proposals for improving equipment performance. Inspect lines and figures for clarity and return erroneous drawings to designer for correction. Analyze test results in relation to design or rated specifications and test objectives and modify or adjust equipment to meet specifications. Evaluate tool drawing designs by measuring drawing dimensions and comparing with original specifications for form and function, using engineering skills. Confer with technicians and submit reports of test results to engineering department and recommend design or material changes. Calculate required capacities for equipment of proposed system to obtain specified performance and submit data to engineering personnel for approval. Record test procedures and results, numerical and graphical data, and recommendations for changes in product or test methods. Read dials and meters to determine amperage, voltage, and electrical output and input at specific operating temperature to analyze parts performance. Estimate cost factors, including labor and material, for purchased and fabricated parts and costs for assembly, testing, or installing. Set up prototype and test apparatus and operate test-controlling equipment to observe and record prototype test results.

Personality Type: Realistic. Realistic occupations frequently involve work activities that include practical, hands-on problems and solutions. They often deal with plants; animals; and real-world materials such as wood, tools, and machinery. Many of the occupations require working outside and do not involve a lot of paperwork or working closely with others.

GOE—Interest Area: 15. Scientific Research, Engineering, and Mathematics. **Work Group:** 15.09. Engineering Technology. **Other Jobs in This Work Group:** Aerospace Engineering and Operations Technicians; Cartographers and Photogrammetrists; Civil Engineering Technicians; Electrical and Electronic Engineering Technicians; Electrical and Electronics Drafters; Electrical Drafters; Electrical Engineering Technicians; Electro-Mechanical Technicians; Electronic Drafters; Electronics Engineering Technicians; Environmental Engineering Technicians; Mapping Technicians; Mechanical Drafters; Surveying and Mapping Technicians; Surveying Technicians.

Skills—Installation: Installing equipment, machines, wiring, or programs to meet specifications. **Troubleshooting:** Determining causes of operating errors and deciding what to do about them. **Technology Design:** Generating or adapting equipment and technology to serve user needs. **Operations Analysis:** Analyzing needs and product requirements to create a design. **Systems Evaluation:** Identifying measures or indicators of system performance and the actions needed to improve or correct performance, relative to the goals of the system. **Equipment Selection:** Determining the kind of tools and equipment needed to do a job.

Education and Training Programs: Mechanical Engineering Related Technologies/Technician Training, Other; Mechanical Engineering/

M

Mechanical Technology/Technician Training. **Related Knowledge/Courses: Engineering and Technology:** The practical application of engineering science and technology. This includes applying principles, techniques, procedures, and equipment to the design and production of various goods and services. **Design:** Design techniques, tools, and principles involved in production of precision technical plans, blueprints, drawings, and models. **Mechanical Devices:** Machines and tools, including their designs, uses, repair, and maintenance. **Physics:** Physical principles, laws, their interrelationships, and applications to understanding fluid, material, and atmospheric dynamics, and mechanical, electrical, atomic, and subatomic structures and processes. **Chemistry:** The chemical composition, structure, and properties of substances and of the chemical processes and transformations that they undergo. This includes uses of chemicals, their danger signs, production techniques, and disposal methods. **Production and Processing:** Raw materials, production processes, quality control, costs, and other techniques for maximizing the effective manufacture and distribution of goods.

Work Environment: Indoors; noisy; contaminants; hazardous equipment; sitting.

Mechanical Engineers

- Education/Training Required: Bachelor's degree
- Annual Earnings: $69,850
- Growth: 4.2%
- Annual Job Openings: 12,394
- Self-Employed: 2.2%
- Part-Time: 11.3%

Level of Stress Tolerance Needed: 59.8 (out of 100)

Most Stressful Aspects: Importance of Being Exact or Accurate (84.7); Duration of Typical Work Week (84.5); Impact of Decisions on Co-workers or Company Results (77.0); Time Pressure (71.7).

Least Stressful Aspects: Deal With Physically Aggressive People (9.0); Pace Determined by Speed of Equipment (21.5); Frequency of Conflict Situations (45.2); Deal With Unpleasant or Angry People (47.5).

Perform engineering duties in planning and designing tools, engines, machines, and other mechanically functioning equipment. Oversee installation, operation, maintenance, and repair of such equipment as centralized heat, gas, water, and steam systems. Read and interpret blueprints, technical drawings, schematics, and computer-generated reports. Confer with engineers and other personnel to implement operating procedures, resolve system malfunctions, and provide technical information. Research and analyze customer design proposals, specifications, manuals, and other data to evaluate the feasibility, cost, and maintenance requirements of designs or applications. Specify system components or direct modification of products to ensure conformance with engineering design and performance specifications. Research, design, evaluate, install, operate, and maintain mechanical products, equipment, systems, and processes to meet requirements, applying knowledge of engineering principles. Investigate equipment failures and difficulties to diagnose faulty operation and to make recommendations to maintenance crew. Assist drafters in developing the structural design of products, using drafting tools or computer-assisted design (CAD) or drafting equipment and software. Provide feedback to design engineers on customer problems and needs. Oversee installation, operation, maintenance, and repair to ensure that machines and equipment are installed and functioning according to specifications. Conduct research that tests and analyzes the feasibility, design, operation, and performance of equipment, components, and systems. Recommend design modifications to eliminate machine or system malfunctions. Develop and test models of alternate designs and processing methods to assess feasibility, operating condition effects, possible new applications, and necessity of modification. Develop, coordinate, and monitor all aspects of production, including selection of manufacturing methods, fabrication, and operation of product designs. Estimate costs and submit bids for engineering, construction, or extraction projects and prepare contract documents. Perform personnel functions such as supervision of production workers, technicians, technologists, and other engineers or design of evaluation programs. Solicit new business and provide technical customer service. Establish and coordinate the maintenance and safety procedures, service schedule, and supply of materials required to maintain machines and equipment in the prescribed condition.

Personality Type: Realistic. Realistic occupations frequently involve work activities that include practical, hands-on problems and solutions. They often deal with plants; animals; and real-world materials such as wood, tools, and machinery. Many of the occupations require working outside and do not involve a lot of paperwork or working closely with others.

GOE—Interest Area: 15. Scientific Research, Engineering, and Mathematics. **Work Group:** 15.07. Research and Design Engineering. **Other Jobs in This Work Group:** Aerospace Engineers; Biomedical Engineers; Chemical Engineers; Civil Engineers; Computer Hardware Engineers; Electrical Engineers; Electronics Engineers, Except Computer; Marine Architects; Marine Engineers; Marine Engineers and Naval Architects; Materials Engineers; Nuclear Engineers.

Skills—Science: Using scientific rules and methods to solve problems. **Operations Analysis:** Analyzing needs and product requirements to create a design. **Installation:** Installing equipment, machines, wiring, or programs to meet specifications. **Complex Problem Solving:** Identifying complex problems and reviewing related information to develop and evaluate options and implement solutions. **Mathematics:** Using mathematics to solve problems. **Systems Analysis:** Determining how a system should work and how changes in conditions, operations, and the environment will affect outcomes.

Education and Training Program: Mechanical Engineering. **Related Knowledge/Courses: Design:** Design techniques, tools, and principles involved in production of precision technical plans, blueprints, drawings, and models. **Engineering and Technology:** The practical application of engineering science and technology. This includes applying principles, techniques, procedures, and equipment to the design and production of various goods and services. **Mechanical Devices:** Machines and tools, including their designs, uses, repair, and maintenance. **Production and Processing:** Raw materials, production processes, quality control, costs, and other techniques for maximizing the effective manufacture and distribution of goods. **Physics:** Physical principles, laws, their interrelationships, and applications to understanding fluid, material, and atmospheric dynamics, and mechanical, electrical, atomic, and subatomic structures and processes. **Administration and Management:** Business and management principles involved in strategic planning, resource allocation, human resources modeling, leadership technique, production methods, and coordination of people and resources.

Work Environment: Indoors; sitting.

M

Metal-Refining Furnace Operators and Tenders

- ◉ Education/Training Required: Moderate-term on-the-job training
- ◉ Annual Earnings: $32,640
- ◉ Growth: –19.0%
- ◉ Annual Job Openings: 5,496
- ◉ Self-Employed: 0.0%
- ◉ Part-Time: 7.2%

Level of Stress Tolerance Needed: 56.0 (out of 100)

Most Stressful Aspects: Duration of Typical Work Week (87.5); Pace Determined by Speed of Equipment (63.0); Level of Competition (60.3).

Least Stressful Aspects: Frequency of Conflict Situations (45.7); Impact of Decisions on Co-workers or Company Results (62.3); Time Pressure (66.0); Importance of Being Exact or Accurate (70.5).

Operate or tend furnaces, such as gas, oil, coal, electric-arc or electric induction, open-hearth, or oxygen furnaces, to melt and refine metal before casting or to produce specified types of steel. Draw smelted metal samples from furnaces or kettles for analysis and calculate types and amounts of materials needed to ensure that materials meet specifications. Drain, transfer, or remove molten metal from furnaces and place it into molds, using hoists, pumps, or ladles. Record production data and maintain production logs. Operate controls to move or discharge metal workpieces from furnaces. Weigh materials to be charged into furnaces, using scales. Regulate supplies of fuel and air or control flow of electric current and water coolant to heat furnaces and adjust temperatures. Inspect furnaces and equipment to locate defects and wear. Observe air and temperature gauges or metal color and fluidity and turn fuel valves or adjust controls to maintain required temperatures. Observe operations inside furnaces, using television screens, to ensure that problems don't occur. Remove impurities from the surface of molten metal, using strainers. Kindle fires and shovel fuel and other materials into furnaces or onto conveyors by hand, with hoists, or by directing crane operators. Sprinkle chemicals over molten metal to bring impurities to the surface. Direct work crews in the cleaning and repair of furnace walls and flooring. Prepare material to load into furnaces, including cleaning, crushing, or applying chemicals, by using crushing machines, shovels, rakes, or sprayers. Scrape accumulations of metal oxides from floors, molds, and crucibles and sift and store them for reclamation.

Personality Type: Realistic. Realistic occupations frequently involve work activities that include practical, hands-on problems and solutions. They often deal with plants; animals; and real-world materials such as wood, tools, and machinery. Many of the occupations require working outside and do not involve a lot of paperwork or working closely with others.

GOE—Interest Area: 13. Manufacturing. **Work Group:** 13.03. Production Work, Assorted Materials Processing. **Other Jobs in This Work Group:** Bakers; Cementing and Gluing Machine Operators and Tenders; Chemical Equipment Operators and Tenders; Cleaning, Washing, and Metal Pickling Equipment Operators and Tenders; Coating, Painting, and Spraying Machine Setters, Operators, and Tenders; Cooling and Freezing Equipment Operators and Tenders; Cutting and Slicing Machine Setters, Operators, and Tenders; Extruding and Forming Machine Setters, Operators, and Tenders, Synthetic and Glass Fibers; Extruding, Forming, Pressing, and Compacting Machine Setters,

Operators, and Tenders; Food and Tobacco Roasting, Baking, and Drying Machine Operators and Tenders; Food Batchmakers; Food Cooking Machine Operators and Tenders; Furnace, Kiln, Oven, Drier, and Kettle Operators and Tenders; Heat Treating Equipment Setters, Operators, and Tenders, Metal and Plastic; Helpers—Production Workers; Meat, Poultry, and Fish Cutters and Trimmers; Mixing and Blending Machine Setters, Operators, and Tenders; Packaging and Filling Machine Operators and Tenders; Plating and Coating Machine Setters, Operators, and Tenders, Metal and Plastic; Pourers and Casters, Metal; Sawing Machine Setters, Operators, and Tenders, Wood; Separating, Filtering, Clarifying, Precipitating, and Still Machine Setters, Operators, and Tenders; Sewing Machine Operators; Shoe Machine Operators and Tenders; Slaughterers and Meat Packers; Team Assemblers; Textile Bleaching and Dyeing Machine Operators and Tenders; Tire Builders; Woodworking Machine Setters, Operators, and Tenders, Except Sawing.

Skills—Operation Monitoring: Watching gauges, dials, or other indicators to make sure a machine is working properly. **Equipment Maintenance:** Performing routine maintenance on equipment and determining when and what kind of maintenance is needed. **Quality Control Analysis:** Conducting tests and inspections of products, services, or processes to evaluate quality or performance. **Operation and Control:** Controlling operations of equipment or systems. **Troubleshooting:** Determining causes of operating errors and deciding what to do about them. **Repairing:** Repairing machines or systems, using the needed tools.

Education and Training Programs: No related CIP programs; this job is learned through informal moderate-term on-the-job training. **Related Knowledge/Courses: Production and Proces-**

sing: Raw materials, production processes, quality control, costs, and other techniques for maximizing the effective manufacture and distribution of goods. **Chemistry:** The chemical composition, structure, and properties of substances and of the chemical processes and transformations that they undergo. This includes uses of chemicals, their danger signs, production techniques, and disposal methods. **Mechanical Devices:** Machines and tools, including their designs, uses, repair, and maintenance. **Engineering and Technology:** The practical application of engineering science and technology. This includes applying principles, techniques, procedures, and equipment to the design and production of various goods and services.

Work Environment: Noisy; very hot or cold; very bright or dim lighting; contaminants; hazardous conditions; minor burns, cuts, bites, or stings.

Meter Readers, Utilities

- Education/Training Required: Short-term on-the-job training
- Annual Earnings: $30,330
- Growth: –10.3%
- Annual Job Openings: 7,328
- Self-Employed: 0.0%
- Part-Time: 32.8%

Level of Stress Tolerance Needed: 63.2 (out of 100)

Most Stressful Aspects: Importance of Being Exact or Accurate (82.7); Time Pressure (77.3); Impact of Decisions on Co-workers or Company Results (71.2); Deal With Physically Aggressive People (27.2).

Least Stressful Aspects: Pace Determined by Speed of Equipment (12.0); Level of

M

Competition (30.5); Consequence of Error (33.0); Frequency of Conflict Situations (34.8).

Read electric, gas, water, or steam consumption meters and enter data in route books or hand-held computers. Walk or drive vehicles along established routes to take readings of meter dials. Upload onto office computers all information collected on hand-held computers during meter rounds or return route books or hand-hand computers to business offices so that data can be compiled. Verify readings in cases where consumption appears to be abnormal and record possible reasons for fluctuations. Inspect meters for unauthorized connections, defects, and damage such as broken seals. Report to service departments any problems such as meter irregularities, damaged equipment, or impediments to meter access, including dogs. Answer customers' questions about services and charges or direct them to customer service centers. Update client address and meter location information. Leave messages to arrange different times to read meters in cases in which meters aren't accessible. Connect and disconnect utility services at specific locations. Collect past-due bills. Report lost or broken keys.

Personality Type: Conventional. Conventional occupations frequently involve following set procedures and routines. These occupations can include working with data and details more than with ideas. Usually, there is a clear line of authority to follow.

GOE—Interest Area: 04. Business and Administration. **Work Group:** 04.07. Records and Materials Processing. **Other Jobs in This Work Group:** Correspondence Clerks; File Clerks; Human Resources Assistants, Except Payroll and Timekeeping; Marking Clerks; Office Clerks, General; Order Fillers, Wholesale and Retail Sales; Postal Service Clerks; Postal Service Mail Sorters, Processors, and Processing Machine Operators; Procurement Clerks; Production, Planning, and Expediting Clerks; Shipping, Receiving, and Traffic Clerks; Stock Clerks and Order Fillers; Stock Clerks, Sales Floor; Stock Clerks—Stockroom, Warehouse, or Storage Yard; Weighers, Measurers, Checkers, and Samplers, Recordkeeping.

Skills—Repairing: Repairing machines or systems, using the needed tools. **Operation Monitoring:** Watching gauges, dials, or other indicators to make sure a machine is working properly. **Installation:** Installing equipment, machines, wiring, or programs to meet specifications. **Systems Evaluation:** Identifying measures or indicators of system performance and the actions needed to improve or correct performance, relative to the goals of the system. **Management of Personnel Resources:** Motivating, developing, and directing people as they work, identifying the best people for the job.

Education and Training Programs: No related CIP programs; this job is learned through informal short-term on-the-job training. **Related Knowledge/Courses: Transportation:** Principles and methods for moving people or goods by air, rail, sea, or road, including the relative costs and benefits. **Public Safety and Security:** Relevant equipment, policies, procedures, and strategies to promote effective local, state, or national security operations for the protection of people, data, property, and institutions.

Work Environment: Outdoors; minor burns, cuts, bites, or stings; standing; walking and running; using hands on objects, tools, or controls; repetitive motions.

Millwrights

- Education/Training Required: Long-term on-the-job training
- Annual Earnings: $45,630
- Growth: 5.8%
- Annual Job Openings: 4,758
- Self-Employed: 3.2%
- Part-Time: 11.1%

Level of Stress Tolerance Needed: 61.8 (out of 100)

Most Stressful Aspects: Time Pressure (81.3); Impact of Decisions on Co-workers or Company Results (78.3); Duration of Typical Work Week (77.5); Importance of Being Exact or Accurate (77.5).

Least Stressful Aspects: Deal With Physically Aggressive People (7.0); Frequency of Conflict Situations (38.2); Deal With Unpleasant or Angry People (49.5).

Install, dismantle, or move machinery and heavy equipment according to layout plans, blueprints, or other drawings. Replace defective parts of machine or adjust clearances and alignment of moving parts. Align machines and equipment, using hoists, jacks, hand tools, squares, rules, micrometers, and plumb bobs. Connect power unit to machines or steam piping to equipment and test unit to evaluate its mechanical operation. Repair and lubricate machines and equipment. Assemble and install equipment, using hand tools and power tools. Position steel beams to support bedplates of machines and equipment, using blueprints and schematic drawings to determine work procedures. Signal crane operator to lower basic assembly units to bedplate and align unit to centerline. Insert shims, adjust tension on nuts and bolts, or position parts, using hand tools and measuring instruments to set specified clearances between moving and stationary parts. Move machinery and equipment, using hoists, dollies, rollers, and trucks. Attach moving parts and subassemblies to basic assembly unit, using hand tools and power tools. Assemble machines and bolt, weld, rivet, or otherwise fasten them to foundation or other structures, using hand tools and power tools. Lay out mounting holes, using measuring instruments, and drill holes with power drill. Bolt parts, such as side and deck plates, jaw plates, and journals, to basic assembly unit. Dismantle machines, using hammers, wrenches, crowbars, and other hand tools. Level bedplate and establish centerline, using straight-edge, levels, and transit. Shrink-fit bushings, sleeves, rings, liners, gears, and wheels to specified items, using portable gas heating equipment. Dismantle machinery and equipment for shipment to installation site, usually performing installation and maintenance work as part of team. Construct foundation for machines, using hand tools and building materials such as wood, cement, and steel. Install robot and modify its program, using teach pendant. Operate engine lathe to grind, file, and turn machine parts to dimensional specifications.

Personality Type: Realistic. Realistic occupations frequently involve work activities that include practical, hands-on problems and solutions. They often deal with plants; animals; and real-world materials such as wood, tools, and machinery. Many of the occupations require working outside and do not involve a lot of paperwork or working closely with others.

GOE—Interest Area: 13. Manufacturing. **Work Group:** 13.13. Machinery Repair. **Other Jobs in This Work Group:** Bicycle Repairers; Control and Valve Installers and Repairers, Except Mechanical Door; Home Appliance Repairers; Industrial Machinery Mechanics; Locksmiths and Safe Repairers; Maintenance Workers, Machinery; Mechanical Door Repairers; Signal and Track Switch Repairers.

Skills—Installation: Installing equipment, machines, wiring, or programs to meet specifications. **Repairing:** Repairing machines or systems, using the needed tools. **Troubleshooting:** Determining causes of operating errors and deciding what to do about them. **Equipment Maintenance:** Performing routine maintenance on equipment and determining when and what kind of maintenance is needed. **Mathematics:** Using mathematics to solve problems. **Equipment Selection:** Determining the kind of tools and equipment needed to do a job.

Education and Training Programs: Heavy/Industrial Equipment Maintenance Technologies, Other; Industrial Mechanics and Maintenance Technology. **Related Knowledge/Courses: Mechanical Devices:** Machines and tools, including their designs, uses, repair, and maintenance. **Building and Construction:** Materials, methods, and the tools involved in the construction or repair of houses, buildings, or other structures such as highways and roads. **Physics:** Physical principles, laws, their interrelationships, and applications to understanding fluid, material, and atmospheric dynamics, and mechanical, electrical, atomic, and subatomic structures and processes. **Engineering and Technology:** The practical application of engineering science and technology. This includes applying principles, techniques, procedures, and equipment to the design and production of various goods and services. **Design:** Design techniques, tools, and principles involved in production of precision technical plans, blueprints, drawings, and models. **Public Safety and Security:** Relevant equipment, policies, procedures, and strategies to promote effective local, state, or national security operations for the protection of people, data, property, and institutions.

Work Environment: Noisy; very hot or cold; very bright or dim lighting; contaminants; hazardous equipment; using hands on objects, tools, or controls.

Mixing and Blending Machine Setters, Operators, and Tenders

- Education/Training Required: Moderate-term on-the-job training
- Annual Earnings: $29,330
- Growth: –5.1%
- Annual Job Openings: 18,661
- Self-Employed: 0.8%
- Part-Time: 15.8%

Level of Stress Tolerance Needed: 60.8 (out of 100)

Most Stressful Aspects: Importance of Being Exact or Accurate (80.5); Duration of Typical Work Week (72.0); Time Pressure (71.5); Consequence of Error (67.5).

Least Stressful Aspects: Frequency of Conflict Situations (38.5); Deal With Unpleasant or Angry People (39.2); Level of Competition (43.8); Impact of Decisions on Co-workers or Company Results (47.8).

Set up, operate, or tend machines to mix or blend materials such as chemicals, tobacco, liquids, color pigments, or explosive ingredients. Weigh or measure materials, ingredients, and products to ensure conformance to requirements. Test samples of materials or products to ensure compliance with specifications, using test equipment. Start machines to mix or blend ingredients; then allow them to mix for specified times. Dump or pour specified amounts of materials into machinery and equipment. Operate or tend machines to mix or blend any of a wide variety of materials such as spices, dough batter, tobacco, fruit juices, chemicals, livestock feed, food products, color pigments, or explosive ingredients. Observe production and monitor equipment to ensure safe and efficient operation. Stop mixing or blending machines when specified product qualities are obtained and open valves and start pumps to transfer mixtures. Collect samples of materials or products for laboratory testing. Add or mix chemicals and ingredients for processing, using hand tools or other devices. Examine materials, ingredients, or products visually or with hands to ensure conformance to established standards. Record operational and production data on specified forms. Transfer materials, supplies, and products between work areas, using moving equipment and hand tools. Tend accessory equipment such as pumps and conveyors to move materials or ingredients through production processes. Read work orders to determine production specifications and information. Compound and process ingredients or dyes according to formulas. Unload mixtures into containers or onto conveyors for further processing. Clean and maintain equipment, using hand tools. Dislodge and clear jammed materials or other items from machinery and equipment, using hand tools. Open valves to drain slurry from mixers into storage tanks.

Personality Type: Realistic. Realistic occupations frequently involve work activities that include practical, hands-on problems and solutions. They often deal with plants; animals; and real-world materials such as wood, tools, and machinery. Many of the occupations require working outside and do not involve a lot of paperwork or working closely with others.

GOE—Interest Area: 13. Manufacturing. **Work Group:** 13.03. Production Work, Assorted Materials Processing. **Other Jobs in This Work Group:** Bakers; Cementing and Gluing Machine Operators and Tenders; Chemical Equipment Operators and Tenders; Cleaning, Washing, and Metal Pickling Equipment Operators and Tenders; Coating, Painting, and Spraying Machine Setters, Operators, and Tenders; Cooling and Freezing Equipment Operators and Tenders; Cutting and Slicing Machine Setters, Operators, and Tenders; Extruding and Forming Machine Setters, Operators, and Tenders, Synthetic and Glass Fibers; Extruding, Forming, Pressing, and Compacting Machine Setters, Operators, and Tenders; Food and Tobacco Roasting, Baking, and Drying Machine Operators and Tenders; Food Batchmakers; Food Cooking Machine Operators and Tenders; Furnace, Kiln, Oven, Drier, and Kettle Operators and Tenders; Heat Treating Equipment Setters, Operators, and Tenders, Metal and Plastic; Helpers—Production Workers; Meat, Poultry, and Fish Cutters and Trimmers; Metal-Refining Furnace Operators and Tenders; Packaging and Filling Machine Operators and Tenders; Plating and Coating Machine Setters, Operators, and Tenders, Metal and Plastic; Pourers and Casters, Metal; Sawing Machine Setters, Operators, and Tenders, Wood; Separating, Filtering, Clarifying, Precipitating, and Still Machine Setters, Operators, and Tenders; Sewing Machine Operators; Shoe Machine Operators and Tenders; Slaughterers and Meat Packers; Team Assemblers; Textile Bleaching and Dyeing Machine Operators and Tenders; Tire Builders; Woodworking Machine Setters, Operators, and Tenders, Except Sawing.

Skills—Operation Monitoring: Watching gauges, dials, or other indicators to make sure a machine is working properly. **Operation and Control:** Controlling operations of equipment or systems. **Equipment Maintenance:** Performing routine maintenance on equipment and determining when and what kind of maintenance is needed. **Repairing:** Repairing machines or systems, using the needed tools.

M

Troubleshooting: Determining causes of operating errors and deciding what to do about them. **Quality Control Analysis:** Conducting tests and inspections of products, services, or processes to evaluate quality or performance.

Education and Training Program: Agricultural and Food Products Processing. **Related Knowledge/Courses: Production and Processing:** Raw materials, production processes, quality control, costs, and other techniques for maximizing the effective manufacture and distribution of goods. **Chemistry:** The chemical composition, structure, and properties of substances and of the chemical processes and transformations that they undergo. This includes uses of chemicals, their danger signs, production techniques, and disposal methods. **Mechanical Devices:** Machines and tools, including their designs, uses, repair, and maintenance. **Physics:** Physical principles, laws, their interrelationships, and applications to understanding fluid, material, and atmospheric dynamics, and mechanical, electrical, atomic, and subatomic structures and processes. **Mathematics:** Arithmetic, algebra, geometry, calculus, statistics, and their applications. **Public Safety and Security:** Relevant equipment, policies, procedures, and strategies to promote effective local, state, or national security operations for the protection of people, data, property, and institutions.

Work Environment: Noisy; contaminants; hazardous conditions; standing; walking and running; using hands on objects, tools, or controls.

Mobile Heavy Equipment Mechanics, Except Engines

- Education/Training Required: Long-term on-the-job training
- Annual Earnings: $40,440
- Growth: 12.3%
- Annual Job Openings: 11,037
- Self-Employed: 5.0%
- Part-Time: 12.7%

Level of Stress Tolerance Needed: 58.5 (out of 100)

Most Stressful Aspects: Time Pressure (81.7); Duration of Typical Work Week (75.0); Impact of Decisions on Co-workers or Company Results (72.3); Consequence of Error (64.0).

Least Stressful Aspects: Level of Competition (43.8); Frequency of Conflict Situations (48.3); Deal With Unpleasant or Angry People (52.7); Importance of Being Exact or Accurate (70.5).

Diagnose, adjust, repair, or overhaul mobile mechanical, hydraulic, and pneumatic equipment, such as cranes, bulldozers, graders, and conveyors, used in construction, logging, and surface mining. Test mechanical products and equipment after repair or assembly to ensure proper performance and compliance with manufacturers' specifications. Repair and replace damaged or worn parts. Diagnose faults or malfunctions to determine required repairs, using engine diagnostic equipment such as computerized test equipment and calibration devices. Operate and inspect machines or heavy equipment to diagnose defects. Dismantle and reassemble heavy equipment, using hoists and hand tools. Clean, lubricate, and perform other routine maintenance work on equipment and vehicles. Examine parts for damage or excessive wear, using micrometers and gauges. Read and understand operating manuals, blueprints, and technical drawings. Schedule maintenance for industrial machines and equipment and keep equipment service records. Overhaul and test machines or equipment to ensure operating efficiency. Assemble gear systems and align frames and gears. Fit bearings to adjust, repair, or overhaul mobile mechanical, hydraulic, and pneumatic equipment. Weld or solder broken parts and structural members, using electric or gas welders and soldering tools. Clean parts by spraying them with grease solvent or immersing them in tanks of solvent. Adjust, maintain, and repair or replace subassemblies, such as transmissions and crawler heads, using hand tools, jacks, and cranes. Adjust and maintain industrial machinery, using control and regulating devices. Fabricate needed parts or items from sheet metal. Direct workers who are assembling or disassembling equipment or cleaning parts.

Personality Type: Realistic. Realistic occupations frequently involve work activities that include practical, hands-on problems and solutions. They often deal with plants; animals; and real-world materials such as wood, tools, and machinery. Many of the occupations require working outside and do not involve a lot of paperwork or working closely with others.

GOE—Interest Area: 13. Manufacturing. **Work Group:** 13.14. Vehicle and Facility Mechanical Work. **Other Jobs in This Work Group:** Aircraft Mechanics and Service Technicians; Aircraft Structure, Surfaces, Rigging, and Systems Assemblers; Automotive Body and Related Repairers; Automotive Glass Installers and Repairers; Automotive Master Mechanics; Automotive Service Technicians and Mechanics; Automotive Specialty Technicians; Bus and Truck Mechanics and Diesel Engine Specialists;

Farm Equipment Mechanics; Fiberglass Laminators and Fabricators; Motorboat Mechanics; Motorcycle Mechanics; Outdoor Power Equipment and Other Small Engine Mechanics; Rail Car Repairers; Recreational Vehicle Service Technicians; Tire Repairers and Changers.

Skills—Installation: Installing equipment, machines, wiring, or programs to meet specifications. **Repairing:** Repairing machines or systems, using the needed tools. **Equipment Maintenance:** Performing routine maintenance on equipment and determining when and what kind of maintenance is needed. **Operation Monitoring:** Watching gauges, dials, or other indicators to make sure a machine is working properly. **Troubleshooting:** Determining causes of operating errors and deciding what to do about them. **Operation and Control:** Controlling operations of equipment or systems.

Education and Training Programs: Agricultural Mechanics and Equipment/Machine Technology; Heavy Equipment Maintenance Technology/Technician Training. **Related Knowledge/Courses: Mechanical Devices:** Machines and tools, including their designs, uses, repair, and maintenance. **Engineering and Technology:** The practical application of engineering science and technology. This includes applying principles, techniques, procedures, and equipment to the design and production of various goods and services. **Physics:** Physical principles, laws, their interrelationships, and applications to understanding fluid, material, and atmospheric dynamics, and mechanical, electrical, atomic, and subatomic structures and processes.

Work Environment: Noisy; contaminants; hazardous equipment; minor burns, cuts, bites, or stings; standing; using hands on objects, tools, or controls.

M

Model Makers, Metal and Plastic

- ◎ Education/Training Required: Long-term on-the-job training
- ◎ Annual Earnings: $42,050
- ◎ Growth: –6.3%
- ◎ Annual Job Openings: 1,801
- ◎ Self-Employed: 4.8%
- ◎ Part-Time: 7.2%

Level of Stress Tolerance Needed: 62.7 (out of 100)

Most Stressful Aspects: Importance of Being Exact or Accurate (84.0); Time Pressure (74.5); Duration of Typical Work Week (68.5); Level of Competition (51.2).

Least Stressful Aspects: Deal With Physically Aggressive People (5.3); Frequency of Conflict Situations (29.0); Deal With Unpleasant or Angry People (35.0); Impact of Decisions on Co-workers or Company Results (53.0).

Set up and operate machines, such as lathes, milling and engraving machines, and jig borers, to make working models of metal or plastic objects. Study blueprints, drawings, and sketches to determine material dimensions, required equipment, and operations sequences. Set up and operate machines such as lathes, drill presses, punch presses, or band saws to fabricate prototypes or models. Inspect and test products to verify conformance to specifications, using precision measuring instruments or circuit testers. Cut, shape, and form metal parts, using lathes, power saws, snips, power brakes and shears, files, and mallets. Lay out and mark reference points and dimensions on materials, using measuring instruments and drawing or scribing tools. Drill, countersink, and ream holes in parts and assemblies for bolts, screws, and other fasteners, using power tools. Grind, file, and sand parts to finished dimensions. Record specifications, production operations, and final dimensions of models for use in establishing operating standards and procedures. Rework or alter component model or parts as required to ensure that products meet standards. Align, fit, and join parts by using bolts and screws or by welding or gluing. Consult and confer with engineering personnel to discuss developmental problems and to recommend product modifications. Assemble mechanical, electrical, and electronic components into models or prototypes, using hand tools, power tools, and fabricating machines. Devise and construct tools, dies, molds, jigs, and fixtures or modify existing tools and equipment. Wire and solder electrical and electronic connections and components.

Personality Type: Realistic. Realistic occupations frequently involve work activities that include practical, hands-on problems and solutions. They often deal with plants; animals; and real-world materials such as wood, tools, and machinery. Many of the occupations require working outside and do not involve a lot of paperwork or working closely with others.

GOE—Interest Area: 13. Manufacturing. **Work Group:** 13.05. Production Machining Technology. **Other Jobs in This Work Group:** Computer-Controlled Machine Tool Operators, Metal and Plastic; Foundry Mold and Coremakers; Lay-Out Workers, Metal and Plastic; Machinists; Numerical Tool and Process Control Programmers; Patternmakers, Metal and Plastic; Tool and Die Makers; Tool Grinders, Filers, and Sharpeners.

Skills—Operation Monitoring: Watching gauges, dials, or other indicators to make sure a machine is working properly. **Repairing:** Repairing machines or systems, using the needed tools. **Quality Control Analysis:** Conducting tests and inspections of products, services, or processes to evaluate quality or performance. **Operation and Control:** Controlling operations of equipment or systems. **Equipment Maintenance:** Performing routine maintenance on equipment and determining when and what kind of maintenance is needed. **Mathematics:** Using mathematics to solve problems.

Education and Training Program: Sheet Metal Technology/Sheetworking. **Related Knowledge/ Courses: Mechanical Devices:** Machines and tools, including their designs, uses, repair, and maintenance. **Design:** Design techniques, tools, and principles involved in production of precision technical plans, blueprints, drawings, and models. **Production and Processing:** Raw materials, production processes, quality control, costs, and other techniques for maximizing the effective manufacture and distribution of goods. **Engineering and Technology:** The practical application of engineering science and technology. This includes applying principles, techniques, procedures, and equipment to the design and production of various goods and services. **Computers and Electronics:** Circuit boards, processors, chips, electronic equipment, and computer hardware and software, including applications and programming. **Mathematics:** Arithmetic, algebra, geometry, calculus, statistics, and their applications.

Work Environment: Indoors; noisy; contaminants; hazardous equipment; standing; using hands on objects, tools, or controls.

Molding and Casting Workers

- Education/Training Required: Moderate-term on-the-job training
- Annual Earnings: $25,010
- Growth: 1.3%
- Annual Job Openings: 5,788
- Self-Employed: 24.2%
- Part-Time: 19.0%

Our sources did not provide separate job openings data for this occupation. The job openings listed here are shared with Glass Blowers, Molders, Benders, and Finishers; Potters, Manufacturing; and Stone Cutters and Carvers, Manufacturing.

Level of Stress Tolerance Needed: 69.0 (out of 100)

Most Stressful Aspects: Time Pressure (73.5); Duration of Typical Work Week (66.0); Consequence of Error (58.2); Pace Determined by Speed of Equipment (57.0).

Least Stressful Aspects: Deal With Physically Aggressive People (8.5); Level of Competition (37.5); Deal With Unpleasant or Angry People (40.8); Frequency of Conflict Situations (42.0).

Perform a variety of duties such as mixing materials, assembling mold parts, filling molds, and stacking molds to mold and cast a wide range of products. Brush or spray mold surfaces with parting agents or insert paper into molds to ensure smoothness and prevent sticking or seepage. Clean, finish, and lubricate molds and mold parts. Separate models or patterns from molds and examine products for accuracy. Pour, pack, spread, or press plaster, concrete, liquid plastic, or other materials into or around models or molds. Operate and adjust controls of heating equipment to melt material or to cure, dry, or

M

bake filled molds. Read work orders or examine parts to determine parts or sections of products to be produced. Load or stack filled molds in ovens, dryers, or curing boxes or on storage racks or carts. Set the proper operating temperature for each casting. Measure and cut products to specified dimensions, using measuring and cutting instruments. Remove excess materials and level and smooth wet mold mixtures. Melt metal pieces, using torches, and cast products such as inlays and crowns, using centrifugal casting machines. Select sizes and types of molds according to instructions. Align and assemble parts to produce completed products, using gauges and hand tools. Trim or remove excess material, using scrapers, knives, or band saws. Bore holes or cut grates, risers, and pouring spouts in molds, using power tools. Withdraw cores and other loose mold members after castings solidify. Construct or form molds for use in casting metal, clay, or plaster objects, using plaster, fiberglass, rubber, casting machines, patterns, or flasks. Verify dimensions of products, using measuring instruments such as calipers, vernier gauges, and protractors. Tap or tilt molds to ensure uniform distribution of materials. Locate and scribe parting lines on patterns, using measuring instruments such as calipers, squares, and depth gauges. Patch broken edges and fractures, using clay or plaster. Smooth surfaces of molds, using scraping tools and sandpaper. Measure ingredients and mix molding, casting material, or sealing compounds to prescribed consistencies according to formulas. Repair mold defects such as cracks and broken edges, using patterns, mold boxes, or hand tools.

Personality Type: Realistic. Realistic occupations frequently involve work activities that include practical, hands-on problems and solutions. They often deal with plants; animals; and real-world materials such as wood, tools, and machinery. Many of the occupations require working outside and do not involve a lot of paperwork or working closely with others.

GOE—Interest Area: 13. Manufacturing. **Work Group:** 13.09. Hands-On Work, Assorted Materials. **Other Jobs in This Work Group:** Coil Winders, Tapers, and Finishers; Cutters and Trimmers, Hand; Fabric and Apparel Patternmakers; Glass Blowers, Molders, Benders, and Finishers; Grinding and Polishing Workers, Hand; Painters, Transportation Equipment; Painting, Coating, and Decorating Workers; Sewers, Hand.

Skills—Quality Control Analysis: Conducting tests and inspections of products, services, or processes to evaluate quality or performance. **Installation:** Installing equipment, machines, wiring, or programs to meet specifications. **Repairing:** Repairing machines or systems, using the needed tools. **Equipment Selection:** Determining the kind of tools and equipment needed to do a job. **Operation Monitoring:** Watching gauges, dials, or other indicators to make sure a machine is working properly.

Education and Training Programs: No related CIP programs; this job is learned through informal moderate-term on-the-job training. **Related Knowledge/Courses: Production and Processing:** Raw materials, production processes, quality control, costs, and other techniques for maximizing the effective manufacture and distribution of goods. **Mechanical Devices:** Machines and tools, including their designs, uses, repair, and maintenance.

Work Environment: Noisy; very hot or cold; contaminants; standing; using hands on objects, tools, or controls; repetitive motions.

Motorcycle Mechanics

- Education/Training Required: Long-term on-the-job training
- Annual Earnings: $30,050
- Growth: 12.5%
- Annual Job Openings: 3,564
- Self-Employed: 21.9%
- Part-Time: 12.7%

Level of Stress Tolerance Needed: 71.5 (out of 100)

Most Stressful Aspects: Impact of Decisions on Co-workers or Company Results (79.3); Consequence of Error (78.3); Importance of Being Exact or Accurate (77.5); Time Pressure (75.8).

Least Stressful Aspects: Pace Determined by Speed of Equipment (14.3); Deal With Unpleasant or Angry People (46.7).

Diagnose, adjust, repair, or overhaul motorcycles, scooters, mopeds, dirt bikes, or similar motorized vehicles. Repair and adjust motorcycle subassemblies such as forks, transmissions, brakes, and drive chains according to specifications. Replace defective parts, using hand tools, arbor presses, flexible power presses, or power tools. Connect test panels to engines and measure generator output, ignition timing, and other engine performance indicators. Listen to engines, examine vehicle frames, and confer with customers to determine nature and extent of malfunction or damage. Reassemble and test subassembly units. Dismantle engines and repair or replace defective parts, such as magnetos, carburetors, and generators. Remove cylinder heads; grind valves; scrape off carbon; and replace defective valves, pistons, cylinders, and rings, using hand tools and power tools. Repair or replace other parts, such as headlights, horns, handlebar controls, gasoline and oil tanks, starters, and mufflers. Disassemble subassembly units and examine condition, movement, or alignment of parts visually or by using gauges. Hammer out dents and bends in frames, weld tears and breaks, and reassemble frames and reinstall engines.

Personality Type: Realistic. Realistic occupations frequently involve work activities that include practical, hands-on problems and solutions. They often deal with plants; animals; and real-world materials such as wood, tools, and machinery. Many of the occupations require working outside and do not involve a lot of paperwork or working closely with others.

GOE—Interest Area: 13. Manufacturing. **Work Group:** 13.14. Vehicle and Facility Mechanical Work. **Other Jobs in This Work Group:** Aircraft Mechanics and Service Technicians; Aircraft Structure, Surfaces, Rigging, and Systems Assemblers; Automotive Body and Related Repairers; Automotive Glass Installers and Repairers; Automotive Master Mechanics; Automotive Service Technicians and Mechanics; Automotive Specialty Technicians; Bus and Truck Mechanics and Diesel Engine Specialists; Farm Equipment Mechanics; Fiberglass Laminators and Fabricators; Mobile Heavy Equipment Mechanics, Except Engines; Motorboat Mechanics; Outdoor Power Equipment and Other Small Engine Mechanics; Rail Car Repairers; Recreational Vehicle Service Technicians; Tire Repairers and Changers.

Skills—Repairing: Repairing machines or systems, using the needed tools. **Installation:** Installing equipment, machines, wiring, or programs to meet specifications. **Troubleshooting:** Determining causes of operating errors and deciding what to do about them. **Equipment Maintenance:** Performing routine maintenance on equipment and determining when and what kind of maintenance is needed. **Science:** Using

M

scientific rules and methods to solve problems. **Technology Design:** Generating or adapting equipment and technology to serve user needs.

Education and Training Program: Motorcycle Maintenance and Repair Technology/ Technician Training. **Related Knowledge/ Courses: Mechanical Devices:** Machines and tools, including their designs, uses, repair, and maintenance. **Design:** Design techniques, tools, and principles involved in production of precision technical plans, blueprints, drawings, and models. **Engineering and Technology:** The practical application of engineering science and technology. This includes applying principles, techniques, procedures, and equipment to the design and production of various goods and services. **Physics:** Physical principles, laws, their interrelationships, and applications to understanding fluid, material, and atmospheric dynamics, and mechanical, electrical, atomic, and subatomic structures and processes. **Transportation:** Principles and methods for moving people or goods by air, rail, sea, or road, including the relative costs and benefits. **Chemistry:** The chemical composition, structure, and properties of substances and of the chemical processes and transformations that they undergo. This includes uses of chemicals, their danger signs, production techniques, and disposal methods.

Work Environment: Indoors; noisy; contaminants; standing; using hands on objects, tools, or controls; bending or twisting the body.

Multiple Machine Tool Setters, Operators, and Tenders, Metal and Plastic

- ◎ Education/Training Required: Moderate-term on-the-job training
- ◎ Annual Earnings: $30,530
- ◎ Growth: 0.3%
- ◎ Annual Job Openings: 15,709
- ◎ Self-Employed: 0.0%
- ◎ Part-Time: 25.0%

Level of Stress Tolerance Needed: 55.5 (out of 100)

Most Stressful Aspects: Duration of Typical Work Week (89.0); Pace Determined by Speed of Equipment (81.7); Importance of Being Exact or Accurate (80.3); Time Pressure (77.0).

Least Stressful Aspects: Deal With Physically Aggressive People (9.3); Frequency of Conflict Situations (46.2); Impact of Decisions on Co-workers or Company Results (49.5).

Set up, operate, or tend more than one type of cutting or forming machine tool or robot. Inspect workpieces for defects and measure workpieces to determine accuracy of machine operation, using rules, templates, or other measuring instruments. Observe machine operation to detect workpiece defects or machine malfunctions; adjust machines as necessary. Read blueprints or job orders to determine product specifications and tooling instructions and to plan operational sequences. Set up and operate machines such as lathes, cutters, shears, borers, millers, grinders, presses, drills, and auxiliary machines to make metallic and plastic workpieces. Position, adjust, and secure stock material or workpieces against stops; on arbors; or in chucks, fixtures, or automatic feeding mechanisms manually or by using hoists. Select, install, and adjust alignment of drills, cutters, dies, guides, and holding devices, using templates, measuring instruments, and hand tools. Change worn machine accessories such as cutting tools and brushes, using hand tools. Make minor electrical and mechanical repairs and adjustments to machines and notify supervisors when major service is required. Start machines and turn handwheels or valves to engage feeding, cooling, and lubricating mechanisms. Perform minor machine maintenance, such as oiling or cleaning machines, dies, or workpieces or adding coolant to machine reservoirs. Select the proper coolants and lubricants and start their flow. Remove burrs, sharp edges, rust, or scale from workpieces, using files, hand grinders, wire brushes, or power tools. Instruct other workers in machine setup and operation. Record operational data such as pressure readings, lengths of strokes, feed rates, and speeds. Extract or lift jammed pieces from machines, using fingers, wire hooks, or lift bars. Set machine stops or guides to specified lengths as indicated by scales, rules, or templates. Move controls or mount gears, cams, or templates in machines to set feed rates and cutting speeds, depths, and angles. Compute data such as gear dimensions and machine settings, applying knowledge of shop mathematics. Align layout marks with dies or blades. Measure and mark reference points and cutting lines on workpieces, using traced templates, compasses, and rules.

Personality Type: Realistic. Realistic occupations frequently involve work activities that include practical, hands-on problems and solutions. They often deal with plants; animals; and real-world materials such as wood, tools, and machinery. Many of the occupations require working outside and do not involve a lot of paperwork or working closely with others.

GOE—Interest Area: 13. Manufacturing. **Work Group:** 13.02. Machine Setup and Operation.

Other Jobs in This Work Group: Crushing, Grinding, and Polishing Machine Setters, Operators, and Tenders; Cutting, Punching, and Press Machine Setters, Operators, and Tenders, Metal and Plastic; Drilling and Boring Machine Tool Setters, Operators, and Tenders, Metal and Plastic; Extruding and Drawing Machine Setters, Operators, and Tenders, Metal and Plastic; Forging Machine Setters, Operators, and Tenders, Metal and Plastic; Grinding, Lapping, Polishing, and Buffing Machine Tool Setters, Operators, and Tenders, Metal and Plastic; Lathe and Turning Machine Tool Setters, Operators, and Tenders, Metal and Plastic; Milling and Planing Machine Setters, Operators, and Tenders, Metal and Plastic; Paper Goods Machine Setters, Operators, and Tenders; Rolling Machine Setters, Operators, and Tenders, Metal and Plastic; Textile Cutting Machine Setters, Operators, and Tenders; Textile Knitting and Weaving Machine Setters, Operators, and Tenders; Textile Winding, Twisting, and Drawing Out Machine Setters, Operators, and Tenders.

Skills—Operation Monitoring: Watching gauges, dials, or other indicators to make sure a machine is working properly. **Repairing:** Repairing machines or systems, using the needed tools. **Quality Control Analysis:** Conducting tests and inspections of products, services, or processes to evaluate quality or performance. **Equipment Maintenance:** Performing routine maintenance on equipment and determining when and what kind of maintenance is needed. **Operation and Control:** Controlling operations of equipment or systems. **Troubleshooting:** Determining causes of operating errors and deciding what to do about them.

Education and Training Programs: Machine Shop Technology/Assistant; Machine Tool Technology/Machinist. **Related Knowledge/Courses: Mechanical Devices:** Machines and

M

tools, including their designs, uses, repair, and maintenance. **Production and Processing:** Raw materials, production processes, quality control, costs, and other techniques for maximizing the effective manufacture and distribution of goods. **Design:** Design techniques, tools, and principles involved in production of precision technical plans, blueprints, drawings, and models. **Engineering and Technology:** The practical application of engineering science and technology. This includes applying principles, techniques, procedures, and equipment to the design and production of various goods and services.

Work Environment: Noisy; contaminants; hazardous equipment; minor burns, cuts, bites, or stings; standing; using hands on objects, tools, or controls.

Museum Technicians and Conservators

- Education/Training Required: Bachelor's degree
- Annual Earnings: $34,340
- Growth: 15.9%
- Annual Job Openings: 1,341
- Self-Employed: 1.3%
- Part-Time: 32.4%

Level of Stress Tolerance Needed: 58.7 (out of 100)

Most Stressful Aspects: Consequence of Error (45.5).

Least Stressful Aspects: Deal With Physically Aggressive People (1.8); Pace Determined by Speed of Equipment (7.2); Level of Competition (21.5); Deal With Unpleasant or Angry People (24.5).

Prepare specimens, such as fossils, skeletal parts, lace, and textiles, for museum collections and exhibits. May restore documents or install, arrange, and exhibit materials. Install, arrange, assemble, and prepare artifacts for exhibition, ensuring the artifacts' safety, reporting their status and condition, and identifying and correcting any problems with the setup. Coordinate exhibit installations, assisting with design; constructing displays, dioramas, display cases, and models; and ensuring the availability of necessary materials. Determine whether objects need repair and choose the safest and most effective method of repair. Clean objects, such as paper, textiles, wood, metal, glass, rock, pottery, and furniture, using cleansers, solvents, soap solutions, and polishes. Prepare artifacts for storage and shipping. Supervise and work with volunteers. Present public programs and tours. Specialize in particular materials or types of object, such as documents and books, paintings, decorative arts, textiles, metals, or architectural materials. Recommend preservation procedures, such as control of temperature and humidity, to curatorial and building staff. Classify and assign registration numbers to artifacts and supervise inventory control. Direct and supervise curatorial and technical staff in the handling, mounting, care, and storage of art objects. Perform on-site fieldwork, which may involve interviewing people, inspecting and identifying artifacts, note-taking, viewing sites and collections, and repainting exhibition spaces. Repair, restore, and reassemble artifacts, designing and fabricating missing or broken parts, to restore them to their original appearance and prevent deterioration. Prepare reports on the operation of conservation laboratories, documenting the condition of artifacts, treatment options, and the methods of preservation and repair used. Study object documentation or conduct standard chemical and physical tests to ascertain the object's age, composition, original appearance, need for treatment or restoration, and appropriate preservation method. Cut and weld metal sections in reconstruction or renovation of exterior structural sections and accessories of exhibits. Perform tests and examinations to establish storage and conservation requirements, policies, and procedures.

Personality Type: Artistic. Artistic occupations frequently involve working with forms, designs, and patterns. They often require self-expression, and the work can be done without following a clear set of rules.

GOE—Interest Area: 05. Education and Training. **Work Group:** 05.05. Archival and Museum Services. **Other Jobs in This Work Group:** Archivists; Audio-Visual Collections Specialists; Curators.

Skills—Management of Material Resources: Obtaining and seeing to the appropriate use of equipment, facilities, and materials needed to do certain work. **Repairing:** Repairing machines or systems, using the needed tools. **Installation:** Installing equipment, machines, wiring, or programs to meet specifications. **Technology Design:** Generating or adapting equipment and technology to serve user needs. **Equipment Maintenance:** Performing routine maintenance on equipment and determining when and what kind of maintenance is needed. **Operations Analysis:** Analyzing needs and product requirements to create a design.

Education and Training Programs: Art History, Criticism and Conservation; Museology/Museum Studies; Public/Applied History and Archival Administration. **Related Knowledge/Courses: History and Archeology:** Historical events and their causes, indicators, and effects on civilizations and cultures. **Fine Arts:** The theory and techniques required to compose, produce, and perform works of music, dance, visual arts, drama, and sculpture. **Sociology and Anthropology:** Group behavior and dynamics, societal trends and influences, human migrations, ethnicity, cultures, and their history and origins. **Design:** Design techniques, tools, and principles involved in production of precision technical plans, blueprints, drawings, and models. **Clerical Practices:** Administrative and clerical procedures and systems such as word processing, managing files and records, stenography and transcription, designing forms, and other office procedures and terminology. **Building and Construction:** Materials, methods, and the tools involved in the construction or repair of houses, buildings, or other structures such as highways and roads.

Work Environment: Indoors; standing; using hands on objects, tools, or controls.

Natural Sciences Managers

- Education/Training Required: Work experience plus degree
- Annual Earnings: $100,080
- Growth: 11.4%
- Annual Job Openings: 3,661
- Self-Employed: 0.6%
- Part-Time: 16.9%

Level of Stress Tolerance Needed: 68.5 (out of 100)

Most Stressful Aspects: Duration of Typical Work Week (87.5); Impact of Decisions on Co-workers or Company Results (77.8); Time Pressure (67.8); Frequency of Conflict Situations (62.0).

Least Stressful Aspects: Deal With Physically Aggressive People (5.8); Pace Determined by Speed of Equipment (13.2); Deal With Unpleasant or Angry People (39.7); Importance of Being Exact or Accurate (69.0).

Plan, direct, or coordinate activities in such fields as life sciences, physical sciences, mathematics, and statistics and research and development in these fields. Confer with scientists, engineers, regulators, and others to plan and review projects and to provide technical assistance. Develop client relationships and communicate with clients to explain proposals, present research findings, establish specifications, or discuss project status. Plan and direct research, development, and production activities. Prepare project proposals. Design and coordinate successive phases of problem analysis, solution proposals, and testing. Review project activities and prepare and review research, testing, and operational reports. Hire, supervise, and evaluate engineers, technicians, researchers, and other staff. Determine scientific and technical goals within broad outlines provided by top management and make detailed plans to accomplish these goals. Develop and implement policies, standards, and procedures for the architectural, scientific, and technical work performed to ensure regulatory compliance and operations enhancement. Develop innovative technology and train staff for its implementation. Provide for stewardship of plant and animal resources and habitats, studying land use; monitoring animal populations; and providing shelter, resources, and medical treatment for animals. Conduct own research in field of expertise. Recruit personnel and oversee the development and maintenance of staff competence. Advise and assist in obtaining patents or meeting other legal requirements. Prepare and administer budget, approve and review expenditures, and prepare financial reports. Make presentations at professional meetings to further knowledge in the field.

Personality Type: Investigative. Investigative occupations frequently involve working with ideas and require an extensive amount of thinking. These occupations can involve searching for facts and figuring out problems mentally.

GOE—Interest Area: 15. Scientific Research, Engineering, and Mathematics. **Work Group:** 15.01. Managerial Work in Scientific Research, Engineering, and Mathematics. **Other Jobs in This Work Group:** Engineering Managers.

Skills—Science: Using scientific rules and methods to solve problems. **Mathematics:** Using mathematics to solve problems. **Management of Personnel Resources:** Motivating, developing, and directing people as they work, identifying the best people for the job. **Active Learning:** Understanding the implications of new information for both current and future problem solving and decision making. **Reading Comprehension:** Understanding written sentences and paragraphs in work-related documents. **Writing:** Communicating effectively in writing as appropriate for the needs of the audience.

Education and Training Programs: Analytical Chemistry; Astronomy; Biology/Biological Sciences; Botany/Plant Biology; Chemistry, General; Entomology; Geology/Earth Science; Inorganic Chemistry; Marine Biology and Biological Oceanography; Mathematics, General; Meteorology; Microbiology; Molecular Biology; Nutrition Sciences; Oceanography, Organic Chemistry; Paleontology; Physics, General; Plant Pathology/Phytopathology; Statistics, General; Theoretical and Mathematical Physics; Toxicology; Virology; Zoology; others. **Related Knowledge/Courses: Biology:** Plant and animal organisms, their tissues, cells, functions, interdependencies, and interactions with each other and the environment. **Chemistry:** The chemical composition, structure, and properties of substances and of the chemical processes and transformations that they undergo. This includes uses of chemicals, their danger signs, production techniques, and disposal methods. **Engineering and Technology:** The practical application of engineering science and technology. This includes applying principles, techniques, procedures, and equipment to the design and production of various goods and services. **Law and Government:** Laws, legal codes, court procedures, precedents, government regulations, executive orders, agency rules, and the democratic political process. **Administration and Management:** Business and management principles involved in strategic planning, resource allocation, human resources modeling, leadership technique, production methods, and coordination of people and resources. **Physics:** Physical principles, laws, their interrelationships, and applications to understanding fluid, material, and atmospheric dynamics, and mechanical, electrical, atomic, and subatomic structures and processes.

Work Environment: Indoors; noisy; sitting.

Nursery and Greenhouse Managers

- ◉ Education/Training Required: Work experience plus degree
- ◉ Annual Earnings: $52,070
- ◉ Growth: 1.1%
- ◉ Annual Job Openings: 18,101
- ◉ Self-Employed: 0.0%
- ◉ Part-Time: 12.1%

Our sources did not provide separate job openings data for this occupation. The job openings listed here are shared with Aquacultural Managers and with Crop and Livestock Managers.

Level of Stress Tolerance Needed: 77.3 (out of 100)

Most Stressful Aspects: Impact of Decisions on Co-workers or Company Results (82.2);

Duration of Typical Work Week (66.0); Level of Competition (52.5); Pace Determined by Speed of Equipment (24.8).

Least Stressful Aspects: Deal With Physically Aggressive People (2.5); Deal With Unpleasant or Angry People (28.3); Frequency of Conflict Situations (30.8); Consequence of Error (33.0).

Plan, organize, direct, control, and coordinate activities of workers engaged in propagating, cultivating, and harvesting horticultural specialties, such as trees, shrubs, flowers, mushrooms, and other plants. Construct structures and accessories such as greenhouses and benches. Prepare soil for planting and plant or transplant seeds, bulbs, and cuttings. Position and regulate plant irrigation systems and program environmental and irrigation control computers. Negotiate contracts such as those for land leases or tree purchases. Inspect facilities and equipment for signs of disrepair and perform necessary maintenance work. Graft plants. Coordinate clerical, record-keeping, inventory, requisitioning, and marketing activities. Confer with horticultural personnel in order to plan facility renovations or additions. Provide information to customers on the care of trees, shrubs, flowers, plants, and lawns. Cut and prune trees, shrubs, flowers, and plants. Determine types and quantities of horticultural plants to be grown, based on budgets, projected sales volumes, and/or executive directives. Determine plant growing conditions, such as greenhouses, hydroponics, or natural settings, and set planting and care schedules. Assign work schedules and duties to nursery or greenhouse staff and supervise their work. Explain and enforce safety regulations and policies. Hire employees and train them in gardening techniques. Identify plants as well as problems such as diseases, weeds, and insect pests. Manage nurseries that grow horticultural plants for sale to trade or retail customers, for display or exhibition, or for research. Select and purchase seeds, plant nutrients, disease control chemicals, and garden and lawn care equipment. Tour work areas to observe work being done, to inspect crops, and to evaluate plant and soil conditions. Apply pesticides and fertilizers to plants.

Personality Type: Enterprising. Enterprising occupations frequently involve starting up and carrying out projects. These occupations can involve leading people and making many decisions. They sometimes require risk taking and often deal with business.

GOE—Interest Area: 01. Agriculture and Natural Resources. **Work Group:** 01.01. Managerial Work in Agriculture and Natural Resources. **Other Jobs in This Work Group:** Aquacultural Managers; Crop and Livestock Managers; Farm Labor Contractors; Farm, Ranch, and Other Agricultural Managers; Farmers and Ranchers; First-Line Supervisors/Managers of Agricultural Crop and Horticultural Workers; First-Line Supervisors/Managers of Animal Husbandry and Animal Care Workers; First-Line Supervisors/Managers of Aquacultural Workers; First-Line Supervisors/Managers of Construction Trades and Extraction Workers; First-Line Supervisors/Managers of Farming, Fishing, and Forestry Workers; First-Line Supervisors/Managers of Landscaping, Lawn Service, and Groundskeeping Workers; First-Line Supervisors/Managers of Logging Workers; Park Naturalists; Purchasing Agents and Buyers, Farm Products.

Skills—Management of Financial Resources: Determining how money will be spent to get the work done and accounting for these expenditures. **Management of Personnel Resources:** Motivating, developing, and directing people as they work, identifying the best people for the job. **Management of Material Resources:** Obtaining and seeing to the appropriate use of equipment, facilities, and materials needed to do certain work. **Science:** Using scientific rules and methods to solve problems. **Systems Evaluation:** Identifying measures or indicators of system performance and the actions needed to improve or correct performance, relative to the goals of the system. **Installation:** Installing equipment, machines, wiring, or programs to meet specifications.

Education and Training Programs: Agribusiness/Agricultural Business Operations; Agricultural Business and Management, General; Greenhouse Operations and Management; Horticultural Science; Ornamental Horticulture; Plant Nursery Operations and Management; Plant Protection and Integrated Pest Management. **Related Knowledge/Courses: Biology:** Plant and animal organisms, their tissues, cells, functions, interdependencies, and interactions with each other and the environment. **Production and Processing:** Raw materials, production processes, quality control, costs, and other techniques for maximizing the effective manufacture and distribution of goods. **Sales and Marketing:** Principles and methods for showing, promoting, and selling products or services. This includes marketing strategy and tactics, product demonstration, sales techniques, and sales control systems. **Chemistry:** The chemical composition, structure, and properties of substances and of the chemical processes and transformations that they undergo. This includes uses of chemicals, their danger signs, production techniques, and disposal methods. **Personnel and Human Resources:** Principles and procedures for personnel recruitment, selection, training, compensation and benefits, labor relations and negotiation, and personnel information systems. **Design:** Design techniques, tools, and principles involved in production of precision technical plans, blueprints, drawings, and models.

Work Environment: More often outdoors than indoors; very hot or cold; contaminants; minor burns, cuts, bites, or stings; standing.

Occupational Health and Safety Specialists

- Education/Training Required: Bachelor's degree
- Annual Earnings: $58,030
- Growth: 8.1%
- Annual Job Openings: 3,440
- Self-Employed: 2.4%
- Part-Time: 28.9%

Level of Stress Tolerance Needed: 73.5 (out of 100)

Most Stressful Aspects: Duration of Typical Work Week (90.0); Impact of Decisions on Co-workers or Company Results (80.8); Consequence of Error (64.5); Frequency of Conflict Situations (55.8).

Least Stressful Aspects: Pace Determined by Speed of Equipment (10.5); Deal With Physically Aggressive People (13.0); Deal With Unpleasant or Angry People (48.5); Time Pressure (66.3).

Review, evaluate, and analyze work environments and design programs and procedures to control, eliminate, and prevent disease or injury caused by chemical, physical, and biological agents or ergonomic factors. May conduct inspections and enforce adherence to laws and regulations governing the health and safety of individuals. May be employed in the public or private sector. Order suspension of activities that pose threats to workers' health and safety. Recommend measures to help protect workers from potentially hazardous work methods, processes, or materials. Investigate accidents to identify causes and to determine how future accidents might be prevented. Investigate the adequacy of ventilation, exhaust equipment, lighting, and other conditions that could affect employee health, comfort, or performance. Develop and maintain hygiene programs such as noise surveys, continuous atmosphere monitoring, ventilation surveys, and asbestos management plans. Inspect and evaluate workplace environments, equipment, and practices to ensure compliance with safety standards and government regulations. Collaborate with engineers and physicians to institute control and remedial measures for hazardous and potentially hazardous conditions or equipment. Conduct safety training and education programs and demonstrate the use of safety equipment. Provide new-employee health and safety orientations and develop materials for these presentations. Collect samples of dust, gases, vapors, and other potentially toxic materials for analysis. Investigate health-related complaints and inspect facilities to ensure that they comply with public health legislation and regulations. Coordinate "right-to-know" programs regarding hazardous chemicals and other substances. Maintain and update emergency response plans and procedures. Develop and maintain medical monitoring programs for employees. Conduct audits at hazardous waste sites or industrial sites and participate in hazardous waste site investigations. Inspect specified areas to ensure the presence of fire prevention equipment, safety equipment, and first-aid supplies. Collect samples of hazardous materials or arrange for sample collection. Maintain inventories of hazardous materials and hazardous wastes, using waste tracking systems to ensure that materials are handled properly. Prepare hazardous, radioactive, and mixed waste samples for transportation and storage by treating, compacting, packaging, and labeling them.

Personality Type: Social. Social occupations frequently involve working with, communicating with, and teaching people. These occupations often involve helping or providing service to others.

GOE—Interest Area: 07. Government and Public Administration. **Work Group:** 07.03. Regulations Enforcement. **Other Jobs in This Work Group:** Agricultural Inspectors; Aviation Inspectors; Compliance Officers, Except Agriculture, Construction, Health and Safety, and Transportation; Construction and Building Inspectors; Environmental Compliance Inspectors; Equal Opportunity Representatives and Officers; Financial Examiners; Fire Inspectors; Fish and Game Wardens; Forest Fire Inspectors and Prevention Specialists; Freight and Cargo Inspectors; Government Property Inspectors and Investigators; Immigration and Customs Inspectors; Licensing Examiners and Inspectors; Nuclear Monitoring Technicians; Occupational Health and Safety Technicians; Tax Examiners, Collectors, and Revenue Agents; Transportation Vehicle, Equipment, and Systems Inspectors, Except Aviation.

Skills—Science: Using scientific rules and methods to solve problems. **Management of Financial Resources:** Determining how money will be spent to get the work done and accounting for these expenditures. **Technology Design:** Generating or adapting equipment and technology to serve user needs. **Systems Analysis:** Determining how a system should work and how changes in conditions, operations, and the environment will affect outcomes. **Management of Personnel Resources:** Motivating, developing, and directing people as they work, identifying the best people for the job. **Persuasion:** Persuading others to change their minds or behavior.

Education and Training Programs: Environmental Health; Industrial Safety Technology/Technician Training; Occupational Health and Industrial Hygiene; Occupational Safety and Health Technology/Technician Training; Quality Control and Safety Technologies/Technician Training, Other. **Related Knowledge/Courses: Chemistry:** The chemical composition, structure, and properties of substances and of the chemical processes and transformations that they undergo. This includes uses of chemicals, their danger signs, production techniques, and disposal methods. **Biology:** Plant and animal organisms, their tissues, cells, functions, interdependencies, and interactions with each other and the environment. **Physics:** Physical principles, laws, their interrelationships, and applications to understanding fluid, material, and atmospheric dynamics, and mechanical, electrical, atomic, and subatomic structures and processes. **Engineering and Technology:** The practical application of engineering science and technology. This includes applying principles, techniques, procedures, and equipment to the design and production of various goods and services. **Public Safety and Security:** Relevant equipment, policies, procedures, and strategies to promote effective local, state, or national security operations for the protection of people, data, property, and institutions. **Psychology:** Human behavior and performance; individual differences in ability, personality, and interests; learning and motivation; psychological research methods; and the assessment and treatment of behavioral and affective disorders.

Work Environment: More often indoors than outdoors; noisy; contaminants; sitting.

Operations Research Analysts

- Education/Training Required: Master's degree
- Annual Earnings: $64,650
- Growth: 10.6%
- Annual Job Openings: 5,727
- Self-Employed: 0.2%
- Part-Time: 2.3%

Level of Stress Tolerance Needed: 55.3 (out of 100)

Most Stressful Aspects: Duration of Typical Work Week (83.5); Impact of Decisions on Co-workers or Company Results (77.0); Importance of Being Exact or Accurate (77.0); Level of Competition (63.5).

Least Stressful Aspects: Pace Determined by Speed of Equipment (2.0); Deal With Physically Aggressive People (2.0); Deal With Unpleasant or Angry People (24.0); Consequence of Error (36.5).

Formulate and apply mathematical modeling and other optimizing methods, using a computer to develop and interpret information that assists management with decision making, policy formulation, or other managerial functions. May develop related software, service, or products. Frequently concentrates on collecting and analyzing data and developing decision-support software. May develop and supply optimal time, cost, or logistics networks for program evaluation, review, or implementation. Formulate mathematical or simulation models of problems, relating constants and variables, restrictions, alternatives, and conflicting objectives and their numerical parameters. Collaborate with others in the organization to ensure successful implementation of chosen problem solutions. Analyze information obtained from management in order to conceptualize and define operational problems. Perform validation and testing of models to ensure adequacy; reformulate models as necessary. Collaborate with senior managers and decision-makers to identify and solve a variety of problems and to clarify management objectives. Define data requirements; then gather and validate information, applying judgment and statistical tests. Study and analyze information about alternative courses of action in order to determine which plan will offer the best outcomes. Prepare management reports defining and evaluating problems and recommending solutions. Break systems into their component parts, assign numerical values to each component, and examine the mathematical relationships between them. Specify manipulative or computational methods to be applied to models. Observe the current system in operation and gather and use various sources to analyze information about each component problem. Design, conduct, and evaluate experimental operational models in cases where models cannot be developed from existing data. Develop and apply time and cost networks in order to plan, control, and review large projects. Develop business methods and procedures, including accounting systems, file systems, office systems, logistics systems, and production schedules.

Personality Type: Investigative. Investigative occupations frequently involve working with ideas, and require an extensive amount of thinking. These occupations can involve searching for facts and figuring out problems mentally.

GOE—Interest Area: 04. Business and Administration. **Work Group:** 04.05. Accounting, Auditing, and Analytical Support. **Other Jobs in This Work Group:** Accountants; Accountants and Auditors; Auditors; Budget Analysts; Industrial Engineering Technicians; Logisticians; Management Analysts.

Skills—Programming: Writing computer programs for various purposes. **Systems Analysis:** Determining how a system should work and how changes in conditions, operations, and the environment will affect outcomes. **Operations Analysis:** Analyzing needs and product requirements to create a design. **Systems Evaluation:** Identifying measures or indicators of system performance and the actions needed to improve or correct performance, relative to the goals of the system. **Mathematics:** Using mathematics to solve problems. **Science:** Using scientific rules and methods to solve problems.

Education and Training Programs: Educational Evaluation and Research; Educational Statistics and Research Methods; Management Science, General; Management Sciences and Quantitative Methods, Other; Operations Research. **Related Knowledge/Courses: Mathematics:** Arithmetic, algebra, geometry, calculus, statistics, and their applications. **Engineering and Technology:** The practical application of engineering science and technology. This includes applying principles, techniques, procedures, and equipment to the design and production of various goods and services. **Computers and Electronics:** Circuit boards, processors, chips, electronic equipment, and computer hardware and software, including applications and programming. **Production and Processing:** Raw materials, production processes, quality control, costs, and other techniques for maximizing the effective manufacture and distribution of goods. **Economics and Accounting:** Economic and accounting principles and practices, the financial markets, banking, and the analysis and reporting of financial data. **Administration and Management:** Business and management principles involved in strategic planning, resource allocation, human resources modeling, leadership technique, production methods, and coordination of people and resources.

Work Environment: Indoors; sitting.

Order Fillers, Wholesale and Retail Sales

- Education/Training Required: Short-term on-the-job training
- Annual Earnings: $20,440
- Growth: −7.7%
- Annual Job Openings: 439,327
- Self-Employed: 0.2%
- Part-Time: 44.2%

Our sources did not provide separate job openings data for this occupation. The job openings listed here are shared with Marking Clerks; Stock Clerks, Sales Floor; and Stock Clerks—Stockroom, Warehouse, or Storage Yard.

Level of Stress Tolerance Needed: 74.8 (out of 100)

Most Stressful Aspects: Time Pressure (85.5); Importance of Being Exact or Accurate (85.2); Duration of Typical Work Week (61.0).

Least Stressful Aspects: Deal With Physically Aggressive People (4.5); Pace Determined by Speed of Equipment (8.3); Consequence of Error (21.3); Level of Competition (34.0).

Fill customers' mail and telephone orders from stored merchandise in accordance with specifications on sales slips or order forms. Duties include computing prices of items; completing order receipts; keeping records of outgoing orders; and requisitioning additional materials, supplies, and equipment. Read orders to ascertain catalog numbers, sizes, colors, and quantities of merchandise. Obtain merchandise from bins or shelves. Compute prices of items or groups of items. Complete order receipts. Keep records of outgoing orders. Place merchandise on conveyors leading to wrapping areas. Requisition additional materials, supplies, and equipment.

Personality Type: Conventional. Conventional occupations frequently involve following set procedures and routines. These occupations can include working with data and details more than with ideas. Usually, there is a clear line of authority to follow.

GOE—Interest Area: 04. Business and Administration. **Work Group:** 04.07. Records and Materials Processing. **Other Jobs in This Work Group:** Correspondence Clerks; File Clerks; Human Resources Assistants, Except Payroll and Timekeeping; Marking Clerks; Meter Readers, Utilities; Office Clerks, General; Postal Service Clerks; Postal Service Mail Sorters, Processors, and Processing Machine Operators; Procurement Clerks; Production, Planning, and Expediting Clerks; Shipping, Receiving, and Traffic Clerks; Stock Clerks and Order Fillers; Stock Clerks, Sales Floor; Stock Clerks—Stockroom, Warehouse, or Storage Yard; Weighers, Measurers, Checkers, and Samplers, Recordkeeping.

Skills—None met the criteria.

Education and Training Program: Retailing and Retail Operations. **Related Knowledge/Courses: Sales and Marketing:** Principles and methods for showing, promoting, and selling products or services. This includes marketing strategy and tactics, product demonstration, sales techniques, and sales control systems. **Production and Processing:** Raw materials, production processes, quality control, costs, and other techniques for maximizing the effective manufacture and distribution of goods.

Work Environment: Indoors; noisy; contaminants; standing; using hands on objects, tools, or controls; repetitive motions.

Outdoor Power Equipment and Other Small Engine Mechanics

- Education/Training Required: Moderate-term on-the-job training
- Annual Earnings: $26,910
- Growth: 5.5%
- Annual Job Openings: 5,130
- Self-Employed: 23.0%
- Part-Time: 12.7%

Level of Stress Tolerance Needed: 65.0 (out of 100)

Most Stressful Aspects: Time Pressure (71.7); Duration of Typical Work Week (61.5); Consequence of Error (45.0).

Least Stressful Aspects: Pace Determined by Speed of Equipment (13.7); Deal With Physically Aggressive People (14.8); Level of Competition (31.5); Frequency of Conflict Situations (44.0).

Diagnose, adjust, repair, or overhaul small engines used to power lawn mowers, chain saws, and related equipment. Sell parts and equipment. Show customers how to maintain equipment. Record repairs made, time spent, and parts used. Grind, ream, rebore, and retap parts to obtain specified clearances, using grinders, lathes, taps, reamers, boring machines, and micrometers. Test and inspect engines to determine malfunctions, to locate missing and broken parts, and to verify repairs, using diagnostic instruments. Replace motors. Repair or replace defective parts such as magnetos, water pumps, gears, pistons, and carburetors, using hand tools. Remove engines from equipment and position and bolt engines to repair stands. Perform routine maintenance such as cleaning and oiling parts, honing cylinders, and tuning ignition systems. Obtain problem descriptions from customers and prepare cost estimates for repairs. Dismantle engines, using hand tools, and examine parts for defects. Adjust points, valves, carburetors, distributors, and spark plug gaps, using feeler gauges. Repair and maintain gasoline engines used to power equipment such as portable saws, lawn mowers, generators, and compressors. Reassemble engines after repair or maintenance work is complete.

Personality Type: Realistic. Realistic occupations frequently involve work activities that include practical, hands-on problems and solutions. They often deal with plants; animals; and real-world materials such as wood, tools, and machinery. Many of the occupations require working outside and do not involve a lot of paperwork or working closely with others.

GOE—Interest Area: 13. Manufacturing. **Work Group:** 13.14. Vehicle and Facility Mechanical Work. **Other Jobs in This Work Group:** Aircraft Mechanics and Service Technicians; Aircraft Structure, Surfaces, Rigging, and Systems Assemblers; Automotive Body and Related Repairers; Automotive Glass Installers and Repairers; Automotive Master Mechanics; Automotive Service Technicians and Mechanics; Automotive Specialty Technicians; Bus and Truck Mechanics and Diesel Engine Specialists; Farm Equipment Mechanics; Fiberglass Laminators and Fabricators; Mobile Heavy Equipment Mechanics, Except Engines; Motorboat Mechanics; Motorcycle Mechanics; Rail Car Repairers; Recreational Vehicle Service Technicians; Tire Repairers and Changers.

Skills—Repairing: Repairing machines or systems, using the needed tools. **Equipment Maintenance:** Performing routine maintenance on equipment and determining when and what kind of maintenance is needed. **Troubleshooting:** Determining causes of operating errors and

deciding what to do about them. **Installation:** Installing equipment, machines, wiring, or programs to meet specifications. **Systems Evaluation:** Identifying measures or indicators of system performance and the actions needed to improve or correct performance, relative to the goals of the system. **Management of Financial Resources:** Determining how money will be spent to get the work done, and accounting for these expenditures.

Education and Training Program: Small Engine Mechanics and Repair Technology/Technician Training. **Related Knowledge/Courses: Mechanical Devices:** Machines and tools, including their designs, uses, repair, and maintenance. **Engineering and Technology:** The practical application of engineering science and technology. This includes applying principles, techniques, procedures, and equipment to the design and production of various goods and services. **Sales and Marketing:** Principles and methods for showing, promoting, and selling products or services. This includes marketing strategy and tactics, product demonstration, sales techniques, and sales control systems. **Physics:** Physical principles, laws, their interrelationships, and applications to understanding fluid, material, and atmospheric dynamics, and mechanical, electrical, atomic, and subatomic structures and processes. **Economics and Accounting:** Economic and accounting principles and practices, the financial markets, banking, and the analysis and reporting of financial data. **Chemistry:** The chemical composition, structure, and properties of substances and of the chemical processes and transformations that they undergo. This includes uses of chemicals, their danger signs, production techniques, and disposal methods.

Work Environment: Indoors; noisy; contaminants; hazardous equipment; standing; using hands on objects, tools, or controls.

Packaging and Filling Machine Operators and Tenders

- Education/Training Required: Short-term on-the-job training
- Annual Earnings: $22,990
- Growth: –5.4%
- Annual Job Openings: 79,540
- Self-Employed: 0.2%
- Part-Time: 16.2%

Level of Stress Tolerance Needed: 58.2 (out of 100)

Most Stressful Aspects: Time Pressure (68.3); Pace Determined by Speed of Equipment (59.8); Duration of Typical Work Week (58.5).

Least Stressful Aspects: Deal With Physically Aggressive People (10.0); Frequency of Conflict Situations (22.5); Level of Competition (27.2); Deal With Unpleasant or Angry People (28.3).

Operate or tend machines to prepare industrial or consumer products for storage or shipment. Includes cannery workers who pack food products. Observe machine operations to ensure quality and conformity of filled or packaged products to standards. Adjust machine components and machine tension and pressure according to size or processing angle of product. Tend or operate machine that packages product. Remove finished packaged items from machine and separate rejected items. Regulate machine flow, speed, or temperature. Stop or reset machines when malfunctions occur, clear machine jams, and report malfunctions to a supervisor. Secure finished packaged items by hand-tying, sewing, gluing, stapling, or attaching fastener. Stock and sort product for packaging or filling machine operation and replenish packaging supplies, such as wrapping paper, plastic sheet, boxes, cartons, glue, ink, or labels. Inspect and remove defective products and packaging material. Clean and remove damaged or otherwise inferior materials to prepare raw products for processing. Sort, grade, weigh, and inspect products, verifying and adjusting product weight or measurement to meet specifications. Clean, oil, and make minor adjustments or repairs to machinery and equipment, such as opening valves or setting guides. Monitor the production line, watching for problems such as pile-ups, jams, or glue that doesn't stick properly. Stack finished packaged items or wrap protective material around each item and pack the items in cartons or containers. Start machine by engaging controls. Count and record finished and rejected packaged items. Package the product in the form in which it will be sent out—for example, filling bags with flour from a chute or spout. Supply materials to spindles, conveyors, hoppers, or other feeding devices and unload packaged product. Attach identification labels to finished packaged items or cut stencils and stencil information on containers, such as lot numbers or shipping destinations. Clean packaging containers, line and pad crates, or assemble cartons to prepare for product packing.

Personality Type: Realistic. Realistic occupations frequently involve work activities that include practical, hands-on problems and solutions. They often deal with plants; animals; and real-world materials such as wood, tools, and machinery. Many of the occupations require working outside and do not involve a lot of paperwork or working closely with others.

GOE—Interest Area: 13. Manufacturing. **Work Group:** 13.03. Production Work, Assorted Materials Processing. **Other Jobs in This Work Group:** Bakers; Cementing and Gluing Machine Operators and Tenders; Chemical Equipment Operators and Tenders; Cleaning, Washing, and

Metal Pickling Equipment Operators and Tenders; Coating, Painting, and Spraying Machine Setters, Operators, and Tenders; Cooling and Freezing Equipment Operators and Tenders; Cutting and Slicing Machine Setters, Operators, and Tenders; Extruding and Forming Machine Setters, Operators, and Tenders, Synthetic and Glass Fibers; Extruding, Forming, Pressing, and Compacting Machine Setters, Operators, and Tenders; Food and Tobacco Roasting, Baking, and Drying Machine Operators and Tenders; Food Batchmakers; Food Cooking Machine Operators and Tenders; Furnace, Kiln, Oven, Drier, and Kettle Operators and Tenders; Heat Treating Equipment Setters, Operators, and Tenders, Metal and Plastic; Helpers—Production Workers; Meat, Poultry, and Fish Cutters and Trimmers; Metal-Refining Furnace Operators and Tenders; Mixing and Blending Machine Setters, Operators, and Tenders; Plating and Coating Machine Setters, Operators, and Tenders, Metal and Plastic; Pourers and Casters, Metal; Sawing Machine Setters, Operators, and Tenders, Wood; Separating, Filtering, Clarifying, Precipitating, and Still Machine Setters, Operators, and Tenders; Sewing Machine Operators; Shoe Machine Operators and Tenders; Slaughterers and Meat Packers; Team Assemblers; Textile Bleaching and Dyeing Machine Operators and Tenders; Tire Builders; Woodworking Machine Setters, Operators, and Tenders, Except Sawing.

Skills—Equipment Maintenance: Performing routine maintenance on equipment and determining when and what kind of maintenance is needed. **Operation and Control:** Controlling operations of equipment or systems. **Operation Monitoring:** Watching gauges, dials, or other indicators to make sure a machine is working properly. **Quality Control Analysis:** Conducting tests and inspections of products, services, or processes to evaluate quality or performance.

Repairing: Repairing machines or systems, using the needed tools. **Troubleshooting:** Determining causes of operating errors and deciding what to do about them.

Education and Training Programs: No related CIP programs; this job is learned through informal short-term on-the-job training. **Related Knowledge/Courses: Production and Processing:** Raw materials, production processes, quality control, costs, and other techniques for maximizing the effective manufacture and distribution of goods. **Mechanical Devices:** Machines and tools, including their designs, uses, repair, and maintenance. **Sociology and Anthropology:** Group behavior and dynamics, societal trends and influences, human migrations, ethnicity, cultures and their history and origins. **Psychology:** Human behavior and performance; individual differences in ability, personality, and interests; learning and motivation; psychological research methods; and the assessment and treatment of behavioral and affective disorders. **Public Safety and Security:** Relevant equipment, policies, procedures, and strategies to promote effective local, state, or national security operations for the protection of people, data, property, and institutions. **Communications and Media:** Media production, communication, and dissemination techniques and methods. This includes alternative ways to inform and entertain via written, oral, and visual media.

Work Environment: Noisy; contaminants; hazardous equipment; standing; using hands on objects, tools, or controls; repetitive motions.

Painters, Construction and Maintenance

- Education/Training Required: Moderate-term on-the-job training
- Annual Earnings: $31,190
- Growth: 11.8%
- Annual Job Openings: 101,140
- Self-Employed: 42.2%
- Part-Time: 21.9%

Level of Stress Tolerance Needed: 54.5 (out of 100)

Most Stressful Aspects: Impact of Decisions on Co-workers or Company Results (77.5); Time Pressure (72.5); Consequence of Error (50.0); Pace Determined by Speed of Equipment (26.7).

Least Stressful Aspects: Deal With Physically Aggressive People (8.5); Frequency of Conflict Situations (38.7); Level of Competition (42.8); Deal With Unpleasant or Angry People (48.3).

Paint walls, equipment, buildings, bridges, and other structural surfaces, using brushes, rollers, and spray guns. May remove old paint to prepare surface prior to painting. May mix colors or oils to obtain desired color or consistency. Cover surfaces with dropcloths or masking tape and paper to protect surfaces during painting. Fill cracks, holes, and joints with caulk, putty, plaster, or other fillers, using caulking guns or putty knives. Apply primers or sealers to prepare new surfaces, such as bare wood or metal, for finish coats. Apply paint, stain, varnish, enamel, and other finishes to equipment, buildings, bridges, and other structures, using brushes, spray guns, or rollers. Calculate amounts of required materials and estimate costs, based on surface measurements and work orders. Read work orders or receive instructions from super-visors or homeowners to determine work requirements. Erect scaffolding and swing gates or set up ladders to work above ground level. Remove fixtures such as pictures, door knobs, lamps, and electric switch covers prior to painting. Wash and treat surfaces with oil, turpentine, mildew remover, or other preparations and sand rough spots to ensure that finishes will adhere properly. Mix and match colors of paint, stain, or varnish with oil and thinning and drying additives to obtain desired colors and consistencies. Remove old finishes by stripping, sanding, wire-brushing, burning, or using water or abrasive blasting. Select and purchase tools and finishes for surfaces to be covered, considering durability, ease of handling, methods of application, and customers' wishes. Smooth surfaces, using sandpaper, scrapers, brushes, steel wool, or sanding machines. Polish final coats to specified finishes. Use special finishing techniques such as sponging, ragging, layering, or faux finishing. Waterproof buildings, using waterproofers and caulking. Spray or brush hot plastics or pitch onto surfaces. Cut stencils and brush and spray lettering and decorations on surfaces. Bake finishes on painted and enameled articles, using baking ovens.

Personality Type: Realistic. Realistic occupations frequently involve work activities that include practical, hands-on problems and solutions. They often deal with plants; animals; and real-world materials such as wood, tools, and machinery. Many of the occupations require working outside and do not involve a lot of paperwork or working closely with others.

GOE—Interest Area: 02. Architecture and Construction. **Work Group:** 02.04. Construction Crafts. **Other Jobs in This Work Group:** Boilermakers; Brickmasons and Blockmasons; Carpet Installers; Cement Masons and Concrete Finishers; Commercial Divers; Construction Carpenters; Crane and Tower Operators; Drywall and Ceiling Tile Installers;

Electricians; Fence Erectors; Floor Layers, Except Carpet, Wood, and Hard Tiles; Floor Sanders and Finishers; Glaziers; Hazardous Materials Removal Workers; Insulation Workers, Floor, Ceiling, and Wall; Insulation Workers, Mechanical; Manufactured Building and Mobile Home Installers; Operating Engineers and Other Construction Equipment Operators; Paperhangers; Paving, Surfacing, and Tamping Equipment Operators; Pile-Driver Operators; Pipe Fitters and Steamfitters; Pipelayers; Plasterers and Stucco Masons; Plumbers; Plumbers, Pipefitters, and Steamfitters; Rail-Track Laying and Maintenance Equipment Operators; Refractory Materials Repairers, Except Brickmasons; Reinforcing Iron and Rebar Workers; Riggers; Roofers; Rough Carpenters; Security and Fire Alarm Systems Installers; Segmental Pavers; Sheet Metal Workers; Stone Cutters and Carvers, Manufacturing; Stonemasons; Structural Iron and Steel Workers; Tapers; Terrazzo Workers and Finishers; Tile and Marble Setters.

Skills—Equipment Maintenance: Performing routine maintenance on equipment and determining when and what kind of maintenance is needed. **Management of Material Resources:** Obtaining and seeing to the appropriate use of equipment, facilities, and materials needed to do certain work. **Management of Personnel Resources:** Motivating, developing, and directing people as they work, identifying the best people for the job. **Repairing:** Repairing machines or systems, using the needed tools. **Equipment Selection:** Determining the kind of tools and equipment needed to do a job. **Monitoring:** Monitoring/assessing performance of yourself, other individuals, or organizations to make improvements or take corrective action.

Education and Training Program: Painting/Painter and Wall Coverer Training. **Related Knowledge/Courses: Building and Construction:** Materials, methods, and the tools involved in the construction or repair of houses, buildings, or other structures such as highways and roads. **Design:** Design techniques, tools, and principles involved in production of precision technical plans, blueprints, drawings, and models. **Transportation:** Principles and methods for moving people or goods by air, rail, sea, or road, including the relative costs and benefits. **Customer and Personal Service:** Principles and processes for providing customer and personal services. This includes customer needs assessment, meeting quality standards for services, and evaluation of customer satisfaction. **Production and Processing:** Raw materials, production processes, quality control, costs, and other techniques for maximizing the effective manufacture and distribution of goods. **Administration and Management:** Business and management principles involved in strategic planning, resource allocation, human resources modeling, leadership technique, production methods, and coordination of people and resources.

Work Environment: Contaminants; standing; climbing ladders, scaffolds, or poles; using hands on objects, tools, or controls; bending or twisting the body; repetitive motions.

Painters, Transportation Equipment

- Education/Training Required: Moderate-term on-the-job training
- Annual Earnings: $35,680
- Growth: 8.4%
- Annual Job Openings: 3,268
- Self-Employed: 3.8%
- Part-Time: 15.8%

Level of Stress Tolerance Needed: 57.0 (out of 100)

Most Stressful Aspects: Time Pressure (81.7); Duration of Typical Work Week (63.5); Level of Competition (46.5); Pace Determined by Speed of Equipment (42.8).

Least Stressful Aspects: Deal With Physically Aggressive People (12.3); Frequency of Conflict Situations (29.0); Consequence of Error (37.3); Deal With Unpleasant or Angry People (40.0).

Operate or tend painting machines to paint surfaces of transportation equipment, such as automobiles, buses, trucks, trains, boats, and airplanes. Dispose of hazardous waste in an appropriate manner. Select paint according to company requirements and match colors of paint following specified color charts. Mix paints to match color specifications or vehicles' original colors; then stir and thin the paints, using spatulas or power mixing equipment. Remove grease, dirt, paint, and rust from vehicle surfaces in preparation for paint application, using abrasives, solvents, brushes, blowtorches, washing tanks, or sandblasters. Pour paint into spray guns and adjust nozzles and paint mixes to get the proper paint flow and coating thickness. Monitor painting operations to identify flaws such as blisters and streaks so that their causes can be corrected. Sand vehicle surfaces between coats of paint or primer to remove flaws and enhance adhesion for subsequent coats. Disassemble, clean, and reassemble sprayers and power equipment, using solvents, wire brushes, and cloths for cleaning duties. Remove accessories from vehicles, such as chrome or mirrors, and mask other surfaces with tape or paper to protect them from paint. Spray prepared surfaces with specified amounts of primers and decorative or finish coatings. Allow the sprayed product to dry and then touch up any spots that may have been missed. Apply rust-resistant undercoats and caulk and seal seams. Select the correct spray gun system for the material being applied. Apply primer over any repairs made to vehicle surfaces. Adjust controls on infrared ovens, heat lamps, portable ventilators, and exhaust units to speed the drying of vehicles between coats. Fill small dents and scratches with body fillers and smooth surfaces to prepare vehicles for painting. Apply designs, lettering, or other identifying or decorative items to finished products, using paint brushes or paint sprayers. Paint by hand areas that cannot be reached with a spray gun or those that need retouching, using brushes. Sand the final finish and apply sealer after a vehicle has dried properly. Buff and wax the finished paintwork. Lay out logos, symbols, or designs on painted surfaces according to blueprint specifications, using measuring instruments, stencils, and patterns.

Personality Type: Realistic. Realistic occupations frequently involve work activities that include practical, hands-on problems and solutions. They often deal with plants; animals; and real-world materials such as wood, tools, and machinery. Many of the occupations require working outside and do not involve a lot of paperwork or working closely with others.

GOE—Interest Area: 13. Manufacturing. **Work Group:** 13.09. Hands-On Work, Assorted Materials. **Other Jobs in This Work Group:** Coil Winders, Tapers, and Finishers; Cutters and Trimmers, Hand; Fabric and Apparel Patternmakers; Glass Blowers, Molders, Benders, and Finishers; Grinding and Polishing Workers, Hand; Molding and Casting Workers; Painting, Coating, and Decorating Workers; Sewers, Hand.

Skills—Repairing: Repairing machines or systems, using the needed tools. **Equipment Maintenance:** Performing routine maintenance on equipment and determining when and what kind of maintenance is needed. **Monitoring:** Monitoring/assessing performance of yourself, other individuals, or organizations to make improvements or take corrective action. **Operation and Control:** Controlling operations

P

of equipment or systems. **Technology Design:** Generating or adapting equipment and technology to serve user needs. **Science:** Using scientific rules and methods to solve problems.

Education and Training Program: Autobody/Collision and Repair Technology/Technician Training. **Related Knowledge/Courses: Chemistry:** The chemical composition, structure, and properties of substances and of the chemical processes and transformations that they undergo. This includes uses of chemicals, their danger signs, production techniques, and disposal methods. **Production and Processing:** Raw materials, production processes, quality control, costs, and other techniques for maximizing the effective manufacture and distribution of goods. **Mechanical Devices:** Machines and tools, including their designs, uses, repair, and maintenance.

Work Environment: Noisy; contaminants; hazardous conditions; standing; using hands on objects, tools, or controls; repetitive motions.

Park Naturalists

- ◎ Education/Training Required: Bachelor's degree
- ◎ Annual Earnings: $54,970
- ◎ Growth: 5.3%
- ◎ Annual Job Openings: 1,161
- ◎ Self-Employed: 3.9%
- ◎ Part-Time: 12.3%

Our sources did not provide separate job openings data for this occupation. The job openings listed here are shared with Range Managers and with Soil and Water Conservationists.

Level of Stress Tolerance Needed: 72.0 (out of 100)

Most Stressful Aspects: Time Pressure (72.8); Impact of Decisions on Co-workers or Company Results (71.7); Deal With Unpleasant or Angry People (61.3); Level of Competition (58.7).

Least Stressful Aspects: Pace Determined by Speed of Equipment (0.7); Consequence of Error (39.7); Duration of Typical Work Week (44.5); Frequency of Conflict Situations (47.3).

Plan, develop, and conduct programs to inform public of historical, natural, and scientific features of national, state, or local park. Provide visitor services by explaining regulations; answering visitor requests, needs, and complaints; and providing information about the park and surrounding areas. Conduct field trips to point out scientific, historic, and natural features of parks, forests, historic sites, or other attractions. Prepare and present illustrated lectures and interpretive talks about park features. Perform emergency duties to protect human life, government property, and natural features of park. Confer with park staff to determine subjects and schedules for park programs. Assist with operations of general facilities, such as visitor centers. Plan, organize, and direct activities of seasonal staff members. Perform routine maintenance on park structures. Prepare brochures and write newspaper articles. Construct historical, scientific, and nature visitor-center displays. Research stories regarding the area's natural history or environment. Interview specialists in desired fields to obtain and develop data for park information programs. Compile and maintain official park photographic and information files. Take photographs and motion pictures for use in lectures and publications and to develop displays. Survey park to determine forest conditions and distribution and abundance of fauna and flora. Plan and develop audiovisual devices for public programs.

Personality Type: Social. Social occupations frequently involve working with, communicating with, and teaching people. These occupations often involve helping or providing service to others.

GOE—Interest Area: 01. Agriculture and Natural Resources. **Work Group:** 01.01. Managerial Work in Agriculture and Natural Resources. **Other Jobs in This Work Group:** Aquacultural Managers; Crop and Livestock Managers; Farm Labor Contractors; Farm, Ranch, and Other Agricultural Managers; Farmers and Ranchers; First-Line Supervisors/Managers of Agricultural Crop and Horticultural Workers; First-Line Supervisors/Managers of Animal Husbandry and Animal Care Workers; First-Line Supervisors/Managers of Aquacultural Workers; First-Line Supervisors/Managers of Construction Trades and Extraction Workers; First-Line Supervisors/Managers of Farming, Fishing, and Forestry Workers; First-Line Supervisors/Managers of Landscaping, Lawn Service, and Groundskeeping Workers; First-Line Supervisors/Managers of Logging Workers; Nursery and Greenhouse Managers; Purchasing Agents and Buyers, Farm Products.

Skills—Management of Personnel Resources: Motivating, developing, and directing people as they work, identifying the best people for the job. **Management of Financial Resources:** Determining how money will be spent to get the work done, and accounting for these expenditures. **Service Orientation:** Actively looking for ways to help people. **Writing:** Communicating effectively in writing as appropriate for the needs of the audience. **Science:** Using scientific rules and methods to solve problems. **Management of Material Resources:** Obtaining and seeing to the appropriate use of equipment, facilities, and materials needed to do certain work.

Education and Training Programs: Forest Management/Forest Resources Management; Forest Sciences and Biology; Forestry, General; Forestry, Other; Land Use Planning and Management/Development; Natural Resources and Conservation, Other; Natural Resources Management and Policy, Other; Natural Resources/Conservation, General; Water, Wetlands, and Marine Resources Management; Wildlife and Wildlands Science and Management. **Related Knowledge/Courses: Biology:** Plant and animal organisms, their tissues, cells, functions, interdependencies, and interactions with each other and the environment. **History and Archeology:** Historical events and their causes, indicators, and effects on civilizations and cultures. **Geography:** Principles and methods for describing the features of land, sea, and air masses, including their physical characteristics, locations, interrelationships, and distribution of plant, animal, and human life. **Sociology and Anthropology:** Group behavior and dynamics, societal trends and influences, human migrations, ethnicity, cultures, and their history and origins. **Communications and Media:** Media production, communication, and dissemination techniques and methods. This includes alternative ways to inform and entertain via written, oral, and visual media. **Customer and Personal Service:** Principles and processes for providing customer and personal services. This includes customer needs assessment, meeting quality standards for services, and evaluation of customer satisfaction.

Work Environment: More often indoors than outdoors; very hot or cold; minor burns, cuts, bites, or stings; sitting; using hands on objects, tools, or controls.

Physicists

- Education/Training Required: Doctoral degree
- Annual Earnings: $94,240
- Growth: 6.8%
- Annual Job Openings: 1,302
- Self-Employed: 0.8%
- Part-Time: 12.4%

Level of Stress Tolerance Needed: 61.3 (out of 100)

Most Stressful Aspects: Duration of Typical Work Week (83.5); Importance of Being Exact or Accurate (79.8); Level of Competition (55.0).

Least Stressful Aspects: Deal With Physically Aggressive People (1.2); Pace Determined by Speed of Equipment (1.5); Deal With Unpleasant or Angry People (26.5); Frequency of Conflict Situations (28.0).

Conduct research into the phases of physical phenomena, develop theories and laws on the basis of observation and experiments, and devise methods to apply laws and theories to industry and other fields. Perform complex calculations as part of the analysis and evaluation of data, using computers. Describe and express observations and conclusions in mathematical terms. Analyze data from research conducted to detect and measure physical phenomena. Report experimental results by writing papers for scientific journals or by presenting information at scientific conferences. Design computer simulations to model physical data so that it can be better understood. Collaborate with other scientists in the design, development, and testing of experimental, industrial, or medical equipment, instrumentation, and procedures. Direct testing and monitoring of contamination of radioactive equipment and recording of per-

sonnel and plant area radiation exposure data. Observe the structure and properties of matter and the transformation and propagation of energy, using equipment such as masers, lasers, and telescopes to explore and identify the basic principles governing these phenomena. Develop theories and laws on the basis of observation and experiments and apply these theories and laws to problems in areas such as nuclear energy, optics, and aerospace technology. Teach physics to students. Develop manufacturing, assembly, and fabrication processes of lasers, masers, and infrared and other light-emitting and light-sensitive devices. Conduct application evaluations and analyze results to determine commercial, industrial, scientific, medical, military, or other uses for electro-optical devices. Develop standards of permissible concentrations of radioisotopes in liquids and gases. Conduct research pertaining to potential environmental impacts of atomic energy–related industrial development to determine licensing qualifications. Advise authorities of procedures to be followed in radiation incidents or hazards and assist in civil defense planning.

Personality Type: Investigative. Investigative occupations frequently involve working with ideas and require an extensive amount of thinking. These occupations can involve searching for facts and figuring out problems mentally.

GOE—Interest Area: 15. Scientific Research, Engineering, and Mathematics. **Work Group:** 15.02. Physical Sciences. **Other Jobs in This Work Group:** Astronomers; Atmospheric and Space Scientists; Chemists; Geographers; Geoscientists, Except Hydrologists and Geographers; Hydrologists; Materials Scientists.

Skills—Programming: Writing computer programs for various purposes. **Science:** Using scientific rules and methods to solve problems. **Mathematics:** Using mathematics to solve problems. **Complex Problem Solving:** Identifying complex problems and reviewing related information to develop and evaluate options and implement solutions. **Systems Analysis:** Determining how a system should work and how changes in conditions, operations, and the environment will affect outcomes. **Management of Financial Resources:** Determining how money will be spent to get the work done, and accounting for these expenditures.

Education and Training Programs: Acoustics; Astrophysics; Atomic/Molecular Physics; Elementary Particle Physics; Health/Medical Physics; Nuclear Physics; Optics/Optical Sciences; Physics, General; Physics, Other; Plasma and High-Temperature Physics; Solid State and Low-Temperature Physics; Theoretical and Mathematical Physics. **Related Knowledge/ Courses: Physics:** Physical principles, laws, their interrelationships, and applications to understanding fluid, material, and atmospheric dynamics and mechanical, electrical, atomic, and subatomic structures and processes. **Mathematics:** Arithmetic, algebra, geometry, calculus, statistics, and their applications. **Engineering and Technology:** The practical application of engineering science and technology. This includes applying principles, techniques, procedures, and equipment to the design and production of various goods and services. **Computers and Electronics:** Circuit boards, processors, chips, electronic equipment, and computer hardware and software, including applications and programming. **English Language:** The structure and content of the English language, including the meaning and spelling of words, rules of composition, and grammar. **Telecommunications:** Transmission, broadcasting, switching, control, and operation of telecommunications systems.

Work Environment: Indoors; sitting.

Pipelayers

- Education/Training Required: Moderate-term on-the-job training
- Annual Earnings: $30,330
- Growth: 8.7%
- Annual Job Openings: 8,902
- Self-Employed: 11.6%
- Part-Time: 16.8%

Level of Stress Tolerance Needed: 73.0 (out of 100)

Most Stressful Aspects: Duration of Typical Work Week (77.0); Pace Determined by Speed of Equipment (58.5); Consequence of Error (51.0).

Least Stressful Aspects: Deal With Physically Aggressive People (9.7); Frequency of Conflict Situations (34.2); Level of Competition (41.5); Deal With Unpleasant or Angry People (47.5).

Lay pipe for storm or sanitation sewers, drains, and water mains. Perform any combination of the following tasks: grade trenches or culverts, position pipe, or seal joints. Check slopes for conformance to requirements, using levels or lasers. Cover pipes with earth or other materials. Cut pipes to required lengths. Connect pipe pieces and seal joints, using welding equipment, cement, or glue. Install and repair sanitary and stormwater sewer structures and pipe systems. Install and use instruments such as lasers, grade rods, and transit levels. Grade and level trench bases, using tamping machines and hand tools. Lay out pipe routes, following written instructions or blueprints and coordinating layouts with supervisors. Align and position pipes to prepare them for welding or sealing. Dig trenches to desired or required depths by hand or using trenching tools. Operate mechanized equipment such as pickup trucks, rollers, tandem dump

P

trucks, front-end loaders, and backhoes. Train others in pipe-laying and provide supervision. Tap and drill holes into pipes to introduce auxiliary lines or devices. Locate existing pipes needing repair or replacement, using magnetic or radio indicators.

Personality Type: Realistic. Realistic occupations frequently involve work activities that include practical, hands-on problems and solutions. They often deal with plants; animals; and real-world materials such as wood, tools, and machinery. Many of the occupations require working outside and do not involve a lot of paperwork or working closely with others.

GOE—Interest Area: 02. Architecture and Construction. **Work Group:** 02.04. Construction Crafts. **Other Jobs in This Work Group:** Boilermakers; Brickmasons and Blockmasons; Carpet Installers; Cement Masons and Concrete Finishers; Commercial Divers; Construction Carpenters; Crane and Tower Operators; Drywall and Ceiling Tile Installers; Electricians; Fence Erectors; Floor Layers, Except Carpet, Wood, and Hard Tiles; Floor Sanders and Finishers; Glaziers; Hazardous Materials Removal Workers; Insulation Workers, Floor, Ceiling, and Wall; Insulation Workers, Mechanical; Manufactured Building and Mobile Home Installers; Operating Engineers and Other Construction Equipment Operators; Painters, Construction and Maintenance; Paperhangers; Paving, Surfacing, and Tamping Equipment Operators; Pile-Driver Operators; Pipe Fitters and Steamfitters; Plasterers and Stucco Masons; Plumbers; Plumbers, Pipefitters, and Steamfitters; Rail-Track Laying and Maintenance Equipment Operators; Refractory Materials Repairers, Except Brickmasons; Reinforcing Iron and Rebar Workers; Riggers; Roofers; Rough Carpenters; Security and Fire Alarm Systems Installers; Segmental Pavers; Sheet Metal Workers; Stone Cutters and Carvers, Manufacturing; Stonemasons; Structural Iron and Steel Workers; Tapers; Terrazzo Workers and Finishers; Tile and Marble Setters.

Skills—Installation: Installing equipment, machines, wiring, or programs to meet specifications. **Quality Control Analysis:** Conducting tests and inspections of products, services, or processes to evaluate quality or performance. **Operation and Control:** Controlling operations of equipment or systems. **Operation Monitoring:** Watching gauges, dials, or other indicators to make sure a machine is working properly. **Equipment Maintenance:** Performing routine maintenance on equipment and determining when and what kind of maintenance is needed. **Repairing:** Repairing machines or systems, using the needed tools.

Education and Training Program: Plumbing Technology/Plumber Training. **Related Knowledge/Courses: Building and Construction:** Materials, methods, and the tools involved in the construction or repair of houses, buildings, or other structures such as highways and roads. **Mechanical Devices:** Machines and tools, including their designs, uses, repair, and maintenance.

Work Environment: Outdoors; noisy; hazardous equipment; standing; using hands on objects, tools, or controls; repetitive motions.

Political Scientists

- ◎ Education/Training Required: Master's degree
- ◎ Annual Earnings: $90,140
- ◎ Growth: 5.3%
- ◎ Annual Job Openings: 318
- ◎ Self-Employed: 7.5%
- ◎ Part-Time: 25.0%

Level of Stress Tolerance Needed: 60.8 (out of 100)

Most Stressful Aspects: Duration of Typical Work Week (89.0); Level of Competition (67.5).

Least Stressful Aspects: Pace Determined by Speed of Equipment (0.0); Deal With Physically Aggressive People (6.7); Consequence of Error (26.2); Deal With Unpleasant or Angry People (36.3).

Study the origin, development, and operation of political systems. Research a wide range of subjects, such as relations between the United States and foreign countries, the beliefs and institutions of foreign nations, or the politics of small towns or a major metropolis. May study topics such as public opinion, political decision making, and ideology. May analyze the structure and operation of governments, as well as various political entities. May conduct public opinion surveys, analyze election results, or analyze public documents. Teach political science. Disseminate research results through academic publications, written reports, or public presentations. Identify issues for research and analysis. Develop and test theories, using information from interviews, newspapers, periodicals, case law, historical papers, polls, and/or statistical sources. Maintain current knowledge of government policy decisions. Collect, analyze, and interpret data such as election results and public opinion surveys; report on findings, recommendations, and conclusions. Interpret and analyze policies; public issues; legislation; and the operations of governments, businesses, and organizations. Evaluate programs and policies and make related recommendations to institutions and organizations. Write drafts of legislative proposals and prepare speeches, correspondence, and policy papers for governmental use. Forecast political, economic, and social trends. Consult with and advise govern-

ment officials, civic bodies, research agencies, the media, political parties, and others concerned with political issues. Provide media commentary and/or criticism related to public policy and political issues and events.

Personality Type: Investigative. Investigative occupations frequently involve working with ideas and require an extensive amount of thinking. These occupations can involve searching for facts and figuring out problems mentally.

GOE—Interest Area: 15. Scientific Research, Engineering, and Mathematics. **Work Group:** 15.04. Social Sciences. **Other Jobs in This Work Group:** Anthropologists; Anthropologists and Archeologists; Archeologists; Economists; Historians; Industrial-Organizational Psychologists; School Psychologists; Sociologists.

Skills—Writing: Communicating effectively in writing as appropriate for the needs of the audience. **Reading Comprehension:** Understanding written sentences and paragraphs in work-related documents. **Critical Thinking:** Using logic and reasoning to identify the strengths and weaknesses of alternative solutions, conclusions or approaches to problems. **Speaking:** Talking to others to convey information effectively. **Active Learning:** Understanding the implications of new information for both current and future problem solving and decision making. **Instructing:** Teaching others how to do something.

Education and Training Programs: American Government and Politics (United States); Canadian Government and Politics; International/Global Studies; Political Science and Government, General; Political Science and Government, Other. **Related Knowledge/Courses: History and Archeology:** Historical events and their causes, indicators, and effects on civilizations and cultures. **Law and Government:** Laws, legal codes, court procedures, precedents, government regulations,

P

executive orders, agency rules, and the democratic political process. **Philosophy and Theology:** Different philosophical systems and religions. This includes their basic principles, values, ethics, ways of thinking, customs, practices, and their impact on human culture. **Sociology and Anthropology:** Group behavior and dynamics, societal trends and influences, human migrations, ethnicity, cultures and their history and origins. **Foreign Language:** The structure and content of a foreign (non-English) language, including the meaning and spelling of words, rules of composition and grammar, and pronunciation. **Geography:** Principles and methods for describing the features of land, sea, and air masses, including their physical characteristics, locations, interrelationships, and distribution of plant, animal, and human life.

Work Environment: Indoors; sitting.

Potters, Manufacturing

- ◎ Education/Training Required: Moderate-term on-the-job training
- ◎ Annual Earnings: $25,010
- ◎ Growth: 1.3%
- ◎ Annual Job Openings: 5,788
- ◎ Self-Employed: 24.2%
- ◎ Part-Time: 19.0%

Our sources did not provide separate job openings data for this occupation. The job openings listed here are shared with Glass Blowers, Molders, Benders, and Finishers; Molding and Casting Workers; and Stone Cutters and Carvers, Manufacturing.

Level of Stress Tolerance Needed: No data available.

Most Stressful Aspects: Pace Determined by Speed of Equipment (35.0).

Least Stressful Aspects: Deal With Physically Aggressive People (0.0); Frequency of Conflict Situations (5.0); Deal With Unpleasant or Angry People (10.0); Consequence of Error (18.3)

Operate production machines such as pug mill, jigger machine, or potter's wheel to process clay in manufacture of ceramic, pottery, and stoneware products. Adjust pressures, temperatures, and trimming tool settings as required. Move pieces from wheels so that they can dry. Teach pottery classes. Maintain supplies of tools, equipment, and materials and order additional supplies as needed. Start machine units and conveyors and observe lights and gauges on panel board to verify operational efficiency. Operate drying chambers to dry or finish molded ceramic ware. Operate jigger machines to form ceramic ware, such as bowls, cups, plates, and saucers. Prepare work for sale or exhibition and maintain relationships with retail, pottery, art, and resource networks that can facilitate sale or exhibition of work. Perform test-fires of pottery to determine how to achieve specific colors and textures. Examine finished ware for defects and measure dimensions, using rule and thickness gauge. Mix and apply glazes and load glazed pieces into kilns for firing. Operate pug mills to blend and extrude clay. Design clay forms and molds and decorations for forms. Adjust wheel speeds according to the feel of the clay as pieces enlarge and walls become thinner. Position balls of clay in centers of potters' wheels and start motors or pump treadles with feet to revolve wheels. Press thumbs into centers of revolving clay to form hollows and press on the inside and outside of emerging clay cylinders with hands and fingers, gradually raising and shaping clay to desired forms and sizes. Pull wires through bases of articles and wheels to separate finished pieces. Raise and shape clay into wares such as vases and pitchers on revolving wheels, using hands, fingers, and thumbs. Smooth surfaces of finished pieces, using rubber scrapers and wet sponges. Verify accuracy of shapes and sizes of objects, using calipers and templates.

Personality Type: Realistic. Realistic occupations frequently involve work activities that include practical, hands-on problems and solutions. They often deal with plants; animals; and real-world materials such as wood, tools, and machinery. Many of the occupations require working outside and do not involve a lot of paperwork or working closely with others.

GOE—Interest Area: 03. Arts and Communication. **Work Group:** 03.04. Studio Art. **Other Jobs in This Work Group:** Craft Artists; Fine Artists, Including Painters, Sculptors, and Illustrators.

Skills—None met the criteria.

Education and Training Program: Crafts/Craft Design, Folk Art and Artisanry. **Related Knowledge/Course: Fine Arts:** The theory and techniques required to compose, produce, and perform works of music, dance, visual arts, drama, and sculpture.

Work Environment: Indoors; sitting; using hands on objects, tools, or controls; bending or twisting the body; repetitive motions.

Pourers and Casters, Metal

- ☺ Education/Training Required: Moderate-term on-the-job training
- ☺ Annual Earnings: $29,570
- ☺ Growth: –17.4%
- ☺ Annual Job Openings: 4,459
- ☺ Self-Employed: 0.0%
- ☺ Part-Time: 7.2%

Level of Stress Tolerance Needed: 65.2 (out of 100)

Most Stressful Aspects: Importance of Being Exact or Accurate (77.3); Duration of Typical Work Week (76.0); Pace Determined by Speed of Equipment (73.3); Consequence of Error (67.5).

Least Stressful Aspects: Deal With Physically Aggressive People (3.5); Level of Competition (32.0); Deal With Unpleasant or Angry People (39.0); Frequency of Conflict Situations (39.7).

Operate hand-controlled mechanisms to pour and regulate the flow of molten metal into molds to produce castings or ingots. Collect samples or signal workers to sample metal for analysis. Pour and regulate the flow of molten metal into molds and forms to produce ingots or other castings, using ladles or hand-controlled mechanisms. Read temperature gauges and observe color changes; then adjust furnace flames, torches, or electrical heating units as necessary to melt metal to specifications. Examine molds to ensure they are clean, smooth, and properly coated. Position equipment such as ladles, grinding wheels, pouring nozzles, or crucibles or signal other workers to position equipment. Skim slag or remove excess metal from ingots or equipment, using hand tools, strainers, rakes, or burners; collect scrap for recycling. Turn valves to circulate water through cores or spray water on filled molds to cool and solidify metal. Add metal to molds to compensate for shrinkage. Pull levers to lift ladle stoppers and to allow molten steel to flow into ingot molds to specified heights. Load specified amounts of metal and flux into furnaces or clay crucibles. Remove solidified steel or slag from pouring nozzles, using long bars or oxygen burners. Assemble and embed cores in casting frames, using hand tools and equipment. Remove metal ingots or cores from molds, using hand tools, cranes, and chain hoists. Transport metal ingots to storage areas, using forklifts. Stencil identifying information on ingots and pigs, using special hand tools. Repair and maintain metal forms and equipment, using hand tools, sledges, and bars.

Personality Type: Realistic. Realistic occupations frequently involve work activities that include practical, hands-on problems and solutions. They often deal with plants; animals; and real-world materials such as wood, tools, and machinery. Many of the occupations require working outside and do not involve a lot of paperwork or working closely with others.

GOE—Interest Area: 13. Manufacturing. **Work Group:** 13.03. Production Work, Assorted Materials Processing. **Other Jobs in This Work Group:** Bakers; Cementing and Gluing Machine Operators and Tenders; Chemical Equipment Operators and Tenders; Cleaning, Washing, and Metal Pickling Equipment Operators and Tenders; Coating, Painting, and Spraying Machine Setters, Operators, and Tenders; Cooling and Freezing Equipment Operators and Tenders; Cutting and Slicing Machine Setters, Operators, and Tenders; Extruding and Forming Machine Setters, Operators, and Tenders, Synthetic and Glass Fibers; Extruding, Forming, Pressing, and Compacting Machine Setters, Operators, and Tenders; Food and Tobacco Roasting, Baking, and Drying Machine Operators and Tenders; Food Batchmakers; Food Cooking Machine Operators and Tenders; Furnace, Kiln, Oven, Drier, and Kettle Operators and Tenders; Heat Treating Equipment Setters, Operators, and Tenders, Metal and Plastic; Helpers—Production Workers; Meat, Poultry, and Fish Cutters and Trimmers; Metal-Refining Furnace Operators and Tenders; Mixing and Blending Machine Setters, Operators, and Tenders; Packaging and Filling Machine Operators and Tenders; Plating and Coating Machine Setters, Operators, and Tenders, Metal and Plastic; Sawing Machine Setters, Operators, and Tenders, Wood; Separating, Filtering, Clarifying, Precipitating, and Still Machine Setters, Operators, and Tenders; Sewing Machine Operators; Shoe Machine Operators and Tenders; Slaughterers and Meat Packers; Team Assemblers; Textile Bleaching and Dyeing Machine Operators and Tenders; Tire Builders; Woodworking Machine Setters, Operators, and Tenders, Except Sawing.

Skills—Repairing: Repairing machines or systems, using the needed tools. **Equipment Maintenance:** Performing routine maintenance on equipment and determining when and what kind of maintenance is needed. **Operation Monitoring:** Watching gauges, dials, or other indicators to make sure a machine is working properly. **Operation and Control:** Controlling operations of equipment or systems. **Troubleshooting:** Determining causes of operating errors and deciding what to do about them. **Management of Material Resources:** Obtaining and seeing to the appropriate use of equipment, facilities, and materials needed to do certain work.

Education and Training Programs: No related CIP programs; this job is learned through informal moderate-term on-the-job training. **Related Knowledge/Course: Production and Processing:** Raw materials, production processes, quality control, costs, and other techniques for maximizing the effective manufacture and distribution of goods.

Work Environment: Noisy; very hot or cold; contaminants; hazardous equipment; minor burns, cuts, bites, or stings; using hands on objects, tools, or controls.

Power Plant Operators

- Education/Training Required: Long-term on-the-job training
- Annual Earnings: $55,000
- Growth: 2.7%
- Annual Job Openings: 1,796
- Self-Employed: 0.0%
- Part-Time: 1.3%

Level of Stress Tolerance Needed: 70.2 (out of 100)

Most Stressful Aspects: Consequence of Error (80.3); Impact of Decisions on Co-workers or Company Results (75.3); Duration of Typical Work Week (74.5); Pace Determined by Speed of Equipment (49.0).

Least Stressful Aspects: Deal With Physically Aggressive People (8.3); Deal With Unpleasant or Angry People (39.7); Frequency of Conflict Situations (43.0); Time Pressure (56.0).

Control, operate, or maintain machinery to generate electric power. Includes auxiliary equipment operators. Monitor and inspect power plant equipment and indicators to detect evidence of operating problems. Adjust controls to generate specified electrical power or to regulate the flow of power between generating stations and substations. Operate or control power-generating equipment, including boilers, turbines, generators, and reactors, using control boards or semi-automatic equipment. Regulate equipment operations and conditions such as water levels based on data from recording and indicating instruments or from computers. Take readings from charts, meters, and gauges at established intervals and take corrective steps as necessary. Inspect records and logbook entries and communicate with other plant personnel to assess equipment operating status. Start or stop generators, auxiliary pumping equipment, turbines, and other power plant equipment and connect or disconnect equipment from circuits. Control and maintain auxiliary equipment, such as pumps, fans, compressors, condensers, feed-water heaters, filters, and chlorinators, to supply water, fuel, lubricants, air, and auxiliary power. Clean, lubricate, and maintain equipment such as generators, turbines, pumps, and compressors to prevent equipment failure or deterioration. Communicate with systems operators to regulate and coordinate transmission loads and frequencies and line voltages. Record and compile operational data, completing and maintaining forms, logs, and reports. Open and close valves and switches in sequence upon signals from other workers to start or shut down auxiliary units. Collect oil, water, and electrolyte samples for laboratory analysis. Make adjustments or minor repairs, such as tightening leaking gland and pipe joints; report any needs for major repairs. Control generator output to match the phase, frequency, and voltage of electricity supplied to panels. Place standby emergency electrical generators on line in emergencies and monitor the temperature, output, and lubrication of the system. Receive outage calls and call in necessary personnel during power outages and emergencies.

Personality Type: Realistic. Realistic occupations frequently involve work activities that include practical, hands-on problems and solutions. They often deal with plants; animals; and real-world materials such as wood, tools, and machinery. Many of the occupations require working outside and do not involve a lot of paperwork or working closely with others.

GOE—Interest Area: 13. Manufacturing. **Work Group:** 13.16. Utility Operation and Energy Distribution. **Other Jobs in This Work Group:** Chemical Plant and System Operators; Gas Compressor and Gas Pumping Station

Operators; Gas Plant Operators; Nuclear Power Reactor Operators; Petroleum Pump System Operators, Refinery Operators, and Gaugers; Power Distributors and Dispatchers; Ship Engineers; Stationary Engineers and Boiler Operators; Water and Liquid Waste Treatment Plant and System Operators.

Skills—Operation Monitoring: Watching gauges, dials, or other indicators to make sure a machine is working properly. **Equipment Maintenance:** Performing routine maintenance on equipment and determining when and what kind of maintenance is needed. **Operation and Control:** Controlling operations of equipment or systems. **Technology Design:** Generating or adapting equipment and technology to serve user needs. **Systems Evaluation:** Identifying measures or indicators of system performance and the actions needed to improve or correct performance, relative to the goals of the system. **Coordination:** Adjusting actions in relation to others' actions.

Education and Training Programs: No related CIP programs; this job is learned through long-term on-the-job training. **Related Knowledge/ Courses: Physics:** Physical principles, laws, their interrelationships, and applications to understanding fluid, material, and atmospheric dynamics, and mechanical, electrical, atomic, and subatomic structures and processes. **Mechanical Devices:** Machines and tools, including their designs, uses, repair, and maintenance. **Chemistry:** The chemical composition, structure, and properties of substances and of the chemical processes and transformations that they undergo. This includes uses of chemicals, their danger signs, production techniques, and disposal methods. **Engineering and Technology:** The practical application of engineering science and technology. This includes applying principles, techniques, procedures, and equipment to the design and production of various

goods and services. **Public Safety and Security:** Relevant equipment, policies, procedures, and strategies to promote effective local, state, or national security operations for the protection of people, data, property, and institutions. **Computers and Electronics:** Circuit boards, processors, chips, electronic equipment, and computer hardware and software, including applications and programming.

Work Environment: Indoors; noisy; very hot or cold; contaminants; high places; hazardous conditions.

Printing Machine Operators

- Education/Training Required: Moderate-term on-the-job training
- Annual Earnings: $30,990
- Growth: –5.7%
- Annual Job Openings: 12,274
- Self-Employed: 2.2%
- Part-Time: 10.4%

Level of Stress Tolerance Needed: 74.3 (out of 100)

Most Stressful Aspects: Pace Determined by Speed of Equipment (81.7); Importance of Being Exact or Accurate (79.5); Time Pressure (74.3); Duration of Typical Work Week (60.0).

Least Stressful Aspects: Deal With Physically Aggressive People (12.0); Frequency of Conflict Situations (46.2); Deal With Unpleasant or Angry People (52.2); Impact of Decisions on Co-workers or Company Results (60.8).

Set up or operate various types of printing machines, such as offset, letterset, intaglio, or gravure presses or screen printers, to produce print on paper or other materials. Inspect and examine printed products for print clarity, color accuracy, conformance to specifications, and external defects. Push buttons, turn handles, or move controls and levers to start and control printing machines. Reposition printing plates, adjust pressure rolls, or otherwise adjust machines to improve print quality, using knobs, handwheels, or hand tools. Set and adjust speed, temperature, ink flow, and positions and pressure tolerances of equipment. Examine job orders to determine details such as quantities to be printed, production times, stock specifications, colors, and color sequences. Select and install printing plates, rollers, feed guides, gauges, screens, stencils, type, dies, and cylinders in machines according to specifications, using hand tools. Monitor feeding, printing, and racking processes of presses to maintain specified operating levels and to detect malfunctions; make any necessary adjustments. Operate equipment at slow speed to ensure proper ink coverage, alignment, and registration. Load, position, and adjust unprinted materials on holding fixtures or in equipment loading and feeding mechanisms. Pour or spread paint, ink, color compounds, and other materials into reservoirs, troughs, hoppers, or color holders of printing units, making measurements and adjustments to control color and viscosity. Repair, maintain, or adjust equipment. Blend and test paint, inks, stains, and solvents according to types of material being printed and work order specifications. Clean and lubricate printing machines and components, using oil, solvents, brushes, rags, and hoses. Remove printed materials from presses, using handtrucks, electric lifts, or hoists, and transport them to drying, storage, or finishing areas. Input instructions to program automated machinery, using a computer keyboard. Place printed items in ovens to dry or set ink. Squeeze or spread ink on plates, pads, or rollers, using putty knives, brushes, or sponges. Measure screens and use measurements to center and align screens in proper positions and sequences on machines, using gauges and hand tools.

Personality Type: Realistic. Realistic occupations frequently involve work activities that include practical, hands-on problems and solutions. They often deal with plants; animals; and real-world materials such as wood, tools, and machinery. Many of the occupations require working outside and do not involve a lot of paperwork or working closely with others.

GOE—Interest Area: 13. Manufacturing. **Work Group:** 13.08. Graphic Arts Production. **Other Jobs in This Work Group:** Bindery Workers; Desktop Publishers; Etchers and Engravers; Job Printers; Photographic Process Workers; Photographic Processing Machine Operators; Prepress Technicians and Workers.

Skills—Operation Monitoring: Watching gauges, dials, or other indicators to make sure a machine is working properly. **Operation and Control:** Controlling operations of equipment or systems. **Equipment Maintenance:** Performing routine maintenance on equipment and determining when and what kind of maintenance is needed. **Repairing:** Repairing machines or systems, using the needed tools. **Quality Control Analysis:** Conducting tests and inspections of products, services, or processes to evaluate quality or performance. **Troubleshooting:** Determining causes of operating errors and deciding what to do about them.

Education and Training Programs: Graphic and Printing Equipment Operator, General Production; Graphic Communications, Other; Printing Management; Printing Press Operator Training. **Related Knowledge/Courses: Mechanical Devices:** Machines and tools, including their designs, uses, repair, and maintenance. **Production and Processing:** Raw materials, production processes, quality control, costs, and other techniques for maximizing the effective manufacture and distribution of goods. **Chemistry:** The chemical composition, structure, and properties of substances and of the chemical processes and transformations that they undergo. This includes uses of chemicals, their danger signs, production techniques, and disposal methods.

Work Environment: Noisy; contaminants; hazardous conditions; hazardous equipment; standing; using hands on objects, tools, or controls.

Product Safety Engineers

- ◎ Education/Training Required: Bachelor's degree
- ◎ Annual Earnings: $66,290
- ◎ Growth: 9.6%
- ◎ Annual Job Openings: 1,105
- ◎ Self-Employed: 1.1%
- ◎ Part-Time: 14.3%

Our sources did not provide separate job openings data for this occupation. The job openings listed here are shared with Fire-Prevention and Protection Engineers and with Industrial Safety and Health Engineers.

Level of Stress Tolerance Needed: 72.5 (out of 100)

Most Stressful Aspects: Duration of Typical Work Week (81.0); Impact of Decisions on Co-workers or Company Results (77.5); Consequence of Error (52.7); Level of Competition (47.5).

Least Stressful Aspects: Pace Determined by Speed of Equipment (4.2); Deal With Physically Aggressive People (5.3); Deal With Unpleasant or Angry People (39.7); Frequency of Conflict Situations (48.3).

Develop and conduct tests to evaluate product safety levels and recommend measures to reduce or eliminate hazards. Report accident investigation findings. Conduct research to evaluate safety levels for products. Evaluate potential health hazards or damage that could occur from product misuse. Investigate causes of accidents, injuries, or illnesses related to product usage in order to develop solutions to minimize or prevent recurrence. Participate in preparation of product usage and precautionary label instructions. Recommend procedures for detection, prevention, and elimination of physical, chemical, or other product hazards.

Personality Type: Investigative. Investigative occupations frequently involve working with ideas and require an extensive amount of thinking. These occupations can involve searching for facts and figuring out problems mentally.

GOE—Interest Area: 15. Scientific Research, Engineering, and Mathematics. **Work Group:** 15.08. Industrial and Safety Engineering. **Other Jobs in This Work Group:** Fire-Prevention and Protection Engineers; Health and Safety Engineers, Except Mining Safety Engineers and Inspectors; Industrial Engineers; Industrial Safety and Health Engineers.

Skills—Science: Using scientific rules and methods to solve problems. **Systems Analysis:** Determining how a system should work and how changes in conditions, operations, and the environment will affect outcomes. **Technology Design:** Generating or adapting equipment and technology to serve user needs. **Quality Control Analysis:** Conducting tests and inspections of products, services, or processes to evaluate quality or performance. **Systems Evaluation:** Identifying measures or indicators of system performance and the actions needed to improve or correct performance, relative to the goals of the system. **Mathematics:** Using mathematics to solve problems.

Education and Training Program: Environmental/Environmental Health Engineering.

Related Knowledge/Courses: **Engineering and Technology:** The practical application of engineering science and technology. This includes applying principles, techniques, procedures, and equipment to the design and production of various goods and services. **Design:** Design techniques, tools, and principles involved in production of precision technical plans, blueprints, drawings, and models. **Physics:** Physical principles, laws, their interrelationships, and applications to understanding fluid, material, and atmospheric dynamics, and mechanical, electrical, atomic, and subatomic structures and processes. **Mechanical Devices:** Machines and tools, including their designs, uses, repair, and maintenance. **Chemistry:** The chemical composition, structure, and properties of substances and of the chemical processes and transformations that they undergo. This includes uses of chemicals, their danger signs, production techniques, and disposal methods. **Public Safety and Security:** Relevant equipment, policies, procedures, and strategies to promote effective local, state, or national security operations for the protection of people, data, property, and institutions.

Work Environment: Indoors; sitting.

Rail Car Repairers

- Education/Training Required: Long-term on-the-job training
- Annual Earnings: $43,320
- Growth: 5.1%
- Annual Job Openings: 1,989
- Self-Employed: 4.0%
- Part-Time: 12.7%

Level of Stress Tolerance Needed: 59.2 (out of 100)

Most Stressful Aspects: Time Pressure (75.3); Duration of Typical Work Week (71.0); Consequence of Error (52.5).

Least Stressful Aspects: Deal With Physically Aggressive People (9.0); Pace Determined by Speed of Equipment (20.2); Deal With Unpleasant or Angry People (30.3); Level of Competition (42.0).

Diagnose, adjust, repair, or overhaul railroad rolling stock, mine cars, or mass-transit railcars. Repair or replace defective or worn parts such as bearings, pistons, and gears, using hand tools, torque wrenches, power tools, and welding equipment. Test units for operability before and after repairs. Remove locomotives, car mechanical units, or other components, using pneumatic hoists and jacks, pinch bars, hand tools, and cutting torches. Record conditions of cars and repair and maintenance work performed or to be performed. Inspect components such as bearings, seals, gaskets, wheels, and coupler assemblies to determine if repairs are needed. Inspect the interior and exterior of railcars coming into rail yards to identify defects and to determine the extent of wear and damage. Adjust repaired or replaced units as needed to ensure proper operation. Perform scheduled maintenance and clean units and components. Repair and maintain electrical and electronic controls for propulsion and braking systems. Repair, fabricate, and install steel or wood fittings, using blueprints, shop sketches, and instruction manuals. Disassemble units such as water pumps, control valves, and compressors so that repairs can be made. Align car sides for installation of car ends and crossties, using width gauges, turnbuckles, and wrenches. Measure diameters of axle wheel seats, using micrometers, and mark dimensions on axles so that wheels can be bored to specified dimensions. Replace defective wiring and insulation and tighten electrical connections, using hand tools. Test electrical systems of cars by operating systems and using testing equipment such as ammeters. Install and repair interior flooring, fixtures, walls, plumbing, steps, and platforms. Examine car roofs for wear and damage and repair defective sections, using roofing material, cement, nails, and waterproof paint. Paint car exteriors, interiors, and fixtures. Repair car upholstery. Repair window sash frames, attach weather stripping and channels to frames, and replace window glass, using hand tools.

Personality Type: Realistic. Realistic occupations frequently involve work activities that include practical, hands-on problems and solutions. They often deal with plants; animals; and real-world materials such as wood, tools, and machinery. Many of the occupations require working outside and do not involve a lot of paperwork or working closely with others.

GOE—Interest Area: 13. Manufacturing. **Work Group:** 13.14. Vehicle and Facility Mechanical Work. **Other Jobs in This Work Group:** Aircraft Mechanics and Service Technicians; Aircraft Structure, Surfaces, Rigging, and Systems Assemblers; Automotive Body and Related Repairers; Automotive Glass Installers and Repairers; Automotive Master Mechanics; Automotive Service Technicians and Mechanics; Automotive Specialty Technicians; Bus and Truck Mechanics and Diesel Engine Specialists; Farm Equipment Mechanics; Fiberglass Laminators and Fabricators; Mobile Heavy Equipment Mechanics, Except Engines; Motorboat Mechanics; Motorcycle Mechanics; Outdoor Power Equipment and Other Small Engine Mechanics; Recreational Vehicle Service Technicians; Tire Repairers and Changers.

Skills—Repairing: Repairing machines or systems, using the needed tools. **Installation:** Installing equipment, machines, wiring, or programs to meet specifications. **Equipment Maintenance:** Performing routine maintenance

on equipment and determining when and what kind of maintenance is needed. **Troubleshooting:** Determining causes of operating errors and deciding what to do about them. **Operation Monitoring:** Watching gauges, dials, or other indicators to make sure a machine is working properly. **Technology Design:** Generating or adapting equipment and technology to serve user needs.

Education and Training Program: Heavy Equipment Maintenance Technology/ Technician Training. **Related Knowledge/ Courses: Mechanical Devices:** Machines and tools, including their designs, uses, repair, and maintenance. **Public Safety and Security:** Relevant equipment, policies, procedures, and strategies to promote effective local, state, or national security operations for the protection of people, data, property, and institutions. **Production and Processing:** Raw materials, production processes, quality control, costs, and other techniques for maximizing the effective manufacture and distribution of goods.

Work Environment: Outdoors; noisy; very hot or cold; contaminants; standing; using hands on objects, tools, or controls.

Rail-Track Laying and Maintenance Equipment Operators

- Education/Training Required: Moderate-term on-the-job training
- Annual Earnings: $40,000
- Growth: 4.8%
- Annual Job Openings: 1,817
- Self-Employed: 0.0%
- Part-Time: 11.5%

Level of Stress Tolerance Needed: 61.0 (out of 100)

Most Stressful Aspects: Time Pressure (73.3); Impact of Decisions on Co-workers or Company Results (69.2); Duration of Typical Work Week (63.5); Consequence of Error (60.5).

Least Stressful Aspects: Level of Competition (36.8); Being Exact or Accurate (75.3).

Lay, repair, and maintain track for standard or narrow-gauge railroad equipment used in regular railroad service or in plant yards, quarries, sand and gravel pits, and mines. Includes ballast-cleaning-machine operators and roadbed-tamping-machine operators. Drive vehicles that automatically move and lay tracks or rails over sections of track to be constructed, repaired, or maintained. Operate track-wrench machines to tighten or loosen bolts at joints that hold ends of rails together. Clean, grade, and level ballast on railroad tracks. Dress and reshape worn or damaged railroad switch points and frogs, using portable power grinders. Push controls to close grasping devices on track or rail sections so that they can be raised or moved. Drive graders, tamping machines, brooms, and ballast cleaning/spreading machines to redistribute gravel and ballast between rails. Adjust controls of machines that spread, shape, raise, level, and align track according to specifications. Engage mechanisms that lay tracks or rails to specified gauges. Grind ends of new or worn rails to attain smooth joints, using portable grinders. Observe leveling indicator arms to verify levelness and alignment of tracks. Operate single- or multiple-head spike-driving machines to drive spikes into ties and secure rails. Operate single- or multiple-head spike pullers to pull old spikes from ties. Operate tie-adzing machines to cut ties and permit insertion of fishplates that hold rails. Drill holes through rails, tie plates, and fishplates for insertion of bolts and spikes, using power drills.

Repair and adjust track switches, using wrenches and replacement parts. Spray ties, fishplates, and joints with oil to protect them from weathering. String and attach wire-guidelines machine to rails so that tracks or rails can be aligned or leveled. Cut rails to specified lengths, using rail saws. Patrol assigned track sections so that damaged or broken track can be located and reported. Paint railroad signs, such as speed limits and gate-crossing warnings. Lubricate machines, change oil, and fill hydraulic reservoirs to specified levels. Clean tracks and clear ice and snow from tracks and switch boxes. Clean and make minor repairs to machines and equipment. Turn wheels of machines, using lever controls, to adjust guidelines for track alignments and grades, following specifications.

Personality Type: Realistic. Realistic occupations frequently involve work activities that include practical, hands-on problems and solutions. They often deal with plants; animals; and real-world materials such as wood, tools, and machinery. Many of the occupations require working outside and do not involve a lot of paperwork or working closely with others.

GOE—Interest Area: 02. Architecture and Construction. **Work Group:** 02.04. Construction Crafts. **Other Jobs in This Work Group:** Boilermakers; Brickmasons and Blockmasons; Carpet Installers; Cement Masons and Concrete Finishers; Commercial Divers; Construction Carpenters; Crane and Tower Operators; Drywall and Ceiling Tile Installers; Electricians; Fence Erectors; Floor Layers, Except Carpet, Wood, and Hard Tiles; Floor Sanders and Finishers; Glaziers; Hazardous Materials Removal Workers; Insulation Workers, Floor, Ceiling, and Wall; Insulation Workers, Mechanical; Manufactured Building and Mobile Home Installers; Operating Engineers and Other Construction Equipment Operators; Painters, Construction and Maintenance;

R

Paperhangers; Paving, Surfacing, and Tamping Equipment Operators; Pile-Driver Operators; Pipe Fitters and Steamfitters; Pipelayers; Plasterers and Stucco Masons; Plumbers; Plumbers, Pipefitters, and Steamfitters; Refractory Materials Repairers, Except Brickmasons; Reinforcing Iron and Rebar Workers; Riggers; Roofers; Rough Carpenters; Security and Fire Alarm Systems Installers; Segmental Pavers; Sheet Metal Workers; Stone Cutters and Carvers, Manufacturing; Stonemasons; Structural Iron and Steel Workers; Tapers; Terrazzo Workers and Finishers; Tile and Marble Setters.

Skills—Repairing: Repairing machines or systems, using the needed tools. **Installation:** Installing equipment, machines, wiring, or programs to meet specifications. **Equipment Maintenance:** Performing routine maintenance on equipment and determining when and what kind of maintenance is needed. **Operation Monitoring:** Watching gauges, dials, or other indicators to make sure a machine is working properly. **Troubleshooting:** Determining causes of operating errors and deciding what to do about them. **Operation and Control:** Controlling operations of equipment or systems.

Education and Training Program: Construction/Heavy Equipment/Earthmoving Equipment Operation. **Related Knowledge/Courses: Building and Construction:** Materials, methods, and the tools involved in the construction or repair of houses, buildings, or other structures such as highways and roads. **Mechanical Devices:** Machines and tools, including their designs, uses, repair, and maintenance. **Transportation:** Principles and methods for moving people or goods by air, rail, sea, or road, including the relative costs and benefits. **Public Safety and Security:** Relevant equipment, policies, procedures, and strategies to promote effective local, state, or national security operations for the protection of people, data, property, and

institutions. **Production and Processing:** Raw materials, production processes, quality control, costs, and other techniques for maximizing the effective manufacture and distribution of goods.

Work Environment: Outdoors; noisy; very hot or cold; hazardous equipment; standing; using hands on objects, tools, or controls.

Range Managers

- Education/Training Required: Bachelor's degree
- Annual Earnings: $54,970
- Growth: 5.3%
- Annual Job Openings: 1,161
- Self-Employed: 3.9%
- Part-Time: 12.3%

Our sources did not provide separate job openings data for this occupation. The job openings listed here are shared with Park Naturalists and with Soil and Water Conservationists.

Level of Stress Tolerance Needed: 67.0 (out of 100)

Most Stressful Aspects: Impact of Decisions on Co-workers or Company Results (72.8); Duration of Typical Work Week (70.0); Frequency of Conflict Situations (59.5); Level of Competition (50.5).

Least Stressful Aspects: Pace Determined by Speed of Equipment (3.5); Consequence of Error (39.0); Deal With Unpleasant or Angry People (50.5); Time Pressure (60.8).

Research or study range land management practices to provide sustained production of forage, livestock, and wildlife. Regulate grazing and help ranchers plan and organize grazing systems to manage, improve, and protect rangelands and maximize their use. Measure and assess vegetation resources for biological assessment companies, environmental impact statements, and rangeland monitoring programs. Maintain soil stability and vegetation for non-grazing uses, such as wildlife habitats and outdoor recreation. Mediate agreements among rangeland users and preservationists as to appropriate land use and management. Study rangeland management practices and research range problems to provide sustained production of forage, livestock, and wildlife. Manage forage resources through fire, herbicide use, or revegetation to maintain a sustainable yield from the land. Offer advice to rangeland users on water management, forage production methods, and control of brush. Plan and direct construction and maintenance of range improvements such as fencing, corrals, stock-watering reservoirs, and soil-erosion control structures. Tailor conservation plans to landowners' goals, such as livestock support, wildlife, or recreation. Develop technical standards and specifications used to manage, protect, and improve the natural resources of rangelands and related grazing lands. Study grazing patterns to determine number and kind of livestock that can be most profitably grazed and to determine the best grazing seasons. Plan and implement revegetation of disturbed sites. Study forage plants and their growth requirements to determine varieties best suited to particular range. Develop methods for protecting range from fire and rodent damage and for controlling poisonous plants. Manage private livestock operations. Develop new and improved instruments and techniques for activities such as range reseeding.

Personality Type: Investigative. Investigative occupations frequently involve working with ideas and require an extensive amount of thinking. These occupations can involve searching for facts and figuring out problems mentally.

GOE—Interest Area: 01. Agriculture and Natural Resources. **Work Group:** 01.02.

Resource Science/Engineering for Plants, Animals, and the Environment. **Other Jobs in This Work Group:** Agricultural Engineers; Animal Scientists; Conservation Scientists; Environmental Engineers; Foresters; Mining and Geological Engineers, Including Mining Safety Engineers; Petroleum Engineers; Soil and Plant Scientists; Soil and Water Conservationists; Zoologists and Wildlife Biologists.

Skills—Negotiation: Bringing others together and trying to reconcile differences. **Science:** Using scientific rules and methods to solve problems. **Management of Financial Resources:** Determining how money will be spent to get the work done, and accounting for these expenditures. **Persuasion:** Persuading others to change their minds or behavior. **Coordination:** Adjusting actions in relation to others' actions. **Systems Evaluation:** Identifying measures or indicators of system performance and the actions needed to improve or correct performance, relative to the goals of the system.

Education and Training Programs: Forest Management/Forest Resources Management; Forest Sciences and Biology; Forestry, General; Forestry, Other; Land Use Planning and Management/Development; Natural Resources and Conservation, Other; Natural Resources Management and Policy; Natural Resources Management and Policy, Other; Natural Resources/Conservation, General; Water, Wetlands, and Marine Resources Management; Wildlife and Wildlands Science and Management. **Related Knowledge/Courses: Biology:** Plant and animal organisms, their tissues, cells, functions, interdependencies, and interactions with each other and the environment. **Geography:** Principles and methods for describing the features of land, sea, and air masses, including their physical characteristics, locations, interrelationships, and distribution of plant, animal, and human life. **Food Production:** Techniques and equipment for planting, growing, and harvesting food products (both plant and animal) for consumption, including storage/handling techniques. **History and Archeology:** Historical events and their causes, indicators, and effects on civilizations and cultures. **Law and Government:** Laws, legal codes, court procedures, precedents, government regulations, executive orders, agency rules, and the democratic political process. **Engineering and Technology:** The practical application of engineering science and technology. This includes applying principles, techniques, procedures, and equipment to the design and production of various goods and services.

Work Environment: More often outdoors than indoors; noisy; very hot or cold; minor burns, cuts, bites, or stings; sitting.

Refuse and Recyclable Material Collectors

- Education/Training Required: Short-term on-the-job training
- Annual Earnings: $28,970
- Growth: 7.4%
- Annual Job Openings: 37,785
- Self-Employed: 6.1%
- Part-Time: 36.0%

Level of Stress Tolerance Needed: 72.5 (out of 100)

Most Stressful Aspects: Duration of Typical Work Week (85.0); Impact of Decisions on Co-workers or Company Results (83.7); Importance of Being Exact or Accurate (79.0); Consequence of Error (78.0).

Least Stressful Aspects: Deal With Physically Aggressive People (7.2); Frequency of Conflict Situations (42.5); Deal With Unpleasant or Angry People (49.3).

Collect and dump refuse or recyclable materials from containers into truck. May drive truck. Inspect trucks prior to beginning routes to ensure safe operating condition. Refuel trucks and add other necessary fluids, such as oil. Fill out any needed reports for defective equipment. Drive to disposal sites to empty trucks that have been filled. Drive trucks along established routes through residential streets and alleys or through business and industrial areas. Operate equipment that compresses the collected refuse. Operate automated or semi-automated hoisting devices that raise refuse bins and dump contents into openings in truck bodies. Dismount garbage trucks to collect garbage and remount trucks to ride to the next collection point. Communicate with dispatchers concerning delays, unsafe sites, accidents, equipment breakdowns, and other maintenance problems. Keep informed of road and weather conditions to determine how routes will be affected. Tag garbage or recycling containers to inform customers of problems such as excess garbage or inclusion of items that are not permitted. Clean trucks and compactor bodies after routes have been completed. Sort items set out for recycling and throw materials into designated truck compartments. Organize schedules for refuse collection. Provide quotes for refuse collection contracts.

Personality Type: Realistic. Realistic occupations frequently involve work activities that include practical, hands-on problems and solutions. They often deal with plants; animals; and real-world materials such as wood, tools, and machinery. Many of the occupations require working outside and do not involve a lot of paperwork or working closely with others.

GOE—Interest Area: 13. Manufacturing. **Work Group:** 13.17. Loading, Moving, Hoisting, and Conveying. **Other Jobs in This Work Group:** Conveyor Operators and Tenders; Hoist and Winch Operators; Industrial Truck and Tractor

Operators; Machine Feeders and Offbearers; Packers and Packagers, Hand; Pump Operators, Except Wellhead Pumpers; Tank Car, Truck, and Ship Loaders.

Skills—Equipment Maintenance: Performing routine maintenance on equipment and determining when and what kind of maintenance is needed. **Operation Monitoring:** Watching gauges, dials, or other indicators to make sure a machine is working properly. **Operation and Control:** Controlling operations of equipment or systems. **Repairing:** Repairing machines or systems, using the needed tools.

Education and Training Programs: No related CIP programs; this job is learned through informal short-term on-the-job training. **Related Knowledge/Courses: Transportation:** Principles and methods for moving people or goods by air, rail, sea, or road, including the relative costs and benefits. **Customer and Personal Service:** Principles and processes for providing customer and personal services. This includes customer needs assessment, meeting quality standards for services, and evaluation of customer satisfaction.

Work Environment: Outdoors; noisy; contaminants; using hands on objects, tools, or controls; bending or twisting the body; repetitive motions.

Reinforcing Iron and Rebar Workers

- ◉ Education/Training Required: Long-term on-the-job training
- ◉ Annual Earnings: $38,220
- ◉ Growth: 11.5%
- ◉ Annual Job Openings: 4,502
- ◉ Self-Employed: 0.0%
- ◉ Part-Time: 16.7%

Level of Stress Tolerance Needed: 69.5 (out of 100)

Most Stressful Aspects: Importance of Being Exact or Accurate (83.0); Time Pressure (79.5); Frequency of Conflict Situations (55.3); Level of Competition (47.5).

Least Stressful Aspects: Deal With Physically Aggressive People (14.8); Impact of Decisions on Co-workers or Company Results (38.2); Deal With Unpleasant or Angry People (45.27); Duration of Typical Work Week (52.5).

Position and secure steel bars or mesh in concrete forms to reinforce concrete. Use a variety of fasteners, rod-bending machines, blowtorches, and hand tools. Space and fasten together rods in forms according to blueprints, using wire and pliers. Cut and fit wire mesh or fabric, using hooked rods, and position fabric or mesh in concrete to reinforce concrete. Cut rods to required lengths, using metal shears, hacksaws, bar cutters, or acetylene torches. Bend steel rods with hand tools and rod-bending machines and weld them with arc-welding equipment. Position and secure steel bars, rods, cables, or mesh in concrete forms, using fasteners, rod-bending machines, blowtorches, and hand tools. Place blocks under rebar to hold the bars off the deck when reinforcing floors. Determine quantities, sizes, shapes, and locations of reinforcing rods from blueprints, sketches, or oral instructions.

Personality Type: Realistic. Realistic occupations frequently involve work activities that include practical, hands-on problems and solutions. They often deal with plants; animals; and real-world materials such as wood, tools, and machinery. Many of the occupations require working outside and do not involve a lot of paperwork or working closely with others.

GOE—Interest Area: 02. Architecture and Construction. **Work Group:** 02.04. Construction Crafts. **Other Jobs in This Work**

Group: Boilermakers; Brickmasons and Blockmasons; Carpet Installers; Cement Masons and Concrete Finishers; Commercial Divers; Construction Carpenters; Crane and Tower Operators; Drywall and Ceiling Tile Installers; Electricians; Fence Erectors; Floor Layers, Except Carpet, Wood, and Hard Tiles; Floor Sanders and Finishers; Glaziers; Hazardous Materials Removal Workers; Insulation Workers, Floor, Ceiling, and Wall; Insulation Workers, Mechanical; Manufactured Building and Mobile Home Installers; Operating Engineers and Other Construction Equipment Operators; Painters, Construction and Maintenance; Paperhangers; Paving, Surfacing, and Tamping Equipment Operators; Pile-Driver Operators; Pipe Fitters and Steamfitters; Pipelayers; Plasterers and Stucco Masons; Plumbers; Plumbers, Pipefitters, and Steamfitters; Rail-Track Laying and Maintenance Equipment Operators; Refractory Materials Repairers, Except Brickmasons; Riggers; Roofers; Rough Carpenters; Security and Fire Alarm Systems Installers; Segmental Pavers; Sheet Metal Workers; Stone Cutters and Carvers, Manufacturing; Stonemasons; Structural Iron and Steel Workers; Tapers; Terrazzo Workers and Finishers; Tile and Marble Setters.

Skills—Installation: Installing equipment, machines, wiring, or programs to meet specifications. **Management of Material Resources:** Obtaining and seeing to the appropriate use of equipment, facilities, and materials needed to do certain work. **Coordination:** Adjusting actions in relation to others' actions. **Management of Personnel Resources:** Motivating, developing, and directing people as they work, identifying the best people for the job. **Equipment Selection:** Determining the kind of tools and equipment needed to do a job. **Mathematics:** Using mathematics to solve problems.

Education and Training Program: Construction Trades, Other. **Related Knowledge/Courses: Building and Construction:** Materials, methods, and the tools involved in the construction or repair of houses, buildings, or other structures such as highways and roads. **Mechanical Devices:** Machines and tools, including their designs, uses, repair, and maintenance. **Public Safety and Security:** Relevant equipment, policies, procedures, and strategies to promote effective local, state, or national security operations for the protection of people, data, property, and institutions. **Transportation:** Principles and methods for moving people or goods by air, rail, sea, or road, including the relative costs and benefits.

Work Environment: Outdoors; contaminants; standing; walking and running; using hands on objects, tools, or controls; repetitive motions.

Rolling Machine Setters, Operators, and Tenders, Metal and Plastic

- ◉ Education/Training Required: Moderate-term on-the-job training
- ◉ Annual Earnings: $31,050
- ◉ Growth: –11.8%
- ◉ Annual Job Openings: 3,075
- ◉ Self-Employed: 3.1%
- ◉ Part-Time: 40.0%

Level of Stress Tolerance Needed: 60.0 (out of 100)

Most Stressful Aspects: Duration of Typical Work Week (84.5); Importance of Being Exact or Accurate (82.7); Pace Determined by Speed of Equipment (81.7); Impact of Decisions on Co-workers or Company Results (70.2).

Least Stressful Aspects: Deal With Physically Aggressive People (6.5); Frequency of Conflict Situations (49.0); Time Pressure (59.8).

Set up, operate, or tend machines to roll steel or plastic, forming bends, beads, knurls, rolls, or plate, or to flatten, temper, or reduce gauge of material. Adjust and correct machine setups to reduce thicknesses, reshape products, and eliminate product defects. Monitor machine cycles and mill operation to detect jamming and to ensure that products conform to specifications. Examine, inspect, and measure raw materials and finished products to verify conformance to specifications. Read rolling orders, blueprints, and mill schedules to determine setup specifications, work sequences, product dimensions, and installation procedures. Manipulate controls and observe dial indicators to monitor, adjust, and regulate speeds of machine mechanisms. Start operation of rolling and milling machines to flatten, temper, form, and reduce sheet metal sections and to produce steel strips. Thread or feed sheets or rods through rolling mechanisms or start and control mechanisms that automatically feed steel into rollers. Set distance points between rolls, guides, meters, and stops according to specifications. Position, align, and secure arbors, spindles, coils, mandrels, dies, and slitting knives. Direct and train other workers to change rolls, operate mill equipment, remove coils and cobbles, and band and load material. Fill oil cups, adjust valves, and observe gauges to control flow of metal coolants and lubricants onto workpieces. Record mill production on schedule sheets. Install equipment such as guides, guards, gears, cooling equipment, and rolls, using hand tools. Signal and assist other workers to remove and position equipment, fill hoppers, and feed materials into machines. Calculate draft space and roll speed for each mill stand to plan rolling sequences and specified dimensions and tempers. Select rolls, dies, roll stands, and chucks from data charts to form specified contours and to fabricate products. Activate shears and grinders to trim workpieces. Remove scratches and polish roll surfaces, using polishing stones and electric buffers. Disassemble sizing mills removed from rolling lines and sort and store parts.

Personality Type: Realistic. Realistic occupations frequently involve work activities that include practical, hands-on problems and solutions. They often deal with plants; animals; and real-world materials such as wood, tools, and machinery. Many of the occupations require working outside and do not involve a lot of paperwork or working closely with others.

GOE—Interest Area: 13. Manufacturing. **Work Group:** 13.02. Machine Setup and Operation. **Other Jobs in This Work Group:** Crushing, Grinding, and Polishing Machine Setters, Operators, and Tenders; Cutting, Punching, and Press Machine Setters, Operators, and Tenders, Metal and Plastic; Drilling and Boring Machine Tool Setters, Operators, and Tenders, Metal and Plastic; Extruding and Drawing Machine Setters, Operators, and Tenders, Metal and Plastic; Forging Machine Setters, Operators, and Tenders, Metal and Plastic; Grinding, Lapping, Polishing, and Buffing Machine Tool Setters, Operators, and Tenders, Metal and Plastic; Lathe and Turning Machine Tool Setters, Operators, and Tenders, Metal and Plastic; Milling and Planing Machine Setters, Operators, and Tenders, Metal and Plastic; Multiple Machine Tool Setters, Operators, and Tenders, Metal and Plastic; Paper Goods Machine Setters, Operators, and Tenders; Textile Cutting Machine Setters, Operators, and Tenders; Textile Knitting and Weaving Machine Setters, Operators, and Tenders; Textile Winding, Twisting, and Drawing Out Machine Setters, Operators, and Tenders.

Skills—Operation Monitoring: Watching gauges, dials, or other indicators to make sure a machine is working properly. **Operation and Control:** Controlling operations of equipment or systems. **Equipment Maintenance:** Performing routine maintenance on equipment and determining when and what kind of maintenance is needed. **Repairing:** Repairing machines or systems, using the needed tools. **Quality Control Analysis:** Conducting tests and inspections of products, services, or processes to evaluate quality or performance. **Troubleshooting:** Determining causes of operating errors and deciding what to do about them.

Education and Training Programs: Machine Tool Technology/Machinist Training; Sheet Metal Technology/Sheetworking. **Related Knowledge/Courses: Mechanical Devices:** Machines and tools, including their designs, uses, repair, and maintenance. **Production and Processing:** Raw materials, production processes, quality control, costs, and other techniques for maximizing the effective manufacture and distribution of goods. **Education and Training:** Principles and methods for curriculum and training design, teaching and instruction for individuals and groups, and the measurement of training effects.

Work Environment: Noisy; contaminants; hazardous equipment; minor burns, cuts, bites, or stings; standing; using hands on objects, tools, or controls.

Rough Carpenters

- ◎ Education/Training Required: Long-term on-the-job training
- ◎ Annual Earnings: $36,550
- ◎ Growth: 10.3%
- ◎ Annual Job Openings: 223,225
- ◎ Self-Employed: 31.8%
- ◎ Part-Time: 15.9%

Our sources did not provide separate job openings data for this occupation. The job openings listed here are shared with Construction Carpenters.

Level of Stress Tolerance Needed: 74.5 (out of 100)

Most Stressful Aspects: Duration of Typical Work Week (69.5); Impact of Decisions on Co-workers or Company Results (68.8); Level of Competition (68.0).

Least Stressful Aspects: Deal With Physically Aggressive People (5.5); Pace Determined by Speed of Equipment (17.8); Consequence of Error (35.8); Deal With Unpleasant or Angry People (42.0).

Build rough wooden structures, such as concrete forms, scaffolds, tunnel, bridge, or sewer supports, billboard signs, and temporary frame shelters, according to sketches, blueprints, or oral instructions. Study blueprints and diagrams to determine dimensions of structure or form to be constructed. Measure materials or distances, using square, measuring tape, or rule to lay out work. Cut or saw boards, timbers, or plywood to required size, using handsaw, power saw, or woodworking machine. Assemble and fasten material together to construct wood or metal framework of structure, using bolts, nails, or screws. Anchor and brace forms and other structures in place, using nails, bolts, anchor rods, steel cables, planks, wedges, and timbers. Mark cutting lines on materials, using pencil and scriber. Erect forms, framework, scaffolds, hoists, roof supports, or chutes, using hand tools, plumb rule, and level. Install rough door and window frames, subflooring, fixtures, or temporary supports in structures undergoing construction or repair. Examine structural timbers and supports to detect decay and replace timbers as required, using hand tools, nuts, and bolts. Bore boltholes in timber, masonry, or concrete walls, using power drill. Fabricate parts, using woodworking and metalworking machines. Dig or direct digging of post holes and set poles to support structures. Build sleds from logs and timbers for use in hauling camp buildings and machinery through wooded areas. Build chutes for pouring concrete.

Personality Type: Realistic. Realistic occupations frequently involve work activities that include practical, hands-on problems and solutions. They often deal with plants; animals; and real-world materials such as wood, tools, and machinery. Many of the occupations require working outside and do not involve a lot of paperwork or working closely with others.

GOE—Interest Area: 02. Architecture and Construction. **Work Group:** 02.04. Construction Crafts. **Other Jobs in This Work Group:** Boilermakers; Brickmasons and Blockmasons; Carpet Installers; Cement Masons and Concrete Finishers; Commercial Divers; Construction Carpenters; Crane and Tower Operators; Drywall and Ceiling Tile Installers; Electricians; Fence Erectors; Floor Layers, Except Carpet, Wood, and Hard Tiles; Floor Sanders and Finishers; Glaziers; Hazardous Materials Removal Workers; Insulation Workers, Floor, Ceiling, and Wall; Insulation Workers, Mechanical; Manufactured Building and Mobile Home Installers; Operating Engineers and Other Construction Equipment Operators; Painters, Construction and Maintenance; Paperhangers; Paving, Surfacing, and Tamping Equipment Operators; Pile-Driver Operators; Pipe Fitters and Steamfitters; Pipelayers; Plasterers and Stucco Masons; Plumbers; Plumbers, Pipefitters, and Steamfitters; Rail-Track Laying and Maintenance Equipment Operators; Refractory Materials Repairers, Except Brickmasons; Reinforcing Iron and Rebar Workers; Riggers; Roofers; Security and Fire Alarm Systems Installers; Segmental Pavers; Sheet Metal Workers; Stone Cutters and Carvers, Manufacturing; Stonemasons; Structural Iron and Steel Workers; Tapers; Terrazzo Workers and Finishers; Tile and Marble Setters.

Skills—Repairing: Repairing machines or systems, using the needed tools. **Installation:** Installing equipment, machines, wiring, or programs to meet specifications. **Management of Personnel Resources:** Motivating, developing, and directing people as they work, identifying the best people for the job. **Equipment Selection:** Determining the kind of tools and equipment needed to do a job. **Mathematics:** Using mathematics to solve problems. **Technology Design:** Generating or adapting equipment and technology to serve user needs.

Education and Training Program: Carpentry/ Carpenter Training. **Related Knowledge/ Courses: Building and Construction:** Materials, methods, and the tools involved in the construction or repair of houses, buildings, or other structures such as highways and roads. **Design:** Design techniques, tools, and principles involved in production of precision technical plans, blueprints, drawings, and models. **Engineering and Technology:** The practical application of engineering science and technology. This includes applying principles, techniques, procedures, and equipment to the design and production of various goods and services. **Mechanical Devices:** Machines and tools, including their designs, uses, repair, and maintenance. **Production and Processing:** Raw materials, production processes, quality control, costs, and other techniques for maximizing the effective manufacture and distribution of goods. **Physics:** Physical principles, laws, their interrelationships, and applications to understanding fluid, material, and atmospheric dynamics, and mechanical, electrical, atomic, and subatomic structures and processes.

Work Environment: Outdoors; noisy; very hot or cold; contaminants; standing; using hands on objects, tools, or controls.

Roustabouts, Oil and Gas

- Education/Training Required: Moderate-term on-the-job training
- Annual Earnings: $25,700
- Growth: –3.2%
- Annual Job Openings: 4,800
- Self-Employed: 0.2%
- Part-Time: 4.9%

Level of Stress Tolerance Needed: 63.7 (out of 100)

Most Stressful Aspects: Duration of Typical Work Week (74.5); Consequence of Error (59.8); Pace Determined by Speed of Equipment (35.5); Deal With Physically Aggressive People (16.5).

Least Stressful Aspects: Frequency of Conflict Situations (28.8); Deal With Unpleasant or Angry People (31.7); Level of Competition (43.8); Impact of Decisions on Co-workers or Company Results (53.8).

Assemble or repair oil-field equipment, using hand and power tools. Perform other tasks as needed. Clean up spilled oil by bailing it into barrels. Unscrew or tighten pipes, casing, tubing, and pump rods, using hand and power wrenches and tongs. Bolt together pump and engine parts. Walk flow lines to locate leaks, using electronic detectors and making visual inspections. Move pipes to and from trucks by hand or by using truck winches and motorized lifts. Dismantle and repair oil-field machinery, boilers, and steam engine parts, using hand tools and power tools. Dig drainage ditches around wells and storage tanks. Keep pipe deck and main deck areas clean and tidy. Guide cranes to move loads about decks. Supply equipment to rig floors as requested and provide assistance to roughnecks. Dig holes, set forms, and mix and pour concrete into forms to make foundations for wood or steel derricks. Cut down and remove trees and brush to clear drill sites, to reduce fire hazards, and to make way for roads to sites. Bolt or nail together wood or steel framework to erect derricks.

Personality Type: Realistic. Realistic occupations frequently involve work activities that include practical, hands-on problems and solutions. They often deal with plants; animals; and real-world materials such as wood, tools, and machinery. Many of the occupations require working outside and do not involve a lot of paperwork or working closely with others.

GOE—Interest Area: 01. Agriculture and Natural Resources. **Work Group:** 01.08. Mining and Drilling. **Other Jobs in This Work Group:** Continuous Mining Machine Operators; Derrick Operators, Oil and Gas; Earth Drillers, Except Oil and Gas; Excavating and Loading Machine and Dragline Operators; Explosives Workers, Ordnance Handling Experts, and Blasters; Helpers—Extraction Workers; Loading Machine Operators, Underground Mining; Mine Cutting and Channeling Machine Operators; Rock Splitters, Quarry; Roof Bolters, Mining; Rotary Drill Operators, Oil and Gas; Service Unit Operators, Oil, Gas, and Mining; Shuttle Car Operators; Wellhead Pumpers.

Skills—Equipment Maintenance: Performing routine maintenance on equipment and determining when and what kind of maintenance is needed. **Installation:** Installing equipment, machines, wiring, or programs to meet specifications. **Operation Monitoring:** Watching gauges, dials, or other indicators to make sure a machine is working properly. **Repairing:** Repairing machines or systems, using the needed tools. **Operation and Control:** Controlling operations of equipment or systems. **Troubleshooting:** Determining causes of operating errors and deciding what to do about them.

Education and Training Program: Heavy/Industrial Equipment Maintenance Technologies, Other. Related Knowledge/Courses: Mechanical Devices: Machines and tools, including their designs, uses, repair, and maintenance. Physics: Physical principles, laws, their interrelationships, and applications to understanding fluid, material, and atmospheric dynamics, and mechanical, electrical, atomic, and subatomic structures and processes. Chemistry: The chemical composition, structure, and properties of substances and of the chemical processes and transformations that they undergo. This includes uses of chemicals, their danger signs, production techniques, and disposal methods. Public Safety and Security: Relevant equipment, policies, procedures, and strategies to promote effective local, state, or national security operations for the protection of people, data, property, and institutions. Production and Processing: Raw materials, production processes, quality control, costs, and other techniques for maximizing the effective manufacture and distribution of goods. Engineering and Technology: The practical application of engineering science and technology. This includes applying principles, techniques, procedures, and equipment to the design and production of various goods and services.

Work Environment: Outdoors; very hot or cold; contaminants; hazardous conditions; standing; using hands on objects, tools, or controls.

Sales Managers

- Education/Training Required: Work experience plus degree
- Annual Earnings: $91,560
- Growth: 10.2%
- Annual Job Openings: 36,392
- Self-Employed: 2.2%
- Part-Time: 8.8%

Level of Stress Tolerance Needed: 50.0 (out of 100)

Most Stressful Aspects: Duration of Typical Work Week (89.5); Impact of Decisions on Co-workers or Company Results (84.7); Time Pressure (81.3); Level of Competition (80.8).

Least Stressful Aspects: Deal With Physically Aggressive People (7.7); Consequence of Error (38.0); Deal With Unpleasant or Angry People (50.0).

Direct the actual distribution or movement of a product or service to the customer. Coordinate sales distribution by establishing sales territories, quotas, and goals and establish training programs for sales representatives. Analyze sales statistics gathered by staff to determine sales potential and inventory requirements and monitor the preferences of customers. Resolve customer complaints regarding sales and service. Monitor customer preferences to determine focus of sales efforts. Direct and coordinate activities involving sales of manufactured products, services, commodities, real estate, or other subjects of sale. Determine price schedules and discount rates. Review operational records and reports to project sales and determine profitability. Direct, coordinate, and review activities in sales and service accounting and record keeping and in receiving and shipping operations. Confer or consult with department heads to plan advertising services and to

S

secure information on equipment and customer specifications. Advise dealers and distributors on policies and operating procedures to ensure functional effectiveness of business. Prepare budgets and approve budget expenditures. Represent company at trade association meetings to promote products. Plan and direct staffing, training, and performance evaluations to develop and control sales and service programs. Visit franchised dealers to stimulate interest in establishment or expansion of leasing programs. Confer with potential customers regarding equipment needs and advise customers on types of equipment to purchase. Oversee regional and local sales managers and their staffs. Direct clerical staff to keep records of export correspondence, bid requests, and credit collections and to maintain current information on tariffs, licenses, and restrictions. Direct foreign sales and service outlets of an organization. Assess marketing potential of new and existing store locations, considering statistics and expenditures.

Personality Type: Enterprising. Enterprising occupations frequently involve starting up and carrying out projects. These occupations can involve leading people and making many decisions. They sometimes require risk taking and often deal with business.

GOE—Interest Area: 14. Retail and Wholesale Sales and Service. **Work Group:** 14.01. Managerial Work in Retail/Wholesale Sales and Service. **Other Jobs in This Work Group:** Advertising and Promotions Managers; First-Line Supervisors/Managers of Non-Retail Sales Workers; First-Line Supervisors/Managers of Retail Sales Workers; Funeral Directors; Marketing Managers; Property, Real Estate, and Community Association Managers; Purchasing Managers.

Skills—Management of Personnel Resources: Motivating, developing, and directing people as they work, identifying the best people for the job. **Negotiation:** Bringing others together and trying to reconcile differences. **Persuasion:** Persuading others to change their minds or behavior. **Service Orientation:** Actively looking for ways to help people. **Operations Analysis:** Analyzing needs and product requirements to create a design. **Time Management:** Managing one's own time and the time of others.

Education and Training Programs: Business Administration and Management, General; Business/Commerce, General; Consumer Merchandising/Retailing Management; Marketing, Other; Marketing/Marketing Management, General. **Related Knowledge/Courses: Sales and Marketing:** Principles and methods for showing, promoting, and selling products or services. This includes marketing strategy and tactics, product demonstration, sales techniques, and sales control systems. **Computers and Electronics:** Circuit boards, processors, chips, electronic equipment, and computer hardware and software, including applications and programming. **Mathematics:** Arithmetic, algebra, geometry, calculus, statistics, and their applications. **Law and Government:** Laws, legal codes, court procedures, precedents, government regulations, executive orders, agency rules, and the democratic political process. **Administration and Management:** Business and management principles involved in strategic planning, resource allocation, human resources modeling, leadership technique, production methods, and coordination of people and resources. **Transportation:** Principles and methods for moving people or goods by air, rail, sea, or road, including the relative costs and benefits.

Work Environment: Indoors; sitting.

Sawing Machine Setters, Operators, and Tenders, Wood

- Education/Training Required: Moderate-term on-the-job training
- Annual Earnings: $24,280
- Growth: 3.8%
- Annual Job Openings: 6,086
- Self-Employed: 8.0%
- Part-Time: 28.6%

Level of Stress Tolerance Needed: 51.7 (out of 100)

Most Stressful Aspects: Time Pressure (80.5); Importance of Being Exact or Accurate (79.5); Pace Determined by Speed of Equipment (76.5); Duration of Typical Work Week (65.0).

Least Stressful Aspects: Deal With Physically Aggressive People (9.7); Frequency of Conflict Situations (33.2); Deal With Unpleasant or Angry People (42.3); Impact of Decisions on Co-workers or Company Results (59.2).

Set up, operate, or tend wood-sawing machines. Includes head sawyers. Adjust saw blades by using wrenches and rulers or by turning handwheels or pressing pedals, levers, or panel buttons. Inspect and measure workpieces to mark for cuts and to verify the accuracy of cuts, using rulers, squares, or caliper rules. Examine logs or lumber to plan the best cuts. Set up, operate, or tend saws and machines that cut or trim wood to specified dimensions, such as circular saws, band saws, multiple-blade sawing machines, scroll saws, ripsaws, and crozer machines. Inspect stock for imperfections and to estimate grades or qualities of stock or workpieces. Operate panelboards of saw and conveyor systems to move stock through processes and to cut stock to specified dimensions. Mount and bolt sawing blades or attachments to machine shafts. Monitor sawing machines, adjusting speed and tension and clearing jams to ensure proper operation. Select saw blades, types and grades of stock, and cutting procedures to be used according to work orders or supervisors' instructions. Guide workpieces against saws, guide saw over workpieces by hand, or operate automatic feeding devices to guide cuts. Adjust bolts, clamps, stops, guides, and table angles and heights, using hand tools. Sharpen blades or replace defective or worn blades and bands, using hand tools. Count, sort, and stack finished workpieces. Lubricate and clean machines, using wrenches, grease guns, and solvents. Clear machine jams, using hand tools. Dispose of waste material after completing work assignments. Measure and mark stock for cuts. Examine blueprints, drawings, work orders, or patterns to determine equipment setup and selection details, procedures to be used, and dimensions of final products. Pull tables back against stops and depress pedals to advance cutterheads that shape stock ends. Trim lumber to straighten rough edges and remove defects, using circular saws. Position and clamp stock on tables, conveyors, or carriages, using hoists, guides, stops, dogs, wedges, and wrenches. Cut grooves, bevels, and miters; saw curved or irregular designs; and sever or shape metals according to specifications or work orders.

Personality Type: Realistic. Realistic occupations frequently involve work activities that include practical, hands-on problems and solutions. They often deal with plants; animals; and real-world materials such as wood, tools, and machinery. Many of the occupations require working outside and do not involve a lot of paperwork or working closely with others.

GOE—Interest Area: 13. Manufacturing. **Work Group:** 13.03. Production Work, Assorted Materials Processing. **Other Jobs in This Work Group:** Bakers; Cementing and Gluing Machine

Operators and Tenders; Chemical Equipment Operators and Tenders; Cleaning, Washing, and Metal Pickling Equipment Operators and Tenders; Coating, Painting, and Spraying Machine Setters, Operators, and Tenders; Cooling and Freezing Equipment Operators and Tenders; Cutting and Slicing Machine Setters, Operators, and Tenders; Extruding and Forming Machine Setters, Operators, and Tenders, Synthetic and Glass Fibers; Extruding, Forming, Pressing, and Compacting Machine Setters, Operators, and Tenders; Food and Tobacco Roasting, Baking, and Drying Machine Operators and Tenders; Food Batchmakers; Food Cooking Machine Operators and Tenders; Furnace, Kiln, Oven, Drier, and Kettle Operators and Tenders; Heat Treating Equipment Setters, Operators, and Tenders, Metal and Plastic; Helpers—Production Workers; Meat, Poultry, and Fish Cutters and Trimmers; Metal-Refining Furnace Operators and Tenders; Mixing and Blending Machine Setters, Operators, and Tenders; Packaging and Filling Machine Operators and Tenders; Plating and Coating Machine Setters, Operators, and Tenders, Metal and Plastic; Pourers and Casters, Metal; Separating, Filtering, Clarifying, Precipitating, and Still Machine Setters, Operators, and Tenders; Sewing Machine Operators; Shoe Machine Operators and Tenders; Slaughterers and Meat Packers; Team Assemblers; Textile Bleaching and Dyeing Machine Operators and Tenders; Tire Builders; Woodworking Machine Setters, Operators, and Tenders, Except Sawing.

Skills—Equipment Maintenance: Performing routine maintenance on equipment and determining when and what kind of maintenance is needed. Repairing: Repairing machines or systems, using the needed tools. Operation Monitoring: Watching gauges, dials, or other indicators to make sure a machine is working

properly. Operation and Control: Controlling operations of equipment or systems. Systems Analysis: Determining how a system should work and how changes in conditions, operations, and the environment will affect outcomes. Installation: Installing equipment, machines, wiring, or programs to meet specifications.

Education and Training Programs: No related CIP programs; this job is learned through informal moderate-term on-the-job training. Related Knowledge/Courses: Mechanical Devices: Machines and tools, including their designs, uses, repair, and maintenance. Production and Processing: Raw materials, production processes, quality control, costs, and other techniques for maximizing the effective manufacture and distribution of goods. Design: Design techniques, tools, and principles involved in production of precision technical plans, blueprints, drawings, and models. Engineering and Technology: The practical application of engineering science and technology. This includes applying principles, techniques, procedures, and equipment to the design and production of various goods and services.

Work Environment: Noisy; contaminants; hazardous equipment; standing; using hands on objects, tools, or controls; repetitive motions.

Secretaries, Except Legal, Medical, and Executive

- Education/Training Required: Moderate-term on-the-job training
- Annual Earnings: $27,450
- Growth: 1.2%
- Annual Job Openings: 239,630
- Self-Employed: 1.4%
- Part-Time: 34.8%

Level of Stress Tolerance Needed: 73.3 (out of 100)

Most Stressful Aspects: Importance of Being Exact or Accurate (83.5); Time Pressure (67.8).

Least Stressful Aspects: Deal With Physically Aggressive People (14.8); Pace Determined by Speed of Equipment (17.0); Consequence of Error (30.0); Level of Competition (36.0).

Perform routine clerical and administrative functions such as drafting correspondence, scheduling appointments, organizing and maintaining paper and electronic files, or providing information to callers. Operate office equipment such as fax machines, copiers, and phone systems and use computers for spreadsheet, word-processing, database management, and other applications. Answer telephones and give information to callers, take messages, or transfer calls to appropriate individuals. Greet visitors and callers, handle their inquiries, and direct them to the appropriate persons according to their needs. Set up and maintain paper and electronic filing systems for records, correspondence, and other material. Locate and attach appropriate files to incoming correspondence requiring replies. Open, read, route, and distribute incoming mail and other material and prepare answers to routine letters. Complete forms in accordance with company procedures. Make copies of correspondence and other printed material. Review work done by others to check for correct spelling and grammar, ensure that company format policies are followed, and recommend revisions. Compose, type, and distribute meeting notes, routine correspondence, and reports. Learn to operate new office technologies as they are developed and implemented. Maintain scheduling and event calendars. Schedule and confirm appointments for clients, customers, or supervisors. Manage projects and contribute to committee and team work. Mail newsletters, promotional material, and other information. Order and dispense supplies. Conduct searches to find needed information, using such sources as the Internet. Provide services to customers, such as order placement and account information. Collect and disburse funds from cash accounts and keep records of collections and disbursements. Prepare and mail checks. Establish work procedures and schedules and keep track of the daily work of clerical staff. Coordinate conferences and meetings. Take dictation in shorthand or by machine and transcribe information. Arrange conferences, meetings, and travel reservations for office personnel. Operate electronic mail systems and coordinate the flow of information both internally and with other organizations. Supervise other clerical staff and provide training and orientation to new staff.

Personality Type: Conventional. Conventional occupations frequently involve following set procedures and routines. These occupations can include working with data and details more than with ideas. Usually, there is a clear line of authority to follow.

GOE—Interest Area: 04. Business and Administration. **Work Group:** 04.04. Secretarial Support. **Other Jobs in This Work Group:** Executive Secretaries and Administrative Assistants; Legal Secretaries; Medical Secretaries.

Skills—Writing: Communicating effectively in writing as appropriate for the needs of the audience.

Education and Training Programs: Administrative Assistant and Secretarial Science, General; Executive Assistant/Executive Secretary Training. **Related Knowledge/Courses: Clerical Practices:** Administrative and clerical procedures and systems such as word processing, managing files and records, stenography and transcription, designing forms, and other office procedures and terminology. **Customer and Personal Service:** Principles and processes for providing customer and personal services. This includes customer needs assessment, meeting quality standards for services, and evaluation of customer satisfaction. **Computers and Electronics:** Circuit boards, processors, chips, electronic equipment, and computer hardware and software, including applications and programming. **Economics and Accounting:** Economic and accounting principles and practices, the financial markets, banking, and the analysis and reporting of financial data. **English Language:** The structure and content of the English language, including the meaning and spelling of words, rules of composition, and grammar. **Personnel and Human Resources:** Principles and procedures for personnel recruitment, selection, training, compensation and benefits, labor relations and negotiation, and personnel information systems.

Work Environment: Indoors; sitting; repetitive motions.

Security and Fire Alarm Systems Installers

- Education/Training Required: Postsecondary vocational training
- Annual Earnings: $34,810
- Growth: 20.2%
- Annual Job Openings: 5,729
- Self-Employed: 7.2%
- Part-Time: 2.6%

Level of Stress Tolerance Needed: 65.0 (out of 100)

Most Stressful Aspects: Impact of Decisions on Co-workers or Company Results (78.8); Importance of Being Exact or Accurate (77.0); Duration of Typical Work Week (74.0); Time Pressure (73.3).

Least Stressful Aspects: Deal With Physically Aggressive People (9.3); Pace Determined by Speed of Equipment (15.0); Frequency of Conflict Situations (36.3); Deal With Unpleasant or Angry People (49.8).

Install, program, maintain, and repair security and fire alarm wiring and equipment. Ensure that work is in accordance with relevant codes. Examine systems to locate problems such as loose connections or broken insulation. Test backup batteries, keypad programming, sirens, and all security features to ensure proper functioning and to diagnose malfunctions. Mount and fasten control panels, door and window contacts, sensors, and video cameras and attach electrical and telephone wiring to connect components. Install, maintain, or repair security systems, alarm devices, and related equipment, following blueprints of electrical layouts and building plans. Inspect installation sites and study work orders, building plans, and installation manuals to determine materials requirements and installation procedures. Feed cables through access holes, roof spaces, and cavity walls to reach fixture outlets; then position and terminate cables, wires, and strapping. Adjust sensitivity of units based on room structures and manufacturers' recommendations, using programming keypads. Test and repair circuits and sensors, following wiring and system specifications. Drill holes for wiring in wall studs, joists, ceilings, and floors. Demonstrate systems for customers and explain details such as the causes and consequences of false alarms. Consult with clients to assess risks and to determine security requirements. Keep informed of new products and developments. Mount raceways and conduits and fasten wires to wood framing, using staplers. Provide customers with cost estimates for equipment installation. Prepare documents such as invoices and warranties. Order replacement parts.

Personality Type: No data available.

GOE—**Interest Area:** 02. Architecture and Construction. **Work Group:** 02.04. Construction Crafts. **Other Jobs in This Work Group:** Boilermakers; Brickmasons and Blockmasons; Carpet Installers; Cement Masons and Concrete Finishers; Commercial Divers; Construction Carpenters; Crane and Tower Operators; Drywall and Ceiling Tile Installers; Electricians; Fence Erectors; Floor Layers, Except Carpet, Wood, and Hard Tiles; Floor Sanders and Finishers; Glaziers; Hazardous Materials Removal Workers; Insulation Workers, Floor, Ceiling, and Wall; Insulation Workers, Mechanical; Manufactured Building and Mobile Home Installers; Operating Engineers and Other Construction Equipment Operators; Painters, Construction and Maintenance; Paperhangers; Paving, Surfacing, and Tamping Equipment Operators; Pile-Driver Operators; Pipe Fitters and Steamfitters; Pipelayers; Plasterers and Stucco Masons; Plumbers; Plumbers, Pipefitters, and Steamfitters; Rail-Track Laying and Maintenance Equipment Operators; Refractory Materials Repairers, Except Brickmasons; Reinforcing Iron and Rebar Workers; Riggers; Roofers; Rough Carpenters; Segmental Pavers; Sheet Metal Workers; Stone Cutters and Carvers, Manufacturing; Stonemasons; Structural Iron and Steel Workers; Tapers; Terrazzo Workers and Finishers; Tile and Marble Setters.

Skills—Installation: Installing equipment, machines, wiring, or programs to meet specifications. **Repairing:** Repairing machines or systems, using the needed tools. **Troubleshooting:** Determining causes of operating errors and deciding what to do about them. **Equipment Maintenance:** Performing routine maintenance on equipment and determining when and what kind of maintenance is needed. **Systems Evaluation:** Identifying measures or indicators of system performance and the actions needed to improve or correct performance, relative to the goals of the system. **Programming:** Writing computer programs for various purposes.

Education and Training Programs: Electrician Training; Security System Installation, Repair, and Inspection Technology/Technician Training. **Related Knowledge/Courses: Telecommunications:** Transmission, broadcasting, switching, control, and operation of telecommunications systems. **Building and Construction:** Materials, methods, and the tools involved in the construction or repair of houses, buildings, or other structures such as highways and roads. **Mechanical Devices:** Machines and tools, including their designs, uses, repair, and maintenance. **Computers and Electronics:** Circuit boards, processors, chips, electronic equipment, and computer hardware and software, including applications and programming. **Public Safety and Security:** Relevant equipment, policies, procedures, and strategies to promote effective local, state, or national security operations for the protection of people, data, property, and institutions. **Design:** Design techniques, tools, and principles involved in production of precision technical plans, blueprints, drawings, and models.

Work Environment: More often indoors than outdoors; noisy; very hot or cold; standing; using hands on objects, tools, or controls.

Segmental Pavers

- ◎ Education/Training Required: Moderate-term on-the-job training
- ◎ Annual Earnings: $28,700
- ◎ Growth: 10.2%
- ◎ Annual Job Openings: 152
- ◎ Self-Employed: 7.8%
- ◎ Part-Time: 11.5%

Level of Stress Tolerance Needed: 62.7 (out of 100)

Most Stressful Aspects: Duration of Typical Work Week (82.5); Time Pressure (75.3); Frequency of Conflict Situations (74.5); Deal With Unpleasant or Angry People (57.7).

Least Stressful Aspects: Pace Determined by Speed of Equipment (17.5); Impact of Decisions on Co-workers or Company Results (67.0); Importance of Being Exact or Accurate (67.0).

Lay out, cut, and paste segmental paving units. Includes installers of bedding and restraining materials for the paving units. Supply and place base materials, edge restraints, bedding sand, and jointing sand. Prepare base for installation by removing unstable or unsuitable materials, compacting and grading the soil, draining or stabilizing weak or saturated soils, and taking measures to prevent water penetration and migration of bedding sand. Sweep sand from the surface prior to opening to traffic. Set pavers, aligning and spacing them correctly. Sweep sand into the joints and compact pavement until the joints are full. Compact bedding sand and pavers to finish the paved area, using a plate compactor. Design paver installation layout pattern and create markings for directional references of joints and stringlines. Resurface an outside area with cobblestones, terra-cotta tiles, concrete, or other materials. Discuss the design with the client. Cut paving stones to size and for edges, using a splitter and a masonry saw. Screed sand level to an even thickness and recheck sand exposed to elements, raking and rescreeding if necessary. Cement the edges of the paved area.

Personality Type: No data available.

GOE—Interest Area: 02. Architecture and Construction. **Work Group:** 02.04. Construction Crafts. **Other Jobs in This Work Group:** Boilermakers; Brickmasons and Blockmasons; Carpet Installers; Cement Masons and Concrete Finishers; Commercial Divers; Construction Carpenters; Crane and Tower Operators; Drywall and Ceiling Tile Installers; Electricians; Fence Erectors; Floor Layers, Except Carpet, Wood, and Hard Tiles; Floor Sanders and Finishers; Glaziers; Hazardous Materials Removal Workers; Insulation Workers, Floor, Ceiling, and Wall; Insulation Workers, Mechanical; Manufactured Building and Mobile Home Installers; Operating Engineers and Other Construction Equipment Operators; Painters, Construction and Maintenance; Paperhangers; Paving, Surfacing, and Tamping Equipment Operators; Pile-Driver Operators; Pipe Fitters and Steamfitters; Pipelayers; Plasterers and Stucco Masons; Plumbers; Plumbers, Pipefitters, and Steamfitters; Rail-Track Laying and Maintenance Equipment Operators; Refractory Materials Repairers, Except Brickmasons; Reinforcing Iron and Rebar Workers; Riggers; Roofers; Rough Carpenters; Security and Fire Alarm Systems Installers; Sheet Metal Workers; Stone Cutters and Carvers, Manufacturing; Stonemasons; Structural Iron and Steel Workers; Tapers; Terrazzo Workers and Finishers; Tile and Marble Setters.

Skills—Negotiation: Bringing others together and trying to reconcile differences. **Management of Personnel Resources:** Motivating, developing, and directing people as they work, identifying the best people for the job. **Equipment Maintenance:** Performing routine maintenance on equipment and determining when and what kind of maintenance is needed. **Management of Material Resources:** Obtaining and seeing to the appropriate use of equipment, facilities, and materials needed to do certain work. **Judgment and Decision Making:** Considering the relative costs and benefits of potential actions to choose the most appropriate one. **Service Orientation:** Actively looking for ways to help people.

Education and Training Program: Concrete Finishing/Concrete Finisher Training. **Related Knowledge/Courses: Building and Construction:** Materials, methods, and the tools involved in the construction or repair of houses, buildings, or other structures such as highways and roads. **Mechanical Devices:** Machines and tools, including their designs, uses, repair, and maintenance. **Transportation:** Principles and methods for moving people or goods by air, rail, sea, or road, including the relative costs and benefits. **Engineering and Technology:** The practical application of engineering science and technology. This includes applying principles, techniques, procedures, and equipment to the design and production of various goods and services.

Work Environment: More often outdoors than indoors; noisy; very hot or cold; walking and running; repetitive motions.

Semiconductor Processors

- Education/Training Required: Associate degree
- Annual Earnings: $32,860
- Growth: −12.9%
- Annual Job Openings: 5,709
- Self-Employed: 0.0%
- Part-Time: 15.8%

Level of Stress Tolerance Needed: 72.3 (out of 100)

Most Stressful Aspects: Importance of Being Exact or Accurate (81.3); Consequence of Error (73.3); Time Pressure (71.5); Duration of Typical Work Week (65.0).

Least Stressful Aspects: Deal With Physically Aggressive People (4.0); Frequency of Conflict Situations (44.2); Deal With Unpleasant or Angry People (45.0); Impact of Decisions on Co-workers or Company Results (54.5).

Perform any or all of the following functions in the manufacture of electronic semiconductors: Load semiconductor material into furnace; saw formed ingots into segments; load individual segment into crystal-growing chamber and monitor controls; locate crystal axis in ingot, using X-ray equipment, and saw ingots into wafers; and clean, polish, and load wafers into series of special-purpose furnaces, chemical baths, and equipment used to form circuitry and change conductive properties. Manipulate valves, switches, and buttons or key commands into control panels to start semiconductor processing cycles. Inspect materials, components, or products for surface defects and measure circuitry, using electronic test equipment, precision measuring instruments, microscope, and standard procedures. Maintain processing, production, and inspection information and reports. Clean semiconductor wafers, using cleaning equipment such as chemical baths, automatic wafer cleaners, or blow-off wands. Study work orders, instructions, formulas, and processing charts to determine specifications and sequence of operations. Load and unload equipment chambers and transport finished product to storage or to area for further processing. Clean and maintain equipment, including replacing etching and rinsing solutions and cleaning bath containers and work area. Place semiconductor wafers in processing containers or equipment holders, using vacuum wand or tweezers. Set, adjust, and readjust computerized or mechanical equipment controls to regulate power level, temperature, vacuum, and rotation speed of furnace, according to crystal-growing specifications. Etch, lap, polish, or grind wafers or ingots to form circuitry and change conductive properties, using etching, lapping, polishing, or grinding equipment. Load semiconductor material into furnace. Monitor operation and adjust controls of processing machines and equipment to produce compositions with specific electronic properties, using computer terminals. Count, sort, and weigh processed items. Calculate etching time based on thickness of material to be removed from wafers or crystals. Inspect equipment for leaks, diagnose malfunctions, and request repairs. Align photo mask pattern on photoresist layer, expose pattern to ultraviolet light, and develop pattern, using specialized equipment. Stamp, etch, or scribe identifying information on finished component according to specifications. Operate saw to cut remelt into sections of specified size or to cut ingots into wafers. Scribe or separate wafers into dice. Connect reactor to computer, using hand tools and power tools.

Personality Type: Realistic. Realistic occupations frequently involve work activities that include practical, hands-on problems and solutions. They often deal with plants; animals; and real-world materials such as wood, tools, and machinery. Many of the occupations require working outside and do not involve a lot of paperwork or working closely with others.

GOE—Interest Area: 13. Manufacturing. **Work Group:** 13.06. Production Precision Work. **Other Jobs in This Work Group:** Bookbinders; Dental Laboratory Technicians; Electrical and Electronic Equipment Assemblers; Electromechanical Equipment Assemblers; Engine and Other Machine Assemblers; Gem and Diamond Workers; Jewelers; Jewelers and Precious Stone and Metal Workers; Medical Appliance Technicians; Molding, Coremaking, and Casting Machine Setters, Operators, and Tenders, Metal and Plastic; Ophthalmic Laboratory Technicians; Precious Metal Workers; Timing Device Assemblers, Adjusters, and Calibrators.

Skills—Operation Monitoring: Watching gauges, dials, or other indicators to make sure a machine is working properly. **Repairing:** Repairing machines or systems, using the needed tools. **Equipment Maintenance:** Performing routine maintenance on equipment and determining when and what kind of maintenance is needed. **Installation:** Installing equipment, machines, wiring, or programs to meet specifications. **Operation and Control:** Controlling operations of equipment or systems. **Troubleshooting:** Determining causes of operating errors and deciding what to do about them.

Education and Training Program: Industrial Electronics Technology/Technician Training. **Related Knowledge/Courses: Production and Processing:** Raw materials, production processes, quality control, costs, and other techniques for maximizing the effective manufacture and distribution of goods. **Chemistry:** The chemical composition, structure, and properties of substances and of the chemical processes and transformations that they undergo. This includes uses of chemicals, their danger signs, production techniques, and disposal methods. **Computers and Electronics:** Circuit boards, processors, chips, electronic equipment, and computer hardware and software, including applications and programming. **English Language:** The structure and content of the English language, including the meaning and spelling of words, rules of composition, and grammar. **Engineering and Technology:** The practical application of engineering science and technology. This includes applying principles, techniques, procedures, and equipment to the design and production of various goods and services.

Work Environment: Indoors; noisy; contaminants; hazardous conditions; standing; using hands on objects, tools, or controls.

Separating, Filtering, Clarifying, Precipitating, and Still Machine Setters, Operators, and Tenders

- ◎ Education/Training Required: Moderate-term on-the-job training
- ◎ Annual Earnings: $34,970
- ◎ Growth: –3.2%
- ◎ Annual Job Openings: 1,238
- ◎ Self-Employed: 1.0%
- ◎ Part-Time: 15.8%

Level of Stress Tolerance Needed: 65.0 (out of 100)

Most Stressful Aspects: Importance of Being Exact or Accurate (80.5); Duration of Typical Work Week (79.5); Time Pressure (79.0); Pace Determined by Speed of Equipment (76.3).

Least Stressful Aspects: Deal With Physically Aggressive People (8.0); Level of Competition (44.7); Deal With Unpleasant or Angry People (50.2).

Set up, operate, or tend continuous flow or vat-type equipment; filter presses; shaker screens; centrifuges; condenser tubes; precipitating, fermenting, or evaporating tanks; scrubbing towers; or batch stills. These machines extract, sort, or separate liquids, gases, or solids from other materials to recover a refined product. Includes dairy-processing equipment operators. Set or adjust machine controls to regulate conditions such as material flow, temperature, and pressure. Monitor material flow and instruments such as temperature and pressure gauges, indicators, and meters to ensure optimal processing conditions. Start agitators, shakers, conveyors, pumps, or centrifuge machines; then turn valves or move controls to admit, drain, separate, filter, clarify, mix, or transfer materials. Examine samples visually or by hand to verify qualities such as clarity, cleanliness, consistency, dryness, and texture. Collect samples of materials or products for laboratory analysis. Maintain logs of instrument readings, test results, and shift production and send production information to computer databases. Test samples to determine viscosity, acidity, specific gravity, or degree of concentration, using test equipment such as viscometers, pH meters, and hydrometers. Measure or weigh materials to be refined, mixed, transferred, stored, or otherwise processed. Clean and sterilize tanks, screens, inflow pipes, production areas, and equipment, using hoses, brushes, scrapers, or chemical solutions. Inspect machines and equipment for hazards, operating efficiency, malfunctions, wear, and leaks. Dump, pour, or load specified amounts of refined or unrefined materials into equipment or containers for further processing or storage. Connect pipes between vats and processing equipment. Communicate processing instructions to other workers. Remove clogs, defects, and impurities from machines, tanks, conveyors, screens, or other processing equipment. Assemble fittings, valves, bowls, plates, disks, impeller shafts, and other parts to equipment to prepare equipment for operation. Install and maintain or repair hoses, pumps, filters, or screens to maintain processing equipment, using hand tools. Turn valves to pump sterilizing solutions and rinsewater through pipes and equipment and to spray vats with atomizers. Remove full bags or containers from discharge outlets and replace them with empty ones. Pack bottles into cartons or crates, using machines.

Personality Type: Realistic. Realistic occupations frequently involve work activities that include practical, hands-on problems and solutions. They often deal with plants; animals; and real-world materials such as wood, tools, and machinery. Many of the occupations require

S

working outside and do not involve a lot of paperwork or working closely with others.

GOE—Interest Area: 13. Manufacturing. **Work Group:** 13.03. Production Work, Assorted Materials Processing. **Other Jobs in This Work Group:** Bakers; Cementing and Gluing Machine Operators and Tenders; Chemical Equipment Operators and Tenders; Cleaning, Washing, and Metal Pickling Equipment Operators and Tenders; Coating, Painting, and Spraying Machine Setters, Operators, and Tenders; Cooling and Freezing Equipment Operators and Tenders; Cutting and Slicing Machine Setters, Operators, and Tenders; Extruding and Forming Machine Setters, Operators, and Tenders, Synthetic and Glass Fibers; Extruding, Forming, Pressing, and Compacting Machine Setters, Operators, and Tenders; Food and Tobacco Roasting, Baking, and Drying Machine Operators and Tenders; Food Batchmakers; Food Cooking Machine Operators and Tenders; Furnace, Kiln, Oven, Drier, and Kettle Operators and Tenders; Heat Treating Equipment Setters, Operators, and Tenders, Metal and Plastic; Helpers—Production Workers; Meat, Poultry, and Fish Cutters and Trimmers; Metal-Refining Furnace Operators and Tenders; Mixing and Blending Machine Setters, Operators, and Tenders; Packaging and Filling Machine Operators and Tenders; Plating and Coating Machine Setters, Operators, and Tenders, Metal and Plastic; Pourers and Casters, Metal; Sawing Machine Setters, Operators, and Tenders, Wood; Sewing Machine Operators; Shoe Machine Operators and Tenders; Slaughterers and Meat Packers; Team Assemblers; Textile Bleaching and Dyeing Machine Operators and Tenders; Tire Builders; Woodworking Machine Setters, Operators, and Tenders, Except Sawing.

Skills—Operation Monitoring: Watching gauges, dials, or other indicators to make sure a machine is working properly. **Repairing:** Repairing machines or systems, using the needed tools. **Equipment Maintenance:** Performing routine maintenance on equipment and determining when and what kind of maintenance is needed. **Operation and Control:** Controlling operations of equipment or systems. **Troubleshooting:** Determining causes of operating errors and deciding what to do about them. **Quality Control Analysis:** Conducting tests and inspections of products, services, or processes to evaluate quality or performance.

Education and Training Programs: No related CIP programs; this job is learned through informal moderate-term on-the-job training. **Related Knowledge/Courses: Chemistry:** The chemical composition, structure, and properties of substances and of the chemical processes and transformations that they undergo. This includes uses of chemicals, their danger signs, production techniques, and disposal methods. **Production and Processing:** Raw materials, production processes, quality control, costs, and other techniques for maximizing the effective manufacture and distribution of goods. **Food Production:** Techniques and equipment for planting, growing, and harvesting food products (both plant and animal) for consumption, including storage/handling techniques. **Mechanical Devices:** Machines and tools, including their designs, uses, repair, and maintenance. **Public Safety and Security:** Relevant equipment, policies, procedures, and strategies to promote effective local, state, or national security operations for the protection of people, data, property, and institutions.

Work Environment: Noisy; very hot or cold; contaminants; high places; hazardous conditions; hazardous equipment.

Septic Tank Servicers and Sewer Pipe Cleaners

- Education/Training Required: Moderate-term on-the-job training
- Annual Earnings: $31,430
- Growth: 10.2%
- Annual Job Openings: 3,156
- Self-Employed: 6.4%
- Part-Time: 11.5%

Level of Stress Tolerance Needed: 68.0 (out of 100)

Most Stressful Aspects: Duration of Typical Work Week (72.5); Impact of Decisions on Co-workers or Company Results (68.0); Level of Competition (66.8); Consequence of Error (55.8).

Least Stressful Aspects: Deal With Physically Aggressive People (8.3); Deal With Unpleasant or Angry People (39.5); Frequency of Conflict Situations (39.7); Time Pressure (64.7).

Clean and repair septic tanks, sewer lines, or drains. May patch walls and partitions of tank, replace damaged drain tile, or repair breaks in underground piping. Drive trucks to transport crews, materials, and equipment. Communicate with supervisors and other workers, using equipment such as wireless phones, pagers, or radio telephones. Prepare and keep records of actions taken, including maintenance and repair work. Operate sewer-cleaning equipment, including power rodders, high-velocity water jets, sewer flushers, bucket machines, wayne balls, and vac-alls. Ensure that repaired sewer line joints are tightly sealed before backfilling begins. Withdraw cables from pipes and examine them for evidence of mud, roots, grease, and other deposits indicating broken or clogged sewer lines. Install rotary knives on flexible cables mounted on machine reels according to the diameters of pipes to be cleaned. Measure excavation sites, using plumbers' snakes, tapelines, or lengths of cutting heads within sewers, and mark areas for digging. Locate problems, using specially designed equipment, and mark where digging must occur to reach damaged tanks or pipes. Start machines to feed revolving cables or rods into openings, stopping machines and changing knives to conform to pipe sizes. Clean and repair septic tanks; sewer lines; or related structures such as manholes, culverts, and catch basins. Service, adjust, and make minor repairs to equipment, machines, and attachments. Inspect manholes to locate sewer line stoppages. Cut damaged sections of pipe with cutters, remove broken sections from ditches, and replace pipe sections, using pipe sleeves. Dig out sewer lines manually, using shovels. Break asphalt and other pavement so that pipes can be accessed, using airhammers, picks, and shovels. Cover repaired pipes with dirt and pack back-filled excavations, using air and gasoline tampers. Requisition or order tools and equipment. Rotate cleaning rods manually, using turning pins. Clean and disinfect domestic basements and other areas flooded by sewer stoppages. Tap mainline sewers to install sewer saddles. Update sewer maps and manhole charts.

Personality Type: Realistic. Realistic occupations frequently involve work activities that include practical, hands-on problems and solutions. They often deal with plants; animals; and real-world materials such as wood, tools, and machinery. Many of the occupations require working outside and do not involve a lot of paperwork or working closely with others.

GOE—Interest Area: 02. Architecture and Construction. **Work Group:** 02.06. Construction Support/Labor. **Other Jobs in This Work Group:** Construction Laborers; Helpers—Brickmasons, Blockmasons, Stonemasons, and

Tile and Marble Setters; Helpers—Carpenters; Helpers—Electricians; Helpers—Installation, Maintenance, and Repair Workers; Helpers—Painters, Paperhangers, Plasterers, and Stucco Masons; Helpers—Pipelayers, Plumbers, Pipefitters, and Steamfitters; Helpers—Roofers; Highway Maintenance Workers.

Skills—Repairing: Repairing machines or systems, using the needed tools. **Equipment Maintenance:** Performing routine maintenance on equipment and determining when and what kind of maintenance is needed. **Operation Monitoring:** Watching gauges, dials, or other indicators to make sure a machine is working properly. **Installation:** Installing equipment, machines, wiring, or programs to meet specifications. **Operation and Control:** Controlling operations of equipment or systems. **Systems Analysis:** Determining how a system should work and how changes in conditions, operations, and the environment will affect outcomes.

Education and Training Program: Plumbing Technology/Plumber Training. **Related Knowledge/Courses: Building and Construction:** Materials, methods, and the tools involved in the construction or repair of houses, buildings, or other structures such as highways and roads. **Mechanical Devices:** Machines and tools, including their designs, uses, repair, and maintenance. **Sales and Marketing:** Principles and methods for showing, promoting, and selling products or services. This includes marketing strategy and tactics, product demonstration, sales techniques, and sales control systems. **Transportation:** Principles and methods for moving people or goods by air, rail, sea, or road, including the relative costs and benefits. **Production and Processing:** Raw materials, production processes, quality control, costs, and other techniques for maximizing the effective manufacture and distribution of goods. **Customer and Personal Service:** Principles and processes for providing customer and personal

services. This includes customer needs assessment, meeting quality standards for services, and evaluation of customer satisfaction.

Work Environment: Outdoors; noisy; very hot or cold; very bright or dim lighting; contaminants; using hands on objects, tools, or controls.

Set and Exhibit Designers

- Education/Training Required: Bachelor's degree
- Annual Earnings: $41,820
- Growth: 17.8%
- Annual Job Openings: 1,402
- Self-Employed: 29.8%
- Part-Time: 32.0%

Level of Stress Tolerance Needed: 70.2 (out of 100)

Most Stressful Aspects: Importance of Being Exact or Accurate (83.7); Impact of Decisions on Co-workers or Company Results (76.5); Duration of Typical Work Week (61.0); Level of Competition (47.8).

Least Stressful Aspects: Deal With Physically Aggressive People (0.0); Pace Determined by Speed of Equipment (5.5); Deal With Unpleasant or Angry People (39.0); Consequence of Error (40.2).

Design special exhibits and movie, television, and theater sets. May study scripts, confer with directors, and conduct research to determine appropriate architectural styles. Examine objects to be included in exhibits to plan where and how to display them. Acquire, or arrange for acquisition of, specimens or graphics required to complete exhibits. Prepare rough drafts and scale working drawings of sets, including floor plans, scenery, and properties to be constructed. Confer with clients and staff to gather information about exhibit space, proposed themes and content, timelines, budgets, materials, and promotion requirements. Estimate set- or exhibit-related costs, including materials, construction, and rental of props or locations. Develop set designs based on evaluation of scripts, budgets, research information, and available locations. Direct and coordinate construction, erection, or decoration activities to ensure that sets or exhibits meet design, budget, and schedule requirements. Inspect installed exhibits for conformance to specifications and satisfactory operation of special effects components. Plan for location-specific issues such as space limitations, traffic flow patterns, and safety concerns. Submit plans for approval and adapt plans to serve intended purposes or to conform to budget or fabrication restrictions. Prepare preliminary renderings of proposed exhibits, including detailed construction, layout, and material specifications and diagrams relating to aspects such as special effects and lighting. Select and purchase lumber and hardware necessary for set construction. Collaborate with those in charge of lighting and sound so that those production aspects can be coordinated with set designs or exhibit layouts. Research architectural and stylistic elements appropriate for the time period to be depicted, consulting experts for information as necessary. Design and produce displays and materials that can be used to decorate windows, interior displays, or event locations such as streets and fairgrounds. Coordinate the removal of sets, props, and exhibits after productions or events are complete. Select set props such as furniture, pictures, lamps, and rugs. Confer with conservators to determine how to handle an exhibit's environmental aspects, such as lighting, temperature, and humidity, so that objects will be protected and exhibits will be enhanced.

Personality Type: Artistic. Artistic occupations frequently involve working with forms, designs and patterns. They often require self-expression, and the work can be done without following a clear set of rules.

GOE—Interest Area: 03. Arts and Communication. **Work Group:** 03.05. Design. **Other Jobs in This Work Group:** Commercial and Industrial Designers; Fashion Designers; Floral Designers; Graphic Designers; Interior Designers; Merchandise Displayers and Window Trimmers.

Skills—Installation: Installing equipment, machines, wiring, or programs to meet specifications. **Management of Personnel Resources:** Motivating, developing, and directing people as they work, identifying the best people for the job. **Management of Material Resources:** Obtaining and seeing to the appropriate use of equipment, facilities, and materials needed to do certain work. **Persuasion:** Persuading others to change their minds or behavior. **Operations Analysis:** Analyzing needs and product requirements to create a design. **Management of Financial Resources:** Determining how money will be spent to get the work done, and accounting for these expenditures.

Education and Training Programs: Design and Applied Arts, Other; Design and Visual Communications, General; Illustration; Technical Theatre/Theatre Design and Technology. **Related Knowledge/Courses: Fine Arts:** The theory and techniques required to compose, produce, and perform works of music, dance, visual arts, drama, and sculpture. **Design:** Design techniques, tools, and principles involved in production of precision technical plans, blueprints, drawings, and models. **History and Archeology:** Historical events and their causes, indicators, and effects on civilizations and cultures. **Communications and Media:** Media production, communication, and dissemination techniques and methods. This includes alternative ways to inform and entertain via written, oral, and visual media.

S

Sociology and Anthropology: Group behavior and dynamics, societal trends and influences, human migrations, ethnicity, cultures and their history and origins. **Computers and Electronics:** Circuit boards, processors, chips, electronic equipment, and computer hardware and software, including applications and programming.

Work Environment: Indoors; sitting; using hands on objects, tools, or controls.

Sheet Metal Workers

- Education/Training Required: Long-term on-the-job training
- Annual Earnings: $37,360
- Growth: 6.7%
- Annual Job Openings: 31,677
- Self-Employed: 4.7%
- Part-Time: 3.0%

Level of Stress Tolerance Needed: 64.5 (out of 100)

Most Stressful Aspects: Importance of Being Exact or Accurate (77.3); Time Pressure (73.0); Duration of Typical Work Week (69.0); Consequence of Error (55.3).

Least Stressful Aspects: Deal With Physically Aggressive People (10.2); Deal With Unpleasant or Angry People (40.0); Frequency of Conflict Situations (48.0); Impact of Decisions on Co-workers or Company Results (63.2).

Fabricate, assemble, install, and repair sheet metal products and equipment, such as ducts, control boxes, drainpipes, and furnace casings. Work may involve any of the following: setting up and operating fabricating machines to cut, bend, and straighten sheet metal; shaping metal over anvils, blocks, or forms, using hammer; operating soldering and welding equipment to join sheet metal parts; and inspecting, assembling, and smoothing seams and joints of burred surfaces. Determine project requirements, including scope, assembly sequences, and required methods and materials, according to blueprints, drawings, and written or verbal instructions. Lay out, measure, and mark dimensions and reference lines on material such as roofing panels according to drawings or templates, using calculators, scribes, dividers, squares, and rulers. Maneuver completed units into position for installation and anchor the units. Convert blueprints into shop drawings to be followed in the construction and assembly of sheet metal products. Install assemblies such as flashing, pipes, tubes, heating and air conditioning ducts, furnace casings, rain gutters, and downspouts in supportive frameworks. Select gauges and types of sheet metal or non-metallic material according to product specifications. Drill and punch holes in metal for screws, bolts, and rivets. Fasten seams and joints together with welds, bolts, cement, rivets, solder, caulks, metal drive clips, and bonds to assemble components into products or to repair sheet metal items. Fabricate or alter parts at construction sites, using shears, hammers, punches, and drills. Finish parts, using hacksaws and hand, rotary, or squaring shears. Trim, file, grind, deburr, buff, and smooth surfaces, seams, and joints of assembled parts, using hand tools and portable power tools. Maintain equipment, making repairs and modifications when necessary. Shape metal material over anvils, blocks, or other forms, using hand tools. Transport prefabricated parts to construction sites for assembly and installation. Develop and lay out patterns that use materials most efficiently, using computerized metalworking equipment to experiment with different layouts. Inspect individual parts, assemblies, and installations for conformance to specifications and building codes, using measuring instruments such as calipers, scales, and micrometers. Secure metal roof panels in place and interlock and fasten grooved panel edges. Fasten roof panel edges and machine-made molding to structures, nailing or welding pieces into place.

Personality Type: Realistic. Realistic occupations frequently involve work activities that include practical, hands-on problems and solutions. They often deal with plants; animals; and real-world materials such as wood, tools, and machinery. Many of the occupations require working outside and do not involve a lot of paperwork or working closely with others.

GOE—Interest Area: 02. Architecture and Construction. **Work Group:** 02.04. Construction Crafts. **Other Jobs in This Work Group:** Boilermakers; Brickmasons and Blockmasons; Carpet Installers; Cement Masons and Concrete Finishers; Commercial Divers; Construction Carpenters; Crane and Tower Operators; Drywall and Ceiling Tile Installers; Electricians; Fence Erectors; Floor Layers, Except Carpet, Wood, and Hard Tiles; Floor Sanders and Finishers; Glaziers; Hazardous Materials Removal Workers; Insulation Workers, Floor, Ceiling, and Wall; Insulation Workers, Mechanical; Manufactured Building and Mobile Home Installers; Operating Engineers and Other Construction Equipment Operators; Painters, Construction and Maintenance; Paperhangers; Paving, Surfacing, and Tamping Equipment Operators; Pile-Driver Operators; Pipe Fitters and Steamfitters; Pipelayers; Plasterers and Stucco Masons; Plumbers; Plumbers, Pipefitters, and Steamfitters; Rail-Track Laying and Maintenance Equipment Operators; Refractory Materials Repairers, Except Brickmasons; Reinforcing Iron and Rebar Workers; Riggers; Roofers; Rough Carpenters; Security and Fire Alarm Systems Installers; Segmental Pavers; Stone Cutters and Carvers, Manufacturing; Stonemasons; Structural Iron and Steel Workers;

Tapers; Terrazzo Workers and Finishers; Tile and Marble Setters.

Skills—Installation: Installing equipment, machines, wiring, or programs to meet specifications. **Repairing:** Repairing machines or systems, using the needed tools. **Equipment Maintenance:** Performing routine maintenance on equipment and determining when and what kind of maintenance is needed. **Mathematics:** Using mathematics to solve problems. **Technology Design:** Generating or adapting equipment and technology to serve user needs. **Troubleshooting:** Determining causes of operating errors and deciding what to do about them.

Education and Training Program: Sheet Metal Technology/Sheetworking. **Related Knowledge/Courses: Building and Construction:** Materials, methods, and the tools involved in the construction or repair of houses, buildings, or other structures such as highways and roads. **Mechanical Devices:** Machines and tools, including their designs, uses, repair, and maintenance. **Physics:** Physical principles, laws, their interrelationships, and applications to understanding fluid, material, and atmospheric dynamics, and mechanical, electrical, atomic, and subatomic structures and processes. **Design:** Design techniques, tools, and principles involved in production of precision technical plans, blueprints, drawings, and models. **Production and Processing:** Raw materials, production processes, quality control, costs, and other techniques for maximizing the effective manufacture and distribution of goods. **Mathematics:** Arithmetic, algebra, geometry, calculus, statistics, and their applications.

Work Environment: Noisy; contaminants; hazardous equipment; minor burns, cuts, bites, or stings; standing; using hands on objects, tools, or controls.

S

Social Science Research Assistants

- ◎ Education/Training Required: Associate degree
- ◎ Annual Earnings: $33,860
- ◎ Growth: 12.4%
- ◎ Annual Job Openings: 3,571
- ◎ Self-Employed: 1.7%
- ◎ Part-Time: 28.9%

Our sources did not provide separate job openings data for this occupation. The job openings listed here are shared with City and Regional Planning Aides.

Level of Stress Tolerance Needed: 61.8 (out of 100)

Most Stressful Aspects: Importance of Being Exact or Accurate (76.3).

Least Stressful Aspects: Deal With Physically Aggressive People (2.0); Pace Determined by Speed of Equipment (2.5); Frequency of Conflict Situations (28.8); Duration of Typical Work Week (30.5).

Assist social scientists in laboratory, survey, and other social research. May perform publication activities, laboratory analysis, quality control, or data management. Normally these individuals work under the direct supervision of a social scientist and assist in those activities that are more routine. Develop and implement research quality-control procedures. Verify the accuracy and validity of data entered in databases; correct any errors. Conduct Internet-based and library research. Provide assistance with the preparation of project-related reports, manuscripts, and presentations. Collect specimens such as blood samples as required by research projects. Supervise the work of survey interviewers. Present research findings to groups of people.

Perform needs assessments and/or consult with clients to determine the types of research and information that are required. Perform data entry and other clerical work as required for project completion. Screen potential subjects to determine their suitability as study participants. Allocate and manage laboratory space and resources. Edit and submit protocols and other required research documentation. Track research participants and perform any necessary follow-up tasks. Code data in preparation for computer entry. Provide assistance in the design of survey instruments such as questionnaires. Prepare, manipulate, and manage extensive databases. Prepare tables, graphs, fact sheets, and written reports summarizing research results. Obtain informed consent of research subjects and their guardians. Design and create special programs for tasks such as statistical analysis and data entry and cleaning. Administer standardized tests to research subjects or interview them to collect research data. Recruit and schedule research participants. Perform descriptive and multivariate statistical analyses of data, using computer software. Track laboratory supplies and expenses such as participant reimbursement.

Personality Type: No data available.

GOE—Interest Area: 15. Scientific Research, Engineering, and Mathematics. **Work Group:** 15.06. Mathematics and Data Analysis. **Other Jobs in This Work Group:** Actuaries; Mathematical Technicians; Mathematicians; Statistical Assistants; Statisticians.

Skills—Programming: Writing computer programs for various purposes. **Science:** Using scientific rules and methods to solve problems. **Writing:** Communicating effectively in writing as appropriate for the needs of the audience. **Mathematics:** Using mathematics to solve problems. **Active Learning:** Understanding the implications of new information for both current and future problem solving and decision making. **Learning Strategies:** Selecting and using training/instructional methods and procedures appropriate for the situation when learning or teaching new things.

Education and Training Program: Social Sciences, General. **Related Knowledge/Courses: Psychology:** Human behavior and performance; individual differences in ability, personality, and interests; learning and motivation; psychological research methods; and the assessment and treatment of behavioral and affective disorders. **Sociology and Anthropology:** Group behavior and dynamics, societal trends and influences, human migrations, ethnicity, cultures and their history and origins. **Clerical Practices:** Administrative and clerical procedures and systems such as word processing, managing files and records, stenography and transcription, designing forms, and other office procedures and terminology. **Computers and Electronics:** Circuit boards, processors, chips, electronic equipment, and computer hardware and software, including applications and programming. **English Language:** The structure and content of the English language, including the meaning and spelling of words, rules of composition, and grammar. **Communications and Media:** Media production, communication, and dissemination techniques and methods. This includes alternative ways to inform and entertain via written, oral, and visual media.

Work Environment: Indoors; sitting.

Sociologists

- ◎ Education/Training Required: Master's degree
- ◎ Annual Earnings: $60,290
- ◎ Growth: 10.0%
- ◎ Annual Job Openings: 403
- ◎ Self-Employed: 0.0%
- ◎ Part-Time: 25.0%

Level of Stress Tolerance Needed: 66.5 (out of 100)

Most Stressful Aspects: Duration of Typical Work Week (89.0); Level of Competition (69.7).

Least Stressful Aspects: Pace Determined by Speed of Equipment (0.7); Deal With Physically Aggressive People (7.0); Deal With Unpleasant or Angry People (27.5); Consequence of Error (33.0).

Study human society and social behavior by examining the groups and social institutions that people form, as well as various social, religious, political, and business organizations. May study the behavior and interaction of groups, trace their origin and growth, and analyze the influence of group activities on individual members. Analyze and interpret data in order to increase the understanding of human social behavior. Prepare publications and reports containing research findings. Plan and conduct research to develop and test theories about societal issues such as crime, group relations, poverty, and aging. Collect data about the attitudes, values, and behaviors of people in groups, using observation, interviews, and review of documents. Develop, implement, and evaluate methods of data collection, such as questionnaires or interviews. Teach sociology. Direct work of statistical clerks, statisticians, and others who compile and evaluate research data. Consult with and advise individuals such as administrators, social workers, and legislators regarding social issues and policies, as well as the implications of research findings. Collaborate with research workers in other disciplines. Develop approaches to the solution of groups' problems based on research findings in sociology and related disciplines. Observe group interactions and role affiliations to collect data, identify problems, evaluate progress, and determine the need for additional change. Develop problem intervention procedures, utilizing techniques such as interviews, consultations, role-playing, and participant observation of group interactions.

Personality Type: Investigative. Investigative occupations frequently involve working with ideas and require an extensive amount of thinking. These occupations can involve searching for facts and figuring out problems mentally.

GOE—Interest Area: 15. Scientific Research, Engineering, and Mathematics. **Work Group:** 15.04. Social Sciences. **Other Jobs in This Work Group:** Anthropologists; Anthropologists and Archeologists; Archeologists; Economists; Historians; Industrial-Organizational Psychologists; Political Scientists; School Psychologists.

Skills—Science: Using scientific rules and methods to solve problems. **Writing:** Communicating effectively in writing as appropriate for the needs of the audience. **Management of Financial Resources:** Determining how money will be spent to get the work done and accounting for these expenditures. **Reading Comprehension:** Understanding written sentences and paragraphs in work-related documents. **Critical Thinking:** Using logic and reasoning to identify the strengths and weaknesses of alternative solutions, conclusions or approaches to problems. **Management of Personnel Resources:** Motivating, developing, and directing people as they work, identifying the best people for the job.

Education and Training Programs: Criminology; Demography and Population Studies; Sociology; Urban Studies/Affairs. **Related Knowledge/Courses: Sociology and Anthropology:** Group behavior and dynamics, societal trends and influences, human migrations, ethnicity, cultures, and their history and origins. **Philosophy and Theology:** Different philosophical systems and religions. This includes their basic principles, values, ethics, ways of thinking, customs, practices, and their impact on human culture. **History and Archeology:** Historical events and their causes, indicators, and effects on civilizations and cultures. **Psychology:** Human behavior and performance; individual differences in ability, personality, and interests; learning and motivation; psychological research methods; and the assessment and treatment of behavioral and affective disorders. **English Language:** The structure and content of the English language, including the meaning and spelling of words, rules of composition, and grammar. **Mathematics:** Arithmetic, algebra, geometry, calculus, statistics, and their applications.

Work Environment: Indoors; sitting.

Soil and Plant Scientists

- Education/Training Required: Bachelor's degree
- Annual Earnings: $56,080
- Growth: 8.4%
- Annual Job Openings: 850
- Self-Employed: 19.5%
- Part-Time: 12.3%

Level of Stress Tolerance Needed: 60.0 (out of 100)

Most Stressful Aspects: Duration of Typical Work Week (81.5); Importance of Being Exact or Accurate (79.3); Level of Competition (57.5).

Least Stressful Aspects: Deal With Physically Aggressive People (5.8); Pace Determined by Speed of Equipment (8.3); Deal With Unpleasant or Angry People (30.8); Consequence of Error (36.3).

Conduct research in breeding, physiology, production, yield, and management of crops and agricultural plants, their growth in soils, and control of pests or study the chemical, physical, biological, and mineralogical composition of soils as they relate to plant or crop growth. May classify and map soils and investigate effects of alternative practices on soil and crop productivity. Communicate research and project results to other professionals and the public or teach related courses, seminars, or workshops. Provide information and recommendations to farmers and other landowners regarding ways in which they can best use land, promote plant growth, and avoid or correct problems such as erosion. Investigate responses of soils to specific management practices to determine the use capabilities of soils and the effects of alternative practices on soil productivity. Develop methods of conserving and managing soil that can be applied by farmers and forestry companies. Conduct experiments to develop new or improved varieties of field crops, focusing on characteristics such as yield, quality, disease resistance, nutritional value, or adaptation to specific soils or climates. Investigate soil problems and poor water quality to determine sources and effects. Study soil characteristics to classify soils on the basis of factors such as geographic location, landscape position, and soil properties. Develop improved measurement techniques, soil conservation methods, soil sampling devices, and related technology. Conduct experiments investigating how soil forms and changes and how it interacts with land-based ecosystems and living organisms.

Identify degraded or contaminated soils and develop plans to improve their chemical, biological, and physical characteristics. Survey undisturbed and disturbed lands for classification, inventory, mapping, environmental impact assessments, environmental protection planning, and conservation and reclamation planning. Plan and supervise land conservation and reclamation programs for industrial development projects and waste management programs for composting and farming. Perform chemical analyses of the microorganism content of soils to determine microbial reactions and chemical mineralogical relationships to plant growth. Provide advice regarding the development of regulatory standards for land reclamation and soil conservation. Develop new or improved methods and products for controlling and eliminating weeds, crop diseases, and insect pests.

Personality Type: Investigative. Investigative occupations frequently involve working with ideas and require an extensive amount of thinking. These occupations can involve searching for facts and figuring out problems mentally.

GOE—Interest Area: 01. Agriculture and Natural Resources. **Work Group:** 01.02. Resource Science/Engineering for Plants, Animals, and the Environment. **Other Jobs in This Work Group:** Agricultural Engineers; Animal Scientists; Conservation Scientists; Environmental Engineers; Foresters; Mining and Geological Engineers, Including Mining Safety Engineers; Petroleum Engineers; Range Managers; Soil and Water Conservationists; Zoologists and Wildlife Biologists.

Skills—Science: Using scientific rules and methods to solve problems. **Management of Financial Resources:** Determining how money will be spent to get the work done, and accounting for these expenditures. **Management of Personnel Resources:** Motivating, developing, and directing people as they work, identifying

S

the best people for the job. **Writing:** Communicating effectively in writing as appropriate for the needs of the audience. **Management of Material Resources:** Obtaining and seeing to the appropriate use of equipment, facilities, and materials needed to do certain work. **Reading Comprehension:** Understanding written sentences and paragraphs in work-related documents.

Education and Training Programs: Soil Chemistry and Physics; Soil Microbiology; Soil Science and Agronomy, General. **Related Knowledge/Courses: Biology:** Plant and animal organisms, their tissues, cells, functions, interdependencies, and interactions with each other and the environment. **Food Production:** Techniques and equipment for planting, growing, and harvesting food products (both plant and animal) for consumption, including storage/handling techniques. **Geography:** Principles and methods for describing the features of land, sea, and air masses, including their physical characteristics, locations, interrelationships, and distribution of plant, animal, and human life. **Chemistry:** The chemical composition, structure, and properties of substances and of the chemical processes and transformations that they undergo. This includes uses of chemicals, their danger signs, production techniques, and disposal methods. **Physics:** Physical principles, laws, their interrelationships, and applications to understanding fluid, material, and atmospheric dynamics, and mechanical, electrical, atomic, and subatomic structures and processes. **Communications and Media:** Media production, communication, and dissemination techniques and methods. This includes alternative ways to inform and entertain via written, oral, and visual media.

Work Environment: More often indoors than outdoors; sitting.

Soil and Water Conservationists

- Education/Training Required: Bachelor's degree
- Annual Earnings: $54,970
- Growth: 5.3%
- Annual Job Openings: 1,161
- Self-Employed: 3.9%
- Part-Time: 12.3%

Our sources did not provide separate job openings data for this occupation. The job openings listed here are shared with Park Naturalists and with Range Managers.

Level of Stress Tolerance Needed: 75.3 (out of 100)

Most Stressful Aspects: Impact of Decisions on Co-workers or Company Results (75.8); Duration of Typical Work Week (66.5); Consequence of Error (54.3); Frequency of Conflict Situations (52.2).

Least Stressful Aspects: Pace Determined by Speed of Equipment (12.0); Deal With Unpleasant or Angry People (47.5); Time Pressure (55.0); Importance of Being Exact or Accurate (58.7).

Plan and develop coordinated practices for soil erosion control, soil and water conservation, and sound land use. Develop and maintain working relationships with local government staff and board members. Advise land users such as farmers and ranchers on conservation plans, problems, and alternative solutions and provide technical and planning assistance. Apply principles of specialized fields of science, such as agronomy, soil science, forestry, or agriculture, to achieve conservation objectives. Plan soil management and conservation practices, such as crop rotation, reforestation, permanent vegetation, contour plowing, or terracing, to maintain soil and conserve water. Visit areas affected by erosion problems to seek sources and solutions. Monitor projects during and after construction to ensure that projects conform to design specifications. Compute design specifications for implementation of conservation practices, using survey and field information technical guides, engineering manuals, and calculator. Revisit land users to view implemented land use practices and plans. Coordinate and implement technical, financial, and administrative assistance programs for local government units to ensure efficient program implementation and timely responses to requests for assistance. Analyze results of investigations to determine measures needed to maintain or restore proper soil management. Participate on work teams to plan, develop, and implement water and land management programs and policies. Develop, conduct, and/or participate in surveys, studies, and investigations of various land uses, gathering information for use in developing corrective action plans. Survey property to mark locations and measurements, using surveying instruments. Compute cost estimates of different conservation practices based on needs of land users, maintenance requirements, and life expectancy of practices. Provide information, knowledge, expertise, and training to government agencies at all levels to solve water and soil management problems and to assure coordination of resource protection activities. Respond to complaints and questions on wetland jurisdiction, providing information and clarification. Initiate, schedule, and conduct annual audits and compliance checks of program implementation by local government.

Personality Type: Investigative. Investigative occupations frequently involve working with ideas and require an extensive amount of think-

ing. These occupations can involve searching for facts and figuring out problems mentally.

GOE—Interest Area: 01. Agriculture and Natural Resources. **Work Group:** 01.02. Resource Science/Engineering for Plants, Animals, and the Environment. **Other Jobs in This Work Group:** Agricultural Engineers; Animal Scientists; Conservation Scientists; Environmental Engineers; Foresters; Mining and Geological Engineers, Including Mining Safety Engineers; Petroleum Engineers; Range Managers; Soil and Plant Scientists; Zoologists and Wildlife Biologists.

Skills—Persuasion: Persuading others to change their minds or behavior. **Operations Analysis:** Analyzing needs and product requirements to create a design. **Science:** Using scientific rules and methods to solve problems. **Quality Control Analysis:** Conducting tests and inspections of products, services, or processes to evaluate quality or performance. **Judgment and Decision Making:** Considering the relative costs and benefits of potential actions to choose the most appropriate one. **Installation:** Installing equipment, machines, wiring, or programs to meet specifications.

Education and Training Programs: Forest Management/Forest Resources Management; Forest Sciences and Biology; Forestry, General; Forestry, Other; Land Use Planning and Management/Development; Natural Resources and Conservation, Other; Natural Resources Management and Policy; Natural Resources Management and Policy, Other; Natural Resources/Conservation, General; Water, Wetlands, and Marine Resources Management; Wildlife and Wildlands Science and Management. **Related Knowledge/Courses: Geography:** Principles and methods for describing the features of land, sea, and air masses, including their physical characteristics, locations, interrelationships, and distribution of plant, animal, and human life. **Biology:** Plant and animal organisms, their tissues, cells, functions, interdependencies, and interactions with each other and the environment. **Engineering and Technology:** The practical application of engineering science and technology. This includes applying principles, techniques, procedures, and equipment to the design and production of various goods and services. **Design:** Design techniques, tools, and principles involved in production of precision technical plans, blueprints, drawings, and models. **History and Archeology:** Historical events and their causes, indicators, and effects on civilizations and cultures. **Physics:** Physical principles, laws, their interrelationships, and applications to understanding fluid, material, and atmospheric dynamics, and mechanical, electrical, atomic, and subatomic structures and processes.

Work Environment: More often outdoors than indoors; contaminants; sitting.

Solderers and Brazers

- Education/Training Required: Postsecondary vocational training
- Annual Earnings: $31,400
- Growth: 5.1%
- Annual Job Openings: 61,125
- Self-Employed: 6.3%
- Part-Time: 7.2%

Our sources did not provide separate job openings data for this occupation. The job openings listed here are shared with Welders, Cutters, and Welder Fitters.

Level of Stress Tolerance Needed: 53.5 (out of 100)

Most Stressful Aspects: Time Pressure (84.7); Importance of Being Exact or Accurate (83.0);

Duration of Typical Work Week (69.0); Level of Competition (57.7).

Least Stressful Aspects: Deal With Physically Aggressive People (3.5); Consequence of Error (39.0); Frequency of Conflict Situations (40.0); Deal With Unpleasant or Angry People (48.3).

Braze or solder together components to assemble fabricated metal parts, using soldering iron, torch, or welding machine and flux. Melt and apply solder along adjoining edges of workpieces to solder joints, using soldering irons, gas torches, or electric-ultrasonic equipment. Heat soldering irons or workpieces to specified temperatures for soldering, using gas flames or electric current. Examine seams for defects and rework defective joints or broken parts. Melt and separate brazed or soldered joints to remove and straighten damaged or misaligned components, using hand torches, irons, or furnaces. Melt and apply solder to fill holes, indentations, and seams of fabricated metal products, using soldering equipment. Clean workpieces to remove dirt and excess acid, using chemical solutions, files, wire brushes, or grinders. Guide torches and rods along joints of workpieces to heat them to brazing temperature, melt braze alloys, and bond workpieces together. Adjust electric current and timing cycles of resistance welding machines to heat metals to bonding temperature. Turn valves to start flow of gases and light flames and adjust valves to obtain desired colors and sizes of flames. Clean equipment parts, such as tips of soldering irons, using chemical solutions or cleaning compounds. Brush flux onto joints of workpieces or dip braze rods into flux to prevent oxidation of metal. Remove workpieces from fixtures, using tongs, and cool workpieces, using air or water. Align and clamp workpieces together, using rules, squares, or hand tools, or position items in fixtures, jigs, or vises. Sweat together workpieces coated with solder. Smooth soldered areas with alternate strokes of paddles and torches, leaving soldered sections slightly higher than surrounding areas for later filing. Remove workpieces from molten solder and hold parts together until color indicates that solder has set. Select torch tips, flux, and brazing alloys from data charts or work orders. Turn dials to set intensity and duration of ultrasonic impulses according to work order specifications. Dip workpieces into molten solder or place solder strips between seams and heat seams with irons to bond items together. Clean joints of workpieces with wire brushes or by dipping them into cleaning solutions.

Personality Type: Realistic. Realistic occupations frequently involve work activities that include practical, hands-on problems and solutions. They often deal with plants; animals; and real-world materials such as wood, tools, and machinery. Many of the occupations require working outside and do not involve a lot of paperwork or working closely with others.

GOE—Interest Area: 13. Manufacturing. **Work Group:** 13.04. Welding, Brazing, and Soldering. **Other Jobs in This Work Group:** Structural Metal Fabricators and Fitters; Welders, Cutters, and Welder Fitters; Welders, Cutters, Solderers, and Brazers; Welding, Soldering, and Brazing Machine Setters, Operators, and Tenders.

Skills—Quality Control Analysis: Conducting tests and inspections of products, services, or processes to evaluate quality or performance. **Installation:** Installing equipment, machines, wiring, or programs to meet specifications. **Operation and Control:** Controlling operations of equipment or systems. **Troubleshooting:** Determining causes of operating errors and deciding what to do about them. **Equipment Selection:** Determining the kind of tools and equipment needed to do a job. **Repairing:** Repairing machines or systems, using the needed tools.

Education and Training Program: Welding Technology/Welder Training. **Related Knowledge/Courses: Production and Processing:** Raw materials, production processes, quality control, costs, and other techniques for maximizing the effective manufacture and distribution of goods. **Mechanical Devices:** Machines and tools, including their designs, uses, repair, and maintenance. **Engineering and Technology:** The practical application of engineering science and technology. This includes applying principles, techniques, procedures, and equipment to the design and production of various goods and services.

Work Environment: Indoors; noisy; contaminants; minor burns, cuts, bites, or stings; using hands on objects, tools, or controls; repetitive motions.

Stock Clerks, Sales Floor

- ◉ Education/Training Required: Short-term on-the-job training
- ◉ Annual Earnings: $20,440
- ◉ Growth: –7.7%
- ◉ Annual Job Openings: 439,327
- ◉ Self-Employed: 0.2%
- ◉ Part-Time: 44.2%

Our sources did not provide separate job openings data for this occupation. The job openings listed here are shared with Marking Clerks; Order Fillers, Wholesale and Retail Sales; and Stock Clerks—Stockroom, Warehouse, or Storage Yard.

Level of Stress Tolerance Needed: 72.5 (out of 100)

Most Stressful Aspects: Time Pressure (74.8); Duration of Typical Work Week (60.5); Pace Determined by Speed of Equipment (37.0).

Least Stressful Aspects: Deal With Physically Aggressive People (11.5); Consequence of Error (31.3); Level of Competition (37.7); Deal With Unpleasant or Angry People (43.8).

Receive, store, and issue sales floor merchandise. Stock shelves, racks, cases, bins, and tables with merchandise and arrange merchandise displays to attract customers. May periodically take physical count of stock or check and mark merchandise. Answer customers' questions about merchandise and advise customers on merchandise selection. Itemize and total customer merchandise selection at checkout counter, using cash register, and accept cash or charge card for purchases. Take inventory or examine merchandise to identify items to be reordered or replenished. Pack customer purchases in bags or cartons. Stock shelves, racks, cases, bins, and tables with new or transferred merchandise. Receive, open, unpack, and issue sales floor merchandise. Clean display cases, shelves, and aisles. Compare merchandise invoices to items actually received to ensure that shipments are correct. Requisition merchandise from supplier based on available space, merchandise on hand, customer demand, or advertised specials. Transport packages to customers' vehicles. Stamp, attach, or change price tags on merchandise, referring to price list. Design and set up advertising signs and displays of merchandise on shelves, counters, or tables to attract customers and promote sales.

Personality Type: Realistic. Realistic occupations frequently involve work activities that include practical, hands-on problems and solutions. They often deal with plants; animals; and real-world materials such as wood, tools, and machinery. Many of the occupations require working outside and do not involve a lot of paperwork or working closely with others.

GOE—Interest Area: 04. Business and Administration. **Work Group:** 04.07. Records and Materials Processing. **Other Jobs in This Work Group:** Correspondence Clerks; File Clerks; Human Resources Assistants, Except Payroll and Timekeeping; Marking Clerks; Meter Readers, Utilities; Office Clerks, General; Order Fillers, Wholesale and Retail Sales; Postal Service Clerks; Postal Service Mail Sorters, Processors, and Processing Machine Operators; Procurement Clerks; Production, Planning, and Expediting Clerks; Shipping, Receiving, and Traffic Clerks; Stock Clerks and Order Fillers; Stock Clerks—Stockroom, Warehouse, or Storage Yard; Weighers, Measurers, Checkers, and Samplers, Recordkeeping.

Skills—None met the criteria.

Education and Training Program: Retailing and Retail Operations. **Related Knowledge/ Courses: Food Production:** Techniques and equipment for planting, growing, and harvesting food products (both plant and animal) for consumption, including storage/handling techniques. **Administration and Management:** Business and management principles involved in strategic planning, resource allocation, human resources modeling, leadership technique, production methods, and coordination of people and resources.

Work Environment: Indoors; standing; walking and running; kneeling, crouching, stooping, or crawling; using hands on objects, tools, or controls; bending or twisting the body.

Stock Clerks—Stockroom, Warehouse, or Storage Yard

- ⊚ Education/Training Required: Short-term on-the-job training
- ⊚ Annual Earnings: $20,440
- ⊚ Growth: –7.7%
- ⊚ Annual Job Openings: 439,327
- ⊚ Self-Employed: 0.2%
- ⊚ Part-Time: 44.2%

Our sources did not provide separate job openings data for this occupation. The job openings listed here are shared with Marking Clerks; Order Fillers, Wholesale and Retail Sales; and Stock Clerks, Sales Floor.

Level of Stress Tolerance Needed: 55.3 (out of 100)

Most Stressful Aspects: Importance of Being Exact or Accurate (79.0); Impact of Decisions on Co-workers or Company Results (71.7); Time Pressure (71.0); Deal With Unpleasant or Angry People (61.5).

Least Stressful Aspects: Deal With Physically Aggressive People (3.5); Consequence of Error (31.0); Duration of Typical Work Week (40.5); Level of Competition (42.3).

Receive, store, and issue materials, equipment, and other items from stockroom, warehouse, or storage yard. Keep records and compile stock reports. Receive and count stock items and record data manually or by using computer. Pack and unpack items to be stocked on shelves in stockrooms, warehouses, or storage yards. Verify inventory computations by comparing them to physical counts of stock and investigate discrepancies or adjust errors. Store items in an orderly and accessible manner in warehouses, tool rooms, supply rooms, or other areas. Mark stock items, using identification tags, stamps, electric marking tools, or other labeling equipment. Clean and maintain supplies, tools, equipment, and storage areas to ensure compliance with safety regulations. Determine proper storage methods, identification, and stock location based on turnover, environmental factors, and physical capabilities of facilities. Keep records on the use and damage of stock or stock-handling equipment. Examine and inspect stock items for wear or defects, reporting any damage to supervisors. Provide assistance or direction to other stockroom, warehouse, or storage yard workers. Dispose of damaged or defective items or return them to vendors. Drive trucks to pick up incoming stock or to deliver parts to designated locations. Prepare and maintain records and reports of inventories, price lists, shortages, shipments, expenditures, and goods used or issued. Sell materials, equipment, and other items from stock in retail settings. Issue or distribute materials, products, parts, and supplies to customers or co-workers based on information from incoming requisitions. Advise retail customers or internal users on the appropriateness of parts, supplies, or materials requested. Purchase new or additional stock or prepare documents that provide for such purchases. Compile, review, and maintain data from contracts, purchase orders, requisitions, and other documents to assess supply needs. Confer with engineering and purchasing personnel and vendors regarding stock procurement and availability. Determine sequence and release of backorders according to stock availability. Prepare products, supplies, equipment, or other items for use by adjusting, repairing, or assembling them as necessary.

Personality Type: Conventional. Conventional occupations frequently involve following set procedures and routines. These occupations can include working with data and details more than with ideas. Usually, there is a clear line of authority to follow.

GOE—Interest Area: 04. Business and Administration. **Work Group:** 04.07. Records and Materials Processing. **Other Jobs in This Work Group:** Correspondence Clerks; File Clerks; Human Resources Assistants, Except Payroll and Timekeeping; Marking Clerks; Meter Readers, Utilities; Office Clerks, General; Order Fillers, Wholesale and Retail Sales; Postal Service Clerks; Postal Service Mail Sorters, Processors, and Processing Machine Operators; Procurement Clerks; Production, Planning, and Expediting Clerks; Shipping, Receiving, and Traffic Clerks; Stock Clerks and Order Fillers; Stock Clerks, Sales Floor; Weighers, Measurers, Checkers, and Samplers, Recordkeeping.

Skills—None met the criteria.

Education and Training Program: Retailing and Retail Operations. **Related Knowledge/ Courses: Food Production:** Techniques and equipment for planting, growing, and harvesting food products (both plant and animal) for consumption, including storage/handling techniques. **Production and Processing:** Raw materials, production processes, quality control, costs, and other techniques for maximizing the effective manufacture and distribution of goods.

Work Environment: Indoors; standing; walking and running; using hands on objects, tools, or controls; bending or twisting the body; repetitive motions.

Stone Cutters and Carvers, Manufacturing

- Education/Training Required: Moderate-term on-the-job training
- Annual Earnings: $25,010
- Growth: 1.3%
- Annual Job Openings: 5,788
- Self-Employed: 24.2%
- Part-Time: 19.0%

Our sources did not provide separate job openings data for this occupation. The job openings listed here are shared with Glass Blowers, Molders, Benders, and Finishers; Molding and Casting Workers; and Potters, Manufacturing.

Level of Stress Tolerance Needed: 64.0 (out of 100)

Most Stressful Aspects: Importance of Being Exact or Accurate (87.0); Time Pressure (75.0); Consequence of Error (66.0); Duration of Typical Work Week (58.0).

Least Stressful Aspects: Deal With Physically Aggressive People (14.0); Frequency of Conflict Situations (32.0); Deal With Unpleasant or Angry People (37.0); Impact of Decisions on Co-workers or Company Results (64.0).

Cut or carve stone according to diagrams and patterns. Carve designs and figures in full and bas relief on stone, employing knowledge of stone-carving techniques and sense of artistry to produce carvings consistent with designers' plans. Verify depths and dimensions of cuts or carvings to ensure adherence to specifications, blueprints, or models, using measuring instruments. Lay out designs or dimensions from sketches or blueprints on stone surfaces, by freehand, or by transferring them from tracing paper, using scribes or chalk and measuring instruments. Study artistic objects or graphic materials such as models, sketches, or blueprints to plan carving or cutting techniques. Drill holes and cut or carve moldings and grooves in stone according to diagrams and patterns. Shape, trim, or touch up roughed-out designs with appropriate tools to finish carvings. Select chisels, pneumatic or surfacing tools, or sandblasting nozzles and determine sequence of use. Move fingers over surfaces of carvings to ensure smoothness of finish. Carve rough designs freehand or by chipping along marks on stone, using mallets and chisels or pneumatic tools. Guide nozzles over stone, following stencil outlines, or chip along marks to create designs or to work surfaces down to specified finishes. Cut, shape, and finish rough blocks of building or monumental stone according to diagrams or patterns. Smooth surfaces of carvings, using rubbing stones. Remove or add stencils during blasting to create differing cut depths; intricate designs; or rough, pitted finishes. Copy drawings on rough clay or plaster models. Load sandblasting equipment with abrasives, attach nozzles to hoses, and turn valves to admit compressed air and activate jets. Dress stone surfaces, using bushhammers.

Personality Type: Realistic. Realistic occupations frequently involve work activities that include practical, hands-on problems and solutions. They often deal with plants; animals; and real-world materials such as wood, tools, and machinery. Many of the occupations require working outside and do not involve a lot of paperwork or working closely with others.

GOE—Interest Area: 02. Architecture and Construction. **Work Group:** 02.04. Construction Crafts. **Other Jobs in This Work Group:** Boilermakers; Brickmasons and Blockmasons; Carpet Installers; Cement Masons and Concrete Finishers; Commercial Divers; Construction Carpenters; Crane and Tower Operators; Drywall and Ceiling Tile Installers; Electricians; Fence Erectors; Floor Layers, Except Carpet, Wood, and Hard Tiles; Floor Sanders and Finishers; Glaziers; Hazardous Materials Removal Workers; Insulation Workers, Floor, Ceiling, and Wall; Insulation Workers, Mechanical; Manufactured Building and Mobile Home Installers; Operating Engineers and Other Construction Equipment Operators; Painters, Construction and Maintenance; Paperhangers; Paving, Surfacing, and Tamping Equipment Operators; Pile-Driver Operators; Pipe Fitters and Steamfitters; Pipelayers; Plasterers and Stucco Masons; Plumbers; Plumbers, Pipefitters, and Steamfitters; Rail-Track Laying and Maintenance Equipment Operators; Refractory Materials Repairers, Except Brickmasons; Reinforcing Iron and Rebar Workers; Riggers; Roofers; Rough Carpenters; Security and Fire Alarm Systems Installers; Segmental Pavers; Sheet Metal Workers; Stonemasons; Structural Iron and Steel Workers; Tapers; Terrazzo Workers and Finishers; Tile and Marble Setters.

Skills—Mathematics: Using mathematics to solve problems. **Equipment Selection:** Determining the kind of tools and equipment needed to do a job. **Repairing:** Repairing machines or systems, using the needed tools. **Equipment Maintenance:** Performing routine maintenance on equipment and determining when and what kind of maintenance is needed. **Quality Control Analysis:** Conducting tests and inspections of products, services, or processes to evaluate quality or performance.

Education and Training Program: Mason Training/Masonry. **Related Knowledge/Courses: Design:** Design techniques, tools, and principles involved in production of precision technical plans, blueprints, drawings, and models. **Fine Arts:** The theory and techniques required to compose, produce, and perform works of music, dance, visual arts, drama, and sculpture. **Building and Construction:** Materials, methods, and the tools involved in the construction or repair of houses, buildings, or other structures such as highways and roads. **Production and Processing:** Raw materials, production processes, quality control, costs, and other techniques for maximizing the effective manufacture and distribution of goods. **Mechanical Devices:** Machines and tools, including their designs, uses, repair, and maintenance. **Mathematics:** Arithmetic, algebra, geometry, calculus, statistics, and their applications.

Work Environment: Noisy; contaminants; hazardous equipment; standing; using hands on objects, tools, or controls; repetitive motions.

Stonemasons

- Education/Training Required: Long-term on-the-job training
- Annual Earnings: $35,960
- Growth: 10.0%
- Annual Job Openings: 2,657
- Self-Employed: 22.8%
- Part-Time: 16.8%

Level of Stress Tolerance Needed: 60.3 (out of 100)

Most Stressful Aspects: Level of Competition (62.5); Deal With Physically Aggressive People (18.3).

Least Stressful Aspects: Consequence of Error (18.3); Pace Determined by Speed of Equipment (22.2); Frequency of Conflict Situations (32.0); Deal With Unpleasant or Angry People (33.7).

Build stone structures, such as piers, walls, and abutments. Lay walks; curbstones; or special types of masonry for vats, tanks, and floors. Lay out wall patterns or foundations, using straight edge, rule, or staked lines. Shape, trim, face, and cut marble or stone preparatory to setting, using power saws, cutting equipment, and hand tools. Set vertical and horizontal alignment of structures, using plumb bob, gauge line, and level. Mix mortar or grout and pour or spread mortar or grout on marble slabs, stone, or foundation. Remove wedges; fill joints between stones; finish joints between stones, using a trowel; and smooth the mortar to an attractive finish, using a tuckpointer. Clean excess mortar or grout from surface of marble, stone, or monument, using sponge, brush, water, or acid. Set stone or marble in place according to layout or pattern. Lay brick to build shells of chimneys and smokestacks or to line or reline industrial furnaces, kilns, boilers, and similar installations. Replace broken or missing masonry units in walls or floors. Smooth, polish, and bevel surfaces, using hand tools and power tools. Drill holes in marble or ornamental stone and anchor brackets in holes. Repair cracked or chipped areas of stone or marble, using blowtorch and mastic, and remove rough or defective spots from concrete, using power grinder or chisel and hammer. Remove sections of monument from truck bed and guide stone onto foundation, using skids, hoist, or truck crane. Construct and install prefabricated masonry units. Dig trench for foundation of monument, using pick and shovel. Position mold along guidelines of wall, press mold in place, and remove mold and paper from wall. Line interiors of molds with treated paper and fill molds with composition-stone mixture.

Personality Type: Realistic. Realistic occupations frequently involve work activities that include practical, hands-on problems and solutions. They often deal with plants; animals; and real-world materials such as wood, tools, and machinery. Many of the occupations require working outside and do not involve a lot of paperwork or working closely with others.

GOE—Interest Area: 02. Architecture and Construction. **Work Group:** 02.04. Construction Crafts. **Other Jobs in This Work Group:** Boilermakers; Brickmasons and Blockmasons; Carpet Installers; Cement Masons and Concrete Finishers; Commercial Divers; Construction Carpenters; Crane and Tower Operators; Drywall and Ceiling Tile Installers; Electricians; Fence Erectors; Floor Layers, Except Carpet, Wood, and Hard Tiles; Floor Sanders and Finishers; Glaziers; Hazardous Materials Removal Workers; Insulation Workers, Floor, Ceiling, and Wall; Insulation Workers, Mechanical; Manufactured Building and Mobile Home Installers; Operating Engineers and Other Construction Equipment Operators; Painters, Construction and Maintenance; Paperhangers; Paving, Surfacing, and Tamping Equipment Operators; Pile-Driver Operators; Pipe Fitters and Steamfitters; Pipelayers; Plasterers and Stucco Masons; Plumbers; Plumbers, Pipefitters, and Steamfitters; Rail-Track Laying and Maintenance Equipment Operators; Refractory Materials Repairers, Except Brickmasons; Reinforcing Iron and Rebar Workers; Riggers; Roofers; Rough Carpenters; Security and Fire Alarm Systems Installers; Segmental Pavers; Sheet Metal Workers; Stone Cutters and Carvers, Manufacturing; Structural Iron and Steel Workers; Tapers; Terrazzo Workers and Finishers; Tile and Marble Setters.

Skills—Installation: Installing equipment, machines, wiring, or programs to meet specifications. **Management of Personnel Resources:** Motivating, developing, and directing people as they work, identifying the best people for the job. **Repairing:** Repairing machines or systems, using the needed tools. **Equipment Maintenance:** Performing routine maintenance on equipment and determining when and what kind of maintenance is needed. **Equipment Selection:** Determining the kind of tools and equipment needed to do a job. **Mathematics:** Using mathematics to solve problems.

Education and Training Program: Mason Training/Masonry. **Related Knowledge/ Courses: Building and Construction:** Materials, methods, and the tools involved in the construction or repair of houses, buildings, or other structures such as highways and roads. **Mechanical Devices:** Machines and tools, including their designs, uses, repair, and maintenance. **Design:** Design techniques, tools, and principles involved in production of precision technical plans, blueprints, drawings, and models. **Mathematics:** Arithmetic, algebra, geometry, calculus, statistics, and their applications. **Public Safety and Security:** Relevant equipment, policies, procedures, and strategies to promote effective local, state, or national security operations for the protection of people, data, property, and institutions. **Education and Training:** Principles and methods for curriculum and training design, teaching and instruction for individuals and groups, and the measurement of training effects.

Work Environment: Outdoors; standing; walking and running; kneeling, crouching, stooping, or crawling; using hands on objects, tools, or controls; bending or twisting the body.

Structural Iron and Steel Workers

- Education/Training Required: Long-term on-the-job training
- Annual Earnings: $40,480
- Growth: 6.0%
- Annual Job Openings: 6,969
- Self-Employed: 5.3%
- Part-Time: 14.3%

Level of Stress Tolerance Needed: 67.3 (out of 100)

Most Stressful Aspects: Importance of Being Exact or Accurate (83.0); Time Pressure (77.8); Consequence of Error (75.3); Duration of Typical Work Week (68.5).

Least Stressful Aspects: Deal With Unpleasant or Angry People (51.0); Impact of Decisions on Co-workers or Company Results (63.7).

Raise, place, and unite iron or steel girders, columns, and other structural members to form completed structures or structural frameworks. May erect metal storage tanks and assemble prefabricated metal buildings. Read specifications and blueprints to determine the locations, quantities, and sizes of materials required. Verify vertical and horizontal alignment of structural-steel members, using plumb bobs, laser equipment, transits, and/or levels. Connect columns, beams, and girders with bolts, following blueprints and instructions from supervisors. Hoist steel beams, girders, and columns into place, using cranes, or signal hoisting equipment operators to lift and position structural-steel members. Bolt aligned structural-steel members in position for permanent riveting, bolting, or welding into place. Ride on girders or other structural-steel members to position them or use rope to guide them into position. Fabricate metal parts such as steel frames, columns, beams, and girders according to blueprints or instructions from supervisors. Pull, push, or pry structural-steel members into approximate positions for bolting into place. Cut, bend, and weld steel pieces, using metal shears, torches, and welding equipment. Fasten structural-steel members to hoist cables, using chains, cables, or rope. Assemble hoisting equipment and rigging, such as cables, pulleys, and hooks, to move heavy equipment and materials. Force structural-steel members into final positions, using turnbuckles, crowbars, jacks, and hand tools. Erect metal and precast concrete components for structures such as buildings, bridges, dams, towers, storage tanks, fences, and highway guardrails. Unload and position prefabricated steel units for hoisting as needed. Drive drift pins through rivet holes to align rivet holes in structural-steel members with corresponding holes in previously placed members. Dismantle structures and equipment. Insert sealing strips, wiring, insulating material, ladders, flanges, gauges, and valves, depending on types of structures being assembled. Catch hot rivets in buckets and insert rivets in holes, using tongs. Place blocks under reinforcing bars used to reinforce floors. Hold rivets while riveters use air-hammers to form heads on rivets.

Personality Type: Realistic. Realistic occupations frequently involve work activities that include practical, hands-on problems and solutions. They often deal with plants; animals; and real-world materials such as wood, tools, and machinery. Many of the occupations require working outside and do not involve a lot of paperwork or working closely with others.

GOE—Interest Area: 02. Architecture and Construction. **Work Group:** 02.04. Construction Crafts. **Other Jobs in This Work Group:** Boilermakers; Brickmasons and Blockmasons; Carpet Installers; Cement Masons and Concrete Finishers; Commercial Divers; Construction Carpenters; Crane and Tower Operators; Drywall and Ceiling Tile Installers; Electricians; Fence Erectors; Floor Layers, Except Carpet, Wood, and Hard Tiles; Floor Sanders and Finishers; Glaziers; Hazardous Materials Removal Workers; Insulation Workers, Floor, Ceiling, and Wall; Insulation Workers, Mechanical; Manufactured Building and Mobile Home Installers; Operating Engineers and Other Construction Equipment Operators; Painters, Construction and Maintenance; Paperhangers; Paving, Surfacing, and Tamping Equipment Operators; Pile-Driver Operators;

Pipe Fitters and Steamfitters; Pipelayers; Plasterers and Stucco Masons; Plumbers; Plumbers, Pipefitters, and Steamfitters; Rail-Track Laying and Maintenance Equipment Operators; Refractory Materials Repairers, Except Brickmasons; Reinforcing Iron and Rebar Workers; Riggers; Roofers; Rough Carpenters; Security and Fire Alarm Systems Installers; Segmental Pavers; Sheet Metal Workers; Stone Cutters and Carvers, Manufacturing; Stonemasons; Tapers; Terrazzo Workers and Finishers; Tile and Marble Setters.

Skills—Equipment Maintenance: Performing routine maintenance on equipment and determining when and what kind of maintenance is needed. **Installation:** Installing equipment, machines, wiring, or programs to meet specifications. **Troubleshooting:** Determining causes of operating errors and deciding what to do about them. **Coordination:** Adjusting actions in relation to others' actions. **Operation Monitoring:** Watching gauges, dials, or other indicators to make sure a machine is working properly. **Equipment Selection:** Determining the kind of tools and equipment needed to do a job.

Education and Training Programs: Construction Trades, Other; Metal Building Assembly/Assembler Training. **Related Knowledge/Courses: Building and Construction:** Materials, methods, and the tools involved in the construction or repair of houses, buildings, or other structures such as highways and roads. **Engineering and Technology:** The practical application of engineering science and technology. This includes applying principles, techniques, procedures, and equipment to the design and production of various goods and services. **Mechanical Devices:** Machines and tools, including their designs, uses, repair, and maintenance. **Production and Processing:** Raw materials, production processes, quality control, costs, and other techniques for maximizing the effective manufacture and distribution of goods.

Design: Design techniques, tools, and principles involved in production of precision technical plans, blueprints, drawings, and models. **Physics:** Physical principles, laws, their interrelationships, and applications to understanding fluid, material, and atmospheric dynamics, and mechanical, electrical, atomic, and subatomic structures and processes.

Work Environment: Outdoors; noisy; very hot or cold; high places; hazardous equipment; using hands on objects, tools, or controls.

Structural Metal Fabricators and Fitters

- Education/Training Required: Moderate-term on-the-job training
- Annual Earnings: $30,290
- Growth: –0.2%
- Annual Job Openings: 20,746
- Self-Employed: 2.0%
- Part-Time: 16.2%

Level of Stress Tolerance Needed: 44.5 (out of 100)

Most Stressful Aspects: Duration of Typical Work Week (73.5); Consequence of Error (53.3); Level of Competition (46.7); Pace Determined by Speed of Equipment (29.5).

Least Stressful Aspects: Deal With Physically Aggressive People (8.0); Deal With Unpleasant or Angry People (33.0); Frequency of Conflict Situations (37.7); Impact of Decisions on Co-workers or Company Results (47.0).

Fabricate, lay out, position, align, and fit parts of structural metal products. Position, align, fit, and weld parts to form complete units or sub-units, following blueprints and layout specifications and using jigs, welding torches, and hand tools. Verify conformance of workpieces to specifications, using squares, rulers, and measuring tapes. Tack-weld fitted parts together. Lay out and examine metal stock or workpieces to be processed to ensure that specifications are met. Align and fit parts according to specifications, using jacks, turnbuckles, wedges, drift pins, pry bars, and hammers. Locate and mark workpiece bending and cutting lines, allowing for stock thickness, machine and welding shrinkage, and other component specifications. Position or tighten braces, jacks, clamps, ropes, or bolt straps or bolt parts in position for welding or riveting. Study engineering drawings and blueprints to determine materials requirements and task sequences. Move parts into position manually or by using hoists or cranes. Set up and operate fabricating machines such as brakes, rolls, shears, flame cutters, grinders, and drill presses to bend, cut, form, punch, drill, or otherwise form and assemble metal components. Hammer, chip, and grind workpieces to cut, bend, and straighten metal. Smooth workpiece edges and fix taps, tubes, and valves. Design and construct templates and fixtures, using hand tools. Straighten warped or bent parts, using sledges, hand torches, straightening presses, or bulldozers. Mark reference points onto floors or face blocks and transpose them to workpieces, using measuring devices, squares, chalk, and soapstone. Set up face blocks, jigs, and fixtures. Remove high spots and cut bevels, using hand files, portable grinders, and cutting torches. Direct welders to build up low spots or short pieces with weld. Lift or move materials and finished products, using large cranes. Heat-treat parts, using acetylene torches. Preheat workpieces to make them malleable, using hand torches or furnaces. Install boilers, containers, and other structures. Erect ladders and scaffolding to fit together large assemblies.

Personality Type: Realistic. Realistic occupations frequently involve work activities that include practical, hands-on problems and solutions. They often deal with plants; animals; and real-world materials such as wood, tools, and machinery. Many of the occupations require working outside and do not involve a lot of paperwork or working closely with others.

GOE—Interest Area: 13. Manufacturing. **Work Group:** 13.04. Welding, Brazing, and Soldering. **Other Jobs in This Work Group:** Solderers and Brazers; Welders, Cutters, and Welder Fitters; Welders, Cutters, Solderers, and Brazers; Welding, Soldering, and Brazing Machine Setters, Operators, and Tenders.

Skills—Quality Control Analysis: Conducting tests and inspections of products, services, or processes to evaluate quality or performance. **Operation Monitoring:** Watching gauges, dials, or other indicators to make sure a machine is working properly. **Equipment Maintenance:** Performing routine maintenance on equipment and determining when and what kind of maintenance is needed. **Installation:** Installing equipment, machines, wiring, or programs to meet specifications. **Repairing:** Repairing machines or systems, using the needed tools. **Operation and Control:** Controlling operations of equipment or systems.

Education and Training Program: Machine Shop Technology/Assistant Training. **Related Knowledge/Courses: Design:** Design techniques, tools, and principles involved in production of precision technical plans, blueprints, drawings, and models. **Building and Construction:** Materials, methods, and the tools involved in the construction or repair of houses, buildings, or other structures such as highways and roads. **Mechanical Devices:** Machines and tools, including their designs, uses, repair, and maintenance. **Production and Processing:** Raw materials, production processes, quality control, costs, and other techniques for maximizing the effective manufacture and distribution of goods.

Work Environment: Noisy; contaminants; hazardous equipment; minor burns, cuts, bites, or stings; standing; using hands on objects, tools, or controls.

Survey Researchers

- Education/Training Required: Bachelor's degree
- Annual Earnings: $33,360
- Growth: 15.9%
- Annual Job Openings: 4,959
- Self-Employed: 6.8%
- Part-Time: 25.0%

Level of Stress Tolerance Needed: 57.2 (out of 100)

Most Stressful Aspects: Impact of Decisions on Co-workers or Company Results (79.3); Duration of Typical Work Week (62.5).

Least Stressful Aspects: Pace Determined by Speed of Equipment (2.0); Deal With Physically Aggressive People (3.7); Consequence of Error (16.0); Frequency of Conflict Situations (23.8).

Design or conduct surveys. May supervise interviewers who conduct the survey in person or over the telephone. May present survey results to client. Prepare and present summaries and analyses of survey data, including tables, graphs, and fact sheets that describe survey techniques and results. Consult with clients in order to identify survey needs and any specific requirements, such as special samples. Analyze data from surveys, old records, and/or case studies, using statistical software programs. Review, classify, and record survey data in preparation for computer analysis. Conduct research in order to gather information about survey topics. Conduct surveys and collect data, using methods such as interviews, questionnaires, focus groups, market analysis surveys, public opinion polls, literature reviews, and file reviews. Collaborate with other researchers in the planning, implementation, and evaluation of surveys. Direct and review the work of staff members, including survey support staff and interviewers who gather survey data. Monitor and evaluate survey progress and performance, using sample disposition reports and response rate calculations. Produce documentation of the questionnaire development process, data collection methods, sampling designs, and decisions related to sample statistical weighting. Determine and specify details of survey projects, including sources of information, procedures to be used, and the design of survey instruments and materials. Support, plan, and coordinate operations for single or multiple surveys. Direct updates and changes in survey implementation and methods. Hire and train recruiters and data collectors. Write training manuals to be used by survey interviewers.

Personality Type: No data available.

GOE—Interest Area: 06. Finance and Insurance. **Work Group:** 06.02. Finance/Insurance Investigation and Analysis. **Other Jobs in This Work Group:** Appraisers and Assessors of Real Estate; Appraisers, Real Estate; Assessors; Claims Adjusters, Examiners, and Investigators; Claims Examiners, Property and Casualty Insurance; Cost Estimators; Credit Analysts; Financial Analysts; Insurance Adjusters, Examiners, and Investigators; Insurance Appraisers, Auto Damage; Insurance Underwriters; Loan Counselors; Loan Officers; Market Research Analysts.

Skills—Management of Personnel Resources: Motivating, developing, and directing people as they work, identifying the best people for the job. **Management of Financial Resources:** Determining how money will be spent to get the work done, and accounting for these expenditures. **Time Management:** Managing one's own time and the time of others. **Writing:** Communicating effectively in writing as appropriate for the needs of the audience. **Persuasion:** Persuading others to change their minds or behavior. **Complex Problem Solving:** Identifying complex problems and reviewing related information to develop and evaluate options and implement solutions.

Education and Training Programs: Applied Economics; Business/Managerial Economics; Economics, General; Marketing Research. **Related Knowledge/Courses: Administration and Management:** Business and management principles involved in strategic planning, resource allocation, human resources modeling, leadership technique, production methods, and coordination of people and resources. **Sociology and Anthropology:** Group behavior and dynamics, societal trends and influences, human migrations, ethnicity, cultures, and their history and origins. **Mathematics:** Arithmetic, algebra, geometry, calculus, statistics, and their applications. **Economics and Accounting:** Economic and accounting principles and practices, the financial markets, banking, and the analysis and reporting of financial data. **Personnel and Human Resources:** Principles and procedures for personnel recruitment, selection, training, compensation and benefits, labor relations and negotiation, and personnel information systems. **Clerical Practices:** Administrative and clerical procedures and systems such as word processing, managing files and records, stenography and transcription, designing forms, and other office procedures and terminology.

Work Environment: Indoors; noisy; sitting.

Tank Car, Truck, and Ship Loaders

- Education/Training Required: Moderate-term on-the-job training
- Annual Earnings: $31,970
- Growth: 9.2%
- Annual Job Openings: 4,519
- Self-Employed: 0.0%
- Part-Time: 29.5%

Level of Stress Tolerance Needed: 68.3 (out of 100)

Most Stressful Aspects: Duration of Typical Work Week (88.0); Time Pressure (81.7); Importance of Being Exact or Accurate (79.3); Pace Determined by Speed of Equipment (75.8).

Least Stressful Aspects: Deal With Physically Aggressive People (10.2); Deal With Unpleasant or Angry People (45.5).

Load and unload chemicals and bulk solids such as coal, sand, and grain into or from tank cars, trucks, or ships, using material moving equipment. May perform a variety of other tasks relating to shipment of products. May gauge or sample shipping tanks and test them for leaks. Verify tank car, barge, or truck load numbers to ensure car placement accuracy based on written or verbal instructions. Observe positions of cars passing loading spouts and swing spouts into the correct positions at the appropriate times. Operate ship loading and unloading equipment, conveyors, hoists, and other specialized material handling equipment such as railroad tank car unloading equipment. Monitor product movement to and from storage tanks, coordinating activities with other workers to ensure constant product flow. Record operating data such as products and quantities pumped, gauge readings, and operating times manually or by using computers. Check conditions and weights of vessels to ensure cleanliness and compliance with loading procedures. Operate industrial trucks, tractors, loaders, and other equipment to transport materials to and from transportation vehicles and loading docks and to store and retrieve materials in warehouses. Connect ground cables to carry off static electricity when unloading tanker cars. Seal outlet valves on tank cars, barges, and trucks. Test samples for specific gravity, using hydrometers, or send samples to laboratories for testing. Remove and replace tank car dome caps or direct other workers in their removal and replacement. Lower gauge rods into tanks or read meters to verify contents, temperatures, and volumes of liquid loads. Clean interiors of tank cars or tank trucks, using mechanical spray nozzles. Operate conveyors and equipment to transfer grain or other materials from transportation vehicles. Test vessels for leaks, damage, and defects and repair or replace defective parts as necessary. Unload cars containing liquids by connecting hoses to outlet plugs and pumping compressed air into cars to force liquids into storage tanks. Copy and attach load specifications to loaded tanks. Start pumps and adjust valves or cables to regulate the flow of products to vessels, utilizing knowledge of loading procedures.

Personality Type: Realistic. Realistic occupations frequently involve work activities that include practical, hands-on problems and solutions. They often deal with plants; animals; and real-world materials such as wood, tools, and machinery. Many of the occupations require working outside and do not involve a lot of paperwork or working closely with others.

GOE—Interest Area: 13. Manufacturing. **Work Group:** 13.17. Loading, Moving, Hoisting, and Conveying. **Other Jobs in This Work Group:** Conveyor Operators and Tenders; Hoist and Winch Operators; Industrial Truck and Tractor Operators; Machine Feeders and Offbearers; Packers and Packagers, Hand; Pump Operators, Except Wellhead Pumpers; Refuse and Recyclable Material Collectors.

Skills—Operation Monitoring: Watching gauges, dials, or other indicators to make sure a machine is working properly. **Operation and Control:** Controlling operations of equipment or systems. **Troubleshooting:** Determining causes of operating errors and deciding what to do about them. **Repairing:** Repairing machines or systems, using the needed tools. **Equipment Maintenance:** Performing routine maintenance on equipment and determining when and what kind of maintenance is needed.

Education and Training Program: Ground Transportation, Other. **Related Knowledge/Courses: Production and Processing:** Raw materials, production processes, quality control, costs, and other techniques for maximizing the effective manufacture and distribution of goods. **Mechanical Devices:** Machines and tools, including their designs, uses, repair, and maintenance. **Transportation:** Principles and methods for moving people or goods by air, rail, sea, or road, including the relative costs and benefits. **Public Safety and Security:** Relevant equipment, policies, procedures, and strategies to promote effective local, state, or national security operations for the protection of people, data, property, and institutions. **Building and Construction:** Materials, methods, and the tools involved in the construction or repair of houses, buildings, or other structures such as highways and roads. **Chemistry:** The chemical composition, structure, and properties of substances and of the chemical processes and transformations that they undergo. This includes uses of chemicals, their danger signs, production techniques, and disposal methods.

Work Environment: Outdoors; noisy; very hot or cold; contaminants; high places; hazardous equipment.

Telecommunications Line Installers and Repairers

- Education/Training Required: Long-term on-the-job training
- Annual Earnings: $46,280
- Growth: 4.6%
- Annual Job Openings: 14,719
- Self-Employed: 3.3%
- Part-Time: 15.0%

Level of Stress Tolerance Needed: 64.0 (out of 100)

Most Stressful Aspects: Importance of Being Exact or Accurate (83.2); Impact of Decisions on Co-workers or Company Results (72.3); Time Pressure (70.2); Duration of Typical Work Week (69.5).

Least Stressful Aspects: Deal With Unpleasant or Angry People (46.7).

String and repair telephone and television cable, including fiber optics and other equipment for transmitting messages or television programming. Travel to customers' premises to install, maintain, and repair audio and visual electronic reception equipment and accessories. Inspect and test lines and cables, recording and analyzing test results, to assess transmission characteristics and locate faults and malfunctions. Splice cables, using hand tools, epoxy, or mechanical equipment. Measure signal strength at utility poles, using electronic test equipment. Set up service for customers, installing, connecting, testing, and adjusting equipment. Place insulation over conductors and seal splices with moisture-proof covering. Access specific areas to string lines and install terminal boxes, auxiliary equipment, and appliances, using bucket trucks or by climbing poles and ladders or entering tunnels, trenches, or crawl spaces. String cables between structures and lines from poles, towers, or trenches and pull lines to proper tension. Install equipment such as amplifiers and repeaters to maintain the strength of communications transmissions. Lay underground cable directly in trenches or string it through conduits running through trenches. Pull up cable by hand from large reels mounted on trucks; then pull lines through ducts by hand or with winches. Clean and maintain tools and test equipment. Explain cable service to subscribers after installation and collect any installation fees that are due. Compute impedance of wires from poles to houses to determine additional resistance needed for reducing signals to desired levels. Use a variety of construction equipment to complete installations, including digger derricks, trenchers, and cable plows. Dig trenches for underground wires and cables. Dig holes for power poles, using power augers or shovels; set poles in place with cranes; and hoist poles upright, using winches. Fill and tamp holes, using cement, earth, and tamping devices. Participate in the construction and removal of telecommunication towers and associated support structures.

Personality Type: Realistic. Realistic occupations frequently involve work activities that include practical, hands-on problems and solutions. They often deal with plants; animals; and real-world materials such as wood, tools, and machinery. Many of the occupations require working outside and do not involve a lot of paperwork or working closely with others.

GOE—Interest Area: 02. Architecture and Construction. **Work Group:** 02.05. Systems and Equipment Installation, Maintenance, and Repair. **Other Jobs in This Work Group:** Electrical and Electronics Repairers,

Powerhouse, Substation, and Relay; Electrical Power-Line Installers and Repairers; Elevator Installers and Repairers; Heating and Air Conditioning Mechanics and Installers; Maintenance and Repair Workers, General; Refrigeration Mechanics and Installers; Telecommunications Equipment Installers and Repairers, Except Line Installers.

Skills—Installation: Installing equipment, machines, wiring, or programs to meet specifications. **Troubleshooting:** Determining causes of operating errors and deciding what to do about them. **Programming:** Writing computer programs for various purposes. **Repairing:** Repairing machines or systems, using the needed tools. **Equipment Maintenance:** Performing routine maintenance on equipment and determining when and what kind of maintenance is needed. **Systems Analysis:** Determining how a system should work and how changes in conditions, operations, and the environment will affect outcomes.

Education and Training Program: Communications Systems Installation and Repair Technology. **Related Knowledge/Courses: Telecommunications:** Transmission, broadcasting, switching, control, and operation of telecommunications systems. **Engineering and Technology:** The practical application of engineering science and technology. This includes applying principles, techniques, procedures, and equipment to the design and production of various goods and services. **Customer and Personal Service:** Principles and processes for providing customer and personal services. This includes customer needs assessment, meeting quality standards for services, and evaluation of customer satisfaction. **Building and Construction:** Materials, methods, and the tools involved in the construction or repair of houses, buildings, or other structures such as highways and roads. **Design:** Design techniques, tools, and principles involved in production of precision technical plans, blueprints, drawings, and models. **Mechanical Devices:** Machines and tools, including their designs, uses, repair, and maintenance.

Work Environment: Outdoors; very hot or cold; contaminants; cramped work space, awkward positions; hazardous equipment; using hands on objects, tools, or controls.

Terrazzo Workers and Finishers

- Education/Training Required: Long-term on-the-job training
- Annual Earnings: $31,630
- Growth: 10.9%
- Annual Job Openings: 1,052
- Self-Employed: 2.3%
- Part-Time: 16.8%

Level of Stress Tolerance Needed: 63.0 (out of 100)

Most Stressful Aspects: Impact of Decisions on Co-workers or Company Results (79.8); Time Pressure (69.7); Duration of Typical Work Week (62.0); Frequency of Conflict Situations (55.8).

Least Stressful Aspects: Deal With Unpleasant or Angry People (48.0); Importance of Being Exact or Accurate (72.5).

Apply a mixture of cement, sand, pigment, or marble chips to floors, stairways, and cabinet fixtures to fashion durable and decorative surfaces. Blend marble chip mixtures and place into panels; then push a roller over the surface to embed the chips. Cut metal division strips and press them into the terrazzo base wherever there is to be a joint or change of color, to form desired designs or patterns, and to help prevent cracks. Measure designated amounts of ingredients for terrazzo or grout according to standard formulas and specifications, using graduated containers and scale, and load ingredients into portable mixer. Mold expansion joints and edges, using edging tools, jointers, and straightedges. Spread, level, and smooth concrete and terrazzo mixtures to form bases and finished surfaces, using rakes, shovels, hand or power trowels, hand or power screeds, and floats. Grind curved surfaces and areas inaccessible to surfacing machine, such as stairways and cabinet tops, with portable hand grinder. Grind surfaces with a power grinder and polish surfaces with polishing or surfacing machines. Position and secure moisture membrane and wire mesh prior to pouring base materials for terrazzo installation. Modify mixing, grouting, grinding, and cleaning procedures according to type of installation or material used. Wash polished terrazzo surface, using cleaner and water, and apply sealer and curing agent according to manufacturer's specifications, using brush or sprayer. Mix cement, sand, and water to produce concrete, grout, or slurry, using hoe, trowel, tamper, scraper, or concrete-mixing machine. Sprinkle colored marble or stone chips, powdered steel, or coloring powder over surface to produce prescribed finish. Wet surface to prepare for bonding, fill holes and cracks with grout or slurry, and smooth, using trowel. Cut out damaged areas, drill holes for reinforcing rods, and position reinforcing rods to repair concrete, using power saw and drill. Clean installation site, mixing and storage areas, tools, machines, and equipment and store materials and equipment. Fill slight depressions left by grinding with a matching grout material and then hand-trowel for a smooth, uniform surface. Chip, scrape, and grind high spots, ridges, and rough projections to finish concrete, using pneumatic chisel, hand chisel, or other hand tools.

Personality Type: Realistic. Realistic occupations frequently involve work activities that include practical, hands-on problems and solutions. They often deal with plants; animals; and real-world materials such as wood, tools, and machinery. Many of the occupations require working outside and do not involve a lot of paperwork or working closely with others.

GOE—Interest Area: 02. Architecture and Construction. **Work Group:** 02.04. Construction Crafts. **Other Jobs in This Work Group:** Boilermakers; Brickmasons and Blockmasons; Carpet Installers; Cement Masons and Concrete Finishers; Commercial Divers; Construction Carpenters; Crane and Tower Operators; Drywall and Ceiling Tile Installers; Electricians; Fence Erectors; Floor Layers, Except Carpet, Wood, and Hard Tiles; Floor Sanders and Finishers; Glaziers; Hazardous Materials Removal Workers; Insulation Workers, Floor, Ceiling, and Wall; Insulation Workers, Mechanical; Manufactured Building and Mobile Home Installers; Operating Engineers and Other Construction Equipment Operators; Painters, Construction and Maintenance; Paperhangers; Paving, Surfacing, and Tamping Equipment Operators; Pile-Driver Operators; Pipe Fitters and Steamfitters; Pipelayers; Plasterers and Stucco Masons; Plumbers; Plumbers, Pipefitters, and Steamfitters; Rail-Track Laying and Maintenance Equipment Operators; Refractory Materials Repairers, Except Brickmasons; Reinforcing Iron and Rebar Workers; Riggers; Roofers; Rough Carpenters; Security and Fire Alarm Systems Installers; Segmental Pavers; Sheet Metal Workers; Stone Cutters and Carvers, Manufacturing; Stonemasons; Structural Iron and Steel Workers; Tapers; Tile and Marble Setters.

Skills—Installation: Installing equipment, machines, wiring, or programs to meet specifications. **Repairing:** Repairing machines or systems, using the needed tools. **Equipment**

Maintenance: Performing routine maintenance on equipment and determining when and what kind of maintenance is needed. **Equipment Selection:** Determining the kind of tools and equipment needed to do a job. **Coordination:** Adjusting actions in relation to others' actions. **Systems Analysis:** Determining how a system should work and how changes in conditions, operations, and the environment will affect outcomes.

Education and Training Program: Building/Construction Finishing, Management, and Inspection, Other. **Related Knowledge/Courses: Building and Construction:** Materials, methods, and the tools involved in the construction or repair of houses, buildings, or other structures such as highways and roads. **Production and Processing:** Raw materials, production processes, quality control, costs, and other techniques for maximizing the effective manufacture and distribution of goods. **Mechanical Devices:** Machines and tools, including their designs, uses, repair, and maintenance. **Administration and Management:** Business and management principles involved in strategic planning, resource allocation, human resources modeling, leadership technique, production methods, and coordination of people and resources. **Sales and Marketing:** Principles and methods for showing, promoting, and selling products or services. This includes marketing strategy and tactics, product demonstration, sales techniques, and sales control systems. **Design:** Design techniques, tools, and principles involved in production of precision technical plans, blueprints, drawings, and models.

Work Environment: Noisy; contaminants; standing; walking and running; using hands on objects, tools, or controls; repetitive motions.

Tile and Marble Setters

- Education/Training Required: Long-term on-the-job training
- Annual Earnings: $36,590
- Growth: 15.4%
- Annual Job Openings: 9,066
- Self-Employed: 33.8%
- Part-Time: 16.8%

Level of Stress Tolerance Needed: 61.5 (out of 100)

Most Stressful Aspects: Impact of Decisions on Co-workers or Company Results (83.7); Importance of Being Exact or Accurate (82.7); Time Pressure (77.5); Level of Competition (51.2).

Least Stressful Aspects: Deal With Physically Aggressive People (4.5); Pace Determined by Speed of Equipment (7.7); Deal With Unpleasant or Angry People (31.5); Consequence of Error (36.3).

Apply hard tile, marble, and wood tile to walls, floors, ceilings, and roof decks. Align and straighten tile, using levels, squares, and straight-edges. Determine and implement the best layout to achieve a desired pattern. Cut and shape tile to fit around obstacles and into odd spaces and corners, using hand- and power-cutting tools. Finish and dress the joints and wipe excess grout from between tiles, using damp sponge. Apply mortar to tile back, position the tile, and press or tap with trowel handle to affix tile to base. Mix, apply, and spread plaster, concrete, mortar, cement, mastic, glue, or other adhesives to form a bed for the tiles, using brush, trowel, and screed. Prepare cost and labor estimates based on calculations of time and materials needed for project. Measure and mark surfaces to be tiled, following blueprints. Level concrete and allow to dry. Build underbeds and install anchor bolts, wires, and brackets. Prepare surfaces for tiling by attaching lath or waterproof paper or by applying a cement mortar coat onto a metal screen. Study blueprints and examine surface to be covered to determine amount of material needed. Cut, surface, polish, and install marble and granite or install pre-cast terrazzo, granite, or marble units. Install and anchor fixtures in designated positions, using hand tools. Cut tile backing to required size, using shears. Remove any old tile, grout, and adhesive, using chisels and scrapers, and clean the surface carefully. Lay and set mosaic tiles to create decorative wall, mural, and floor designs. Assist customers in selection of tile and grout. Remove and replace cracked or damaged tile. Measure and cut metal lath to size for walls and ceilings, using tin snips. Select and order tile and other items to be installed, such as bathroom accessories, walls, panels, and cabinets, according to specifications. Mix and apply mortar or cement to edges and ends of drain tiles to seal halves and joints. Spread mastic or other adhesive base on roof deck to form base for promenade tile, using serrated spreader. Apply a sealer to make grout stain- and water-resistant. Brush glue onto manila paper on which design has been drawn and position tiles, finished side down, onto paper.

Personality Type: Realistic. Realistic occupations frequently involve work activities that include practical, hands-on problems and solutions. They often deal with plants; animals; and real-world materials such as wood, tools, and machinery. Many of the occupations require working outside and do not involve a lot of paperwork or working closely with others.

GOE—Interest Area: 02. Architecture and Construction. **Work Group:** 02.04. Construction Crafts. **Other Jobs in This Work Group:** Boilermakers; Brickmasons and Blockmasons; Carpet Installers; Cement Masons and Concrete Finishers; Commercial Divers; Construction Carpenters; Crane and Tower Operators; Drywall and Ceiling Tile Installers; Electricians; Fence Erectors; Floor Layers, Except Carpet, Wood, and Hard Tiles; Floor Sanders and Finishers; Glaziers; Hazardous Materials Removal Workers; Insulation Workers, Floor, Ceiling, and Wall; Insulation Workers, Mechanical; Manufactured Building and Mobile Home Installers; Operating Engineers and Other Construction Equipment Operators; Painters, Construction and Maintenance; Paperhangers; Paving, Surfacing, and Tamping Equipment Operators; Pile-Driver Operators; Pipe Fitters and Steamfitters; Pipelayers; Plasterers and Stucco Masons; Plumbers; Plumbers, Pipefitters, and Steamfitters; Rail-Track Laying and Maintenance Equipment Operators; Refractory Materials Repairers, Except Brickmasons; Reinforcing Iron and Rebar Workers; Riggers; Roofers; Rough Carpenters; Security and Fire Alarm Systems Installers; Segmental Pavers; Sheet Metal Workers; Stone Cutters and Carvers, Manufacturing; Stonemasons; Structural Iron and Steel Workers; Tapers; Terrazzo Workers and Finishers.

Skills—Installation: Installing equipment, machines, wiring, or programs to meet specifications. **Management of Financial Resources:** Determining how money will be spent to get the work done, and accounting for these expenditures. **Mathematics:** Using mathematics to solve problems. **Management of Material Resources:** Obtaining and seeing to the appropriate use of equipment, facilities, and materials needed to do certain work. **Equipment Selection:** Determining the kind of tools and equipment needed to do a job. **Technology Design:** Generating or adapting equipment and technology to serve user needs.

Education and Training Program: Mason Training/Masonry. **Related Knowledge/ Courses: Building and Construction:** Materials, methods, and the tools involved in the construction or repair of houses, buildings, or other structures such as highways and roads. **Design:** Design techniques, tools, and principles involved in production of precision technical plans, blueprints, drawings, and models. **Production and Processing:** Raw materials, production processes, quality control, costs, and other techniques for maximizing the effective manufacture and distribution of goods. **Economics and Accounting:** Economic and accounting principles and practices, the financial markets, banking, and the analysis and reporting of financial data. **Administration and Management:** Business and management principles involved in strategic planning, resource allocation, human resources modeling, leadership technique, production methods, and coordination of people and resources. **Transportation:** Principles and methods for moving people or goods by air, rail, sea, or road, including the relative costs and benefits.

Work Environment: Noisy; contaminants; cramped work space, awkward positions; standing; using hands on objects, tools, or controls; bending or twisting the body.

Tour Guides and Escorts

- Education/Training Required: Moderate-term on-the-job training
- Annual Earnings: $20,420
- Growth: 21.2%
- Annual Job Openings: 15,027
- Self-Employed: 20.1%
- Part-Time: 31.4%

Level of Stress Tolerance Needed: 70.7 (out of 100)

Most Stressful Aspects: None greater than average.

Least Stressful Aspects: Pace Determined by Speed of Equipment (0.7); Deal With Physically Aggressive People (2.0); Duration of Typical Work Week (7.0); Level of Competition (10.2).

Escort individuals or groups on sightseeing tours or through places of interest such as industrial establishments, public buildings, and art galleries. Conduct educational activities for schoolchildren. Escort individuals or groups on cruises; on sightseeing tours; or through places of interest such as industrial establishments, public buildings, and art galleries. Describe tour points of interest to group members and respond to questions. Monitor visitors' activities to ensure compliance with establishment or tour regulations and safety practices. Greet and register visitors and issue any required identification badges or safety devices. Distribute brochures, show audiovisual presentations, and explain establishment processes and operations at tour sites. Provide directions and other pertinent information to visitors. Provide for physical safety of groups, performing such activities as providing first aid and directing emergency evacuations. Research environmental conditions and clients' skill and ability levels to plan appropriate expeditions, instruction, and commentary. Provide information about wildlife varieties and habitats, as well as any relevant regulations, such as those pertaining to hunting and fishing. Collect fees and tickets from group members. Teach skills, such as proper climbing methods, and demonstrate and advise on the use of equipment. Select travel routes and sites to be visited based on knowledge of specific areas. Solicit tour patronage and sell souvenirs. Speak foreign languages to communicate with foreign visitors.

Assemble and check the required supplies and equipment prior to departure. Perform clerical duties such as filing, typing, operating switchboards, and routing mail and messages. Drive motor vehicles to transport visitors to establishments and tour site locations.

Personality Type: Social. Social occupations frequently involve working with, communicating with, and teaching people. These occupations often involve helping or providing service to others.

GOE—Interest Area: 09. Hospitality, Tourism, and Recreation. **Work Group:** 09.03. Hospitality and Travel Services. **Other Jobs in This Work Group:** Baggage Porters and Bellhops; Concierges; Flight Attendants; Hotel, Motel, and Resort Desk Clerks; Janitors and Cleaners, Except Maids and Housekeeping Cleaners; Maids and Housekeeping Cleaners; Reservation and Transportation Ticket Agents and Travel Clerks; Transportation Attendants, Except Flight Attendants and Baggage Porters; Travel Agents; Travel Guides.

Skills—Speaking: Talking to others to convey information effectively. **Reading Comprehension:** Understanding written sentences and paragraphs in work-related documents.

Education and Training Program: Tourism and Travel Services Management. **Related Knowledge/Courses: History and Archeology:** Historical events and their causes, indicators, and effects on civilizations and cultures. **Fine Arts:** The theory and techniques required to compose, produce, and perform works of music, dance, visual arts, drama, and sculpture. **Philosophy and Theology:** Different philosophical systems and religions. This includes their basic principles, values, ethics, ways of thinking, customs, practices, and their impact on human culture. **Sociology and Anthropology:** Group behavior and dynamics, societal trends and influences, human migrations, ethnicity, cultures, and their history and origins. **Communications and Media:** Media production, communication, and dissemination techniques and methods. This includes alternative ways to inform and entertain via written, oral, and visual media. **Customer and Personal Service:** Principles and processes for providing customer and personal services This includes customer needs assessment, meeting quality standards for services, and evaluation of customer satisfaction.

Work Environment: Standing.

Travel Agents

- Education/Training Required: Postsecondary vocational training
- Annual Earnings: $29,210
- Growth: 1.0%
- Annual Job Openings: 13,128
- Self-Employed: 13.4%
- Part-Time: 51.3%

Level of Stress Tolerance Needed: 68.0 (out of 100)

Most Stressful Aspects: Importance of Being Exact or Accurate (83.0); Level of Competition (71.5); Impact of Decisions on Co-workers or Company Results (70.0); Duration of Typical Work Week (63.5).

Least Stressful Aspects: Deal With Physically Aggressive People (8.3); Pace Determined by Speed of Equipment (14.5); Frequency of Conflict Situations (48.8); Deal With Unpleasant or Angry People (51.0).

Plan and sell transportation and accommodations for travel agency customers. Converse with customers to determine destination,

modes of transportation, travel dates, costs, and accommodations required. Collect payment for transportation and accommodations from customer. Compute cost of travel and accommodations, using calculator, computer, carrier tariff books, and hotel rate books, or quote package tour's costs. Book transportation and hotel reservations, using computer terminal or telephone. Plan, describe, arrange, and sell itinerary tour packages and promotional travel incentives offered by various travel carriers. Provide customers with brochures and publications containing travel information, such as local customs, points of interest, or foreign country regulations. Print or request transportation carrier tickets, using computer printer system or system link to travel carrier.

Personality Type: Enterprising. Enterprising occupations frequently involve starting up and carrying out projects. These occupations can involve leading people and making many decisions. They sometimes require risk taking and often deal with business.

GOE—Interest Area: 09. Hospitality, Tourism, and Recreation. **Work Group:** 09.03. Hospitality and Travel Services. **Other Jobs in This Work Group:** Baggage Porters and Bellhops; Concierges; Flight Attendants; Hotel, Motel, and Resort Desk Clerks; Janitors and Cleaners, Except Maids and Housekeeping Cleaners; Maids and Housekeeping Cleaners; Reservation and Transportation Ticket Agents and Travel Clerks; Tour Guides and Escorts; Transportation Attendants, Except Flight Attendants and Baggage Porters; Travel Guides.

Skills—Service Orientation: Actively looking for ways to help people. **Persuasion:** Persuading others to change their minds or behavior. **Active Listening:** Giving full attention to what other people are saying, taking time to understand the points being made, asking questions as appro-priate, and not interrupting at inappropriate times. **Speaking:** Talking to others to convey information effectively. **Management of Personnel Resources:** Motivating, developing, and directing people as they work, identifying the best people for the job. **Negotiation:** Bringing others together and trying to reconcile differences.

Education and Training Programs: Selling Skills and Sales Operations; Tourism and Travel Services Marketing Operations. **Related Knowledge/Courses: Geography:** Principles and methods for describing the features of land, sea, and air masses, including their physical characteristics, locations, interrelationships, and distribution of plant, animal, and human life. **Sales and Marketing:** Principles and methods for showing, promoting, and selling products or services. This includes marketing strategy and tactics, product demonstration, sales techniques, and sales control systems. **Clerical Practices:** Administrative and clerical procedures and systems such as word processing, managing files and records, stenography and transcription, designing forms, and other office procedures and terminology. **Transportation:** Principles and methods for moving people or goods by air, rail, sea, or road, including the relative costs and benefits. **Economics and Accounting:** Economic and accounting principles and practices, the financial markets, banking, and the analysis and reporting of financial data. **Customer and Personal Service:** Principles and processes for providing customer and personal services. This includes customer needs assessment, meeting quality standards for services, and evaluation of customer satisfaction.

Work Environment: Indoors; sitting.

Tree Trimmers and Pruners

- ◎ Education/Training Required: Short-term on-the-job training
- ◎ Annual Earnings: $28,250
- ◎ Growth: 11.1%
- ◎ Annual Job Openings: 9,621
- ◎ Self-Employed: 28.9%
- ◎ Part-Time: 32.8%

Level of Stress Tolerance Needed: 61.0 (out of 100)

Most Stressful Aspects: Importance of Being Exact or Accurate (81.7); Time Pressure (81.5); Impact of Decisions on Co-workers or Company Results (78.8); Duration of Typical Work Week (73.0).

Least Stressful Aspects: Frequency of Conflict Situations (47.5); Deal With Unpleasant or Angry People (47.8).

Cut away dead or excess branches from trees or shrubs to maintain right-of-way for roads, sidewalks, or utilities or to improve appearance, health, and value of tree. Prune or treat trees or shrubs, using handsaws, pruning hooks, shears, and clippers. May use truck-mounted lifts and power pruners. May fill cavities in trees to promote healing and prevent deterioration. Supervise others engaged in tree-trimming work and train lower-level employees. Transplant and remove trees and shrubs and prepare trees for moving. Climb trees, using climbing hooks and belts, or climb ladders to gain access to work areas. Operate boom trucks, loaders, stump chippers, brush chippers, tractors, power saws, trucks, sprayers, and other equipment and tools. Operate shredding and chipping equipment and feed limbs and brush into the machines. Remove broken limbs from wires, using hooked extension poles. Prune, cut down, fertilize, and spray trees as directed by tree surgeons. Spray trees to treat diseased or unhealthy trees, including mixing chemicals and calibrating spray equipment. Clean, sharpen, and lubricate tools and equipment. Trim, top, and reshape trees to achieve attractive shapes or to remove low-hanging branches. Cable, brace, tie, bolt, stake, and guy trees and branches to provide support. Clear sites, streets, and grounds of woody and herbaceous materials, such as tree stumps and fallen trees and limbs. Collect debris and refuse from tree trimming and removal operations into piles, using shovels, rakes, or other tools. Load debris and refuse onto trucks and haul it away for disposal. Inspect trees to determine whether they have diseases or pest problems. Cut away dead and excess branches from trees or clear branches around power lines, using climbing equipment or buckets of extended truck booms and/or chain saws, hooks, handsaws, shears, and clippers. Apply tar or other protective substances to cut surfaces to seal surfaces and to protect them from fungi and insects. Split logs or wooden blocks into bolts, pickets, posts, or stakes, using hand tools such as ax wedges, sledgehammers, and mallets. Trim jagged stumps, using saws or pruning shears. Water, root-feed, and fertilize trees. Harvest tanbark by cutting rings and slits in bark and stripping bark from trees, using spuds or axes. Install lightning protection on trees. Plan and develop budgets for tree work and estimate the monetary value of trees. Provide information to the public regarding trees, such as advice on tree care.

Personality Type: Realistic. Realistic occupations frequently involve work activities that include practical, hands-on problems and solutions. They often deal with plants; animals; and real-world materials such as wood, tools, and machinery. Many of the occupations require working outside and do not involve a lot of paperwork or working closely with others.

GOE—Interest Area: 01. Agriculture and Natural Resources. **Work Group:** 01.05.

Nursery, Groundskeeping, and Pest Control. **Other Jobs in This Work Group:** Landscaping and Groundskeeping Workers; Nursery Workers; Pest Control Workers; Pesticide Handlers, Sprayers, and Applicators, Vegetation.

Skills—Equipment Maintenance: Performing routine maintenance on equipment and determining when and what kind of maintenance is needed. **Repairing:** Repairing machines or systems, using the needed tools. **Equipment Selection:** Determining the kind of tools and equipment needed to do a job. **Management of Personnel Resources:** Motivating, developing, and directing people as they work, identifying the best people for the job. **Operation Monitoring:** Watching gauges, dials, or other indicators to make sure a machine is working properly. **Operation and Control:** Controlling operations of equipment or systems.

Education and Training Program: Applied Horticulture/Horicultural Business Services, Other. **Related Knowledge/Courses: Biology:** Plant and animal organisms, their tissues, cells, functions, interdependencies, and interactions with each other and the environment. **Mechanical Devices:** Machines and tools, including their designs, uses, repair, and maintenance. **Transportation:** Principles and methods for moving people or goods by air, rail, sea, or road, including the relative costs and benefits. **Physics:** Physical principles, laws, their interrelationships, and applications to understanding fluid, material, and atmospheric dynamics, and mechanical, electrical, atomic, and subatomic structures and processes. **Public Safety and Security:** Relevant equipment, policies, procedures, and strategies to promote effective local, state, or national security operations for the protection of people, data, property, and institutions. **Sales and Marketing:** Principles and methods for showing, promoting, and selling products or services. This includes marketing strategy and tactics, product demonstration, sales techniques, and sales control systems.

Work Environment: Outdoors; noisy; contaminants; hazardous equipment; minor burns, cuts, bites, or stings; using hands on objects, tools, or controls.

Water and Liquid Waste Treatment Plant and System Operators

- Education/Training Required: Long-term on-the-job training
- Annual Earnings: $36,070
- Growth: 13.8%
- Annual Job Openings: 9,575
- Self-Employed: 1.3%
- Part-Time: 3.8%

Level of Stress Tolerance Needed: 55.0 (out of 100)

Most Stressful Aspects: Impact of Decisions on Co-workers or Company Results (84.0); Importance of Being Exact or Accurate (79.8); Duration of Typical Work Week (79.5); Consequence of Error (72.5).

Least Stressful Aspects: Deal With Physically Aggressive People (8.8); Level of Competition (34.8); Frequency of Conflict Situations (35.8); Deal With Unpleasant or Angry People (39.7).

Operate or control an entire process or system of machines, often through the use of control boards, to transfer or treat water or liquid waste. Add chemicals such as ammonia, chlorine, or lime to disinfect and deodorize water and other liquids. Operate and adjust controls on equipment to purify and clarify water, process or dispose of sewage, and generate power. Inspect equipment or monitor operating conditions, meters, and gauges to determine load requirements and detect malfunctions. Collect and test water and sewage samples, using test equipment and color analysis standards. Record operational data, personnel attendance, or meter and gauge readings on specified forms. Maintain, repair, and lubricate equipment, using hand tools and power tools. Clean and maintain tanks and filter beds, using hand tools and power tools. Direct and coordinate plant workers engaged in routine operations and maintenance activities.

Personality Type: Realistic. Realistic occupations frequently involve work activities that include practical, hands-on problems and solutions. They often deal with plants; animals; and real-world materials such as wood, tools, and machinery. Many of the occupations require working outside and do not involve a lot of paperwork or working closely with others.

GOE—Interest Area: 13. Manufacturing. **Work Group:** 13.16. Utility Operation and Energy Distribution. **Other Jobs in This Work Group:** Chemical Plant and System Operators; Gas Compressor and Gas Pumping Station Operators; Gas Plant Operators; Nuclear Power Reactor Operators; Petroleum Pump System Operators, Refinery Operators, and Gaugers; Power Distributors and Dispatchers; Power Plant Operators; Ship Engineers; Stationary Engineers and Boiler Operators.

Skills—Operation Monitoring: Watching gauges, dials, or other indicators to make sure a machine is working properly. **Operation and Control:** Controlling operations of equipment or systems. **Installation:** Installing equipment, machines, wiring, or programs to meet specifications. **Troubleshooting:** Determining causes of operating errors and deciding what to do about them. **Management of Material Resources:** Obtaining and seeing to the appropriate use of equipment, facilities, and materials needed to do certain work. **Operations Analysis:** Analyzing needs and product requirements to create a design.

Education and Training Program: Water Quality and Wastewater Treatment Management and Recycling Technology/Technician Training. **Related Knowledge/Courses: Biology:** Plant and animal organisms, their tissues, cells, functions, interdependencies, and interactions with each other and the environment. **Chemistry:** The chemical composition, structure, and properties of substances and of the chemical processes and transformations that they undergo. This includes uses of chemicals, their danger signs, production techniques, and disposal methods. **Physics:** Physical principles, laws, their interrelationships, and applications to understanding fluid, material, and atmospheric dynamics, and mechanical, electrical, atomic, and subatomic structures and processes. **Public Safety and Security:** Relevant equipment, policies, procedures, and strategies to promote effective local, state, or national security operations for the protection of people, data, property, and institutions. **Mechanical Devices:** Machines and tools, including their designs, uses, repair, and maintenance. **Law and Government:** Laws, legal codes, court procedures, precedents, government regulations, executive orders, agency rules, and the democratic political process.

Work Environment: More often outdoors than indoors; noisy; very hot or cold; contaminants; minor burns, cuts, bites, or stings.

Welders, Cutters, and Welder Fitters

- Education/Training Required: Postsecondary vocational training
- Annual Earnings: $31,400
- Growth: 5.1%
- Annual Job Openings: 61,125
- Self-Employed: 6.3%
- Part-Time: 7.2%

Our sources did not provide separate job openings data for this occupation. The job openings listed here are shared with Solderers and Brazers.

Level of Stress Tolerance Needed: 68.5 (out of 100)

Most Stressful Aspects: Importance of Being Exact or Accurate (76.8); Duration of Typical Work Week (67.0); Level of Competition (59.5); Pace Determined by Speed of Equipment (37.5).

Least Stressful Aspects: Deal With Physically Aggressive People (5.0); Deal With Unpleasant or Angry People (26.0); Frequency of Conflict Situations (26.7); Consequence of Error (42.5).

Use hand-welding or flame-cutting equipment to weld or join metal components or to fill holes, indentations, or seams of fabricated metal products. Operate safety equipment and use safe work habits. Weld components in flat, vertical, or overhead positions. Ignite torches or start power supplies and strike arcs by touching electrodes to metals being welded, completing electrical circuits. Clamp, hold, tack-weld, heat-bend, grind, or bolt component parts to obtain required configurations and positions for welding. Detect faulty operation of equipment or defective materials and notify supervisors. Operate manual or semi-automatic welding equipment to fuse metal segments, using processes such as gas tungsten arc, gas metal arc, flux-cored arc, plasma arc, shielded metal arc, resistance welding, and submerged arc welding. Monitor the fitting, burning, and welding processes to avoid overheating of parts or warping, shrinking, distortion, or expansion of material. Examine workpieces for defects and measure workpieces with straightedges or templates to ensure conformance with specifications. Recognize, set up, and operate hand and power tools common to the welding trade, such as shielded metal arc and gas metal arc welding equipment. Lay out, position, align, and secure parts and assemblies prior to assembly, using straightedges, combination squares, calipers, and rulers. Chip or grind off excess weld, slag, or spatter, using hand scrapers or power chippers, portable grinders, or arc-cutting equipment. Analyze engineering drawings, blueprints, specifications, sketches, work orders, and material safety data sheets to plan layout, assembly, and welding operations. Connect and turn regulator valves to activate and adjust gas flow and pressure so that desired flames are obtained. Weld separately or in combination, using aluminum, stainless steel, cast iron, and other alloys. Determine required equipment and welding methods, applying knowledge of metallurgy, geometry, and welding techniques. Mark or tag material with proper job number, piece marks, and other identifying marks as required. Prepare all material surfaces to be welded, ensuring that no loose or thick scale, slag, rust, moisture, grease, or other foreign matter is present.

Personality Type: Realistic. Realistic occupations frequently involve work activities that include practical, hands-on problems and solutions. They often deal with plants; animals; and real-world materials such as wood, tools, and machinery. Many of the occupations require working outside and do not involve a lot of paperwork or working closely with others.

W

GOE—**Interest Area:** 13. Manufacturing. **Work Group:** 13.04. Welding, Brazing, and Soldering. **Other Jobs in This Work Group:** Solderers and Brazers; Structural Metal Fabricators and Fitters; Welders, Cutters, Solderers, and Brazers; Welding, Soldering, and Brazing Machine Setters, Operators, and Tenders.

Skills—Repairing: Repairing machines or systems, using the needed tools. **Equipment Maintenance:** Performing routine maintenance on equipment and determining when and what kind of maintenance is needed. **Installation:** Installing equipment, machines, wiring, or programs to meet specifications. **Quality Control Analysis:** Conducting tests and inspections of products, services, or processes to evaluate quality or performance. **Operation and Control:** Controlling operations of equipment or systems.

Education and Training Program: Welding Technology/Welder Training. **Related Knowledge/Courses: Building and Construction:** Materials, methods, and the tools involved in the construction or repair of houses, buildings, or other structures such as highways and roads. **Mechanical Devices:** Machines and tools, including their designs, uses, repair, and maintenance. **Design:** Design techniques, tools, and principles involved in production of precision technical plans, blueprints, drawings, and models. **Engineering and Technology:** The practical application of engineering science and technology. This includes applying principles, techniques, procedures, and equipment to the design and production of various goods and services.

Work Environment: Noisy; contaminants; minor burns, cuts, bites, or stings; standing; using hands on objects, tools, or controls; repetitive motions.

Welding, Soldering, and Brazing Machine Setters, Operators, and Tenders

- Education/Training Required: Postsecondary vocational training
- Annual Earnings: $30,980
- Growth: 3.0%
- Annual Job Openings: 7,707
- Self-Employed: 6.7%
- Part-Time: 7.2%

Level of Stress Tolerance Needed: 66.0 (out of 100)

Most Stressful Aspects: Time Pressure (80.3); Importance of Being Exact or Accurate (78.3); Pace Determined by Speed of Equipment (75.8); Duration of Typical Work Week (72.5).

Least Stressful Aspects: Deal With Physically Aggressive People (8.5); Level of Competition (41.5); Frequency of Conflict Situations (49.5); Impact of Decisions on Co-workers or Company Results (60.0).

Set up, operate, or tend welding, soldering, or brazing machines or robots that weld, braze, solder, or heat-treat metal products, components, or assemblies. Turn and press knobs and buttons or enter operating instructions into computers to adjust and start welding machines. Set up, operate, and tend welding machines that join or bond components to fabricate metal products or assemblies. Load or feed workpieces into welding machines to join or bond components. Correct problems by adjusting controls or by stopping machines and opening holding devices. Give directions to other workers regarding machine setup and use. Inspect, measure, or test completed metal workpieces to ensure conformance to specifications, using measuring and testing devices. Record operational information on specified production reports. Start, monitor, and adjust robotic welding production lines. Read blueprints, work orders, and production schedules to determine product or job instructions and specifications. Assemble, align, and clamp workpieces into holding fixtures to bond, heat-treat, or solder fabricated metal components. Lay out, fit, or connect parts to be bonded, calculating production measurements as necessary. Conduct trial runs before welding, soldering or brazing; make necessary adjustments to equipment. Dress electrodes, using tip dressers, files, emery cloths, or dressing wheels. Remove workpieces and parts from machinery after work is complete, using hand tools. Observe meters, gauges, and machine operations to ensure that soldering or brazing processes meet specifications. Select, position, align, and bolt jigs, holding fixtures, guides, and stops onto machines, using measuring instruments and hand tools. Compute and record settings for new work, applying knowledge of metal properties, principles of welding, and shop mathematics. Select torch tips, alloys, flux, coil, tubing, and wire according to metal types and thicknesses, data charts, and records. Clean, lubricate, maintain, and adjust equipment to maintain efficient operation, using air hoses, cleaning fluids, and hand tools. Prepare metal surfaces and workpieces, using hand-operated equipment such as grinders, cutters, or drills. Set dials and timing controls to regulate electrical current, gas flow pressure, heating and cooling cycles, and shutoff.

Personality Type: Realistic. Realistic occupations frequently involve work activities that include practical, hands-on problems and solutions. They often deal with plants; animals; and real-world materials such as wood, tools, and machinery. Many of the occupations require working outside and do not involve a lot of paperwork or working closely with others.

GOE—Interest Area: 13. Manufacturing. **Work Group:** 13.04. Welding, Brazing, and Soldering. **Other Jobs in This Work Group:** Solderers and Brazers; Structural Metal Fabricators and Fitters; Welders, Cutters, and Welder Fitters; Welders, Cutters, Solderers, and Brazers.

Skills—Equipment Maintenance: Performing routine maintenance on equipment and determining when and what kind of maintenance is needed. **Operation Monitoring:** Watching gauges, dials, or other indicators to make sure a machine is working properly. **Operation and Control:** Controlling operations of equipment or systems. **Repairing:** Repairing machines or systems, using the needed tools. **Installation:** Installing equipment, machines, wiring, or programs to meet specifications. **Quality Control Analysis:** Conducting tests and inspections of products, services, or processes to evaluate quality or performance.

Education and Training Program: Welding Technology/Welder. **Related Knowledge/Courses: Production and Processing:** Raw materials, production processes, quality control, costs, and other techniques for maximizing the effective manufacture and distribution of goods. **Mechanical Devices:** Machines and tools, including their designs, uses, repair, and maintenance. **Engineering and Technology:** The practical application of engineering science and technology. This includes applying principles, techniques, procedures, and equipment to the design and production of various goods and services. **Design:** Design techniques, tools, and principles involved in production of precision technical plans, blueprints, drawings, and models. **Personnel and Human Resources:** Principles and procedures for personnel recruitment, selection, training, compensation and benefits, labor relations and negotiation, and personnel information systems. **Public Safety and Security:** Relevant equipment, policies, procedures, and strategies to promote effective local, state, or national security operations for the protection of people, data, property, and institutions.

Work Environment: Noisy; contaminants; standing; using hands on objects, tools, or controls; bending or twisting the body; repetitive motions.

Wellhead Pumpers

- Education/Training Required: Moderate-term on-the-job training
- Annual Earnings: $36,150
- Growth: –11.9%
- Annual Job Openings: 2,517
- Self-Employed: 2.2%
- Part-Time: 29.5%

Level of Stress Tolerance Needed: 57.2 (out of 100)

Most Stressful Aspects: Duration of Typical Work Week (78.5); Impact of Decisions on Co-workers or Company Results (78.0); Consequence of Error (73.3); Time Pressure (67.8).

Least Stressful Aspects: Deal With Physically Aggressive People (6.0); Frequency of Conflict Situations (30.8); Deal With Unpleasant or Angry People (32.7); Level of Competition (44.5).

Operate power pumps and auxiliary equipment to produce flow of oil or gas from wells in oil field. Monitor control panels during pumping operations to ensure that materials are being pumped at the correct pressure, density, rate, and concentration. Operate engines and pumps to shut off wells according to production schedules and to switch flow of oil into storage tanks.

Perform routine maintenance on vehicles and equipment. Repair gas and oil meters and gauges. Unload and assemble pipes and pumping equipment, using hand tools. Attach pumps and hoses to wellheads. Start compressor engines and divert oil from storage tanks into compressor units and auxiliary equipment to recover natural gas from oil. Open valves to return compressed gas to bottoms of specified wells to repressurize them and force oil to surface. Supervise oil pumpers and other workers engaged in producing oil from wells. Drive trucks to transport high-pressure pumping equipment and chemicals, fluids, or gases to be pumped into wells. Prepare trucks and equipment necessary for the type of pumping service required. Control pumping and blending equipment to acidize, cement, or fracture gas or oil wells and permeable rock formations. Mix acids, chemicals, or dry cement as required for a specific job.

Personality Type: Realistic. Realistic occupations frequently involve work activities that include practical, hands-on problems and solutions. They often deal with plants; animals; and real-world materials such as wood, tools, and machinery. Many of the occupations require working outside and do not involve a lot of paperwork or working closely with others.

GOE—Interest Area: 01. Agriculture and Natural Resources. **Work Group:** 01.08. Mining and Drilling. **Other Jobs in This Work Group:** Continuous Mining Machine Operators; Derrick Operators, Oil and Gas; Earth Drillers, Except Oil and Gas; Excavating and Loading Machine and Dragline Operators; Explosives Workers, Ordnance Handling Experts, and Blasters; Helpers—Extraction Workers; Loading Machine Operators, Underground Mining; Mine Cutting and Channeling Machine Operators; Rock Splitters, Quarry; Roof Bolters, Mining; Rotary Drill Operators, Oil and Gas;

Roustabouts, Oil and Gas; Service Unit Operators, Oil, Gas, and Mining; Shuttle Car Operators.

Skills—Repairing: Repairing machines or systems, using the needed tools. **Operation Monitoring:** Watching gauges, dials, or other indicators to make sure a machine is working properly. **Equipment Maintenance:** Performing routine maintenance on equipment and determining when and what kind of maintenance is needed. **Installation:** Installing equipment, machines, wiring, or programs to meet specifications. **Operation and Control:** Controlling operations of equipment or systems. **Systems Analysis:** Determining how a system should work and how changes in conditions, operations, and the environment will affect outcomes.

Education and Training Program: Mechanic and Repair Technologies/Technician Training, Other. **Related Knowledge/Courses: Mechanical Devices:** Machines and tools, including their designs, uses, repair, and maintenance. **Physics:** Physical principles, laws, their interrelationships, and applications to understanding fluid, material, and atmospheric dynamics, and mechanical, electrical, atomic, and subatomic structures and processes. **Production and Processing:** Raw materials, production processes, quality control, costs, and other techniques for maximizing the effective manufacture and distribution of goods. **Chemistry:** The chemical composition, structure, and properties of substances and of the chemical processes and transformations that they undergo. This includes uses of chemicals, their danger signs, production techniques, and disposal methods. **Engineering and Technology:** The practical application of engineering science and technology. This includes applying principles, techniques, procedures, and equipment to the design and production of various goods and services. **Design:** Design techniques, tools, and principles

involved in production of precision technical plans, blueprints, drawings, and models.

Work Environment: Outdoors; very hot or cold; contaminants; high places; hazardous conditions; hazardous equipment.

Woodworking Machine Setters, Operators, and Tenders, Except Sawing

- Education/Training Required: Moderate-term on-the-job training
- Annual Earnings: $23,940
- Growth: 6.4%
- Annual Job Openings: 11,860
- Self-Employed: 2.7%
- Part-Time: 26.3%

Level of Stress Tolerance Needed: 56.7 (out of 100)

Most Stressful Aspects: Importance of Being Exact or Accurate (83.7); Time Pressure (78.3); Pace Determined by Speed of Equipment (71.0); Duration of Typical Work Week (65.5).

Least Stressful Aspects: Deal With Physically Aggressive People (4.5); Frequency of Conflict Situations (26.0); Deal With Unpleasant or Angry People (28.3); Impact of Decisions on Co-workers or Company Results (59.0).

Set up, operate, or tend woodworking machines, such as drill presses, lathes, shapers, routers, sanders, planers, and wood-nailing machines. Start machines, adjust controls, and make trial cuts to ensure that machinery is operating properly. Determine product specifications and materials, work methods, and machine setup requirements according to blueprints, oral or written instructions, drawings, or work orders. Feed stock through feed mechanisms or conveyors into planing, shaping, boring, mortising, or sanding machines to produce desired components. Adjust machine tables or cutting devices and set controls on machines to produce specified cuts or operations. Set up, program, operate, or tend computerized or manual woodworking machines, such as drill presses, lathes, shapers, routers, sanders, planers, and wood-nailing machines. Monitor operation of machines and make adjustments to correct problems and ensure conformance to specifications. Select knives, saws, blades, cutter heads, cams, bits, or belts according to workpiece, machine functions, and product specifications. Examine finished workpieces for smoothness, shape, angle, depth of cut, and conformity to specifications and verify dimensions visually and by using hands, rules, calipers, templates, or gauges. Install and adjust blades, cutterheads, boring bits, or sanding belts, using hand tools and rules. Inspect and mark completed workpieces and stack them on pallets, in boxes, or on conveyors so that they can be moved to the next workstation. Push or hold workpieces against, under, or through cutting, boring, or shaping mechanisms. Change alignment and adjustment of sanding, cutting, or boring machine guides to prevent defects in finished products, using hand tools. Inspect pulleys, drive belts, guards, and fences on machines to ensure that machines will operate safely. Remove and replace worn parts, bits, belts, sandpaper, and shaping tools. Secure woodstock against a guide or in a holding device, place woodstock on a conveyor, or dump woodstock in a hopper to feed woodstock into machines. Clean and maintain products, machines, and work areas. Attach and adjust guides, stops, clamps, chucks, and feed mechanisms, using hand tools. Examine raw woodstock for defects and to ensure conformity to size and other specification standards.

Personality Type: Realistic. Realistic occupations frequently involve work activities that include practical, hands-on problems and solutions. They often deal with plants; animals; and real-world materials such as wood, tools, and machinery. Many of the occupations require working outside and do not involve a lot of paperwork or working closely with others.

GOE—Interest Area: 13. Manufacturing. **Work Group:** 13.03. Production Work, Assorted Materials Processing. **Other Jobs in This Work Group:** Bakers; Cementing and Gluing Machine Operators and Tenders; Chemical Equipment Operators and Tenders; Cleaning, Washing, and Metal Pickling Equipment Operators and Tenders; Coating, Painting, and Spraying Machine Setters, Operators, and Tenders; Cooling and Freezing Equipment Operators and Tenders; Cutting and Slicing Machine Setters, Operators, and Tenders; Extruding and Forming Machine Setters, Operators, and Tenders, Synthetic and Glass Fibers; Extruding, Forming, Pressing, and Compacting Machine Setters, Operators, and Tenders; Food and Tobacco Roasting, Baking, and Drying Machine Operators and Tenders; Food Batchmakers; Food Cooking Machine Operators and Tenders; Furnace, Kiln, Oven, Drier, and Kettle Operators and Tenders; Heat Treating Equipment Setters, Operators, and Tenders, Metal and Plastic; Helpers—Production Workers; Meat, Poultry, and Fish Cutters and Trimmers; Metal-Refining Furnace Operators and Tenders; Mixing and Blending Machine Setters, Operators, and Tenders; Packaging and Filling Machine Operators and Tenders; Plating and Coating Machine Setters, Operators, and Tenders, Metal and Plastic; Pourers and Casters, Metal; Sawing Machine Setters, Operators, and Tenders, Wood; Separating, Filtering, Clarifying, Precipitating, and Still Machine Setters, Operators, and Tenders; Sewing

Machine Operators; Shoe Machine Operators and Tenders; Slaughterers and Meat Packers; Team Assemblers; Textile Bleaching and Dyeing Machine Operators and Tenders; Tire Builders.

Skills—Equipment Maintenance: Performing routine maintenance on equipment and determining when and what kind of maintenance is needed. **Operation Monitoring:** Watching gauges, dials, or other indicators to make sure a machine is working properly. **Operation and Control:** Controlling operations of equipment or systems. **Repairing:** Repairing machines or systems, using the needed tools. **Troubleshooting:** Determining causes of operating errors and deciding what to do about them. **Quality Control Analysis:** Conducting tests and inspections of products, services, or processes to evaluate quality or performance.

Education and Training Programs: No related CIP programs; this job is learned through informal moderate-term on-the-job training. **Related Knowledge/Courses: Production and Processing:** Raw materials, production processes, quality control, costs, and other techniques for maximizing the effective manufacture and distribution of goods. **Mechanical Devices:** Machines and tools, including their designs, uses, repair, and maintenance. **Design:** Design techniques, tools, and principles involved in production of precision technical plans, blueprints, drawings, and models. **Mathematics:** Arithmetic, algebra, geometry, calculus, statistics, and their applications.

Work Environment: Noisy; contaminants; hazardous equipment; standing; using hands on objects, tools, or controls; repetitive motions.

Word Processors and Typists

- Education/Training Required: Moderate-term on-the-job training
- Annual Earnings: $29,430
- Growth: –11.6%
- Annual Job Openings: 32,279
- Self-Employed: 9.2%
- Part-Time: 44.9%

Level of Stress Tolerance Needed: 56.3 (out of 100)

Most Stressful Aspects: Importance of Being Exact or Accurate (84.5).

Least Stressful Aspects: Deal With Physically Aggressive People (5.3); Pace Determined by Speed of Equipment (19.2); Duration of Typical Work Week (30.5); Consequence of Error (32.7).

Use word processor/computer or typewriter to type letters, reports, forms, or other material from rough draft, corrected copy, or voice recording. May perform other clerical duties as assigned. Check completed work for spelling, grammar, punctuation, and format. Perform other clerical duties such as answering telephone, sorting and distributing mail, running errands, or sending faxes. Gather, register, and arrange the material to be typed, following instructions. File and store completed documents on computer hard drive or disk and maintain a computer filing system to store, retrieve, update, and delete documents. Type correspondence, reports, text, and other written material from rough drafts, corrected copies, voice recordings, dictation, or previous versions, using a computer, word processor, or typewriter. Print and make copies of work. Keep records of work performed. Compute and verify totals on report

W

forms, requisitions, or bills, using adding machine or calculator. Collate pages of reports and other documents prepared. Electronically sort and compile text and numerical data, retrieving, updating, and merging documents as required. Reformat documents, moving paragraphs or columns. Search for specific sets of stored, typed characters in order to make changes. Adjust settings for format, page layout, line spacing, and other style requirements. Address envelopes or prepare envelope labels, using typewriter or computer. Operate and resupply printers and computers, changing print wheels or fluid cartridges; adding paper; and loading blank tapes, cards, or disks into equipment. Transmit work electronically to other locations. Work with technical material, preparing statistical reports, planning and typing statistical tables, and combining and rearranging material from different sources. Use data-entry devices, such as optical scanners, to input data into computers for revision or editing. Transcribe stenotyped notes of court proceedings.

Personality Type: Conventional. Conventional occupations frequently involve following set procedures and routines. These occupations can include working with data and details more than with ideas. Usually there is a clear line of authority to follow.

GOE—Interest Area: 04. Business and Administration. **Work Group:** 04.08. Clerical Machine Operation. **Other Jobs in This Work Group:** Billing, Posting, and Calculating Machine Operators; Data Entry Keyers; Mail Clerks and Mail Machine Operators, Except Postal Service; Office Machine Operators, Except Computer; Switchboard Operators, Including Answering Service.

Skills—Installation: Installing equipment, machines, wiring, or programs to meet specifica-

tions. **Social Perceptiveness:** Being aware of others' reactions and understanding why they react as they do. **Writing:** Communicating effectively in writing as appropriate for the needs of the audience. **Equipment Selection:** Determining the kind of tools and equipment needed to do a job.

Education and Training Programs: General Office Occupations and Clerical Services; Word Processing. **Related Knowledge/Courses: Clerical Practices:** Administrative and clerical procedures and systems such as word processing, managing files and records, stenography and transcription, designing forms, and other office procedures and terminology. **Computers and Electronics:** Circuit boards, processors, chips, electronic equipment, and computer hardware and software, including applications and programming. **Customer and Personal Service:** Principles and processes for providing customer and personal services. This includes customer needs assessment, meeting quality standards for services, and evaluation of customer satisfaction. **English Language:** The structure and content of the English language including the meaning and spelling of words, rules of composition, and grammar.

Work Environment: Indoors; sitting.

Zoologists and Wildlife Biologists

- Education/Training Required: Bachelor's degree
- Annual Earnings: $53,300
- Growth: 8.7%
- Annual Job Openings: 1,444
- Self-Employed: 2.6%
- Part-Time: 12.3%

Level of Stress Tolerance Needed: 61.0 (out of 100)

Most Stressful Aspects: Impact of Decisions on Co-workers or Company Results (72.0); Time Pressure (69.7); Duration of Typical Work Week (61.5); Frequency of Conflict Situations (57.5).

Least Stressful Aspects: Pace Determined by Speed of Equipment (3.7); Deal With Physically Aggressive People (5.3); Consequence of Error (41.3); Deal With Unpleasant or Angry People (46.7).

Study the origins, behavior, diseases, genetics, and life processes of animals and wildlife. May specialize in wildlife research and management, including the collection and analysis of biological data to determine the environmental effects of present and potential use of land and water areas. Study animals in their natural habitats, assessing effects of environment and industry on animals, interpreting findings, and recommending alternative operating conditions for industry. Inventory or estimate plant and wildlife populations. Analyze characteristics of animals to identify and classify them. Make recommendations on management systems and planning for wildlife populations and habitat, consulting with stakeholders and the public at large to explore options. Disseminate information by writing reports and scientific papers or journal articles and by making presentations and giving talks for schools, clubs, interest groups, and park interpretive programs. Study characteristics of animals such as origin, interrelationships, classification, life histories and diseases, development, genetics, and distribution. Perform administrative duties such as fundraising, public relations, budgeting, and supervision of zoo staff. Organize and conduct experimental studies with live animals in controlled or natural surroundings. Oversee the care and distribution of zoo animals, working with curators and zoo directors to determine the best way to contain animals, maintain their habitats, and manage facilities. Coordinate preventive programs to control the outbreak of wildlife diseases. Prepare collections of preserved specimens or microscopic slides for species identification and study of development or disease. Raise specimens for study and observation or for use in experiments. Collect and dissect animal specimens and examine specimens under microscope.

Personality Type: Investigative. Investigative occupations frequently involve working with ideas, and require an extensive amount of thinking. These occupations can involve searching for facts and figuring out problems mentally.

GOE—Interest Area: 01. Agriculture and Natural Resources. **Work Group:** 01.02. Resource Science/Engineering for Plants, Animals, and the Environment. **Other Jobs in This Work Group:** Agricultural Engineers; Animal Scientists; Conservation Scientists; Environmental Engineers; Foresters; Mining and Geological Engineers, Including Mining Safety Engineers; Petroleum Engineers; Range Managers; Soil and Plant Scientists; Soil and Water Conservationists.

Skills—Science: Using scientific rules and methods to solve problems. **Management of Financial Resources:** Determining how money will be spent to get the work done, and accounting for these expenditures. **Writing:** Communicating effectively in writing as appropriate for the needs of the audience. **Coordination:** Adjusting actions in relation to others' actions. **Management of Personnel Resources:** Motivating, developing, and directing people as they work, identifying the best people for the job. **Persuasion:** Persuading others to change their minds or behavior.

Education and Training Programs: Animal Behavior and Ethology; Animal Physiology; Cell/Cellular Biology and Anatomical Sciences,

Other; Ecology; Entomology; Wildlife and Wildlands Science and Management; Wildlife Biology; Zoology/Animal Biology; Zoology/Animal Biology, Other. **Related Knowledge/Courses: Biology:** Plant and animal organisms, their tissues, cells, functions, interdependencies, and interactions with each other and the environment. **Geography:** Principles and methods for describing the features of land, sea, and air masses, including their physical characteristics, locations, interrelationships, and distribution of plant, animal, and human life. **Law and Government:** Laws, legal codes, court procedures, precedents, government regulations, executive orders, agency rules, and the democratic political process. **English Language:** The structure and content of the English language, including the meaning and spelling of words, rules of composition, and grammar. **Administration and Management:** Business and management principles involved in strategic planning, resource allocation, human resources modeling, leadership technique, production methods, and coordination of people and resources. **Computers and Electronics:** Circuit boards, processors, chips, electronic equipment, and computer hardware and software, including applications and programming.

Work Environment: More often indoors than outdoors; sitting.

APPENDIX A

Resources for Further Exploration

The facts and pointers in this book provide a good beginning to the subject of low-stress jobs. If you want additional details, we suggest you consult some of the resources listed here.

Facts About Careers

Occupational Outlook Handbook (or the *OOH*) (JIST): Updated every two years by the U.S. Department of Labor, this book provides descriptions for 270 major jobs covering more than 85 percent of the workforce. A concise version, the *EZ Occupational Outlook Handbook*, is also available.

Enhanced Occupational Outlook Handbook (JIST): Includes all descriptions in the *OOH* plus descriptions of more than 6,100 more-specialized jobs related to them.

O*NET Dictionary of Occupational Titles (JIST): The only printed source of the more than 900 jobs described in the U.S. Department of Labor's Occupational Information Network database. It covers all the jobs in the book you're now reading, but it offers more topics than we were able to fit here.

New Guide for Occupational Exploration (JIST): An important career reference that allows you to explore all major O*NET jobs based on your interests. (An outline of the Interest Areas and Work Groups included appears in Appendix B.)

Career Decision Making and Planning

Overnight Career Choice, by Michael Farr (JIST): This book can help you choose a career goal based on a variety of criteria, including skills, interests, and values. It is part of the *Help in a Hurry* series, so it is designed to produce quick results.

50 Best Jobs for Your Personality by Michael Farr and Laurence Shatkin, Ph.D. (JIST): Built around the six Holland personality types, this book includes an assessment to help you identify your dominant and secondary personality types, plus lists and descriptions of high-paying and high-growth jobs linked to those personality types.

Job Hunting

Same-Day Resume, by Michael Farr (JIST): Learn in an hour how to write an effective resume. This book includes dozens of sample resumes from professional writers and even offers advice on cover letters, online resumes, and more.

The *Magic* series (JIST): The four books in this series—*Résumé Magic, Interview Magic,* and *Job Search* Magic, by Susan Britton Whitcomb, and *Cover Letter Magic,* by Wendy S. Enelow and Louise M. Kursmark—offer tips, before-and-after examples, and step-by-step advice on all aspects of the job search.

The Ultimate Job Search, by Richard H. Beatty (JIST): Find the inside scoop on networking, interviewing, negotiating job offers, and more with this book's intelligent strategies to help readers through the job search process.

Job Banks by Occupation: This is a set of links offered by America's Career InfoNet. At www.acinet.org, find the Career Tools box, click Career Resource Library, then Job & Resume Banks. The Job Banks by Occupation link leads you to groups of jobs such as "Construction and Extraction Occupations" and "Arts, Design, Entertainment, Sports and Media Occupations," which in turn lead you to more specific job titles and occupation-specific job-listing sites maintained by various organizations.

APPENDIX B

GOE Interest Areas and Work Groups

A s Part III explains, the GOE is a way of organizing the world of work into large Interest Areas and more specific Work Groups containing jobs that have a lot in common. Part II defines the 16 GOE Interest Areas, and Part III also identifies the Work Groups for each job described. We thought you would want to see the complete GOE taxonomy so you would understand how any job that interests you fits into this structure.

Interest Areas have two-digit code numbers; Work Groups have four-digit code numbers beginning with the code number for the Interest Area in which they are classified. These are the 16 GOE Interest Areas and 117 Work Groups:

01 Agriculture and Natural Resources

    01.01 Managerial Work in Agriculture and Natural Resources

    01.02 Resource Science/Engineering for Plants, Animals, and the Environment

    01.03 Resource Technologies for Plants, Animals, and the Environment

    01.04 General Farming

    01.05 Nursery, Groundskeeping, and Pest Control

    01.06 Forestry and Logging

    01.07 Hunting and Fishing

    01.08 Mining and Drilling

02 Architecture and Construction

    02.01 Managerial Work in Architecture and Construction

    02.02 Architectural Design

    02.03 Architecture/Construction Engineering Technologies

    02.04 Construction Crafts

    02.05 Systems and Equipment Installation, Maintenance, and Repair

    02.06 Construction Support/Labor

03 Arts and Communication

      03.01 Managerial Work in Arts and Communication

      03.02 Writing and Editing

      03.03 News, Broadcasting, and Public Relations

      03.04 Studio Art

      03.05 Design

      03.06 Drama

      03.07 Music

      03.08 Dance

      03.09 Media Technology

      03.10 Communications Technology

      03.11 Musical Instrument Repair

04 Business and Administration

      04.01 Managerial Work in General Business

      04.02 Managerial Work in Business Detail

      04.03 Human Resources Support

      04.04 Secretarial Support

      04.05 Accounting, Auditing, and Analytical Support

      04.06 Mathematical Clerical Support

      04.07 Records and Materials Processing

      04.08 Clerical Machine Operation

05 Education and Training

      05.01 Managerial Work in Education

      05.02 Preschool, Elementary, and Secondary Teaching and Instructing

      05.03 Postsecondary and Adult Teaching and Instructing

      05.04 Library Services

      05.05 Archival and Museum Services

      05.06 Counseling, Health, and Fitness Education

06 Finance and Insurance

      06.01 Managerial Work in Finance and Insurance

      06.02 Finance/Insurance Investigation and Analysis

      06.03 Finance/Insurance Records Processing

      06.04 Finance/Insurance Customer Service

      06.05 Finance/Insurance Sales and Support

07 Government and Public Administration

      07.01 Managerial Work in Government and Public Administration

      07.02 Public Planning

      07.03 Regulations Enforcement

      07.04 Public Administration Clerical Support

08 Health Science

      08.01 Managerial Work in Medical and Health Services

      08.02 Medicine and Surgery

      08.03 Dentistry

      08.04 Health Specialties

      08.05 Animal Care

      08.06 Medical Technology

      08.07 Medical Therapy

      08.08 Patient Care and Assistance

      08.09 Health Protection and Promotion

09 Hospitality, Tourism, and Recreation

      09.01 Managerial Work in Hospitality and Tourism

      09.02 Recreational Services

      09.03 Hospitality and Travel Services

      09.04 Food and Beverage Preparation

      09.05 Food and Beverage Service

      09.06 Sports

      09.07 Barber and Beauty Services

10 Human Service

      10.01 Counseling and Social Work

      10.02 Religious Work

      10.03 Child/Personal Care and Services

      10.04 Client Interviewing

11 Information Technology

      11.01 Managerial Work in Information Technology

      11.02 Information Technology Specialties

      11.03 Digital Equipment Repair

12 Law and Public Safety

      12.01 Managerial Work in Law and Public Safety

      12.02 Legal Practice and Justice Administration

      12.03 Legal Support

12.04 Law Enforcement and Public Safety

12.05 Safety and Security

12.06 Emergency Responding

12.07 Military

13 Manufacturing

13.01 Managerial Work in Manufacturing

13.02 Machine Setup and Operation

13.03 Production Work, Assorted Materials Processing

13.04 Welding, Brazing, and Soldering

13.05 Production Machining Technology

13.06 Production Precision Work

13.07 Production Quality Control

13.08 Graphic Arts Production

13.09 Hands-On Work, Assorted Materials

13.10 Woodworking Technology

13.11 Apparel, Shoes, Leather, and Fabric Care

13.12 Electrical and Electronic Repair

13.13 Machinery Repair

13.14 Vehicle and Facility Mechanical Work

13.15 Medical and Technical Equipment Repair

13.16 Utility Operation and Energy Distribution

13.17 Loading, Moving, Hoisting, and Conveying

14 Retail and Wholesale Sales and Service

14.01 Managerial Work in Retail/Wholesale Sales and Service

14.02 Technical Sales

14.03 General Sales

14.04 Personal Soliciting

14.05 Purchasing

14.06 Customer Service

15 Scientific Research, Engineering, and Mathematics

15.01 Managerial Work in Scientific Research, Engineering, and Mathematics

15.02 Physical Sciences

15.03 Life Sciences

15.04 Social Sciences

15.05 Physical Science Laboratory Technology

15.06 Mathematics and Data Analysis

Index

I

J–L

M